10TH EDITION

MACROECONOMICS
for Today

Irvin B. Tucker
University of North Carolina at Charlotte

 CENGAGE

Australia • Brazil • Mexico • Singapore • United Kingdom • United States

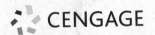

**Macroeconomics for Today,
Tenth Edition**

Irvin B. Tucker

Contributing Authors: Douglas W. Copeland, Johnson County Community College and Joseph P. McGarrity, University of Central Arkansas

Senior Vice President, Higher Ed Product, Content, and Market Development: Erin Joyner

Product Director: Jason Fremder

Sr. Product Manager: Michael Parthenakis

Sr. Content Developer: Julia Chase

Executive Marketing Manager: John Carey

Sr. Content Project Manager: Colleen Farmer

Production Service: Lumina Datamatics, Inc.

Sr. Art Director: Michelle Kunkler

Cover and Internal Designer: Red Hangar Design

Cover Image: Andrew Koturanov/Shutterstock.com

Intellectual Property

   Analyst: Diane Garrity

   Project Manager: Sarah Shainwald

Internal Image Credit Lines:
   dencg/Shutterstock.com;
   Andrii Symonenko/Shutterstock.com;
   mkos83/Shutterstock.com;
   Nelson Marques/Shutterstock.com;
   Intrepix/Shutterstock.com;
   Jezper/Shutterstock.com

For product information and technology assistance, contact us at **Cengage Customer & Sales Support, 1-800-354-9706 or support.cengage.com.**

For permission to use material from this text or product, submit all requests online at **www.cengage.com/permissions**

Library of Congress Control Number: 2017963567

ISBN: 978-1-337-61305-7

Cengage
20 Channel Center Street
Boston, MA 02210
USA

Cengage is a leading provider of customized learning solutions with employees residing in nearly 40 different countries and sales in more than 125 countries around the world. Find your local representative at **www.cengage.com.**

Cengage products are represented in Canada by Nelson Education, Ltd.

To learn more about Cengage platforms and services, visit **www.cengage.com**

To register or access your online learning solution or purchase materials for your course, visit **www.cengagebrain.com**

Printed in the United States of America
Print Number: 01   Print Year: 2018

ABOUT THE AUTHOR

IRVIN B. TUCKER

IRVIN B. TUCKER was a longtime leader in economic education with over 30 years of experience teaching introductory economics at the University of North Carolina at Charlotte. He earned his B.S. in economics at N.C. State University and his M.A. and Ph.D. in economics from the University of South Carolina. Dr. Tucker served as executive director of the S.C. Council of Education and director of the Center for Economic Education at the University of North Carolina at Charlotte. Dr. Tucker is recognized for his ability to relate basic principles to economic issues and public policy. His work has received national recognition by being awarded the Meritorious Levy Award for Excellence in Private Enterprise Education, the Federation of Independent Business Award for Postsecondary Educator of the Year in Entrepreneurship and Economic Education, and the Freedom Foundation's George Washington Medal for Excellence in Economic Education. In addition, his research has been published in numerous professional economics journals on a wide range of topics including industrial organization, entrepreneurship, and economics of education. Dr. Tucker is also the author of the highly successful *Survey of Economics*, tenth edition, a text for the one-semester principles of economics courses, published by Cengage Learning.

BRIEF CONTENTS

CONTENTS

PART 3 MACROECONOMICS FUNDAMENTALS   129

AVAILABLE VERSIONS

The Four Versions of This Book

Economics for Today	Economics for Today	Microeconomics for Today	Macroeconomics for Today	Survey of Economics
1 Introducing the Economic Way of Thinking	X	X	X	X
2 Production Possibilities, Opportunity Cost, and Economic Growth	X	X	X	X
3 Market Demand and Supply	X	X	X	X
4 Markets in Action	X	X	X	X
5 Price Elasticity of Demand and Supply	X	X		X
6 Consumer Choice Theory	X	X		
7 Production Costs	X	X		X
8 Perfect Competition	X	X		X
9 Monopoly	X	X		X
10 Monopolistic Competition and Oligopoly	X	X		X
11 Labor Markets	X	X		X
12 Income Distribution, Poverty, and Discrimination	X	X		X
13 Antitrust and Regulation	X	X		
14 Environmental Economics	X	X		
15 Gross Domestic Product	X		X	X
16 Business Cycles and Unemployment	X		X	X
17 Inflation	X		X	X
18 The Keynesian Model	X		X	
19 The Keynesian Model in Action	X		X	
20 Aggregate Demand and Supply	X		X	X
21 Fiscal Policy	X		X	X
22 The Public Sector	X		X	X
23 Federal Deficits, Surpluses, and the National Debt	X		X	X
24 Money and the Federal Reserve System	X		X	X
25 Money Creation	X		X	X
26 Monetary Policy	X		X	X
27 The Phillips Curve and Expectations Theory	X		X	
28 International Trade and Finance	X	X	X	X
29 Economies in Transition	X	X	X	X
30 Growth and the Less-Developed Countries	X	X	X	X

Note: Chapter numbers refer to the complete book, *Economics for Today.*

PREFACE

TEXT WITH A MISSION

The purpose of *Economics for Today,* tenth edition, is to teach, in an engaging style, the basic operations of the U.S. economy to students who will take a two-term economics course. Rather than taking an encyclopedic approach to economic concepts, *Economics for Today* focuses on the most important tools in economics and applies these concepts to clearly explain real-world economic issues and events.

Every effort has been made to make *Economics for Today* the most student-friendly text on the market. This text was written because so many others expose students to a confusing array of economic analyses that force students to simply memorize in order to pass the course. Instead, *Economics for Today* presents a straightforward and unbiased approach that effectively teaches the application of basic economic principles. After reading this text, the student should be able to say, "Now that economics stuff in the news makes sense."

HOW IT FITS TOGETHER

This text presents the core principles of microeconomics, macroeconomics, and international economics. The first 14 chapters introduce the logic of economic analysis and develop the core of microeconomic analysis. Here, students learn the role of demand and supply in determining prices in competitive markets versus monopolistic markets. Within these chapters, the book explores such issues as minimum wage laws, rent control, and pollution. The next 13 chapters develop the macroeconomics part of the text. Using the modern yet simple aggregate demand and aggregate supply model, the text explains measurement of and changes in the price level, national output, and employment in the economy. The study of macroeconomics also includes how the supply of and the demand for money influences the economy. Finally, this text concludes with three chapters devoted entirely to global issues. For example, students will learn how the supply of and demand for currencies determine exchange rates and what the implications are for a strong or a weak dollar on our nation's economy.

TEXT FLEXIBILITY

The full version of *Economics for Today* is easily adapted to an instructor's preference for the sequencing of microeconomics and macroeconomics topics. This text can be used in a macroeconomic–microeconomic sequence by teaching the first four chapters and then Parts 5 through 7. Next, microeconomics is covered in Parts 2 through 4. Finally, the course can be completed with Part 8, consisting of three chapters devoted to international economics.

An important design of this text is that it accommodates the two major approaches for teaching principles of macroeconomics: those who cover both the Keynesian Cross and AD/AS models, and those who skip the Keynesian model and cover only the AD/AS model. For instructors who prefer the former, *Economics for Today* moves smoothly in Chapters 18–19 (*Macroeconomics for Today* Chapters 8–9) from the Keynesian model (based on the Great Depression) to the AD/AS model in Chapter 20 (*Macroeconomics for Today* Chapter 10). For instructors using the latter approach, this text is written so that instructors can skip the Keynesian model in Chapters 18–19 (*Macroeconomics for Today* Chapters 8–9) and proceed from Chapter 17 (*Macroeconomics for Today* Chapter 7) to Chapter 20 (*Macroeconomics for Today* Chapter 10) without losing anything. For example, the spending multiplier is completely covered both in the Keynesian and AD/AS model chapters.

For instructors who want to teach the self-correcting AD/AS model, emphasis can be placed on the appendixes to Chapters 20 (*Macroeconomics for Today* Chapter 10) and 26 (*Macroeconomics for Today* Chapter 16). Instructors who choose not to cover this model can simply skip these appendixes. In short, *Economics for Today* provides more comprehensive and flexible coverage of macroeconomics models than is available in other texts. Also, a customized text might meet your needs. If so, contact your Cengage learning consultant for information.

HOW NOT TO STUDY ECONOMICS

To some students, studying economics is a little frightening because many chapters are full of graphs. Students often make the mistake of preparing for tests by trying to memorize the lines of graphs. When their graded tests are returned, the students using this strategy will probably exclaim, "What happened?" The answer to this question is that the students should have learned the economic concepts *first;* then they would understand the graphs as *illustrations* of these underlying concepts. Stated simply, superficial cramming for economics quizzes does not work.

For students who are anxious about using graphs, the Appendix to Chapter 1 provides a brief review of graphical analysis. In addition, Graph Builder in the Tucker MindTap product contains step-by-step features on how to construct and interpret graphs. Moreover, and new to this edition, Videos entitled "GuideMe Videos" (A Graphing Tutorial for Students) are found in the Tucker MindTap product that explain numerous key graphs throughout the textbook.

CHANGES TO THE TENTH EDITION

The basic layout of the tenth edition remains the same. The following are changes:

- Chapter 1, Introducing the Economic Way of Thinking, recognizes that students taking introductory, college-level economics courses are considering their major. One reason to select economics is that the average starting salary for an undergraduate economics major is higher compared to many other majors. To aid their decision, current average starting salary figures for selected majors have been updated. In addition, the *You're the Economist* feature on the Minimum Wage has been updated with the positive and normative arguments both for and against the minimum wage.
- Chapter 2, Production Possibilities, Opportunity Cost, and Economic Growth has an updated discussion on how public investment in infrastructure can promote economic growth and enhance the average absolute standard of living for a nation.
- Chapter 4, Markets in Action, has updated the *You're the Economist* feature entitled "Rigging the Market for Milk" to reflect the latest changes in government's attempts at supporting farm incomes.

- Chapter 5, Gross Domestic Product, has updated data on all components of GDP.
- Chapter 6, Business Cycles and Unemployment, includes updated business cycles and unemployment data. This chapter also includes updated unemployment data by demographic groups with a section on the impacts of globalization on unemployment. This chapter also features a new *You're the Economist* examining the potential impact of artificial intelligence and other technological advancements on unemployment in the future.
- Chapter 7, Inflation, updates data on inflation including a global comparison of annual inflation rates. A new *You're the Economist* feature reports on the high inflation rates for health care in the United States and examines the impact on households, businesses, and government. In addition, a couple of *Checkpoints* provide an application for adjusting the price of going to college and the price of gasoline for inflation over time. Here students can also enjoy learning how Babe Ruth's 1932 salary is converted into today's dollars.
- Chapter 8, The Keynesian Model, has updated data on all personal consumption, disposable income and investment.
- Chapter 9, The Keynesian Model in Action, has a new *You're the Economist* feature on infrastructure spending that allows students to test their understanding of spending and tax multipliers.
- Chapter 12, The Public Sector, highlights the important current issue of the changing economic character of the United States with global comparisons to other countries. Here, for example, updated data and exhibits trace the growth of U.S. government expenditures and taxes since the Great Depression. And global comparison of spending and taxation exhibits have been revised.
- Chapter 13, Federal Deficits, Surpluses, and the National Debt, focuses on the current "hot button" issue of federal deficits and the national debt using updated data and exhibits. This chapter includes global comparisons of the deficit and national debt as a percentage of GDP.
- Chapter 14, Money and the Federal Reserve System, has updated money supply figures and an updated listing of the top 10 U.S. banks by asset size. This chapter also features a new *Checkpoint* that examines the role of bitcoins as money, and a new *You're the Economist* entitled "Should the Fed be Independent?"
- Chapter 15, Money Creation, has a new *Checkpoint* that asks students to determine how the Fed could utilize its tools to combat unemployment.
- Chapter 16, Monetary Policy, features a new *Checkpoint* that tests students' understanding of how the Fed could push interest rates down.
- Chapter 18, International Trade and Finance, has updated data for international balance of payments and trade.
- Chapter 19, Economies in Transition, has greater clarification on the differences between capitalism and socialism and why all real-world economies are mixed economies. This chapter also features a new *You're the Economist* entitled "The unrealistic path to communism." In addition, there is a new *Global Economics* section that points to a satellite photo of North Korea as perhaps a compelling testimony to the long-run failure of undemocratic command economies. Students should find this interesting.
- Chapter 20, Growth and the Less-Developed Countries, presents updated data ranking countries by their GDP per capita. It also presents updated data comparing regions of the world by their average GDP per capita. Here, updated data is used

to explain the link between economic freedom and quality-of-life indicators. There is a new *You're the Economist* section entitled "India and China's Economic Growth: An Updated Version of Aesop's Tale" that probes the ingredients for sustained economic growth.

ALTERNATIVE VERSIONS OF THE BOOK

For instructors who want to spend various amounts of time for their courses and offer different topics of this text:

* *Economics for Today.* This complete version of the book contains all 30 chapters. It is designed for two-semester introductory courses that cover both microeconomics and macroeconomics.
* *Microeconomics for Today.* This version contains 17 chapters and is designed for one-semester courses in introductory microeconomics.
* *Macroeconomics for Today.* This version contains 20 chapters and is designed for one-semester courses in introductory macroeconomics.
* *Survey of Economics.* This version of the book contains 23 chapters. It is designed for one-semester courses that cover the basics of both microeconomics and macroeconomics.

The Available Versions accompanying table on page xxi shows precisely which chapters are included in each book. Instructors who want more information about these alternative versions should contact their local Cengage learning consultant.

MOTIVATIONAL PEDAGOGICAL FEATURES

Economics for Today strives to motivate and advance the boundaries of pedagogy with the following features:

Part Openers

Each part begins with a statement of the overall mission of the chapters in the part. In addition, there is a nutshell introduction of each chapter in relation to the part's learning objective.

Chapter Previews

Each chapter begins with a preview designed to pique the student's interest and reinforce how the chapter fits into the overall scheme of the book. Each preview appeals to students' "Sherlock Holmes" impulses by posing several economics puzzles that can be solved by understanding the material presented in the chapter.

Margin Definitions and Flashcards

Key concepts introduced in the chapter are highlighted in bold type and then defined with the definitions again in the margins. This feature therefore serves as a quick reference. Key terms are also defined on the Tucker MindTap product with a flashcard feature that is great for learning terms.

You're the Economist

Each chapter includes boxed inserts that provide the acid test of "relevance to everyday life." This feature gives the student an opportunity to encounter timely, real-world extensions of economic theory. For example, students read about Fred Smith as he writes an economics term paper explaining his plan to create FedEx. To ensure that the student wastes no time figuring out which concepts apply to the article, applicable concepts are listed after each title. Several of these boxed features include quotes from newspaper articles over a period of years demonstrating that economic concepts remain relevant over time. Many of these boxed features have been updated or changed in the tenth edition to reflect the latest issues, developments, and relevant applications of economics for students today.

Conclusion Statements

Throughout the chapters, highlighted conclusion statements of key concepts appear at the ends of sections and tie together the material just presented. Students will be able to see quickly if they have understood the main points of the section. A summary of these conclusion statements is provided at the end of each chapter.

Global Economics

Today's economic environment is global. *Economics for Today* carefully integrates international topics throughout the text and presents the material using a highly readable and accessible approach designed for students with no training in international economics. All sections of the text that present global economics are identified by a special global icon in the text margin and in the *Global Economics* boxes. In addition, the final three chapters of the book are devoted entirely to international economics.

Analyze the Issue

This feature follows each *You're the Economist* and *Global Economics* feature and asks specific questions that require students to test their knowledge of how the material in the boxed insert is relevant to the applicable concept. To allow these questions to be used in classroom discussions or homework assignments, answers are provided in the Instructor's Manual rather than in the text.

Checkpoint

Watch for these! Who said learning economics can't be fun? This feature is a unique approach to generating interest and critical thinking. These questions spark students to check their progress by asking challenging economics puzzles in game-like style. Students enjoy thinking through and answering the questions, and then checking the answers at the end of the chapter. Students who answer correctly earn the satisfaction of knowing they have mastered the concepts. Many of these have been updated for the tenth edition to pique interest and to apply to the experiences of students today.

Exhibits

Attractive large graphical presentations with grid lines and real-world numbers are essential for any successful economics textbook. Each exhibit has been carefully analyzed to ensure that the key concepts being represented stand out clearly. Brief descriptions are included with graphs to provide guidance for students as they study the graph. The MindTap course brings these exhibits to life:

- Students can interact with selected exhibits via Graph Builder.
- Students can watch detailed explanations of selected exhibits via GuideMe Videos (A graphing tutorial for students.)

Causation Chain Game

This will be one of your favorites. The highly successful causation chains are included under many graphs throughout the text. This pedagogical device helps students visualize complex economic relationships in terms of simple box diagrams that illustrate how one change causes another change. Each exhibit has a causation chain in the text, and a correlating in the animated causation chain game exercise in the Tucker MindTap product. Arrange the blocks correctly to win the game.

Key Concepts

Key concepts introduced in the chapter are listed at the end of each chapter and defined in the margins. Visit the Tucker MindTap to access for interactive flashcards.

Visual Summaries

Each chapter ends with a brief point-by-point summary of the key concepts. Many of these summarized points include miniaturized versions of the important graphs and causation chains that illustrate many of the key concepts. These are intended to serve as visual reminders for students as they finish the chapters and are also useful in reviewing and studying for quizzes and exams.

Study Questions and Problems

These end-of-chapter questions and problems offer a variety of levels ranging from straightforward recall to deeply thought-provoking applications. The answers to odd-numbered questions and problems are found in Appendix A in the back of the text. This feature gives students immediate feedback without requiring the instructor to check their work. The even-numbered answers are found in the Instructor's Manual.

End-of-Chapter Sample Quizzes

These particular assessments are a great help before quizzes. Many instructors test students using multiple-choice questions. For this reason, the final section of each chapter provides the type of multiple-choice questions given in the test bank. The answers are readily available to students to help them learn the material and are found in Appendix B at the end of the textbook. In addition to the end-of-chapter sample quizzes, each section quiz appears in the Tucker MindTap product. Each quiz contains multiple questions like those found on a typical exam. Feedback is included for each answer so that you may know instantly why you have answered correctly or incorrectly. Between this feature and the end-of-chapter sample quizzes, students are well prepared for tests. Finally, the Instructor's Manual also contains four to five multiple choice questions per chapter that can also be used to engage students with the material.

Road Maps

This feature concludes each sectioned part with review questions listed by chapter from the particular part. To reinforce the concepts, each set of questions relates to the interactive causation chain game that is available in the Tucker MindTap product. This makes learning fun. Answers to the questions are also found in Appendix C in the back of the text.

A SUPPLEMENTS PACKAGE DESIGNED FOR SUCCESS

Tucker is known for its unequaled resources for instructors and students. To access additional course material for *Economics for Today,* visit www.cengagebrain.com. At the CengageBrain.com home page, search for "Tucker" using the search box on the page. This will take you to the product page where these resources can be found. For additional information, contact your Cengage learning consultant.

INSTRUCTORS RESOURCES

Tucker Companion Site

The Tucker website at www.cengagebrain.com provides open access to PowerPoint chapter review slides; an instructor's manual prepared by Douglas Copeland of Johnson County Community College, available in various formats; updates to the text, describing key concepts relevant to the current states of economics and the world today; Power-Point lecture tools elaborating on key concepts and exhibits, which can be used as supplies or can be customized for instructor intentions; and test banks in various downloadable formats.

STUDENT RESOURCES

MindTap for Tucker

MindTap engages students and aids them in consistently producing their best work. By seamlessly integrating course material with interactive media, step-by-step graphing, activities, apps, and much more, MindTap creates a unique learning path for courses that foster increased comprehension and efficiency of material.

- MindTap delivers real-world relevance with activities, assignments, homework, media, and study tools that help students build critical thinking and analytic skills that will carry over to their professional lives.
- MindTap helps students stay organized and efficient with a single destination that reflects what's important to the instructor and the tools to master that content.

MindTap empowers students to get their "game face on" by motivating them with competitive benchmarks in performance.

- Relevant readings, multimedia, and activities are designed to take students up the levels of learning from basic knowledge to analysis and application.
- Graph Builder exercises enable students to practice building their own graphs and honing the skills to do so for application both in the course and real-life situations.
- Students can watch detailed explanations of selected exhibits via GuideMe Videos (A Graphing Tutorial for Students) that explain numerous key graphs throughout the textbook.
- Analytics and reports provide a snapshot of class progress, time in course, engagement and completion rates.
- Homework and the Math & Graphing Tutorial, both powered by Aplia, as well as videos that explain key graphs round out the student learning experience within MindTap that enable students to master course content.

Acknowledgments

A deep debt of gratitude is owed to the reviewers of all ten editions for their expert assistance. All comments and suggestions were carefully evaluated and served to improve the final product.

Special Thanks

Much appreciation goes to Michael Parthenakis, Senior Product Manager. Thanks also to Clara Goosman, Content Development Manager, Julia Chase, Content Developer, Colleen Farmer, Senior Content Project Manager; Michelle Kunkler, Senior Art Director; Derek Drifmeyer, Senior Digital Project Manager; Drew Gaither, Media Producer; and Denisse Zavala-Rosalez, Product Assistant. I am also grateful to John Carey for his skillful marketing. Finally, I give my sincere thanks for a job well done to the entire team at Cengage.

A Tribute to Irvin B. Tucker

The contributing authors and the entire Cengage team want to express our heartfelt gratitude for the opportunity and the privilege to have been able to work with Irvin Tucker and this textbook over all these years. Some of us have had the honor of working with Irvin from the beginning, when this book was just a manuscript. We know of few, if any, other authors who have consistently demonstrated such a firm commitment and tireless dedication to teaching and learning. Irvin has always believed that knowledge of economics can enhance people's lives and should therefore be made accessible to everyone. And Irvin has displayed the rare ability to translate complex concepts into easily understood principles that have enriched the lives of countless numbers of students across the globe. He has made economics not only accessible but fun to learn. For this, he has distinguished himself among the very best economists of our time! He is a true complement to the profession of economics and to the noble cause of education. Beyond having earned our respect as a superb economist and author, Irvin has also been such a joy to work with. He has always been kind to everyone, willing to listen to any new ideas or suggestions, and has consistently made everyone feel needed and appreciated.

We would be remiss if we did not also make a tribute to Irvin's wife, Nonie. Nonie also possesses the traits of those you feel blessed to work with. She has also made countless meaningful contributions to this title from the very beginning. Irvin and Nonie have always been known to be "quite the team!" Thank you Irvin, and thank you Nonie! You have made the world a better place!

This edition is dedicated to Irvin B. Tucker.

MACROECONOMICS
for Today

PART 1

Introduction to Economics

The first two chapters introduce you to a foundation of economic knowledge vital to understanding the other chapters in the text. In these introductory chapters, you will begin to learn a valuable reasoning approach to solving economics puzzles that economists call "the economic way of thinking." Part 1 develops the cornerstone of this type of logical analysis by presenting basic economic models that explain such important topics as scarcity, opportunity cost, production possibilities, and economic growth.

CHAPTER 1

Introducing the Economic Way of Thinking

CHAPTER PREVIEW

You and I know that navigating the complex social environment in which we live as we strive to be successful and happy is not easy. However, understanding the important economic, social (cultural), and political (legal) elements at play and how they interact can certainly help. In fact, all headline-grabbing issues of our times can be viewed from these three perspectives. Perhaps all too often the economic perspective is the least understood. So, what is this *economic perspective*? What is the economic way of thinking?

In this text, you will learn what it means to think economically. You will discover that the world is full of economics problems requiring more powerful tools than just common sense. Just to give a sneak preview, in later chapters, you will discover the shortcomings of government price fixing for gasoline and health care. You will also find out why colleges and universities charge students different tuitions for the same education. You

will investigate whether you should worry if the federal government fails to balance its budget. You will learn that the island of Yap uses large stones with holes in the center as money. In the final chapter, you will study why some countries grow rich while others remain poor and less developed. And the list of fascinating and relevant topics continues throughout each chapter. As you read these pages, your efforts will be rewarded by an understanding of just how much economic theories and policies affect our daily lives past, present, and future.

Chapter 1 acquaints you with the foundation of the economic way of thinking. The first building blocks joined are the concepts of scarcity and choice. The next building blocks are the steps in the model-building process that economists use to study the choices people make. Then we look at some pitfalls of economic reasoning and explain why economists might disagree with one another. The chapter concludes with a discussion of why you may want to be an economics major.

IN THIS CHAPTER, YOU WILL LEARN TO SOLVE THESE ECONOMICS PUZZLES:

- Can you prove there is no person worth a trillion dollars?
- Why would you purchase more Coca-Cola when its price increases?
- How can the relationship between the Super Bowl winner and changes in the stock market be explained?

1-1 THE PROBLEM OF SCARCITY

At the heart of the economic way of thinking is the fact that we live in a world of scarcity. **Scarcity** is the condition in which human wants are forever greater than the available supply of time, goods, and resources. Because of scarcity, we are unable to have as much as we would like. It is impossible to satisfy every desire. Pause for a moment to list some of your unsatisfied wants. Perhaps you would like a big home, gourmet meals, designer clothes, clean air, better health care, shelter for the homeless, more leisure time, and so on. Unfortunately, nature does not offer the Garden of Eden, where every desire is fulfilled. Instead, there are always limits on the economy's ability to satisfy unlimited wants. Alas, scarcity is pervasive, so "you can't have it all."

You may think your scarcity problem would disappear if you were rich, but wealth does not solve the problem. No matter how affluent an individual is, the wish list continues to grow. We are familiar with the "rich and famous" who never seem to have enough. Although they live well, they still desire finer homes, faster planes, and larger yachts. In short, the condition of scarcity means all individuals, whether rich or poor, are dissatisfied with their material well-being and would like more. What is true for individuals also applies to society. Even Uncle Sam can't escape the problem of scarcity because the federal government never has enough money to spend for education, highways, police, national defense, Social Security, and all the other programs it wants to fund.

Scarcity is a fact of life throughout the world. In much of South America, Africa, and Asia, the problem of scarcity is often life-threatening. On the other hand, North America, Western Europe, and some parts of Asia have achieved substantial economic growth and development. Although life is much less "gruelling" in the more developed countries, the problem of scarcity still exists because individuals and countries never have as much of all the goods and services as they would like to have. As a result of scarcity, every nation must decide what combination of products to produce, how much to produce, and who is going to get those goods and services. These economic choices have profound social and political implications.

Scarcity
The condition in which human wants are forever greater than the available supply of time, goods, and resources.

> The problems of scarcity and choice are basic economic problems faced by every society.

CONCLUSION

1-2 SCARCE RESOURCES AND PRODUCTION

Because of the economic problem of scarcity, no society has enough resources to produce all the goods and services necessary to satisfy all human wants. **Resources** are the basic categories of inputs used to produce goods and services. Resources are also called *factors of production*. Economists divide resources into three categories: *land, labor,* and *capital* (see Exhibit 1).

1-2a Land

Land is a shorthand expression for any natural resource provided by nature that is used to produce a good or service. *Land* includes those resources or raw materials that are gifts of

Resources
The basic categories of inputs used to produce goods and services. Resources are also called *factors of production*. Economists divide resources into three categories: *land, labor,* and *capital*.

Land
Any natural resource provided by nature that is used to produce a good or service.

EXHIBIT 1 Three Categories of Resources

Resources are the basic categories of inputs organized by entrepreneurship (a special type of labor) to produce goods and services. Economists divide resources into the three categories of land, labor, and capital.

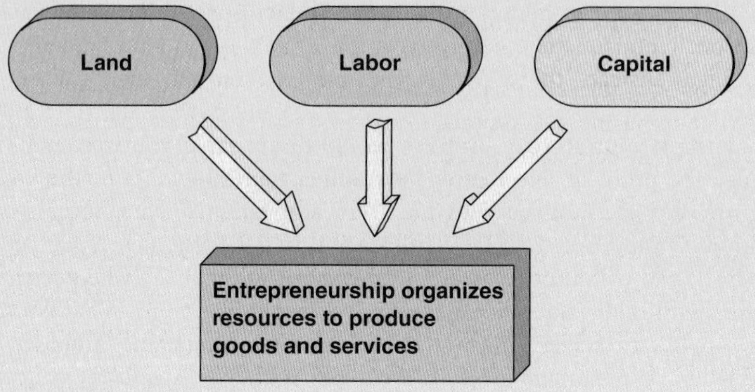

```
Land          Labor          Capital
```

Entrepreneurship organizes resources to produce goods and services

nature available for use in the production process. Farming, building factories, and constructing oil refineries would be impossible without land. Land includes anything natural above or below the ground, such as forests, gold, diamonds, oil, coal, wind, and the ocean. Two broad categories of natural resources are *renewable resources* and *nonrenewable resources*. Renewable resources are basic inputs that nature can automatically replace. Examples include crops, clean air, and the water and fish in lakes. Nonrenewable resources are basic inputs that nature cannot automatically replace. There is only so much coal, oil, and natural gas in the world. If these fossil fuels disappear, we must use substitutes.

1-2b Labor

Labor
The mental and physical capacity of workers to produce goods and services.

Labor is the mental and physical capacity of workers to produce goods and services. The services of farmers, assembly-line workers, lawyers, professional football players, and economists are all *labor*. The labor resource is measured both by the number of people available for work and by the skills or quality of workers. One reason nations differ in their ability to produce is that human characteristics, such as the education, experience, health, and motivation of workers, differ among nations.

Entrepreneurship
The creative ability of individuals to seek profits by taking risks and combining resources to produce innovative products.

Entrepreneurship is a special type of labor. **Entrepreneurship** is the creative ability of individuals to seek profits by taking risks and combining resources to produce innovative products. An *entrepreneur* is a motivated person who seeks profits by undertaking risky activities such as starting new businesses, creating new products, or inventing new ways of accomplishing tasks. Entrepreneurs are often successful when they embrace new or existing technologies (using their "know-how") in creative ways. For example, consider all of the amazing apps created for use with Androids and the iPhone. Entrepreneurship is a scarce human resource because relatively few people are willing or able to innovate and make decisions involving a high likelihood of failure. An important benefit of entrepreneurship is that it creates a growing economy.

Entrepreneurs are the agents of change who bring material progress to society. The birth of the Levi Strauss Company is a classic entrepreneurial success story. In 1853, at the age of 24, Levi Strauss, who was born in Bavaria, sailed from New York to join the California Gold Rush. His intent was not to dig for gold but to sell cloth. By the time he arrived in San Francisco, he had sold most of his cloth to other people on the ship. The only cloth he had left was a roll of canvas for tents and covered wagons. On the dock, he met a miner who wanted sturdy pants that would last while digging for gold, so Levi made a pair from the canvas. Later, a customer gave Levi the idea of using little copper rivets to strengthen the seams. Presto! Strauss knew a good thing when he saw it, so he hired workers, built factories, and became one of the largest pants makers in the world. As a reward for taking business risks, organizing production, and introducing a product, the Levi Strauss Company earned profits, and Strauss became rich and famous.

1-2c Capital

Capital can be defined as a human-made good used to produce other goods and services; for example, capital includes the physical plants, machinery, and equipment used to produce other goods. Capital can be privately or publicly owned. Private capital is owned by private companies and consists of factories, office buildings, warehouses, robots, trucks, and distribution facilities. Public (or social) capital, also known as *infrastructure*, is provided by government through taxes and is collectively owned. It consists of roads, bridges, dams, airports, harbors, and public universities and other government buildings. The term *capital*, as it is used in the study of economics, can be confusing. Economists know that capital in everyday conversations means money or the money value of paper assets, such as stocks, bonds, or a deed to a house. This is actually *financial* capital. In the study of economics, capital does not refer to money assets. Capital in economics means a factor of production, such as a factory or machinery. Stated simply, you must pay special attention to this point: Money is not capital and is, therefore, not a resource. Instead, money is used to purchase land, labor, or capital, as well as many consumer goods and services.

Capital
A human-made good used to produce other goods and services.

> Money by itself does not produce goods and services; instead, it is only a means to facilitate the purchase and sale of resources and consumer products.

CONCLUSION

1-3 ECONOMICS: THE STUDY OF SCARCITY AND CHOICE

The perpetual problem of scarcity forcing people to make choices is the basis for the definition of economics. **Economics** is the study of how society chooses to allocate its scarce resources to satisfy unlimited wants. You may be surprised by this definition. People often think economics means studying supply and demand, the stock market, money, and banking. Well, those are certainly parts, but economics is more all-encompassing. It is the study of the choices we make because we are faced with scarcity—because we are unable to have as much as we would like.

Society makes two broad levels of choices: economy-wide, or macro choices, and individual, or micro choices. The prefixes *macro* and *micro* come from the Greek words

Economics
The study of how society chooses to allocate its scarce resources to the production of goods and services to satisfy unlimited wants.

meaning "large" and "small," respectively. Reflecting the macro and micro perspectives, economics consists of two main branches: *macroeconomics* and *microeconomics*.

1-3a Macroeconomics

Macroeconomics
The branch of economics that studies decision making for the economy as a whole.

The old saying "Looking at the forest rather than the trees" describes **macroeconomics**, which is the branch of economics that studies decision making for the economy as a whole. Macroeconomics applies an overview perspective to an economy by examining economy-wide variables, such as inflation, unemployment, economic growth, the money supply, and the national incomes of different countries. Macroeconomic decision making considers such "big picture" policies as the effect that federal tax cuts will have on unemployment and the effect that a change in the money supply will have on inflation.

1-3b Microeconomics

Microeconomics
The branch of economics that studies decision making by a single individual, household, firm, industry, or level of government.

Examining individual trees, leaves, and pieces of bark, rather than surveying the forest, illustrates microeconomics. **Microeconomics** is the branch of economics that studies decision making by a single individual, household, firm, industry, or level of government. It applies a microscope to study specific parts of an economy, as one would examine cells in the body. The focus is on small economic units, such as economic decisions of particular groups of consumers and businesses. An example of microeconomic analysis would be to study economic units involved in the market for ostrich eggs. Will suppliers decide to supply more, less, or the same quantity of ostrich eggs to the market in response to price changes? Will individual consumers of these eggs decide to buy more, less, or the same quantity at a new price?

We have described macroeconomics and microeconomics as two separate branches, but they are related. Because the overall economy is the sum, or aggregation, of its parts, micro changes affect the macro economy, and macro changes produce micro changes.

1-4 THE METHODOLOGY OF ECONOMICS

As used by other disciplines, such as criminology, biology, chemistry, and physics, economists employ a step-by-step procedure for solving problems by identifying the problem, developing a model, gathering data, and testing whether the data are consistent with the theory. Based on this analysis, economists formulate a conclusion. Exhibit 2 summarizes the model-building process.

1-4a Problem Identification

The first step in applying the economic method is to define the issue. Suppose an economist wishes to investigate the microeconomic problem of why U.S. motorists cut back on gasoline consumption in a given year from, for example, 400 million gallons per day in May to 300 million gallons per day in December.

Model
A simplified description of reality used to understand and predict the relationship between variables.

1-4b Model Development

The second step in our hypothetical example toward finding an explanation is for the economist to build a model. A **model** is a simplified description of reality used to

EXHIBIT 2 The Steps in the Model-Building Process

The first step in developing a model is to identify the problem. The second step is to select the critical variables necessary to formulate a model that explains the problem under study. Eliminating other variables that complicate the analysis requires simplifying assumptions. In the third step, the researcher collects data and tests the model. If the evidence supports the model, the conclusion is to accept the model. If the evidence doesn't support the model, the model is rejected.

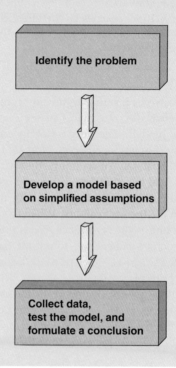

understand and predict the relationship between variables. The terms *model* and *theory* are interchangeable. A model emphasizes only those variables that are most important to explaining an event. As Albert Einstein said, "Theories should be as simple as possible, but not more so." The purpose of a model is to construct an abstraction from real-world complexities and make events understandable. Consider a model airplane that is placed in a wind tunnel to test the aerodynamics of a new design. For this purpose, the model must represent only the shapes of the wings and fuselage, but it does not need to include tiny seats, electrical wiring, or other interior design details. A highway map is another example. To find the best route to drive between two distant cities, you do not want extraneous information on the location of all roads, streets, potholes, telephone lines, trees, stoplights, schools, hospitals, and firehouses. This would be too much detail, and the complexity would make it difficult to choose the best route.

A map is a model because it is an abstraction from reality.

To be useful, a model requires simplified assumptions. Someone must decide, for example, whether a map will include only symbols for the major highways or the details of hiking trails through mountains. In our gasoline consumption example, several variables might be related to the quantity of gasoline consumed, including the price of gasoline, consumer incomes, the fuel economy of cars, and weather conditions. Because a theory focuses only on the main or critical variables, the economist must be a "Sherlock Holmes" and use a keen sense of observation to form a model. Using his or her expertise, the economist must select the variables that are related to gasoline consumption and reject variables that have only a slight or no relationship to gasoline consumption. In this simple case, the economist removes the cloud of complexity by formulating a theory, which states that increases in the price of gasoline *cause* the quantity of gasoline consumed to decrease during the time period.

1-4c Testing a Theory

An economic model can be stated as a verbal argument, numerical table, graph, or mathematical equation. You will soon discover that a major part of this book is devoted to building and using economic models. The purpose of an economic model is to *forecast* or *predict* the results of various changes in variables. Note that the appendix to this chapter provides a review of graphical analysis. An economic theory can be expressed in the form "If *X*, then *Y*, all other things held constant." An economic model is useful only if it yields accurate predictions. When the evidence is consistent with the theory that *X* causes outcome *Y*, there is confidence in the theory's validity. When the evidence is inconsistent with the theory that *X* causes outcome *Y*, the researcher rejects this theory.

In this third step, the economist gathers data to test the theory that if the price of gasoline *rises*, then gasoline purchases *fall*—all other relevant factors held constant. Suppose the investigation reveals that the price of gasoline rose sharply between May and December of the given year. The data, therefore, appear to support the theory that the quantity of gasoline consumed per month falls when its price rises, assuming no other relevant factors change. Thus, the conclusion is that the theory is valid if, for example, consumer incomes or the fuel economy of cars does not change at the same time that gasoline prices rise.

CHECKPOINT

Can You Prove There Is No Trillion-Dollar Person?
Suppose a theory says that no U.S. citizen is worth $1 trillion. You decide to test this theory and send researchers to all corners of the nation to check financial records to see whether someone qualifies by owning assets valued at $1 trillion or more. After years of checking, the researchers return and report that not a single person is worth at least $1 trillion. Do you conclude that the evidence proves the theory? Explain.

1-5 HAZARDS OF THE ECONOMIC WAY OF THINKING

Models help us understand and predict the impact of changes in economic variables. A model is an important tool in the economist's toolkit, but it must be handled with care. The economic way of thinking seeks to avoid reasoning mistakes. Two of the most common pitfalls to clear thinking are

1. failing to understand the *ceteris paribus assumption.*
2. confusing *association* and *causation.*

1-5a The Ceteris Paribus Assumption

As you work through a model, try to think of a host of relevant variables assumed to be "standing still," or "held constant." **Ceteris paribus** is a Latin phrase that means while certain variables change, "all other things remain unchanged." In short, the ceteris paribus assumption allows us to isolate or focus attention on selected variables. In the gasoline example discussed earlier, a key simplifying assumption of the model is that changes in consumer incomes and certain other variables do not occur and complicate the analysis. The ceteris paribus assumption holds everything else constant and therefore allows us to concentrate on the relationship between two key variables: changes in the price of gasoline and the quantity of gasoline purchased per month.

Ceteris paribus
A Latin phrase that means while certain variables change, "all other things remain unchanged."

Now suppose an economist examines a model explaining the relationship between the price and quantity purchased of Coca-Cola. The theory is "If the price increases, then the quantity of Coca-Cola purchased decreases, ceteris paribus." Now assume you observe that the price of Coca-Cola increased one summer and some people actually bought more, not less. Based on this real-world observation, you might declare that the theory is incorrect. Think again! Perhaps the reason the model appeared flawed is because another factor—for example a sharp rise in the temperature—*caused* people to buy more Coca-Cola in spite of its higher price. However, if the temperature and all other factors were held constant, and the ceteris paribus assumption is satisfied, we would find that as the price of Coca-Cola rises, people will indeed buy less Coca-Cola, as the model predicts.

A theory cannot be tested legitimately unless its ceteris paribus assumption is satisfied.

CONCLUSION

1-5b Association versus Causation

Another common error in reasoning is confusing *association* (or correlation) and *causation* between variables. Stated differently, you err when you read more into a relationship between variables than is actually there. A model is valid only when a cause-and-effect relationship is stable or dependable over time, rather than being an association that occurs by chance and eventually disappears. Suppose a witch doctor performs a voodoo dance during three different months and stock market prices skyrocket during each of these months. The voodoo dance is *associated* with the increase in stock prices, but this does not mean the dance *caused* the event. Even though there is a statistical relationship between these two variables in a number of observations, eventually the voodoo dance will be performed, and stock prices will fall or remain unchanged. The reason is that there is no true systematic economic relationship between voodoo dances and stock prices.

Further investigation may reveal that stock prices actually responded to changes in interest rates during the months that the voodoo dances were performed. Changes in interest rates affect borrowing and spending, which in turn impacts corporate profits and stock prices. In contrast, there is no real economic relationship between voodoo dances and stock prices, and therefore, the voodoo model is not valid.

CONCLUSION   The fact that one event follows another does not necessarily mean that the first event caused the second event.

CHECKPOINT

Should Nebraska State Join a Big-Time Athletic Conference?
Nebraska State (a mythical university) stood by while Penn State, Florida State, the University of Miami, and the University of South Carolina joined big-time athletic conferences. Now Nebraska State officials are pondering whether to remain independent or to pursue membership in a conference noted for high-quality football and basketball programs. An editorial in the newspaper advocates joining and cites a study showing that universities belonging to major athletic conferences have higher graduation rates than nonmembers. Because educating its students is the number one goal of Nebraska State, will this evidence persuade Nebraska State officials to join a big-time conference? Why or why not?

Throughout this book, you will study economic models or theories that include variables linked by stable cause-and-effect relationships. For example, the theory that a change in the price of a good *causes* a change in the quantity purchased is a valid microeconomic model. The theory that a change in the money supply *causes* a change in interest rates is an example of a valid macroeconomic model. The You're the Economist gives some amusing examples of the "association means causation" reasoning pitfall.

1-6 WHY DO ECONOMISTS DISAGREE?

Why might one economist say a clean environment should be our most important priority and another economist say economic growth should be our most important goal? If economists share the economic way of thinking and carefully avoid reasoning pitfalls, then why do they disagree? Why are economists known for giving advice by saying, "On the one hand, if you do this, then *A* results, and, on the other hand, doing this causes result *B*?" In fact, President Harry Truman once jokingly exclaimed, "Find me an economist with only one hand." George Bernard Shaw offered another famous line in the same vein: "If you took all the economists in the world and laid them end to end, they would never reach a conclusion." These famous quotes imply that economists should agree, but the quotes ignore the fact that physicists, doctors, business executives, lawyers, and other professionals often disagree as well.

Economists may appear to disagree more than other professionals partly because it is more interesting to report disagreements than agreements. Actually, economists agree

YOU'RE THE ECONOMIST

Applicable Concept: Association versus Causation

Mops and Brooms, the Boston Snow Index, the Super Bowl, and Other Economic Indicators

Although the Commerce Department, the Wharton School, the Federal Reserve Board, and other organizations publish economic forecasts and data on key economic indicators, they are not without armchair competition. For example, the chief executive of Standex International Corporation, Daniel E. Hogan, reported that his company can predict economic downturns and recoveries from sales reports of its National Metal Industries subsidiary in Springfield, Massachusetts. National makes metal parts for about 300 U.S. manufacturers of mops and brooms. A drop in National's sales always precedes a proportional fall in consumer spending. The company's sales always pick up slightly before consumer spending does.[1]

The Boston Snow Index (BSI) is the brainchild of a vice president of a New York securities firm. It predicts a rising economy for the next year if there is snow on the ground in Boston on Christmas Day. The BSI predicted correctly about 73 percent of the time over a 30-year period. However, its creator, David L. Upshaw, did not take it too seriously and views it as a spoof of other forecasters' methods.

Greeting card sales are another tried and true indicator, according to a vice president of American Greetings. Before a recession sets in, sales of higher-priced greeting cards rise. It seems that people substitute the cards for gifts, and since there is no gift, the card must be fancier.

A Super Bowl win by a National Football Conference (NFC) team predicts that in the following December the stock market will be higher than the year before. A win by an old American Football League (AFL) team predicts a dip in the stock market.

Several other less well-known indicators have also been proposed. For example, one economist suggested that the surliness of servers is a countercyclical indicator. If they are nice, expect that bad times are coming, but if they are rude, expect an upturn. Servers on the other hand, counter that a fall in the average tip usually precedes a downturn in the economy.

Finally, Anthony Chan, chief economist for Bank One Investment Advisors, studied marriage trends over a 34-year period. He discovered that when the number of marriages increases, the economy rises significantly, and a slowdown in marriages is followed by a decline in the economy. Chan explains that there is usually about a one-year lag between a change in the marriage rate and the economy.[2]

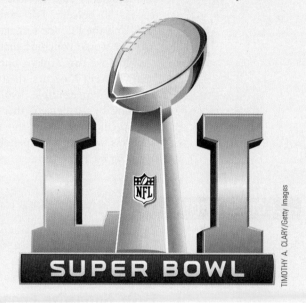

TIMOTHY A. CLARY/Getty Images

ANALYZE THE ISSUE

Which of the above indicators are examples of causation? Explain.

---

1. "Economic Indicators, Turtles, Butterflies, Monks, and Waiters," *The Wall Street Journal*, August 27, 1979, pp. 1, 16.
2. Sandra Block, "Worried? Look at Wedding Bell Indicator," *The Charlotte Observer*, April 15, 1995, p. 8A.

on a wide range of issues. Many economists, for example, agree that the benefits from free trade outweigh the costs, that a market-driven healthcare delivery system has many flaws, and that government deficit spending (which adds to the national debt) can be a good thing if we want to recover more quickly from a recession. When disagreements do exist, the reason can often be explained by the difference between *positive economics* and *normative economics*.

1-6a Positive Economics

Positive economics deals with facts and therefore addresses "what is" true or false about how the economy really works. **Positive economics** is an analysis limited to statements that are verifiable. Positive statements can be proven either true or false. Often a positive statement is expressed: "If *X*, then *Y*." For example, if the national unemployment rate rises to 9 percent, then teenage unemployment exceeds 80 percent. This is a positive "if-then" prediction, which may or may not be correct. Accuracy is not the criterion for a statement to be positive. The key consideration is whether the statement is *testable* and not whether it is true or false. Suppose the data show that when the nation's overall unemployment rate is close to 9 percent, the unemployment rate for teenagers never reaches 80 percent. For example, the overall unemployment rate was 9.6 percent in 2010, and the rate for teenagers was 25.9 percent—far short of 80 percent. Based on the facts, we would conclude that this positive statement is false.

Now we can explain one reason why economists' forecasts can diverge. The statement "If event *X* occurs, then event *Y* follows" can be thought of as a *conditional* positive statement. For example, two economists may agree that if the federal government cuts spending by 10 percent this year, prices will fall about 2 percent next year. However, their predictions about the fall in prices may differ because one economist assumes Congress will not cut spending, while the other economist assumes Congress will cut spending by 10 percent.

Positive economics
An analysis limited to statements that are verifiable.

CONCLUSION

Economists' forecasts can differ because using the same methodology; economists can agree that event *X* causes event *Y*, but disagree over the assumption that event *X* will occur.

1-6b Normative Economics

Instead of using objective statements, an argument can be phrased subjectively. Normative economics attempts to determine "what should be." **Normative economics** is an analysis based on subjective value judgments. Normative statements express an individual or collective opinion on a subject and cannot be proven by facts to be true or false. Certain words or phrases, such as *good*, *bad*, *need*, *should*, and *ought to*, tell us clearly that we have entered the realm of normative economics.

The point here is that these subjective value judgments are the result of ever-present social and political influences that shape our opinions. An animal rights activist says that no one *should* purchase a fur coat. Someone else may argue that government *ought to* take steps to ensure a more *fair* distribution of income and wealth. Others argue that health care is a basic human right that *needs* to be made available to all regardless of their ability to pay.

Normative economics
An analysis based on subjective value judgments.

CONCLUSION

When opinions or points of view are not based on facts, they are scientifically untestable.

YOU'RE THE ECONOMIST

Applicable Concepts: Positive and Normative Analyses

Does the Minimum Wage Really Help the Working Poor?

Minimum wages exist in more than 100 countries. In 1938, Congress enacted the federal Fair Labor Standards Act, commonly known as the "minimum-wage law." Today, a minimum wage worker who works full-time still earns a deplorably low annual income. One approach to help the working poor earn a living wage might be to raise the minimum wage.

The dilemma for Congress is that a higher minimum wage for the employed is enacted at the expense of jobs for unskilled workers. Opponents forecast that the increased labor cost from a large minimum wage hike would jeopardize hundreds of thousands of unskilled jobs. For example, employers may opt to purchase more capital and less expensive labor. Restaurants can use iPads instead of servers to take orders and install robotic burger flippers. The fear of such sizable job losses forces Congress to perform a difficult balancing act to ensure that a minimum wage increase is large enough to help the working poor, but not so large as to threaten their jobs.

Some politicians claim that raising the minimum wage is a way to help the working poor without cost to taxpayers. Others believe the cost is hidden in inflation and lost employment opportunities for marginal workers, such as teenagers, the elderly, and minorities. One study by economists, for example, examined 60 years of data and concluded that minimum wage increases resulted in reduced employment and hours of work for low-skilled workers.[1]

Another problem with raising the minimum wage to aid the working poor is that the minimum wage is a blunt weapon for redistributing wealth. Some studies show that only a small percentage of minimum wage earners are full-time workers whose family income falls below the poverty line. This means that most increases in the minimum wage go to workers who are not poor. For example, many minimum wage workers are students living at home or workers whose spouse earns a much higher income. To help only the working poor, some economists argue that the government should target only those who need assistance, rather than using the "shotgun" approach of raising the minimum wage.

Supporters of raising the minimum wage are not convinced by these arguments. They say it just isn't right that a worker who works full-time should live in poverty. They point to the fact that the minimum wage has not kept pace with the typical worker's wage or with the cost of living. As a result, a growing underclass has to rely on some form of public assistance, like food stamps. And this, they argue, only adds to income inequality as taxpayers end up subsidizing profitable companies who don't pay their workers a living wage.

Tony Stock/Shutterstock.com

Moreover, people on this side of the debate believe that opponents exaggerate many of their claims, especially the extent to which unemployment and higher prices result from a higher minimum wage. They provide evidence that the benefits from a higher minimum wage may more than offset these costs.[2] For example, when earning a higher wage, workers will spend more money, generating a need for companies to expand production and to hire even more workers. In addition, the gain from these higher incomes far exceed the cost of higher prices, leaving workers better off. To proponents, increasing the minimum wage is a win-win proposition. We return to this issue in Chapter 4 as an application of supply and demand analysis.

ANALYZE THE ISSUE

1. Identify two positive and two normative statements given above concerning raising the minimum wage. List other minimum wage arguments not discussed in this You're the Economist and classify them as either positive or normative economics.

2. Give a positive and a normative argument why a business leader would oppose raising the minimum wage. Give a positive and a normative argument why a labor leader would favor raising the minimum wage.

3. Explain your position on this issue. Identify positive and normative reasons for your decision. Are there alternative ways to aid the working poor? Explain.

---

1. David Neumark and William Wascher, *Minimum Wages*, Cambridge, MA, The MIT Press, 2008.
2. Economic Policy Institute, "The impact of raising the federal minimum wage to $12 by 2020 on workers, businesses, and the economy." Testimony before the U.S. House Committee on Education and the Workforce Member Forum. April 27, 2016, found at http://www.epi.org/publication/the-impact-of-raising-the-federal-minimum-wage-to-12-by-2020-on-workers-businesses-and-the-economy-testimony-before-the-u-s-house-committee-on-education-and-the-workforce-member-forum/.

When considering a debate, make sure to separate the arguments into their positive and normative components. This distinction allows you to determine whether you are choosing a course of action based on factual evidence or on opinion. The material presented in this textbook, like most of economics, takes pains to stay within the boundaries of positive economic analysis. In our everyday lives, however, politicians, business executives, relatives, and friends use mostly normative statements to discuss economic issues. Economists may also associate themselves with a political position and use normative arguments for or against some economic policy. When using value judgments, an economist's normative arguments may have no greater validity than those of other people. Biases or preconceptions can cloud an economist's thinking about deficit spending or whether to increase taxes on gasoline. Like beginning economics students, economists are human.

1-7 CAREERS IN ECONOMICS

The author of this text entered college more years ago than I would like to admit. In those days, economics was not taught in high school, so I knew nothing of the subject. Like many students taking this course, I was uncertain about which major to pursue, but selected electrical engineering because I was an amateur radio operator and enjoyed building radio receivers and transmitters. My engineering curriculum required a course in economics. I signed up thinking that "econ is boring." Instead, it was an eye-opening experience that inspired me to change my major to economics and pursue an economics teaching career.

The study of economics has attracted a number of well-known people. For example, The Rolling Stones' Mick Jagger attended the London School of Economics, and other famous people who majored in economics include four presidents—George H. W. Bush, Ronald Reagan, Gerald Ford, and Donald Trump.

An economics major can choose many career paths. Most economics majors work for business firms. Because economists are trained in analyzing financial matters, they find good jobs in management, sales, or as a market analyst interpreting economic conditions relevant to a firm's market. For those with an undergraduate degree, private-sector job opportunities exist in banking, securities brokering, management consulting, computer and data processing firms, the power industry, market research, finance, health care, and many other industries. Other economics majors work for government agencies and in colleges and universities.

Government economists work for federal, state, and local governments. For example, a government economist might compile and report national statistics for economic growth or work on projects such as how to improve indexes to measure trends in consumer prices. Economists in academe not only enjoy the challenge of teaching economics but also have great freedom in selecting research projects.

Studying economics is also an essential preparation for other careers. Those preparing for law school, for example, find economics an excellent major because of its emphasis on a logical approach to problem solving. Economics is also great preparation for an MBA. In fact, students majoring in any field will benefit throughout their lives from learning how to apply the economic way of thinking to analyze real-world economic issues.

Finally, economics majors shine in salary offers upon graduation. Exhibit 3 shows average yearly salaries for some bachelor's degrees with 0–5 years of experience for 2016–2017.

EXHIBIT 3 Average Yearly Salary for Selected Bachelor Majors with 0–5 Years of Experience

Bachelor's major	Median salary with 0–5 years of experience, 2016–2017
Petroleum engineering	96,700
Nuclear engineering	68,500
Computer science	65,300
Nursing	57,500
Economics	53,900
Finance	53,300
International business	48,800
Accounting	48,300
Business administration	46,100
Chemistry	45,700
Marketing	45,300
Philosophy	44,700
Communications	42,100
Human resources	41,900
Journalism	41,200
Biology	40,800
Sociology	40,400
Psychology	37,800
Criminal justice	37,000
Animal science	35,800
Early childhood education	30,700

SOURCE: www.payScale.com/college-salary-report.

Key Concepts

Scarcity	Entrepreneurship	Macroeconomics	Ceteris paribus
Resources	Capital	Microeconomics	Positive economics
Land	Economics	Model	Normative economics
Labor			

Summary

- **Scarcity** is the fundamental economic problem that human wants exceed the availability of time, goods, and resources. Individuals and society therefore can never have everything they desire.

- **Resources** are factors of production classified as land, labor, and capital. Entrepreneurship is a special type of labor. An entrepreneur seeks profits by taking risks and combining resources to produce innovative products.

- **Economics** is the study of how individuals and society choose to allocate scarce resources to satisfy unlimited wants. Faced with unlimited wants and scarce resources, we must make choices among alternatives.

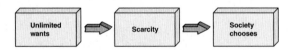

- **Macroeconomics** applies an economy-wide perspective that focuses on such issues as inflation, unemployment, and the growth rate of the economy.

- **Microeconomics** examines individual decision-making units within an economy, such as a consumer's response to changes in the price of coffee and the reasons for changes in the market price of personal computers.

- **Models** are simplified descriptions of reality used to understand and predict economic events. An economic model can be stated verbally or in a table, a graph, or an equation. If the event is not consistent with the model, the model is rejected.

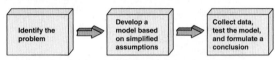

- **Ceteris paribus** holds "all other factors unchanged" that might affect a particular relationship. If this assumption is violated, a model cannot be tested. Another reasoning pitfall is to think that *association* means *causation.*

- Use of positive versus normative economic analysis is a major reason for disagreements among economists. **Positive economics** uses testable statements. Often a positive argument is expressed as an *if-then* statement. **Normative economics** is based on value judgments or opinions and uses words such as *good, bad, ought to,* and *should.*

Summary of Conclusion Statements

- The problems of scarcity and choice are basic economic problems faced by every society.

- Money by itself does not produce goods and services; instead, it is only a means to facilitate the purchase and sale of resources and consumer products.

- A theory cannot be tested legitimately unless its ceteris paribus assumption is satisfied.

- The fact that one event follows another does not necessarily mean that the first event caused the second event.

- Economists' forecasts can differ because using the same methodology, economists can agree that event X causes event Y, but disagree over the assumption that event X will occur.

- When opinions or points of view are not based on facts, they are scientifically untestable.

Study Questions and Problems

Please see Appendix A for answers to the odd-numbered questions. Your instructor has access to the answers for even-numbered questions.

1. Explain why both nations with high living standards and nations with low living standards face the problem of scarcity. If you won $1 million in a lottery, would you escape the scarcity problem?

2. Why isn't money considered capital in economics?

3. Explain the difference between macroeconomics and microeconomics. Give examples of the areas of concern to each branch of economics.

4. Which of the following are microeconomic issues? Which are macroeconomic issues?
   a. How will an increase in the price of Coca-Cola affect the quantity of Pepsi Cola sold?
   b. What will cause the nation's inflation rate to fall?
   c. How does a quota on textile imports affect the textile industry?
   d. Does a large federal budget deficit reduce the rate of unemployment in the economy?

5. Explain why it is important for an economic model to be an abstraction from the real world.

6. Explain the importance of the ceteris paribus assumption for an economic model.

7. Suppose Congress cuts spending for the military, and then unemployment rises in the U.S. defense industry. Is there causation in this situation, or are we observing an association between events?

8. Analyze the positive versus normative arguments in the following case. What statements of positive economics are used to support requiring air bags? What normative reasoning is used?

Should the Government Require Air Bags?
Technological advances continuously provide new high-tech options to save lives that add to the price of cars, such as cameras, radar, and airbags. Air bag advocates say air bags will save lives and the government should require them in all cars. Air bags add an estimated $600 to the cost of a car, compared to about $100 for a set of regular seat belts. Opponents argue that air bags are electronic devices subject to failure and have produced injuries and death. For example, air bags have killed both adults and children whose heads were within the inflation zone at the time of deployment. Opponents therefore believe the government should leave the decision of whether to spend an extra $600 or so for an air bag to the consumer. The role of the government should be limited to providing information on the risks of having versus not having air bags.

 CHECKPOINT ANSWERS

Can You Prove There Is No Trillion-Dollar Person?

How can researchers ever be certain they have found all the rich people in the United States? There is always the possibility that somewhere there is a person who qualifies. If the researchers had found one, you could have rejected the theory. Because they did not, you cannot reject the theory. If you said that the evidence can support but never prove the theory, **YOU ARE CORRECT**.

Should Nebraska State Join a Big-Time Athletic Conference?

Suppose universities that belong to big-time athletic conferences do indeed have higher graduation rates than nonmembers. This is not the only possible explanation for the statistical correlation (or association) between the graduation rate and membership in a big-time athletic conference. A more plausible explanation is that improving academic variables, such as tuition, quality of faculty, and student-faculty ratios, and not athletic conference membership, increase the graduation rate. If you said correlation, does not mean causation, and therefore Nebraska State officials will not necessarily accept the graduation rate evidence, **YOU ARE CORRECT**.

Sample Quiz

Please see Appendix B for answers to Sample Quiz questions.

1. Which of the following illustrates the concept of scarcity?
   a. More clean air is wanted than is available in large polluted metropolitan areas such as Mexico City.
   b. There is usually more than one use of your "free" time in the evening.
   c. There are many competing uses for the annual budget of your city, county, or state.
   d. All of the above are correct.

2. Which of the following are factors of production?
   a. The outputs generated by the production process transforming land, labor, and capital into goods and services
   b. Resources restricted to the land, such as natural resources that are unimproved by human economic activity
   c. Land (natural resources), labor (human capital, entrepreneurship), and capital (constructed inputs such as factories)
   d. Just labor and capital in industrialized countries, where natural resources are no longer used to produce goods and services

3. Which of the following is *not* an example of a capital input?
   a. A person's skills and abilities, which can be employed to produce valuable goods and services
   b. Factories and offices where goods and services are produced
   c. Tools and equipment
   d. Computers used by a company to record inventory, sales, and payroll

4. Which of the following is the best definition of economics?
   a. Economics is the study of how to manage corporations to generate the greatest return on shareholder investment.
   b. Economics is the study of how to manage city and county government to generate the greatest good to its citizens.

   c. Economics is the study of how society chooses to allocate its scarce resources.
   d. Economics is the study of how to track revenues and costs in a business.

5. Which of the following *best* illustrates the application of the model-building process to economics?
   a. On a Sunday morning talk show, two economists with differing political agendas argue about the best way to solve the Social Security problem.
   b. A labor economist notices that unemployment tends to be higher among teenagers than more experienced workers, develops a model, and gathers data to test the hypotheses in the model.
   c. A Ph.D. student in economics makes up data on the lumber market and develops a model for his dissertation that seems to be consistent with the data.
   d. Economists come to believe that some economic models are true simply because prominent leading economists say they are true.

6. Which of the following represents causality rather than association?
   a. In years that fashion dictates wider lapels on men's jackets, the stock market grows by at least 5 percent.
   b. Interest rates are higher in years ending with a 1 or a 6.
   c. Unemployment falls when the AFC champion wins the Super Bowl.
   d. Quantity demanded goes up when price falls because lower prices increase consumer purchasing power and because some consumers of substitute goods switch.

7. Which of the following describes the ceteris paribus assumption?
   a. If we increase the price of a good, reduce consumer income, and lower the price of substitutes and if quantity demanded is

observed to fall, we know that the price increase caused the decline in quantity demanded.

b. If the federal government increases government spending and the Federal Reserve Bank lowers interest rates, we know that the increase in government spending caused unemployment to fall.

c. If a company reduces its labor costs, negotiates lower materials costs from its vendors, and advertises, we know that the reduced labor costs are why the company's profits are higher.

d. If we decrease the price of a good and observe that there is an increase in the quantity demanded, holding all other factors that influence this relationship constant.

8. The condition of scarcity
   a. cannot be eliminated.
   b. prevails in poor economies.
   c. prevails in rich economies.
   d. all of the above are correct.

9. Which of the following *best* describes an entrepreneur?
   a. A person who works as an office clerk at a major corporation
   b. A person who combines the factors of production to produce innovative products
   c. A special type of capital
   d. Wealthy individuals who provide savings that stimulates the economy

10. Which of the following is *true* about renewable natural resources?
    a. They are a type of land resource (for example, oil, coal, and natural gas) that has a fixed stock.
    b. They are a type of capital resource (for example, irrigation networks and wastewater treatment plants) that utilize water.
    c. They are a type of capital resource (for example, air filtration systems in buildings) that renew and refresh polluted air from the outside.
    d. They are a type of land resource (for example, forests, rangelands, and marine fisheries) that naturally regenerate and thus can tolerate a sustained harvest but can be depleted from excessive harvest.

11. Because of scarcity,
    a. it is impossible to satisfy every desire and choices must be made.
    b. the available supply of time, goods, and resources is greater than human wants.
    c. every desire is fulfilled.
    d. there are no limits on the economy's ability to satisfy unlimited wants.

12. Which of the following represents positive economics?
    a. Policy X is fair.
    b. Outcome Y is the best objective to achieve.
    c. If policy X is followed, then outcome Y results.
    d. All of the above are positive economic analyses.

13. Which of the following is the last step in the model-building process?
    a. Collect data and test the model.
    b. Develop a model based on simplified assumptions.
    c. Identify the problem.
    d. Formulate an assumption.

14. Which of the following is *not* a type of economic analysis?
    a. Positive
    b. Resources
    c. Normative
    d. None of the above

15. Which word indicates that an economist is using positive economics?
    a. Good
    b. Bad
    c. If-then
    d. Should

16. Which of the following would eliminate scarcity as an economic problem?
    a. Moderation of people's competitive instincts
    b. Discovery of new, sufficiently large energy reserves
    c. Resumption of steady productivity growth
    d. None of the above is correct

17. Which resource is *not* an example of capital?
    a. Equipment
    b. Machinery
    c. Physical plants
    d. Stocks and bonds

18. Which of the following is the second step in the model-building process?
    a. Collect data and test the model.
    b. Develop a model based on simplified assumptions.
    c. Identify the problem.
    d. Include all possible variables that affect the model.

19. Which of the following is a type of economic analysis?
    a. Positive
    b. Resources
    c. Association
    d. None of the above is correct.

20. Which of the following careers could result from majoring in economics?
    a. Management
    b. Banking
    c. Government
    d. All of the above is correct.

Applying Graphs to Economics

Economists are famous for their use of graphs. The reason is "a picture is worth a thousand words." Graphs are used throughout this text to present economics models. By drawing a line, you can use a two-dimensional illustration to analyze the effects of a change in one variable on another. You could describe the same information using other model forms, such as verbal statements, tables, or equations, but a graph is the simplest way to present and understand the relationship between economic variables.

Don't be worried that graphs will "throw you for a loop." Relax! This appendix explains all the basic graphical language you will need. The following illustrates the simplest use of graphs for economic analysis.

A-1 A DIRECT RELATIONSHIP

Basic economic analysis typically concerns the relationship between two variables, both having positive values. Hence, we can confine our graphs to the upper-right (northeast) quadrant of the coordinate number system. In Exhibit A-1, notice that the scales on the horizontal axis (*x*-axis) and the vertical axis (*y*-axis) do not necessarily measure the same numerical values.

The horizontal axis in Exhibit A-1 measures annual income, and the vertical axis shows the amount spent per year for a personal computer (PC). The intersection of the horizontal and vertical axes is the *origin* and the point at which both income and expenditure are zero. In Exhibit A-1, each point is a coordinate that matches the dollar value of income and the corresponding expenditure for a PC. For example, point *A* on the graph shows that people with an annual income of $10,000 spent $1,000 per year for a PC. Other incomes are associated with different expenditure levels. For example, at $30,000 per year (point *C*), $3,000 will be spent annually for a PC.

The straight line in Exhibit A-1 allows us to determine the direction of change in PC expenditure as annual income changes. This relationship is *positive* because PC expenditure, measured along the vertical axis, and annual income, measured along the horizontal axis, move in the same direction. PC expenditure increases as annual income increases. As income declines, so does the amount spent on a PC. Thus, the straight line representing the relationship between income and PC expenditure is a direct relationship. A **direct relationship** is a positive association between two variables. When one variable increases, the other variable increases, and when one variable decreases, the other variable decreases. In short, both variables change in the *same* direction.

Finally, an important point to remember: A two-variable graph, like any model, isolates the relationship between two variables and holds all other variables constant under the

Direct relationship
A positive association between two variables. When one variable increases, the other variable increases, and when one variable decreases, the other variable decreases.

EXHIBIT **A-1** Direct Relationship between Variables

The line with a positive slope shows that the expenditure per year for a personal computer has a direct relationship to annual income, ceteris paribus. As annual income increases along the horizontal axis, the amount spent on a PC also increases, as measured by the vertical axis. Along the line, each 10-unit increase in annual income results in a 1-unit increase in expenditure for a PC. Because the slope is constant along a straight line, we can measure the same slope between any two points. Between points *A* and *D*, the slope $= \Delta Y/\Delta X = +3/+30 = +1/+10 = 1/10$.

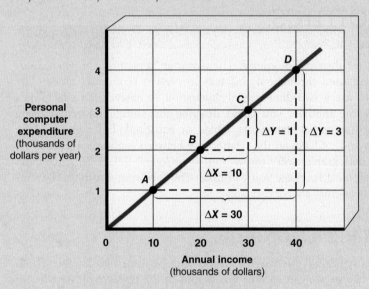

Expenditure for a Personal Computer at Different Annual Incomes		
Point	**Personal computer expenditure** (thousands of dollars per year)	**Annual income** (thousands of dollars)
A	$1	$10
B	2	20
C	3	30
D	4	40

ceteris paribus assumption. In Exhibit A-1, for example, factors such as the prices of PCs and education are held constant by assumption. In Chapter 3, you will learn that allowing variables not shown in the graph to change can shift the position of the line or curve.

A-2 AN INVERSE RELATIONSHIP

Now consider the relationship between the price of compact discs (CDs) and the quantity consumers will buy per year, shown in Exhibit A-2. These data indicate an *inverse* (or *negative*) relationship between the price and quantity variables. When the price is low, consumers purchase a greater quantity of CDs than when the price is high.

In Exhibit A-2, there is an inverse relationship between the price per CD and the quantity consumers buy. An **inverse relationship** is a negative association between two variables. When one variable increases, the other variable decreases, and when one variable decreases, the other variable increases. Stated simply, the variables move in *opposite* directions.

The line drawn in Exhibit A-2 is an inverse relationship. By long-established tradition, economists put price on the vertical axis and quantity on the horizontal axis. In Chapter 3, we will study in more detail the relationship between the price and the quantity demanded called the *law of demand*.

Inverse relationship
A negative association between two variables. When one variable increases, the other variable decreases, and when one variable decreases, the other variable increases.

EXHIBIT A-2 An Inverse Relationship between Variables

The line with a negative slope shows an inverse relationship between the price per compact disc and the quantity of CDs consumers purchase, ceteris paribus. As the price of a CD rises, the quantity of CDs purchased falls. A lower price for CDs is associated with more CDs purchased by consumers. Along the line, with each $5 decrease in the price of CDs, consumers increase the quantity purchased by 25 units. The slope $= \Delta Y / \Delta X = -5/+25 = -1/5$.

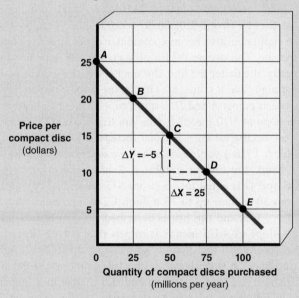

The Quantity of Compact Discs Consumers Purchase at Different Prices

Point	Price per compact disc	Quantity of compact discs purchased (millions per year)
A	$25	0
B	20	25
C	15	50
D	10	75
E	5	100

In addition to observing the inverse relationship (negative slope), you must interpret the *intercept* at point *A* in the exhibit. The intercept in this case means that at a price of $25 no consumer is willing to buy a single CD.

A-3 THE SLOPE OF A STRAIGHT LINE

Slope
The ratio of the change in the variable on the vertical axis (the rise or fall) to the change in the variable on the horizontal axis (the run).

Plotting numbers provides a clear visual expression of the relationship between two variables, but it is also important to know how much one variable changes as another variable changes. To find out, we calculate the slope. The **slope** is the ratio of the change in the variable on the vertical axis (the rise or fall) to the change in the variable on the horizontal axis (the run). Algebraically, if *Y* is on the vertical axis and *X* is on the horizontal axis, the slope is expressed as follows (the delta symbol, Δ, means "change in"):

$$\textbf{Slope} = \frac{\textbf{rise}}{\textbf{run}} = \frac{\textbf{change in vertical axis}}{\textbf{change in horizontal axis}} = \frac{\Delta Y}{\Delta X}$$

Consider the slope between points *B* and *C* in Exhibit A-1. The change in expenditure for a PC, *Y*, is equal to +1 (from $2,000 to $3,000 per year), and the change in annual income, *X*, is equal to +10 (from $20,000 to $30,000 per year). The slope is therefore +1/+10 = 0.10. The sign is positive because computer expenditure is directly, or positively, related to annual income. The steeper the line, the greater the slope because the ratio of ΔY to ΔX rises. Conversely, the flatter the line, the smaller the slope. Exhibit A-1 also illustrates that the slope of a straight line is constant. That is, the slope between any two points along the line, such as between points *A* and *D*, is equal to +3/ + 30 = 1/10 = 0.10

What does the slope of 1/10 mean? It tells you that a $1,000 increase (decrease) in PC expenditure each year occurs for each $10,000 increase (decrease) in annual income. The line plotted in Exhibit A-1 has a *positive slope,* and we describe the line as "upward-sloping."

On the other hand, the line in Exhibit A-2 has a *negative slope*. The change in *Y* between points *C* and *D* is equal to −5 (from $15 down to $10), and the change in *X* is equal to +25 (from 50 million up to 75 million CDs purchased per year). The slope is therefore −5/ + 25 = −1/5, and this line is described as "downward-sloping."

What does this slope of −1/5 mean? It means that raising (lowering) the price per CD by $1 decreases (increases) the quantity of CDs purchased by 5 million per year.

Suppose we calculate the slope between any two points on a flat line—for example, points *B* and *C* in Exhibit A-3. In this case, there is no change in *Y* (expenditure for toothpaste) as *X* (annual income) increases. Consumers spend $20 per year on toothpaste regardless of annual income. It follows that $\Delta Y = 0$ for any ΔX, so the slope is equal to 0. The two variables along a flat line (horizontal or vertical) have an independent relationship. An **independent relationship** is a zero association between two variables. When one variable changes, the other variable remains unchanged.

Independent relationship
A zero association between two variables. When one variable changes, the other variable remains unchanged.

A-4 A THREE-VARIABLE RELATIONSHIP IN ONE GRAPH

The two-variable relationships drawn so far conform to a two-dimensional flat piece of paper. For example, the vertical axis measures the price per CD variable, and the horizontal axis measures the quantity of CDs purchased variable. All other factors, such as

EXHIBIT **A-3** An Independent Relationship between Variables

The flat line with a zero slope shows that the expenditure per year for toothpaste is unrelated to annual income. As annual income increases along the horizontal axis, the amount spent each year for toothpaste remains unchanged at 20 units. If annual income increases 10 units, the corresponding change in expenditure is zero. The Slope $= \Delta Y / \Delta X = 0/ + 10 = 0$

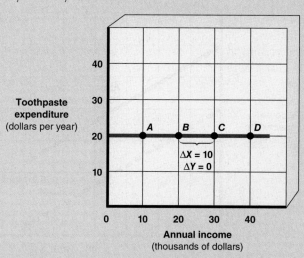

Expenditure for Toothpaste at Different Annual Incomes

Point	Toothpaste expenditure (dollars per year)	Annual income (thousands of dollars)
A	$20	$10
B	20	20
C	20	30
D	20	40

consumer income, that may affect the relationship between the price and quantity variables are held constant by the ceteris paribus assumption. But reality is frequently not so accommodating. Often a model must take into account the impact of changes in a third variable (consumer income) drawn on a two-dimensional piece of paper.

Economists' favorite method of depicting a three-variable relationship is shown in Exhibit A-4. As explained earlier, the cause-and-effect relationship between price and quantity of CDs determines the downward-sloping curve. A change in the price per CD causes a movement downward along either of the two separate curves. As the price falls, consumers increase the quantity of CDs demanded. The location of each curve on the graph, however, depends on the annual income of consumers. As the annual income variable increases from $30,000 to $60,000 and consumers can afford to purchase more at any price, or pay more at any quantity, the price–quantity demanded curve shifts rightward. Conversely, as the annual income variable decreases and consumers have less to spend, the price–quantity demanded curve shifts leftward.

EXHIBIT A-4 Changes in Price, Quantity, and Income in Two Dimensions

Economists use a multicurve graph to represent a three-variable relationship in a two-dimensional graph. A decrease in the price per CD causes a movement downward along each curve. As the annual income of consumers rises, there is a shift rightward in the position of the demand curve.

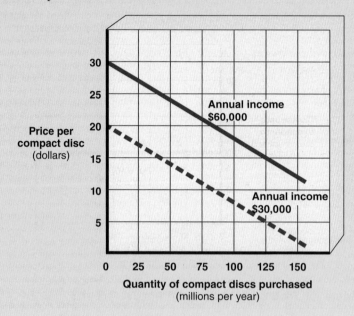

This is an extremely important concept that you must understand: Throughout this text, you must distinguish between *movements along* and *shifts in* a curve. Here's how to tell the difference. A change in one of the variables shown on either of the coordinate axes of the graph causes *movement along* a curve. On the other hand, a change in a variable not shown on one of the coordinate axes of the graph causes a *shift* in a curve's position on the graph.

CONCLUSION   A shift in a curve occurs only when the ceteris paribus assumption is relaxed and a third variable not shown on either axis of the graph is allowed to change.

A-5 A HELPFUL STUDY HINT FOR USING GRAPHS

To some students, studying economics is a little frightening because many chapters are full of graphs. Just remember that a graph is simply a visual aid that illustrates the relationship between economic variables. Noting these relationships is the ticket to understanding how the economy really works. So, keep in mind that all inverse (negative) relationships are expressed as downward sloping curves (or lines), and all direct (positive) relationships are expressed as upward sloping curves. This will help you to do well on tests!

Key Concepts

Direct relationship
Inverse relationship

Slope
Independent relationship

Summary

- **Graphs** provide a means to clearly show economic relationships in two-dimensional space. Economic analysis is often concerned with two variables confined to the upper-right (northeast) quadrant of the coordinate number system.

- A **direct relationship** occurs when two variables change in the *same* direction.

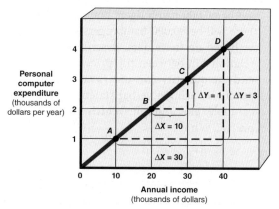

- An **inverse relationship** occurs when two variables change in *opposite* directions.

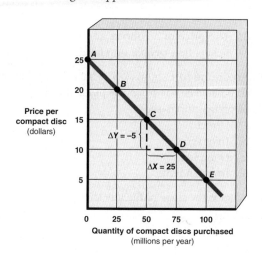

- An **independent relationship** occurs when two variables are unrelated.

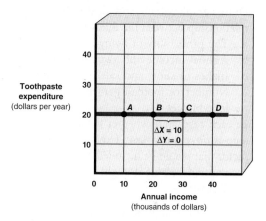

- A **three-variable relationship** is depicted by a graph showing a shift in a curve when the ceteris paribus assumption is relaxed and a third variable (such as annual income) not on either axis of the graph is allowed to change.

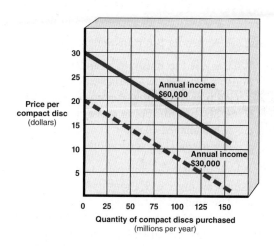

Summary of Conclusion Statement

- A shift in a curve occurs only when the ceteris paribus assumption is relaxed and a third vari-able not shown on either axis of the graph is allowed to change.

Study Questions and Problems

Please see Appendix A for answers to the odd-numbered questions. Your instructor has access to the answers for even-numbered questions.

1. Draw a graph without specific data for the expected relationship between the following variables:
   a. The probability of living and age
   b. Annual income and years of education
   c. Inches of snow and sales of bathing suits
   d. Number of football games won and the ath-letic budget

   In each case, state whether the expected relation-ship is *direct* or *inverse*. Explain an additional factor that would be included in the *ceteris paribus* assumption because it might change and influence your theory.

2. Assume a research firm collects survey sales data that reveal the relationship between the possible selling prices of hamburgers and the quantity of hamburgers consumers would purchase per year at alternative prices. The report states that if the price of a hamburger is $4, then 20,000 will be bought. However, at a price of $3, there will be 40,000 hamburgers bought. At $2, there will be 60,000 hamburgers bought, and at $1, there will be 80,000 hamburgers purchased.

   Based on these data, describe the relevant relationship between the price of a hamburger and the quantity consumers are willing to purchase, using a verbal statement, a numeri-cal table, and a graph. Which model do you prefer? Why?

Sample Quiz

Please see Appendix B for answers to Sample Quiz questions.

1. What is used to illustrate an independent rela-tionship between two variables?
   a. An upward-sloping curve
   b. A downward-sloping curve
   c. A hill-shaped curve
   d. A horizontal or vertical line

2. Which of the following pairs is *most* likely to exhibit an inverse relationship?
   a. The amount of time you study and your grade point average
   b. People's annual income and their expenditure on personal computers
   c. Baseball players' salaries and their batting averages

   d. The price of a concert and the number of tickets that people purchase

3. According to Exhibit A-5, what is the relation-ship between the price per pizza and the quantity of pizzas purchased?
   a. Direct
   b. Inverse
   c. Complex
   d. Independent

4. What is the slope of the line shown in Exhibit A-5?
   a. −1
   b. −1/2
   c. −1/4
   d. 0

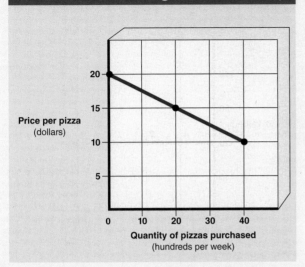

EXHIBIT A-5 Straight Line Relationship

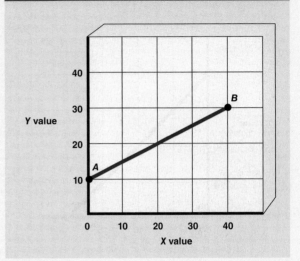

EXHIBIT A-6 Straight Line Relationship

5. Which of the following would cause a leftward shift in the relationship shown in Exhibit A-5?
   a. A fall in household incomes
   b. A fall in the price of pizza
   c. A fall in the quantity of pizza that people want to purchase
   d. All of the above would shift the line in the graph

6. Suppose two variables are directly related. If one variable rises, the other variable
   a. also rises.
   b. falls.
   c. remains unchanged.
   d. reacts unpredictably.

7. When an inverse relationship is graphed, the resulting line or curve is
   a. horizontal.
   b. vertical.
   c. upward-sloping.
   d. downward-sloping.

8. Straight line AB in Exhibit A-6 shows that
   a. increasing values for X decreases the values of Y.
   b. decreasing values for X increases the values of Y.

   c. there is a direct relationship between X and Y.
   d. all of the above are true.

9. In Exhibit A-6, what is the slope of straight line AB?
   a. Positive
   b. Zero
   c. Negative
   d. Variable

10. In Exhibit A-6, what is the slope of straight line AB?
   a. 1
   b. 5
   c. 1/2
   d. −1

11. As shown in Exhibit A-6, the slope of straight line AB
   a. decreases with increases in X.
   b. increases with increases in X.
   c. increases with decreases in X.
   d. remains constant with changes in X.

12. In Exhibit A-6, as X increases along the horizontal axis, the Y values increase. What is the relationship between the X and Y variables?
   a. Direct
   b. Inverse

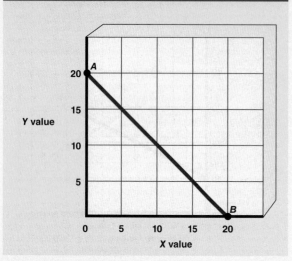

EXHIBIT **A-7** Straight Line Relationship

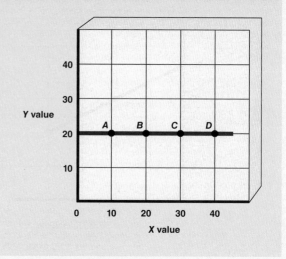

EXHIBIT **A-8** Straight Line Relationship

c. Independent
d. Variable

13. In Exhibit A-7, as *X* increases along the horizontal axis, the *Y* values decrease. What is the relationship between the *X* and *Y* variables?
   a. Direct
   b. Inverse
   c. Independent
   d. Variable

14. Straight line AB in Exhibit A-7 shows that
   a. increasing values for *X* reduces the value of *Y*.
   b. decreasing values for *X* increases the value of *Y*.
   c. there is an inverse relationship between *X* and *Y*.
   d. all of the above are true.

15. As shown in Exhibit A-7, the slope of straight line AB
   a. decreases with increases in *X*.
   b. increases with increases in *X*.
   c. increases with decreases in *X*.
   d. remains constant with changes in *X*.

16. In Exhibit A-7, what is the slope for straight line AB?
   a. 3
   b. 1

c. −1
d. −5

17. In Exhibit A-7, what is the slope of straight line AB?
   a. Positive
   b. Zero
   c. Negative
   d. Variable

18. In Exhibit A-8, as *X* increases along the horizontal axis, corresponding to points A–D on the line, the *Y* values remain unchanged at 20 units. What is the relationship between the *X* and *Y* variables?
   a. Direct
   b. Inverse
   c. Independent
   d. Undefined

19. In Exhibit A-8, what is the slope of straight line A–D?
   a. Greater than 1
   b. Equal to 1
   c. Less than 1
   d. Zero

20. Exhibit A-9 represents a three-variable relationship. As the annual income of consumers falls
from $50,000 (line A) to $30,000 (line B), the
result is a(n)
a. upward movement along each curve.
b. downward movement along each
curve.
c. leftward shift in curve A to curve B.
d. rightward shift in curve A to
curve B.

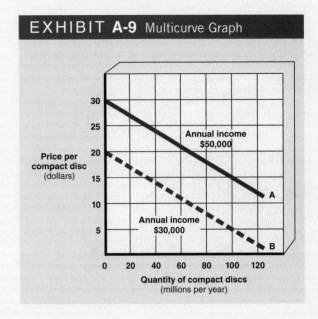

EXHIBIT **A-9** Multicurve Graph

CHAPTER 2

Production Possibilities, Opportunity Cost, and Economic Growth

CHAPTER PREVIEW

 This chapter continues building on the foundation laid in the preceding chapter. Having learned that *scarcity* forces *choices*, here you will study the choices people make in more detail. This chapter begins by examining the three basic choices: *What*, *How*, and *For Whom* to produce. The process of answering these basic questions introduces two other key building blocks in the economic way of thinking—*opportunity cost* and *marginal analysis*. Once you understand these important concepts stated in words, it will be easier to interpret our first formal economic model, the *production possibilities curve*. This model illustrates how economists use graphs as a powerful tool to supplement words and develop an understanding of basic economic principles. You will discover that the production possibilities model teaches many of the most important concepts in economics, including scarcity, the law of increasing opportunity costs, efficiency, investment, and economic growth. For example, this chapter applies the production possibilities curve to explain why developing countries find it difficult to achieve economic growth and thereby reach a higher standard of living for their people.

IN THIS CHAPTER, YOU WILL LEARN TO SOLVE THESE ECONOMICS PUZZLES:

- Why do so few rock stars and movie stars go to college?

- Why would you spend an extra hour reading this text rather than going to a movie or sleeping?

- Why are investment and economic growth so important?

- What does a war on terrorism really mean?

2-1 THREE FUNDAMENTAL ECONOMIC QUESTIONS

Because of the problem of scarcity, whether rich or poor, every nation must answer the same three fundamental economic questions:

1. *What* products will be produced?
2. *How* will they be produced? and
3. *For Whom* will they be produced?

Later, the chapter on economies in transition introduces various types of economic systems and describes how each deals with these three economic choices.

2-1a What to Produce?

The *What* question requires an economy to decide the mix and quantity of goods and services it will produce. Should society devote more of its limited resources to producing more health care and fewer military goods? Should society produce more iPods and fewer Blu-rays? Should more capital goods be produced instead of consumer goods, or should more small hybrid cars and fewer SUVs be produced? The problem of scarcity restricts our ability to produce everything we want during a given period, so the choice to produce "more" of one good requires producing "less" of another good. In the United States, consumer sovereignty answers the *What* question. In Cuba and North Korea, for example, the government and not the consumer answers this question.

2-1b How to Produce?

After deciding *what* products to make, the second question for society to decide is *how* to mix technology and scarce resources in order to produce these goods. For instance, a towel can be sewn primarily by hand (labor), partially by hand and partially by machine (labor and capital), or primarily by machine (capital). In short, the *How* question asks whether a production technique will be more or less capital-intensive. The *How* question also concerns choices among resources for production. Should electricity be produced from oil, solar power, or nuclear power?

Education plays an important role in answering the *How* question. Education improves the ability of workers to perform their work. Variation in the quality and quantity of education among nations is one reason economies differ in their capacities to apply resources and technology to answer the *How* question. For example, the United States is striving to catch up with Japan in the use of robotics. Answering the question *How do we improve our robotics*? requires engineers and employees with the proper training in the installation and operation of robots.

2-1c For Whom to Produce?

After the *What* and *How* questions are resolved, the third question is *For Whom*. Among all those desiring the produced goods, who actually receives them? This question concerns how the economic pie is divided. Who is fed well? Who drives a Mercedes? Who receives organ transplants? Should economics professors earn a salary of $1 million a year and others pay higher taxes to support economists? The *For Whom* question means that society must have a method to decide who will be "rich and famous" and who will be "poor and unknown."

2-2 OPPORTUNITY COST

Because of scarcity, the three basic questions cannot be answered without sacrifice or cost. But what does the term *cost* really mean? The common response would be to say that the purchase price is the cost. A movie ticket *costs* $8, or a shirt *costs* $50. Applying the economic way of thinking, however, *cost* is defined differently. A well-known phrase from Nobel Prize–winning economist Milton Friedman says, *There is no such thing as a free lunch.* This expression captures the links among the concepts of scarcity, choice, and cost. Because of scarcity, people must make choices, and each choice incurs a cost (sacrifice). Once one option is chosen, another option is given up. The money you spend on a movie ticket cannot also buy a Blu-ray. A business may purchase a new textile machine to manufacture towels, but this same money cannot be used to buy a new recreation facility for employees.

The Blu-ray and recreation facility examples illustrate that the true cost of these decisions is the opportunity cost of a choice, not the purchase price. **Opportunity cost** is the best alternative sacrificed for a chosen alternative. Stated differently, it is the cost of not choosing the next best alternative. This principle states that some highly valued opportunity must be forgone in all economic decisions. The highest-valued good or use of time given up for the chosen good or use of time measures the opportunity cost. We may omit the *opportunity* before the word *cost,* but the concept remains the same. Exhibit 1 illustrates the causation chain linking scarcity, choice, and opportunity cost.

Examples are endless, but let's consider a few. Suppose your economics professor decides to become a rock star in the Rolling in Dough band. Now all his or her working hours are devoted to creating hit music, and the opportunity cost is the educational services no longer provided. Now a personal example: The opportunity cost of dating a famous model or movie star (name your favorite) might be the loss of your current girlfriend or boyfriend. Opportunity cost also applies to national economic decisions. Suppose the federal government decides to spend tax revenues on a space station. The opportunity cost depends on the next best program *not* funded. Assume roads and bridges are the highest-valued projects not built as a result of the decision to construct the space station. Then the opportunity cost of the decision to devote resources to the space station is the forgone roads and bridges and not the money actually spent to build the space station.

Opportunity cost
The best alternative sacrificed for a chosen alternative.

EXHIBIT 1 The Links between Scarcity, Choice, and Opportunity Cost

Scarcity means that no society has enough resources to produce all the goods and services necessary to satisfy all human wants. As a result, society is always confronted with the problem of making choices. This concept is captured in Milton Friedman's famous phrase, "There is no such thing as a free lunch." This means that each decision has a sacrifice in terms of an alternative choice that has to be foregone.

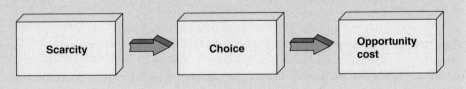

To personalize the relationship between time and opportunity cost, ask yourself what you would be doing if you were not reading this text. Your answer might be watching television or sleeping. If sleeping is your choice, the opportunity cost of studying this text is the sleep you sacrifice. Rock stars and movie stars, on the other hand, must forfeit a large amount of income to attend college. Now you know why you see so few of these stars in class.

Decisions often involve sacrifice of *both* goods and time. Suppose you decide to see a movie at a theater located 15 minutes from campus. If you had not spent the money at the movie theater, you could have purchased a Blu-ray and watched a movie at home. And the time spent traveling to and from the movie and sitting through it could have been devoted to studying for your economics exam. The opportunity cost of the movie consists of giving up a Blu-ray as well as the study time needed to score higher on the economics exam.

2-3 MARGINAL ANALYSIS

Marginal analysis
An examination of the effects of additions to or subtractions from a current situation.

At the heart of all rational decision-making is marginal analysis. **Marginal analysis** examines the effects of additions to or subtractions from a current situation. This is a very valuable tool in the economic way of thinking toolkit because it considers the "marginal" effects of change. The rational decision maker decides on an option only if the marginal benefit exceeds the marginal cost. For example, you must decide how to use your scarce time. Should you devote an extra hour to reading this text, going to a movie, watching television, texting, or sleeping? Which of your many options do you choose? The answer depends on marginal analysis. If you decide the benefit of a higher grade in economics exceeds the opportunity cost of, say sleep, then you allocate the extra hour to studying economics. Excellent choice!

Businesses use marginal analysis. Hotels, for example, rent space to student groups for dances and other events. Assume you are the hotel manager, and a student group offers to pay $400 to use the ballroom for a party. To decide whether to accept the offer requires marginal analysis. The marginal benefit of renting otherwise vacant space is $400, and the marginal cost is $300 for extra electricity and cleaning services. Since the marginal benefit exceeds the marginal cost, the manager sensibly accepts the offer.

Similarly, farmers use marginal analysis. For example, a farmer must decide whether to add more fertilizer when growing corn. Using marginal analysis, the farmer estimates that the corn revenue yield will be about $75 per acre with the current amount of fertilizer usage and about $100 per acre using one more application of fertilizer. If the cost of fertilizer is $20 per acre, marginal analysis tells the farmer to add one more application of fertilizer. The addition of fertilizer will increase profit by $5 per acre because fertilizing adds $25 to the value of each acre at a cost of $20 per acre.

Marginal analysis is an important concept when the government considers changes in various programs. For example, as demonstrated in the next section, it is useful to know that an increase in the production of military goods will result in an opportunity cost of fewer consumer goods produced.

2-4 THE PRODUCTION POSSIBILITIES CURVE

The economic problem of scarcity means that society's capacity to produce combinations of goods is constrained by its limited resources. This condition can be represented in a model called the production possibilities curve (*PPC*). The **production possibilities curve** shows the maximum combinations of two outputs that an economy can produce in a given period of time with its available resources and technology. Three basic assumptions underlie the production possibilities curve model:

1. **Fixed Resources.** The quantities and qualities of all resource inputs remain unchanged during the time period. But the "rules of the game" do allow an economy to shift any resource from the production of one output to the production of another output. For example, an economy might shift workers from producing consumer goods to producing capital goods. Although the number of workers remains unchanged, this transfer of labor will produce fewer consumer goods and more capital goods.

2. **Fully Employed Resources.** The economy operates with all its factors of production fully employed and producing the greatest output possible without waste or mismanagement.

3. **Technology Unchanged.** Holding existing technology fixed creates limits, or constraints, on the amounts and types of goods any economy can produce. **Technology** is the body of knowledge applied to how goods are produced.

Exhibit 2 shows a hypothetical economy that has the capacity to manufacture any combination of military goods (guns) and consumer goods (butter) per year along its production possibilities curve (*PPC*), including points *A*, *B*, *C*, and *D*. For example, if this economy uses all its resources to make military goods, it can produce a *maximum* of 160 billion units of military goods and zero units of consumer goods (combination *A*). Another possibility is for the economy to use all its resources to produce a *maximum* of 100 billion units of consumer goods and zero units of military goods (point *D*). Between the extremes of points *A* and *D* lie other production possibilities for combinations of military and consumer goods. If combination *B* is chosen, the economy will produce 140 billion units of military goods and 40 billion units of consumer goods. Another possibility (point *C*) is to produce 80 billion units of military goods and 80 billion units of consumer goods.

What happens if the economy does not use all its resources to their capacity? For example, some workers may not find work, or plants and equipment may be idle for any number of reasons. The result is that our hypothetical economy fails to reach any of the combinations along the *PPC*. In Exhibit 2, point *U* illustrates an *inefficient* output level for any economy operating without all its resources fully employed. At point *U*, our model economy is producing 80 billion units of military goods and 40 billion units of consumer goods per year. Such an economy is underproducing because it could satisfy more of society's wants if it were producing at some point along the *PPC*.

Even if an economy fully employs all its resources, it is impossible to produce certain output quantities. Any point outside the production possibilities curve is *currently unattainable* because it is beyond the economy's present production capabilities. Point *Z*, for example, represents an unattainable output of 140 billion units of military goods and 80 billion units of consumer goods. Society would prefer this combination to any combination along, or inside, the *PPC*, but the economy cannot reach this point with its existing resources and technology.

Production possibilities curve
A curve that shows the maximum combinations of two outputs an economy can produce in a given period of time with its available resources and technology.

Technology
The body of knowledge applied to how goods are produced.

Scarcity limits an economy to points on or below its production possibilities curve.

CONCLUSION

Because all the points along the curve are *maximum* output levels with the given resources and technology, they are all called *efficient* points. A movement between any two efficient points on the curve means that *more* of one product is produced only by producing *less* of the other product. In Exhibit 2, moving from point *A* to point *B* produces

---

EXHIBIT 2 The Production Possibilities Curve for Military Goods and Consumer Goods

All points along the production possibilities curve (*PPC*) are maximum possible combinations of military goods and consumer goods. One possibility, point *A*, would be to produce 160 billion units of military goods and zero units of consumer goods each year. At the other extreme, point *D*, the economy uses all its resources to produce 100 billion units of consumer goods and zero units of military goods each year. Points *B* and *C* are obtained by using some resources to produce each of the two outputs. If the economy fails to utilize its resources fully and has some unemployment, the result is an inefficient combination given by a point inside the *PPC*, like point *U*. Any point outside the *PPC*, like point *Z*, lies beyond the economy's present production capabilities and is currently unattainable.

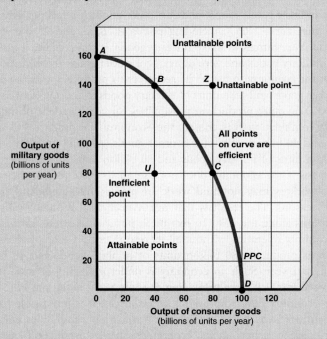

Production Possibilities Schedule for Military and Consumer Goods per Year				
Output	**Production possibilities**			
(billions of units per year)	**A**	**B**	**C**	**D**
Military goods	160	140	80	0
Consumer goods	0	40	80	100

40 billion additional units of consumer goods per year, but only at a cost of sacrificing 20 billion units of military goods. Thus, a movement between any two efficient points graphically illustrates opportunity cost and that "There is no such thing as a free lunch."

	CONCLUSION
The production possibilities curve consists of all efficient output combinations at which an economy can produce more of one good only by producing less of the other good.	

2-5 THE LAW OF INCREASING OPPORTUNITY COSTS

Why is the production possibilities curve shaped the way it is? Exhibit 3 will help us answer this question. It presents a production possibilities curve for a hypothetical economy that must choose between producing tanks and producing sailboats. Consider expanding the production of sailboats in 20,000-unit increments. Moving from point *A* to point *B*, the *opportunity cost* is 10,000 tanks; between points *B* and *C*, the *opportunity cost* is 20,000 tanks; and the *opportunity cost* of producing at point *D*, rather than point *C*, is 50,000 tanks.

Exhibit 3 illustrates the **law of increasing opportunity costs**, which states that the opportunity cost increases as production of one output expands. Holding the stock of resources and technology constant (ceteris paribus), the law of increasing opportunity costs causes the production possibilities curve to display a *bowed-out* shape.

Why must our hypothetical economy sacrifice larger and larger amounts of tank output in order to produce each additional 20,000 sailboats? The reason is that resources, like workers, are not equally suited to producing one good compared to another good. For example, expanding the output of sailboats requires the use of more resources, like workers who may be less suited to producing sailboats than producing tanks. Suppose our hypothetical economy produces no sailboats (point *A*) and then decides to produce them. At first, the least-skilled tank workers are transferred to making sailboats, and 10,000 tanks are sacrificed at point *B*. As the economy moves from point *B* to point *C*, more highly skilled tank makers become sailboat makers, and the opportunity cost rises to 20,000 tanks. Finally, the economy can decide to move from point *C* to point *D*, and the opportunity cost increases even more—to 50,000 tanks. Now the remaining tank workers, who are superb tank makers, but poor sailboat makers, must adapt to the techniques of sailboat production.

Finally, it should be noted that the production possibilities curve model could assume that resources are equally well-suited to producing all goods and the opportunity cost remains constant. In this case, the production possibilities curve would be a straight line, which is the model employed in the chapter on international trade and finance.

Law of increasing opportunity costs
The principle that the opportunity cost increases as production of one output expands.

	CONCLUSION
Because resources are not equally well-suited to producing all products, it's common to experience increasing opportunity costs and a bowed-out production possibilities curve.	

EXHIBIT 3 The Law of Increasing Opportunity Costs

A hypothetical economy produces equal increments of 20,000 sailboats per year as we move from point *A* through point *D* on the production possibilities curve (*PPC*). If the economy moves from point *A* to point *B*, the opportunity cost of 20,000 sailboats is a reduction in tank output of 10,000 per year. This opportunity cost rises to 20,000 tanks if the economy moves from point *B* to point *C*. Finally, production at point *D*, rather than point *C*, results in an opportunity cost of 50,000 tanks per year. The opportunity cost rises because workers are not equally suited to making tanks and sailboats.

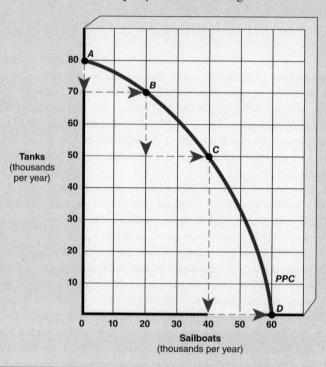

Production Possibilities Schedule for Tanks and Sailboats per Year				
Output	Production possibilities			
(thousands per year)	**A**	**B**	**C**	**D**
Tanks	80	70	50	0
Sailboats	0	20	40	60

2-6 SOURCES OF ECONOMIC GROWTH

Economic growth
The ability of an economy to produce greater levels of output, represented by an outward shift of its production possibilities curve.

The economy's production capacity is not permanently fixed. If either the resource base increases or technology advances, the economy experiences economic growth, and the production possibilities curve shifts outward. **Economic growth** is the ability of an economy to produce greater levels of output, represented by an outward shift of its production possibilities curve. Exhibit 4 illustrates the importance of an outward shift. (Note the

EXHIBIT 4 An Outward Shift of the Production Possibilities Curve for Computers and Pizzas

The economy begins with the capacity to produce combinations along the first production possibilities curve PPC_1. Growth in the resource base or technological advances can shift the production possibilities curve outward from PPC_1 to PPC_2. Points along PPC_2 represent new production possibilities that were previously impossible. This outward shift permits the economy to produce greater quantities of output. Instead of producing combination A, the economy can produce, for example, more computers at point B or more pizzas at point C. If the economy grows and produces at a point between B and C, more of both pizzas and computers can be produced, compared to point A.

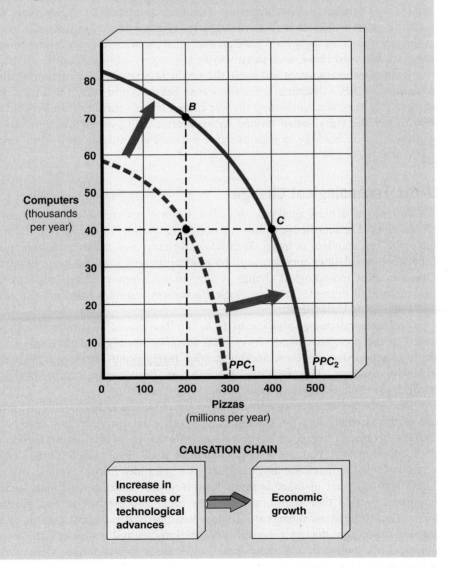

CAUSATION CHAIN

Increase in resources or technological advances ⟹ Economic growth

causation chain, which is often used in this text to focus on a model's cause-and-effect relationship.) At point A on PPC$_1$, a hypothetical full-employment economy produces 40,000 computers and 200 million pizzas per year. If the curve shifts outward to the new curve PPC$_2$, the economy can expand its full-employment output options. One option is to produce at point B and increase computer output to 70,000 per year. Another possibility is to increase pizza output to 400 million per year. Yet another choice is to produce more of both at some point between points B and C on PPC$_2$.

2-6a Changes in Resources

One way to accelerate economic growth is to obtain more resources. Any increase in resources, for example, more natural resources, a baby boom, or more factories will shift the production possibilities curve outward. In Exhibit 4, assume curve PPC_1 represents Japan's production possibilities for computers and pizzas in a given year. Suddenly, Japan discovers within its borders new sources of labor and other resources. As a result of the new resources, Japan will have an expanded capacity to produce any combination along an expanded curve, such as curve PPC_2.

Reductions in resources will cause the production possibilities curve to shift inward. Assume curve PPC_2 describes Japan's economy before World War II and the destruction of its factors of production during the war caused Japan's curve to shift leftward to curve PPC_1. Over the years, Japan trained its workforce, built new factories and equipment, and used new technology to shift its curve outward and surpass its original production capacity at curve PPC_2.

2-6b Technological Change

Another way to achieve economic growth is through research and development of new technologies. The knowledge of how to transform a stone into a wheel vastly improved the prehistoric standard of living. Technological change also makes it possible to shift the production possibilities curve outward by producing more from the same resources base. One source of technological change is *invention*. Computer chips, satellites, and the Internet are all examples of technological advances resulting from the use of science and engineering knowledge.

Technological change also results from the innovations of entrepreneurship, introduced in the previous chapter. Innovation involves creating and developing new products or productive processes. Seeking profits, entrepreneurs create new, better, or less expensive products. This requires organizing an improved mix of resources, which expands the production possibilities curve.

One entrepreneur, Henry Ford, changed auto industry technology by pioneering the use of the assembly line for making cars. Another entrepreneur, law student Chester Carlson, became so frustrated copying documents that he worked on his own to develop photocopying. After years of disappointment, a small firm named Xerox Corporation accepted Carlson's invention and transformed a good idea into a revolutionary product. These and a myriad of other business success stories illustrate that entrepreneurs are important because they transform their new ideas into production and practical use. Throughout history, technological advances have fostered economic growth by increasing our nation's productive power. Today, the Internet and computers are "new" technologies, but railroads, electricity, and automobiles, for example, were also "new" technologies in their time.

YOU'RE THE ECONOMIST

Applicable Concept: Entrepreneurship

FedEx Wasn't an Overnight Success

Frederick W. Smith is a classic entrepreneurial success story. Young Fred went to Yale University, had a good new idea, secured venture capital, worked like crazy, and made a fortune, and the Smithsonian Institution rendered its ultimate accolade. It snapped up an early Federal Express jet for its collection, displaying it for a time in the National Air and Space Museum in Washington, D.C., not far from the Wright brothers' first airplane.

Smith's saga began with a college economics term paper that spelled out a nationwide overnight parcel delivery system that would be guaranteed to "absolutely, positively" beat the pants off the U.S. Postal Service. People, he said, would pay much more if their packages arrived at their destination the next morning. To accomplish his plan, planes would converge nightly on Memphis, Tennessee, carrying packages accepted at any location throughout the nation. Smith chose this city for its central U.S. location and because its airport has little bad weather to cause landing delays. In the morning hours, all items would be unloaded, sorted, and rerouted to other airports, where vans would battle rush-hour traffic to make deliveries before the noon deadline.

Smith's college term paper only got a C grade. Perhaps the professor thought the idea was too risky, and lots of others certainly agreed. In 1969, after college and a tour as a Marine pilot in Vietnam, the 24-year-old Smith began pitching his parcel delivery plan to mostly skeptical financiers. Nevertheless, with $4 million of his family's money, he persuaded a few venture capitalists to put up $80 million. At the time, this was the largest venture capital package ever assembled. In 1973, delivery service began with 33 jets connecting 25 cities, but on the first night, only 86 packages showed up.

pio3/Shutterstock.com

It was years before Smith looked like a genius. The company posted a $27 million loss the first year, turned the corner in 1976, and then took off, helped by a 1981 decision to add letters to its basic package delivery service. Today, Smith's basic strategy hasn't changed, but the scale of the operation has exploded. FedEx is the world's largest express transportation company serving over 200 countries.

ANALYZE THE ISSUE Draw a production possibilities curve for an economy producing only pizzas and computers. Explain how Fred Smith and other successful entrepreneurs affect the curve.

What Does a War on Terrorism Really Mean?

With the disappearance of the former Soviet Union and the end of the Cold War, the United States became the world's only superpower and no longer engaged in an intense competition to build up its military. As a result, in the 1990s, Congress and the White House had the opportunity to reduce the military's share of the budget and spend more funds for nondefense goods. This situation was referred to as the "peace dividend." Now consider that the need to combat terrorism diverts resources back to military and security output. Does the peace dividend or a reversal to more military spending represent a possible shift of the production possibilities curve or a movement along it?

CHECKPOINT

2-7 PRESENT INVESTMENT AND THE FUTURE PRODUCTION POSSIBILITIES CURVE

When the decision for an economy involves choosing between capital goods and consumer goods, the output combination chosen for the present period can determine future production capacity. Exhibit 5 compares two countries producing different combinations of capital and consumer goods. Part (a) shows the production possibilities curve for the low-investment economy of Alpha. This economy was producing combination A in 2000, which is an output of C_a of consumer goods and an output of K_a of capital goods per year. This economy is currently producing relatively few capital goods and lots of consumer goods. Let's assume K_a is just enough capital output to replace the capital being worn out each year (depreciation). As a result, Alpha fails to accumulate the net gain of factories and equipment required to expand its production possibilities

---

EXHIBIT 5 Alpha's and Beta's Present and Future Production Possibilities Curves

In part (a), each year Alpha produces only enough capital (K_a) to replace existing capital that has worn out. Without more capital, and assuming other resources remain fixed as well, Alpha is unable to grow and shift its production possibilities curve outward. In part (b), each year Beta produces K_b capital, which is more than the amount required to replenish its depreciated capital. In 2018, this expanded capital provides Beta with the extra production capacity to shift its production possibilities curve to the right (outward). If Beta chooses point B on its curve, it has the production capacity to increase the amount of consumer goods from C_b to C_c without producing fewer capital goods. Because it now has more consumer goods, the country has increased its standard of living.

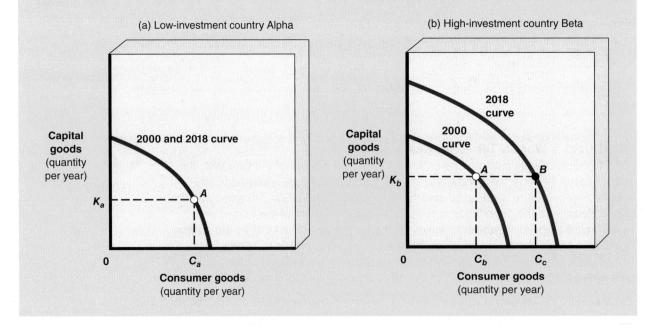

GLOBAL ECONOMICS

How Does Public Capital Affect a Nation's Curve?

Applicable Concept: Economic Growth

iStock.com/Robert Hackett

The discussion of low-investment country Alpha versus high-investment country Beta explained that sacrificing production of consumer goods for an increase in capital goods output can result in economic growth and a higher standard of living. Stated differently, there was a long-run benefit from the accumulation of capital that offset the short-run opportunity cost in terms of consumer goods foregone. Here the analysis was in terms of investment in private capital such as factories, machines, and inventories. However, public or government capital can also influence a nation's production possibilities over time.

For example, according to Josh Bivens at the Economic Policy Institute: "Public investment by federal, state, and local governments builds the nation's capital stock by devoting resources to the basic physical infrastructure (such as roads, bridges, rail lines, airports, and water distribution), innovative activity (basic research), green investments (clean power sources and weatherization), and education (both primary and advanced, as well as job training) that leads to higher productivity and/or higher living standards." Moreover, …"investments in public capital have significant positive impacts on private-sector productivity, with estimated rates of return ranging from 15 percent to upwards of 45 percent," and "public investment has benefits that extend beyond simply increasing [overall production]: It also offers benefits that are more broadly shared by all… such as safer water and cleaner air."[1]

Finally, economic growth and development is a major goal of countries throughout the world, and there are numerous factors that cause some countries to experience greater economic growth compared to other countries. Note that this topic is discussed in more depth in the last chapter of the text.

ANALYZE THE ISSUE Construct a production possibilities curve for a hypothetical country. Put public capital goods per year on the vertical axis and consumer goods per year on the horizontal axis. Not shown directly in your graph, assume that this country produces just enough private capital per year to replace its depreciated capital. Assume further that this country is without public capital and is operating at point *A*, where consumer goods are at a maximum. Based on the above research and using a production possibilities curve, show and explain what happens to this country's private capital, production possibilities curve, and standard of living if it increases its output of public capital.

---

1. "Public Investment: The Next 'New Thing' for Powering Economic Growth," report by Josh Bivens, April 18, 2012, Economic Policy Institute, found at http://www.epi.org/publication/bp338-public-investments/. See also "The Short- and Long-Term Impact of Infrastructure Investments on Employment and Economic Activity in the U.S. Economy," report by Josh Bivens, July 1, 2014, Economic Policy Institute, found at http://www.epi.org/publication/impact-of-infrastructure-investments/. See also "The Macroeconomic and Budgetary Effects of Federal Investment," Congressional Budget Office, June 2016, found at https://www.cbo.gov/sites/default/files/114th-congress-2015-2016/reports/51628-Federal_Investment-OneCol.pdf.

curve outward in future years.[1] Why wouldn't Alpha simply move up along its production curve by shifting more resources to capital goods production? The problem is that sacrificing consumer goods for capital formation causes a lower standard of living, which can be unpopular.

---

[1]Recall from the Appendix to Chapter 1 that a third variable can affect the variables measured on the vertical and horizontal axes. In this case, the third variable is the quantity of capital worn out per year.

Investment
The accumulation of capital, such as factories, machines, and inventories, used to produce goods and services.

Comparing Alpha to Beta illustrates the importance of being able to do more than just replace worn out capital. Beta operated in 2000 at point *A* in part (b), which is an output of C_b of consumer goods and K_b of capital goods. Assuming K_b is more than enough to replenish worn-out capital, Beta is a high-investment economy, adding to its capital stock and creating extra production capacity. This process of accumulating capital (*capital formation*) is investment. **Investment** is the accumulation of capital, such as factories, machines, and inventories, used to produce goods and services. Newly built factories and machines in the present provide an economy with the capacity to expand its production options in the future. For example, the outward shift of its curve allows Beta to produce C_c consumer goods at point *B* in 2018. This means Beta will be able to improve its standard of living by producing $C_c - C_b$ extra consumer goods, while Alpha's standard of living remains unchanged because the production of consumer goods remains unchanged.

CONCLUSION   A nation can accelerate economic growth by increasing its production of capital goods in excess of the capital being worn out in the production process.

Key Concepts

What, How, and For
  Whom questions

Opportunity cost

Marginal analysis

Production possibilities
  curve

Technology

Law of increasing
  opportunity costs

Economic growth

Investment

Summary

- **Three fundamental economic questions** facing any economy are *What*, *How*, and *For Whom* to produce goods. The *What* question asks exactly which goods are produced and in what quantities. The *How* question requires society to decide the resource mix used to produce goods. The *For Whom* problem concerns the division of limited output among society's unlimited wants.

- **Opportunity cost** is the best alternative forgone for a chosen option. This means no decision can be made without cost.

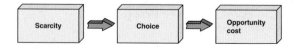

- **Marginal analysis** examines the impact of changes from a current situation and is a technique used extensively in economics. The basic approach is to compare the additional benefits of a change with the additional costs of the change.

- A **production possibilities curve** illustrates an economy's capacity to produce goods, subject to the constraint of scarcity. The production possibilities curve is a graph of the maximum possible combinations of two outputs that can be produced in a given period of time, subject to three conditions: (1) All resources are fully employed. (2) The resource base is not allowed to vary during the time period. (3) **Technology**, which is the body of knowledge applied to the production of goods, remains constant.

- **Inefficient** production occurs at any point inside the production possibilities curve. All points along the curve are **efficient** points because each point represents a maximum output possibility.

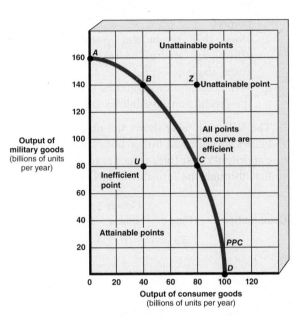

- The **law of increasing opportunity costs** states that the opportunity cost increases as the production of output expands. The explanation for this law is that the suitability of resources declines sharply as greater amounts are transferred from producing one output to producing another output.

- **Economic growth** is represented by the production possibilities curve shifting outward as the result of an increase in resources or an advance in technology. Economic growth is desired because it increases standards of living.

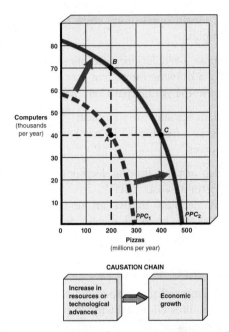

- **Investment** means that an economy is producing and accumulating capital. Investment consists of factories, machines, and inventories (capital) produced in the present that are used to shift the production possibilities curve outward in the future.

Summary of Conclusion Statements

- Scarcity limits an economy to points on or below its production possibilities curve.

- The production possibilities curve consists of all efficient output combinations at which an economy can produce more of one good only by producing less of the other good.

- Because resources are not equally well-suited to producing all products, it's common to

experience increasing opportunity costs and a bowed-out shaped production possibilities curve.

- A nation can accelerate economic growth by increasing its production of capital goods in excess of the capital being worn out in the production process.

Study Questions and Problems

Please see Appendix A for answers to the odd-numbered questions. Your instructor has access to the answers for even-numbered questions.

1. Explain why scarcity forces individuals and society to incur opportunity costs. Give specific examples.

2. Suppose a retailer promotes its store by advertising a drawing for a "free car." Is this car *free* because the winner pays *zero* for it?

3. Explain verbally the statement "There is no such thing as a free lunch" in relation to scarce resources.

4. Which of the following decisions has the greater opportunity cost? Why?
   a. A decision to use an undeveloped lot in Tokyo's financial district for an apartment building.
   b. A decision to use a square mile in the desert for a gas station.

5. Attending college is expensive, time consuming, and requires effort. So why do people decide to attend college?

6. The following is a set of hypothetical production possibilities for a nation.

Combination	Automobiles (thousands)	Beef (thousands of tons)
A	0	10
B	2	9
C	4	7
D	6	4
E	8	0

   a. Plot these production possibilities data. What is the opportunity cost of the first 2,000 automobiles produced? Between which points is the opportunity cost per thousand automobiles highest? Between which points is the opportunity cost per thousand tons of beef highest?
   b. Label a point *F* inside the curve. Why is this an inefficient point? Label a point *G* outside the curve. Why is this point unattainable? Why are points *A* through *E* all efficient points?
   c. Does this production possibilities curve reflect the law of increasing opportunity costs? Explain.
   d. What assumptions could be changed to shift the production possibilities curve?

7. The following table shows the production possibilities for pies and flower boxes. Fill in the opportunity cost (pies forgone) of producing the first through the fifth flower box.

Combination	Pies	Flower boxes	Opportunity cost
A	30	0	____
B	26	1	____
C	21	2	____
D	15	3	____
E	8	4	____
F	0	5	____

8. Why does a production possibilities curve have a bowed-out shape?

9. Interpret the phrases "There is no such thing as a free lunch" and "A free lunch is possible" in terms of the production possibilities curve.

10. Suppose, unfortunately, your mathematics and economics professors have decided to give tests two days from now and you can spend a total of only twelve hours studying for both exams. After some thought, you conclude that dividing your study time equally between each subject will give you an expected grade of C in each course. For each additional three hours of study time for one of the subjects, your grade will increase one letter for that subject, and your grade will fall one letter for the other subject.

a. Construct a table for the production possibilities and corresponding number of hours of study in this case.
b. Plot these production possibilities data in a graph.
c. Does this production possibilities curve reflect the law of increasing opportunity costs? Explain.

11. Draw a production possibilities curve for a hypothetical economy producing capital goods and consumer goods. Suppose a major technological breakthrough occurs in the capital goods industry and the new technology is widely adopted only in this industry. Draw the new production possibilities curve. Now assume that a technological advance occurs in consumer goods production, but not in capital goods production. Draw the new production possibilities curve.

12. The present choice between investing in capital goods and producing consumer goods now affects the ability of an economy to produce in the future. Explain.

 CHECKPOINT ANSWERS

What Does a War on Terrorism Really Mean?
A "peace dividend" suggests resources are allocated away from military production and used for greater nonmilitary production. The war on terrorism arguably shifts resources in the opposite direction. If you said that this phrase represents a movement along the production possibilities curve, **YOU ARE CORRECT**.

Sample Quiz

Please see Appendix B for answers to Sample Quiz questions.

1. Which of the following *best* describes the three fundamental economic questions?
   a. What to produce, when to produce, and where to produce
   b. What time to produce, what place to produce, and how to produce
   c. What to produce, when to produce, and for whom to produce
   d. What to produce, how to produce, and for whom to produce

2. Suppose the alternative uses of an hour of your time in the evening, ranked from best to worst, are (1) study economics, (2) watch two half-hour sitcoms, (3) play video games, and (4) jog around town. You can choose only one activity. What is the opportunity cost of studying economics for one hour given this information?
   a. Jogging around town
   b. Watching two half-hour TV sitcoms
   c. Playing video games
   d. The sum of watching two half-hour TV sitcoms, playing pool, and doing your laundry

3. Which word or phrase *best* completes the following sentence? Marginal analysis means evaluating _____ changes from a current situation.
   a. positive or negative
   b. infinite
   c. no
   d. maximum

4. Which of the following is an example of an organization using marginal analysis?
   a. A hotel manager calculating the average cost per guest for the past year
   b. A farmer hoping for rain
   c. A government official considering the effect an increase in military goods

production will have on the production of consumer goods

   d. A businessperson calculating economic profits

5. A production possibilities curve shows the various combinations of two outputs that
   a. consumers would like to consume.
   b. producers would like to produce.
   c. an economy can produce.
   d. an economy should produce.

6. A production possibilities curve is drawn based on which of the following assumptions?
   a. Resources are fixed and fully employed, and technology advances at the rate of growth of the economy overall.
   b. Resources such as nonrenewable resources will decline, but labor remains fully employed and technology is unchanged.
   c. Resources can vary; most resources experience times of unemployment; and technology advances, particularly during wartime.
   d. Resources such as labor and capital will grow and are fully employed, and technology is unchanged.
   e. None of the answers correct.

7. If an economy can produce various combinations of food and shelter along a production possibilities curve (PPC), then if we increase the production of shelter along the PPC, which of the following is true?
   a. We also increase the production of food.
   b. We must decrease the production of food. This forgone food production represents the opportunity cost of the increase in shelter.
   c. We cannot change the production of food.
   d. The concept of opportunity cost does not apply along PPC.

8. An economy can produce various combinations of food and shelter along a production possibilities curve (PPC). First, increase the production of shelter along the PPC; then continue to shift more and more production to shelter. Which of the following will most likely happen to the opportunity cost of a unit of shelter?
   a. Opportunity cost will increase because as more and more shelter is produced, labor and capital that is highly productive at producing food is being shifted to shelter production, and so more and more food is being given up to produce a unit of shelter.
   b. Opportunity cost is the amount of labor (but not capital) that is used to produce the extra shelter.
   c. Opportunity cost must stay constant if we are to stay on the production possibilities curve (PPC).
   d. Opportunity cost includes all options given up to produce shelter.

9. An economy can produce various combinations of food and shelter along a production possibilities curve (PPC). Suppose a technological innovation resulted in a new, higher-yielding crop that generated more bushels of grain for a given set of land, labor, and capital resources. If this innovation did not affect the productivity of shelter production, which of the following would be *true*?
   a. The PPC will shift outward equally along both axes of the graph.
   b. The PPC will rotate inward along the food axis, but will not shift on the shelter axis.
   c. The PPC will rotate outward along the food axis, but will not shift on the shelter axis.
   d. The PPC will not change.

10. If a production possibilities curve (PPC) has capital on the vertical axis and consumer goods on the horizontal axis, which of the following is *true*?
   a. There is a trade-off between emphasizing the production of capital today to benefit people today versus emphasizing the production of consumer goods today that will generate benefits in the future.
   b. Greater emphasis on the production of capital today leads to future inward shifts in the

PPC, thus decreasing the wealth of people in the future.

c. Greater emphasis on the production of consumer goods today leads to greater outward shifts in the PPC, thus increasing the wealth of people in the future.

d. Greater emphasis on the production of capital today leads to greater outward shifts in the PPC, thus increasing the wealth of people in the future.

11. Which of the following reasons could explain why an economy would be operating inside its production possibilities curve (PPC)?
a. Because shrinking population has reduced the number of productive workers in the economy
b. Because technological innovations have increased the productivity of labor and capital
c. Because damage to natural resources, such as damage caused by deforestation leading to erosion of topsoil, has shrunk the land resource
d. Because of unemployment or underemployment of labor, perhaps due to discrimination against employing workers of a certain race or gender

12. Combinations of goods outside the production possibilities curve (PPC) have which of the following characteristics?
a. They are attainable today only if we employ all unemployed or underemployed resources.
b. They are not attainable given our existing stock of resources and technology.
c. They imply that some resources, such as labor, are unemployed or underemployed.
d. None of the answers is correct.

13. Suppose an economy can produce various combinations of fish and bread. If more people with strong fishing skills became employed in this economy, how would the production possibilities curve (PPC) change?
a. The PPC would shift outward on the fish axis, but would not change on the bread axis.

b. The PPC would shift outward equally along both the fish and bread axes.
c. The PPC would shift inward on the bread axis, but would not change on the fish axis.
d. The PPC would shift inward equally along both the fish and bread axes.

14. Three different economies have made choices about the production of capital goods. Which of the following is most likely to produce the greatest growth in the production possibilities curve (PPC)?
a. Capital goods produced at the exact rate needed to replace worn-out capital.
b. Greater production of capital goods than what is needed to replace worn-out capital.
c. Less production of capital goods than what is needed to replace worn-out capital.
d. More production of consumption goods that replace worn-out capital.

15. In the study of economics, investment means
a. the accumulation of capital that is used to produce goods and services.
b. owning stocks and bonds.
c. the principle that the opportunity cost increases as the production of one output expands.
d. the effect of stock prices on the production possibilities curve.

16. Which of the following is *not* one of the three fundamental economic questions?
a. What happens when you add to or subtract from a current situation?
b. For whom to produce?
c. How to produce?
d. What to produce?

17. Opportunity cost
a. represents the best alternative sacrificed for a chosen alternative.
b. has no relationship to the various alternatives that must be given up when a choice is made in the context of scarcity.
c. represents the worst alternative sacrificed for a chosen alternative.
d. represents all alternatives not chosen.

18. Which words best complete the following sentence? A rational decision maker always chooses the option for which marginal benefit is _____ marginal cost.
    a. less than
    b. equal to
    c. unrelated to
    d. more than

19. The principle that the opportunity cost increases as the production of one output expands is the

    a. law of increasing opportunity costs.
    b. law of demand.
    c. law of supply.
    d. law of increasing returns to scale.

20. The ability of an economy to produce greater levels of output per time period is called
    a. positive economics.
    b. negative economics.
    c. economic growth.
    d. the law of specialization.

PART 1
Introduction to Economics

This road map feature helps you tie together material in the part as you travel the Economic Way of Thinking Highway. The following are review questions listed by chapter from the previous part. The key concept in each question is given for emphasis, and each question or set of questions concludes with an interactive game to reinforce the concepts. The correct answers to the multiple choice questions are given in Appendix C. If your instructor has included MindTap in your course, visit MindTap to play the interactive Causation Chain Game.

Chapter 1: Introducing the Economic Way of Thinking

1. Key Concept: Scarcity

Economists believe that scarcity forces everyone to

a. satisfy all wants.
b. abandon consumer sovereignty.
c. lie about their wants.
d. create unlimited resources.
e. make choices.

2. Key Concept: Economics

The subject of economics is primarily the study of

a. the government decision-making process.
b. how to operate a business successfully.
c. decision making because of the problem of scarcity.
d. how to make money in the stock market.

CAUSATION CHAIN GAME
The Relationship between Scarcity and Decision Making

3. Key Concept: Model

When building a model, an economist must

a. adjust for exceptional situations.
b. provide a complete description of reality.
c. make simplifying assumptions.
d. develop a set of behavioral equations.

4. Key Concept: Ceteris paribus

If the price of a textbook rises and students purchase fewer textbooks, an economic model can show a cause-and-effect relationship only if which of the following conditions holds?

a. Students' incomes fall.
b. Tuition decreases.
c. The number of students increases.
d. Everything else is constant.
e. The bookstore no longer accepts used book trade-ins.

5. Key Concept: Association versus causation

Someone notices that sunspot activity is high just prior to recessions and concludes that sunspots cause recessions. This person has

a. confused association and causation.
b. misunderstood the ceteris paribus assumption.
c. used normative economics to answer a positive question.
d. built an untestable model.

 CAUSATION CHAIN GAME
The Steps in the Model-Building Process—Exhibit 2

Chapter 2: Production Possibilities, Opportunity Cost, and Economic Growth

6. Key Concept: Production possibilities curve

Which of the following is *not* true about a production possibilities curve? The curve

a. indicates the combinations of goods and services that can be produced with a given technology.
b. indicates the efficient production points.
c. indicates the nonefficient production points.
d. indicates the feasible (attainable) and nonfeasible production points.
e. indicates which production point will be chosen.

7. Key Concept: Production possibilities curve

Which of the following is *true* about the production possibilities curve when a technological progress occurs?

a. Shifts inward to the left
b. Becomes flatter at one end and steeper at the other end
c. Becomes steeper
d. Shifts outward to the right
e. Does not change

8. Key Concept: Shifting the production possibilities curve

An outward shift of an economy's production possibilities curve is caused by

a. entrepreneurship.
b. an increase in labor.
c. an advance in technology.
d. all of the above.

9. Key Concept: Shifting the production possibilities curve

Which would be *least* likely to cause the production possibilities curve to shift to the right?

a. An increase in the labor force
b. Improved methods of production
c. An increase in the education and training of the labor force
d. A decrease in unemployment

10. Key Concept: Investment

A nation can accelerate its economic growth by

a. reducing the number of immigrants allowed into the country.
b. adding to its stock of capital.
c. printing more money.
d. imposing tariffs and quotas on imported goods.

 CAUSATION CHAIN GAME
Economic Growth and Technology—Exhibit 4

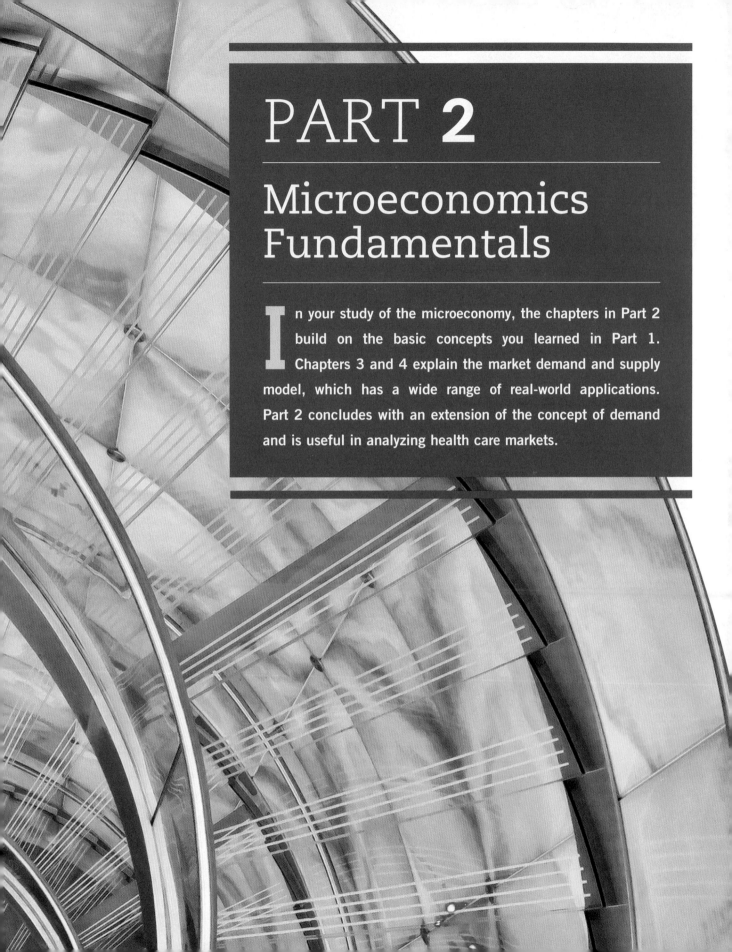

PART **2**

Microeconomics Fundamentals

In your study of the microeconomy, the chapters in Part 2 build on the basic concepts you learned in Part 1. Chapters 3 and 4 explain the market demand and supply model, which has a wide range of real-world applications. Part 2 concludes with an extension of the concept of demand and is useful in analyzing health care markets.

CHAPTER 3

Market Demand and Supply

CHAPTER PREVIEW

A cornerstone of the U.S. economy is the use of markets to answer the basic economic questions discussed in the previous chapter. Consider baseball cards, Blu-rays, physical fitness, gasoline, soft drinks, and sneakers. In a *market economy*, each is bought and sold by individuals coming together as buyers and sellers in markets. This chapter is extremely important because it introduces basic supply and demand analysis. This technique will prove to be valuable because it is applicable to a multitude of real-world choices of buyers and sellers facing the

problem of scarcity. For example, the Global Economics feature asks you to consider the highly controversial issue of international trade in human organs.

Demand represents the choice-making behavior of consumers, whereas supply represents the choices of producers. The chapter begins by looking closely at demand and then at supply. Finally, it combines these forces to see how prices and quantities traded are determined in the marketplace. Market demand and supply analysis are the basic tools of microeconomic analysis.

IN THIS CHAPTER, YOU WILL LEARN TO SOLVE THESE ECONOMICS PUZZLES:

- What is the difference between a "change in quantity demanded" and a "change in demand"?

- Can Congress repeal the law of supply to control oil prices?

- Does the price system eliminate scarcity?

3-1 THE LAW OF DEMAND

Economics might be referred to as "graphs and laughs" because economists are so fond of using graphs to illustrate demand, supply, and many other economic concepts. Unfortunately, some students taking economics courses say they miss the laughs.

Exhibit 1 reveals an important "law" in economics called the law of demand. The **law of demand** states there is an inverse relationship between the price of a good and the quantity buyers are willing to purchase in a defined time period, ceteris paribus. The law of demand makes good sense. At a "sale," consumers buy more when the price of merchandise is cut.

In Exhibit 1, the *demand curve* is formed by the line connecting the possible price and quantity purchased responses of an individual consumer. The demand curve, therefore,

Law of demand
The principle that there is an inverse relationship between the price of a good and the quantity buyers are willing to purchase in a defined time period, ceteris paribus.

EXHIBIT 1 An Individual Buyer's Demand Curve for Blu-Rays

Bob's demand curve shows how many Blu-rays he is willing to purchase at different possible prices. As the price of Blu-rays declines, the quantity demanded increases, and Bob purchases more Blu-rays. The inverse relationship between price and quantity demanded conforms to the law of demand.

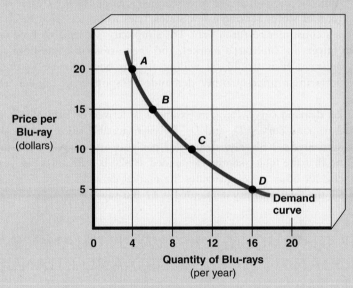

An Individual Buyer's Demand Schedule for Blu-rays

Point	Price per Blu-ray	Quantity demanded (per year)
A	$20	4
B	15	6
C	10	10
D	5	16

allows you to find the quantity demanded by a buyer at any possible selling price by moving along the curve. For example, Bob, a sophomore at Marketplace College, enjoys watching Blu-ray movies. Bob's demand curve shows that at a price of $15 per Blu-ray, his quantity demanded is six Blu-rays purchased annually (point *B*). At the lower price of $10, Bob's quantity demanded increases to ten Blu-rays per year (point *C*). Following this procedure, other price and quantity possibilities for Bob are read along the demand curve.

Note that until we know the actual price determined by both demand and supply, we do not know how many Blu-rays Bob will actually purchase annually. The demand curve is simply a summary of Bob's buying intentions. After we know the market price, a quick look at the demand curve tells us how many Blu-rays Bob will buy.

CONCLUSION	*Demand curve* is a curve or schedule showing the various quantities of a product consumers are willing to purchase at possible prices during a specified period of time, ceteris paribus.

Demand curve
A curve or schedule showing the various quantities of product consumers are willing to purchase at possible prices during a specified period of time, ceteris paribus.

3-1a Market Demand

To make the transition from an individual demand curve to a market demand curve, we total, or sum, the individual demand schedules. Suppose the owner of ZapMart, a small retail chain of stores serving a few states, tries to decide what to charge for Blu-rays and hires a consumer research firm. For simplicity, we assume Fred and Mary are the only two buyers in ZapMart's market, and they are sent a questionnaire that asks how many Blu-rays each would be willing to purchase at several possible prices. Exhibit 2 reports their price-quantity demanded responses in tabular and graphical form.

The market demand curve, D_{total}, in Exhibit 2 is derived by summing *horizontally* the two individual demand curves, D_1 and D_2, for each possible price. At a price of $20, for example, we sum Fred's 2 Blu-rays demanded per year and Mary's 1 Blu-ray demanded per year to find that the total quantity demanded at $20 is 3 Blu-rays per year. Repeating the same process for other prices generates the market demand curve, D_{total}. For example, at a price of $5, the total quantity demanded is 12 Blu-rays.

3-2 THE DISTINCTION BETWEEN CHANGES IN QUANTITY DEMANDED AND CHANGES IN DEMAND

Price is not the only variable that determines how much of a good or service consumers will buy. Recall from Exhibit A-4 of Appendix 1 that the price and quantity variables in our model are subject to the ceteris paribus assumption. If we relax this assumption and allow other variables held constant to change, a variety of factors can influence the position of the demand curve. Because these factors are not the price of the good itself, these variables are called *nonprice determinants*, or simply, *demand shifters*. The major nonprice determinants include (1) the number of buyers; (2) tastes and preferences; (3) income; (4) expectations of future changes in prices, income, and availability of goods; and (5) prices of related goods.

EXHIBIT 2 The Market Demand Curve for Blu-Rays

Individual demand curves differ for consumers Fred and Mary. Assuming they are the only buyers in the market, the market demand curve, D_{total}, is derived by summing horizontally the individual demand curves, D_1 and D_2.

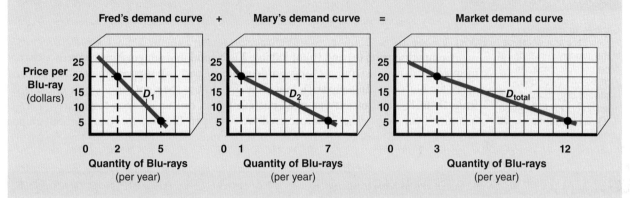

Market Demand Schedule for Blu-rays

	Quantity demanded per year				
Price per Blu-ray	Fred	+	Mary	=	Total demand
$25	1		0		1
20	2		1		3
15	3		3		6
10	4		5		9
5	5		7		12

Before discussing these nonprice determinants of demand, we must pause to explain an important and possibly confusing distinction in terminology. We have been referring to a change in quantity demanded, which results solely from a change in the price. A **change in quantity demanded** is a movement between points along a stationary demand curve, ceteris paribus. In Exhibit 3(a), at the price of $15, the quantity demanded is 20 million Blu-rays per year. This is shown as point A on the demand curve, D. At a lower price of, say, $10, the quantity demanded increases to 30 million Blu-rays per year, shown as point B. Verbally, we describe the impact of the price decrease as an increase in the quantity demanded of 10 million Blu-rays per year. We show this relationship on the demand curve as a movement down along the curve from point A to point B.

Change in quantity demanded
A movement between points along a stationary demand curve, ceteris paribus.

Under the law of demand, any decrease in price along the vertical axis will cause an increase in quantity demanded, measured along the horizontal axis, and appears as a movement along the demand curve.

CONCLUSION

A **change in demand** is an increase (rightward shift) or a decrease (leftward shift) in the quantity demanded at each possible price. If ceteris paribus no longer applies and if one of the five major nonprice factors changes, the location of the demand curve shifts.

CONCLUSION	Changes in nonprice determinants can produce only a shift in the demand curve and not a movement along the demand curve.

Change in demand
An increase or a decrease in the quantity demanded at each possible price. An increase in demand is a rightward shift in the entire demand curve. A decrease in demand is a leftward shift in the entire demand curve.

Comparing parts (a) and (b) of Exhibit 3 is helpful in distinguishing between a change in quantity demanded and a change in demand. In part (b), suppose the market demand curve for Blu-rays is initially at D_1 and there is a shift to the right (an increase in demand) from D_1 to D_2. This means that at all possible prices, consumers wish to purchase a larger quantity than before the shift occurred. At $15 per Blu-ray, for example, 30 million Blu-rays (point B) will be purchased each year, rather than 20 million Blu-rays (point A).

EXHIBIT 3 Movement along a Demand Curve versus a Shift in Demand

Part (a) shows the demand curve, D, for Blu-rays per year. If the price is $15 at point A, the quantity demanded by consumers is 20 million Blu-rays. If the price decreases to $10 at point B, the quantity demanded increases from 20 million to 30 million Blu-rays.

Part (b) illustrates an increase in demand. A change in some nonprice determinant can cause an increase in demand from D_1 to D_2. At a price of $15 on D_1 (point A), 20 million Blu-rays is the quantity demanded per year. At this price on D_2 (point B), the quantity demanded increases to 30 million.

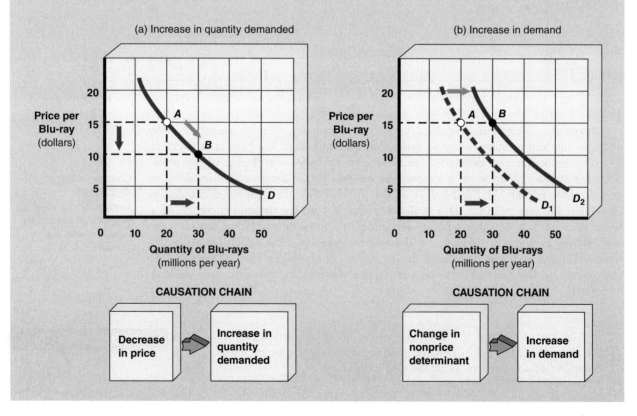

Now suppose a change in some nonprice factor causes demand curve D_1 to shift leftward (a decrease in demand). The interpretation in this case is that at *all* possible prices consumers will buy a smaller quantity than before the shift occurred.

Exhibit 4 summarizes the terminology for the effects of changes in price and non-price determinants on the demand curve.

3-3 NONPRICE DETERMINANTS OF DEMAND

Distinguishing between a change in quantity demanded and a change in demand requires some patience and practice. The following discussion of specific changes in nonprice factors, or demand shifters, will clarify how each nonprice variable affects demand.

EXHIBIT 4 Terminology for Changes in Price and Nonprice Determinants of Demand

Caution! It is important to distinguish between a change in quantity demanded, which is a movement along a demand curve (D_1) caused by a change in price, and a change in demand, which is a shift in the demand curve. An increase in demand (shift to D_2) or a decrease in demand (shift to D_3) is not caused by a change in price. Instead, a shift is caused by a change in one of the nonprice determinants.

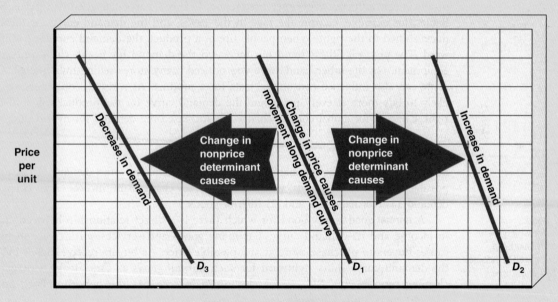

Change	Effect	Terminology
Price increases	Upward movement along the demand curve	Decrease in the quantity demanded
Price decreases	Downward movement along the demand curve	Increase in the quantity demanded
Nonprice determinant	Leftward or rightward shift in the demand curve	Decrease or increase in demand

3-3a **Number of Buyers**

Look back at Exhibit 2 and imagine the impact of adding more individual demand curves to the individual demand curves of Fred and Mary. At all possible prices, there is extra quantity demanded by the new customers, and the market demand curve for Blu-rays shifts rightward (an increase in demand). Population growth therefore tends to increase the number of buyers, which shifts the market demand curve for a good or service rightward. Conversely, a population decline shifts most market demand curves leftward (a decrease in demand).

The number of buyers can be specified to include both foreign and domestic buyers. Suppose the market demand curve D_1 in Exhibit 3(b) is for Blu-rays purchased in the United States by customers at home and abroad. Also assume that Japan restricts the import of Blu-rays into Japan. What would be the effect of Japan removing this trade restriction? The answer is that the demand curve shifts rightward from D_1 to D_2 when Japanese consumers add their individual demand curves to the U.S. market demand for Blu-rays.

3-3b **Tastes and Preferences**

A favorable or unfavorable change in consumer tastes or preferences means more or less of a product is demanded at each possible price. Fads, fashions, advertising, and new products can influence consumer preferences to buy a particular good or service. Beanie Babies, for example, became the rage in the 1990s, and the demand curve for these products shifted to the right. When people tire of a product, the demand curve will shift leftward. The physical fitness trend has increased the demand for health clubs and exercise equipment. On the other hand, have you noticed many stores selling hula hoops? Advertising can also influence consumers' taste for a product. As a result, consumers are more likely to buy more at every price, and the demand curve for the product will shift to the right. Concern for global climate change has increased the demand for hybrid cars.

3-3c **Income**

Most students are all too familiar with how changes in income affect demand. There are two possible categories of goods when it comes to changes in income and changes in demand: (1) Normal goods and (2) Inferior goods

Normal good
Any good for which there is a direct relationship between changes in income and its demand curve.

A **normal good** is any good for which there is a direct relationship between changes in income and its demand curve. For many goods and services, an increase in income causes buyers to purchase more at any possible price. As buyers receive higher incomes, the demand curve shifts rightward for such *normal goods* as cars, steaks, vintage wine, cleaning services, and Blu-rays. A decline in income has the opposite effect, and the demand curve shifts leftward.

Inferior good
Any good for which there is an inverse relationship between changes in income and its demand curve.

An **inferior good** is any good for which there is an inverse relationship between changes in income and its demand curve. A rise in income can result in reduced purchases of a good or service at any possible price. This might happen with such *inferior goods* as generic brands, Spam, discount clothes, and used cars. Instead of buying these inferior goods, consumers with higher incomes buy brand-name products, steaks, designer clothes, or new cars. Conversely, a fall in income causes the demand curve for inferior goods to shift rightward.

3-3d **Expectations of Buyers**

What is the effect on demand in the present when consumers anticipate future changes in prices, incomes, or availability? What happens when a war breaks out in the Middle East?

Expectations that there will be a shortage of gasoline induce consumers to say "fill 'er up" at every opportunity, and demand increases. Suppose students learn that the prices of the textbooks for several courses they plan to take next semester will double soon. Their likely response is to buy now, which causes an increase in the demand curve for these textbooks. Another example is a change in the weather, which can indirectly cause expectations to shift demand for some products. Suppose severe weather destroys a substantial portion of the peach crop. Consumers reason that the reduction in available supply will soon drive up prices, and they dash to stock up before it is too late. This change in expectations causes the demand curve for peaches to increase. For example, when a hurricane is expected to hit a major U.S. city, the sales of batteries and flashlights soar.

3-3e Prices of Related Goods

Possibly the most confusing nonprice factor is the influence of other prices on the demand for a particular good or service. The term *nonprice* seems to forbid any shift in demand resulting from a change in the price of *any* product. This confusion exists when one fails to distinguish between changes in quantity demanded and changes in demand. Remember that ceteris paribus holds all prices of other goods constant. Therefore, movement along a demand curve occurs solely in response to changes in the price of a product, that is, its "own" price. When we draw the demand curve for Coca-Cola, for example, we assume that the prices of Pepsi-Cola and other colas remain unchanged. What happens if we relax the ceteris paribus assumption and the price of Pepsi rises? Many Pepsi buyers switch to Coca-Cola, and the demand curve for Coca-Cola shifts rightward (an increase in demand). Coca-Cola and Pepsi-Cola are one type of related goods called substitute goods. A **substitute good** competes with another good for consumer purchases. As a result, there is a direct relationship between a price change for one good and the demand for its "competitor" good. Other examples of substitutes include margarine and butter, domestic cars and foreign cars, and Blu-rays and Internet movie downloads.

Blu-rays and Blu-ray players illustrate a second type of related goods called complementary goods. A **complementary good** is jointly consumed with another good. As a result, there is an inverse relationship between a price change for one good and the demand for its "go together" good. Although buying a Blu-ray and buying a Blu-ray player can be separate decisions, these two purchases are related. The more Blu-ray players consumers buy, the greater the demand for Blu-rays. What happens when the price of Blu-ray players falls sharply? The market demand curve for Blu-rays shifts rightward (an increase in demand) because new owners of players add their individual demand curves to those of people already owning players and buying Blu-rays. Conversely, a sharp rise in the price of desk jet printers would decrease the demand for ink cartridges.

Exhibit 5 summarizes the relationship between changes in the nonprice determinants of demand and the demand curve, accompanied by examples for each type of nonprice factor change.

Substitute good
A good that competes with another good for consumer purchases. As a result, there is a direct relationship between a price change for one good and the demand for its "competitor" good.

Complementary good
A good that is jointly consumed with another good. As a result, there is an inverse relationship between a price change for one good and the demand for its "go together" good.

Can Gasoline Become an Exception to the Law of Demand?
Suppose war in the Middle East threatened oil supplies, and gasoline prices began rising. Consumers feared future oil shortages, so they rushed to fill up their gas tanks. In this case, as the price of gas increased, consumers bought more, not less. Is this an exception to the law of demand?

CHECKPOINT

EXHIBIT 5 Summary of the Impact of Changes in Nonprice Determinants of Demand on the Demand Curve

Nonprice determinant of demand	Relationship to changes in demand curve	Shift in the demand curve	Examples
1. Number of buyers	Direct		• Immigration from Mexico increases the demand for Mexican food products in grocery stores. • A decline in the birthrate reduces the demand for baby clothes.
2. Tastes and preferences	Direct		• For no apparent reason, consumers want Beanie Babies and demand increases. • After a while, the fad dies and demand declines.
3. Income a. Normal goods	Direct		• Consumers' incomes increase, and the demand for steaks increases. • A decline in income decreases the demand for air travel.
b. Inferior goods	Inverse		• Consumers' incomes increase, and the demand for hamburger decreases. • A decline in income increases the demand for bus service.

(Continued)

Continued from previous page

Nonprice determinant of demand	Relationship to changes in demand curve	Shift in the demand curve	Examples
4. Expectations of buyers	Direct		• Consumers expect that gasoline will be in short supply next month and that prices will rise sharply. Consequently, consumers fill the tanks in their cars this month, and there is an increase in demand for gasoline. • Months later, consumers expect the price of gasoline to fall soon, and the demand for gasoline decreases.
5. Prices of related Goods a. Substitute goods	Direct		• A reduction in the price of tea decreases the demand for coffee. • An increase in the price of airfares causes higher demand for bus transportation.
b. Complementary goods	Inverse		• A decline in the price of cellular service increases the demand for cell phones. • A higher price for peanut butter decreases the demand for jelly.

3-4 THE LAW OF SUPPLY

In everyday conversations, the term *supply* refers to a specific quantity. A "limited supply" of golf clubs at a sporting goods store means there are only so many clubs for sale and that's all. This interpretation of supply is *not* the economist's definition. To economists, supply is the relationship between ranges of possible prices and quantities supplied, which is stated as the law of supply. The **law of supply** states there is a direct relationship between the price of a good and the quantity sellers are willing to offer for sale in a defined time period, ceteris paribus. Interpreting the individual *supply curve* for ZapMart shown in Exhibit 6 is basically the same as interpreting Bob's demand curve shown in Exhibit 1. Each point on the **supply curve** represents a quantity supplied (measured along the horizontal axis) at a particular price (measured along the vertical axis). For example, at a price of $10 per Blu-ray (point *C*), the quantity supplied by the seller,

Law of supply
The principle that there is a direct relationship between the price of a good and the quantity sellers are willing to offer for sale in a defined time period, ceteris paribus.

Supply curve
A curve or schedule showing the various quantities of a product sellers are willing to produce and offer for sale at possible prices during a specified period of time, ceteris paribus.

EXHIBIT 6   An Individual Seller's Supply Curve for Blu-Rays

The supply curve for an individual seller, such as ZapMart, shows the quantity of Blu-rays offered for sale at different possible prices. As the price of Blu-rays rises, a retail store has an incentive to increase the quantity of Blu-rays supplied per year. The direct relationship between price and quantity supplied conforms to the law of supply.

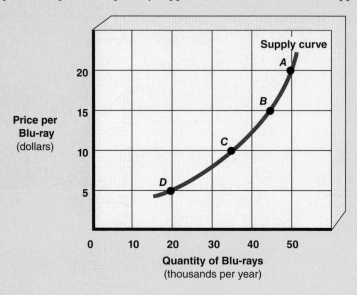

An Individual Seller's Supply Schedule for Blu-rays

Point	Price per Blu-ray	Quantity supplied (thousands per year)
A	$20	50
B	15	45
C	10	35
D	5	20

ZapMart, is 35,000 Blu-rays per year. At the higher price of $15, the quantity supplied increases to 45,000 Blu-rays per year (point *B*).

CONCLUSION   Supply curve is a curve or schedule showing the various quantities of a product sellers are willing to produce and offer for sale at possible prices during a specified period of time, ceteris paribus.

Why are sellers willing to sell more at a higher price? Suppose Farmer Brown is trying to decide whether to devote more of his land, labor, and barn space to the production of soybeans. Recall from Chapter 2 the production possibilities curve and the concept of increasing opportunity cost developed in Exhibit 3. If Farmer Brown devotes few of his resources to producing soybeans, the opportunity cost of, say, producing milk is small. But increasing soybean production means a higher opportunity cost, measured by the quantity of milk not produced. The logical question is: What would induce Farmer Brown to produce more soybeans for sale and overcome the higher opportunity cost of producing less milk? You guessed it! There must be the *incentive* of a higher price for soybeans.

Only at a higher price will it be profitable for sellers to incur the higher opportunity cost associated with producing and supplying a larger quantity.	**CONCLUSION**

CHECKPOINT

Can the Law of Supply Be Repealed for the Oil Market?
The United States experienced two oil shocks during the 1970s in the aftermath of Middle East tensions. Congress said no to high oil prices by passing a law prohibiting prices above a legal limit. Supporters of such price controls said this was a way to ensure adequate supply without allowing oil producers to earn excess profits. Did price controls increase, decrease, or have no effect on U.S. oil production during the 1970s?

3-4a Market Supply

To construct a market supply curve, we follow the same procedure used to derive a market demand curve. That is, we *horizontally* sum all the quantities supplied at various prices that might prevail in the market.

Let's assume that Entertain City and High Vibes are the only two firms selling Blu-rays in a given market. As you can see in Exhibit 7, the market supply curve, S_{total}, slopes upward to the right. At a price of $25, Entertain City will supply 25,000 Blu-rays per year, and High Vibes will supply 35,000 Blu-rays per year. Thus, summing the two individual supply curves, S_1 and S_2, *horizontally*, the total of 60,000 Blu-rays is plotted at this price on the market supply curve, S_{total}. Similar calculations at other prices along the price axis generate a market supply curve, telling us the total amount of Blu-rays these businesses offer for sale at different selling prices.

3-5 THE DISTINCTION BETWEEN CHANGES IN QUANTITY SUPPLIED AND CHANGES IN SUPPLY

As with demand, the price of a product is not the only factor that influences how much sellers offer for sale. Once we relax the ceteris paribus assumption, there are six principal *nonprice determinants* (also called *supply shifters*) that can shift the supply curve's

EXHIBIT 7 The Market Supply Curve for Blu-Rays

Entertain City and High Vibes are two businesses selling Blu-rays. If these are the only two firms in the Blu-ray market, the market supply curve, S_{total}, can be derived by summing horizontally the individual supply curves, S_1 and S_2.

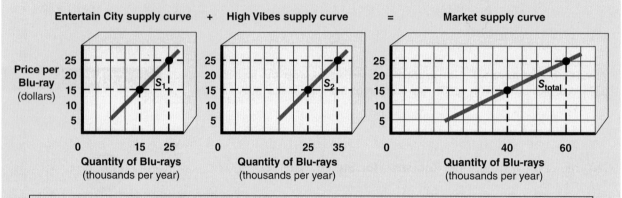

The Market Supply Schedule for Blu-rays

Price per Blu-ray	Quantity supplied (thousands per year)				
	Entertain City	+	High Vibes	=	Total supply
$25	25		35		60
20	20		30		50
15	15		25		40
10	10		20		30
5	5		15		20

position: (1) The number of sellers, (2) Technology, (3) Resource prices, (4) Taxes and subsidies, (5) Expectations, and (6) Prices of other goods the firm can produce.

We will discuss these nonprice determinants in more detail momentarily, but first we must distinguish between a *change in quantity supplied* and a *change in supply*.

Change in quantity supplied

A movement between points along a stationary supply curve, ceteris paribus.

A **change in quantity supplied** is a movement between points along a stationary supply curve, ceteris paribus. In Exhibit 8(a), at the price of $10, the quantity supplied is 30 million Blu-rays per year (point A). At the higher price of $15, sellers offer a larger "quantity supplied" of 40 million Blu-rays per year (point B). Economists describe the effect of the rise in price as an increase in the quantity supplied of 10 million Blu-rays per year.

CONCLUSION

Under the law of supply, any increase in price along the vertical axis will cause an increase in the quantity supplied, measured along the horizontal axis, and appears as a movement along the supply curve.

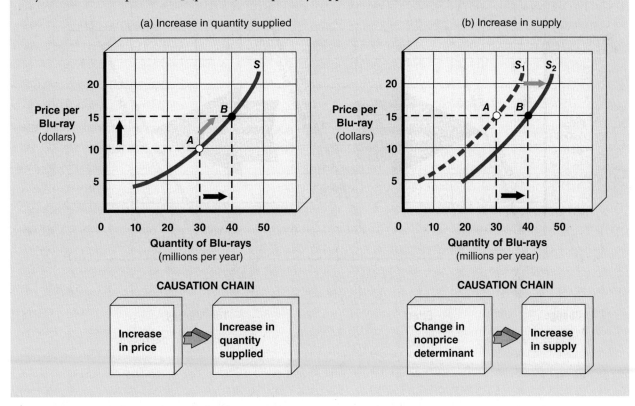

EXHIBIT 8 Movement along a Supply Curve versus a Shift in Supply

Part (a) presents the market supply curve, S, for Blu-rays per year. If the price is $10 at point A, the quantity supplied by firms will be 30 million Blu-rays. If the price increases to $15 at point B, the quantity supplied will increase from 30 million to 40 million Blu-rays.

Part (b) illustrates an increase in supply. A change in some nonprice determinant can cause an increase in supply from S_1 to S_2. At a price of $15 on S_1 (point A), the quantity supplied per year is 30 million Blu-rays. At this same price on S_2 (point B), the quantity supplied increases to 40 million.

A **change in supply** is an increase (rightward shift) or a decrease (leftward shift) in the quantity supplied at each possible price. If ceteris paribus no longer applies and if one of the six nonprice factors changes, the impact is to alter the supply curve's location.

Changes in nonprice determinants can produce only a shift in the supply curve and not a movement along the supply curve.

CONCLUSION

Change in supply
An increase or a decrease in the quantity supplied at each possible price. An increase in supply is a rightward shift in the entire supply curve. A decrease in supply is a leftward shift in the entire supply curve.

In Exhibit 8(b), the rightward shift (an increase in supply) from S_1 to S_2 means that at all possible prices, sellers offer a greater quantity for sale. At $15 per Blu-ray, for instance, sellers provide 40 million for sale annually (point B), rather than 30 million (point A). On the other hand, if some nonprice factor changes in a way that causes a leftward shift (a decrease in supply) from supply curve S_1, a smaller quantity will be offered for sale at any price.

EXHIBIT 9 Terminology for Changes in Price and Nonprice Determinants of Supply

Caution! As with demand curves, you must distinguish between a change in quantity supplied, which is a movement along a supply curve (S_1) in response to a change in price, and a shift in the supply curve. An increase in supply (shift to S_2) or a decrease in supply occurs (shift to S_3) is caused by a change in some nonprice determinant and not by a change in the price.

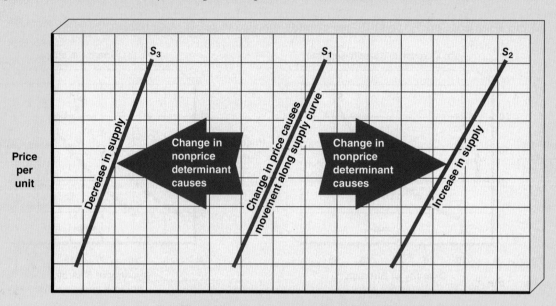

Quantity of good or service per unit of time

Change	Effect	Terminology
Price increases	Upward movement along the supply curve	Increase in the quantity supplied
Price decreases	Downward movement along the supply curve	Decrease in the quantity supplied
Nonprice determinant	Leftward or rightward shift in the supply curve	Decrease or increase in supply

Exhibit 9 summarizes the terminology for the effects of changes in price and non-price determinants on the supply curve.

3-6 NONPRICE DETERMINANTS OF SUPPLY

Now we turn to how each of the six basic nonprice factors affects supply.

3-6a Number of Sellers

What happens when a severe drought destroys wheat or a frost ruins the orange crop? The damaging effect of the weather may force orange growers out of business, and supply decreases. When the government eases restrictions on hunting alligators, the number of alligator hunters increases, and the supply curve for alligator meat and skins increases. Internationally, the United States may decide to lower trade barriers on textile imports, and this action increases supply by allowing new foreign firms to add their individual supply curves to the U.S. market supply curve for textiles. Conversely, higher U.S. trade barriers on textile imports shift the U.S. market supply curve for textiles leftward.

3-6b Technology

Never has society experienced such an explosion of new production techniques. Throughout the world, new and more efficient technology is making it possible to manufacture more products at any possible selling price. New, more powerful personal computers (PCs) reduce production costs and increase the supply of all sorts of goods and services. For example, computers are now milking cows. Computers admit the cows into the milking area and then activate lasers to guide milking cups into place. Dairy farmers no longer must wake up at 5:30 a.m., and cows get milked whenever they wish, day or night. As this technology spreads across the United States, it will be possible to offer more milk for sale at each possible price, and the entire supply curve for milk will shift to the right.

3-6c Resource Prices

Natural resources, labor, capital, and entrepreneurship are all required to produce products, and the prices of these resources affect supply. Suppose many firms are competing for computer programmers to design their software, and the salaries of these highly skilled workers increase. This increase in the price of labor adds to the cost of production. Along the original supply curve, extra costs must be added to each possible price. As a result, the supply of computer software shifts leftward (decreases) because sellers must charge more than before for any quantity supplied. Any reduction in production cost caused by a decline in the price of resources will have an opposite effect on the supply curve and it shifts rightward (increases). Along the original supply curve, cost declines, so the price can be reduced at each possible quantity supplied.

3-6d Taxes and Subsidies

Certain taxes, such as excise taxes imposed on sellers, have the same effect on supply as does an increase in the price of a resource. The impact of an excise tax (or "per unit" tax) that must be paid by sellers is similar to a rise in the cost of a microprocessor. The excise tax imposes an additional production cost on, for example, Blu-rays, and the supply curve shifts leftward. Conversely, a payment from the government for each Blu-ray produced (an unlikely subsidy) would have the same effect as lower prices for resources or a technological advance. That is, the supply curve for Blu-rays shifts rightward.

3-6e Expectations of Producers

Expectations affect both current demand and current supply. Suppose a war in the Middle East causes oil producers to believe that oil prices will rise dramatically.

Their initial response could be to hold back a portion of the oil in their storage tanks so that they can sell more and make greater profits later when oil prices rise. One approach used by the major oil companies might be to limit the amount of gasoline delivered to independent distributors. This response by the oil industry shifts the current supply curve to the left. Now suppose farmers anticipate that the price of wheat will soon fall sharply. The reaction is to sell their inventories stored in silos today before the price declines tomorrow. Such a response shifts the supply curve for wheat to the right.

3-6f Prices of Other Goods the Firm Could Produce

Businesses are always considering shifting resources from producing one good to producing another good. A rise in the price of one product relative to the prices of other products signals to suppliers that switching production to the product with the higher relative price yields higher profit. Suppose the price of corn rises because of government incentives to grow corn for ethanol while the price of wheat remains the same; then many farmers will divert more of their land to corn and less to wheat. The result is an increase in the supply of corn and a decrease in the supply of wheat. This happens because the opportunity cost of growing wheat, measured in forgone corn profits, increases.

Exhibit 10 summarizes the relationship between changes in the nonprice determinants of supply and the supply curve, accompanied by examples for each type of nonprice factor change.

EXHIBIT 10 Summary of the Impact of Changes in Nonprice Determinants of Supply on the Supply Curve

Nonprice determinant of supply	Relationship to changes in supply curve	Shift in the supply curve	Examples
1. Number of sellers	Direct		• The United States lowers trade restrictions on foreign textiles, and the supply of textiles in the United States increases.
			• A severe drought destroys the orange crop, and the supply of oranges decreases.
2. Technology	Direct		• New methods of producing automobiles reduce production costs, and the supply of automobiles increases.
			• Technology is destroyed in war, and production costs increase; the result is a decrease in the supply of good X.

(Continued)

Continued from previous page

Nonprice determinant of supply	Relationship to changes in supply curve	Shift in the supply curve	Examples
3. Resource prices	Inverse		• A decline in the price of computer chips increases the supply of computers.
			• An increase in the cost of farm equipment decreases the supply of soybeans.
4. Taxes and subsidies	Inverse		• An increase in the per-pack tax on cigarettes reduces the supply of cigarettes.
	Direct		• A government payment to dairy farmers based on the number of gallons produced increases the supply of milk.
5. Expectations	Inverse		• Oil companies anticipate a substantial rise in future oil prices, and this expectation causes these companies to decrease their current supply of oil.
			• Farmers expect the future price of wheat to decline, so they increase the present supply of wheat.
6. Prices of other goods and services	Inverse		• A rise in the price of brand-name drugs causes drug companies to decrease the supply of generic drugs.
			• A decline in the price of tomatoes causes farmers to increase the supply of cucumbers.

3-7 A MARKET SUPPLY AND DEMAND ANALYSIS

"Teach a parrot to say 'supply and demand' and you've got an economist." Drum roll, please! Buyer and seller actors are on center stage to perform a balancing act in a market. A **market** is any arrangement in which buyers and sellers interact to determine the price and quantity of goods and services exchanged. Let's consider the retail market for

Market
Any arrangement in which buyers and sellers interact to determine the price and quantity of goods and services exchanged.

YOU'RE THE **ECONOMIST**

Applicable Concept: Nonprice Determinants of Demand and Supply

PC Prices: How Low Can They Go?

Farknot Architect/Shutterstock.com

Radio was in existence for 38 years before 50 million people tuned in. Television took 13 years to reach that benchmark. Sixteen years after the first PC kit was introduced, 50 million people were using one. When available to the public, the Internet crossed that line in four years.[1] Before 1999, there were no blogs, and now there are millions. Today approximately 85 percent of U.S. households have a computer. Following are quotes from articles that illustrate changes in supply and demand for computers over time.

An Associated Press article reported in 1998:

Personal computers, which tumbled below the $1,000-price barrier just 18 months ago, now are breaking through the $400 price mark—putting them within reach of the average U.S. family. The plunge in PC prices reflects declining wholesale prices for computer parts, such as microprocessors, memory chips, and hard drives. "We've seen a massive transformation in the PC business," said Andrew Peck, an analyst with Cowen & Co., based in Boston.[2]

In 2001, an article in *The New York Times* described a computer price war:

We reached a situation where the market was saturated in 2000. People who needed computers had them. Vendors are living on sales of replacements, at least in the United States. But that doesn't give you the kind of growth these companies were used to. In the past, most price cuts came from falling prices for processors and other components. In addition, manufacturers have been narrowing profit margins for the last couple years. But when demand dried up last fall, the more aggressive manufacturers decided to try to gain market share by cutting prices to the bone. This is an all-out battle for market share.[3]

In 2016, analysts at *MarketWatch* observed the following decline in PC sales:

PCs are being left in the dust by the more preferred mobile devices such as smartphones and tablets. Worldwide growth of smartphone shipments skyrocketed by 1,000% between 2007 and 2015. PCs, meanwhile, have been on the decline since peaking at 362 million [in sales] in 2011, dropping by more than 20% over the past four years alone…[4]

Finally, Wikipedia reports that over time changes in supply and demand have continued to reduce PC prices. In 1982, for example, Dell offered a $3,000 PC. By 1998, the average selling price was below $1,000. Today, computers selling for less than $300 outperform computers from only a few years previously.

> **ANALYZE** THE ISSUE   Identify changes in quantity demanded, changes in demand, changes in quantity supplied, or changes in supply described in the article. For any change in demand or supply, also identify the nonprice determinant causing the change.

1. The Emerging Digital Economy (U.S. Department of Commerce, 1998), Chapter 1, P. 1.
2. David E. Kalish, "Pc Prices Fall Below $400, Luring Bargain-Hunters," Associated Press/Charlotte Observer, August 25, 1998, p. 3D.
3. Barnaby J. Feder, "Five Questions for Martin Reynolds: A Computer Price War Leaves Buyers Smiling," The New York Times, May 13, 2001.
4. Jon Swartz and Adam Ganucheau, "PCs Hang in, Tables … Don't," USA Today, "The Rise and Fall of the PC in One Chart," http://www.marketwatch.com/story/one-chart-shows-how-mobile-has-crushed-pcs-2016-04-20, April 24, 2016.

EXHIBIT 11 Demand, Supply, and Equilibrium for Sneakers (Pairs per Year)

(1) Price per pair	(2) Quantity demanded	(3) Quantity supplied	(4) Difference (3)–(2)	(5) Market condition	(6) Pressure on price
$105	25,000	75,000	+50,000	Surplus	Downward
90	30,000	70,000	+40,000	Surplus	Downward
75	40,000	60,000	+20,000	Surplus	Downward
60	50,000	50,000	0	Equilibrium	Stationary
45	60,000	35,000	−25,000	Shortage	Upward
30	80,000	20,000	−60,000	Shortage	Upward
15	100,000	5,000	−95,000	Shortage	Upward

sneakers. Exhibit 11 displays hypothetical market demand and supply data for this product. Notice in column 1 of the exhibit that price serves as a common variable for both supply and demand relationships. Columns 2 and 3 list the quantity demanded and the quantity supplied for pairs of sneakers per year.

The important question for market supply and demand analysis is this: Which selling price and quantity will prevail in the market? Let's start by asking what will happen if retail stores supply 75,000 pairs of sneakers and charge $105 a pair. At this relatively high price for sneakers, consumers are willing and able to purchase only 25,000 pairs. As a result, 50,000 pairs of sneakers remain as unsold inventory on the shelves of sellers (column 4), and the market condition is a surplus (column 5). A **surplus** is a market condition existing at any price where the quantity supplied is greater than the quantity demanded.

How will retailers react to a surplus? Competition forces sellers to bid down their selling price to attract more sales (column 6). If they cut the selling price to $90, there will still be a surplus of 40,000 pairs of sneakers, and pressure on sellers to cut their selling price will continue. If the price falls to $75, there will still be an unwanted surplus of 20,000 pairs of sneakers remaining as inventory, and pressure to charge a lower price will persist.

Now let's assume sellers slash the price of sneakers to $15 per pair. This price is very attractive to consumers, and the quantity demanded is 100,000 pairs of sneakers each year. However, sellers are willing and able to provide only 5,000 pairs at this price. The good news is that some consumers buy these 5,000 pairs of sneakers at $15. The bad news is that potential buyers are willing to purchase 95,000 more pairs at that price, but cannot because the shoes are not on the shelves for sale. This out-of-stock condition signals the existence of a shortage. A **shortage** is a market condition existing at any price where the quantity supplied is less than the quantity demanded.

In the case of a shortage, unsatisfied consumers compete to obtain the product by bidding to pay a higher price. Because sellers are seeking the higher profits that higher prices make possible, they gladly respond by setting a higher price of, say, $30 and increasing the quantity supplied to 20,000 pairs annually. At the price of $30, the shortage persists because the quantity demanded still exceeds the quantity supplied. Thus, a price of $30 will also be temporary because the unfulfilled quantity demanded provides an incentive for sellers to raise their selling price further and offer more sneakers for sale.

Surplus
A market condition existing at any price where the quantity supplied is greater than the quantity demanded.

Shortage
A market condition existing at any price at where the quantity supplied is less than the quantity demanded.

Suppose the price of sneakers rises to $45 a pair. At this price, the shortage falls to 25,000 pairs, and the market still gives sellers the message to move upward along their market supply curve and sell for a higher price.

3-7a Equilibrium Price and Quantity

Equilibrium
A market condition that occurs at any price and quantity at which the quantity demanded and the quantity supplied are equal.

Assuming sellers are free to sell their products at any price, trial and error will make all possible price-quantity combinations unstable except at equilibrium. **Equilibrium** occurs at any price and quantity where the quantity demanded and the quantity supplied are equal. Economists also refer to equilibrium as market clearing.

In Exhibit 11, $60 is the *equilibrium* price, and 50,000 pairs of sneakers is the *equilibrium* quantity per year. Equilibrium means that the forces of supply and demand are "in balance" or "at rest" and there is no reason for price or quantity to change, ceteris paribus. In short, all prices and quantities except a unique equilibrium price and quantity are temporary. Once the price of sneakers is $60, this price will not change unless a non-price factor changes demand or supply.

English economist Alfred Marshall (1842–1924) compared supply and demand to a pair of scissor blades. He wrote, "We might as reasonably dispute whether it is the upper or the under blade of a pair of scissors that cuts a piece of paper, as whether value is governed by utility [demand] or cost of production [supply]."[1] Joining market supply and market demand in Exhibit 12 allows us to clearly see the "two blades," that is, the demand curve, *D*, and the supply curve, *S*. We can measure the amount of any surplus or shortage by the horizontal distance between the demand and supply curves. At any price *above* the equilibrium—say, $90—there is an *excess quantity supplied* (surplus) of 40,000 pairs of sneakers. For any price *below* equilibrium—$30, for example—the horizontal distance between the curves tells us there is an *excess quantity demanded* (shortage) of 60,000 pairs. When the price per pair is $60, the market supply curve and the market demand curve intersect at point *E* and the quantity demanded equals the quantity supplied at 50,000 pairs per year. At this price, there is neither a shortage nor a surplus of sneakers.

CONCLUSION

Graphically, the intersection of the supply curve and the demand curve is the market equilibrium price-quantity point. When all other nonprice factors are held constant, this is the only stable coordinate on the graph.

3-7b Rationing Function of the Price System

Price system
A mechanism that uses the forces of supply and demand to create an equilibrium through rising and falling prices.

Our analysis leads to an important conclusion. The predictable or stable outcome in the sneakers example is that the price will eventually come to rest at $60 per pair. All other factors held constant, the price may be above or below $60, but the forces of surplus or shortage guarantee that any price other than the equilibrium price is temporary. This is the theory of how the price system operates, and it is the cornerstone of microeconomic analysis. The **price system** is a mechanism that uses the forces of supply and demand to create equilibrium through rising and falling prices. Stated simply, price plays a *rationing* role. The price system is important because it is a mechanism for distributing scarce goods and services. At the equilibrium price of $60, only those consumers willing to pay $60 per pair get sneakers, and there are no shoes for buyers unwilling to pay that price.

[1]Alfred Marshall, Principles of Economics, 8th ed. New York: Macmillan, 1982, p. 348.

EXHIBIT **12** The Supply and Demand for Sneakers

The supply and demand curves represent a market for sneakers. The intersection of the demand curve, *D*, and the supply curve, *S*, at point *E* indicates the equilibrium price of $60 and the equilibrium quantity of 50,000 pairs bought and sold per year. At any price above $60, a surplus prevails and pressure exists to push the price downward. At $90, for example, the excess quantity supplied of 40,000 pairs remains unsold. At any price below $60, a shortage provides pressure to push the price upward. At $30, for example, the excess quantity demanded of 60,000 pairs encourages consumers to bid up the price.

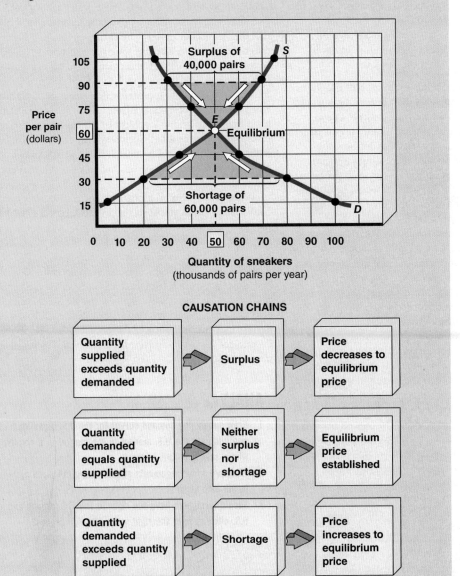

CAUSATION CHAINS

Quantity supplied exceeds quantity demanded	⇨	Surplus	⇨	Price decreases to equilibrium price
Quantity demanded equals quantity supplied	⇨	Neither surplus nor shortage	⇨	Equilibrium price established
Quantity demanded exceeds quantity supplied	⇨	Shortage	⇨	Price increases to equilibrium price

GLOBAL ECONOMICS

The Market Approach to Organ Shortages

Applicable Concept: Price System

There is a global market in human organs in spite of attempts to prevent these transactions. For example, China banned organ sales in 2006, and India did the same in 1994. Conversely, in Iran regulated kidney sales for profit are legal and currently there is no waiting list. The National Transplant Organ Act of 1984 made sale of organs illegal in the United States. Economist James R. Rinehart wrote the following on this subject:

> If you were in charge of a kidney transplant program with more potential recipients than donors, how would you allocate the organs under your control? Life and death decisions cannot be avoided. Some individuals are not going to get kidneys regardless of how the organs are distributed because there simply are not enough to go around. Persons who run such programs are influenced in a variety of ways. It would be difficult not to favor friends, relatives, influential people, and those who are championed by the press.
>
> The selection process frequently takes the form of having the patient wait at home until a suitable donor is found. What this means is that, at any given point in time, many potential recipients are just waiting for an organ to be made available. In essence, the organs are rationed to those who are able to survive the wait. In many situations, patients are simply screened out because they are not considered to be suitable candidates for a transplant. For instance, patients with heart disease and overt psychosis often are excluded. Others with end-stage liver disorders are denied new organs on the grounds that the habits that produced the disease may remain to jeopardize recovery...
>
> Under the present arrangements, owners receive no monetary compensation; therefore, suppliers are willing to supply fewer organs than potential recipients want. Compensating a supplier monetarily would encourage more people to offer their organs for sale. It also would be an excellent incentive for us to take better care of our organs. After all, who would want an enlarged liver or a weak heart...?[1]

The following illustrates the controversy: Apple CEO Steve Jobs had a temporary deliverance from death thanks to a liver transplant. This illustrates how the organ-donations system can be heavily weighted against poor potential recipients. Affluent patients like Steve Jobs can win the "transplant lottery" by listing simultaneously in different regions to increase their odds of finding a donor. In this case, a Palo Alto, Californian found his organ donor in Tennessee. The rules require that a prospective patient must be able to get to a center within seven or eight hours when an organ becomes available. This means a patient must be able to afford a private jet on standby and rent a place nearby the hospital. Such a system can be considered highly unfair. It should be noted that it is not known if Jobs was on more than one list, but this was allowed under the rules.

Based on altruism, the organ donor distribution system continues to result in shortages. In 2017, over 117,000 patients were on the waiting list for organs. When the price system is not allowed to allocate scarce items, alternative methods are often used to alleviate the shortage. For example, some European countries such as Spain, Belgium, and Austria have implemented an "opt out" organ donation system. In the opt out system, people are automatically considered as organ donors unless they officially declare that they do not wish to donate. Also, Facebook, encourages users to advertise their donor status on their pages.

ANALYZE THE ISSUE

1. Draw supply and demand curves for the U.S. organ market and compare the U.S. market to the market in a country where selling organs is legal.
2. What are some arguments against using the price system to allocate organs?
3. Should foreigners have the right to buy U.S. organs and U.S. citizens have the right to buy foreign organs?

---

1.   James R. Rinehart, "The Market Approach to Organ Shortages," *Journal of Health Care Marketing 8*, no. 1, March 1988, pp. 72–75.

Why would you prefer a world with all markets in equilibrium? If all markets were in equilibrium, there would be no shortages or surpluses for any good or service. In this world, consumers are not frustrated because they want to buy something and it is not on the shelf. Sellers are not upset because unsold merchandise is not piling up in their storerooms. Everyone is happy!

CHECKPOINT

Can the Price System Eliminate Scarcity?
You visit Cuba and observe that at "official" prices, there is a constant shortage of consumer goods in government stores. People explain that in Cuba, scarcity is caused by low prices combined with low production quotas set by the government. Many Cuban citizens say that the condition of scarcity would be eliminated if the government would allow markets to respond to supply and demand. Can the price system eliminate scarcity?

Key Concepts

Law of demand

Demand curve

Change in quantity demanded

Change in demand

Normal good

Inferior good

Substitute good

Complementary good

Law of supply

Supply curve

Change in quantity supplied

Change in supply

Market

Surplus

Shortage

Equilibrium

Price system

Summary

- The **law of demand** states there is an inverse relationship between the price and the quantity demanded, ceteris paribus. A market demand curve is the horizontal summation of individual demand curves.

- A **change in quantity demanded** is a movement along a stationary demand curve caused by a change in price.

- A **change in demand** occurs when any of the nonprice determinants of demand change, which causes the demand curve to shift. An *increase in demand* (rightward shift) or a *decrease in demand* (leftward shift) is caused by a change in one of the nonprice determinants.

Change in Quantity Demanded

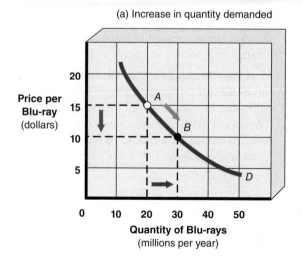

Change in Demand

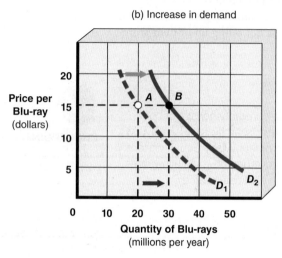

(b) Increase in demand

Change in Quantity Supplied

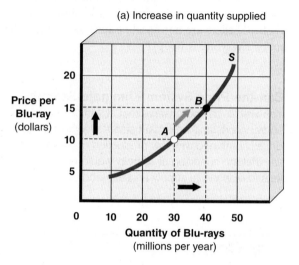

(a) Increase in quantity supplied

- **Nonprice determinants of demand** are as follows:
  a. Number of buyers
  b. Tastes and Preferences
  c. Income (normal and inferior goods)
  d. Expectations of future price and income changes
  e. Prices of related goods (substitutes and complements)

- The **law of supply** states there is a direct relationship between the price and the quantity supplied, ceteris paribus. The market supply curve is the horizontal summation of individual supply curves.

- A **change in quantity supplied** is a movement along a stationary supply curve caused by a change in price.

- A **change in supply** occurs when any of the nonprice determinants of supply change, which shifts the supply curve. An *increase in supply* (rightward shift) or a *decrease in supply* (leftward shift) is caused by a change in one of the nonprice determinants.

Change in Supply

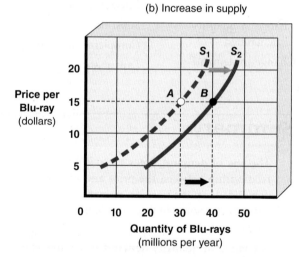

(b) Increase in supply

- **Nonprice determinants of supply** are as follows:
  a. Number of sellers
  b. Technology

c.   Resource prices
d.   Taxes and subsidies
e.   Expectations of future price changes
f.   Prices of other goods and services

- A **surplus** or **shortage** exists at any price where the quantity demanded and the quantity supplied are not equal. When the price of a good is higher than the equilibrium price, there is an excess quantity supplied, or *surplus*. When the price is less than the equilibrium price, there is an excess quantity demanded, or *shortage*.

- **Equilibrium** is the unique price and quantity established at the intersection of the supply and demand curves. Only at equilibrium does quantity demanded equal quantity supplied.

Equilibrium

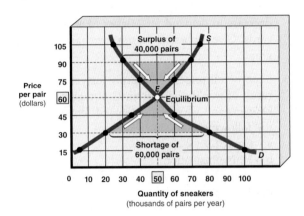

- The **price system** is the supply and demand mechanism that establishes equilibrium through the ability of prices to rise and fall.

Summary of Conclusion Statements

- **Demand curve** is a curve or schedule showing the various quantities of a product consumers are willing to purchase at possible prices during a specified period of time, ceteris paribus.

- Under the law of demand, any decrease in price along the vertical axis will cause an increase in quantity demanded, measured along the horizontal axis, and appears as a movement along the demand curve.

- Changes in nonprice determinants can produce only a shift in the demand curve and not a movement along the demand curve.

- **Supply curve** is a curve or schedule showing the various quantities of a product sellers are willing to produce and offer for sale at possible prices during a specified period of time, ceteris paribus.

- Only at a higher price will it be profitable for sellers to incur the higher opportunity cost associated with producing and supplying a larger quantity.

- Under the law of supply, any increase in price along the vertical axis will cause an increase in the quantity supplied, measured along the horizontal axis, and appears as a movement along the supply curve.

- Changes in nonprice determinants can produce only a shift in the supply curve and not a movement along the supply curve.

- Graphically, the intersection of the supply curve and the demand curve is the market equilibrium price-quantity point. When all other nonprice factors are held constant, this is the only stable coordinate on the graph.

Study Questions and Problems

Please see Appendix A for answers to the odd-numbered questions. Your instructor has access to the answers for even-numbered questions.

1. Some people will pay a higher price for brand-name goods. For example, some people buy Rolls Royce cars and Rolex watches to impress others. Does knowingly paying higher prices for certain items just to be a "snob" violates the law of demand?

2. Draw graphs to illustrate the difference between a decrease in the quantity demanded and a decrease in demand for Mickey Mantle baseball cards. Give a possible reason for change in each graph.

3. Suppose oil prices rise sharply for years as a result of war in the Persian Gulf region. What happens and why to the demand for each of the following?
   a. Cars
   b. Home insulation
   c. Coal
   d. Tires

4. Draw graphs to illustrate the difference between a decrease in quantity supplied and a decrease in supply for condominiums. Give a possible reason for change in each graph.

5. Use supply and demand analysis to explain why the quantity of word processing software exchanged increases from one year to the next.

6. Predict the direction of change for either supply or demand in the following situations:
   a. Several new companies enter the cell phone industry.
   b. Consumers suddenly decide SUVs are unfashionable.
   c. The U.S. surgeon general issues a report stating that tomatoes prevent colds.
   d. Frost threatens to damage the coffee crop, and consumers expect the price to rise sharply in the future.
   e. The price of tea falls. What is the effect on the coffee market?
   f. The price of sugar rises. What is the effect on the coffee market?
   g. Tobacco lobbyists convince Congress to remove the tax paid by sellers on each carton of cigarettes sold.
   h. A new type of robot is invented that will pick peaches.
   i. Nintendo anticipates that the future price of its games will fall much lower than the current price.

7. Explain the effect of the following situations:
   a. Population growth surges rapidly.
   b. The prices of resources used in the production of good X increase.
   c. The government is paying a $1-per-unit subsidy for each unit of a good produced.
   d. The incomes of consumers of normal good X increase.
   e. The incomes of consumers of inferior good Y decrease.
   f. Farmers are deciding what crop to plant and learn that the price of corn has fallen relative to the price of cotton.

8. Explain why the market price may not be the same as the equilibrium price.

9. If a new breakthrough in manufacturing technology reduces the cost of producing Blu-ray players by half, what will happen to the each of the following?
   a. Supply of Blue-ray players.
   b. Demand for Blu-ray players.
   c. Equilibrium price and quantity of Blu-ray players.
   d. Demand for Blu-rays.

10. The U.S. Postal Service is facing increased competition from firms providing overnight delivery of packages and letters. Additional competition has emerged because communications can be sent by emails, fax machine, and text messaging. What will be the effect of this competition on the market demand for mail delivered by the post office?

11. There is a shortage of college basketball and football tickets for some games, and a surplus occurs for other games. Why do shortages and surpluses exist for different games? Assume ticket prices are the same for all of a team's home games during a season.

12. Explain the statement "People respond to incentives and disincentives" in relation to the demand curve and supply curve for good X.

CHECKPOINT ANSWERS

Can Gasoline Become an Exception to the Law of Demand?

As the price of gasoline began to rise, the expectation of still higher prices caused buyers to buy more now, and therefore, demand increased. As shown in Exhibit 13, suppose the price per gallon of gasoline was initially at P_1 and the quantity demanded was Q_1 on demand curve D_1 (point A). Then war in the Middle East caused the demand curve to shift rightward to D_2. Along the new demand curve, D_2, consumers increased their quantity demanded to Q_2 at the higher price of P_2 per gallon of gasoline (point B). The increased demand caused more to be purchased even though the price increased.

The expectation of rising gasoline prices in the future caused "an increase in demand," rather than "an increase in quantity demanded." If you said this is not an exception to the law of demand, **YOU ARE CORRECT**.

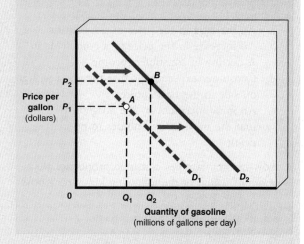

EXHIBIT 13 Increase in Demand

Can the Law of Supply Be Repealed for the Oil Market?

There is not a single quantity of oil—say, 3 million barrels—for sale in the world on a given day. The supply curve for oil is not vertical. As the law of supply states, higher oil prices will cause greater quantities of oil to be offered for sale. At lower prices, oil producers have less incentive to drill deeper for oil that is more expensive to discover.

The government cannot repeal the law of supply. Price controls discourage producers from oil exploration and production, which causes a reduction in the quantity supplied. If you said U.S. oil production decreased in the 1970s when the government put a lid on oil prices, **YOU ARE CORRECT**.

Can the Price System Eliminate Scarcity?

Recall from Chapter 1 that scarcity is the condition in which human wants are forever greater than the resources available to satisfy those wants. Using markets free from government interference will not solve the scarcity problem. Scarcity exists at any price for a good or service. This means scarcity occurs at any

disequilibrium price at which a shortage or surplus exists, and scarcity remains at any equilibrium price at which no shortage or surplus exists.

Although the price system can eliminate shortages (or surpluses), if you said it cannot eliminate scarcity, **YOU ARE CORRECT**.

Sample Quiz

Please see Appendix B for answers to Sample Quiz questions.

1. Which of the following causes the demand for veggie burgers to increase?
   a. A decline in the price of veggie burgers
   b. An increase in the price of tofu burgers, perceived as a substitute by veggie burger consumers

c. An increase in the price of burger buns

d. A technological innovation that lowers the cost of producing veggie burgers

2. Which of the following would *not* cause market demand for a normal good to decline?

a. An increase in the price of a substitute

b. An increase in the price of a complement

c. A decline in consumer income

d. Consumer expectations that the good will go on sale in the near future

e. An announcement by the Surgeon General that the product contributes to premature death

3. Low-income families consume proportionately more of which of the following kinds of goods?

a. Luxury goods

b. Substitute goods

c. Normal goods

d. Inferior goods

4. Suppose each of the seven dwarfs buys four mugs of ginger ale per week from Snow White's café, when the price per mug is $2. If the seven dwarfs are the entire market demand for Snow White's ginger ale, which of the following is the correct value for market quantity demanded of ginger ale per week at a price of $2?

a. 4

b. 8

c. 28

d. 7

5. Which of the following increases the supply of corn?

a. The farm workers' union successfully negotiates a pay increase for corn harvest workers.

b. The Surgeon General announces that eating corn contributes to heart disease.

c. Congress and the President eliminate subsidies formerly paid to corn farmers.

d. Farmers who grow soybeans can also grow corn, and the price of soybeans drops by 75 percent.

6. With an upward-sloping supply curve, which of the following is *true*?

a. An increase in price results in a decrease in quantity supplied.

b. An increase in price results in an increase in supply.

c. A decrease in price results in a decrease in quantity supplied.

d. A decrease in price results in an increase in supply.

7. A rightward shift in the demand curve is called a(an)

a. decrease in output.

b. decrease in demand.

c. increase in demand.

d. increase in income.

8. A surplus occurs when

a. the quantity demanded exceeds the quantity supplied.

b. price is below the equilibrium price.

c. price is at the equilibrium.

d. price is above the equilibrium.

9. A shortage occurs when

a. the quantity supplied exceeds the quantity demanded.

b. price is below the equilibrium price.

c. price is at the equilibrium.

d. price is above the equilibrium.

10. Which of the following decreases supply in the market for pizza?

a. Pizza shop employees successfully organize a union and negotiate a pay increase.

b. The Surgeon General announces that eating pizza reduces the incidence of stomach cancer.

c. Cheese prices drop because price supports for dairy farmers are removed.

d. Some hot sandwich shops can also make and sell pizzas, and consumer demand for hot sandwiches declines sharply, reducing the profitability of producing hot sandwiches.

11. Which of the following results from an increase in the price of a one-week vacation at beach resorts on the coast of Mexico?

a. An increase in the supply of bicycle tires in Toledo, Ohio

b. An increase in the demand for vacations at resorts on Caribbean islands

c. An increase in the supply of vacation opportunities at resorts on the coast of Mexico

d. A decrease in the demand for vacations at resorts on Caribbean islands

12. There is news that the price of Tucker's Root Beer will increase significantly next week. If the demand for Tucker's Root Beer reacts *only* to this factor and shifts to the right, the position of this demand curve has reacted to a change in
    a. tastes.
    b. income levels.
    c. the prices of related goods.
    d. the number of buyers.
    e. expectations.

13. Which of the following causes a shortage to become larger?
    a. An increase in market price
    b. An increase in supply
    c. A decrease in demand
    d. A decrease in price

14. Which of the following is *true* in ski towns such as Crested Butte, Colorado, and Whistler, British Columbia during the peak winter ski season as compared to May and June?
    a. Demand for motel rooms is higher.
    b. Demand for motel rooms is lower.
    c. There is a surplus of motel rooms.
    d. The price of motel rooms will be lower.

15. In moving from a shortage toward the market equilibrium, which of the following is *true*?
    a. Price falls.
    b. Price rises.
    c. Quantity demanded increases.
    d. Quantity supplied decreases.

16. The law of demand is the principle that there is _____ relationship between the price of a good and the quantity buyers are willing to purchase in a defined time period, ceteris paribus.
    a. a direct
    b. no
    c. an inverse
    d. an independent

17. A curve that is derived by summing horizontally individual demand curves is called

a. aggregate supply.
b. market supply.
c. aggregate demand.
d. market demand.

18. A leftward shift in the demand curve is called a(an)
    a. decrease in demand.
    b. decrease in quantity demanded.
    c. increase in demand.
    d. increase in quantity demanded.

19. Under the law of demand, any increase in price will cause _____ in quantity demanded.
    a. a decrease
    b. an increase
    c. no change
    d. constant change

20. The law of supply is the principle that the relationship between the price of a good and the quantity sellers are willing to offer for sale in a defined time period, ceteris paribus, is
    a. inverse.
    b. direct.
    c. no relationship.
    d. independent.

EXHIBIT 14 Demand and Supply Data for Video Games

Price	Quantity demanded of video games	Quantity supplied of video games
$75	400	900
70	450	850
65	500	800
60	550	750
55	600	700
50	650	650
45	700	600
40	750	550

21. Exhibit 14 presents supply and demand data for the video game market. If the price of video games was currently $70, there would be an _____ of _____ video games in this market.
    a. excess demand; 450
    b. excess demand; 500
    c. excess supply; 400
    d. excess supply; 850
    e. excess demand; 400

22. In Exhibit 14, if the price of video games was currently $45, there would be an _____ of _____ video games in this market.
    a. excess demand; 700
    b. excess demand; 500
    c. excess supply; 100
    d. excess supply; 600
    e. excess demand; 100

23. In Exhibit 14, at any market price of video games above $50, a(n) _____ would result, causing price to _____.

    a. excess demand; rise
    b. excess supply; rise
    c. excess demand; fall
    d. excess supply; fall
    e. shortage; rise

24. In Exhibit 14, at any market price of video games below $50, a(n) _____ would result, causing price to _____.
    a. excess demand; rise
    b. excess supply; rise
    c. excess demand; fall
    d. excess supply; fall
    e. surplus; rise

25. In Exhibit 14, if there is a shortage of video games of 200 units, the current price of video games must be
    a. $60.
    b. $55.
    c. $50.
    d. $45.
    e. $40.

Consumer Surplus, Producer Surplus, and Market Efficiency

This chapter explained how the market forces of demand and supply establish the equilibrium price and output. Here it will be demonstrated that the equilibrium price and quantity determined in a competitive market are desirable because the result is *market efficiency*. To understand this concept, we use the area between the market price and the demand and supply curves to measure gains or losses from market transactions for consumers and producers.

3A-1 CONSUMER SURPLUS

Consider the market demand curve shown in Exhibit A-1(a). The height of this demand curve shows the maximum willingness of consumers to purchase ground beef at various prices per pound. At a price of $4.00 (point *X*), no one will purchase ground beef. But if the price drops to $3.50 at point *A*, consumers will purchase 1 million pounds of ground beef per year. Moving downward along the demand curve to point *B*, consumers will purchase an additional million pounds of ground beef per year at a lower price of $3.00 per pound. If the price continues to drop to $2.50 per pound at point *C* and lower, consumers are willing to purchase more pounds of ground beef consistent with the law of demand.

Assuming the market equilibrium price for ground beef is $2.00 per pound, we can use the demand curve to measure the net benefit, or *consumer surplus*, in this market. **Consumer surplus** is the value of the difference between the price consumers are willing to pay for a product on the demand curve and the price actually paid for it. At point *A*, consumers are willing to pay $3.50 per pound, but they actually pay the equilibrium price of $2.00. Thus, consumers earn a surplus of $1.50 ($3.50 − $2.00) per pound multiplied by 1 million pounds purchased, which is a $1.5 million consumer surplus. This value is represented by the gray shaded vertical rectangle formed at point *A* on the demand curve. At point *B*, consumers who purchase an additional million pounds of ground beef at $3.00 per pound receive a lower extra consumer surplus than at point *A*, represented by a rectangle of lower height. At point *C*, the marginal consumer surplus continues to fall until at equilibrium point *E*, where there is no consumer surplus.

The total value of consumer surplus can be interpreted from the explanation given above. As shown in Exhibit A-1(b), begin at point *X* and instead of selected prices, now imagine offering ground beef to consumers at each possible price downward along the demand curve until the equilibrium price of $2.00 is reached at point *E*. The result is that the entire green triangular area between the demand curve and the horizontal line at the equilibrium price represents total consumer surplus. Note that a rise in the

Consumer surplus
The value of the difference between the price consumers are willing to pay for a product on the demand curve and the price actually paid for it.

EXHIBIT A-1 Market Demand Curve and Consumer Surplus

As illustrated in part (a), consumers are willing at point *A* on the market demand curve to pay $3.50 per pound to purchase 1 million pounds of ground beef per year. Since the equilibrium price is $2.00, this means they receive a consumer surplus of $1.50 for each pound of ground beef and the vertical gray shaded rectangular area is the consumer surplus earned only at point *A*. Others who pay less at points *B*, *C*, and *E* receive less consumer surplus and the height of the corresponding rectangles falls at each of these prices. In part (b), moving downward along all possible prices on the demand curve yields the green shaded triangle, which is equal to total consumer surplus (net benefit).

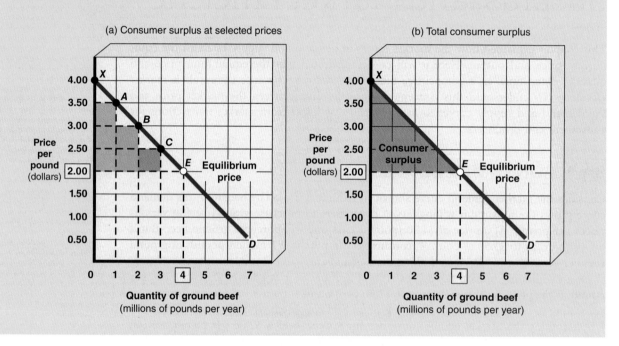

equilibrium price decreases total consumer surplus and a fall in the equilibrium price increases total consumer surplus.

CONCLUSION   Total consumer surplus measured in dollars is represented by the total area under the market demand curve and above the equilibrium price.

3A-2 PRODUCER SURPLUS

Similar to the concept of consumer surplus, the height of the market supply curve in Exhibit A-2(a) shows the producers' minimum willingness to accept payment for ground beef offered for sale at various prices per pound. At point *X*, firms offer no ground beef for sale at a price of zero and they divert their resources to an alternative use. At a price of $0.50 per pound (point *A*), the supply curve tells us that 1 million pounds will be

EXHIBIT **A-2** Market Supply Curve and Producer Surplus

In part (a), firms are willing at $0.50 (point *A*) to supply 1 million pounds of ground beef per year. Because $2.00 is the equilibrium price, the sellers earn a producer surplus of $1.50 per pound of ground beef sold. The first vertical shaded rectangle is the producer surplus earned only at point *A*. At points *B*, *C*, and *E*, sellers receive less producer surplus at each of these higher prices and the sizes of the rectangles fall. In part (b), moving upward along all possible selling prices on the supply curve yields the red-shaded triangle that is equal to total producer surplus (net benefit).

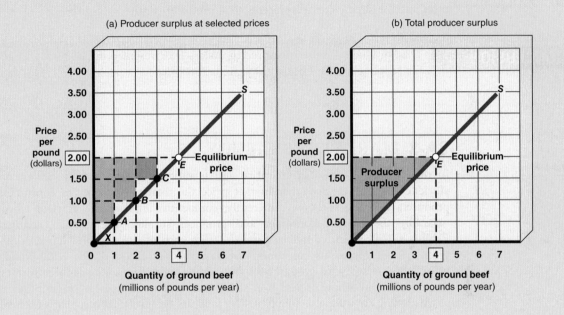

offered for sale. Moving upward along the supply curve to point *B*, firms will offer an additional million pounds of ground beef for sale at the higher price of $1.00 per pound. If the price rises to $1.50 at point *C* and higher, firms allocate more resources to ground beef production and another million pounds will be supplied along the supply curve.

Again, we will assume the equilibrium price is $2.00 per pound, and the supply curve can be used to measure the net benefit, or *producer surplus*. **Producer surplus** is the value of the difference between the actual selling price of a product and the price producers are willing to sell it for on the supply curve. Now assume the first million pounds of ground beef is sold at point *A* on the supply curve. In this case, producer surplus is the difference between the equilibrium selling price of $2.00 and the $0.50 price that is the minimum price that producers will accept to supply this quantity of ground beef. Thus, producer surplus is equal to $1.50 ($2.00−$0.50) per pound multiplied by 1 million pounds sold, which is a $1.5 million producer surplus. This value is represented by the vertical gray shaded rectangle formed at point *A* on the supply curve. The second million pounds of ground beef offered for sale at point *B* also generates a producer surplus because the selling price of $2.00 exceeds the $1.00

Producer surplus
The value of the difference between the actual selling price of a product and the price producers are willing to sell it for on the supply curve.

price at which firms are willing to supply this additional quantity of ground beef. Note that producer surplus is lower at point *B* compared to point *A*, and marginal producer surplus continues to fall at point *C* until it reaches zero at the equilibrium point *E*.

The total value of producer surplus is represented in Exhibit A-2(b). Start at point *X*, where none of the product will be supplied at the price of zero. Now consider the quantities of ground beef producers are willing to offer for sale at each possible price upward along the supply curve until the equilibrium price of $2.00 is reached at point *E*. The result is that the entire red triangular area between the horizontal line at the equilibrium price and the supply curve represents total producer surplus.

CONCLUSION Total producer surplus measured in dollars is represented by the total area above the supply curve and below the equilibrium price.

3A-3 MARKET EFFICIENCY

In this section, the equilibrium price and quantity will be shown to achieve market efficiency because at any other market price the total net benefits to consumers and producers will be less. Stated differently, competitive markets are efficient when they maximize the sum of consumer and producer surplus. The analysis continues in Exhibit A-3(a), which combines parts (b) from each of the two previous exhibits. The green triangle represents consumer surplus earned in excess of the $2.00 equilibrium price consumers pay for ground beef. The red triangle represents producer surplus producers receive by selling ground beef at $2.00 per pound in excess of the minimum price at which they are willing to supply it. The total net benefit (total surplus) is therefore the entire triangular area consisting of both the green consumer surplus and red producer surplus triangles.

Now consider in Exhibit A-3(b) the consequences to market efficiency of producers devoting fewer resources to ground beef production and only 2 million pounds being bought and sold per year compared with 4 million pounds at the equilibrium price of $2.00. The result is a deadweight loss. **Deadweight loss** is the net loss of consumer and producer surplus from underproduction or overproduction of a product. In Exhibit A-3 (b), the deadweight loss is equal to the gray triangle *ABE*, which represents the total surplus of green and red triangles in part (a) that is not obtained because the market is operating below equilibrium point *E*.

Exhibit A-3(c) illustrates that a deadweight loss of consumer and producer surplus can also result from overproduction. Now suppose more resources are devoted to production and 6 million pounds of ground beef are bought and sold at the equilibrium price. However, from the producers' side of the market, the equilibrium selling price is only $2.00 and is below any possible selling price on the supply curve between points *E* and *C*. Therefore, firms have a net loss for each pound sold beyond 4 million pounds, represented by the area under the supply curve and bounded below by the horizontal equilibrium price line. Similarly, consumers pay the equilibrium price of $2.00, but this price exceeds any price consumers are willing to pay between points *E* and *D* on the demand curve. This means consumers experience a total net benefit

Deadweight loss
The net loss of consumer and producer surplus from underproduction or over-production of a product.

EXHIBIT A-3 Comparison of Market Efficiency and Deadweight Loss

In part (a), the green triangle represents consumer surplus and the red triangle represents producer surplus. The total net benefit, or total surplus, is the entire triangle consisting of the consumer and producer surplus triangles.

In part (b), too few resources are used to produce 2 million pounds of ground beef compared to 4 million pounds at equilibrium point *E*. The market is inefficient because the deadweight loss gray triangle *ABE* is no longer earned by either consumers or producers. As shown in part (c), overproduction at the equilibrium price of $2.00 can also be inefficient. If 6 million pounds of ground beef are offered for sale, too many resources are devoted to this product and a deadweight loss of area *EDC* occurs.

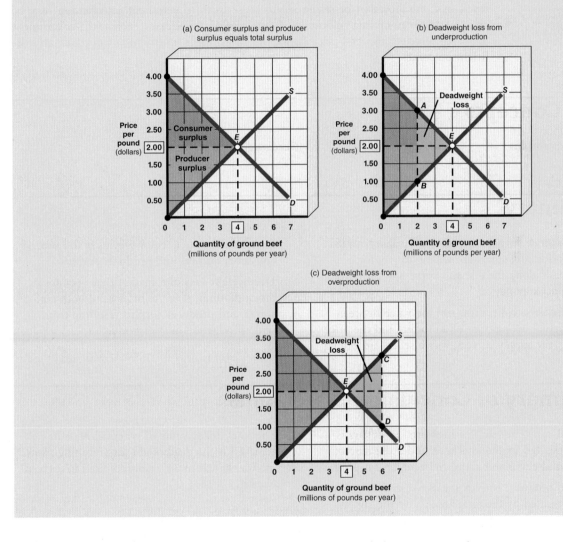

loss for each pound purchased, represented by the portion of the gray area above the demand curve but below the horizontal equilibrium price line. The total net loss of consumer and producer surplus (deadweight loss) is equal to the gray-shaded area *EDC*.

> **CONCLUSION** The total dollar value of potential benefits not achieved is the deadweight loss resulting from too few or too many resources used in a given market.

Looking ahead, the conclusion drawn from this appendix is that market equilibrium is efficient, but this conclusion is not always the case. In the next chapter, the topic of *market failure* will be discussed, in which market equilibrium under certain conditions can result in too few or too many resources being used to produce goods and services. For example, the absence of a competitive market, the existence of pollution, or vaccinations to prevent a disease can establish equilibrium conditions which are inefficient and result in a misallocation of resources. In these cases, government intervention may be able to achieve an optimal allocation of resources. In other cases, such as the government imposing price ceilings and price floors, the government intervention can create an inefficient outcome.

Key Concepts

Consumer surplus   Producer surplus   Deadweight loss

Summary

- **Consumer surplus** measures the value between the price consumers are willing to pay for a product along the demand curve and the price they actually pay.

- **Producer surplus** measures the value between the actual selling price of a product and the price along the supply curve at which sellers are willing

to sell the product. Total surplus is the sum of consumer surplus and producer surplus.

- **Deadweight loss** of a market that operates in disequilibrium. It is the net loss of both consumer and producer surplus resulting from underproduction or overproduction of a product.

Summary of Conclusion Statements

- Total consumer surplus measured in dollars is represented by the total area under the market demand curve and above the equilibrium price.

- Total producer surplus measured in dollars is represented by the total area above the supply curve and below the equilibrium price.

- The total dollar value of potential benefits not achieved is the deadweight loss resulting from too few or too many resources used in a given market.

Study Questions and Problems

Please see Appendix A for answers to the odd-numbered questions. Your instructor has access to the answers for even-numbered questions.

1. Consider the market for used textbooks. Use Exhibit A-4 to calculate the total consumer surplus.

EXHIBIT A-4 Used Textbook Market

Potential buyer	Willingness to pay	Market price
Brad	$60	$30
Juan	45	30
Sue	35	30
Jamie	25	30
Frank	10	30

2. Consider the market for used textbooks. Use Exhibit A-5 to calculate the total producer surplus.

EXHIBIT A-5 Used Textbook Market

Potential seller	Willingness to sell	Market price
Forest	$60	$30
Betty	45	30
Alan	35	30
Paul	25	30
Alice	10	30

3. Using Exhibits A-4 and A-5 above, calculate the total surplus. Then calculate the effect on consumer surplus, producer surplus, and total surplus of a fall in the equilibrium price of textbooks from $30 to $15 each. Explain the meaning of your calculations.

4. Using Exhibit A-6, and assuming the market is in equilibrium at Q_E, identify areas *ACD*, *DCE*, and *ACE*. Now explain the result of underproduction at *Q* in terms of areas *BCG*, *GCF*, and *BCF*.

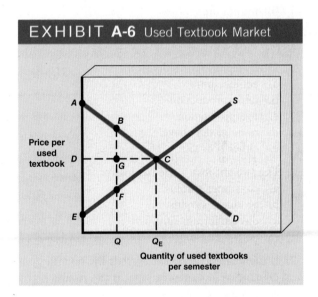

EXHIBIT A-6 Used Textbook Market

Sample Quiz

Please see Appendix B for answers to Sample Quiz questions.

1. Consumer surplus measures the value between the price consumers are willing to pay and the
   a. producer surplus price.
   b. deadweight gain price.
   c. actual price paid.
   d. preference price.

2. If Sam is willing to pay $50 for one good X, $30 for a second, $20 for a third, $8 for a fourth, and

the market price is $10. What is Sam's consumer surplus?
a. $10
b. $40
c. $70
d. $100

3. Suppose Tucker Inc. is willing to sell one gizmo for $10, a second gizmo for $15, a third for $20, and the market price is $25. What is Tucker Inc.'s producer surplus?
a. $10
b. $15
c. $30
d. $50

4. In an efficient market, deadweight loss is
a. maximum.
b. minimum.
c. constant.
d. zero.

5. Deadweight loss results from
a. equilibrium.
b. underproduction.
c. overproduction.
d. none of the above.
e. either b or c.

6. Deadweight loss is the net loss of
a. consumer surplus.
b. producer surplus.
c. disequilibrium surplus.
d. both a and b.

7. If the quantity supplied exceeds the quantity demanded in a market, what is the result?
a. Deadweight loss
b. Inefficiency
c. Overproduction
d. All of the above answers are correct

8. Suppose a consumer is willing to pay $20 for one good X, $10 for a second, and $5 for a third, and the market price is $4. What is the consumer surplus?
a. $16
b. $6
c. $1
d. $23

9. Producer surplus measures the value between the actual selling price and the
a. price sellers are willing to sell the product.
b. deadweight loss price.
c. lowest price sellers are willing to sell the product.
d. profit-maximization price.

10. Suppose seller X is willing to sell one good X for $5, a second good X for $10, a third for $16, a fourth for $25, and the market price is $20. What is seller X's producer surplus?
a. $15
b. $20
c. $22
d. $29

11. Deadweight loss is the result of
a. disequilibrium.
b. underproduction.
c. overproduction.
d. all of the above.

12. Deadweight loss is computed as the net of
a. consumer surplus minus producer surplus.
b. disequilibrium surplus plus consumer surplus.
c. producer surplus minus disequilibrium surplus.
d. consumer surplus plus producer surplus.

13. Deadweight loss is *not* the result of
a. an efficient market.
b. an inefficient market.
c. zero consumer surplus.
d. zero producer surplus.

14. At the equilibrium price, deadweight loss is
a. minimized.
b. zero.
c. maximized.
d. equal to the equilibrium price multiplied by the quantity exchanged.

15. If the quantity demanded exceeds the quantity supplied in a market, what is the result?
a. Deadweight loss
b. Inefficiency
c. Underproduction
d. All of the above answers are correct

EXHIBIT A-7 Comparison of Market Efficiency and Dead-weight Loss

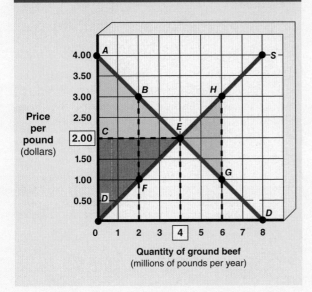

Quantity of ground beef
(millions of pounds per year)

16. As shown in Exhibit A-7, if the market is in equilibrium, _____ represents consumer surplus.
    a. *ABEC*
    b. *AED*
    c. *EGH*
    d. *BEF*

17. As shown in Exhibit A-7, if the market is in equilibrium, _____ represents producer surplus.

    a. *ADFB*
    b. *CEFD*
    c. *EGH*
    d. *BEF*

18. As shown in Exhibit A-7, if the quantity supplied is 2 million pounds of ground beef per year, what is the result?
    a. Deadweight loss
    b. Inefficiency
    c. Underproduction
    d. All of the above
    e. None of the above

19. As shown in Exhibit A-7, if the quantity supplied is 6 million pounds of ground beef per year, what is the result?
    a. Deadweight loss
    b. Inefficiency
    c. Overproduction
    d. All of the above
    e. None of the above

20. As shown in Exhibit A-7, if the quantity supplied is 2 million pounds of ground beef per year, the result is a deadweight loss represented by area
    a. *ABEC.*
    b. *CEFD.*
    c. *EGH.*
    d. *BEF.*

CHAPTER 4

Markets in Action

CHAPTER PREVIEW

When you understand how buyers and sellers respond to changes in equilibrium prices, you begin to understand the economic way of thinking. This chapter starts by showing that changes in supply and demand influence the equilibrium price and quantity of goods and services exchanged around you every day. For example, you will study the impact of changes in supply and demand curves on the markets for Caribbean cruises, new homes, and AIDS vaccinations. Then you will see why the laws of supply and demand cannot be repealed. Using market supply and demand analysis, you will learn that government policies to control markets have predictable consequences. For example, you will understand what happens when the government limits the maximum rent landlords can charge and who benefits and who loses from the federal minimum-wage law.

In this chapter, you will also study situations in which the market mechanism fails. Have you visited a city and lamented the smog that blankets the beautiful surroundings? Or have you ever wanted to swim or fish in a stream, but could not because of industrial waste? These are obvious cases in which market-system magic failed and the government must consider cures to reach socially desirable results.

IN THIS CHAPTER, YOU WILL LEARN TO SOLVE THESE ECONOMICS PUZZLES:

- How can a spotted owl affect the price of homes?

- How do demand and supply affect the price of high-definition televisions?

- Why might government warehouses overflow with cheese and milk?

- What do ticket scalping and rent controls have in common?

- Can vouchers fix our schools?

4-1 CHANGES IN MARKET EQUILIBRIUM

Using market supply and demand analysis is like putting on glasses if you are near-sighted. Suddenly, the fuzzy world around you comes into clear focus. Many people believe that prices are set by sellers adding a certain percentage to their costs. If costs rise, sellers simply raise their prices by that percentage. In free markets, there is more to the story. In the following examples, you will open your eyes and see that economic theory has something important to say about so many things in the real world.

4-1a Changes in Demand

The Caribbean cruise market shown in Exhibit 1(a) assumes market supply, S, is constant and market demand increases from D_1 to D_2. Why has the demand curve shifted rightward in the figure? We will assume the popularity of cruises to these vacation islands has suddenly risen sharply due to extensive advertising that influenced tastes and preferences. Given supply curve S and demand curve D_1, the initial equilibrium price is $600 per cruise, and the initial equilibrium quantity is 8,000 cruises per year, shown as point E_1. After the impact of advertising, the new equilibrium point, E_2, becomes 12,000 cruises per year at a price of $900 each. Thus, the increase in demand causes both the equilibrium price and the equilibrium quantity to increase.

It is important to understand the force that caused the equilibrium to shift from E_1 to E_2. When demand initially increased from D_1 to D_2, there was a temporary shortage of 8,000 cruises (16,000–8,000) at $600 per cruise. Firms in the cruise business responded to the excess demand by hiring more workers, offering more cruises to the Caribbean, and raising the price. The cruise lines therefore move upward along the supply curve (increasing quantity supplied, but not changing supply). During some period of trial and error, Caribbean cruise sellers increase their price and quantity supplied until a shortage no longer exists at point E_2. Therefore, the increase in demand causes both the equilibrium price and the equilibrium quantity to increase.

What will happen to the demand for gas-guzzling automobiles (for example, SUVs) if the price of gasoline triples? Because gasoline and automobiles are complements, a rise in the price of gasoline decreases the demand for gas guzzlers from D_1 to D_2 in Exhibit 1(b). At the initial equilibrium price of $30,000 per gas guzzler ($E_1$), the quantity supplied now exceeds the quantity demanded by 20,000 automobiles per month (30,000–10,000). This unwanted inventory forces automakers to reduce the price and quantity supplied. As a result of this movement downward on the supply curve, market equilibrium changes from E_1 to E_2. The equilibrium price falls from $30,000 to $20,000, and the equilibrium quantity falls from 30,000 to 20,000 gas guzzlers per month.

4-1b Changes in Supply

Now reverse the analysis by assuming demand remains constant and allow some non-price determinant to shift the supply curve. In Exhibit 2(a), begin at point E_1 in a market for babysitting services at an equilibrium price of $9 per hour and 4,000 babysitters hired per month. Then assume there is a population shift and the number of people available to babysit rises. This increase in the number of sellers shifts the market supply curve rightward from S_1 to S_2 and creates a temporary surplus of 4,000 babysitters (8,000–4,000) at

EXHIBIT 1 The Effects of Shifts in Demand on Market Equilibrium

In part (a), demand for Caribbean cruises increases because of extensive advertising and the demand curve shifts rightward from D_1 to D_2. This shift in demand causes a temporary shortage of 8,000 cruises per year at the initial equilibrium of E_1. This disequilibrium condition encourages firms in the cruise business to move upward along the supply curve to a new equilibrium at E_2.

Part (b) illustrates a decrease in the demand for gas-guzzling automobiles (SUVs) caused by a sharp rise in the price of gasoline (a complement). This leftward shift in demand from D_1 to D_2 results in a temporary surplus of 20,000 gas guzzlers per month at the initial equilibrium of E_1. This disequilibrium condition forces sellers of these cars to move downward along the supply curve to a new equilibrium at E_2.

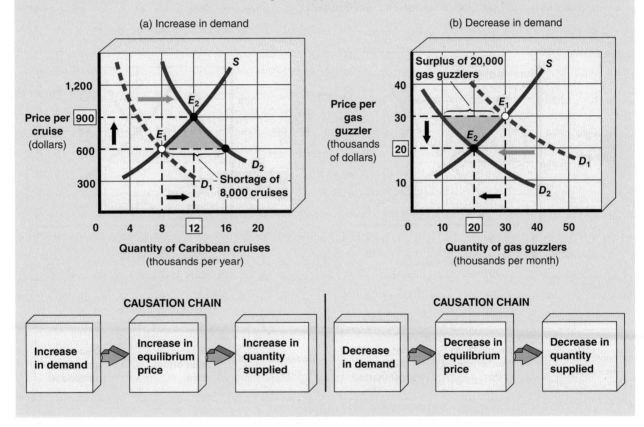

point E_1 who offer their services but are not hired. The unemployed babysitters respond by reducing the price and the number of babysitters available for hire, which is a movement downward along S_2. As the price falls, buyers move down along their demand curve and hire more babysitters per month. When the price falls to $6 per hour, the market is in equilibrium again at point E_2, instead of E_1, and consumers hire 6,000 babysitters per month.

Exhibit 2(b) illustrates the market for lumber. Suppose this market is at equilibrium at point E_1, where the going price is $400 per thousand board feet, and 8 billion board feet are bought and sold per year. Now suppose a new Endangered Species Act is passed, and the federal government sets aside huge forest resources to protect the

EXHIBIT 2 The Effects of Shifts in Supply on Market Equilibrium

In part (a), begin at equilibrium E_1 in the market for babysitters, and assume an increase in the number of babysitters shifts the supply curve rightward from S_1 to S_2. This shift in supply causes a temporary surplus of 4,000 unemployed babysitters per month. This disequilibrium condition causes a movement downward along the demand curve to a new equilibrium at E_2. At E_2, the equilibrium price declines, and the equilibrium quantity rises.

In part (b), steps to protect the environment cause the supply curve for lumber to shift leftward from S_1 to S_2. This shift in supply results in a temporary shortage of 4 billion board feet per year. Customer bidding for the available lumber raises the price. As a result, the market moves upward along the demand curve to a new equilibrium at E_2, and the quantity demanded falls.

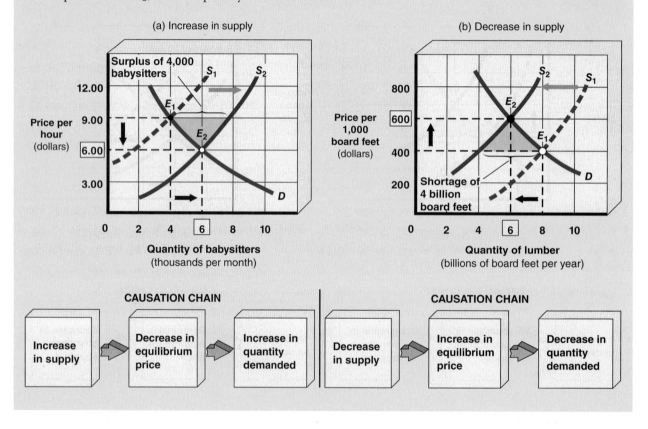

spotted owl and other wildlife. This means the market supply curve shifts leftward from S_1 to S_2, and a temporary shortage of 4 billion board feet of lumber exists (8 billion–4 billion) at point E_1. Suppliers respond by hiking their price from $400 to $600 per thousand board feet, and a new equilibrium is established at E_2, where the quantity is 6 billion board feet per year. This higher cost of lumber, in turn, raises the price of a new home.

Exhibit 3 gives a concise summary of the impact of changes in demand or supply on market equilibrium.

EXHIBIT 3 The Effects of Shifts in Supply on Market Equilibrium

Change	Effect on equilibrium price	Effect on equilibrium quantity
Demand increases	Increases	Increases
Demand decreases	Decreases	Decreases
Supply increases	Decreases	Increases
Supply decreases	Increases	Decreases

CHECKPOINT

Why the Lower Price for Big-Screen High-Definition Televisions?

Suppose more consumers were willing and able to purchase more big-screen high-definition televisions because of their increased popularity, and at the same time, producers manufactured more of these sets. Within one year, the price of big-screen hi-def televisions would fall dramatically. During this period, which would increase more—demand, supply, or neither?

4-1c Trend of Equilibrium Prices over Time

Basic demand and supply analysis allows us to explain a trend in prices over a number of years. Exhibit 4 shows the effect of changes in nonprice determinants that increase both the demand and supply curves for good *X* between 2010, 2015, and 2020. A line connects the equilibrium prices for each year in order to summarize the trend of equilibrium price and quantity changes over this time period. In this case, the observed prices trace an upward-sloping trend line.

4-2 CAN THE LAWS OF SUPPLY AND DEMAND BE REPEALED?

The government intervenes in some markets with the objective of preventing prices from rising to the equilibrium price. In other markets, the government's goal is to intervene and maintain a price higher than the equilibrium price. Market supply and demand analysis is a valuable tool for understanding what happens when the government fixes prices. There are two types of price controls: *price ceilings* and *price floors*.

4-2a Price Ceilings

Case 1: Rent Controls

What happens if the government prevents the price system from setting a market price "too high" by mandating a price ceiling? A **price ceiling** is a legally established maximum price a seller can charge. Rent controls are an example of the imposition of a price

Price ceiling
A legally established maximum price a seller can charge.

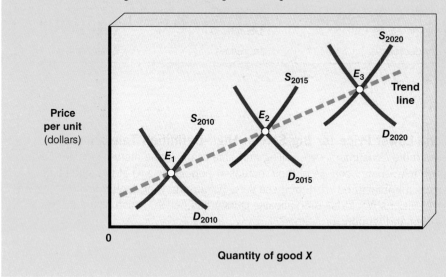

EXHIBIT 4 Trend of Equilibrium Prices over Time

Nonprice determinants of demand and supply for good X have caused both the demand and supply curves to shift rightward between 2010 and 2020. As a result, the equilibrium price and quantity in this example rise along the upward-sloping trend line connecting each observed equilibrium price.

ceiling in the market for rental units. New York City, Washington, D.C., Los Angeles, San Francisco, and other communities in the United States have some form of rent control. Since World War I, rent controls have been widely used in Europe. The rationale for rent controls is to provide an "essential service" that would otherwise be unaffordable by many people at the equilibrium rental price. Let's see why most economists believe that rent controls are counterproductive.

Exhibit 5 is a supply and demand diagram for the quantity of rental units demanded and supplied per month in a hypothetical city. We begin the analysis by assuming no rent controls exist and equilibrium is at point *E*, with a monthly rent of $1,200 per month and 6 million units occupied. Next, assume the city council imposes a rent control (ceiling price) that by law forbids any landlord from renting a unit for more than $800 per month. What does market supply and demand theory predict will happen? At the low rent ceiling of $800, the quantity demanded of rental units will be 8 million, but the quantity supplied will be only 4 million. Consequently, the price ceiling creates a persistent market shortage of 4 million rental units because suppliers cannot raise the rental price without being subjected to legal penalties.

Note that a rent ceiling at or above $1,200 per month would have no effect. If the ceiling is set at the equilibrium rent of $1,200, the quantity of rental units demanded and the quantity of rental units supplied are equal regardless of the rent control. If the rent ceiling is set above the equilibrium rent, the quantity of rental units supplied exceeds the quantity of rental units demanded, and this surplus will cause the market to adjust to the equilibrium rent of $1,200.

EXHIBIT 5 Rent Control Results in a Shortage of Rental Units

If no rent controls exist, the equilibrium rent for a hypothetical apartment is $1,200 per month at point *E*. However, if the government imposes a rent ceiling of $800 per month, a shortage of 4 million rental units occurs. Because rent cannot rise by law, one outcome is that consumers must search for available units instead of paying a higher rent. Other outcomes include a black market, bribes, discrimination, and other illegal methods of dealing with a shortage of 4 million rental units per month.

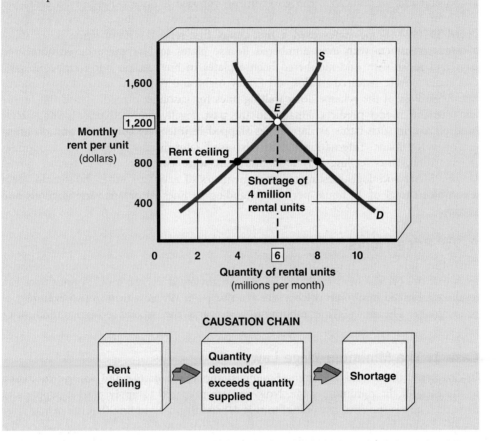

What is the impact of rent controls on consumers? First, as a substitute for paying higher prices, consumers must spend more time on waiting lists and searching for housing. This means consumers incur an *opportunity cost* added to the $800 rent set by the government. Second, an illegal market, or *black market*, can arise because of the excess quantity demanded. Because the price of rental units is artificially low, the profit motive encourages tenants to risk breaking the law by subletting their unit to the highest bidder over $800 per month.

From the seller's perspective, rent control encourages two undesirable effects. First, faced with a mandated low rent, landlords may cut maintenance expenses, and housing deterioration will reduce the stock of rental units in the long run. Second, landlords may use discriminatory practices to replace the price system. Once owners realize there is an excess quantity demanded for rentals at the controlled price, they may resort to preferences based on pet ownership or family size to determine how to allocate scarce rental space.

Case 2: Gasoline Price Ceiling

The government placed ceilings on most nonfarm prices during World War II and, to a lesser extent, during the Korean War. In 1971, President Nixon "froze" virtually all wages, prices, and rents until 1973 in an attempt to control inflation. As a result of an oil embargo in late 1973, the government imposed a price ceiling of 55 cents per gallon of gasoline. To deal with the shortage, nonprice rationing schemes were introduced in 1974. Some states used a first-come, first-served system, while other states allowed consumers with even-numbered license plates to buy gas on even-numbered days and those with odd-numbered license plates to buy gas on odd-numbered days. Gas stations were required to close on Friday night and not open until Monday morning. Regardless of the scheme, long waiting lines for gasoline formed, just as the supply and demand model predicts. Finally, in the past, legally imposed price ceilings have been placed on such items as natural gas shipped in interstate commerce and on interest rates for loans. Internationally, as discussed later in the chapter on economies in transition, price ceilings on food and rent were common in the former Soviet Union. Soviet sociologists estimated that members of a typical urban household spent a combined total of 40 hours per week standing in lines to obtain various goods and services.

4-2b Price Floors

Price floor
A legally established minimum price a seller can be paid.

The other side of the price-control coin is a price floor set by government because it fears that the price system might establish a price viewed as "too low." A **price floor** is a legally established minimum price a seller can be paid. We now turn to two examples of price floors. The first is the minimum wage, and the second is agricultural price supports.

Case 1: The Minimum-Wage Law

In Chapter 1, the second *You're the Economist* applied *normative* and *positive* reasoning to the issue of the minimum wage. Now you are prepared to apply market supply and demand analysis (positive reasoning) to this debate. Begin by noting that the demand for unskilled labor is a downward-sloping curve as shown in Exhibit 6. The wage rate on the vertical axis is the price of unskilled labor, and the amount of unskilled labor employers are willing to hire varies inversely with the wage rate. At a higher wage rate, businesses will hire fewer workers. At a lower wage rate, they will employ a larger quantity of workers.

On the supply side, the wage rate determines the number of unskilled workers willing and able to work per year. At higher wages, workers will give up leisure or schooling to work, and at lower wages, fewer workers will be available for hire. The upward-sloping curve in Exhibit 6 is the supply of labor.

Assuming the freedom to bargain, the price system will establish an equilibrium wage rate of W_e and an equilibrium quantity of labor employed of Q_e. But suppose the government enacts a minimum wage, W_m, which is a price floor above the equilibrium wage, W_e. The intent of the legislation is to "wave a carrot" in front of people

EXHIBIT 6 A Minimum Wage Results in a Surplus of Labor

When the federal or state government sets a wage-rate floor above the equilibrium wage, a surplus of unskilled labor develops. The supply curve is the number of workers offering their labor services per year at possible wage rates. The demand curve is the number of workers employers are willing and able to hire at various wage rates. Equilibrium wage, W_e, will result if the price system is allowed to operate without government interference. At the minimum wage of W_m, there is a surplus of unemployed workers, $Q_s - Q_d$.

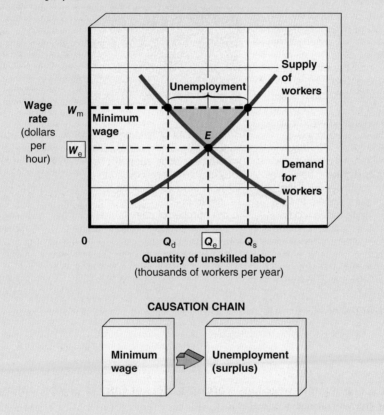

CAUSATION CHAIN

Minimum wage ⇨ Unemployment (surplus)

who will not work at W_e and to make lower-paid workers better off with a higher wage rate. But consider the undesirable consequences. One result of an artificially high minimum wage is that the number of workers willing to offer their labor increases upward along the supply curve to Q_s, but there are fewer jobs because the number of workers firms are willing to hire decreases to Q_d on the demand curve. The predicted outcome is a labor surplus of unskilled workers, $Q_s - Q_d$, who are unemployed. Moreover, employers are encouraged to substitute machines and skilled labor for the unskilled labor previously employed at equilibrium wage W_e. The minimum wage is therefore considered counterproductive because employers lay off the lowest-skilled workers, who ironically are the type of workers minimum wage legislation intends to help.

YOU'RE THE ECONOMIST

Rigging the Market for Milk

For many years the milk industry faced an important question: What does the federal government plan to do about its dairy price support program, which has helped boost farmers' income since 1949? Under the price support program, the federal government agrees to buy storable milk products, such as cheese, butter, and dry milk. If the farmers cannot sell all their products to consumers at a price exceeding the price support level, the federal government will purchase any unsold grade A milk production. Although state-run dairy commissions set their own minimum prices for milk, these legal minimums were similar to the federally set prices. To reduce the interstate price competition for milk, each state set its minimum milk price within 3 percent of the prices set by bordering states. The result has been that government essentially bought up surplus production at supported prices—prices above what would otherwise exist in the market.

These federal price supports on dairy products, as well as other agricultural products, have been controversial. Critics argue that price support programs force consumers to face considerably higher prices for milk and milk-based foods. They also argue that these programs waste taxpayer money. For example, each year the federal government pays billions of dollars to dairy farmers for milk products that sometimes are destroyed or held in storage at a huge cost. Moreover, the problem is compounded because the federal government encourages dairy farmers to use ultramodern farming techniques to increase the production per cow. Another concern

smereka/Shutterstock.com

is that instead of helping small family farmers, these price supports are a corporate welfare program, and the biggest government price support checks go to the largest farmers. This enables these corporate farms to buy smaller, less-efficient farmers, pushing up land values that prevent young people from entering farming and contributing to the decline in the number of dairy farmers. Finally, opponents of the dairy price support program argue that the market for milk is inherently a competitive industry and that consumers and taxpayers would be better served without government price supports for milk.

Perhaps as a result of the critics, Congress did take action with the passage of the Agricultural Act of 2014, which repealed price supports on dairy products. This legislation,

Also, loss of minimum wage jobs represents a loss of entry-level jobs to those who seek to enter the workforce.

Supporters of the minimum wage are quick to point out that those employed (Q_d) are better off. Moreover, when their additional income is spent, it generates more sales, more production, and some job creation that can offset at least some of the initial unemployment over a period of time. Even though the minimum wage causes a reduction in employment, some economists argue that a more equal or fairer income distribution is worth the loss of some jobs. Moreover, the shape of the labor demand curve may be much more vertical than shown in Exhibit 6. If this is the case, the unemployment effect of a rise in the minimum wage would be small. In addition, they claim opponents ignore the possibility that unskilled workers lack bargaining power versus employers.

Finally, a minimum wage set at or below the equilibrium wage rate is ineffective. If the minimum wage is set at the equilibrium wage rate of W_e, the quantity of labor demanded and the quantity of labor supplied are equal regardless of the minimum

"I always wondered how the government set milk prices."

charged farmers). The Dairy Product Donation Program (DPDP) requires the Secretary of Agriculture to purchase dairy products for donation to low-income groups when the dairy margin falls below $4.00.

The Agricultural Act of 2014 is due to expire December 31, 2018. We will have to see what the future holds as government balances the interests of farmers, consumers, and taxpayers.

ANALYZE THE ISSUE

1. Draw a supply and demand graph to illustrate the problem of a price support on milk described in the case study.
2. Who benefits and who is hurt by dairy price supports?
3. What do you think the impact is on dairy farmers, consumers, and taxpayers as a result of the Margin Protection Program for Dairy (MPP-Dairy)? Is this an improvement over the price support program?
4. What do you think the impact is on dairy farmers, consumers, and taxpayers as a result of the Dairy Product Donation Program (DPDP)? Is this an improvement over the price support program?

however, has not stopped government from trying to assist farmers. Two new government programs were established with this act: the Margin Protection Program for Dairy (MPP-Dairy) and the Dairy Product Donation Program (DPDP).

The Margin Protection Program for Dairy (MPP-Dairy) offers dairy producers catastrophic insurance coverage at virtually no cost to them, and some additional insurance at their expense, should the difference between current market prices and the costs of production fall below a certain amount (called the "margin"—currently between $4, which is the basic catastrophic amount, and up $8, where a premium is

wage. If the minimum wage is set below the equilibrium wage, the forces of supply of and demand for labor establish the equilibrium wage regardless of the minimum wage rate.

Case 2: Agricultural Price Supports

A farm price support is a well-known example of a price floor, which results in government purchases of surplus food and in higher food prices. Agricultural price support programs began in the 1930s as a means of raising the income of farmers, who were suffering from low market prices during the Great Depression. Under these programs, the government guarantees a minimum price above the equilibrium price and agrees to purchase any quantity the farmer is unable to sell at the legal price.

A few of the crops that have received price supports are corn, peanuts, soybeans, wheat, cotton, rice, tobacco, and dairy products. As predicted by market supply and demand analysis, a price support above the equilibrium price causes surpluses. Government warehouses therefore often overflow with such perishable products as butter, cheese, and dry milk purchased with taxpayers' money. The previous "You're the Economist" section on the dairy industry examines one of the best-known examples of U.S. government interference with agricultural market prices.

CONCLUSION A price ceiling or price floor prevents market adjustment in which competition among buyers and sellers bids the price upward or downward to the equilibrium price.

CHECKPOINT

Is There Price Fixing at the Ticket Window?
At sold-out concerts, sports contests, and other events, some ticket holders try to resell their tickets for more than they paid—a practice known as scalping. For scalping to occur, must the original ticket price be legally set by a price floor, at the equilibrium price, or by a price ceiling?

4-3 MARKET FAILURE

In this chapter and the previous chapter, you gained an understanding of how markets operate. Through the price system, society coordinates economic activity, but markets are not always "Prince Charmings" that achieve *market efficiency* without a misallocation of resources. It is now time to step back with a critical eye and consider markets that become "ugly frogs" by allocating resources inefficiently. **Market failure** occurs when market equilibrium results in too few or too many resources being used in the production of a good or service. In this section, you will study four important cases of market failure: lack of competition, externalities, public goods, and income inequality. Market failure is discussed in more detail in the chapter on environmental economics, except for the macroeconomics version of the text.

Market failure
A situation in which market equilibrium results in too few or too many resources being used in the production of a good or service. This inefficiency may justify government intervention.

4-3a Lack of Competition

There must be competition among both producers and consumers for markets to function properly. But what happens if the producers fail to compete? In *The Wealth of Nations*, Adam Smith stated, "People of the same trade seldom meet together, even for merriment and diversion, but the conversation ends in a conspiracy against the public, or in some diversion to raise prices."[1] This famous quotation clearly underscores the fact that in the real world businesses seek ways to replace consumer sovereignty with "big business sovereignty." What happens when a few firms rig the market and they become the market's boss? By restricting supply through artificial limits on the output of a good,

---

[1]Adam Smith, *An Inquiry into the Nature and Causes of the Wealth of Nations*, 1776; reprint, New York: Random House, The Modern Library, 1937, p. 128.

firms can enjoy higher prices and profits. As a result, firms may waste resources and retard technology and innovation.

Exhibit 7 illustrates how IBM, Apple, Gateway, Dell, and other suppliers of personal computers (PCs) could benefit from rigging the market. Without collusive action, the competitive price for PCs is $1,500, the quantity of 200,000 per month is sold, and efficient equilibrium prevails at point E_1. It is in the best interest of sellers, however, to take steps that would make PCs artificially scarce and raise the price. Graphically, the sellers wish to shift the competitive supply curve, S_1, leftward to the restricted supply curve, S_2. This could happen for a number of reasons, including an agreement among sellers to restrict supply (collusion) and government action. For example, the sellers could lobby the government to pass a law allowing an association of PC suppliers to set production quotas. The proponents might argue this action raises prices, revenues, and, in turn, profits. Higher profits enable the industry to invest in new capital and become more competitive in world markets.

EXHIBIT 7 Rigging the PC Market

At efficient equilibrium point E_1, sellers compete. As a result, the price charged per PC is $1,500, and the quantity of PCs exchanged is 200,000. Suppose suppliers use collusion, government intervention, or other means to restrict the supply of this product. The decrease in supply from S_1 to S_2 establishes inefficient market equilibrium E_2. At E_2, firms charge the higher price of $2,500, and the equilibrium quantity of PCs falls to 150,000. Thus, the outcome of restricted supply is that the market fails because firms use too few resources to produce fewer than the optimal number of PCs, while charging an artificially high price.

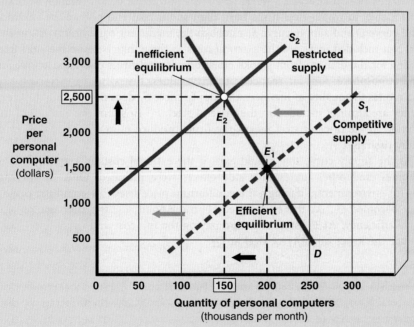

Opponents of artificially restricted supply argue that, although the producers benefit, the lack of competition means the economy loses. The result of restricting supply is that the efficient equilibrium point, E_1, changes to the inefficient equilibrium point, E_2. At point E_2, the higher price of \$2,500 is charged, and the lower equilibrium quantity means that firms devote too few resources to producing PCs and charge an artificially high price. Note that under U.S. antitrust laws, the Justice Department is responsible for prosecuting firms that collude to restrict supply to force higher prices.

4-3b Externalities

Externality

A cost or benefit imposed on people other than the consumers and producers of a good or service.

Even when markets are competitive, some markets may still fail because they suffer from the presence of side effects economists call externalities. An **externality** is a cost or benefit imposed on people other than the consumers and producers of a good or service. Externalities are also called *spillover effects* or *neighborhood effects*. People other than consumers and producers who are affected by these side effects of market exchanges are called *third parties*. Externalities may be either negative or positive; that is, they may be detrimental or beneficial. Suppose you are trying to study and your roommate is listening to Steel Porcupines at full blast. The action of your roommate is imposing an unwanted *external cost* or *negative externality* on you and other third parties who are trying to study or sleep. Externalities can also result in an *external benefit* or *positive externality* to nonparticipating parties. When a community proudly displays its neat lawns, gorgeous flowers, and freshly painted homes, visitors are third parties who did none of the work, but enjoy the benefit of the pleasant scenery.

A Graphical Analysis of Pollution

Exhibit 8 provides a graphical analysis of two markets that fail to include externalities in their market prices unless the government takes corrective action. Exhibit 8(a) shows a market for steel in which steel firms burn high-sulfur coal and pollute the environment. Demand curve D and supply curve S_1 establish the inefficient equilibrium, E_1, in the steel market. Not included in S_1 are the *external costs* to the public because the steel firms are not paying for the damage from smoke emissions. If steel firms discharge smoke and ash into the atmosphere, foul air reduces property values, raises health care costs, and, in general, erodes the quality of life. Because supply curve S_1 does not include these external costs, they are also not included in the price of steel, P_1. In short, the absence of the cost of pollution in the price of steel means the firms produce more steel and pollution than is socially desirable.

S_2 is the supply curve that would exist if the external costs of respiratory illnesses, dirty homes, and other undesirable side effects were included. Once S_2 includes the charges for environmental damage, the equilibrium price rises to P_2, and the equilibrium quantity becomes Q_2. At the efficient equilibrium point, E_2, the steel market achieves allocative efficiency. At E_2, steel firms are paying the full cost and using fewer resources to produce the lower quantity of steel at Q_2.

CONCLUSION

When the supply curve fails to include external costs, the equilibrium price is artificially low, and the equilibrium quantity is artificially high. External costs cause the market to overallocate resources.

EXHIBIT 8 Externalities in the Steel and AIDS Vaccination Markets

In part (a), resources are overallocated at inefficient market equilibrium E_1 because steel firms do not include the cost per ton of pollution in the cost per ton of steel. Supply curve S_2 includes the external costs of pollution. If firms are required to purchase equipment to remove the pollution or to pay a tax on pollution, the economy achieves the efficient equilibrium of E_2.

Part (b) demonstrates that external benefits cause an underallocation of resources. The efficient output at equilibrium point E_2 is obtained if people are required to purchase AIDS shots or if the government pays a subsidy equal to the external benefit per shot.

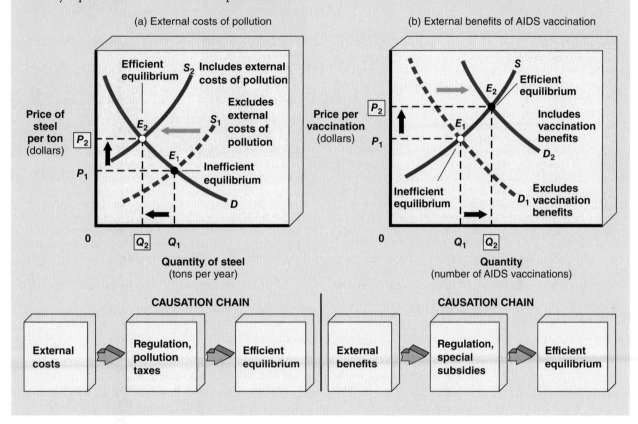

Regulation and pollution taxes are two ways society can correct the market failure of pollution:

1. **Regulation.** Legislation can set standards that force firms to clean up their emissions as a condition of remaining in business. This means firms must buy, install, and maintain pollution-control equipment. When the extra cost of the pollution equipment is added to the production cost per ton of steel, the initial supply curve, S_1, in Exhibit 8(a), shifts leftward to supply curve S_2. This means regulation has forced the market equilibrium to change from E_1 to E_2. At point E_2, the firms use fewer resources to produce Q_2 compared to Q_1 output of steel per year, and S_2 reflects all costs of production, including the external costs; therefore, the firms operate efficiently.

Can Vouchers Fix Our Schools?

In their book *Free to Choose*, published in 1980, economists Milton Friedman and his wife Rose Friedman proposed a voucher plan for schools.[1] The objective of their proposal was to retain government financing, but give parents greater freedom to choose the schools their children attend. The Friedmans pointed out that under the current system parents face a strong incentive not to remove their children from the public schools. The reason is because if parents decide to withdraw their children from a public school and send them to a private school, they must pay private tuition in addition to the taxes that finance children enrolled in the public schools.

To remove the financial penalty that limits the freedom of parents to choose schools, the government could give parents a voucher, which is a piece of paper redeemable for a sum of money payable to any approved school. For example, if the government spends $8,000 per year to educate a student, then the voucher could be for this amount. The voucher plan embodies the same principle as the GI Bill that provides educational benefits to military veterans. The veteran receives a voucher good only for educational expenses and is free to choose the school where it is used, provided the school satisfies certain standards.

The Friedmans argue that parents could, and should, be permitted to use the vouchers not only at private schools, but also at other public schools—and not only at schools in their own

Marjorie Kamys Cotera/Bob Daemmrich Photography/Alamy Stock Photo

district, city, or state, but at any school that is willing to accept their child. That option would give every parent a greater opportunity to choose and at the same time would require public schools to charge tuition. The tuition would be competitive because public schools must compete for students both with other public schools and with private schools. It is important to note that this plan relieves no one of the burden of taxation to pay for schooling. It simply gives parents a wider choice as to which competing schools their children can attend, given the

2. **Pollution Taxes.** Another approach would be for the government to levy a tax per ton of steel equal to the external cost imposed on society when the firm emits pollution into the air. This action inhibits production by imposing an additional production cost per ton of steel from the pollution taxes and shifts the supply curve leftward from S_1 to S_2 as shown in Exhibit 8(a). Again, the objective is to change the equilibrium from E_1 to E_2 and eliminate the overuse of resources devoted to steel production and its pollution. The tax revenue could be used to compensate those damaged by the pollution.

A Graphical Analysis of AIDS Vaccinations

As explained earlier, the supply curve may not include the *external costs* of a product. Now you will see that the demand curve may not include the *external benefits* of a product. Suppose a vaccination is discovered that prevents AIDS. Exhibit 8(b) illustrates the market for immunization against AIDS. Demand curve D_1 reflects the price consumers would pay for shots to receive the benefit of a reduced probability of infection by AIDS. Supply curve S shows the quantities of shots suppliers offer for sale at different prices.

amount of funding per student that the community has obligated itself to provide. The plan also does not affect the present standards imposed on private schools to ensure that students attending them satisfy the compulsory attendance laws.

In 1990, Milwaukee began an experiment with school vouchers. The program gave selected children from low-income families taxpayer-funded vouchers to allow them to attend private schools. There has been a continuing heated debate among parents, politicians, and educators over the results. In 1998, Wisconsin's highest court ruled in a 4–2 decision that without violating the constitutional separation of church and state, Milwaukee could use public money for vouchers for students who attend religious schools.

A 2002 article in *USA Today* reported:

Opponents of vouchers have repeatedly argued that they would damage the public schools, draining them of resources and better students. A recent study of the Milwaukee voucher program by Caroline Hoxby, a Harvard economist, suggests just the opposite. She wrote that "schools that faced the most potential competition from vouchers had the best productivity response." No doubt, the nation's experience with vouchers is limited, yet the evidence cited in a recent Brookings Institution report shows that they do seem to benefit African-American youngsters.[2]

The controversy continues: For example, in a 2002 landmark case, the U.S. Supreme Court ruled that government vouchers for private or parochial schools are constitutional. In 2003, however, a Denver judge struck down Colorado's new school voucher law, ruling that it violated the state's constitution by stripping local school boards of their control over education. In 2006, the Florida Supreme Court ruled that Florida's voucher program for students in the lowest-rated public schools was unconstitutional. Then in 2010, Florida legislated a tax-credit voucher plan for low-income students. In 2013 the Indiana Supreme Court upheld the state's voucher program, which is the nation's broadest school voucher program. And in the 2014–2015 school year, North Carolina awarded vouchers to students whose families meet certain income requirements. In 2017, a renewed debate was sparked by President Trump's appointment of Betsy DeVos, a long-time supporter of school vouchers, as Secretary of Education.

ANALYZE THE ISSUE

1. In recent years, school choice has been a hotly debated issue. Explain whether education is a public good. If education is not a public good, why should the government provide it?

2. The Friedmans present a one-sided view of the benefits of a voucher system. Other economists disagree about the potential effectiveness of vouchers. Do you support a voucher system for education? Explain your reasoning.

1. Milton Friedman and Rose Friedman, *Free to Choose: A Personal Statement*, New York: Harcourt Brace Jovanovich, 1980, pp. 160–161.
2. Robert J. Bresler, "Vouchers and The Constitution," *USA Today*, May 2002, p. 15.

At equilibrium point E_1, the market fails to achieve an efficient allocation of resources. The reason is that when buyers are vaccinated, other people who do not purchase AIDS shots (called *free riders*) also benefit because this disease is less likely to spread. Once demand curve D_2 includes external benefits to nonconsumers of AIDS vaccinations (increase in the number of buyers), the efficient equilibrium of E_2 is established. At Q_2, sellers devote greater resources to AIDS vaccinations, and the underallocation of resources is eliminated.

How can society prevent the market failure of AIDS vaccinations? Two approaches follow:

1. **Regulation.** The government can boost consumption and shift the demand curve rightward by requiring all citizens to purchase AIDS shots each year. This approach to capturing external benefits in market demand explains why all school-age children must have polio and other shots before entering school.

2. **Special Subsidies.** Another possible solution would be for the government to increase consumer income by paying consumers for each AIDS vaccination. This would mean the government pays each citizen a dollar payment equal to the amount

of external benefits per shot purchased. Because the subsidy amount is payable at any price along the demand curve, the demand curve shifts rightward until the efficient equilibrium price and quantity are reached.

CONCLUSION When the demand curve fails to include external benefits the equilibrium price is artificially low, and the equilibrium quantity is artificially low. External benefits cause the market to underallocate resources.

4-3c Public Goods

Public good
A good or service with two properties: (1) users collectively consume benefits, and (2) there is no way to bar people who do not pay (free riders) from consuming the good or service.

Private goods are produced through the price system. In contrast, national defense is an example of a public good provided by the government because of its special characteristics. A **public good** is a good or service that, once produced, has two properties: (1) Users collectively consume benefits, (2) There is no way to bar people who do not pay (free riders) from consuming the good or service.

To see why the marketplace fails, imagine that Patriot Missiles Inc. offers to sell missile defense systems to people who want private protection against attacks from incoming missiles. First, once the system is operational, everyone in the defense area benefits from increased safety. Second, the *nonexclusive* nature of a public good means it is impossible or very costly for any owner of a Patriot missile defense system to prevent nonowners, the free riders, from reaping the benefits of its protection.

Given the two properties of a public good, why would any private individual purchase a Patriot missile defense system? Why not take a free ride and wait until someone else buys a missile system? Thus, each person wants a Patriot system, but does not want to bear the cost of the system when everyone shares in the benefits. As a result, the market fails to provide Patriot missile defense systems, and everyone hopes no missile attacks occur before someone finally decides to purchase one. Government can solve this public goods problem by producing Patriot missiles and taxing the public to pay. Unlike a private citizen, the government can use force to collect payments and prevent the free-rider problem. Other examples of public goods include global agreements to reduce emissions, the judicial system, the national emergency warning system, air traffic control, prisons, dams, city roads, and traffic lights.

CONCLUSION If public goods are available only in the marketplace, people wait for someone else to pay, and the result is an underproduction or zero production of public goods.

4-3d Income Inequality

In the cases of insufficient competition, externalities, and public goods, the marketplace allocates too few or too many resources to producing output. The market may also result in a very unequal distribution of income, thereby raising a very controversial issue. Under the impersonal price system, movie stars earn huge incomes for acting in movies, while homeless people roam the streets penniless. The controversy is therefore over how equal the distribution of income should be and how much government intervention is required to achieve this goal. Some people wish to remove most inequality of income. Others argue for the government to provide a "safety net" minimum income level for all citizens. Still others see high income as an incentive and a "fair" reward for productive resources.

To create a more equal distribution of income, the government uses various programs to transfer money from people with high incomes to those with low incomes. Unemployment compensation and food stamps are examples of such programs. The federal minimum wage is another example of a government attempt to raise the earnings of low-income workers.

Should There Be a War on Drugs?
The U.S. government fights the use of drugs, such as marijuana and cocaine, in a variety of ways, including spraying crops with poisonous chemicals; imposing jail sentences for dealers and users; and confiscating drug-transporting cars, boats, and planes. Which market failure motivates the government to interfere with the market for drugs: lack of competition, externalities, public goods, or income inequality?

CHECKPOINT

Key Concepts

Price ceiling	Market failure	Public good
Price floor	Externalities	

Summary

- **Price ceilings** and **price floors** are maximum and minimum prices enacted by law, rather than allowing the forces of supply and demand to determine prices. A *price ceiling* is a maximum price mandated by government, and a *price floor*, or *support price,* is a minimum legal price. If a price ceiling is set below the equilibrium price, a shortage will persist. If a price floor is set above the equilibrium price, a surplus will persist.

Price Ceiling

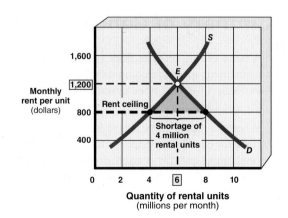

Price Floor

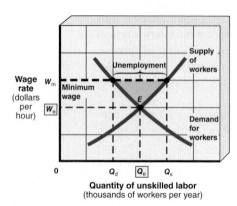

Wage rate (dollars per hour)

Quantity of unskilled labor
(thousands of workers per year)

Externalities

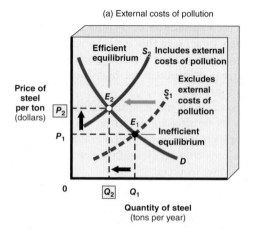

(a) External costs of pollution

Price of steel per ton (dollars)

Quantity of steel
(tons per year)

- **Market failure** occurs when the market mechanism does not achieve an efficient allocation of resources. Sources of market failure include lack of competition, externalities, public goods, and income inequality. Although controversial, government intervention is a possible way to correct market failure.

- An **externality** is a cost or benefit of a good imposed on people who are not buyers or sellers of that good. Pollution is an example of an *external cost,* which means too many resources are used to produce the product responsible for the pollution. Two basic approaches to solve this market failure are regulation and pollution taxes. Vaccinations provide *external benefits,* which means sellers devote too few resources to producing this product. Two basic solutions to this type of market failure are laws to require consumption of shots and special subsidies.

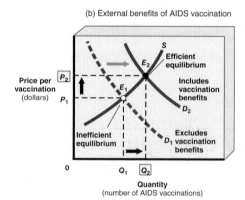

(b) External benefits of AIDS vaccination

Price per vaccination (dollars)

Quantity
(number of AIDS vaccinations)

- **Public goods** are goods that are consumed by all people in a society regardless of whether they pay or not. National defense, air traffic control, and other public goods can benefit many individuals simultaneously and are provided by the government.

Summary of Conclusion Statements

- A price ceiling or price floor prevents market adjustment in which competition among buyers and sellers bids the price upward or downward to the equilibrium price.

- When the supply curve fails to include external costs, the equilibrium price is artificially low, and the equilibrium quantity is artificially high. External costs cause the market to overallocate resources.

- When the demand curve fails to include external benefits, the equilibrium price and the equilibrium quantity are artificially low. External benefits cause the market to underallocate resources.

- If public goods are available only in the marketplace, people wait for someone else to pay, and the result is an underproduction or zero production of public goods.

Study Questions and Problems

Please see Appendix A for answers to the odd-numbered questions. Your instructor has access to the answers for even-numbered questions.

1. Market researchers have studied the market for milk, and their estimates for the supply of and the demand for milk per month are as follows:

Price per gallon	Quantity demanded (millions of gallons)	Quantity supplied (millions of gallons)
$10.00	100	500
8.00	200	400
6.00	300	300
4.00	400	200
2.00	500	100

a. Using the data, graph the demand for and the supply of milk. Identify the equilibrium point as *E*, and use dotted lines to connect *E* to the equilibrium price on the price axis and the equilibrium quantity on the quantity axis.

b. Suppose the government enacts a milk price support of $8 per gallon. Indicate this action on your graph, and explain the effect on the milk market. Why would the government establish such a price support?

c. Now assume the government decides to set a price ceiling of $4 per gallon. Show and explain how this legal price affects your graph of the milk market. What objective could the government be trying to achieve by establishing such a price ceiling?

2. Use a graph to show the impact on the price of Japanese cars sold in the United States if the United States imposes import quotas and other trade restrictions that decrease the supply of Japanese cars. Now draw another graph to show how the change in the price of Japanese cars affects the price of American-made cars in the United States. Explain the market outcome in each graph and the link between the two graphs.

3. Using market supply and demand analysis, explain why labor union leaders are strong advocates of raising the minimum wage above the equilibrium wage.

4. What are the advantages and disadvantages of the price system?

5. Suppose a market is in equilibrium and both demand and supply curves increase. What happens to the equilibrium price if demand increases more than supply?

6. Consider this statement: "*Government involvement in markets is inherently inefficient.*" Do you agree or disagree? Explain.

7. Suppose coal-burning firms are emitting excessive pollution into the air. Suggest two ways the government can deal with this market failure.

8. Explain the impact of external costs and external benefits on resource allocation.

9. Why are public goods not produced in sufficient quantities by private markets?

10. Which of the following are public goods?
    a. Air bags
    b. Pencils
    c. Cycle helmets
    d. City streetlights
    e. Contact lenses

CHECKPOINT ANSWERS

Why the Lower Price for Big-Screen High-Definition Televisions?

As shown in Exhibit 9, an increase in demand leads to higher TV prices, while an increase in supply leads to lower prices. Because the overall direction of the market price of TVs was down, the increase in supply must have been larger than the increase in demand. If you said supply increased by more than demand, **YOU ARE CORRECT**.

Is There Price Fixing at the Ticket Window?

Scalpers are evidence of a shortage whereby buyers are unable to find tickets at the official price. As shown in Exhibit 10, scalpers (often illegally) profit from the shortage by selling tickets above the official price. Shortages result when prices are restricted below equilibrium, as is the case when there is a price ceiling. If you said scalping occurs when there is a price ceiling because scalpers charge more than the official maximum price, **YOU ARE CORRECT**.

Should There Be a War on Drugs?

Drug use often affects not only the person using the drugs, but also other members of society as well. For example, higher crime rates are largely attributable to increased drug usage, and AIDS is often spread when users inject drugs using nonsterile needles. When one person's actions affect others not involved in the decision to buy or sell, the market fails to operate efficiently. If you said the market failure motivating government intervention in the drug market is externalities because drug users impose costs on nonusers, **YOU ARE CORRECT**.

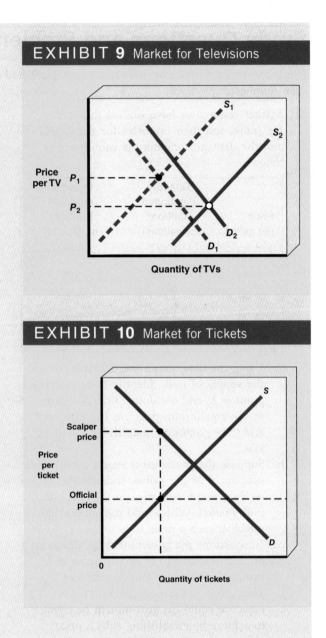

EXHIBIT 9 Market for Televisions

EXHIBIT 10 Market for Tickets

Sample Quiz

Please see Appendix B for answers to Sample Quiz questions.

1. A decrease in demand with the supply held constant leads to a(an)
   a. increased equilibrium price and an increased equilibrium quantity.
   b. decreased equilibrium price and a decreased equilibrium quantity.
   c. decreased equilibrium price and an increased equilibrium quantity.
   d. increased equilibrium price and a decreased equilibrium quantity.

2. An increased equilibrium price and a decreased equilibrium quantity results from a(an)

a. decrease in demand.
b. increase in supply.
c. decrease in supply.
d. increase in demand.

3. Assume no price ceiling exists in a market. Then a price ceiling is established below the market equilibrium. What would result?
   a. Shortage
   b. Equilibrium
   c. Surplus
   d. Exchange price

4. Which of the following is *not* an example of market failure?
   a. Lack of competition
   b. Externalities
   c. Efficient equilibrium
   d. Extreme income inequality

5. A cost imposed on people other than the consumers of a good or service is a
   a. price floor.
   b. negative externality.
   c. positive externality.
   d. price ceiling.

6. Suppose X and Y are substitutes. If the price of Y increases, how will this change the market equilibrium for X?
   a. Both equilibrium price and quantity decline.
   b. Both equilibrium price and quantity rise.
   c. Equilibrium price declines, and equilibrium quantity rises.
   d. Equilibrium price rises, and equilibrium quantity falls.

7. If the cost of producing a good rises for sellers, how will this affect the market equilibrium for that good?
   a. Price will rise, and quantity will fall.
   b. Price will fall, and quantity will rise.
   c. Both price and quantity will rise.
   d. Both price and quantity will fall.

8. If goods A and B are complements, and the price of good B rises, how will this affect the market equilibrium for good A?
   a. Price will rise, and quantity will fall.
   b. Price will fall, and quantity will rise.
   c. Both price and quantity will rise.
   d. Both price and quantity will fall.

9. Suppose Big-Cat and Fat-Cat are rival cat food brands and the price of Fat-Cat is reduced. Following this price drop, is there a shortage or a surplus of Big-Cat at the old price of Big-Cat?
   a. Shortage
   b. Surplus

c. Neither because equilibrium exists
d. Neither because a price drop cannot cause a shortage or a surplus

10. Suppose the average equilibrium monthly rental price of apartments and rooms in a college town has been steady at $600, but then the college expands enrollment from 10,000 to 12,000. Suddenly, there is a shortage of rental housing at the prevailing price of $600. Which of the following is *most* likely true?
    a. The shortage occurred because demand increased, and a new market equilibrium will feature higher rental prices and more rental units available on the market.
    b. The shortage occurred because supply increased, and a new market equilibrium will feature lower rental prices and fewer rental units available on the market.
    c. The shortage occurred because demand decreased, and a new market equilibrium will feature lower rental prices and fewer rental units available on the market.
    d. The shortage occurred because demand increased, and a new market equilibrium will feature higher rental prices and fewer rental units available on the market.

11. If a price ceiling is set at $10, and the equilibrium market price is $8, which price will consumers actually pay?
    a. $10
    b. $8
    c. $18
    d. $2

12. Suppose the state of California imposes a minimum wage of $15 per hour. In the entry-level labor market in California fast-food restaurants, the quantity of labor demanded at $15 per hour is 800,000 and the quantity of labor supplied is 1.2 million. Which of the following is true?
    a. There is a shortage of 800,000 workers in the labor market.
    b. There is a surplus of 400,000 workers in the labor market.
    c. There is a shortage of 400,000 workers in the labor market.
    d. There is a surplus of 1.2 million workers in the labor market.

13. Suppose the federal government imposes a price floor (support price) in the milk market at a price of $6 per gallon. If market quantity demanded at $6 is 1 billion gallons, and market

quantity supplied is 1.5 billion gallons, which of the following is true?

a. There is a shortage of 500 million gallons of milk, and the federal government will buy 1 billion gallons to maintain the $6 price.

b. There is a surplus of 500 million gallons of milk, and the federal government will buy these 500 million gallons to maintain the $6 price.

c. There is a shortage of 500 million gallons of milk, and the federal government will buy an additional 500 million gallons to maintain the $6 price.

d. There is a surplus of 1 billion gallons of milk, and the federal government will buy 1.5 billion gallons to maintain the $6 price.

14. Suppose the city of Arcata, California, imposes rent control so that rents cannot exceed $1,000 per month on one-bedroom rental units. Suppose $1,000 had also been the equilibrium rental price in Arcata before a huge new apartment complex was built in the nearby town of McKinleyville, where rents are $800 per month. Which of the following is *most* likely true?

a. There will be a shortage of rental housing in Arcata at the rent control price of $1,000.

b. There will be a lasting surplus of rental housing in Arcata after the new apartment complex is built in McKinleyville.

c. The equilibrium rental price in Arcata will fall below $1,000; thus, rent control will not affect the rental market in Arcata.

d. The equilibrium price of $1,000 per month in Arcata will not change.

15. Suppose the federal government provides wheat farmers with a price floor above the market equilibrium price of wheat, creating a surplus. Which of the following causes a reduction in the surplus of wheat?

a. Elimination of the price floor

b. An increase in the price of wheat

c. A decrease in the demand for wheat

d. An increase in the supply of wheat

16. If society allows firms to freely pollute the environment, which of the following is *true*?

a. Market equilibrium output will be too high relative to the efficient output level.

b. Market equilibrium output will be too low relative to the efficient output level.

c. Market equilibrium output will be equivalent to the efficient output level.

d. The efficient output level can be achieved by giving firms a subsidy for the pollution they generate.

17. If there are external benefits for good X, which of the following is true?

a. The socially efficient amount of good X can be achieved if society taxes consumers of good X.

b. The socially efficient amount of good X can be achieved if society subsidizes consumers of good X.

c. The socially efficient amount of good X will be equivalent to the free market equilibrium quantity.

d. The socially efficient amount of good X does not exist.

18. Suppose the federal government imposes a new pollution tax of $0.01 per kilowatt-hour of electricity on coal-fired power producers. Which of the following describes how this tax will affect the market for electricity served by these power plants?

a. Demand for electricity will decrease.

b. Demand for electricity will increase.

c. The supply of electricity will decrease.

d. The supply of electricity will increase.

19. Why don't competitive markets do a good job providing public goods?

a. Because people do not receive benefits from public goods

b. Because firms cannot produce enough goods to satisfy market demand

c. Because public goods generate negative externalities and pollution taxes reduce the incentive for firms to supply public goods

d. Because it is difficult to exclude people from gaining benefits from public goods without paying for them; so market demand does not reflect the benefits to society from the public good

20. Which of the following is *not* an example of market failure?

a. Lack of competition

b. Externalities

c. Efficient equilibrium

d. Extreme income inequality

Applying Supply and Demand Analysis to Health Care

One out of every six dollars spent in the United States is spent for health care services. This is a greater percentage than in any other industrialized country.[1] And in 2010, historic health care legislation (the Affordable Care Act, commonly called Obamacare) was enacted to dramatically reform the U.S. system. The topic of health care arouses deep emotions and generates intense media coverage. How can we understand many of the important health care issues? One approach is to listen to the normative statements made by politicians and other concerned citizens. Another approach is to use supply and demand theory to analyze the issue. Here again the objective is to bring textbook theory to life and use it to provide you with a deeper understanding of third-party health service markets.

4A-1 THE IMPACT OF HEALTH INSURANCE

There is a downward-sloping demand curve for health care services just as there is for other goods and services. Following the same law of demand that applies to cars, clothing, entertainment, and other goods and services, movements along the demand curve for health care occur because consumers respond to changes in the price of health care. As shown in Exhibit A-1, we assume that health care, including doctor visits, medicine, hospital bills, and other medical services, can be measured in units of health care. Without health insurance, consumers buy Q_1 units of health care services per year at a price of P_1 per unit. Assuming supply curve S represents the quantity supplied, the market is in equilibrium at point A. At this point, the total cost of health care can be computed by the price of health care (P_1) times the quantity demanded (Q_1) or represented geometrically by the rectangle $0P_1AQ_1$.

Analysis of the demand curve for health care is complicated by the way health care is financed. About 80 percent of all health care is paid for by *third parties*, including private insurance companies and government programs, such as Medicare and Medicaid. The price of health care services paid by patients, therefore, depends on the *copayment rate*, which is the percentage of the cost of services consumers pay out of pocket. To understand the impact, it is more realistic to assume consumers are insured and extend the analysis represented in Exhibit A-1. Because patients pay only 20 percent of the bill, the quantity of health care demanded in the figure increases to Q_2 at a lower

---

[1]Source Bureau of Economic Analysis, *Health Care Satellite Account*, http://www.bea.gov/industry/index.htm.

EXHIBIT A-1 The Impact of Insurance on the Health care Market

Without health insurance, the market is in equilibrium at point A, with a price of P_1 and a quantity demanded of Q_1. Total spending is $0P_1AQ_1$. With copayment health insurance, consumers pay the lower price of P_2, and the quantity demanded increases to Q_2. Total health care costs rise to $0P_3CQ_2$, with $0P_2BQ_2$ paid by consumers and P_2P_3CB paid by insurers. As a result, the quantity supplied increases from point A to point C, where it equals the quantity demanded of Q_2.

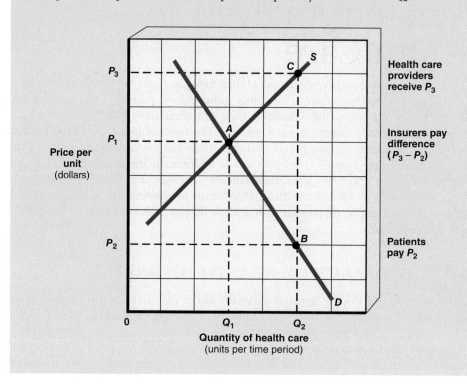

price of P_2. At point B on the demand curve, insured consumers pay an amount equal to rectangle $0P_2BQ_2$, and insurers pay an amount represented by rectangle P_2P_3CB. Health care providers respond by increasing the quantity supplied from point A to point C on the supply curve S, where the quantity supplied equals the quantity demanded of Q_2. The reason that there is no shortage in the health care market is that the combined payments from the insured consumers and insurers equal the total payment required for the movement upward along the supply curve. Stated in terms of rectangles, the total health care payment of $0P_3CQ_2$ equals $0P_2BQ_2$ paid by consumers plus P_2P_3CB paid by insurers.

CONCLUSION

Compared to a health care market without insurance, the quantity demanded, the quantity supplied, and the total cost of health care are increased by copayment health care insurance.

Finally, note that Exhibit A-1 represents an overall or general model of the health care market. Individual health care markets are subject to *market failure*. For example, there would be a lack of competition if hospitals, doctors, or drug companies conspired to fix prices. Externalities provide another source of market failure, as illustrated previously for vaccinations in Exhibit 8(b). We are also concerned that health care should be distributed in a fair way. This concern explains why the government Medicare and Medicaid programs help the elderly and poor afford health care. In fact, as a result of market failure, some nations have chosen to have their governments provide health care to all that is paid for through taxes.

4A-2 SHIFTS IN THE DEMAND FOR HEALTH CARE

While changes in the price of health care cause movements along the demand curve, other factors can cause the demand curve to shift. The following are some of the non-price determinants that can change the demand for health care.

4A-2a Number of Buyers

As the population increases, the demand for health care increases. In addition to the total number of people, the distribution of older people in the population is important. As more people move into the 65-and-older age group, the demand for health care services becomes greater because older people have more frequent and prolonged spells of illness. An increase in substance abuse involving alcohol, tobacco, or drugs also increases the demand for health care. For example, if the percentage of babies born into drug-prone families increases, the demand for health care will shift rightward.

4A-2b Tastes and Preferences

Changes in consumer attitudes toward health care can also change demand. For example, television, movies, magazines, and advertising may be responsible for changes in people's preferences for cosmetic surgery. Moreover, medical science has improved so much that we believe there must be a cure for most ailments. As a result, consumers are willing to buy larger quantities of medical services at each possible price.

Doctors also influence consumer preferences by prescribing treatment. It is often argued that some doctors guard against malpractice suits or boost their incomes by ordering more tests or office visits than are really needed. Some estimates suggest that fraud and abuse account for as much as 10 percent of total health care spending. These studies reveal that as many as one-third of some procedures are inappropriate.

4A-2c Income

Health care is a normal good. Rising inflation-adjusted incomes of consumers in the United States cause the demand curve for health care services to shift to the right. On the other hand, if real median family income remains unchanged, there is no influence on the demand curve.

4A-2d Prices of Substitutes

The prices of medical goods and services that are substitutes can change and, in turn, influence the demand for other medical services. For example, treatment of a back problem by a chiropractor is an alternative for many of the treatments provided by orthopedic doctors. If the price of orthopedic therapy rises, then some people will switch to treatment by a chiropractor. As a result, the demand curve for chiropractic therapy shifts rightward.

4A-3 SHIFTS IN THE SUPPLY OF HEALTH CARE

Changes in the following nonprice factors change the supply of health care.

4A-3a Number of Sellers

Sellers of health care include hospitals, nursing homes, physicians in private practice, drug companies, chiropractors, psychologists, and a host of other suppliers. To ensure the quality and safety of health care, virtually every facet of the industry is regulated and licensed by the government or controlled by the American Medical Association (AMA). Primarily through medical school accreditation and licensing requirements, the AMA limits the number of people practicing medicine. The federal Food and Drug Administration (FDA) requires testing that delays the introduction of new drugs. Tighter restrictions on the number of sellers shift the health care supply curve leftward and reduced restrictions shift the supply curve rightward.

4A-3b Resource Prices

An increase in the costs of resources underlying the supply of health care shifts the supply curve leftward. By far the single most important factor behind increasing health care spending has been technological change. New diagnostic, surgical, and therapeutic equipment is used extensively in the health care industry, and the result is higher costs. Wages, salaries, and other costs, such as the costs of malpractice suits, also influence the supply curve. If hospitals, for example, are paying higher prices for inputs used to produce health care, the supply curve shifts to the left because the same quantities may be supplied only at higher prices.

ROAD MAP

PART 2
Microeconomics Fundamentals

This road map feature helps you tie together material in the part as you travel the Economic Way of Thinking Highway. The following are review questions listed by chapter from the previous part. The key concept in each question is given for emphasis, and each question or set of questions concludes with an interactive game to reinforce the concepts. The correct answers to the multiple choice questions are given in Appendix C. If your instructor has included MindTap in your course, visit MindTap to play the interactive Causation Chain Game.

Chapter 3: Market Demand and Supply

1. Key Concept: Movement along versus shift in demand
Which of the following would shift the demand curve for autos to the right?

a. A fall in the price of autos
b. A fall in the price of auto insurance

c. A fall in consumers' incomes
d. A fall in the price of steel

 CAUSATION CHAIN GAME
Movement along a Demand Curve versus a Shift in Demand—Exhibit 3

2. Key Concept: Movement along versus shift in supply
Assuming that both soybeans and tobacco can be grown on the same land, a decrease in the price of tobacco, other things being equal, causes a(an)

a. rightward shift of the supply curve for tobacco.
b. upward movement along the supply curve for soybeans.
c. rightward shift in the supply curve for soybeans.
d. leftward shift in the supply curve for soybeans.

 CAUSATION CHAIN GAME
Movement along a Supply Curve versus a Shift in Supply—Exhibit 8

3. Key Concept: Surplus
Assume Q_s represents the quantity supplied at a given price and Q_d represents the quantity demanded at the same given price. Which of the following market conditions produce a downward movement of the price?

a. $Q_s = 1,000, Q_d = 750$
b. $Q_s = 750, Q_d = 750$

c. $Q_s = 750, Q_d = 1,000$
d. $Q_s = 1,000, Q_d = 1,000$

4. Key Concept: Shortage
Which of the following situations results from a ticket price to a concert set below the equilibrium price?

a. A long line of people wanting to purchase tickets to the concert
b. No line of people wanting to buy tickets to the concert

c. Tickets available at the box office, but no line of people wanting to buy them
d. None of the above

CAUSATION CHAIN GAME
Supply and Demand for Sneakers—Exhibit 12

Chapter 4: Markets in Action

5. Key Concept: Change in demand

A decrease in consumer income decreases the demand for compact discs. As a result of the change to a new equilibrium, there is a(an)

a. leftward shift of the supply curve.
b. rightward shift of the supply curve.
c. upward movement along the supply curve.
d. downward movement along the supply curve.

CAUSATION CHAIN GAME
The Effects of Shifts in Demand on Market Equilibrium—Exhibit 1

6. Key Concept: Change in supply

Consider the market for grapes. An increase in the wage paid to grape pickers will cause the

a. demand curve for grapes to shift to the right, resulting in a higher equilibrium price for grapes and a reduction in the quantity consumed.
b. demand curve for grapes to shift to the left, resulting in a lower equilibrium price for grapes and an increase in the quantity consumed.
c. supply curve for grapes to shift to the left, resulting in a lower equilibrium price for grapes and a decrease in the quantity consumed.
d. supply curve for grapes to shift to the left, resulting in a higher equilibrium price for grapes and a decrease in the quantity consumed.

CAUSATION CHAIN GAME
The Effects of Shifts in Supply on Market Equilibrium—Exhibit 2

7. Key Concept: Rent control

Rent controls create distortions in the housing market by

a. increasing rents received by landlords.
b. raising property values.
c. encouraging landlords to overspend for maintenance.
d. discouraging new housing construction.
e. increasing the supply of housing in the long run.

CAUSATION CHAIN GAME
Rent Control—Exhibit 5

8. Key Concept: Minimum wage

Which of the following is a good example of a price floor?

a. Rent controls on apartments in major cities
b. General admission tickets to concerts
c. The minimum wage law
d. Food stamp regulations
e. Rock concert tickets

CAUSATION CHAIN GAME
Minimum Wage—Exhibit 6

PART **3**

Macroeconomics Fundamentals

The three chapters in this part explain key measures of how well the macro economy is performing. Knowledge of this material is vital to the discussion of macro theory and policy in the next part. The first chapter in this part explains GDP computation. The next chapter begins by teaching how to measure business cycles and concludes with an examination of unemployment. The final chapter in this part explores the measurement and consequences of inflation.

CHAPTER 5

Gross Domestic Product

CHAPTER PREVIEW

Measuring the performance of the economy is an important part of life. Suppose one candidate for president of the United States proclaims that the economy's performance is the best in a generation, and the opposing presidential candidate argues that the economy could perform better. Which statistics would you seek to determine how well the economy is doing? The answer requires understanding some of the nuts and bolts of *national income accounting*. National income accounting is the system used to measure the aggregate income and expenditures for a nation. Despite certain limitations, the national income accounting system provides a valuable indicator of an economy's performance. For example, you can visit the Internet and check the annual *Economic*

Report of the President to compare the size or growth of the U.S. economy between years.

Prior to the Great Depression, there were no national accounting procedures for estimating the data required to assess the economy's performance. To provide accounting methodologies for macro data, the late economist Simon Kuznets published a small report in 1934 titled *National Income, 1929–32*. For his pioneering work, Kuznets, the "father of GDP," earned the 1971 Nobel Prize in Economics. Today, thanks in large part to Kuznets, most countries use common national accounting methods. National income accounting serves a nation similar to the manner in which accounting serves a business or household. In each case, accounting methodology is vital for identifying economic problems and formulating plans for achieving goals.

IN THIS CHAPTER, YOU WILL LEARN TO SOLVE THESE ECONOMICS PUZZLES:

- Why doesn't economic growth include increases in spending for welfare, Social Security, and unemployment programs?

- Can one newscaster report that the economy grew while another reports that for the same year the economy declined, and both reports be correct?

- How is the calculation of national output affected by environmental damage?

5-1 GROSS DOMESTIC PRODUCT

The most widely reported measure throughout the world of a nation's economic performance is **gross domestic product (GDP)**, which is the market value of all final goods and services produced in a nation during a period of time, usually a year. GDP therefore excludes production abroad by U.S. businesses. For example, GDP excludes Microsoft's earnings on its foreign operations. On the other hand, GDP includes Toyota's profits from its car plants in the United States. Why is GDP important? It tells a country how well its economy is doing. One advantage of GDP is that it avoids the "apples and oranges" measurement problem. If an economy produces 10 apples one year and 10 oranges the next, can we say that the value of output has changed in any way? To answer this question, we must attach price tags in order to evaluate the relative monetary value of apples and oranges to society. This is the reason GDP measures value using dollars, rather than listing the number of cars, heart transplants, legal cases, toothbrushes, and tanks produced. Instead, the market-determined dollar value establishes the monetary importance of production. In GDP calculations, "money talks." That is, GDP relies on markets to establish the relative value of goods and services.

GDP is compiled by the Bureau of Economic Analysis (BEA), which is an agency of the Department of Commerce. GDP requires that the following two points receive special attention: (1) GDP counts only new domestic production and (2) It counts only final goods.

Gross domestic product (GDP)
The market value of all final goods and services produced in a nation during a period of time, usually a year.

5-1a GDP Counts Only New Domestic Production

National income accountants calculating GDP carefully exclude transactions in two major areas: secondhand transactions and nonproductive financial transactions.

Secondhand Transactions

GDP includes only current transactions. It does not include the sale of a used car or the sale of a home constructed some years ago. Such transactions are merely exchanges of previously produced goods and not *current* production of new goods that add to the existing stock of cars and homes. Used items were counted previously in GDP for the year when they were newly produced. However, the sales commission on a used car or a home produced in another GDP period counts in current GDP because the salesperson performed a service during the present period of time.

Nonproductive Financial Transactions

GDP does not count purely private or public financial transactions, such as giving private gifts, buying and selling stocks and bonds, and making transfer payments. A **transfer payment** is a government payment to individuals not in exchange for goods or services currently produced. Welfare, Social Security, veterans' benefits, and unemployment benefits are transfer payments. These transactions are considered nonproductive because they do not represent production of any new or *current* output. Transfer payments are made to people who are entitled to them—perhaps because they are poor or they have reached a certain age. Similarly, stock market transactions represent only the exchange of certificates of ownership (stocks) or indebtedness (bonds) and not actual new production.

Transfer payment
A government payment to individuals not in exchange for goods or services currently produced.

5-1b GDP Counts Only Final Goods

Final goods
Finished goods and services produced for the ultimate user.

Intermediate goods
Goods and services used as inputs for the production of final goods.

The popular press usually defines GDP as simply "the value of all goods and services produced." This is technically incorrect because GDP counts only **final goods**, which are finished goods and services produced for the ultimate user. Including all goods and services produced would inflate GDP by *double counting* (counting many items more than once). In order to count only final goods and avoid overstating GDP, national income accountants must take care not to include intermediate goods. **Intermediate goods** are goods and services used as inputs for the production of final goods. Stated differently, intermediate goods are not produced for consumption by the ultimate user. Instead, they are produced for further processing or for resale.

Suppose a wholesale distributor sells glass to an automaker. This transaction is not included in GDP. The glass is an intermediate good used in the production of cars. When a customer buys a new car from the car dealer, the value of the glass is included in the car's selling price, which is the value of a final good counted in GDP. Let's consider another example. A wholesale distributor sells glass to a hardware store. GDP does not include this transaction because the hardware store is not the final user. When a customer buys the glass from the hardware store to repair a broken window, the final purchase price of the glass is added to GDP as a consumer expenditure.

5-2 MEASURING GDP

GDP is like an enormous puzzle with many pieces to fit together, including markets for products, markets for resources, consumers spending and earning money, and businesses spending and earning money. How can one fit all these puzzle pieces together? One way to understand how all these concepts fit together is to use a simple macroeconomic model called the circular flow model. The **circular flow model** shows the exchange of money, products, and resources between households and businesses. In exchange for these products and resources, money payments flow between businesses and households. Exhibit 1 shows the circular flow in a hypothetical economy with no government, no financial markets, and no foreign trade. In this ultra-simple pure market economy, only the households and the businesses make decisions.

Circular flow model
A diagram showing the exchange of money, products, and resources between households and businesses.

5-2a The Circular Flow Model

The upper half of the diagram in Exhibit 1 represents *product markets*, in which households exchange money for goods and services produced by firms. The red *supply* arrow in the top loop represents all finished products and the value of services produced, sold, and delivered to consumers. The blue *demand* arrow in the top loop shows why the businesses make this effort to satisfy the consuming households. When consumers decide to buy products, they are actually voting with their dollars. This flow of consumption expenditures from households is sales revenues to businesses and expenses from the viewpoint of households. Notice that the box labeled *product markets* contains a supply and demand graph. This means the forces of supply and demand in individual markets determine the price and quantity of each product exchanged without government interference.

The bottom half of the circular flow diagram consists of the *factor markets*, in which firms *demand* the natural resources, labor, capital, and entrepreneurship needed to

EXHIBIT 1 The Basic Circular Flow Model

In this simple economy, households spend all their income in the upper loop and demand consumer goods and services from businesses. Businesses seek profits by supplying goods and services to households through the product markets. Prices and quantities in individual markets are determined by the market supply and demand model. In the factor markets in the lower loop, resources (land, labor, and capital) are owned by households and supplied to businesses that demand these factors in return for money payments. The forces of supply and demand determine the returns to the factors, for example, wages and the quantity of labor supplied. Overall, goods and services flow clockwise, and the corresponding payments flow counterclockwise.

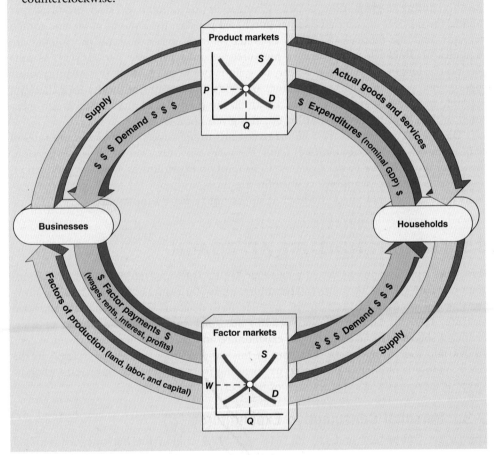

produce the goods and services sold in the product markets. Our hypothetical economy is capitalistic, and the model assumes for simplicity that households own the factors of production. Businesses therefore must purchase all their resources from the households. The red *supply* arrow in the bottom loop represents this flow of resources from households to firms, and the blue *demand* arrow is the flow of money payments to households for these resources. These payments are also income earned by households in the form of wages, rents, interest, and profits. As in the product markets, market supply and demand determine the price and quantity of factor payments.

This simple model also assumes all households live from hand to mouth. That is, households spend all the income they earn in the factor markets on products. Households, therefore, do not save. Likewise, all firms spend all their income earned in the product markets on resources from the factor markets. The simple circular flow model therefore fails to mirror the real world. But it does aid your understanding of the relationships among product markets, factor markets, the flow of money, and the theory behind GDP measurement.

5-2b Flow versus Stock

Flow
A rate of change in a quantity during a given time period, such as dollars per year. For example, income and consumption are flows that occur per week, per month, or per year.

Stock
A quantity measured at one point in time. For example, an inventory of goods or the amount of money in a checking account.

The arrows in Exhibit 1 are flows, rather than stocks. A **flow** is a rate of change in a quantity during a given time period. Changes in the amount of steel produced per month, the number of computer games purchased per day, the amount of income earned per year, and the number of gallons of water pouring into a bathtub per minute are examples of flows. Flows are always measured in units per time period, such as tons per month, billions of dollars per year, or gallons per hour. A **stock** is a quantity measured at one point in time. An inventory of goods, the amount of money in a checking account, and the amount of water in a bathtub are examples of stocks. Stocks are measured in tons, dollars, gallons, and so on, at a given point in time.

The important point is this: *All measurements in the circular flow model are rates of change (flows) and tell us nothing about the total amounts (stocks) of goods, services, money, or anything else in the economy.* Consumption expenditures, business production, wages, rents, interest payments, and profits are flows of money for newly produced products or resources that affect the level of stocks not shown in the model.

5-3 THE EXPENDITURE APPROACH

Expenditure approach
The national income accounting method that measures GDP by adding all the spending for final goods during a period of time.

How does the government actually calculate GDP? One way national income accountants calculate GDP is to use the expenditure approach to measure total spending flowing through product markets in the circular flow diagram. The **expenditure approach** measures GDP by adding all the spending for final goods during a period of time. Exhibit 2 shows 2016 GDP using the expenditure approach, which breaks down expenditures into four components. The data in this exhibit show that all production in the U.S. economy is ultimately purchased by spending from households, businesses, government, or foreigners. Let's discuss each of these expenditure categories.

5-3a Personal Consumption Expenditures (*C*)

The largest component of GDP in 2016 was $12.8 trillion for the category national income accountants call *personal consumption expenditures*, represented by the letter *C*. Personal consumption expenditures is household spending for durable goods, nondurable goods, and services. Durable goods include items such as automobiles, appliances, and furniture because they last longer than three years. Food, clothing, soap, and gasoline are examples of nondurables, because they are considered used up or consumed in less than three years. Services, which is the largest category, include recreation, legal advice, medical treatment, education, and any transaction not in the form of a tangible object. This is why the U.S. economy is often referred to as a service economy.

EXHIBIT 2 Gross Domestic Product Using the Expenditure Approach, 2016

National income account		Amount (trillions of dollars)	Percentage of GDP
Personal consumption expenditures (**C**)		$12.8	69%
Durable goods	$1.4		
Nondurable goods	2.7		
Services	8.7		
Gross private domestic investment (**I**)		3.036	16
Fixed investment	3.015		
Change in business inventories	0.021		
Government consumption expenditures and gross investment (**G**)		3.27	18
Federal	1.24		
State and local	2.03		
Net exports of goods and services (**X − M**)		−0.5	−3
Exports (X)	2.2		
Imports (M)	2.7		
Gross domestic product (**GDP**)		$18.6	100%

SOURCE: Bureau of Economic Analysis, *National Economic Accounts*, http://www.bea.gov/iTable/index_nipa.cfm, Table 1.1.5.

5-3b Gross Private Domestic Investment (*I*)

In 2016, a little over $3 trillion was spent for what is officially called *gross private domestic investment* (*I*). This national income account includes "gross" (all) "private" (not government) "domestic" (not foreign) spending by businesses for investment in capital assets that are expected to earn profits in the future. Gross private domestic investment is the sum of two components: (1) *Fixed investment* expenditures for newly produced capital goods, such as commercial and residential structures, machinery, equipment, tools, and computers and (2) Change in *business inventories*, which is the net change in spending for unsold finished goods

Note that gross private domestic investment is simply the national income accounting category for "investment," defined in Chapter 2. The only difference is that investment in Exhibit 5 in Chapter 2 was in physical capital, such as manufacturing plants, oil wells, or fast-food restaurants, rather than the dollar value of capital used here. Also, note that gross domestic investment does not include *personal investments* in stocks, bonds, and other financial assets. Recall that these personal investments are not included in the expenditure approach to GDP because they are unproductive financial transactions.

Now we will take a closer look at gross private domestic investment. Note that national income accountants include the rental value of newly constructed residential housing in the $3.015 trillion spent for fixed investment. A new factory, warehouse, or robot is surely a form of investment, but why include residential housing as business investment rather than consumption by households? The debatable answer is that a new home is considered investment because it provides services in the future that the owner can rent for financial return. For this reason, all newly produced housing is considered investment whether the owner rents or occupies the property. Also note that starting from July 2013 intellectual property products that include research and development (R&D) spending are added to gross domestic investment.

Finally, the $0.021 trillion change in business inventories means this amount of net dollar value of unsold finished goods and raw materials was added to the stock of inventories during 2016. A decline in inventories would reduce GDP because households consumed more output than firms produced during this year. When businesses have more on their shelves this year than last, more new production has taken place than has been consumed during this year.

5-3c Government Consumption Expenditures and Gross Investment (*G*)

This official category simply called *government spending* includes the value of goods and services government at all levels purchased measured by their costs. For example, spending for police and state university professors enters the GDP accounts at the prices the government pays for them. In addition, the government spends for investment additions to its stock of capital, such as tanks, schools, highways, bridges, and government buildings. In 2016, federal, state, and local government spending (*G*) totaled $3.27 trillion. As the figures in Exhibit 2 reveal, government purchases by state and local governments far exceeded those of the federal government. It is important to understand that the government spending category of GDP excludes *transfer payments* because, as explained at the beginning of the chapter, they do not represent newly produced goods and services. Instead, transfer payments are paid to those entitled to Social Security benefits, veterans' benefits, welfare, unemployment compensation, and benefits from other programs.

5-3d Net Exports (*X* − *M*)

The last GDP account is net exports, expressed in the formula (*X* − *M*). Exports (*X*) are spending by foreigners for U.S. domestically produced goods. Imports (*M*) are the dollar amount of U.S. purchases for goods produced abroad, like for Japanese automobiles, French wine, and clothes from China. The positive sign (+*X*) means that money flows into the United States from foreigners to pay for our exports. The negative sign (−*M*) indicates dollars are flowing out of the United States to pay for imports. In 2016, export spending was $2.2 trillion and import spending was −$2.7 trillion. Net exports were therefore −$0.5 trillion. What is the effect of a negative sign for net exports? It means the United States is spending more dollars to purchase foreign products than it is receiving from abroad for U.S. goods sold to foreigners. The effect of a negative net exports figure is to reduce U.S. GDP. Stated another way, higher exports (*X*) relative to imports (*M*) increases GDP. Prior to the early 1980s, the United States was a consistent net exporter, selling more goods and services to the rest of the world than we purchased from abroad. Since 1983, the United States has been a net importer. International trade is discussed in more detail in the last section of the text.

5-3e A Formula for GDP

Using the expenditure approach, GDP is expressed mathematically in trillions of dollars as

$$GDP = C + I + G + (X - M)$$

For 2016 (see Exhibit 2),

$$\$18.6 = \$12.8 + \$3.036 + \$3.27 + (\$2.2 - 2.7)$$

This simple equation plays a central role in macroeconomics. It is the basis for analyzing macro problems and formulating macro policy. When economists study the macro economy, they can apply this equation to predict the behavior of the major sectors of the economy: consumption (C) is spending by households, investment (I) is spending by firms, government spending (G) is spending by the government, and net exports ($X - M$) is net spending by foreigners.

5-4 THE INCOME APPROACH

The second, somewhat more complex approach to measuring GDP is the income approach. The **income approach** measures GDP by adding all the incomes earned by households in exchange for the factors of production during a period of time. Both the expenditure approach and the income approach yield identical GDP calculations. As shown in the basic circular flow model, each dollar of expenditure paid by households to businesses in the product markets means a dollar of income flows to households through the factor markets as a payment for the land, labor, and capital required to produce the product. Using the income approach, GDP is expressed as follows:

Income approach
The national income accounting method that measures GDP by adding all incomes during a period of time, including compensation of employees, rents, net interest, and profits.

$$\text{GDP} = \textbf{compensation of employees} + \textbf{rents} + \textbf{profits} + \textbf{net interest}$$
$$+ \textbf{indirect taxes} + \textbf{depreciation}$$

In practice, it is necessary to add depreciation (capital consumption allowance) to factor payments so that national income equals GDP. Exhibit 3 presents actual 2016 GDP calculated following the income approach and then each component is discussed in turn.

5-4a Compensation of Employees

Employees' compensation is the largest of the national income accounts. About 54 percent of GDP in 2016 ($10.07 trillion) was income earned from wages, salaries, and certain supplements paid by firms and government to suppliers of labor. Since labor services play such an important role in production, it is not surprising that employee compensation represents the largest share of the GDP income pie. The supplements consist of employer taxes for Social Security and unemployment insurance. Also included are fringe benefits from a variety of private health insurance and pension plans.

EXHIBIT 3 Gross Domestic Product Using the Income Approach, 2016

National income account		Amount (trillions of dollars)	Percentage of GDP
Compensation of employees		$10.07	54%
Rental income		0.7	4
Profits		3.51	19
Proprietors' income	1.42		
Corporate profits	2.09		
Net interest		0.5	3
Indirect business taxes		1.3	7
Depreciation		2.5	13
Gross domestic product (GDP)		$18.6	100%

SOURCE: Bureau of Economic Analysis, *National Income Accounts*, http://www.bea.gov/iTable/index_nipa.cfm, Tables 1.7.5 and 2.1.

5-4b Rental Income

The smallest source of income is from rent and royalties received by property owners who permit others to use their assets during a time period. For example, this category includes house and apartment rents received by landlords. In 2016, $0.7 trillion was earned in rental income.

5-4c Profits

Proprietors' Income

All forms of income earned by unincorporated businesses totaled $1.42 trillion in 2016. Self-employed proprietorships and partnerships simultaneously own their businesses and pay themselves for their labor services to their firms.

Corporate Profits

This income category includes all income earned by the stockholders of corporations regardless of whether stockholders receive it. The $2.09 trillion of corporate profits in 2016 was the sum of three sources: (1) Dividends, (2) Undistributed corporate profits (retained earnings for expanding plant and equipment), (3) Corporate income taxes

Thus, corporate profits using the income approach are "before taxes."

5-4d Net Interest

Households both receive and pay interest. Persons who make loans to businesses earn interest income. Suppose you purchase a bond issued by Apple. When Apple pays interest on its bonds, the interest payments are included in the national income accounts. Households also received interest from savings accounts and certificates of deposits (CDs). On the other hand, households borrow money and pay interest on, for example, credit cards, installment loans, and mortgage loans. The net interest of $0.5 trillion in 2016 is the difference between interest income earned and interest payments.

5-4e Indirect Business Taxes

As reported in Exhibit 3, $1.3 trillion was collected by government in the form of indirect business taxes. Why do national income accountants include business taxes in the income approach to GDP competition? **Indirect business taxes** are levied as a percentage of the prices of goods sold and therefore become part of the revenue received by firms. These taxes include sales taxes, federal excise taxes, license fees, business property taxes, and customs duties. Indirect taxes are not income payments to suppliers of resources. Instead, firms collect indirect taxes and send these funds to the government. Suppose you purchased a new automobile for $20,000, including a $1,000 federal excise tax and state sales tax. These taxes are included in the price, but are income for the government, which represents the public interest of households.

Indirect business taxes Taxes levied as a percentage of the prices of goods sold and therefore collected as part of the firm's revenue. Firms treat such taxes as production costs. Examples include general sales taxes, excise taxes, and customs duties.

5-4f Depreciation

To reconcile the above income accounts with GDP requires adding the category labeled *consumption of fixed capital*. Consumption of fixed capital is an estimate of the depreciation of capital. This somewhat imposing term is simply an allowance for the portion of capital worn out producing GDP. Over time, capital goods, such as buildings, machines, and equipment, wear out and become less valuable. Depreciation (capital consumption allowance) is therefore a portion of GDP that is not available for income payments. Because it is impossible to measure depreciation precisely, an estimate is entered. In 2016, $2.5 trillion was the estimated amount of GDP attributable to depreciation during the year.

Exhibit 4 presents the conceptual frameworks of the expenditure and income approaches to computing GDP.

EXHIBIT 4 Expenditure and Income Approaches to GDP

Expenditure approach		Income approach
Consumption (*C*) expenditures by households plus Investment (*I*) expenditures by businesses plus Government consumption expenditures and gross investment (*G*) plus Net exports (*X* – *M*) expenditures by foreign economies	= GDP =	Compensation of employees plus Rents plus Profits plus Net interest plus Indirect business taxes plus Depreciation

How Much Does Mario Add to GDP?
Mario works part-time at Pizza Hut and earns an annual wage plus tips of $15,000. He sold 4,000 pizzas at $15 per pizza during the year. He was unemployed part of the year, so he received unemployment compensation of $3,000. During the past year, Mario bought a used car for $5,000. Using the expenditure approach, how much has Mario contributed to GDP?

5-4g GDP in Other Countries

Global Economics Image Exhibit 5 compares GDP for selected countries in 2016. The United States had the world's highest GDP, and China had the second largest GDP. U.S. GDP, for example, was over 1.6 times the size of China's GDP.

5-5 GDP SHORTCOMINGS

For various reasons, GDP omits certain measures of overall economic well-being. Because GDP is the basis of government economic policies, there is concern that GDP may be giving us a false impression of the nation's material well-being. GDP is a less-than-perfect measure of the nation's economic pulse because it excludes the following factors.

5-5a Nonmarket Transactions

Because GDP counts only market transactions, it excludes certain unpaid activities, such as homemaker production, child rearing, and do-it-yourself home repairs and services. For example, if you take your dirty clothes to the laundry, GDP increases by the amount of the cleaning bill paid. But GDP ignores the value of laundering these same clothes if you wash them yourself at home.

There are two reasons for excluding nonmarket activities from GDP; first, it would be extremely imprecise to attempt to collect data and assign a dollar value to services people provide for themselves or others without compensation. Second, it is difficult to decide which nonmarket activities to exclude and which ones to include. Perhaps repairing your own roof, painting your own house, and repairing your own car should be included. Now consider the value of washing your car. GDP does include the price of cleaning your car if you purchase that service at a car wash, so it could be argued that GDP should include the value of you washing your car at home.

The issue of unpaid do-it-yourself activities affects comparisons of the GDPs of different nations. One reason some less-developed nations have lower GDPs than major industrialized nations is that a greater proportion of people in less-developed nations farm, clean, make repairs, and perform other tasks for their families rather than hire someone else to do the work.

EXHIBIT 5 An International Comparison of GDPs, 2016

This exhibit shows GDPs in 2016 for selected countries. The United States had the world's highest GDP, and China has the second largest GDP. U.S. GDP, for example, is over 1.6 times the size of China's GDP.

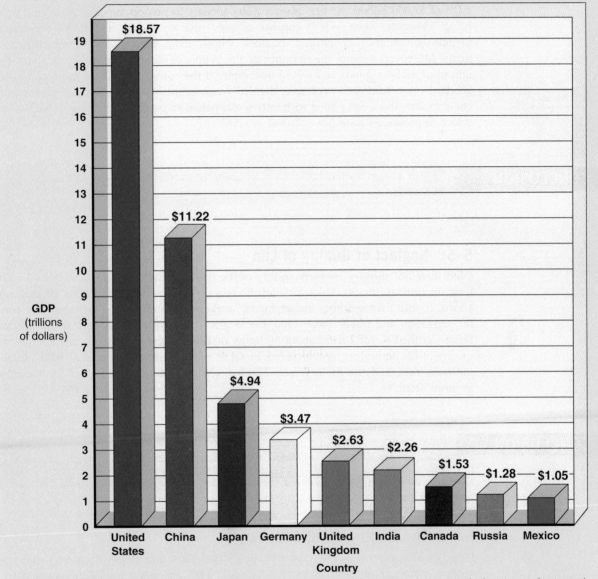

SOURCE: International Monetary Fund, *World Economic Outlook Database*, http://www.imf.org/external/index.htm. Found at http://www.imf.org/external/datamapper/NGDPD@WEO/OEMDC/ADVEC/WEOWORLD

5-5b Distribution, Kind, and Quality of Products

GDP is blind to whether a small fraction of the population consumes most of a country's GDP or consumption is evenly divided. GDP also wears a blindfold with respect to the quality and kinds of goods and services that make up a nation's GDP. Consider the fictional economies of Zuba and Econa. Zuba has a GDP of $2,000 billion, and Econa has a GDP of $1,000 billion. At first glance, Zuba appears to possess superior economic well-being. However, Zuba's GDP consists of only military goods, and Econa's products include computers, cell phones, tractors, wheat, milk, houses, and other consumer items. Moreover, assume the majority of the people of Zuba could care less about the output of military goods and would be happier if the country produced more consumer goods. Now consider, for example, the difference in quality between a cell phone purchased today and a cell phone with only few capabilities purchased years ago. Such qualitative improvements are not reflected in GDP.

CONCLUSION GDP is a quantitative, rather than a qualitative, measure of the output of goods and services.

5-5c Neglect of Quality of Life

GDP does not directly measure quality-of-life or "happiness" variables such as leisure time. In general, the wealthier a nation becomes, the more leisure time its citizens can afford. Rather than working longer hours, workers often choose to increase their time for recreation and travel. Since 1900, the length of the typical workweek in the United States declined steadily from about 50 hours in 1900 to about 34 hours in 2017.[1] Other quality-of-life indicators not included in GDP include life expectancy at birth, infant mortality rate, and the literacy rate. The last chapter discusses quality-of-life variables in more detail.

CONCLUSION It can be argued that GDP understates national well-being because no allowance is made for variables such as leisure time, life expectancy, infant mortality, literacy rate and other quality-of-life variables.

5-5d The Underground Economy

Illegal gambling, prostitution, loan-sharking, illegal guns, and illegal drugs are goods and services that meet all the requirements for GDP. They are final goods with a value determined in "black" markets, but GDP does not include unreported criminal activities because no record is made of these transactions. The "underground" economy also includes tax evasion. One way to avoid paying taxes on a legal activity is to trade or

---

[1]Bureau of Labor Statistics, http://www.bls.gov/data/, Table B–2.

barter goods and services rather than selling them. One person fixes a neighbor's car in return for babysitting services, and the value of the exchange is unreported. Other individuals and businesses make legal sales for cash and do not report the income earned to the Internal Revenue Service.

Estimates of the size of this subterranean economy vary. Some studies by economists estimate the size of the underground sector is about 9 percent of GDP. This range of estimates is slightly less than the estimated size of the underground economy in most European countries.

> **CONCLUSION**
> If the underground economy is sizable, GDP will understate an economy's performance by a sizable amount.

5-5e Economic Bads

More production means a larger GDP, regardless of the level of pollution created in the process. Recall from Chapter 4 the discussion of *negative externalities,* such as pollution caused by steel mills, chemical plants, and cigarettes. Air, water, and noise pollution are *economic bads* that impose costs on society not reflected in private market prices and quantities bought and sold. When a polluting company sells its product, this transaction increases GDP. However, critics of GDP argue that it fails to account for the diminished quality of life from the "bads" not reported in GDP.

Stated another way, if production results in pollution and environmental damage, GDP overstates the nation's well-being.

> **CONCLUSION**
> Since the costs of negative by-products are not deducted, GDP overstates the national well-being.

5-5f GDP Alternatives

There are alternative measures for GDP that have been developed to value more diverse economic activities. The Measure of Economic Welfare (MEW) and the Genuine Progress Indicator (GPI) expand the range of economic activities counted, such as nonmarket work and leisure. MEW, for example, discounts spending on so-called wasteful activities like the military, as well as making adjustments for environmental damage, while giving value to home production and leisure activity. The GPI puts weight on income distribution. Another measure is the Human Development Index (HDI) that includes life expectancy and education. However, the HDI does not include any measure of environmental sustainability. The Happy Planet Index (HPI) is distinctive because it provides no measure of market transactions. Instead the HDI places heavy weight on health systems, schools, and environmental sustainability. Using the HDI, Norway has consistently ranked highest. Switzerland, Australia, Germany, Denmark and Singapore followed in 2015. The United States was tied with Canada for tenth place.

5-6 OTHER NATIONAL INCOME ACCOUNTS

In addition to GDP, the media often report several other national income accounts because they are necessary for studying the macro economy. We now take a brief look at each.

5-6a National Income (NI)

It can be argued that depreciation should be subtracted from GDP. Recall that GDP is not entirely a measure of newly produced output because it includes an estimated value of capital goods required to replace those worn out in the production process. The measurement designed to correct this deficiency is **national income (NI)**, which is the gross domestic product minus depreciation of the capital worn out in producing output. Stated as a formula

$$NI = GDP - depreciation \text{ (consumption of fixed capital)}$$

In 2016, $2.5 trillion was the estimated amount of GDP attributable to depreciation during the year. Exhibit 6 shows the actual calculation of NI from GDP in 2016. NI measures how much income is *earned* by households that own and supply resources. It includes the total flow of payments to the owners of the factors of production, including wages, rents, interest, and profits. Another way to compute national income is to add compensation of employees, rents, profits, net interest, and indirect business taxes using the income approach demonstrated in Exhibit 3. Exhibit 7 illustrates the transition from GDP to NI and two other measures of the macro economy.[2]

5-6b Personal Income (PI)

National income measures the total amount of money *earned*, but determining the amount of income actually *received* by households (not businesses) requires a measurement of personal income. **Personal income (PI)** is the total income received by households that is available for consumption, saving, and payment of personal taxes. Suppose we want to measure the total amount of money individuals receive that they can use to consume products, save, and pay taxes. National income is not the appropriate measure for

National income (NI)
The total income earned by resource owners, including wages, rents, interest, and profits. NI is calculated as gross domestic product minus depreciation of the capital worn out in producing output.

Personal income (PI)
The total income received by households that is available for consumption, saving, and payment of personal taxes.

EXHIBIT 6 National Income Calculated from Gross Domestic Product, 2016

	Amount (trillions of dollars)
Gross domestic product (GDP)	$18.6
Depreciation	−2.5
National income (NI)	$16.1

SOURCE: Bureau of Economic Analysis, *National Economic Accounts*, http://www.bea.gov/iTable/index_nipa.cfm, Table 1.7.5.

---

[2]As a result of a revision in national income accounting, the only difference between net domestic product (NDP) and national income (NI) is a statistical discrepancy. Since NI is more widely reported in the media, and to simplify, NDP is not calculated here.

YOU'RE THE **ECONOMIST**

Applicable Concept: National Income Accounting
"Goods" and "Bads"

Is GDP a False Beacon Steering Us into the Rocks?

Suppose a factory in your community has been dumping hazardous wastes into the local water supply and people develop cancer and other illnesses from drinking polluted water. The Environmental Protection Agency (EPA) discovers this pollution and, under the federal "Superfund" law, orders a cleanup and imposes a fine for the damages. The company defends itself against the EPA by hiring lawyers and experts to take the case to court. After years of trial, the company loses the case and has to pay for the cleanup and damages.

In terms of GDP, an amazing "good" result occurs. The primary measure of national economic output, GDP, increases. GDP counts the millions of dollars spent to clean up the water supply. GDP even includes the health care expenses of anyone who develops cancer or other illnesses caused by drinking polluted water. GDP also includes the money spent by the company on lawyers and experts to defend itself against the EPA. And GDP includes the money spent by the EPA to regulate the polluting company.

Now consider what happens when trees are cut down and oil and minerals are used to produce houses, cars, and other goods. The value of the wood, oil, and minerals is an intermediate good implicitly computed in GDP because the value of the final goods is explicitly computed in GDP. Using scarce resources to produce goods and services therefore raises GDP and is considered a "good" result. On the other hand, don't we lose the value of trees, oil, and minerals in the production process, so isn't this a "bad" result?

The Bureau of Economic Analysis (BEA) is an agency of the U.S. Department of Commerce. The BEA is the nation's economic accountant, and it is the source of GDP data cited throughout this text. Critics have called for a new measure designed to estimate the kinds of damage described above. These new accounts would adjust for changes in air and water quality and depletion of oil and minerals. These accounts would also adjust for changes in the stock of renewable natural resources, such as forests and fish stocks. In addition, accounts should be created to measure the effects of global warming and the destruction of the ozone layer.

haak78/Shutterstock.com

As explained in this chapter, a dollar estimate of capital depreciation is subtracted from GDP to compute national income (NI). The argument here is that a dollar estimate of the damage to the environment should also be subtracted. To ignore measuring such environmental problems, critics argue, threatens future generations. In short, are we really better off producing more things if that results in a less pristine environment? Perhaps conventional GDP perpetuates a false dichotomy suggesting there is a trade-off between economic growth and progress, and environmental protection and sustainability

Critics of this approach argue that assigning a dollar value to environmental damage and resource depletion requires a methodology that is extremely subjective and complex. For example, how do you measure the lost value of an extinct species? Nevertheless, national income accountants have not ignored these criticisms, and the National Academy of Sciences has reviewed BEA proposals for ways to account for interactions between the environment and the economy.

ANALYZE THE ISSUE   Suppose a nuclear power plant disaster occurs. How could GDP be a false beacon in this case?

two reasons. First, NI excludes transfer payments, which constitute unearned income that can be spent, saved, or used to pay taxes. Second, NI includes corporate profits, but stockholders do not receive all these profits. A portion of corporate profits is paid in corporate taxes. Also, retained earnings are not distributed to stockholders, but are channeled back into business operations.

Exhibit 7 illustrates the relationship between personal income and national income, and Exhibit 8 gives the figures for 2016. National income accountants adjust national

EXHIBIT 7 Four Measures of the Macro Economy

The four bars show major measurements of the U.S. macro economy in 2016 in trillions of dollars. Beginning with gross domestic product, depreciation is subtracted to obtain national income. Next, personal income equals national income minus corporate profits and contributions for Social Security insurance (FICA payments) plus transfer payments and other income. Subtracting personal taxes from personal income yields disposable personal income.

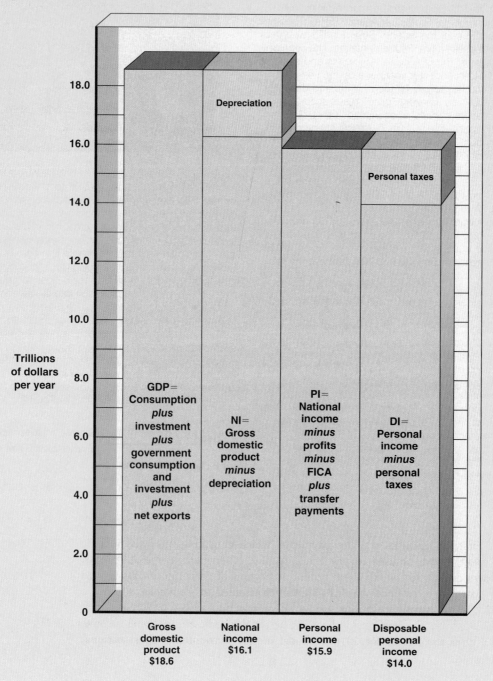

EXHIBIT 8 Personal Income Calculated from National Income, 2016

	Amount (trillions of dollars)
National income (NI)	$16.1
Corporate profits	−2.1
Contributions for Social Security (FICA)	−1.2
Transfer payments and other income	3.1
Personal income (PI)	$15.9

SOURCE: Bureau of Economic Analysis, *National Economic Accounts*, http://www.bea.gov/iTable/index_nipa.cfm, Table 1.7.5.

EXHIBIT 9 Disposable Personal Income Calculated from Personal Income, 2016

	Amount (trillions of dollars)
Personal income (PI)	$15.9
Personal taxes	−1.9
Disposable personal income (DI)	$14.0

SOURCE: Bureau of Economic Analysis, *National Economic Accounts*, http://www.bea.gov/iTable/index_nipa.cfm, Table 2.1.

income by subtracting corporate profits and payroll taxes for Social Security (FICA deductions). Next, *transfer payments* and other income individuals receive from net interest and dividends are added. The net result is the personal income received by households, which in 2016 amounted to $15.9 trillion.

5-6c Disposable Personal Income (DI)

One final measure of national income is shown at the far right of Exhibit 7. **Disposable personal income (DI)** is the amount of income that households actually have to spend or save after payment of personal taxes. Disposable, or *after-tax*, income is equal to personal income minus personal taxes paid to federal, state, and local governments. Personal taxes consist of personal income taxes, personal property taxes, and inheritance taxes. As tabulated in Exhibit 9, disposable personal income in 2016 was $14.0 trillion.

Disposable personal income (DI)
The amount of income that households actually have to spend or save after payment of personal taxes.

5-7 CHANGING NOMINAL GDP TO REAL GDP

So far, GDP has been expressed as nominal GDP. **Nominal GDP** is the value of all final goods based on the prices existing during the time period of production. Nominal GDP

Nominal GDP
The value of all final goods based on the prices existing during the time period of production.

is also referred to as *current-dollar* or *money GDP*. Nominal GDP grows in three ways. First, output rises and prices remain unchanged. Second, prices rise and output is constant. Third, in the typical case, both output and prices rise. The problem, then, is how to adjust GDP so it reflects only changes in output and not changes in prices. This adjusted GDP allows meaningful comparisons over time when prices are changing.

Changing prices can have a huge impact on how we compare dollar figures. Suppose a newspaper headline reports that a film titled *The History of Economic Thought* is the biggest box-office sales movie of all time. You ask, "How can this be? What about *Gone with the Wind*?" Reading the article reveals that this claim is based on the nominal measure of gross box-office receipts. This gives a recent movie with higher ticket prices an advantage over a movie released in 1939 when the average ticket price was about $1. A better measure of popularity would be to compare "real" (or inflation-adjusted) box-office receipts by multiplying actual attendance figures for each movie by a base year movie price.

Measuring the difference between changes in output and changes in the price level involves making an important distinction between nominal GDP and real GDP. **Real GDP** is the value of all final goods produced during a given time period based on the prices existing in a selected base year. The U.S. Department of Commerce currently uses 2009 prices as the base year. Real GDP is also referred to as *constant dollar GDP*.

Real GDP
The value of all final goods produced during a given time period based on the prices existing in a selected base year.

5-7a The GDP Chain Price Index

The most broadly based measure used to take the changes-in-the-price-level "air" out of the nominal GDP "balloon" and compute real GDP is officially called the GDP chain price index. This index is also called GDP price index or simply GDP deflator. The **GDP chain price index** is a measure that compares changes in the prices of all final goods produced during a given time period relative to the prices of those goods in a base year. The GDP chain price index is a broad "deflator" index calculated by a complex chain-weighted geometric series (you are spared the details). It is highly inclusive because it measures not only price changes of consumer goods, but also price changes of business investment, government purchases, exports, and imports. Do not confuse the GDP chain price index with the *consumer price index* (CPI), which is widely reported in the news media. The CPI is a different index, measuring only consumer prices, which we will discuss in the chapter on inflation.

GDP chain price index
A measure that compares changes in the prices of all final goods during a given year relative to the prices of those goods in a base year. This index is also called GDP price index or simply GDP deflator.

Now it's time to see how the GDP chain price index works. We begin with the following conversion equation:

$$\text{Real GDP} = \frac{\text{nominal GDP}}{\text{GDP chain price index}} \times 100$$

Using 2009 as the base year, suppose you are given the 2016 nominal GDP of $18,569 billion and the 2016 GDP chain price index of 111.44. To calculate 2016 real GDP, use the above formula as follows:

$$\$16,662 \text{ billion} = \frac{\$18,569 \text{ billion}}{111.44} \times 100$$

Exhibit 10 shows actual U.S. nominal GDP, real GDP, and the GDP chain price index for selected years. Column (1) reports nominal GDP, column, column (2) gives real GDP figures for these years, column (3) lists corresponding GDP chain price indexes.

EXHIBIT 10 Nominal GDP, Real GDP, and the GDP Chain Price Index for Selected Years

Real GDP reflects output valued at 2009 base-year prices, but nominal GDP is annual output valued at prices prevailing during the current year. The intersection of real and nominal GDP occurs in 2009 because in the base year, both nominal GDP and real GDP measure the same output at 2009 prices. Note that the nominal GDP curve has risen more sharply than the real GDP curve as a result of inflation included in the nominal figures.

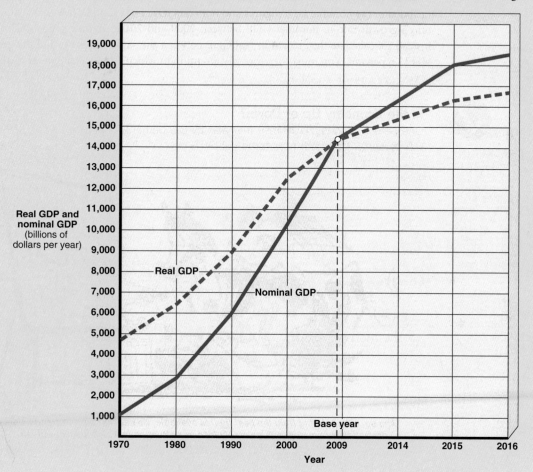

Year	(1) Nominal GDP (billions of dollars)	(2) Real GDP (billions of 2009 dollars)	(3) GDP Deflator (2009 = 100)
1970	1,076	4,718	22.8
1980	2,862	6,443	44.4
1990	5,980	8,945	66.8
2000	10,290	12,565	81.9
2009	14,418	14,418	100.0
2014	17,419	16,086	108.29
2015	18,037	16,397	110.0
2016	18,569	16,662	111.44

SOURCE: Bureau of Economic Analysis, *National Economic Accounts*, http://www.bea.gov/iTable/index_nipa.cfm, Tables 1.1.5, 1.1.6, and 1.1.9.

Notice that the GDP chain price index exceeds 100 in years beyond 2009. This means that prices, on average, have risen since 2009, causing the real purchasing power of the dollar to fall. In years before 2009, the GDP chain price index is less than 100, which means the real purchasing power of the dollar was higher relative to the 2009 base year. At the base year of 2009, nominal and real GDP are identical, and the GDP price index equals 100.

The graph in Exhibit 10 traces real GDP and nominal GDP for the U.S. economy since 1970. Note that nominal GDP usually grows faster than real GDP because inflation is included in the nominal GDP figures and not real GDP. For example, if we calculate the economy's growth rate in nominal GDP between 2009 and 2016, we find it was 28.8 percent. If instead we calculate the growth in real GDP between the same years, we find the growth rate was 15.6 percent. You must therefore pay attention to which GDP is being used in an analysis.

CHECKPOINT

Is the Economy Up or Down?
One person reports, "GDP rose this year by 8.5 percent." Another says, "GDP fell by 0.5 percent." Can both reports be right?

"And so, extrapolating from the best figures available, we see that current trends, unless dramatically reversed, will inevitably lead to a situation in which the sky will fall."

Key Concepts

Gross domestic product (GDP)

Transfer payment

Final goods

Intermediate goods

Circular flow model

Flow

Stock

Expenditure approach

Income approach

Indirect business taxes

National income (NI)

Personal income (PI)

Disposable personal income (DI)

Nominal GDP

Real GDP

GDP chain price index

Summary

- **Gross domestic product (GDP)** is the most widely used measure of a nation's economic performance. GDP is the market value of all **final goods** produced in the United States during a period of time. Secondhand and financial transactions are not counted in GDP. To avoid double counting, GDP also does not include **intermediate goods**. GDP is calculated by either the expenditure approach or the income approach.

- The **circular flow model** is a diagram representing the flow of products and resources between businesses and households in exchange for money payments. **Flows** must be distinguished from **stocks**. Flows are measured in units per time period—for example, dollars per year. Stocks are quantities that exist at a given point in time.

of employees, rents, profits, net interest, **indirect business taxes**, and depreciation. Indirect business taxes are levied as a percentage of product prices and include sales taxes, excise taxes, and customs duties.

- **National income (NI)** is total income *earned* by households that own and supply resources. It is calculated as GDP minus depreciation.

- **Personal income (PI)** is the total income *received* by households and is calculated as NI minus corporate taxes and Social Security taxes plus transfer payments and other income.

- **Disposable personal income (DI)** is personal income minus personal taxes. DI is the amount of income a household has available to consume or save.

Circular Flow Model

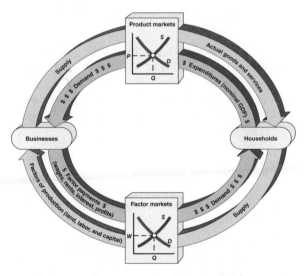

- The **expenditure approach** sums the four major spending components of GDP consumption, investment, government spending, and net exports. Algebraically,
  $GDP = C + I + G + (X - M)$, where X equals foreign spending for domestic exports and M equals domestic spending for foreign products.

- The **income approach** sums the major income components of GDP, consisting of compensation

Measures of the Macro Economy

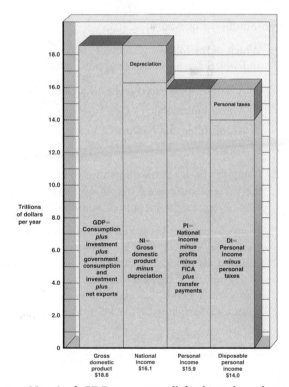

- **Nominal GDP** measures all final goods and services produced in a given time period valued at the prices existing during the time period of production.

- **Real GDP** measures all final goods and services produced in a given time period valued at the prices existing in a base year.

- The **GDP chain price index** is a broad price index used to convert nominal GDP to real GDP.

The GDP chain price index measures changes in the prices of consumer goods, business investment, government spending, exports, and imports. Real GDP is computed by dividing nominal GDP for year X by year X's GDP chain price index and then multiplying the result by 100.

Summary of Conclusion Statements

- GDP is a quantitative, rather than a qualitative, measure of the output of goods and services.

- It can be argued that GDP understates national well-being because no allowance is made for people working fewer hours than they once did.

- If the underground economy is sizable, GDP will understate an economy's performance by a sizeable amount.

- Because the costs of negative by-products are not deducted, GDP overstates our national well-being.

Study Questions and Problems

Please see Appendix A for answers to the odd-numbered questions. Your instructor has access to the answers for even-numbered questions.

1. Which of the following are final goods or services, and which are intermediate goods or services?

   a. A haircut purchased from a hair salon
   b. A new automobile
   c. An oil filter purchased in a new automobile
   d. Crude oil

2. Using the basic circular flow model, explain why the value of businesses' output of goods and services equals the income of households.

3. A small economy produced the following final goods and services during a given month: 3 million pounds of food, 50,000 shirts, 20 houses, 50,000 hours of medical services, 1 automobile plant, and 2 tanks. Calculate the value of this output at the following market prices:

   - $1 per pound of food
   - $20 per shirt
   - $50,000 per house
   - $20 per hour of medical services
   - $1 million per automobile plant
   - $500,000 per tank

4. An economy produces final goods and services with a market value of $5,000 billion in a given year, but only $4,500 billion worth of goods and services is sold to domestic or foreign buyers. Is this nation's GDP $5,000 billion or $4,500 billion? Explain your answer.

5. Explain why a new forklift sold for use in a warehouse is a final good even though it is fixed investment (capital) used to produce other goods. Is there a double-counting problem if this sale is added to GDP?

6. Explain why the government spending (G) component of GDP falls short of actual government expenditures.

7. Explain how net exports affect the U.S. economy. Describe both positive and negative impacts on GDP. Why do national income accountants use net exports to compute GDP, rather than simply adding exports to the other expenditure components of GDP?

8. Suppose the data in Exhibit 11 are for a given year from the annual *Economic Report of the President*. Calculate GDP using the expenditure and income approaches.

EXHIBIT 11 National Income Data

	Amount (billions of dollars)
Corporate profits	$ 305
Depreciation	479
Gross private domestic investment	716
Personal taxes	565
Personal saving	120
Government spending	924
Imports	547
Net interest	337
Compensation of employees	2,648
Rental income	19
Exports	427
Personal consumption expenditures	2,966
Indirect business taxes	370
Contributions for Social Security (FICA)	394
Transfer payments and other income	967
Proprietors' income	328

9. Using the data in Exhibit 11, compute national income (NI) by making the required subtraction from GDP. Explain why NI might be a better measure of economic performance than GDP.

10. Again using the data from Exhibit 11, derive personal income (PI) from national income (NI). Then make the required adjustments to PI to obtain disposable personal income (DI).

11. Suppose U.S. nominal GDP increases from one year to the next year. Can you conclude that these figures present a misleading measure of economic growth? What alternative method would provide a more accurate measure of the rate of growth?

12. Which of the following are counted in this year's GDP? Explain your answer in each case.
    a. Flashy Car Company sold a used car.
    b. Juanita Jones cooked meals for her family.
    c. IBM paid interest on its bonds.
    d. José Suarez purchased 100 shares of Microsoft stock.
    e. Bob Smith received a welfare payment.
    f. Carriage Realty earned a brokerage commission for selling a previously owned house.
    g. The government makes interest payments to persons holding government bonds.
    h. Air and water pollution increase.
    i. Gambling is legalized in all states.
    j. A retired worker receives a Social Security payment.

13. Explain why comparing the GDPs of various nations might not tell you which nations are better off.

 CHECKPOINT ANSWERS

How Much Does Mario Add to GDP?

Measuring GDP by the expenditure approach, Mario's output production is worth $60,000 because consumers purchased 4,000 pizzas at $15 each. Transfer payments and purchases of goods produced in other years are excluded from GDP. The $3,000 in unemployment compensation received and the $5,000 spent for a used car are therefore not counted in GDP. Mario's income of $15,000 is also not counted using the expenditure approach. If you said using the expenditure approach to measure GDP, Mario contributed $60,000 to GDP, **YOU ARE CORRECT**.

Is the Economy Up or Down?

Between 1973 and 1974, for example, nominal GDP rose from $1,428 to $1,549 billion—an 8.5 percent increase. During the same period, real GDP fell from $5,424 to $5,396 billion—a 0.5 percent decrease. If you said both reports can be correct because of the difference between nominal and real GDP, **YOU ARE CORRECT**.

Sample Quiz

Please see Appendix B for answers to Sample Quiz questions.

1. Gross domestic product is officially measured by adding together the
   a. quantity of each good and service produced by U.S. residents.
   b. market value of all final goods and services produced within the borders of a nation.
   c. quantity of goods and services produced by companies owned by U.S. citizens.
   d. None of the answers above are correct.

2. Which of the following items is included in the calculation of GDP?
   a. Purchase of 100 shares of Microsoft stock
   b. Purchase of a used car
   c. The value of a homemaker's services
   d. Sale of Gulf War military surplus
   e. None of the above would be included.

3. Which of the following expenditures would *not* be included in GDP?
   a. Purchase of a new lawnmower
   b. Purchase of a silver cup previously sold new in 1950
   c. Purchase of a ticket to the latest movie
   d. All of the above would be counted in GDP.

4. Gross domestic product (GDP) includes
   a. intermediate as well as final goods.
   b. foreign goods as well as domestically produced goods.
   c. used goods sold in the current time period.
   d. only final goods and services.

5. GDP includes
   a. the negative attributes in our quest for more goods and services, such as soil erosion and deforested landscape.
   b. all quality improvements resulting from higher-quality goods replacing inferior goods.
   c. the cleanup expenses associated with pollution.
   d. the value of leisure time.

6. The largest component of GDP is
   a. personal consumption expenditures.
   b. government spending.
   c. durable goods.
   d. net exports.

7. The circular flow of economic activity is a model of the
   a. flow of goods, resources, payments, and expenditures between the sectors of the economy.
   b. influence of government on business behavior.
   c. influence of business on consumers.
   d. role of unions and government in the economy.

8. All final goods and services that make up GDP can be expressed as
   a. $GDP = C + I - G + (X + M)$
   b. $GDP = C + I + G + (X + M)$
   c. $GDP = C + I + G + (X - M)$
   d. $GDP = C + I + (X - M)$
   e. $GDP = C + I + G$

9. The expenditure approach for the calculation of GDP includes spending on
   a. consumption, investment, durable goods and exports.
   b. consumption, gross private domestic investment, government spending for goods and services, and exports.
   c. consumption, gross private domestic investment, government spending for goods and services, and net exports.
   d. consumption, net private domestic investment, government spending for goods and services, and net exports.
   e. consumption, gross private domestic investment, all government spending including transfer payments, and net exports.

10. Which of the following is a shortcoming of GDP?
    a. GDP excludes changes in inventories.
    b. GDP includes an estimate of illegal transactions.
    c. GDP excludes nonmarket transactions.
    d. GDP excludes business investment spending.

11. National income (NI) is calculated by adjusting GDP for
    a. depreciation.
    b. investment and net exports.
    c. Social Security insurance contributions and transfer payments.
    d. corporate and personal income taxes.

12. Which of the following is included in personal income but *not* in national income?
    a. Compensation for workers
    b. Proprietors' income
    c. Corporate profits
    d. Social Security payments

13. Which national income account should be examined to discover trends in the after-tax income that people have to save and spend?
    a. Gross domestic product (GDP)
    b. Gross national product (GNP)
    c. National income (NI)
    d. Disposable personal income (DI)

14. The equation for determining real GDP for year X is
    a. $\dfrac{\text{nominal GDP for year } X}{\text{average nominal GDP}}.$
    b. $\dfrac{\text{nominal GDP for year } X}{\text{GDP for year } X} - 100.$
    c. $\dfrac{\text{nominal GDP for year } X}{\text{GDP chain price index for year } X} \times 100.$
    d. $\dfrac{\text{nominal GDP for year } X}{\text{average family income}} \times 100.$

15. The most broadly based price index is the
    a. real GDP price index.
    b. consumer price index.
    c. producer price index.
    d. GDP chain price index.

16. Which of the following would be counted as a final good for inclusion in GDP?
    a. A piece of glass bought this year by a consumer to fix a broken window.
    b. A sheet of glass produced this year by Ford to use for windows in a new car.
    c. A tire produced this year and sold to a car maker for a new car sold this year.
    d. None of the answers are correct.

17. Based on the circular flow model, money flows from households to businesses in
    a. factor markets.
    b. product markets.
    c. neither factor nor product markets.
    d. both factor and product markets.

18. If the underground economy is sizable, GDP will
    a. understate the economy's performance.
    b. overstate the economy's performance.
    c. fluctuate unpredictably.
    d. accurately reflect this subterranean activity.

19. The income that people earn in resource or factor markets is called
    a. national income.
    b. personal income.
    c. disposable personal income.
    d. transfer payments.
    e. net national product.

20. Increased production, but *not* increased inflation, will result in higher
    a. nominal GDP.
    b. money GDP.
    c. real GDP.
    d. current dollar GDP.

A Four-Sector Circular Flow Model

Sound the trumpets! This exhibit is going to put all the puzzle pieces together. Exhibit A-1 presents a more complex circular flow model by adding three sectors: financial markets, government, and foreign markets. In addition to the spending of

EXHIBIT A-1 The Circular Flow Model of an Open Economy

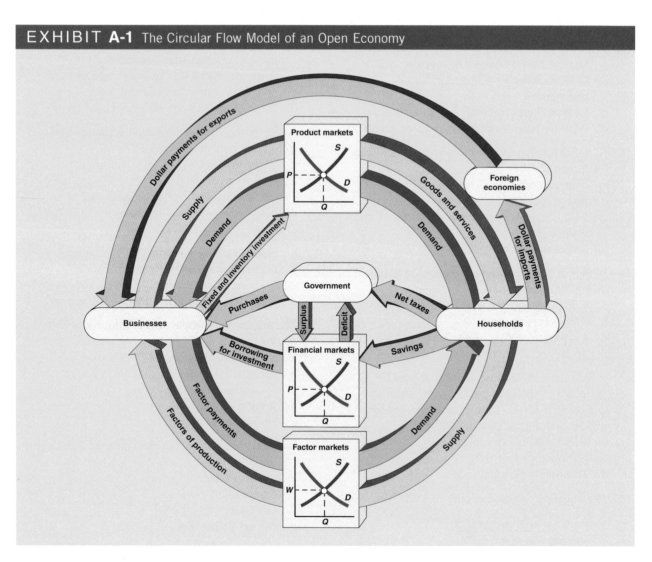

households for the output of firms shown in the simplified model in Exhibit 1, these additions add three *leakages* from the amount of income paid to households. First, part of households' income is saved. Second, part of it is taxed. Third, part of the income is spent on imports. On the other hand, this model includes three sources of spending *injections* for firms' output other than from households. First, firms purchase new plants, equipment, and inventories (investment) from other firms. Second, government consumption purchases are for goods and services from firms. Third, foreigners purchase exports from the firms.

This exhibit presents a circular flow model for an economy, such as the United States, that engages in international trade. The theoretical model includes links between the product and factor markets in the domestic economy and the financial markets, government, and foreign economies. To simplify the model, only dollar payments are shown for the foreign sector.

CHAPTER 6

Business Cycles and Unemployment

CHAPTER PREVIEW

 The headline in the morning newspaper reads, "The Economy is in Deep Recession." Later in the day, a radio announcer begins the news by saying, "The unemployment rate rose for the tenth consecutive month." On television, the evening news broadcasts an interview with several economists who predict that the slump will last for another year. Next, a presidential candidate appears on the screen and says, "It's time for change," and the media are a-buzz with speculation on the political implications. The growth rate of the economy and the unemployment rate are headline-catching news. Indeed, these measures of macroeconomic instability are important because they affect your future. When real GDP rises

and the economy "booms," jobs are more plentiful. A fall in real GDP means a "bust" because the economy forces some firms into bankruptcy and workers lose their jobs. Not being able to find a job when you want one is a painful experience not easily forgotten.

This chapter looks behind the macroeconomy at a story that touches each of us. It begins by discussing the business cycle. How are the expansions and contractions of business cycles measured? And what causes the business-cycle roller coaster? Finally, you will learn what the types of unemployment are, what "full employment" is, and what the monetary, nonmonetary, and demographic costs of unemployment are.

IN THIS CHAPTER, YOU WILL LEARN TO SOLVE THESE ECONOMICS PUZZLES:

- What is the difference between a recession and a depression?

- Is a worker who has given up searching for work counted as unemployed?

- Can an economy produce more output than its potential?

6-1 THE BUSINESS–CYCLE ROLLER COASTER

Business cycle
Alternating periods of economic growth and contraction, which can be measured by changes in real GDP.

A central concern of macroeconomics is the upswings and downswings in the level of real output called the business cycle. The **business cycle** consists of alternating periods of economic growth and contraction. Business cycles are inherent in market economies. Market-based economies are driven by ever-changing forces of supply and demand. A key measure of cycles is the rise and fall in real GDP, which mirrors changes in employment and other key measures of the macroeconomy. Recall from the previous chapter that changes in real GDP measure changes in the value of national output, while ignoring changes in the price level. This is important because jobs are impacted by changes in output.

6-1a The Four Phases of the Business Cycle

Exhibit 1(a) illustrates a theoretical business cycle. Although business cycles vary in duration and intensity, each cycle is divided into four phases: *peak, recession, trough,* and *recovery*. The business cycle looks like a roller coaster. It begins at a peak, drops to a bottom, climbs steeply, and then reaches another peak. After the peak is reached, another business cycle begins. Although forecasters cannot precisely predict the timing of the phases of a cycle, the economy is always operating along one of these phases. Over time, there has been a long-term upward trend with shorter-term cyclical fluctuations around the long-run trend.

Peak
The phase of the business cycle in which real GDP reaches its maximum after rising during a recovery.

Two peaks are illustrated in Exhibit 1(a). At each of these peaks, the economy is close to or at full employment. At a **peak**, real GDP reaches its maximum after rising during a recovery (*expansion* or *upturn*) in the business cycle. That is, as explained in Chapter 2, the economy is operating near its production possibilities curve, and real GDP is at its highest level relative to recent years. However, a peak is a temporary high point. A macro setback called a recession (a *contraction* or *downturn*) follows each peak. A **recession** is a downturn in the business cycle during which real GDP declines, business sales and profits fall, the percentage of the workforce without jobs rises, and production capacity is underutilized. A general rule is that a recession consists of at least two consecutive quarters (six months) in which there is a decline in real GDP. Stated differently, during a recession, the economy is functioning inside and farther away from its production possibilities curve.

Recession
A downturn in the business cycle during which real GDP declines, and the unemployment rate rises. Also called a *contraction*.

What is the difference between a *recession* and a *depression*? According to the old saying, "A recession is when your neighbor loses his or her job, and a depression is when you also lose your job!" This one-liner is close to the true distinction between these two concepts because economists have never really clearly distinguished between them. The term *depression* is primarily a historical reference to the Great Depression from 1929 to 1933. Hopefully, we will never again experience such an extremely deep and long recession. The Great Depression is discussed at the end of this chapter, the chapter on aggregate demand and supply, and the chapter on monetary policy.

Trough
The phase of the business cycle in which real GDP reaches its minimum after falling during a recession.

The **trough** is where the level of real GDP "bottoms out" after falling during a recession. The length of time between the peak and the trough is the duration of the recession. Since the end of World War II, recessions in the United States have averaged 11 months. As shown in Exhibit 2, the last recession, called the Great Recession, lasted 18 months, from December 2007 to June 2009. The percentage decline in real GDP was 4.1 percent, and the national unemployment rate hit a high of 9.7 percent. The Great Recession is the longest recession since the Great Depression.

EXHIBIT 1   Hypothetical and Actual Business Cycles

Part (a) illustrates a hypothetical business cycle consisting of four phases: peak, recession, trough, and recovery. These fluctuations of real GDP can be measured by a growth trend line, which shows that over time, real GDP has trended upward. In reality, the fluctuations are not so clearly defined as those in this graph.

Part (b) illustrates actual ups and downs of the business cycle. After a recession in 2001, an upswing continued until the Great Recession began in 2007. The economy has been expanding since 2010.

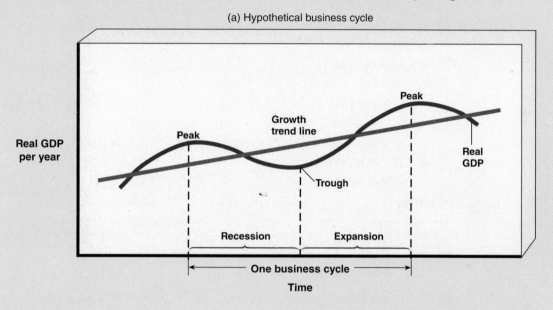

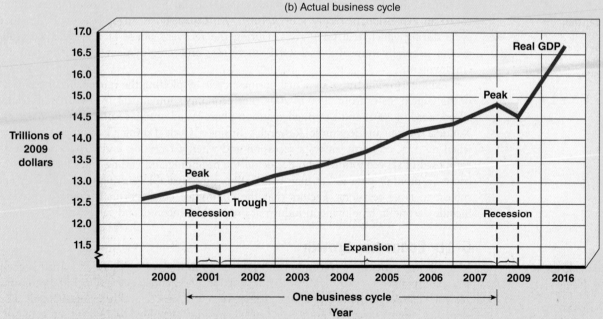

SOURCE: Bureau of Economic Analysis, *National Income Accounts*, http://www.bea.gov/iTable/index_nipa.cfm, Table 1.1.2.

EXHIBIT 2 Severity of Post–World War II Recessions

Recession dates	Duration (months)	Percentage decline in real GDP	Peak unemployment rate
Nov. 1948–Oct. 1949	11	−1.7%	7.9%
July 1953–May 1954	10	−2.7	5.9
Aug. 1957–Apr. 1958	8	−1.2	7.4
Apr. 1960–Feb. 1961	10	−1.6	6.9
Dec. 1969–Nov. 1970	11	−0.6	5.9
Nov. 1973–Mar. 1975	16	−3.1	8.6
Jan. 1980–July 1980	6	−2.2	7.8
July 1981–Nov. 1982	16	−2.9	10.8
July 1990–Mar. 1991	8	−1.3	6.8
Mar. 2001–Nov. 2001	8	−0.5	5.6
Dec. 2007–June 2009	18	−4.1	9.7
Average	**11**	**−2.0**	**7.6**

SOURCE: National Bureau of Economic Research, Business Cycle Expansion and Contractions, http://www.nber.org /cycles/cyclesmain.html. Real GDP and unemployment rate data added by author.

The trough is both bad news and good news. It is simultaneously the bottom of the "valley" of the downturn and the foot of the "hill" of improving economic conditions called an expansion (a *recovery* or *upturn*). An **expansion** is an upturn in the business cycle during which real GDP rises. During the recovery phase of the cycle, sales and profits generally improve, real GDP increases, and employment moves toward full employment.

Expansion
An upturn in the business cycle during which real GDP rises. Also called a *recovery*.

Exhibit 1(b) illustrates an actual business cycle by plotting the movement of real GDP in the United States from 2000 to 2007. The economy's initial peak, recession, and trough all occurred in 2001, and a strong expansion phase lasted until a second peak in 2007. The National Bureau of Economic Research's Business Cycle Dating Committee determines when the U.S. economy enters a recession and when a recession ends. This committee is composed of six economists who decide on the beginning and ending dates for a recession based on monthly data rather than real GDP because real GDP is measured quarterly and subject to large revisions. Factors that the committee considers in defining a recession include decline in employment, industrial production, income, and sales.

6-1b Economic Growth

Economic growth
An expansion in national output measured by the annual percentage increase in a nation's real GDP.

We will now expand the definition of **economic growth** given in Chapter 2. In this chapter, recall that an outward shift of the production possibilities curve illustrated economic growth. Also recall that factors such as increases in resources and technological advances were key reasons for economic growth. Here the expanded definition of economic growth is explained. Economic growth is defined by economists as an expansion in national output measured by the annual percentage increase in a nation's real GDP. The growth trend line in the hypothetical model in Exhibit 1(a) illustrates that over time, our real GDP tends to rise. This general, long-term upward trend in real GDP persists in spite of the peaks, recessions, troughs, and recoveries. As shown by the dashed line in Exhibit 3, since 1930, real GDP in the United States has grown at an average annual rate of 3.34 percent. This annual change may seem small, but about 3 percent annual growth will lead to a doubling of real GDP in only 24 years. The largest expansion in U.S. history occurred over 10 years from 1991 to 2001.

> We value economic growth as one of our nation's economic goals because it increases our standard of living—it creates a bigger "economic pie."

CONCLUSION

Closer examination of Exhibit 3 reveals that the growth path of the U.S. economy over time is not a smooth, rising trend, but instead is a series of year-to-year variations in real GDP growth rates. Following the Great Recession beginning in 2007, the growth rate was a negative 2.8 percent in 2009 before rising to positive percentages since 2010. The growth rate has remained positive but below the long-term average of 3.34 percent. In 2016, the growth rate was only 1.6 percent, down from 2.6 percent in 2015.

EXHIBIT 3 A Historical Record of Business Cycles in the United States, 1929–2016

Real GDP has increased at an average annual growth rate of 3.34 percent since 1930. Above-average annual growth rates have alternated with below-average annual growth rates. Following the Great Recession of 2007, the annual growth rate was a negative 2.8 percent in 2009 before rising to positive percentages since 2010.

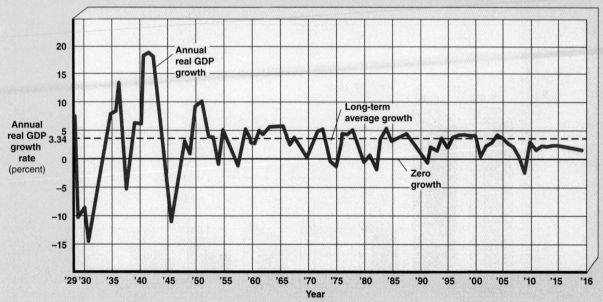

SOURCE: Bureau of Economic Analysis, *National Economic Accounts*, http://www.bea.gov/iTable/index_nipa.cfm, Table 1.1.2.

Where Are We on the Business-Cycle Roller Coaster?

Suppose the economy is in a recession, and everyone is asking when the economy will recover. To find an answer to the state of the economy's health, a television reporter interviews Terrence Carter, a local car dealer. Carter says, "I do not see any recovery. The third and fourth quarters of this year we sold more cars than in the second quarter, but sales in these last two quarters were far below the first quarter." Is Mr. Carter correct? Are his observations consistent with the peak, recession, trough, or expansion phase of the business cycle?

GLOBAL ECONOMICS

6-1c Real GDP Growth Rates in Other Countries

Exhibit 4 presents real GDP growth rates for selected countries in 2016. India and China had the largest rates of growth at 6.8 and 6.7 percent, respectively. The United States and other countries throughout the world had lower growth rates, with Greece having a 0.1 percent rate.

EXHIBIT 4 Global Comparison of Real GDP Growth Rates, 2016

The exhibit shows that India and China had the largest rates of growth at 6.8 and 6.7 percent, respectively. In contrast, the United States and other countries had lower growth rates for the year, with Greece the lowest at 0.1 percent.

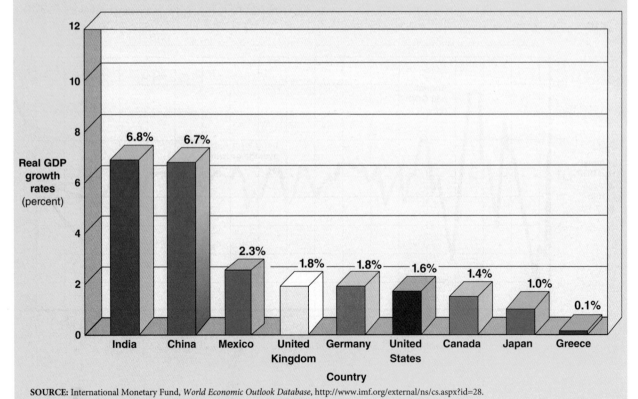

SOURCE: International Monetary Fund, *World Economic Outlook Database*, http://www.imf.org/external/ns/cs.aspx?id=28.

6-1d Business-Cycle Indicators

In addition to changes in real GDP, the media often report several other macro variables that measure business activity and are published by the U.S. Department of Commerce in *Business Conditions Digest*. These economic *indicator* variables are classified in three categories: leading indicators, coincident indicators, and lagging indicators. Exhibit 5 lists the variables corresponding to each indicator series.

The government's chief forecasting gauge for business cycles is the index of leading indicators. **Leading indicators** are key variables that change before real GDP changes. This index captures the headlines when there is concern over swings in the economy. The first set of 10 variables in Exhibit 5 is used to forecast the business cycle months in advance. For example, a slump ahead is signaled when declines exceed advances in the components of the leading indicators' data series. But beware! The leading indicators may rise for two consecutive months and then fall for the next three consecutive months. Economists are therefore cautious and wait for the leading indicators to move in a new direction for several months before forecasting a change in the cycle.

Leading indicators
Variables that change before real GDP changes.

Is a recession near or when will a recession end? The Conference Board's Consumer Confidence Index is often reported in the news as a key measure of the economy's health. It is based on a survey of households who are asked their expectations of how well the economy will perform over the next six months. Prolonged consumer pessimism can result in less consumer spending and contribute to slowing economic growth. Stated differently, persistent consumer pessimism can result in lower personal consumption expenditures (*C*) and business investment (*I*) because businesses reduce investment when consumers' purchases of their products fall. This can trigger a recession because when spending falls, sales fall, and workers are laid off which results in less income and still further cutbacks in spending.

The second data series of key variables listed in Exhibit 5 are four coincident indicators. **Coincident indicators** are variables that change at the same time that real

Coincident indicators
Variables that change at the same time real GDP changes.

EXHIBIT 5 Business-Cycle Indicators

Leading indicators	
Average workweek	**Coincident indicators**
Unemployment claims	Nonagricultural payrolls
New consumer goods orders	Personal income minus transfer payments
Delayed deliveries	Industrial production
New orders for plant and equipment	Manufacturing and trade sales
New building permits	**Lagging indicators**
Stock prices	Unemployment rate
Money supply	Duration of unemployment
Interest rates	Labor cost per unit of output
Consumer expectations	Consumer price index for services
	Commercial and industrial loans
	Consumer-credit-to-personal-income ratio
	Prime rate

GDP changes. For example, as real GDP rises, economists expect employment, personal income, industrial production, and sales to rise.

The third group of variables listed in Exhibit 5 are lagging indicators. **Lagging indicators** are seven variables that change after real GDP changes. For example, the duration of unemployment is a lagging indicator. As real GDP increases, the average time workers remain unemployed does not fall until months after the beginning of the expansion. Similar time lags are observed for the other lagging indicators.

Lagging indicators
Variables that change after real GDP changes.

6-1e Total Spending and the Business Cycle

The uneven historical pattern of economic growth for the U.S. economy gives rise to the following question: What causes business cycles? The theory generally accepted by economists today is that changes in total or aggregate expenditures are the cause of variations in real GDP. Recall from the previous chapter that aggregate expenditures refer to total spending for *final goods* by households, businesses, government, and foreign buyers. Expressed as a formula:

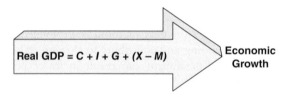

$$\text{Real GDP} = C + I + G + (X - M)$$

Economic Growth

Why do changes in total spending cause the level of real GDP to rise during an expansion? Suppose consumers are optimistic about the economic future. If consumer spending (C) increases, then business sales and production rise and these companies find it profitable to increase investment (I) in plants and equipment. When firms produce more goods and services, they use more land, labor, and capital. Such increased spending leads to an expansion in output, employment, and incomes. Economic growth can also occur when government spending (G) increases, or from increases in spending for exports (X), or decreases in import spending (M). On the other hand, a recession is the result of declines in the total expenditures (spending) components of real GDP. For example, assume consumers become pessimistic about their economic future. If consumer spending (C) decreases, then business sales, production and profits fall, and businesses decrease investment (I) in plants and equipment. When businesses produce less, they require fewer resources, such as workers, and unemployment rises. Real GDP can also fall if government spending (G) decreases, export spending (X) falls, or import spending (M) rises.

6-2 UNEMPLOYMENT

Since the abyss of the Great Depression, a major economic goal of the United States has been to achieve a high level of employment. The *Employment Act of 1946* declared it the responsibility of the federal government to use all practical means consistent with free competitive enterprise to create conditions under which all able individuals who are willing to work and seeking work will be afforded useful employment opportunities. Later, Congress amended this act with the *Full Employment and Balanced*

Growth Act of 1978, which established specific goals for unemployment and the level of prices.

Each month the Bureau of Labor Statistics (BLS) of the U.S. Department of Labor, in conjunction with the Bureau of the Census, conducts a survey of a random sample of about 60,000 households in the United States. Each member of the household who is 16 years of age or older is asked whether he or she is employed or unemployed. If a person works at least 1 hour per week for pay or at least 15 hours per week as an unpaid worker in a family business, he or she is counted as employed. If the person is not employed, the question then is whether he or she has looked for work in the last month. If so, the person is said to be unemployed. Based on its survey data, the BLS publishes the unemployment rate and other employment-related statistics monthly.

The **unemployment rate** is the percentage of people in the civilian labor force who are without jobs and are actively seeking jobs. But who is actually counted as an unemployed worker, and which people belong to the labor force? Certainly, all people without jobs are not classified as unemployed. Babies, full-time students, and retired persons are not counted as unemployed. Likewise, individuals who are ill or severely disabled are not included as unemployed. And there are other groups not counted.

Turn to Exhibit 6. The **civilian labor force** is the number of people 16 years of age and over who are either employed or unemployed (remember, these people are actively seeking jobs), excluding members of the armed forces, homemakers, discouraged workers and other groups listed in the "persons not in labor force" category. Based on survey data, the BLS computes the *civilian unemployment rate* using the following formula:

$$\text{Unemployment rate} = \frac{\text{unemployed}}{\text{civilian labor force}} \times 100$$

In 2016, the unemployment rate was

$$4.9\% = \frac{7.769 \text{ million persons}}{159.1 \text{ million persons}} \times 100$$

Exhibit 7 charts a historical record of the U.S. unemployment rate since 1929. Note that the highest unemployment rate was 25 percent in 1933 during the Great Depression. At the other extreme, the lowest unemployment rate we have attained was 1.2 percent in 1944. Following the Great Recession, the unemployment rate surged to 9.6 percent in 2010, which was the highest annual rate since 1983. In 2016, the unemployment rate was 4.9 percent.

6-2a Unemployment in Other Countries

Exhibit 8 shows unemployment rates for selected countries in 2016. South Africa and Greece had unemployment rates higher than the United States. Other industrialized countries such as Japan and China had unemployment rates much lower than the United States.

Unemployment rate
The percentage of people in the civilian labor force who are without jobs and are actively seeking jobs.

Civilian labor force
The number of people 16 years of age and older who are employed or who are actively seeking a job, excluding armed forces, homemakers, discouraged workers, and other persons not in the labor force.

GLOBAL **ECONOMICS**

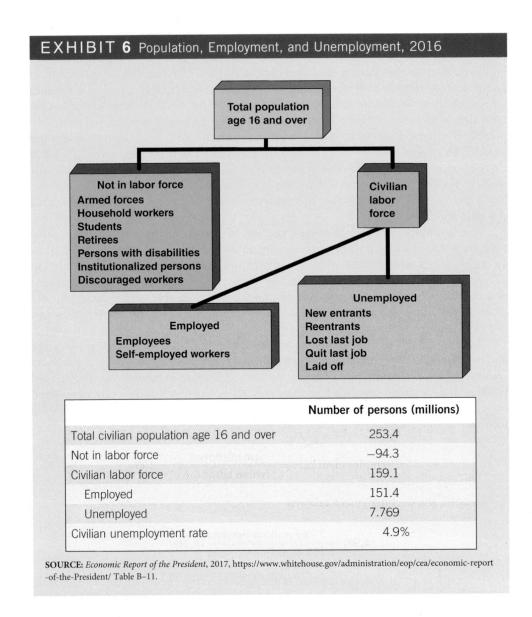

EXHIBIT 6 Population, Employment, and Unemployment, 2016

Total population age 16 and over

Not in labor force
Armed forces
Household workers
Students
Retirees
Persons with disabilities
Institutionalized persons
Discouraged workers

Civilian labor force

Employed
Employees
Self-employed workers

Unemployed
New entrants
Reentrants
Lost last job
Quit last job
Laid off

	Number of persons (millions)
Total civilian population age 16 and over	253.4
Not in labor force	−94.3
Civilian labor force	159.1
Employed	151.4
Unemployed	7.769
Civilian unemployment rate	4.9%

SOURCE: *Economic Report of the President*, 2017, https://www.whitehouse.gov/administration/eop/cea/economic-report -of-the-President/ Table B–11.

6-2b Unemployment Rate Criticisms

The unemployment rate is criticized for both understating and overstating the "true" unemployment rate. An example of *overstating* the unemployment rate occurs when respondents to the BLS survey falsely report they are seeking employment. The motivation may be that their eligibility for unemployment compensation or welfare benefits depends on actively pursuing a job. Or possibly an individual is "employed" in illegal activities.

The other side of the coin is that the official definition of unemployment *understates* the unemployment rate by not counting so-called discouraged workers. A **discouraged worker** is a person who wants to work, but has given up searching for work because he

Discouraged worker
A person who wants to work, but who has given up searching for work because he or she believes there will be no job offers.

EXHIBIT 7   The U.S. Unemployment Rate, 1929–2016

This exhibit shows fluctuations in the civilian unemployment rate since 1929. The unemployment rate reached a high point of 25 percent in 1933 during the Great Depression. The lowest unemployment rate of 1.2 percent was achieved during World War II in 1944. In 2010, the unemployment rate was 9.6 percent, which was the highest annual rate since 1983. In 2016, the unemployment rate was 4.9 percent.

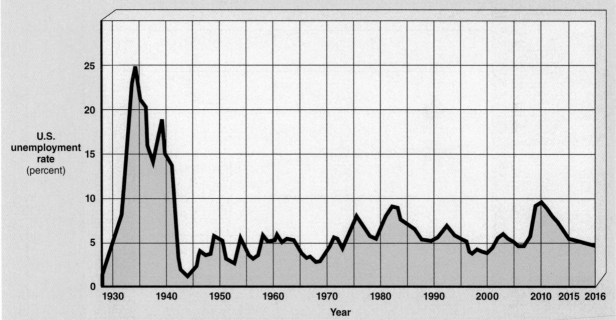

SOURCE: *Economic Report of the President*, 2017, https://www.whitehouse.gov/administration/eop/cea/economic-report-of-the-President/ Table B–11.

or she believes there will be no job offers. After repeated rejections, discouraged workers often turn to their families, friends, and public welfare for support. The BLS counts a discouraged worker as anyone who has looked for work within the last 12 months, but is no longer actively looking. The BLS simply includes discouraged workers in the "not in labor force" category listed in Exhibit 6. Because the number of discouraged workers rises during a recession, the underestimation of the official unemployment rate increases during a downturn.

Another example of *understating* the unemployment rate occurs because the official BLS data include all part-time workers as fully employed. These workers are actually partially employed, and many would rather work full-time if they could find full-time employment. The unemployment rate does not measure *underemployment*. If jobs are scarce and a college graduate takes a job not requiring his or her level of skills, a human resource is underutilized. Or suppose an employer cuts an employee's hours of work from 40 to 20 per week. Such losses of work potential are greater during a recession, but are not reflected in the unemployment rate.

EXHIBIT 8 Unemployment Rates for Selected Nations, 2016

In 2016, some nations shown had a higher unemployment rate than the United States. For example, Greece's unemployment rate was 23.8 percent. This is similar to the unemployment rate experienced in the United States during the darkest days of the Great Depression. In 2016, the United States had an unemployment rate of 4.9 percent, while other nations, like China and Japan had lower rates.

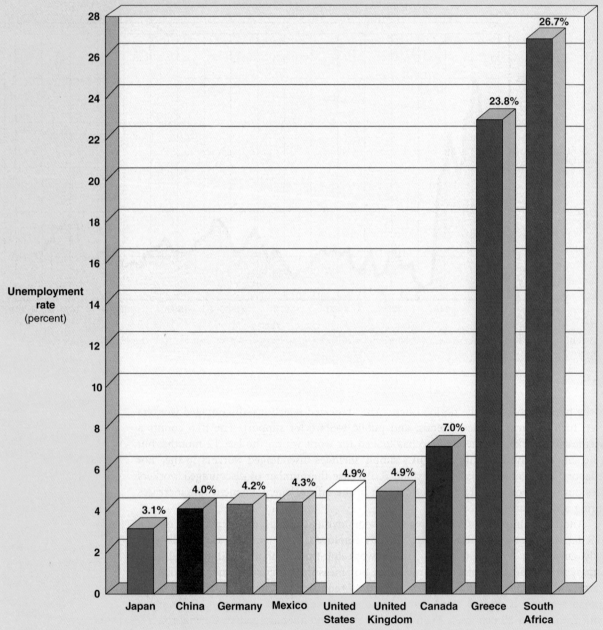

SOURCE: International Monetary Fund, *World Economic Outlook Database*, http://www.imf.org/external/ns/cs.aspx?id=28.

6-3 TYPES OF UNEMPLOYMENT

The unemployment rate is determined by three different types of unemployment: *frictional*, *structural*, and *cyclical*. Understanding these conceptual categories of unemployment aids in understanding and formulating policies to ease the burden of unemployment. In fact, each type of unemployment requires a different policy prescription to reduce it.

6-3a Frictional Unemployment

For some unemployed workers, the absence of a job is only temporary. At any given time, some people with marketable skills are fired, and others voluntarily quit jobs to accept or look for new ones. And there are always young people who leave school and search for their first job. Workers in some industries such as construction experience short periods of unemployment between projects, and temporary layoffs are common. Other workers are "seasonally unemployed." For example, ski resort workers will be employed in the winter, but not in the summer, and certain crops are harvested "in season." Because jobs requiring the skills of these unemployed workers are available, the unemployed workers and the job vacancies are matched and such workers are therefore considered "between jobs." This type of unemployment is called frictional unemployment, and it is not of great concern. **Frictional unemployment** is temporary unemployment caused by the time required for workers to move from one job to another. Frictional unemployment is unemployment caused by the normal search time required by workers with marketable skills who are changing jobs, initially entering the labor force, or reentering the labor force. The cause of frictional unemployment is either the transition time to a new job or the lack of information required to match a job applicant immediately with a job vacancy. For this reason, frictional unemployment is sometimes called *transitional unemployment* or *search unemployment*.

> **Frictional unemployment**
> Temporary unemployment caused by the time required of workers to move from one job to another.

The fact that job market information is imperfect and operates with "friction" causes frictional unemployment in the economy. Because it takes time to search for the information required to match employer and employees, some workers will always be frictionally unemployed. Frictional unemployment is therefore a normal condition in an economic system permitting freedom of job choice. Improved methods of distributing job information through job listings on the Internet help unemployed workers find jobs more quickly and reduce frictional unemployment.

6-3b Structural Unemployment

Unlike frictional unemployment, structural unemployment is not a short-term situation. Instead, it is long-term, or possibly permanent, unemployment. **Structural unemployment** is unemployment caused by a mismatch of the skills of workers who are out of work and the skills required for existing job opportunities. Note that changing jobs and lack of job information are *not* problems for structurally unemployed workers. Unlike frictionally unemployed workers who have marketable skills, structurally unemployed workers require additional education or retraining. The following are four causes of structural unemployment.

> **Structural unemployment**
> Unemployment caused by a mismatch of the skills of workers out of work and the skills required for existing job opportunities.

Lack of Education

Workers may face joblessness because they lack the education or the job-related skills to perform available jobs. This type of structural unemployment particularly affects teenagers and minority groups, but other groups of workers can be affected as well. For example, environmental concerns, such as protecting the spotted owl by restricting trees from being cut, cost some loggers their jobs. Reducing such structural unemployment requires retraining loggers for new jobs as, say, forest rangers.

Changes in Consumer Demand

The consuming public may decide to increase the demand for computer products and decrease the demand for Chevrolet Corvettes. This shift in demand would cause U.S. autoworkers who lose their jobs in Bowling Green, Kentucky, to become structurally unemployed. To regain employment, these unemployed autoworkers must retrain and find job openings in other industries, for example, manufacturing printers in North Carolina. Another example involves the reduction in defense spending after a war. This situation creates structural unemployment for discharged military personnel who require retraining after a war for, say, teaching, nursing, or police jobs.

Technological Advances

Implementation of the latest technology may also increase the pool of structural unemployment in a particular industry and region. For example, the U.S. textile industry, located primarily in the South, can fight less expensive foreign textile imports by installing modern machinery. This new capital may replace textile workers. But suppose these unemployed textile workers do not wish to move to a new location where new types of jobs are available. The costs of moving, fear of the unknown, and family ties are understandable reasons for being reluctant to move, and instead, the workers become structurally unemployed until they are retrained for other jobs.

Globalization

Outsourcing
The practice of a company having its work done by another company in another country.

Certain jobs can be globally resourced, which means they can be performed anywhere in the world. U.S. companies sometimes use outsourcing of U.S. jobs to India, China, and other countries. **Outsourcing** is the practice of a company having its work done by another company in another country. As a result, U.S. workers can lose their jobs and require retraining for other jobs. It can be argued that outsourcing allows U.S. companies to reduce their costs, lower the prices of U.S. goods, and therefore be more competitive in global markets. In short, some jobs are saved from being lost to more efficient competitors, and consumers benefit from lower prices.

Offshoring
The practice of work for a company performed by the company's employees located in another country.

A company also has the choice of having a job performed by its own employees in the United States, where the product is sold, or in another country. **Offshoring** occurs when a U.S. company hires employees from another country to perform jobs once done by the company's American employees. Suppose, for example, a U.S. company hires engineers in India to do jobs once done for this company in the United States. Assume the result is that the average salary paid by the company to these engineers drops $50,000 per year. A benefit is that the company reduces it costs to remain globally competitive or to increase its profits, although some Americans may lose their jobs and must find new jobs.

To summarize, there are many causes of structural unemployment, including poor schools, new products, new technology, foreign competition, geographic differences, restricted entry into jobs, and shifts in government priorities. Because of the numerous sources of mismatching between skills and jobs, economists consider a certain level of structural unemployment inevitable. Public and private programs that train employees to fill existing job openings decrease structural unemployment. Conversely, one of the concerns about the minimum wage is that it may contribute to structural unemployment. In Exhibit 6 of Chapter 4, we demonstrated that a minimum wage set by legislation above the equilibrium wage causes unemployment. One approach intended to offset such undesirable effects of the minimum wage is a subminimum wage paid during a training period to give employers an incentive to hire unskilled workers.

In conclusion, there will always be mismatching between skills and jobs. Economists, therefore, consider a level of structural unemployment inevitable.

6-3c Cyclical Unemployment

Cyclical unemployment is directly attributable to the lack of jobs caused by the business cycle. **Cyclical unemployment** is unemployment caused by the lack of jobs during a recession. When real GDP falls, companies close, jobs disappear, and workers scramble for fewer available jobs. Similar to the game of musical chairs, there are not enough chairs (jobs) for the number of players (workers) in the game.

The Great Depression is a dramatic example of cyclical unemployment. There was a sudden decline in consumption, investment, government spending, and net exports. As a result of this striking fall in total spending, real GDP fell dramatically, and the unemployment rate rose to about 25 percent (see Exhibit 7). Now notice what happened to the unemployment rate when total spending and real GDP rose sharply during World War II. The Great Recession beginning in 2007 is another example of cyclical unemployment. Falling home prices and a plunge in stock prices caused households to cut back on consumption spending and, in combination with a fall in business investment spending, caused a negative growth rate and a sharp rise in the unemployment rate to a high of 9.7 percent at the end of the Great Recession in 2009. Cyclical unemployment is considered the most unacceptable type of unemployment. As a result, most of the focus of macroeconomic policy is on minimizing cyclical unemployment.

Cyclical unemployment
Unemployment caused by the lack of jobs during a recession.

CHECKPOINT

What Kind of Unemployment Did the Invention of the Wheel Cause?

"But Egor, what about the effect on labor?"

Did the invention of the wheel cause frictional, structural, or cyclical unemployment?

"Courtesy of Irvin Tucker"

6-4 THE GOAL OF FULL EMPLOYMENT

In this section, we take a closer look at the meaning of full employment, also called the *natural rate of unemployment*. Because both frictional and structural unemployment are present in good and bad times, *full employment* does not mean "zero" percent unemployment. **Full employment** is the situation in which an economy operates at an unemployment rate equal to the sum of the frictional and structural unemployment rates. Full employment therefore is the rate of unemployment that exists without cyclical unemployment.

Unfortunately, economists cannot state with certainty what percentages of the labor force are frictionally and structurally unemployed at any particular point in time. In practice, therefore, full employment is difficult to define. Moreover, the full-employment rate of unemployment, or natural rate of unemployment, changes over time. In the 1960s, 4 percent unemployment was generally considered to represent full employment. In the 1980s, the accepted rate was 6 percent. Currently, the consensus among economists is that the natural rate is close to 5 percent with a frictional unemployment rate of 3 percent and a structural unemployment of 2 percent.

Several reasons are given for why full employment is not fixed. One reason is that between the early 1960s and the early 1980s, the participation of women and teenagers in the labor force increased. This change in the labor force composition increased the full-employment rate of unemployment because both women and young workers (under age 25) typically experience higher unemployment rates than men. Another frequently cited and controversial reason for the rise in the full-employment rate of unemployment is that larger unemployment compensation payments, food stamps, welfare, and Social Security benefits from the government make unemployment less painful. In the 1990s, the natural rate of unemployment declined somewhat because the entry of females and teenagers into the labor force slowed. Also, the baby boom generation has aged, and middle-aged workers have lower unemployment rates.

6-4a The GDP Gap

When people in an economy are unemployed, society forfeits the production of some goods and services. To determine the dollar value of how much society loses if the economy fails to reach the natural rate of unemployment, economists estimate the GDP gap. The **GDP gap** is the difference between actual real GDP and full-employment real GDP. The level of GDP that could be produced at full employment is also called *potential real GDP*. Expressed as a formula:

$$\text{GDP gap} = \text{actual real GDP} - \text{potential real GDP}$$

The GDP gap can be either positive if actual real GDP exceeds potential real GDP or negative if actual real GDP is less than potential real GDP. Because the GDP gap is calculated on the basis of the difference between GDP at the actual unemployment rate and estimated GDP at the full-employment rate of unemployment, the GDP gap measures the cost of cyclical unemployment. A positive GDP gap measures a boom in the economy when workers are employed overtime, and a negative GDP gap increases during a recession. Exhibit 9 shows the size of the GDP gap (in 2009 prices) from 1998 to 2016, based on potential real GDP and actual real GDP for each of these years. Prior to the recession that began in 2007, the economy operated above its potential (positive GDP gap). Beginning in 2008, the economy operated below its potential (negative gap). And since the Great Recession's beginning in 2007, the U.S. economy has experienced large but shrinking negative GDP gaps. If this trend continues, hopefully we will experience positive GDP gaps soon.

Full employment
The situation in which an economy operates at an unemployment rate equal to the sum of the frictional and structural unemployment rates. Also called the *natural rate of unemployment*.

GDP gap
The difference between actual real GDP and potential or full-employment real GDP.

YOU'RE THE ECONOMIST   Applicable Concept: Types of Unemployment

What Kind of Unemployment Do Robots and Artificial Intelligence Cause?

Technological advances continue to enhance our productivity, enabling us to enjoy a greater quantity, quality, and variety of products that significantly elevate our standard of living as a nation. Every day we witness incredible new technologies in computing, social media, business management systems, modes of learning, sustainable energy, and an array of truly amazing life-saving advances in medicine. Robots can now undertake tasks faster and better than humans ever imagined. Advanced global positioning systems (GPS) enable drones to monitor traffic congestion and may soon be able to deliver packages to our doors. 3-D virtual reality and 3-D printing opens up many new possibilities for satisfying human needs and wants. And recent developments in artificial intelligence make it possible for machines to learn by doing, to recognize speech, and to diagnose disease.

Although we embrace all these wonderful new goods and services, many worry that robots and artificial intelligence may be coming for our jobs! This concern is not new. In the early nineteenth century, Luddites, a group of textile workers in England, smashed weaving machines because they feared this new automation would threaten their livelihoods. This Luddite-type reasoning is not without merit. A widely cited paper published by Carl Frey and Michael Osborn of Oxford University claim that "47 percent of U.S. workers have a high probability of seeing their jobs automated over the next 20 years."[1]

Some jobs look especially ripe for automation, like those of assembly-line workers, clerks, tellers, and call-center operators. Self-driving technology alone could cause many of America's approximately 3.5 million truck drivers to be out of work. Technology has also fuelled globalization, which makes it possible to outsource jobs to their least-cost locations wherever they may be on the globe. Firms faced with this more intense foreign competition may lose market share and downsize, or they may go out of business altogether, creating some unemployment that puts downward pressure on these workers' wages and benefits.

Despite the scary projections, there is no need to panic and to start smashing machines! The Luddite-type reasoning is only one side of the story. At the same time that technology destroys jobs, it creates new ones. Someone will have to create, develop, produce, and monitor all these new robots and artificial intelligence. But, these new jobs will be much different than the old ones. They will require new skill sets. The challenge facing many workers today will be to obtain the necessary education, skills, and training that will enable them to fill the new jobs of tomorrow.

Pixabay

Although there is a tug of war between job destruction and job creation associated with technological advances, the transition can be rocky. Typically the brunt of the job destruction comes before the job creation is fully realized. It takes time for workers to hone their skill sets in response to shifting labor market demand. In the meantime, the promise of new, better, higher-paying jobs for skilled workers in the future is often of little comfort to those who are currently unemployed.

ANALYZE THE ISSUE

1. What type of unemployment does technological development cause? Explain.
2. What solution would you propose for any worker threatened by new technologies?
3. Can you think of any public policies that might help offset this unemployment?

---

1. Carl Benedikt Frey and Michael A. Osborne, "The Future of Employment: How Susceptible are Jobs to Computerisation?" September 17, 2013. Found at: http://www.oxfordmartin.ox.ac.uk/downloads/academic/The_Future_of_Employment.pdf.

EXHIBIT 9 Actual and Potential GDP, 1998–2016

The GDP gap is the difference between actual real GDP and potential real GDP. Potential GDP is GDP when the economy operates at full employment. A positive GDP gap measures a boom in the economy when workers are employed overtime and actual GDP exceeds potential GDP. Between 1998 and 2007, the U.S. economy experienced positive GDP gaps. The recession that began in 2007 reversed the GDP gap, and the economy began in 2008 with large but shrinking negative GDP gaps below potential.

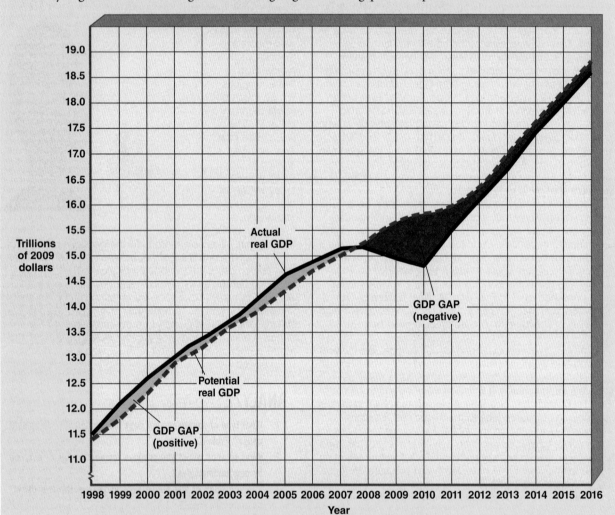

SOURCE: International Monetary Fund, *World Economic Outlook Database*, http://www.imf.org/external/ns/cs.aspx?id=28.

CONCLUSION The gap between actual and potential real GDP measures the monetary losses of real goods and services to the nation from operating at less than full employment.

6-5 NONMONETARY AND DEMOGRAPHIC CONSEQUENCES OF UNEMPLOYMENT

The burden of unemployment is more than the loss of potential output measured by the GDP gap. Unemployment also has many social and political costs. Some people endure unemployment pretty well because they have substantial savings to draw on, but others sink into despair. Without work, many people lose their feeling of worth. A person's self-image suffers when he or she cannot support a family and be a valuable member of society. Research has associated high unemployment with suicides, crime, mental illness, heart attacks, and other maladies. Moreover, severe unemployment causes despair, family breakups, and political unrest.

Various labor market groups share the impact of unemployment unequally. Exhibit 10 presents the unemployment rates experienced by selected demographic groups. In 2016, the overall unemployment rate was 4.9 percent, but the figures in the exhibit reveal the unequal burden by gender, race, age, and educational attainment. First, it is interesting to note that the unemployment rate for males was greater than

EXHIBIT 10 Civilian Unemployment Rates by Selected Demographic Groups, 2016

Demographic group	Unemployment rate (percent)
Overall	4.9%
Gender	
Male	4.9
Female	4.8
Race	
White	4.3
Hispanic	5.8
African American	8.5
Teenagers (16–19 years old)	
All	15.8
White	14.1
Hispanics	17.1
African American	26.5
Education (25 years and over)	
Less than high school diploma	7.5
High school graduates, no college	5.2
Bachelor's degree and higher	2.5

SOURCE: Economic Report of the President, 2017, https://www.whitehouse.gov/administration/eop/cea/economic-report-of-the-President/Table B–11. Bureau of Labor Statistics, Current Population Survey, http://stats.bls.gov/cps/cpsatabs.htm, Tables A-1 thru A-4.

YOU'RE THE ECONOMIST

Applicable Concept: Human Costs of Unemployment

Brother Can You Spare a Dime?

The unemployment rate does not measure the full impact of unemployment on individuals. Prolonged unemployment not only means lost wages, but it also impairs health and social relationships. The United States fought its most monstrous battle against unemployment during the Great Depression of the 1930s. Return to Exhibit 7 and note that the unemployment rate stayed at 20 percent or more from 1932 through 1935. In 1933, it reached almost 25 percent of the civilian labor force; that is, about one out of every four people who wanted to work could not. This meant 16 million Americans were out of work when our country's population was less than half its present size.[1]

But these statistics tell only part of the horror story. Millions of workers were "discouraged workers" who had simply given up looking for work because there was no work available, and these people were not counted. People were standing in line for soup kitchens, selling apples on the street, and living in cardboard shacks. "Brother can you spare a dime?" was a common greeting. Some people jumped out of windows, and others roamed the country trying valiantly to survive. John Steinbeck's great novel *The Grapes of Wrath* described millions of Midwesterners who drove in caravans to California after being wiped out by drought in what became known as the Dust Bowl.

A 1992 study estimated the frightening impact of sustained unemployment that is not reflected in official unemployment data. Mary Merva, a University of Utah economist, authored a study of unemployment in 30 selected big cities from 1976 to 1990. This research found that a 1 percentage point increase in the national unemployment rate resulted in the following:

- 6.7 percent more murders
- 3.1 percent more deaths from stroke
- 5.6 percent more deaths from heart disease
- 3.9 percent increase in suicides[2]

Hard times during the recession of 2007 caused people to cut back on their medical care. According to a survey by the American Heart Association (AHA), 42 percent of the respondents said they trimmed health-related expenses, 32 percent skipped some preventive care, such as a mammogram or an annual physical, and 10 percent stopped or diminished the

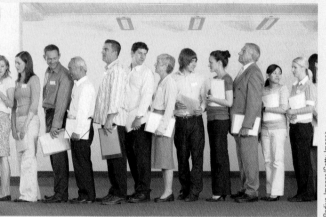

Radius Images/Getty Images

use of medicine for chronic conditions. And a 2011 article in *The New York Times* reported the finding in a Harvard School of Public Health survey that workers who lost a job through no fault of their own were twice as likely to report developing a new ailment such as high blood pressure, diabetes, or heart disease over the next year and a half, compared with people who were continuously employed.[3] The *Atlantic* magazine reported in 2014 that "those who have been looking for work for half a year or more are more than three times as likely to be suffering from depression as those with jobs."[4]

Although these estimates are subject to statistical qualifications, they underscore the notion that prolonged unemployment poses a real danger to many individuals. As people attempt to adjust to layoffs, cutbacks, and a sudden inability to support their families, many Americans find themselves clinically depressed. In fact, Federal Reserve Chair Janet Yellen has reported before Congress on the "exceptional psychological trauma" of being unemployed.[5]

ANALYZE THE ISSUE What are other social and political problems that can result from unemployment?

---

1. U.S. Bureau of the Census, *Historical Statistics of the United States, Colonial Times to 1957* (Washington, D.C.: U.S. Government Printing Office, 1960), Series D46–47, p. 73.
2. Robert Davis, "Recession's Cost: Lives," *USA Today*, Oct. 16, 1992, p. 1A.
3. Roni Caryn Rabin, "Losing Job May Be Hazardous to Health," *The New York Times*, May 9, 2011.
4. Rebecca J. Rosen, "The Mental Health Consequences of Unemployment," *The Atlantic*, June 9, 2014.
5. "Yellen on Human Toll of Unemployment," *CNN Money*, July 15, 2014. Video found at: http://money.cnn.com/video/news/economy/2014/07/15/janet-yellen-federal-reserve-chair-on-human-toll-of-unemployment.cnnmoney/

for females. Second, the unemployment rate for African Americans was more than twice the rate for whites and higher than the rate for Hispanics. Third, teenagers experienced a high unemployment rate because they are new entrants to the workforce who have little employment experience, high quit rates, and little job mobility. Again, race is a strong factor, and the unemployment rate for African-American teenagers was greater than for white teenagers. Among the explanations are discrimination; the concentration of African Americans in the inner city where job opportunities for less skilled (blue-collar) workers are inadequate; and the minimum wage law.

Finally, comparison of the unemployment rates in 2016 by educational attainment reveals the importance of education as an insurance policy against unemployment. Firms are much less likely to lay off a higher-skilled worker with a college education, in whom they have a greater investment in terms of training and salaries, than a worker with only a high school diploma.

Key Concepts

Business cycle	Leading indicators	Frictional unemployment	Cyclical unemployment
Peak	Coincident indicators		Full employment
Recession	Lagging indicators	Structural unemployment	GDP gap
Trough	Unemployment rate	Outsourcing	
Expansion	Civilian labor force	Offshoring	
Economic growth	Discouraged worker		

Summary

- **Business cycles** are recurrent rises and falls in real GDP over a period of years. Business cycles vary greatly in duration and intensity. A cycle consists of four phases: peak, recession, trough, and recovery. The generally accepted theory today is that changes in total spending cause business cycles. A **recession** is generally defined as at least two consecutive quarters of real GDP decline and is caused by a decrease in total spending. A **trough** is the turning point in national output between recession and recovery. During an **expansion**, there is an upturn in the business cycle, during which real GDP rises as a result of an increase in aggregate expenditures. A **peak** occurs when real GDP reaches its maximum level during a recovery.

Hypothetical Business Cycle

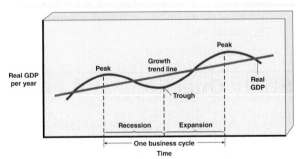

- **Economic growth** is measured by the annual percentage change in real GDP in a nation. The long-term average annual growth rate since 1930 in the United States is 3.5 percent.

- **Leading**, **coincident**, and **lagging indicators** are economic variables that change before, at the same time as, and after changes in real GDP, respectively.

- The **unemployment rate** is the ratio of the number of unemployed to the number in the civilian labor force multiplied by 100. The nation's **civilian labor force** consists of people who are employed plus those who are out of work, but seeking employment.

- **Discouraged workers** are a reason critics say the unemployment rate is *understated*. Discouraged workers are persons who want to work, but have given up searching for work. Another criticism of the unemployment rate is that it *overstates* unemployment because respondents can falsely report they are seeking a job.

- **Frictional**, **structural**, and **cyclical unemployment** are different types of unemployment. **Frictional unemployment**, including seasonal unemployment, results when workers are seeking new jobs that exist. The problem is that imperfect information prevents matching the applicants with the available jobs. **Structural unemployment** is long-term unemployment caused by

factors in the economy, including lack of education, changes in consumer demand, technological change, and globalization. Outsourcing and offshoring can occur as part of globalization. **Outsourcing** is the practice of a company having its work done by another company in another country. **Offshoring** occurs when a U.S. company hires employees from another country to perform jobs once done by the company's American employees. **Cyclical unemployment** is unemployment resulting from insufficient aggregate demand (total spending).

- **Full employment** occurs when the unemployment rate is equal to the total of the frictional and structural unemployment rates. Currently, the full-employment rate of unemployment (natural rate of unemployment) in the United States is considered to be close to 5 percent. At this rate of unemployment, the economy is producing at its maximum potential.

- The **GDP gap** is the difference between actual real GDP and full employment, or potential real GDP. Therefore, the GDP gap measures the loss of output due to cyclical unemployment.

Summary of Conclusion Statements

- We value economic growth as one of our nation's economic goals because it increases our standard of living—it creates a bigger "economic pie."

- The gap between actual and potential real GDP measures the monetary losses of real goods and services to the nation from operating at less than full employment.

Study Questions and Problems

Please see Appendix A for answers to the odd-numbered questions. Your instructor has access to the answers for even-numbered questions.

1. What is the basic cause of the business cycle?

2. Following are real GDP figures for 10 quarters:

Quarter	Real GDP (billions of dollars)
1	$ 400
2	500
3	300
4	200
5	300
6	500
7	800
8	900
9	1000
10	500

Plot these data points, and identify the four phases of the business cycle. Give a theory that may explain the cause of the observed business cycle. What are some of the consequences of a prolonged decline in real GDP? Is the decline in real GDP from $1,000 billion to $500 billion a recession?

3. In a given year, there are 10 million unemployed workers and 120 million employed workers in an economy. Excluding members of the armed forces and persons in institutions and assuming these figures include only civilian workers, calculate the civilian unemployment rate.

4. Describe the relevant criteria that government statisticians use to determine whether a person is "unemployed."

5. How has the official unemployment rate been criticized for overestimating and underestimating unemployment?

6. Why is frictional unemployment inevitable in an economy characterized by imperfect job information?

7. How does structural unemployment differ from cyclical unemployment?

8. Is it reasonable to expect the unemployment rate to fall to zero for an economy? What is the relationship of frictional, structural, and cyclical unemployment to the full-employment rate of unemployment, or natural rate of unemployment?

9. In the 1960s, economists used 4 percent as their approximation for the natural rate of unemployment. Currently, full employment is on the order of 5 percent unemployment. What is the major factor accounting for this rise?

10. Speculate on why teenage unemployment rates exceed those for the overall labor force.

11. Explain the GDP gap.

 CHECKPOINT ANSWERS

Where Are We on the Business-Cycle Roller Coaster?

The car dealer's sales in the first quarter conformed to the recession phase of the business cycle, and those in the second quarter, to the trough. Then car sales in the third and fourth quarters, although below those in the first quarter, indicate an increase over the second quarter. Therefore, the economy has been in a recovery for the last two quarters. If you said the economy is expanding and that real GDP during an expansion can be lower than real GDP during a recession, **YOU ARE CORRECT**.

What Kind of Unemployment Did the Invention of the Wheel Cause?

The invention of the wheel represented a new technology for primitive people. Even in the primitive era, many workers who transported goods lost their jobs to the more efficient cart with wheels. If you said the invention of the wheel caused structural unemployment, **YOU ARE CORRECT**.

Sample Quiz

Please see Appendix B for answers to Sample Quiz questions.

1. A business cycle is the
   a. period of time in which expansion and contraction of economic activity are equal.
   b. period of time in which there are three phases: peak, depression, and expansion.
   c. recurring growth and decline in real GDP.
   d. period of time in which a business is established and ceases operations.

2. A business cycle is the period of time in which
   a. a business is established and ceases operations.
   b. there are four phases: peak, recession, trough, and expansion.
   c. the price level changes.
   d. expansion and contraction of economic activity are equal.

3. What phase of the business cycle immediately follows a recession?
   a. Expansion
   b. Unemployment
   c. Peak
   d. Trough

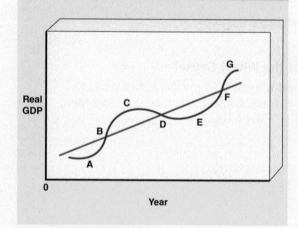

EXHIBIT 11 Business Cycle

4. In Exhibit 11 the expansion phase of the business cycle is represented by points
   a. *A* and *C*
   b. *B* and *F*
   c. *B* and *D*
   d. *C* and *G*

5. A general rule is that an economy is experiencing a recession when
   a. real GDP declines for at least three months.
   b. real GDP declines for at least nine months.
   c. nominal GDP declines for at least nine months.
   d. real GDP declines for at least six months.

6. A person who has given up searching for work is called
   a. frictionally unemployed.
   b. structurally unemployed.
   c. a discouraged worker.
   d. unemployed.

7. John Steinbeck's *Cannery Row* describes a character who takes his own life because of poor job prospects. If he was an unemployed person who gave up looking for work, he would be considered
   a. chronically unemployed.
   b. a discouraged worker.
   c. a member of the labor force.
   d. frictionally unemployed.

8. Unemployment that is of a short duration to allow a person time to find a new job is
   a. structural unemployment.
   b. cyclical unemployment.
   c. frictional unemployment.
   d. durational unemployment.

9. A person who voluntarily quits their job in New York and expects to get a similar job in Los Angeles is an example of
   a. structural unemployment.
   b. cyclical unemployment.
   c. durational unemployment.
   d. frictional unemployment.

10. Frictional unemployment refers to
    a. people who are out of work and have no job skills.
    b. short periods of unemployment needed to match jobs and job seekers.
    c. people who spend relatively long periods out of work.
    d. unemployment related to the ups and downs of the business cycle.

11. Sam is a musician who is out of work because electronic equipment replaced live musicians. This is an example of
    a. frictional unemployment.
    b. cyclical unemployment.
    c. structural unemployment.
    d. involuntary unemployment.

12. Louise is unemployed due to a decrease in the demand for workers with knowledge of a certain word processing language. This is an example of
    a. cyclical unemployment.
    b. frictional unemployment.
    c. involuntary unemployment.
    d. structural unemployment.

13. Consider a broom factory that permanently closes because of foreign competition. If the broom factory's workers cannot find new jobs because their skills are no longer marketable, they are classified as
    a. seasonally unemployed.
    b. frictionally unemployed.
    c. structurally unemployed.
    d. cyclically unemployed.

14. The increase in unemployment associated with a recession is called
    a. structural unemployment.
    b. frictional unemployment.
    c. discouraged unemployment.
    d. cyclical unemployment.

15. Which of the following is true?
    a. The GDP gap is the difference between full-employment real GDP and actual real GDP.
    b. We desire economic growth because it increases the nation's standard of living.

c. Economic growth is measured by the annual percentage increase in a nation's real GDP.
    d. Discouraged workers are a reason critics say the unemployment rate is understated.
    e. All of the above answers are correct.

16. What stage of the business cycle immediately follows the trough?
    a. Peak
    b. Recovery
    c. Recession
    d. Depression

17. The government's chief forecasting gauge for business cycles is the
    a. unemployment rate.
    b. real GDP.
    c. personal income index.
    d. index of leading indicators.

18. Which of the following is *not* a lagging indicator?
    a. Duration of unemployment
    b. Stock prices
    c. Commercial and industrial loans
    d. Prime rate

19. Suppose the official unemployment rate is 10 percent. We can conclude without question that
    a. the same 10 percent of the people in the economy were out of work for the entire year.
    b. 1 out of every 10 people in the civilian labor force is currently unemployed.
    c. the same 10 percent of the people in the civilian labor force was out of work for the entire year.
    d. every person in the civilian labor force was out of work for 10 percent of the year.

20. Sally lost her job when her company went out of business because of a recession. This is an example of
    a. frictional unemployment.
    b. structural unemployment.
    c. cyclical unemployment.
    d. technological unemployment.

CHAPTER 7

Inflation

CHAPTER PREVIEW

In addition to the goals of full employment and economic growth discussed in the previous chapter, keeping prices stable is another one of the most important economic goals facing a nation. In the United States, the Great Depression of the 1930s and the Great Recession of 2007 produced profound changes in people's lives from the consequences of unemployment. Similarly, the "Great Inflation" of the 1970s and early 1980s left memories of the miseries of inflation. In fact, every American president since Franklin Roosevelt has resolved to keep the price level stable. Politicians are aware that, as with high unemployment, voters are quick to blame any administration that fails to keep inflation rates under control.

This chapter explains what inflation is: What does it mean when a 50 percent hike in the price of gasoline causes pain at the pump, eggs jump by 35 percent, a gallon of milk is up 23 percent, a loaf of bread climbs 16 percent, and around the world others feel the pinch of higher prices? Here you will study how the government actually measures changes in the price level and computes the rate of inflation. The chapter concludes with a discussion of the consequences and root causes of inflation. It explains who the winners are and who the losers are. For example, you will see what happened in Zimbabwe when the inflation rate reached 231,000,000 percent. After studying this chapter, you will have a much clearer understanding of why inflation is so feared.

IN THIS CHAPTER, YOU WILL LEARN TO SOLVE THESE ECONOMICS PUZZLES:

- What is the inflation rate of your college education?

- Can a person's income fall even though he or she received a raise?

- What would Babe Ruth's salary be worth today?

- What is the real price of gasoline?

- Can an interest rate be negative?

- Does inflation harm everyone equally?

7-1 MEANING AND MEASUREMENT OF INFLATION

Inflation
An increase in the general (average) price level of goods and services in the economy.

Deflation
A decrease in the general (average) price level of goods and services in the economy.

After World War II, a 12-ounce bottle of Pepsi sold for 5 cents. Today, a 12-ounce can of Pepsi sells for more than 20 times that much. This is not inflation. **Inflation** is an increase in the *general* (average) price level of goods and services in the economy. Inflation's opposite is deflation. **Deflation** is a decrease in the *general* (average) price level of goods and services in the economy. Note that inflation does not mean that *all* prices of *all* products in the economy rise during a given period of time. For example, the annual percentage change in the average overall price level during the 1970s reached double digits, but the prices of pocket calculators and digital watches actually declined. The reason that the average price level rose in the 1970s was that the rising prices of Pepsi, houses, and other goods outweighed the falling prices of pocket calculators, digital watches, and other goods.

CONCLUSION Inflation is an increase in the overall average level of prices and not an increase in the price of any specific product.

7-1a The Consumer Price Index

Consumer price index (CPI)

An index that measures changes in the average prices of consumer goods and services.

The most widely reported measure of inflation is the **consumer price index (CPI)**, which measures changes in the average prices of consumer goods and services. The CPI is sometimes called the *cost-of-living index*. It includes only consumer goods and services in order to determine how rising prices affect the purchasing power of consumers' incomes. Unlike the *GDP chain price index* explained in the previous chapter on GDP, the CPI does not consider items purchased by businesses and government.

The Bureau of Labor Statistics (BLS) of the Department of Labor prepares the CPI. Each month the bureau's "price collectors" contact retail stores, homeowners, and tenants in selected cities throughout the United States. Based on these monthly inquiries, the BLS records average prices for a "market basket" of different items purchased by the typical *urban* family. These items are included under the following categories: food, housing, apparel, transportation, medical care, entertainment, and other expenditures. Exhibit 1 presents a more detailed breakdown of these categories and shows the relative importance of each as a percentage of total expenditures. The survey reveals, for example, that 33 cents out of each consumer dollar is spent for housing and 17 cents for transportation. The composition of the market basket generally remains unchanged from one period to the next, so the CPI is called a *fixed-weight price index*. If 33 percent of consumer spending was on housing during a given base year, the assumption is that 33 percent of spending is still spent on housing in, say, 2018. Over time, particular items in the CPI change. For example, personal computers, digital cameras, and cell phones have been added. The base period is changed periodically.

7-1b How the CPI Is Computed

Exhibit 2 illustrates the basic idea behind the CPI using hypothetical data to show how this price index measures inflation. Suppose, in 1982, a typical family in the United States lived a very meager existence and purchased a market basket of only hamburgers, gasoline, and jeans. Column 1 shows the quantity purchased for each of these items, and column 2

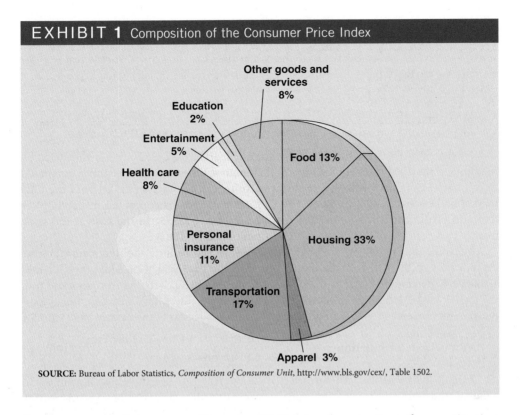

EXHIBIT 1 Composition of the Consumer Price Index

Other goods and services 8%

Education 2%

Entertainment 5%

Health care 8%

Food 13%

Personal insurance 11%

Housing 33%

Transportation 17%

Apparel 3%

SOURCE: Bureau of Labor Statistics, *Composition of Consumer Unit*, http://www.bls.gov/cex/, Table 1502.

lists the corresponding average selling price. Multiplying the price times the quantity gives the market basket cost in column 3 of each consumer product purchased in 1982.

The total cost paid by our typical family for the market basket, based on 1982 prices and quantities purchased, is $245.

EXHIBIT 2 A Hypothetical Consumer Price Index for a Simple Economy

Products in consumers' market basket	(1) 1982 quantity purchased	(2) 1982 price	(3) Market basket cost in 1982 [(1) × (2)]	(4) 2000 price	(5) Market basket cost in 2000 [(1) × (4)]
Hamburgers	50	$ 0.80	$ 40	$ 1.00	$ 50
Gallons of gasoline	250	0.70	175	0.90	225
Jeans	2	15.00	30	30.00	60
			Total 1982 cost = $245		Total 2000 cost = $335

$$2000 \text{ CPI} = \frac{2000 \text{ market basket cost}}{1982 \text{ market basket cost}} \times 100$$

$$2000 \text{ CPI} = \frac{\$335}{\$245} \times 100 = 136.7$$

Years later it is 2000, and we wish to know the impact of rising prices on consumer purchases. To calculate the CPI, we determine the cost of the *same* market basket, valued at 2000 *current-year prices*, and compare this to the cost at 1982 *base-year prices*. A **base year** is a year chosen as a reference point for comparison with some earlier or later year. Expressed as a general formula:

Base year
A year chosen as a reference point for comparison with some earlier or later year.

$$CPI = \frac{\text{cost of market basket of products at current-year (2000) prices}}{\text{cost of same market basket of products at base-year (1982) prices}} \times 100$$

As shown in Exhibit 2, the 2000 cost for our market basket example is calculated by multiplying the 2000 price for each item in column 4 times the 1982 quantity purchased in column 1. Column 5 lists the result for each item in the market basket, and the total market basket cost in 2000 is $335. The CPI value of 136.7 is computed in Exhibit 2 as the ratio of the current 2000 cost of the market basket ($335) to the cost of the same market basket in the 1982 base year ($245) multiplied by 100.

The value of the CPI in the base year is always 100 because the numerator and the denominator of the CPI formula are the same in the base year. Currently, the CPI uses 1982–1984 spending patterns as its base year. Once the BLS selects the base year and uses the market basket technique to generate the CPI numbers, the annual *inflation rate* is computed as the percentage change in the official CPI from one year to the next. Mathematically,

$$\text{Annual rate of inflation} = \frac{\text{CPI in given year} - \text{CPI in previous year}}{\text{CPI in previous year}} \times 100$$

Exhibit 3 lists actual CPI for selected years. You can use the above formula and calculate the inflation rate for any given year using the base year of 1982–84 = 100.

EXHIBIT 3 Consumer Price Indexes and Percentage Changes, Selected Years

Year	CPI	Inflation rate
1931	15.2	−9.0%
1932	13.7	−9.9
1979	72.6	11.3
1980	82.4	13.5
2000	172.2	3.4
2001	177.1	2.8
2002	179.9	1.6
2008	215.3	3.8
2009	214.5	−0.4
2013	233.0	1.5
2014	236.7	1.6
2015	237.0	0.1
2016	240.0	1.3

SOURCE: Bureau of Labor Statistics, Consumer Price Index, http://data.bls.gov/cgi-bin/surveymost?cu.

In 2016, for example, the CPI was 240.0, while in 2015, it was 237.0. The rate of inflation for 2016 is computed as follows:

$$1.3\% = [(240 - 237)/237] \times 100$$

The negative inflation rate of 9.9 percent for 1932 was deflation, and the 13.5 percent inflation rate for 1980 illustrates a relatively high rate in recent U.S. history. The fall in the inflation rate from 2.8 percent to 1.6 percent between 2001 and 2002 was disinflation. **Disinflation** is a reduction in the rate of inflation. Disinflation does not mean that prices are falling; rather, it means that the rate of increases in prices is falling. The negative inflation rate of −0.4 percent in 2009 was the first U.S. deflation since 1955.

Disinflation
A reduction in the rate of inflation.

The College Education Price Index

Suppose your *market basket* for a college education consisted of only the four items listed in the following table:

Item	2015	2016
Tuition and fees[1]	$4,500	$5,000
Room and board[2]	6,000	6,200
Books[3]	1,000	1,200
Soft drinks[4]	150	200

[1]Tuition for two semesters.
[2]Payment for nine months.
[3]Ten textbooks.
[4]Two hundred 12-ounce Coca-Colas.

Using 2015 as your base year, what is the percentage change in the college education price index in 2016?

CHECKPOINT

7-1c History of U.S. Inflation Rates

Exhibit 4 shows how prices have changed in the United States since 1929, as measured by annual changes in the CPI. During the early years of the Great Depression, the nation experienced *deflation*, and the CPI declined at almost a double-digit rate. In contrast, the CPI reached a double-digit inflation rate during and immediately following World War II. After 1950, the inflation rate generally remained below 3 percent until the inflationary pressures from the Vietnam War in the late 1960s. In fact, the average inflation rate between 1950 and 1968 was only 2 percent. During the 1973–1982 period, the average annual inflation rate was 8.8 percent, reaching a high of 13.5 percent in 1980. Following the 1990–1991 recession, the annual inflation rate moderated, and it averaged 2.5 percent between 1992 and 2010. In 2009 during the Great Recession, the deflation rate was −0.4 percent in 2009. In 2016, the inflation rate was 1.3 percent.

EXHIBIT 4 The U.S. Inflation Rate, 1929–2016

During the Great Depression, the economy experienced deflation as prices plunged. During and immediately after World War II, the annual rate of inflation reached the double-digit level. After 1950, the inflation rate was generally below 3 percent until the inflationary pressures from the Vietnam War in the late 1960s. During the 1950–1968 period the average inflation rate was only 2 percent. In contrast, the inflation rate climbed sharply to an average of 7.6 percent between 1969 and 1982. Between 1992 and 2009, inflation moderated and averaged 2.6 percent annually. In 2009 during the Great Recession, the deflation rate was −0.4 percent. In 2016, the inflation rate was 1.3 percent.

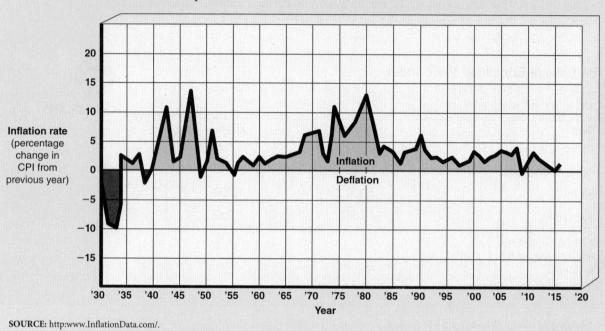

SOURCE: http:www.InflationData.com/.

7-1d Consumer Price Index Criticisms

Just as there is criticism of the unemployment rate, the CPI is not a perfect measure of inflation, and it has been the subject of much public debate. There are reasons for this criticism:

1. Changes in the CPI are based on a typical market basket of products that does not match the actual market basket purchased by many consumers. Suppose you spend your nominal annual income entirely on lemonade, hot dogs, and jeans. During this year, the inflation rate is 5 percent, but assume the prices of lemonade, hot dogs, and jeans actually fall. In this case, your real income (or *purchasing power* of your income) will rise, and the official inflation rate based on the CPI will *overstate* the impact of inflation on your standard of living. Consider another example. Retired persons generally buy a bundle of products that differs from that of the "typical" family. Because retired persons purchase proportionally more medical services than the typical family, and because the cost of medical care usually increases faster than the prices of other products, then the inflation rate may *understate* the impact of inflation on older persons.

2. Also, the BLS has difficulty adjusting the CPI for changes in *quality*. Compare a car made in the past with a new car. The new car may cost more, but it is much better than the old car. A portion of the price increase, therefore, reflects better quality instead of simply a higher price for the same item. If the quality of items improves, increases in the CPI *overstate* inflation. Similarly, deteriorating quality *understates* inflation. The BLS attempts to make adjustments for quality changes in automobiles, electronic equipment, and other products in the market basket, but these adjustments are difficult to determine accurately.

3. Finally, the use of a single base-year market basket ignores the law of demand. If the price of a product rises, consumers purchase substitutes, and a smaller quantity is demanded. Suppose orange growers suffer from severe frosts and the supply of oranges decreases. Consequently, the price of oranges increases sharply. According to the *law of demand*, consumers will decrease the quantity demanded of oranges and substitute consumption of, say, apples for oranges. Because the market basket does not automatically change by reducing the percentage or weight of oranges and increasing the percentage of apples, the CPI will *overstate* the impact of higher prices for oranges on the price level. To deal with this *substitution* bias problem, the BLS takes annual surveys to keep up with changing consumption patterns and correct for the fixed market basket limitations of the CPI.

7-2 CONSEQUENCES OF INFLATION

We will now turn from measuring inflation to examining its effects on people's income and wealth. Why should inflation cause concern? You will learn in this section that inflation is feared because it can significantly alter one's standard of living. You will see that inflation can create winners, who enjoy a larger slice of the national income pie, and losers, who receive a smaller slice as a result of inflation.

7-2a Inflation Shrinks Income

Economist Arthur Okun once stated, "This society is built on implicit and explicit contracts… They are linked to the idea that the dollar means something. If you cannot depend on the value of the dollar, this system is undermined. People will constantly feel they've been fooled and cheated." When prices rise, people worry whether the rise in their income will keep pace with inflation. And the more quickly prices rise, the more people suffer from the stresses of inflation and its uncertainties.

Inflation tends to reduce your standard of living through declines in the purchasing power of money. The greater the rate of inflation, the greater the decline in the quantity of goods we can purchase with a given *nominal income*, or *money income*. **Nominal income** is the actual number of dollars received over a period of time. The source of income can be wages, salary, rent, dividends, interest, or pensions.

Nominal income does not measure your real purchasing power. Finding out if you are better or worse off over time requires converting nominal income to real income. **Real income** is the actual number of dollars received (nominal income) adjusted for changes in the CPI. Real income measures the amount of goods and services that can be purchased with one's nominal income. If the CPI increases and your nominal income remains the same, your real income (purchasing power) falls. In short, if your nominal income fails to keep pace with inflation, your standard of living falls.

Nominal income
The actual number of dollars received over a period of time.

Real income
The actual number of dollars received (nominal income) adjusted for changes in the CPI.

Suppose your nominal income in Year 1 was $50,000 and the CPI value for this year is 228.9. Your real income relative to a base year is

$$\textbf{Real income} = \frac{\textbf{nominal income}}{\textbf{CPI (as decimal, or CPI/100)}}$$

$$\textbf{Year 1 real income} = \frac{\$50{,}000}{2.289} = \$21{,}844$$

Now assume your nominal income rises in the next year (Year 2) by 10 percent, from $50,000 to $55,000, and the CPI increases by 1.5 percent, from 228.9 to 232.4. Thus, you earn $5,000 more money, but how much are you really better off? To answer this question, you must compute your Year 2 real income as follows:

$$\textbf{Year 2 real income} = \frac{\$55{,}000}{2.324} = \$23{,}666$$

Using the two computed real-income figures, the percentage change in your real income between Year 1 and Year 2 was 8.3 percent ($1,822/$21,844 × 100). This means that your standard of living has risen because you have an extra $1,822 to spend on entertainment, clothes, or travel. Even though the general price level has risen, your purchasing power has increased because the percentage rise in nominal income more than offsets the rate of inflation. Instead of precisely calculating this relationship, a good approximation can be obtained through the following simple formula:

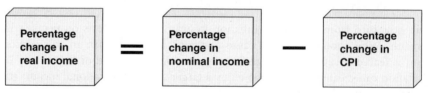

It should be noted that workers with union contracts might be largely unaffected by inflation if their contacts include a *cost-of-living adjustment (COLA),* where wages automatically increase with increases in the CPI. For example, with a COLA, an inflation rate of 3 percent in a given year would automatically increase wages by 3 percent.

CONCLUSION People whose nominal incomes rise faster than the rate of inflation gain purchasing power, while people whose nominal incomes do not keep pace with inflation lose purchasing power.

Now suppose someone asks you the following question: In 1932, Babe Ruth, the New York Yankees home run slugger, earned $80,000. How much did he earn in 2016 dollars? Economists convert a past salary into a salary today by using this formula:

$$\textbf{Salary in given year} = \textbf{salary in previous year} \times \frac{\textbf{CPI in given year}}{\textbf{CPI in previous year}}$$

$$\textbf{Salary in 2016 dollars} = \$80{,}000 \times \frac{240.0}{13.7} = \$1{,}401{,}460$$

In other words, a salary of $80,000 in 1932 was equivalent to a salary of about $1.4 million in 2016.

What Is the Real Price of Gasoline?

In 1981, consumers were shocked when the average price for gasoline reached $1.35 per gallon because only a few years previously, gasoline was selling for one-half this price. If the CPI in 1981 was 90.9 and the CPI in 2016 was 240.0, what is the average inflation adjusted price in 2016 dollars?

CHECKPOINT

*"I've called the family together to announce that, because of inflation,
I'm going to have to let two of you go."*

Joseph Farris The New Yorker Collection/The Cartoon Bank

7-2b Inflation and Wealth

Income is one measure of economic well-being, and wealth is another. Income is a flow of money earned by selling factors of production. **Wealth** is the value of the stock of assets owned at some point in time. Wealth includes real estate, stocks, bonds, bank accounts, life insurance policies, cash, and automobiles. A person can have a high income and little wealth or great wealth and little income.

Inflation can benefit holders of wealth because the value of assets tends to increase as prices rise. Consider a home purchased for $200,000 that sells ten years later for $300,000. This 50 percent increase can be largely the result of inflation. People who own forms of wealth that increase in value faster than the inflation rate, such as real estate and stocks, are winners. On the other hand, the impact of inflation on wealth penalizes people without it. Consider younger couples wishing to purchase a home. As prices rise, it becomes more difficult for them to buy a home or acquire other assets.

Wealth
The value of the stock of assets owned at some point in time.

7-2c Inflation and the Real Interest Rate

Nominal interest rate
The actual rate of interest without adjustment for the inflation rate.

Borrowers and savers may be winners or losers, depending on the rate of inflation. Understanding how this might happen requires making a distinction between the *nominal interest rate* and the *real interest rate*. The **nominal interest rate** is the actual rate of interest earned over a period of time. The nominal interest rate, for example, is the interest rate specified on a loan or savings account. If you borrow $10,000 from a bank at a 5 percent annual interest rate for five years, this is more accurately called a 5 percent annual nominal interest rate. Similarly, a $10,000 certificate of deposit that yields 5 percent annual interest is said to have a 5 percent annual nominal interest rate.

Real interest rate
The nominal rate of interest minus the inflation rate.

The **real interest rate** is the nominal interest rate minus the inflation rate. Expressed as an equation:

$$\text{Real interest rate} = \text{Nominal interest rate} - \text{Inflation rate}$$

The occurrence of inflation means that the real rate of interest will be less than the nominal rate. Suppose the inflation rate during the year is 2 percent. This means that a 5 percent annual nominal interest rate paid on a $10,000 loan amounts to a 3 percent *real interest rate* and a certificate of deposit that yields 5 percent annual nominal interest also earns 3 percent *real interest.*

To understand how inflation can make those who borrow winners, suppose you receive a one-year loan from your parents to start a business. Earning a profit is not your parents' motive, and they know you will repay the loan. Their only concern is that you replace the decline in purchasing power of the money they loaned you. Both you and your parents anticipate the inflation rate will be 2 percent during the year; so the loan is made, and you agree to repay the principal plus the 2 percent to offset inflation. In short, both parties assume payment of a zero real interest rate (the 2 percent nominal interest rate minus the 2 percent rate of inflation). Now consider what happens if the inflation rate is actually 5 percent during the year of the loan. The clear unintentional winner is you, the debtor, because your creditor parents are paid the principal plus 2 percent interest, but their purchasing power still falls by 3 percent because the actual inflation rate is 5 percent. Stated differently, instead of zero, the real interest rate paid on the loan was −3 percent (the 2 percent nominal interest rate minus the 5 percent rate of inflation). In real terms, your parents paid you to borrow from them.

Adjustable-rate mortgage (ARMs)
A home loan that adjusts the nominal interest rate to changes in an index rate, such as rates on Treasury securities.

During the late 1970s, the rate of inflation rose frequently. This forced mortgage lenders to protect themselves against declining real interest rates on their loans by offering *adjustable-rate mortgages* in addition to conventional fixed-rate mortgages. **Adjustable-rate mortgage (ARMs)** are home loans that adjust the nominal interest rate to changes in an index, such as rates on Treasury securities that reflect changes in inflation. If inflation rises, then the interest rate on ARMS increases. This pushes up monthly loan payments. A *subprime loan crisis* associated with the Great Recession of 2007 resulted in large part from homeowners who were unable to make payments as the interest rate rose on their ARMs. This subject is discussed in more depth in the chapter on monetary policy.

A nest egg in the form of a savings account set aside for a rainy day is also affected by inflation. For example, if the interest rate on a one-year $10,000 certificate of deposit is fixed at 5 percent and the inflation rate is zero (5 percent real interest rate), the certificate holder will earn a 5 percent return on his or her savings. If the inflation rate exceeds the fixed nominal rate of interest, the real interest rate is negative, and the saver is hurt because the interest earned does not keep pace with the inflation rate. This is the reason: Suppose, after one year, the saver withdraws the original $10,000 plus the $500 interest earned and the inflation rate during the year has been 10 percent.

The real value of $10,500 adjusted for loss of purchasing power is only $9,500 [$10,000 + ($10,000 × −0.05)]. Finally, it is important to note that the nominal interest rate is never negative, but the real interest rate can be either positive or negative.

> When the real rate of interest is negative, lenders and savers lose because interest earned does not keep up with the inflation rate.

CONCLUSION

7-2d Inflation in Other Countries

Exhibit 5 reveals that inflation rates vary widely among nations. In 2016, Angola, Sudan, and other countries experienced very high rates of inflation. In contrast, the United States had a relatively low inflation rate of 1.3 percent.

GLOBAL ECONOMICS

EXHIBIT 5 Annual Inflation Rates in Selected Countries, 2016

As shown by the bars, inflation was a serious problem in 2016 for Angola, Sudan, and other countries. The United States experienced a low inflation rate of 1.3 percent.

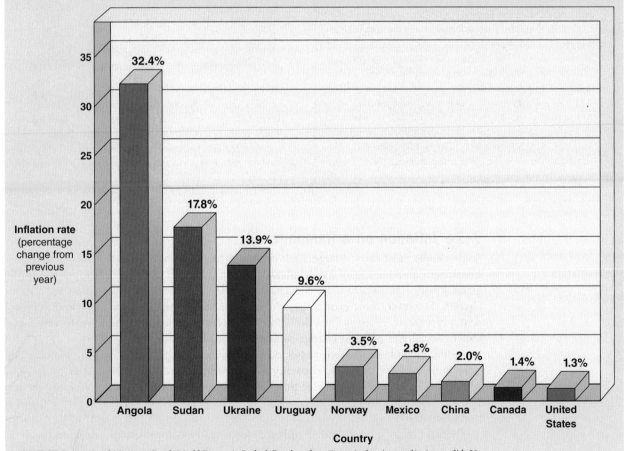

SOURCE: International Monetary Fund, *World Economic Outlook Database*, http://www.imf.org/external/ns/cs.aspx?id=28.

GLOBAL ECONOMICS

Who Wants to Be a Trillionaire?

Applicable Concept: Hyperinflation

The following articles are two historical examples of hyperinflation:

The first is a *Wall Street Journal* article from 1985 that describes hyperinflation in La Paz, Bolivia; the second article is from the San Francisco Chronicle article that reported on hyperinflation in Zimbabwe. The *Wall Street Journal* states:

A courier stumbles into Banco Boliviano Americano, struggling under the weight of a huge bag of money he is carrying on his back. He announces that the sack contains 32 million pesos, and a teller slaps on a notation to that effect. The courier pitches the bag into a corner. "We don't bother counting the money anymore," explains Max Lowes Stah, a loan officer standing nearby. "We take the client's word for what's in the bag." Pointing to the courier's load, he says, "That's a small deposit." At that moment the 32 million pesos—enough bills to stuff a mail sack—were worth only $500. Today, less than two weeks later, they are worth at least $180 less. Life's like that with quadruple-digit inflation....

Prices go up by the day, the hour or the customer. If the pace continues all year it would mean an annual rate of 116,000 percent. The 1,000-peso bill, the most commonly used, costs more to print than it purchases. To purchase an average-size television set with

1,000-peso bills, customers have to haul money weighing more than 68 pounds into the showroom. Inflation makes use of credit cards impossible here, and merchants generally can't take checks, either. Restaurant owners often covered their menus with cellophane and changed prices several times daily using a dry-erase marker.[1]

© Taigi/Shutterstock.com

7-2e Inflation on a Rampage

Hyperinflation
An extremely rapid rise in the general price level.

Some people must carry a large stack of money to pay for a chocolate bar because of the disastrous consequences of hyperinflation. **Hyperinflation** is an extremely rapid rise in the general price level. There is no consensus on when a particular rate of inflation becomes "hyper." However, most economists would agree that an inflation rate of about 100 percent per year or more is hyperinflation. Runaway inflation is conducive to rapid and violent social and political change stemming from four causes.

First, individuals and businesses develop an *inflation psychosis*, causing them to buy quickly today in order to avoid paying even more tomorrow. Everyone feels pressure to spend their earnings before their purchasing power deteriorates. Regardless of whether you are paid once, twice, or any number of times per day, you will be eager to spend it immediately.

Second, huge unanticipated inflation jeopardizes debtor–lender contracts, such as credit cards, home mortgages, life insurance policies, pensions, bonds, and other forms

And the *San Francisco Chronical* article shows:

What is happening is no laughing matter. (In 2008, the annual inflation rate was 231 million percent.) For untold numbers of Zimbabweans, bread, margarine, meat and even the morning cup of tea have become unimaginable luxuries. The city suffers rolling electrical blackouts because the state cannot afford parts or technicians to fix broken down power turbines. Mounds of uncollected garbage pile up on the streets of slums. Public-school fees and other ever-rising government surcharges have begun to exceed the monthly incomes of many urban families lucky enough to work. Those with spare cash put it not in banks, but in gilt-edged investments like bags of cornmeal and sugar, guaranteed not to lose their value.[2]

In 2010, Zimbabwe's central bank announced the introduction of new 100 trillion, 50 trillion, 20 trillion, and 10 trillion notes. Want to be a trillionaire? Buy Zimbabwe notes.

Hyperinflation is not just a thing of the past. Currently, Venezuela is projected to see its inflation rate skyrocket from 255 percent in 2016 to 800 percent in 2017, and then to around 2,000 percent rate in 2018, and 3,500 percent in 2019. All the while, its GDP is falling precipitously, creating untold stories of human hardship.[3]

A *Newsweek* article made the following thoughtful observation:

Hyperinflation is the worst economic malady that can befall a nation, wiping out the value of money, savings, assets, and thus work. It is worse even than a deep recession. Hyperinflation robs you of what you have now (savings), whereas a recession robs you of what you might have had (higher standards of living if the economy had grown). That's why it so often toppled governments and produced revolution. Recall that it was not the Great Depression that brought the Nazis to power in Germany but rather hyperinflation, which destroyed the middle class of that country by making its savings worthless.[4]

ANALYZE THE ISSUE

1. Can you relate inflation psychosis to these excerpts? Give an example of a debtor–lender relationship that is jeopardized by hyperinflation.

2. Explain why the workers in Bolivia were striking, even though wages rose at an annual rate of 1,500 percent. Do you see any connection between hyperinflation and the political system?

1. Sonia L. Nazario, "When Inflation Rate Is 116,000 Percent, Prices Change by the Hour," *The Wall Street Journal,* February 7, 1985, p. 1.
2. Michale Wines, "Zimbabwe: Inflation Capitol," *San Francisco Chronicle,* May 2, 2006, p. A-2.
3. International Monetary Fund, *World Economic Outlook Database,* http://www.imf.org/external/ns/cs.aspx?id=28.
4. Fareed Zakaria, "Is This the End of Inflation? Turkey's Currency Crisis May Be the Last Battle in the Global War Against Hyperinflation," *Newsweek,* March 19, 2001, p. 38.

of savings. For example, if nominal interest rates rise unexpectedly in response to higher inflation, borrowers find it more difficult to make their monthly payments.

Third, hyperinflation sets a wage-price spiral in motion. A **wage-price spiral** occurs in a series of steps when increases in nominal wage rates are passed on in higher prices, which, in turn, result in even higher nominal wage rates and prices. A wage-price spiral continues when management believes it can boost prices faster than the rise in labor costs. As the cost of living moves higher, however, labor must again demand even higher wage increases. Each round yields higher and higher prices as wages and prices chase each other in an upward spiral.

Fourth, because the future rate of inflation is difficult or impossible to anticipate, people turn to more speculative investments that might yield higher financial returns. To hedge against the high losses of purchasing power from hyperinflation, funds flow into gold, silver, stamps, jewels, art, antiques, and other currencies, rather than into new factories, machinery, and technological research that expand an economy's production possibilities curve.

Wage-price spiral
A situation that occurs when increases in nominal wage rates are passed on in higher prices, which, in turn, result in even higher nominal wage rates and prices.

YOU'RE THE ECONOMIST

Applicable Concepts: Demand-Pull and Cost-Push Inflation

Why the High Cost of Health Care?

The inflation rate for health care in the United States has consistently exceeded the overall rate of inflation over the last half century. According to the Bureau of Labor Statistics, in 2016, the costs of health care increased by 4 percent, while the overall inflation rate was 1.3 percent. Americans now spend almost twice as much on health care compared to other developed nations.[1] Our per capita spending is currently over $9,000 per year, bringing total U.S. spending on health care to about $3 trillion a year. And the growth rate on healthcare spending in the U.S. continues to spiral upward at a faster rate than the growth rate of the economy at large. Healthcare expenditures were 9 percent of GDP in 1980, but have skyrocketed to over a 17 percent share of GDP in 2016.

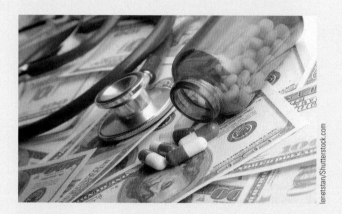

lenetstan/Shutterstock.com

The accelerating costs of health care has created many challenges for the U.S. economy. It impacts government, businesses, and households alike. About half of all healthcare dollars are spent by government as it provides for Medicare, Medicaid, and veteran's healthcare needs. The sheer magnitude of these expenditures ensures that when more is spent on these programs, less money is available for other programs, like on Social Security and national defense; unless taxes are increased to pay for these additional expenditures. Higher taxes would certainly put the squeeze on taxpayers' budgets. If taxes are not increased and other government programs are not cut, then government will be forced to run larger deficits, which are financed by borrowing, which will add to the national debt. None of these options are attractive. Businesses face challenges, too. Employers that do provide health insurance benefits to their workers face higher costs of production as health insurance premiums rise. This reduces their ability to compete in the global economy. Many businesses are cutting back on healthcare benefits provided to their workers for just this reason. Households are also hurt by rising healthcare costs. Increasingly individuals are having to pick up a larger share of financing their health insurance, and rising premiums puts a real pinch on the amount of other goods and services they

History reveals numerous hyperinflation examples. One of the most famous occurred during the 1920s in the German Weimar Republic. Faced with huge World War I reparations payments, the Weimar government simply printed money to pay its bills. By late 1923, the annual inflation rate in Germany had reached 35,000 percent per month. Prices rose frequently, sometimes increasing in minutes, and German currency became so worthless that it was used as kindling for stoves. No one was willing to make new loans, and credit markets collapsed. Wealth was redistributed because those who were heavily in debt easily paid their debts, and people's savings were wiped out.

Finally, hyperinflation is invariably the result of a government's ill-advised decision to increase a country's money supply too much. Moreover, hyperinflation is not a historical relic, as illustrated in the Global Economics article that appears on page 196.

7-3 DEMAND-PULL AND COST-PUSH INFLATION

Economists distinguish between two basic types of inflation, depending on whether it originates from the buyers' or the sellers' side of the market. The analysis presented in this section returns to the cause-and-effect relationship between total spending and the business cycle discussed in the previous chapter.

can afford to purchase. Worse yet, health insurance premiums continue to outpace wage growth resulting in declining real incomes.

What has caused this high rate of inflation for health care? Like the price of anything, it is a function of demand and supply. Simply put, demand has increased faster than supply over time. Demand has been rising due to many factors, including a growing and aging population, as well as rising incomes. Technological advances in medicine has also increased the demand for health care as many people seek out these opportunities to enhance their well-being. At the same time, the supply of hospitals, clinics, physicians, nurses, and medical technologists has not kept pace with the growth in demand.

What can be done to contain runaway healthcare costs? Policy recommendations are plentiful. But, if any measures are to be successful they will have to address the root causes. The following is a list of some more-commonly cited reasons for the high costs for health care.

- High administrative costs
- Rising drug costs
- "Defensive medicine," where unnecessary treatments are undertaken to minimize malpractice suits
- Overutilization of expensive specialists
- Overuse of medically unnecessary expensive technology

- Price-gouging by hospitals and nursing homes, as well as drug and insurance companies
- Fraud and abuse of Medicare and Medicaid

Complicating any attempts at cost containment is the presence of two other important goals common to all countries' healthcare systems. First, there is the desire to maximize accessibility to health care, to ensure that those who need health care will have access to it in a timely and appropriate manner. Second, everyone wants to maximize public health outcomes, like extending average life expectancy, minimizing infant mortality rates, and a whole host of other public health goals. The catch is that there is a trade-off between the goals of minimizing costs, maximizing accessibility, and maximizing public health outcomes. Nevertheless, any country's healthcare system is often judged based on its ability to achieve these goals.

ANALYZE THE ISSUE

1. Which of the causes of healthcare inflation discussed here could be considered demand-pull causes? Which are elements of cost-push inflation?
2. Can you think of any other causes for the rising costs of health care?

---

1. Organization for Economic Co-operation and Development, *OECD Health Statistics*, http://www.oecd-ilibrary.org/social-issues-migration-health/data/oecd -health-statistics_health-data-en.

7-3a Demand-Pull Inflation

Perhaps the most familiar type of inflation is **demand-pull inflation**, which is a rise in the general price level resulting from an excess of total spending (demand). Demand-pull inflation is often expressed as "too much money chasing too few goods." When sellers are unable to supply all the goods and services buyers demand, sellers respond by raising prices. In short, the general price level in the economy is "pulled up" by the pressure from buyers' total expenditures.

Demand-pull inflation
A rise in the general price level resulting from an excess of total spending (demand).

Demand-pull inflation occurs at or close to full employment, when the economy is operating at or near full capacity. Recall that at full employment, all but the frictionally and structurally unemployed are working and earning income. Therefore, total, or aggregate demand for goods and services is high. Businesses find it profitable to expand their plants and production to meet the buyers' demand, but cannot in the short run. As a result, national output remains fixed, and prices rise as buyers try to outbid one another for the limited supply of goods and services. If total spending subsides, so will the pressure on the available supply of products, and prices will not rise as rapidly or may even fall.

A word of caution: Consumers may not be the only villain in the demand-pull story. Recall that total aggregate spending includes consumer spending (*C*), business investment (*I*), government spending (*G*), and net exports (*X–M*). Even foreigners may contribute to inflation by bidding up the price of U.S. exports.

7-3b Cost-Push Inflation

An excess of total spending is not the only possible explanation for rising prices. For example, suppose the Organization of the Petroleum Exporting Countries (OPEC) sharply increases the price of oil. This action means a significant increase in the cost of producing goods and services. The result could be cost-push inflation. **Cost-push inflation** is a rise in the general price level resulting from an increase in the cost of production.

Cost-push inflation
An increase in the general price level resulting from an increase in the cost of production.

The source of cost-push inflation is not always such a dramatic event as an OPEC price hike. Any sharp increase in costs to businesses can be a potential source of cost-push inflation. This means that upward pressure on prices can be caused by cost increases for labor, raw materials, construction, equipment, borrowing, and so on. Businesses can also contribute to cost-push inflation by raising prices to increase profits.

The influence of *expectations* on both demand-pull and cost-push inflation is an important consideration. Suppose buyers see prices rise and believe they should purchase that new house or car today before these items cost much more tomorrow. At or near full employment, this demand-pull results in a rise in prices. On the suppliers' side, firms might expect their production costs to rise in the future, so they raise prices in anticipation of the higher costs. The result is cost-push inflation.

Here you should take note of coming attractions. The chapter on aggregate demand and supply develops a modern macro model that you can use to analyze with more precision the factors that determine national output, employment, and the price level. In particular, the last section of this chapter applies the aggregate demand and supply model to the concepts of demand-pull and cost-push inflation. Also, the chapter on monetary policy will discuss the theory that inflation is the result of increases in the money supply in excess of increases in the production of goods and services.

Key Concepts

Inflation	Disinflation	Nominal interest rate	Wage-price spiral
Deflation	Nominal income	Real interest rate	Demand-pull inflation
Consumer price index (CPI)	Real income	Adjustable-rate mortgage (ARM)	Cost-push inflation
Base year	Wealth	Hyperinflation	

Summary

- **Inflation** is an increase in the general (average) price level of goods and services in the economy.

- **Deflation** is a decrease in the general level of prices. During the early years of the Great Depression, there was deflation, and the CPI declined at about a double-digit rate.

- The **consumer price index (CPI)** is the most widely known price-level index. It measures the cost of purchasing a market basket of goods and services by a typical household during a time period relative to the cost of the same bundle during a base year. The annual rate of inflation is computed using the following formula:

Annual rate of inflation =

$$\frac{\text{CPI in given year} - \text{CPI in previous year}}{\text{CPI in previous year}} \times 100$$

- The **base year** is chosen as a reference point for comparison with some earlier or later year.

- **Disinflation** is a reduction in the inflation rate. This does not mean that prices were falling, only that the inflation rate fell.

- The *inflation rate* determined by the CPI is criticized because (1) it is not representative, (2) it has difficulty adjusting for quality changes, and (3) it ignores the relationship between price changes and the importance of items in the market basket.

- **Nominal income** is income measured in actual money amounts. Measuring your purchasing power requires converting nominal income into **real income**, which is nominal income adjusted for inflation.

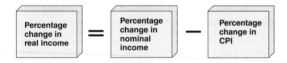

- **Wealth** is the value of the stock of assets owned at some point in time.

- The **nominal interest rate** is the actual rate of interest earned over a period of time. The **real interest rate** is the *nominal interest rate* adjusted for inflation. If real interest rates are negative, lenders incur losses.

- An **adjustable-rate mortgage** is a home loan that adjusts the nominal interest rate to changes in an index rate, such as rates on Treasury securities that reflect changes in inflation.

- **Hyperinflation** can seriously disrupt an economy by causing inflation psychosis, credit market collapses, a wage-price spiral, and speculation. A **wage-price spiral** occurs when increases in nominal wages cause higher prices, which, in turn, cause higher wages and prices.

- **Demand-pull inflation** is caused by upward pressure on prices originating from the buyers' side of the market. In contrast, **cost-push inflation** is caused by upward pressure on prices originating from the sellers' side of the market.

Summary of Conclusion Statements

- Inflation is an increase in the overall average level of prices and not an increase in the price of any specific product.

- People whose nominal incomes rise faster than the rate of inflation gain purchasing power, while people whose nominal incomes do not keep pace with inflation lose purchasing power.

- When the real rate of interest is negative, lenders and savers lose because interest earned does not keep up with the inflation rate.

Study Questions and Problems

Please see Appendix A for answers to the odd-numbered questions. Your instructor has access to the answers for even-numbered questions.

1. Consider this statement: "When the price of a good or service rises, the inflation rate rises." Do you agree or disagree? Explain.

2. Suppose, in the base year, a typical market basket purchased by an urban family cost $250. In Year 1, the same market basket cost $950.

What is the consumer price index (CPI) for Year 1? If the same market basket cost $1,000 in Year 2, what is the CPI for Year 2? What was the Year 2 rate of inflation?

3. What are three criticisms of the CPI?

4. Suppose you earned $100,000 in a given year. Calculate your real income, assuming the CPI is 200 for this year.

5. Explain how a person's purchasing power can decline in a given year even though he or she received a salary increase.

6. Who loses from inflation? Who wins from inflation?

7. Suppose you borrow $100 from a bank at 5 percent interest for one year and the inflation rate that year is 10 percent. Was this loan advantageous to you or to the bank?

8. Suppose the annual nominal rate of interest on a bank certificate of deposit is 12 percent. What would be the effect of an inflation rate of 13 percent?

9. When the economy approaches full employment, why does demand-pull inflation become a problem?

10. How does demand-pull inflation differ from cost-push inflation?

11. Explain this statement: "If everyone expects inflation to occur, it will."

 CHECKPOINT ANSWERS

The College Education Price Index

$$2015 \text{ college education price index} = \frac{\text{market basket cost at 2015 prices}}{\text{market basket cost at base-year (2015) prices}} \times 100$$

$$= \frac{\$11,650}{\$11,650} \times 100 = 100$$

$$2016 \text{ college education price index} = \frac{\text{market basket cost at 2016 prices}}{\text{market basket cost at base-year (2015) prices}} \times 100$$

$$= \frac{\$12,600}{\$11,650} \times 100 = 108.1$$

$$\text{Percentage change in price level of college education} = \frac{108.1 - 100}{100} \times 100 = 8.1\%$$

If you said the price of a college education increased 8.1 percent in 2016, **YOU ARE CORRECT**.
To update this calculation, click on the CPI Inflation Calculator athttps://data.bls.gov/cgi-bin/cpicalc.pl.

What Is the Real Price of Gasoline?

$$\text{Average gasoline price in 2016 dollars} = \$1.35 \times \frac{240.0}{90.9} = \$3.56$$

If you said the price of $1.35 per gallon for gasoline in 1981 was $3.56 per gallon in 2016 after adjusting for inflation over these years, **YOU ARE CORRECT**.
To update this calculation, click on the CPI Inflation Calculator at http://data.bls.gov/cgi-bin/cpicalc.pl.

Sample Quiz

Please see Appendix B for answers to Sample Quiz questions.

1. Inflation is defined as an increase in
   a. real wages of workers.
   b. real GDP.
   c. the average price level.
   d. all consumer products.

2. Inflation is measured by an increase in
   a. homes, autos, and basic resources.
   b. prices of all products in the economy.
   c. the consumer price index (CPI).
   d. None of the answers above are correct.

3. Which one of the following groups benefits from inflation?
   a. Borrowers
   b. Savers
   c. Landlords
   d. Lenders

4. Price indexes such as the CPI are calculated using a base year. The term *base year* refers to
   a. the first year that price data are available.
   b. any year in which inflation is higher than 5 percent.
   c. the most recent year in which the business cycle hit the trough.
   d. an arbitrarily chosen reference year.

5. If the consumer price index (CPI) in Year 1 was 200 and the CPI in Year 2 was 215, the rate of inflation is
   a. 215 percent.
   b. 15 percent.
   c. 5 percent.
   d. 7.5 percent.
   e. 8 percent.

6. Which of the following statements is true?
   a. Deflation is an increase in the general level of prices.
   b. The consumer price index (CPI) measures changes in the average prices of consumer goods and services.
   c. Disinflation is an increase in the rate of inflation.
   d. Real income is the actual number of dollars received over a period of time.

7. Suppose the price of bananas rises over time and consumers respond by buying fewer bananas. This situation contributes to which bias in the consumer price index?
   a. Substitution bias
   b. Transportation bias
   c. Quality bias
   d. Indexing bias

8. Deflation means a decrease in
   a. the rate of inflation.
   b. the prices of all products in the economy.
   c. homes, autos, and basic resources.
   d. the general level of prices in the economy.

9. Real income in Year X is equal to
   a. $\dfrac{\text{Year } X \text{ nominal income}}{\text{Year } X \text{ real GDP}}$.
   b. $\dfrac{\text{Year } X \text{ nominal income}}{\text{Year } X \text{ real output}} - 100$.
   c. $\dfrac{\text{Year } X \text{ nominal income}}{\text{CPI}/100}$.
   d. Year X nominal income $\times$ CPI.

10. The real interest rate is defined as the
    a. actual interest rate.
    b. fixed rate on consumer loans.
    c. nominal interest rate minus the inflation rate.
    d. expected interest rate minus the inflation rate.

11. If the inflation rate exceeds the nominal rate of interest,
    a. the real interest rate is negative.
    b. lenders lose.
    c. savers lose.
    d. All of the above answers are correct.

12. Suppose you place $10,000 in a retirement fund that earns a nominal interest rate of 8 percent. If you expect inflation to be 5 percent or lower, then you are expecting to earn a real interest rate of at least
    a. 1.6 percent.
    b. 3 percent.

c. 4 percent.

d. 5 percent.

13. Which of the following can create demand-pull inflation?

a. Excessive aggregate spending

b. Sharply rising oil prices

c. Higher labor costs

d. Recessions and depressions

14. Which of the following statements is true?

a. Demand-pull inflation is caused by excess total spending.

b. Cost-push inflation is caused by an increase in resource costs.

c. If nominal interest rates remain the same and the inflation rate falls, real interest rates increase.

d. If real interest rates are negative, lenders incur losses.

e. All of these answers are correct.

15. Cost-push inflation is due to

a. labor cost increases.

b. energy cost increases.

c. raw material cost increases.

d. All of the above answers are correct.

16. During periods of hyperinflation, which of the following is the most likely response of consumers?

a. Save as much as possible

b. Spend money as fast as possible

c. Invest as much as possible

d. Lend money

17. The base year in the consumer price index (CPI) is

a. given a value of zero.

b. a year chosen as a reference for prices in all other years.

c. always the first year in the current decade.

d. established by law.

18. Deflation

a. was prevalent during the oil shocks of the 1970s.

b. will cause consumers' purchasing power to shrink under current trends.

c. has been persistent in the U.S. economy since the Great Depression.

d. refers to none of these answers.

19. As the price of gasoline rose during the 1970s, consumers cut back on their use of gasoline relative to other consumer goods. This situation contributed to which bias in the consumer price index?

a. Substitution bias

b. Transportation bias

c. Quality bias

d. Indexing bias

20. If the rate of inflation in a given time period turns out to be lower than lenders and borrowers anticipated, then the effect will be a

a. redistribution of wealth from borrowers to lenders.

b. redistribution of wealth from lenders to borrowers.

c. net loss in purchasing power for lenders relative to borrowers.

d. net gain in purchasing power for borrowers relative to lenders.

PART 3

Macroeconomics Fundamentals

This road map feature helps you tie together material in the part as you travel the Economic Way of Thinking Highway. The following are review questions listed by chapter from the previous part. The key concept in each question is given for emphasis, and each question or set of questions concludes with an interactive game to reinforce the concepts. The correct answers to the multiple choice questions are given in Appendix C. If your instructor has included MindTap in your course, visit MindTap to play the interactive Causation Chain Game.

Chapter 5: Gross Domestic Product

1. Key Concept: Gross Domestic Product

Which of the following items is included in the calculation of GDP?

a. Purchase of 100 shares of Apple stock.
b. Purchase of a used car.
c. The value of a homemaker's services.
d. Sale of Gulf War military surplus.
e. None of the above would be included.

2. Key Concept: Expenditure Approach

Using the expenditure approach, GDP equals

a. $C + I + G + (X - M)$.
b. $C + I + G + (X + M)$.
c. $C + I - G + (X - M)$.
d. $C + I + G - (X - M)$.

3. Key Concept: GDP Shortcomings

If the underground economy is sizable, then GDP will

a. understate the economy's performance.
b. overstate the economy's performance.
c. fluctuate unpredictably.
d. accurately reflect this underground activity.

4. Key Concept: Real GDP

The equation for determining real GDP for year X is

a. $\dfrac{\text{nominal GDP for year } X}{\text{average nominal GDP}}$.

b. $\dfrac{\text{nominal GDP for year } X}{\text{GDP for year } X} - 100$.

c. $\dfrac{\text{nominal GDP for year } X}{\text{GDP chain price index for year } X} \times 100$.

d. $\dfrac{\text{nominal GDP for year } X}{\text{average family income } X} \times 100$.

Chapter 6: Business Cycles and Unemployment

5. Key Concept: Business Cycle

A business cycle is the

a. period of time in which expansion and contraction of economic activity are equal.
b. period of time in which there are three phases which are: peak, depression, and expansion.
c. recurring growth and decline in real GDP.
d. period of time in which a business is established and ceases operations.

6. Key Concept: Business Cycle

A business cycle is the period of time in which

a. a business is established and ceases operations.
b. there are four phases which are: peak, recession, trough, and expansion.
c. the price level varies with real GDP.
d. expansion and contraction of economic activity are equal.
e. None of the answers above are correct.

7. Key Concept: Unemployment

John Steinbeck's *Cannery Row* describes a character who takes his own life because of poor job prospects. If he was an unemployed person who gave up looking for work, he would be considered

a. chronically unemployed.
b. a discouraged worker.
c. a member of the labor force.
d. frictionally unemployed.

8. Key Concept: Unemployment

Consider a broom factory that permanently closes because of foreign competition. If the broom factory's workers cannot find new jobs because their skills are no longer marketable, then they are classified as

a. a seasonally unemployed.
b. frictionally unemployed.

c. structurally unemployed.
d. cyclically unemployed.

Chapter 7: Inflation

9. Key Concept: Inflation

Inflation is measured by an increase in

a. homes, autos, and basic resources.
b. prices of all products in the economy.
c. the consumer price index (CPI).
d. None of the answers above are correct.

10. Key Concept: Consumer Price Index Bias

As the price of gasoline rose during the 1970s, consumers cut back on their use of gasoline relative to other consumer goods. This situation contributed to which bias in the consumer price index?

a. Substitution bias
b. Transportation bias
c. Quality bias
d. Indexing bias

11. Key Concept: Real Income

Real income in Year X is equal to

a. $\dfrac{\text{Year } X \text{ nominal income}}{\text{Year } X \text{ real GDP}} \times 100.$

b. $\dfrac{\text{Year } X \text{ nominal income}}{\text{Year } X \text{ real output}} \times 100.$

c. $\dfrac{\text{Year } X \text{ nominal income}}{\text{CPI}/100}.$

d. Year X nominal income $\times$ CPI.

12. Key Concept: Cost-push Inflation

Cost-push inflation is due to

a. labor cost increases.
b. energy cost increases.
c. raw material cost increases.
d. All of these answers are correct.

PART 4

Macroeconomics Theory and Policy

This part begins with two chapters that present a theoretical model originating in a book published in 1936 by British economist John Maynard Keynes. The purpose of the Keynesian model is to understand the causes and cures of the Great Depression. The next chapter explains another theoretical macro model based on aggregate demand and aggregate supply. The following chapter discusses the federal government's taxing and spending policies, and the next chapter explains actual data measures of government spending and taxation patterns. The part concludes with a chapter on hotly debated topics: federal deficits, surpluses, and the national debt.

CHAPTER 8

The Keynesian Model

CHAPTER PREVIEW

In U.S. history, the 1920s are known as the "Roaring 20s." It was a time of optimism and prosperity. The spirit of the times was captivated in the lyrics of a popular song of the day: *Nothing but blue skies do I see*. Between 1920 and 1929, real GDP rose by 42 percent. Stock prices soared year after year and made many investors rich. As business boomed, companies invested in new factories, and the U.S. economy was a job-creating machine. People bought fine clothes, had parties, and danced the popular Charleston. Then the business cycle took an abrupt downturn on October 29, 1929, Black Tuesday. The most severe recession in recent U.S. history had begun. During the Great Depression, stock prices fell. Wages fell. Real output fell. Banks failed. Businesses closed their doors, and the unemployment rate soared to 25 percent. Unemployed workers would fight over a job, sell apples on the corner to survive, and walk the streets in bewilderment.

The misery of the Great Depression created a revolution in economic thought. Prior to the Great Depression, economists recognized that over the years, business downturns would interrupt the nation's prosperity, but they

believed these episodes were temporary. They argued that in a short time, the price system would automatically restore an economy to full employment without government intervention.

Why didn't the economy self-correct to its 1929 level of real GDP? What went wrong? The stage was set for a new idea offered by British economist **John Maynard Keynes** (pronounced "canes"). Keynes argued that the economy was not self-correcting and therefore could indeed remain below full employment indefinitely because of inadequate aggregate spending. Keynes's work not only explained the crash, but also offered cures requiring the government to play an active rather than a passive role in the economy.

Whether or not economists agree with Keynes's ideas, this famous economist still influences macroeconomics today. This chapter begins with a discussion of classical economic theory before Keynes. Then you will learn what determines the level of consumption and investment expenditures, which are the first two components of Keynes's aggregate expenditures model. In the next chapter, these two components are added to government spending and net exports to form the complete Keynesian aggregate expenditures model.

IN THIS CHAPTER, YOU WILL LEARN TO SOLVE THESE ECONOMICS PUZZLES:

- Why did economists believe the Great Depression was impossible?

- According to Keynes, what determines a family's spending for consumption?

- Why did Keynes believe that "animal spirits" and government policy were important to maintain full employment?

8-1 INTRODUCING CLASSICAL THEORY AND THE KEYNESIAN REVOLUTION

Prior to the Great Depression of the 1930s, a group of economists known as the **classical economists** dominated economic thinking.[1] The founder of the classical school of economics was Adam Smith (discussed in the chapter on economies in transition). Macroeconomics had not developed as a separate economic theory, and classical economics was therefore based primarily on microeconomic market equilibrium theory. The classical school of economics was mainstream economics from the 1770s to the Great Depression era. The classical economists believed in the *laissez-faire* "leave it alone" theory that our economy was self-regulating and would correct itself without government interference. The classical economists believed, as you studied in Chapter 4, that the forces of supply and demand naturally achieve full employment in the economy because flexible prices (including wages and interest rates) in competitive markets bring all markets to full-employment equilibrium. After a temporary adjustment period, markets always clear because firms sell all goods and services offered for sale. In short, recessions would naturally cure themselves because the capitalistic price system would automatically restore full employment. The classical model is explained in more detail in the chapter on aggregate demand and supply.

John Maynard Keynes
British economist (1883–1946) whose influential work offered an explanation of the Great Depression and suggested, as a cure, that the government should play an active role in the economy.

Classical economists
A group of economists whose theory dominated economic thinking from the 1770s to the Great Depression. They believed recessions would naturally cure themselves because the price system would automatically restore full employment.

> The classical economists believed that a continuing depression is impossible because markets eliminate persistent shortages or surpluses.

CONCLUSION

The simple idea known as Say's Law, developed in the early 1800s by Jean-Baptiste Say, convinced classical economists that a prolonged depression was impossible. **Say's Law** is the theory that supply creates its own demand. Say's Law was the cornerstone of classical economics. Simply put, this theory states that long-term underspending is impossible because the production of goods and services (supply) generates an equal amount of total spending (demand) for these goods and services. Recall the circular flow model explained in the chapter on GDP. Suppose a firm produces $1 worth of bread in the product market. This supply decision creates $1 of income to the household sector through the factor markets. In other words, Say's Law is a theory that a glut of unsold products causing workers to lose their jobs is a temporary problem because there is just the right amount of income in the economy to purchase all products produced without layoffs.

Say's Law
The theory that supply creates its own demand.

> In the classical view, unemployment is the result of a short-lived adjustment period in which wages and prices decline or people voluntarily choose not to work. Thus, there is a natural tendency for the economy to restore full employment over time.

CONCLUSION

---

[1]The classical economists included Adam Smith, J. B. Say, David Ricardo, John Stuart Mill, Thomas Malthus, Alfred Marshall, and others.

In 1936, seven years after the beginning of the Great Depression and three years before the beginning of World War II, John Maynard Keynes published *The General Theory of Employment, Interest, and Money.*[2] Keynes, a Cambridge University economist, wrote in a time of great uncertainty and instability. His book established macroeconomics as a separate field of economics and challenged the baffled classical economists by turning Say's Law upside down. Keynesian theory argues that "demand creates its own supply." Keynes explained that *aggregate expenditures (demand)* can be forever inadequate for an economy to achieve full employment. Aggregate expenditures are the sum of consumption (*C*), investment (*I*), government spending (*G*), and net exports (*X−M*). Aggregate expenditures are also known as *aggregate spending, aggregate demand,* or *total spending.* Recall from the chapter on GDP that *C*, *I*, *G*, and (*X−M*) are national accounting categories used to calculate GDP following the expenditures approach.

8-1a The Consumption Function

Consumption function
The graph or table that shows the amount households spend for goods and services at different levels of real disposable income.

What determines your family's spending for food, clothing, automobiles, education, and other consumer goods and services? According to Keynes, the most important factor is disposable income (personal income to spend after taxes; see Exhibit 9 in the chapter on GDP). Keynes argued it is a fundamental psychological law that if take-home pay increases, consumers will increase their spending and saving. Keynes's focus on the relationship between consumption and real disposable income is represented by the consumption function. The **consumption function** shows the amount households spend for goods and services at different levels of real disposable income. Recall from Exhibit 2 in the chapter on GDP that consumption is the largest single component of aggregate expenditures.

Exhibit 1 provides data on real disposable income (Y_d) in column (1), consumption (*C*) in column (2), and saving (*S*) in column (3) for a hypothetical economy. Since households spend each dollar of real disposable income either for consumption or for saving, the formula for saving is

$$S = Y_d - C$$

From this equation, it follows that

$$Y_d = C + S$$

Autonomous consumption
Consumption that is independent of the level of real disposable income.

Dissaving
The amount by which real personal consumption expenditures exceed real disposable income.

Note that if real disposable income is zero, consumption expenditures will be $1 trillion of autonomous consumption. **Autonomous consumption** is consumption spending that is independent of the level of real disposable income. It is the amount of consumption expenditures that occur even when real disposable income is zero. At other low levels of real disposable income, households also spend more on consumer goods and services than they earn in income during the year. If annual real disposable income is any level below $4 trillion, households dissave. **Dissaving** is the amount by which real personal consumption expenditures exceed real disposable income. Negative saving, or dissaving, is financed by drawing down previously accumulated financial assets, such as savings accounts, stocks, and bonds, or by borrowing. At a real disposable income

---

[2]John Maynard Keynes, *The General Theory of Employment, Interest, and Money,* New York, Harcourt, Brace, and World, 1936.

EXHIBIT 1 The Consumption Function

This exhibit shows the consumption function for a hypothetical economy. The break-even income is $4 trillion real disposable income, where households spend each dollar of real disposable income, $C = Y_d$, and savings are zero. Below $4 trillion, households spend more than their real disposable income by borrowing or withdrawing from past savings. Above the break-even income, households spend less than their real disposable income, and saving occurs. The marginal propensity to consume (MPC) is 0.75 because the slope of the consumption schedule shows that for each dollar increase in income (ΔY_d), consumption increases (ΔC) by 75 cents, and the remaining 25 cents is saved.

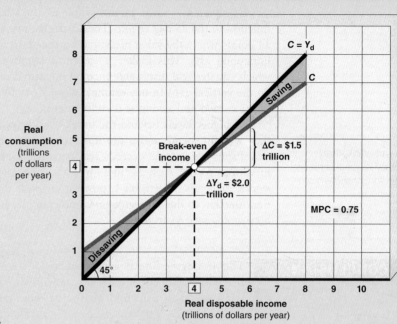

Consumption, Dissaving, Saving, MPC, and MPS Data

(1) Real disposable income (Y_d)	(2) Consumption (C)	(3) Dissaving (−) or saving (+) (S)	(4) Marginal propensity to consume (MPC) [$\Delta C/\Delta Y_d$ or $\Delta 2/\Delta 1$]	(5) Marginal propensity to save (MPS) [$\Delta S/\Delta Y_d$ or $\Delta 3/\Delta 1$]
$0	$1.00	−$1.00	—	—
1.00	1.75	−0.75	0.75	0.25
2.00	2.50	−0.50	0.75	0.25
3.00	3.25	−0.25	0.75	0.25
4.00	4.00	0	0.75	0.25
5.00	4.75	0.25	0.75	0.25
6.00	5.50	0.50	0.75	0.25
7.00	6.25	0.75	0.75	0.25
8.00	7.00	1.00	0.75	0.25

NOTE: All amounts are in trillions of dollars per year.

of $2 trillion per year, for example, families spend $2.5 trillion and thereby dissave $0.5 trillion.

Dissaving is shown in the graph as the vertical distance below the consumption function to the *45-degree line*. The 45-degree line is a geometric construct that represents all points where the value measured on the vertical axis equals the value measured on the horizontal axis. This makes it easier to identify the *break-even, or no-saving income*, which equates real disposable income measured on the horizontal axis and consumption on the vertical axis. In our example, $C = Y_d$ at $4 trillion, where households spend every dollar earned and saving is therefore zero.

At higher levels beyond the break-even income, households earn more income than they wish to spend, and a portion of income is saving. **Saving** is the amount by which real disposable income exceeds real personal consumption expenditures. Savings can be in various forms, such as funds in a passbook savings account, a certificate of deposit, stocks, or bonds. In Exhibit 1, positive saving is the vertical distance above the consumption function to the 45-degree line. For example, at a real disposable income of $8 trillion, households save $1 trillion.

Saving
The part of disposable income households do not spend for consumer goods and services.

CONCLUSION

The 45-degree line is a geometric construct. It indicates all points where real disposable income (measured on the horizontal axis) and real consumption (measured on the vertical axis) are equal. Consequently, the 45-degree line makes it easier to identify the break-even, or no-saving, income level.

8-1b Marginal Propensities to Consume and Save

Keynes argued that as income grows, so does consumption, but by less than income. This crucial concept is called the marginal propensity to consume. The **marginal propensity to consume (MPC)** is "the change" or "extra" in consumption resulting from a given change in real disposable income. Stated differently, the MPC is the ratio of the change in real consumption (ΔC) to the change in real disposable income (ΔY_d). The Greek letter Δ (delta) means "a change in." Mathematically,

Marginal propensity to consume (MPC)
The change in consumption resulting from a given change in real disposable income.

$$\text{MPC} = \frac{\textbf{change in consumption}}{\textbf{change in real disposable income}} = \frac{\Delta C}{\Delta Y_d}$$

As shown in column (4) of Exhibit 1, the MPC is 0.75. This means for every dollar increase (decrease) in disposable income (ΔY_d), consumption (ΔC) increases (decreases) 75 cents. In each model developed throughout this text, we assume the MPC is constant for all income levels. In our numerical example, real disposable income rises by $1 trillion between each level of income listed in column (1) of Exhibit 1, and consumption rises by $0.75 trillion. Mathematically,

$$\text{MPC} = \frac{\Delta C}{\Delta Y_d} = \frac{\textbf{\$0.75 trillion}}{\textbf{\$1 trillion}} = 0.75$$

Marginal propensity to save (MPS)
The change in saving resulting from a given change in real disposable income.

What do households do with an extra dollar of real disposable income if they do not spend it? There is only one other choice—they save it. The **marginal propensity to save (MPS)** is the change in saving resulting from a given change in real disposable income. That is, the

MPS is the ratio of the change in saving (ΔS) to the change in real disposable income (ΔY_d). Mathematically,

$$\text{MPS} = \frac{\textbf{change in saving}}{\textbf{change in real disposable income}} = \frac{\Delta S}{\Delta Y_d}$$

The MPS given in column (5) of Exhibit 1 is 0.25. Each dollar increase (decrease) in disposable income (ΔY_d) yields a rise (fall) of 25 cents in the amount of savings (ΔC). Mathematically,

$$\text{MPC} = \frac{\Delta S}{\Delta Y_d} = \frac{\textbf{\$0.25 trillion}}{\textbf{\$1 trillion}} = 0.25$$

As derived previously, $Y_d = C + S$, so it follows that $\Delta C + \Delta S = \Delta Y_d$. Dividing both sides of this equation by ΔY_d yields

$$\frac{\Delta C}{\Delta Y_d} + \frac{\Delta S}{\Delta Y_d} = \frac{\Delta Y_d}{\Delta Y_d}$$

or

$$\text{MPC} + \text{MPS} = 1$$

In our example, $0.75 + 0.25 = 1$, which means any change in real disposable income is divided between changes in consumption and changes in saving. Hence, if you know the MPC, you can calculate the MPS and vice versa.

8-1c Graphical Analysis of MPC

Exhibit 1 shows a graphic representation of the MPC. The consumption function has a positive slope because consumption spending increases with real disposable income. The MPC (slope) of the consumption function, C, for example, between the break-even income of \$4 trillion and \$6 trillion is measured by dividing $\Delta C = \$1.5$ trillion (the rise) by $\Delta Y_d = \$2.0$ trillion (the run). Since the MPC is constant, the ratio $\Delta C/\Delta Y_d$ between any two levels of real disposable income is 0.75. As a formula:

$$\textbf{Slope of consumption function} = \frac{\textbf{rise}}{\textbf{run}} = \frac{\Delta C}{\Delta Y_d} = \frac{\textbf{\$1.5 trillion}}{\textbf{\$2.0 trillion}} = 0.75$$

The points along the consumption function, C, in Exhibit 1 can be expressed by the following equation:

$$C = a + bY_d$$

where a is autonomous consumption (the value of the y-axis intercept) and b is the MPC (the slope of the line), which falls between 0 and 1. Keynes used this basic equation to derive consumption (C), and it is called the Keynesian consumption function.

Using this equation,

$$C = \$1 \textbf{ trillion} + 0.75 \ Y_d$$

For example, at $Y_d = \$4$ trillion,

$$C = \$1 \textbf{ trillion} + 0.75 \ (\$4 \textbf{ trillion})$$
$$C = \$4 \textbf{ trillion}$$

To demonstrate how changes in MPC affect the consumption function, Exhibit 2 shows two consumption functions with the same autonomous consumption of $1 trillion, but each has a different slope. C_1 has an MPC of 0.50, and C_2 has a larger MPC of 0.75. Thus, the higher the marginal propensity to consume, the steeper the consumption function.

How do changes in taxes cause movements along the consumption function? Suppose there is an income-tax cut. As a result, real disposable income (Y_d) increases and, in turn, induces higher consumption represented by an upward movement along the

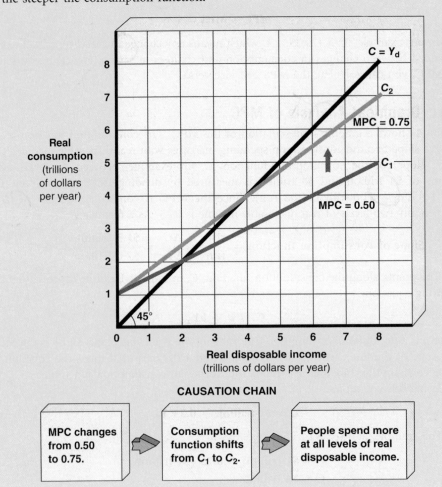

EXHIBIT 2 Consumption Functions for Two Marginal Propensities to Consume

The MPC is the slope of the consumption function. Here two consumption functions are shown for MPCs of 0.50 and 0.75. The autonomous consumption of $1 trillion is the same for both consumption functions. The higher the MPC, the steeper the consumption function.

CAUSATION CHAIN

| MPC changes from 0.50 to 0.75. | Consumption function shifts from C_1 to C_2. | People spend more at all levels of real disposable income. |

consumption function. An income-tax hike, on the other hand, reduces real disposable income and causes less consumption shown by a downward movement along the consumption function.

Exhibit 3 provides recent empirical evidence that supports Keynes's theoretical consumption function. Each point in the exhibit represents a pair of values for real personal consumption spending and real disposable income in the United States for years since 2000. Note that the relationship is close to an upward-sloping linear line. As real disposable income rises, real consumption spending also rises.

There is a direct relationship between changes in real disposable income and changes in consumption spending.

CONCLUSION

EXHIBIT 3 U.S. Personal Consumption and Disposable Income, 2000–2016

Keynes argued that a fundamental psychological law exists whereby real disposable income strongly influences real consumption. Actual data on real personal consumption expenditures and real disposable income are consistent with Keynes's theory.

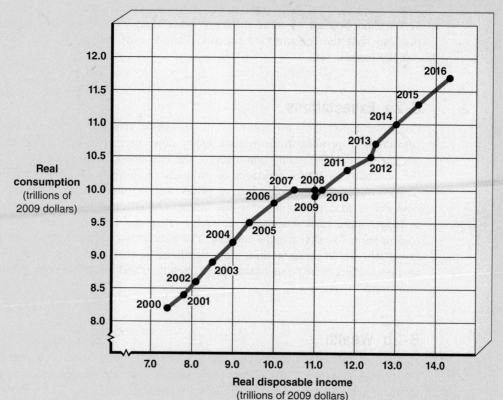

SOURCE: Bureau of Economic Research, *National Economic Accounts*, http://www.bea.gov/national/nipaweb/SelectTable.asp?Selected=Y, Tables 1.1.6 and 2.1.

What's Your MPC?
As your income increases over time, your marginal propensity to consume (MPC) can remain constant, or it can change. Would you expect your MPC to increase, decrease, or remain constant as your income increases throughout your career?

8-2 REASONS THE CONSUMPTION FUNCTION SHIFTS

Just as nonprice factors in the market supply and demand model, such as consumer tastes and income, shift the demand curve, changes in certain *nonincome* factors cause the consumption function to *shift*. Exhibit 4 uses hypothetical data to illustrate this difference in terminology. The sole cause of the change in consumption spending from $3 trillion (point *A*) to $4 trillion (point *B*), which is movement along the stable consumption schedule, C_1, is a $2 trillion change in the level of real disposable income. A change in a nonincome determinant, on the other hand, can cause the consumption schedule to shift upward from $C_1 = a_1 + bY_d$ to $C_2 = a_2 + bY_d$. As a result, households spend an extra $1 trillion $(a_2 - a_1)$ at each point along C_2. This means that the level of autonomous consumption has increased by $1 trillion from $1.5 trillion to $2.5 trillion because of some influence other than current Y_d. Nonincome variables that can shift the consumption function include expectations, wealth, the price level, and the interest rate.

8-2a Expectations

Consumer expectations are optimistic or pessimistic views of the future that can change consumption spending in the present. Expectations may involve the future inflation rate, the likelihood of becoming unemployed, the likelihood of receiving higher income, or the possibility of future shortages of products resulting from a war or other circumstances. Suppose households believe prices will be much higher next year and buy now, rather than paying more in the future. The effect of such expectations would be to trigger more current spending at each level of real disposable income and shift the consumption function parallel upward. The anticipation of a recession and fears about losing jobs would make families more tightfisted in their current spending. This means an autonomous decrease in consumption spending, and the consumption function shifts downward.

8-2b Wealth

Holding all other factors constant, the more wealth households accumulate, the more they spend at any level of real disposable income, causing the consumption function to shift upward. Wealth owned by households includes both *real* assets, such as homes, automobiles, and land, and *financial* assets, including cash, savings accounts, stocks, bonds, insurance policies, and pensions. Changes in prices of stocks, real estate, and other assets affect the value of wealth and, in turn, can shift the nation's consumption

EXHIBIT 4   Movement along and Shifts in the Consumption Function

The movement from real consumption spending of $3 trillion (point A) to $4 trillion (point B) along the stable consumption schedule, C_1, is a change in real consumption caused by a $2 trillion change in the level of real disposable income (Y_d). A change in a nonincome determinant causes the consumption function to shift. For example, some nonincome factors may increase autonomous consumption by $1 trillion from a_1 to a_2. As a result, the entire consumption function shifts upward from C_1 to C_2. Nonincome factors include changes in expectations, wealth, the price level, and the interest rate.

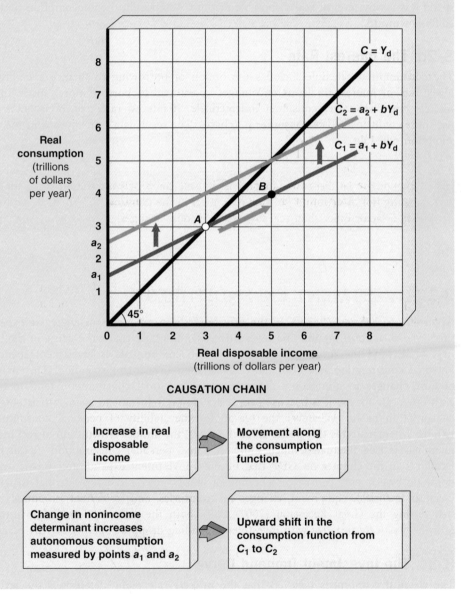

CAUSATION CHAIN

Increase in real disposable income	→	Movement along the consumption function

Change in nonincome determinant increases autonomous consumption measured by points a_1 and a_2	→	Upward shift in the consumption function from C_1 to C_2

Wealth effect
A shift in the consumption function caused by a change in the value of real and financial assets.

function. A so-called **wealth effect** occurred in the 1990s when stock values rose and households increased their spending. And during the financial turmoil in 2008, the fall in stock prices and housing prices was a significant factor in depressing consumption.

8-2c The Price Level

Any change in the general price level shifts the consumption schedule by reducing or enlarging the *purchasing power* of financial assets (wealth) with fixed nominal value. Suppose you own a $100,000 government bond or certificate of deposit. If the price level increases by, say, 10 percent, this same financial asset will buy approximately 10 percent less. Once the real value of financial wealth falls, families are poorer and spend less at any level of real disposable income. As a result, the consumption function shifts downward.

8-2d The Interest Rate

The consumption schedule includes the option of borrowing to finance spending. A lower rate of interest on loans encourages consumers to borrow more, and a higher interest rate discourages consumer indebtedness. If interest rates fall, households may use more credit to finance consumer purchases. The result is a shift upward in the consumption schedule.

CONCLUSION A change in real disposable income is the sole cause of a movement along the consumption function. A shift or relocation in the consumption schedule occurs when a factor other than real disposable income changes.

8-3 INVESTMENT EXPENDITURES

According to Keynes, changes in the private-sector components of aggregate expenditures (personal consumption and investment spending) are the major cause of the business cycle. And the more volatile of these two components is investment spending. Personal consumption has been more stable than investment spending. This may be because changes in nonincome determinants of personal consumption tend to offset each other. Or maybe it is because people are simply reluctant to change their personal consumption habits. Whatever the reason for the stability of personal consumption, Exhibit 5 demonstrates this point. Over the years, the annual growth rate of real investment has indeed fluctuated much more than real personal consumption. Recall from Exhibit 2 in the chapter on GDP that business investment expenditures (gross private domestic investment) consist of spending on newly produced nonresidential structures (such as factories), equipment, changes in inventories, and residential structures. Note that during the Great Recession (2007–2009), both the consumption and investment growth rates were negative with investment spending dropping sharply to −24 percent.

8-3a The Investment Demand Curve

The classical economists believed that the interest rate alone determines the level of investment spending. Keynes disputed this idea. Instead, Keynes argued that expectations

EXHIBIT 5   A Comparison of the Volatility of Real Investment and Real Consumption, 1965–2016

Real investment spending is highly volatile compared to real personal consumption. The data since 1965 confirm that the annual growth rate of real investment (gross private domestic investment) fluctuates much more than the annual growth rate of real personal consumption.

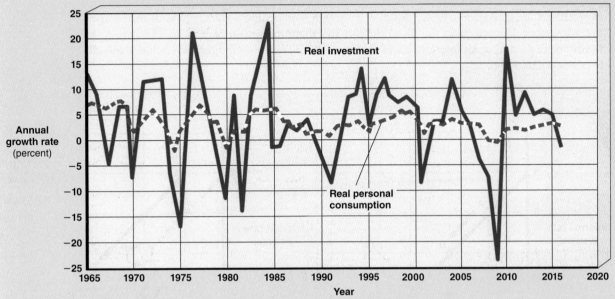

SOURCE: Bureau of Economic Analysis, *National Economic Accounts*, http://www.bea.gov/national/nipaweb/SelectTable.asp?Selected=Y, Table 1.1.1.

of future profits are the primary factor in determining investment, and the interest rate is the financing cost of any investment proposal.

Using a micro example to illustrate the investment decision-making process, suppose a consulting firm plans to purchase a new computer program for $1,000 that will be obsolete in a year. It anticipates that the new software will increase the firm's revenue by $1,100. Thus, assuming no taxes or expenses exist, the expected rate of return or profit is 10 percent. Now consider the impact of the cost of borrowing funds to finance the software investment. If the interest rate is less than 10 percent, the business will earn a profit, so it will make the investment expenditure to buy the computer program. On the other hand, a rate of interest higher than 10 percent means the software investment will be a loss, so this project will not be undertaken.

Understanding a single firm's investment decision from a micro perspective allows us to develop the investment demand curve from the macro vantage point. The **investment demand curve** shows the amount businesses spend for investment goods at different possible rates of interest. Exhibit 6 expresses the interest rate as annual percentages on the vertical axis. As shown in part (a), changes in the interest rate generate movements along the firm's investment demand curve. If the interest rate falls from, say, 6 percent at point *A* to 4 percent at point *B*, an additional $5 million of real investment spending occurs because *marginal* planned projects become profitable. Stated another way, as a

Investment demand curve
The curve that shows the amount businesses spend for investment goods at different possible rates of interest.

EXHIBIT 6 Movement along and a Shift in a Firm's Investment Demand

Part (a) shows that investment spending by a hypothetical business firm depends on the interest rate. Ceteris paribus, lowering the interest rate from 6 percent at point *A* to 4 percent at point *B* increases the quantity of real investment purchases from $5 million to $10 million during the year.

Keynes argued that investment spending is unstable because a change in volatile factors, such as expectations, technological change, capacity utilization, and business taxes, can shift the location of the investment demand curve. As shown in part (b), the initial investment demand curve, I_1, has shifted rightward to I_2, and at an interest rate of 4 percent, $5 million in additional investment spending occurs between points *B* and *C*.

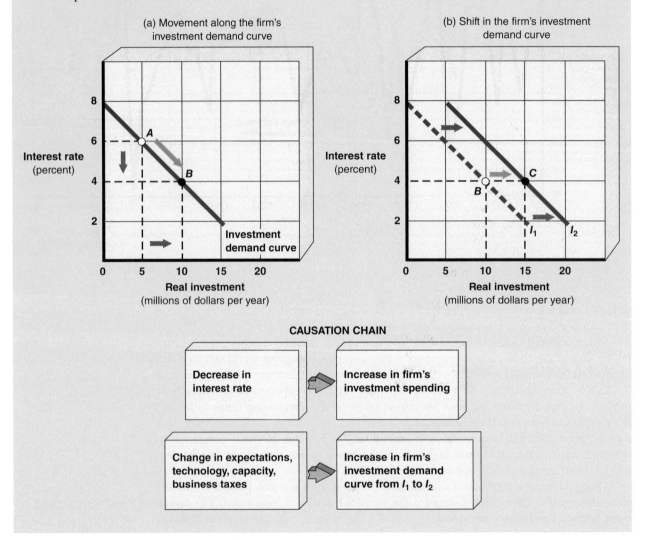

result of this fall in the rate of interest, the firm's real investment increases from $5 million to $10 million.

The relationship among the expected rate of profit, the interest rate, and investment follows this investment rule: *Businesses will undertake all planned investment projects for which the expected rate of profit exceeds or equals the interest rate.*

8-4 WHY INVESTMENT DEMAND IS UNSTABLE

Why did Keynes view investment spending as so susceptible to ups and downs? The reason is there are several volatile determinants that cause the investment demand curve to be quite unstable. In short, any factor that changes the expected rate of profit shifts the investment demand curve and thereby changes the investment spending component of aggregate expenditures. As shown in Exhibit 6(b), the initial investment demand curve, I_1, has shifted rightward to I_2, and at an interest rate of 4 percent, $5 million of additional investment spending occurs between points *B* and *C*. The next sections discuss major factors that can shift the investment demand curve.

8-4a Expectations

Keynes argued that swings in "animal spirits" cause volatile investment expenditures. Translated this means businesspersons are quite susceptible to moods of optimism and pessimism about future economic conditions. Their expectations about the future impacts estimates of future sales, future costs, and future profitability of investment projects. These forecasts involve a clouded crystal ball, requiring a degree of intuition or normative analysis. There are always many ever-changing factors, such as government spending and tax policies, world events, population growth, and stock market conditions that make forecasting difficult.

When a wave of pessimism becomes pervasive, businesspeople reduce their expectations for profitability at each rate of interest. Such a pessimistic attitude can become contagious and shift the investment demand curve leftward. This was the case during the Great Depression, when the outlook was dismal. At other times, such as during the 1990s, businesspersons become very optimistic and revise upward their expected rate of profit for investment at each interest rate. If so, the investment demand curve shifts rightward. Thus, Keynes viewed changes in business confidence (expectations) as a major cause of investment spending volatility.

8-4b Technological Change

Technological progress includes the introduction of new products and new ways of doing things. Robots, personal computers, iPhones, the Internet, and similar new inventions provide less costly ways of production. New technologies create a flurry of investment spending as firms buy the latest innovations in order to improve their production capabilities and remain competitive, thereby causing the investment demand curve to shift rightward.

8-4c Capacity Utilization

During the Great Depression and the Great Recession, many businesses operated at far less than full capacity. Capacity is defined as the maximum possible output of a firm or

YOU'RE THE ECONOMIST

Applicable Concept: Consumption and Investment

Does a Stock Market Crash Cause Recession?

The stock market soared during the "Roaring 20s." Lavish spending was in style as people enjoyed their new wealth. Then, on October 29, 1929, Black Tuesday, the stock market crashed. During the Great Depression, banks failed, businesses closed their doors, real GDP plummeted, and unemployment soared. Over the years, much debate has occurred over whether the 1929 stock market crash was merely a symptom or a major cause of the downturn. Evidence exists that the 1929 stock market crash only reflected an economic decline already in progress. For example, months before Black Tuesday, national production had already fallen.

The argument over the impact of a stock market crash on the economy was renewed in 2001. The National Association for Business Economics (NABE) was holding its annual meeting in the World Trade Center when disaster struck the building on September 11, 2001. "The chandeliers shook, we heard a concussive sound, and as we were herding out, we could see that one tower was burning," said Carl Tannenbaum, the chief economist of LaSalle Bank in Chicago, who was attending the meeting.[1] Just the day before, a panel of NABE economists predicted slow growth for the economy, but no recession. That forecast

© mdd/Shutterstock.com

became obsolete the moment the first plane hit. Analysts predicted a recession, and one reason was that they expected the stock market would dive as profit expectations fell due to uncertainty. Indeed, as a result of the September terrorist attacks, the stock market suffered its worst one-week loss since the Great Depression. In the immediate aftermath, equities losses were estimated to be an extraordinary $1.2 trillion in value.[2]

Prior to the September attacks, the Dow Jones Industrial Average had reached a high of about 11,500 in May, but it had already fallen almost 2,000 points to a low of 9,431 on September 10, 2001. During this period

an industry. When much of the nation's capital stock stands idle, firms have little incentive to buy more. As a result, the investment demand curve shifts far to the left. Conversely, firms may be operating their plants at a high rate of capacity utilization, and the outlook for sales growth is optimistic. To satisfy this anticipated greater demand for their products, firms will need to invest in more plants and equipment, and the investment demand curve shifts to the right.

8-4d Business Taxes

As explained earlier, changes in income taxes on individuals affect disposable income and the level of consumption. Similarly, taxes on business firms can shift the investment demand curve. Business decisions, in reality, depend on the expected *after-tax* rate of profit. An increase in business taxes therefore would lower profitability and shift the investment demand curve to the left. On the other hand, the U.S. government may want to encourage investment by allowing, say, a *tax credit* for new investment. A 10 percent *investment tax credit* means that if ExxonMobil decides to invest $10 million in a new plant, the corporation's tax bill to the IRS will be cut by $1 million. The effect

of time, the economy was plagued by the implosion of the dot-com companies and sharp declines in high-tech stocks. After the attacks, the stock market closed for the remainder of the week and reopened the following Monday, September 17, 2001, with the famous statue of the Wall Street Bull decorated with American flags and the National Guard patrolling the streets. The result of trading was a huge sell-off and another loss of 1,371 points during the week. Throughout the remainder of the year, the Dow Jones Industrial Average gradually rose toward its pre-September 11 levels, closing at 10,022 on December 31, 2001. Real GDP contracted at a 1.3 percent annual rate in the third quarter of 2001 and then rose in the final three months of 2001 by 1.7 percent, which was a surprisingly strong performance under the circumstances. The six-member panel at the National Bureau of Economic Research (NBER), which is considered the nation's arbiter of U.S. business cycles, declared in November 2001 that a recession had begun in March and ended eight months later in November of that year.

Stock market plunges are widely reported headline news. The latest major plunge occurred with the global financial collapse in October 2008. One result of these plunges is that many Americans feel poorer because of the threat to their life's savings. In only a few hours, spectacular paper losses reduce the wealth that people are counting on to pay for homes, automobiles, college tuition, or retirement. Although not all U.S. households own stock, everyone fears a steep downhill ride on the Wall Street roller coaster. If a stock market crash leads to a recession, it will cause layoffs and cuts in profit sharing and pension funds. Businesses fear that many families will postpone buying major consumer items in case they need their cash to tide them over the difficult economic times ahead. Reluctance of consumers to spend lowers aggregate demand, and, in turn, prices and profits fall. Falling sales and anxiety about a recession may lead many business executives to postpone modernization plans. Rather than buying new factories and equipment, businesses continue with used plants and machinery, which means lower private investment spending, employment, output, and income for the overall economy.

ANALYZE THE ISSUE Immediately following the attack on the United States on September 11, 2001, the stock market plunged and many observers predicted a recession. Using the consumption and investment functions, explain their predictions.

1. "Worldwide, Hope for Recovery Dims," *Business Week*, September 24, 2001, p. 42.
2. "Economy under Siege," *Fortune*, October 15, 2001, p. 86.

of this tax policy is that the government increases the profitability of new investment projects by 10 percent and the investment demand curve shifts to the right.

8-4e Investment as an Autonomous Expenditure

Assuming none of the above factors changes in the short run, Keynes argued that investment spending is an autonomous expenditure. An **autonomous expenditure** is spending that does not vary with the level of real disposable income. Stated simply, autonomous expenditures in the Keynesian model remain a fixed amount, regardless of the level of disposable income. Exhibit 7 shows how the rate of interest determines the aggregate level of autonomous investment for all firms in an economy, regardless of or external to the level of real disposable income. In part (a), at an interest rate of 4 percent, *all* businesses, when considered together, spend $1 trillion for capital goods and inventory. Part (b) shows that this $1 trillion in *aggregate* investment spending (when the interest rate is 4 percent) does not vary with changes in the level of real disposable income. However, if the rate of interest is lower, investment increases, and the horizontal investment spending curve shifts vertically upward. Alternatively, a higher rate of interest discourages investment and shifts the horizontal investment spending curve vertically downward.

Autonomous expenditure
Spending that does not vary with the level of real disposable income.

EXHIBIT 7 The Aggregate Investment Demand and Autonomous Investment Spending Curves

In part (a), the level of real investment for all firms in an economy is determined by the investment rule that all investment projects for which the expected rate of profit exceeds or equals the interest rate will be undertaken. If the interest rate is 4 percent, real autonomous investment will be $1 trillion, shown as point *A* on the investment demand curve, *I*.

In part (b), autonomous real investment expenditures are shown to be independent of the level of real disposable income per year. This means firms will collectively spend $1 trillion regardless of the level of real disposable income per year.

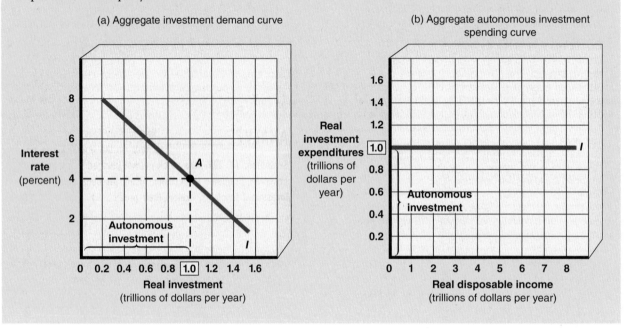

(a) Aggregate investment demand curve

(b) Aggregate autonomous investment spending curve

Key Concepts

John Maynard Keynes

Classical economists

Say's Law

Consumption function

Autonomous consumption

Dissaving

Saving

Marginal propensity to consume (MPC)

Marginal propensity to save (MPS)

Wealth effect

Investment demand curve

Autonomous expenditure

Summary

• **Say's Law** is the classical theory that "supply creates its own demand," and therefore, the Great Depression was impossible. Say's Law is the theory that the value of production generates an equal amount of income and, in turn, total spending. The classical economists rejected the argument that underconsumption is possible because they believed flexible prices, wages, and interest rates would quickly re-establish a balance between supply and demand.

- **John Maynard Keynes** rejected the classical theory that the economy quickly self-corrects to return the economy to full employment. The key in Keynesian theory is aggregate demand, rather than the classical economists' focus on aggregate supply. Unless aggregate spending is adequate, the economy can experience prolonged and severe unemployment.

- The **consumption function (C)** is determined by changes in the level of real disposable income. **Autonomous consumption** is consumption spending that occurs even if real disposable income equals zero. Changes in such nonincome determinants as expectations, wealth, the price level, and interest rates can cause shifts in the consumption function.

- The **marginal propensity to save (MPS)** is the change in saving associated with a given change in real disposable income. The MPS measures how much of an additional dollar of disposable income households will save.

- The **wealth effect** occurs when the value of households' assets increase (decrease). This causes people to spend more (less) at any level of real disposable income, and the consumption function shifts upward (downward).

- The **investment demand curve (I)** shows the amount businesses spend for investment goods at different possible rates of interest. The determinants of this schedule are the expected rate of profit and rate of interest. Shifts in the investment demand curve result from changes in expectations, technology, capacity utilization, and business taxes.

Consumption Function

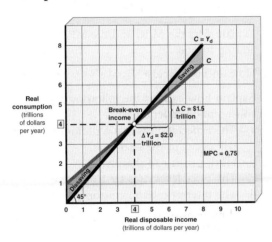

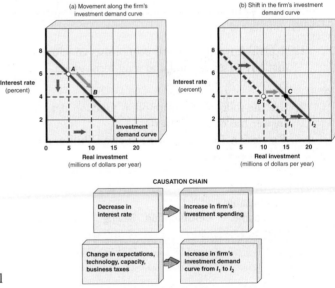

- **Dissaving** is the amount by which real personal consumption expenditures exceed real disposable income. **Saving** is the amount by which real disposable income exceeds real personal consumption expenditures.

- The **marginal propensity to consume (MPC)** is the change in consumption spending associated with a given change in real disposable income. The MPC tells how much of an additional dollar of disposable income households will spend for consumption.

- An **autonomous expenditure** is spending that does not vary with the level of real disposable income. The Keynesian model applies this simplifying assumption to investment. As a result, the aggregate autonomous investment spending curve is a fixed amount determined by the rate of profit and the interest rate.

Summary of Conclusion Statements

- The classical economists believed that a continuing depression is impossible because markets eliminate persistent shortages or surpluses.

- In the classical view, unemployment is the result of a short-lived adjustment period in which wages and prices decline or people voluntarily choose not to work. Thus, there is a natural tendency for the economy to restore full employment over time.

- The 45-degree line is a geometric construct. It indicates all points where real disposable income (measured on the horizontal axis) and real consumption (measured on the vertical axis) are equal. Consequently, the 45-degree line makes it easier to identify the break-even or no-saving income level.

- There is a direct relationship between changes in real disposable income and changes in consumption spending.

- A change in real disposable income is the sole cause of a movement along the consumption function. A shift or relocation in the consumption schedule occurs when a factor other than real disposable income changes.

Study Questions and Problems

Please see Appendix A for answers to the odd-numbered questions. Your instructor has access to the answers for even-numbered questions.

1. Explain how the classical economists concluded that Say's Law is valid and long-term unemployment is impossible.

2. Use the following consumption function data to answer the questions next.
   Keynesian Consumption Function (billions of dollars per year)

Real disposable income	Consumption	Saving	MPC	MPS
$100	$150	$___	___	___
200	200	___	___	___
300	250	___	___	___
400	300	___	___	___
500	350	___	___	___

   a. Calculate the saving schedule.
   b. Determine the marginal propensities to consume (MPC) and save (MPS).
   c. Determine the break-even income.
   d. What is the relationship between the MPC and the MPS?

3. Explain why the MPC and the MPS must always add up to one.

4. How do households "dissave"?

5. Explain how each of the following affects the consumption function:
   a. The expectation is that a prolonged recession will occur in the next year.
   b. Stock prices rise sharply.
   c. The price level rises by 10 percent.
   d. The interest rate on consumer loans rises sharply.
   e. Income taxes increase.

6. Your college is considering investing $6 million to add 10,000 seats to its football stadium. The athletic department forecasts it can sell all these extra seats at each game for a ticket price of $20 per seat, and the team plays six home games per year. If the school can borrow at an interest rate of 14 percent, should the school undertake this project? What would happen if the school expected a losing season and could sell tickets for only half of the 10,000 seats?

7. Why is the investment demand curve less stable than the consumption and saving schedules? What are the basic determinants that can shift the investment demand curve?

8. Suppose most business executives expect a slowdown in the economy. How might this situation affect the economy?

9. The levels of real disposable income and aggregate expenditures for a two-sector economy (consumption and investment) are given in the following table:

Real disposable income (trillions of dollars per year)	Consumption (C) (trillions of dollars per year)
$0	$3.00
1	3.25
2	3.50
3	3.75

Real disposable income (trillions of dollars per year)	Consumption (C) (trillions of dollars per year)
4	4.00
5	4.25
6	4.50
7	4.75
8	5.00

a. Construct a graph of the consumption function (C).

b. Determine the autonomous consumption, MPC, and MPS for this hypothetical economy.

c. What is the break-even income consumption of real disposable income?

d. What is the amount of dissavings at $2 trillion real disposable income and the savings at $7 trillion?

 CHECKPOINT ANSWERS

What's Your MPC?

Early in your career when your income is relatively low, you are likely to spend your entire income, and perhaps even dissave, just to afford necessities. During this stage of your life, your MPC will be close to 1. As your income increases and you have purchased the necessities, additional income can go to luxuries. If you become wealthier, you have a higher marginal propensity to save and consequently a lower marginal propensity to consume. If you said your MPC will probably decrease as your income increases, **YOU ARE CORRECT**.

Sample Quiz

Please see Appendix B for answers to Sample Quiz questions.

1. The popular theory prior to the Great Depression that the economy will automatically adjust to achieve full employment in the long run is
   a. supply-side economics.
   b. Keynesian economics.
   c. classical economics.
   d. mercantilism.

2. The French economist Jean-Baptiste Say transformed the equality of total output and total spending into a law that can be expressed as
   a. unemployment is not possible in the short run.
   b. demand and supply are never equal.
   c. supply creates its own demand.
   d. demand creates its own supply.

3. If the economy is experiencing less than full employment equilibrium, the Keynesian school recommends that the government
   a. do nothing to stimulate the economy.
   b. undertake fiscal policy to stimulate aggregate demand.
   c. undertake fiscal policy to stimulate aggregate supply.
   d. balance the budget to stimulate aggregate demand.

4. The school of thought that emphasizes the natural tendency for an economy to move toward a full employment equilibrium is known as the
   a. Keynesian school.
   b. supply-side school.
   c. noninterventionist school.
   d. classical school.

5. What is the title of the John Maynard Keynes's book published in 1936 that challenged the classical self-correction economic theory?
   a. *In the Long Run, We Are All Dead.*
   b. *Classical Economics Revised.*
   c. *General Theory of Employment, Interest, and Money.*
   d. *A Keynesian Approach to Economic Policy.*

6. What is the vertical intercept of the consumption function that represents the portion of consumption expenditure *not* associated with a level of disposable income?
   a. Consumption intercept
   b. Disposable income intercept
   c. Autonomous consumption
   d. Automatic consumption line

7. John Maynard Keynes's central proposition that a dollar increase in disposable income would increase consumption, but by less than the increase in disposable income, implies a marginal propensity to consume (MPC) that is
   a. greater than or equal to one.
   b. equal to one.
   c. less than one but greater than zero.
   d. negative.

8. The marginal propensity to consume (MPC) is the slope of the
   a. GDP curve.
   b. disposable income curve.
   c. consumption function.
   d. autonomous consumption curve.

9. The sum of the marginal propensity to consume (MPC) and the marginal propensity to save (MPS) always equals
   a. 1.
   b. 0.
   c. the interest rate.
   d. the marginal propensity to invest (MPI).

10. The relationship between MPC and MPS is
    a. $1 + MPC = MPS$.
    b. $1 - MPC = MPS$.
    c. $1 + MPS = MPC$.
    d. $MPC - MPS = 1$.

11. If the marginal propensity to consume = 0.75, then
    a. the marginal propensity to save = 0.75.
    b. the marginal propensity to save = 1.33.
    c. the marginal propensity to save = 0.20.
    d. the marginal propensity to save = 0.25.

12. As shown in Exhibit 8, autonomous consumption is
    a. 0.
    b. $2 trillion.
    c. $4 trillion.
    d. $6 trillion.
    e. $8 trillion.

13. As shown in Exhibit 8, savings occurs
    a. at 0.
    b. between 0 and $4 trillion.
    c. where disposable income is greater than $4 trillion.
    d. at $2 trillion.

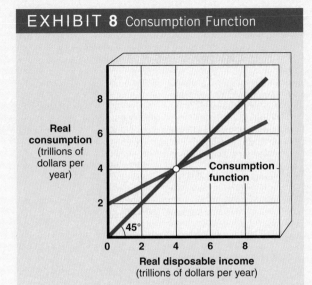

EXHIBIT 8 Consumption Function

Real consumption (trillions of dollars per year)

Consumption function

45°

Real disposable income (trillions of dollars per year)

14. As shown in Exhibit 8, dissaving occurs
    a. at $5 trillion.
    b. between 0 and $4 trillion.
    c. where disposable income is greater than $4 trillion.
    d. at $8 trillion.

15. As shown in Exhibit 8, the marginal propensity to consume (MPC) is
    a. 0.33.
    b. 0.50.
    c. 0.67.
    d. 0.75.

16. As shown in Exhibit 8, the break-even income is
    a. $2 trillion.
    b. $4 trillion.
    c. $6 trillion.
    d. $8 trillion.

17. As shown in Exhibit 8, the 45° line represents
    a. autonomous consumption.
    b. real consumption spending.
    c. real disposable income.
    d. all points where real consumption equals real disposable income.

18. The consumption function is drawn on a graph with disposable income on the horizontal axis. Assume autonomous consumption increases. The effect is
    a. an upward adjustment in the vertical intercept.
    b. no change in the adjustment in the vertical intercept.
    c. an increase in the slope of the consumption function.
    d. a decrease in the slope of the consumption function.

19. The investment demand curve shows the amount businesses spend for investment goods at different possible
    a. price levels.
    b. levels of GDP.
    c. rates of interest.
    d. levels of taxation.

20. A rightward shift of the investment demand curve would be caused by a(an)
    a. increase in the expected rate of return on investment caused by an increase in business confidence.
    b. decrease in the expected rate of return on investment caused by a decrease in business confidence.
    c. increase in the rate of interest.
    d. decrease in the rate of interest.

CHAPTER 9

The Keynesian Model in Action

CHAPTER PREVIEW

In 1935, George Bernard Shaw received a letter from John Maynard Keynes, which stated, "I believe myself to be writing a book [*The General Theory*] on economic theory which will largely revolutionize—not, I suppose, at once but in the course of the next ten years—the way the world thinks about economic problems." Indeed, Keynes's macroeconomic theory offered powerful ideas whose time had come during the Great Depression. Building on the foundation of the previous chapter, this chapter describes how Keynes conceived the economy as driven by aggregate demand that can be separated and analyzed under the individual components of consumption (*C*), investment (*I*), government spending (*G*), and net exports (*X* − *M*).

You must keep in mind that during the Great Depression era, plants had idle capacity and unemployment was massive. Under these conditions, inflation was not the problem. The Keynesian model, therefore, generally ignores price level changes and focuses instead on how full-employment output can be achieved by changes in aggregate expenditures.

Like adding icing to a cake, this chapter begins by adding government spending and global trade to the consumption function and autonomous investment spending curve introduced in the previous chapter. The result is the complete aggregate expenditures model. Next, you will learn how the economy gravitates to an equilibrium where aggregate expenditures equal aggregate output (real GDP). And you will look at the link between the equilibrium real GDP and the level of employment in an economy. The analysis will make clear why Keynes argued that there is no self-correction mechanism that eventually moves the nation to the full-employment equilibrium output.

Finally, you will understand one of Keynes's most powerful ideas—the spending multiplier. At the very heart of Keynesian theory is the concept that an initial increase in aggregate spending of $1 in an economy can increase equilibrium output by more than $1. Thus, Keynesian economics offers a cure for an economy in deep recession: government policies that expand aggregate demand, raise national output, create jobs, and restore full employment.

IN THIS CHAPTER, YOU WILL LEARN TO SOLVE THESE ECONOMICS PUZZLES:

- Why did Keynes reject the classical theory that "supply creates its own demand"?

- Why did Keynes argue that the government should adopt active policies, rather than allowing the market system to prevail?

233

9-1 ADDING GOVERNMENT AND GLOBAL TRADE TO THE KEYNESIAN MODEL

In this chapter, we continue our study of the Keynesian model begun in the previous chapter. Consumption and investment are not the only forms of spending. As shown earlier in the chapter on GDP (Exhibit 2), consumption and investment represent 85 percent of total spending, while government spending and net exports account for the remaining 15 percent of GDP.

9-1a Government Spending

Government spending is the second largest component of aggregate expenditures in the United States. Like investment, government spending can be considered an autonomous expenditure. The reasoning is that government spending is primarily the result of political decisions made independent of the level of national output.

Exhibit 1(a) shows hypothetical government spending as a horizontal line labeled G at $1 trillion. If government officials increase government spending, the G line shifts vertically upward at each possible level of real GDP to G_1, and reduced government spending shifts the G line vertically downward at each possible level of real GDP to G_2. The amount of the shift is equal to the amount of change in government spending.

Here we must pause to take special note of the change from real disposable income to real GDP on the horizontal axis of the graph. Does it make a difference? No, it makes little difference. In the previous chapter, real disposable income was used following the theory Keynes himself developed. However, it is important to connect aggregate output and income measures. Recall from Exhibit 7 in the chapter on GDP the adjustments required to convert GDP into disposable income (Y_d). As it turns out, real disposable income is a sizable portion of real GDP. Over the last decade, real disposable income, on average, has consistently been about 70 percent of real GDP. If we assume that real disposable income remains the same high proportion of real GDP each year, then we can substitute real GDP for real disposable income in the Keynesian model. Changes in real GDP, therefore, reflect changes in both real national output and income (real disposable income).

GLOBAL ECONOMICS

9-1b Net Exports

Like investment and government spending, exports and imports can be treated as autonomous expenditures unaffected by a nation's domestic level of real GDP. Economic conditions in the countries that buy U.S. products affect the level of our exports. On the other hand, the level of imports purchased by U.S. citizens is influenced by economic conditions in the United States. As shown in Exhibit 1(b), net exports, $(X - M)$, can be positive, zero, or negative. The level of net exports, or the $(X - M)$ line, is horizontal because net exports are assumed to be independent of the level of real GDP. Since for many years the value of imports we have purchased from foreigners has exceeded the value of exports we have been selling them, the model assumes net exports are negative at line $(X - M)_1$. If exports and imports are equal, the net exports line shifts upward to zero at line $(X - M)$. If exports exceed imports, the positive $(X - M)$ line shifts farther upward to line $(X - M)_2$.

EXHIBIT 1 Autonomous Government Spending and Net Exports Curves

In part (a), government spending (G) is assumed to be determined by the political decision-making process. The autonomous government spending line, G, is therefore a horizontal line indicating that government spending is independent of the level of real GDP. An increase in government spending shifts G upward to G_1. A decrease shifts G downward to G_2.

Part (b) also shows that net exports are assumed to be independent of the level of GDP. Horizontal line $(X - M)_1$ is negative because imports exceed exports. If exports equal imports, then the net export line shifts upward to $(X - M)$. If exports exceed imports, the net exports line is represented by a positive net exports line, $(X - M)_2$.

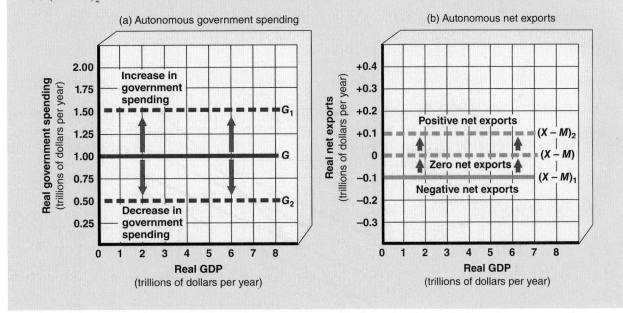

(a) Autonomous government spending

(b) Autonomous net exports

9-2 THE AGGREGATE EXPENDITURES MODEL

Keynes countered classical theory by developing an alternative theory that explained how a depressed economy can be stuck forever in a below-full-employment equilibrium without adequate aggregate expenditures. In this section, a basic Keynesian model is developed to explain what Keynes meant by his famous saying, "In the long run, we are all dead."

9-2a The Aggregate Expenditures Function (AE)

A little drum roll please! Now we are ready to tie together concepts and point the spotlight on an important concept called the aggregate expenditures function necessary to understand Keynes's cure for the Great Depression. The **aggregate expenditures function (AE)** is the total spending in an economy at different levels of real GDP. The AE function or line is conceptually derived graphically in Exhibit 2 by vertically summing $C + I + G + (X - M)$ at each level of real GDP on the horizontal axis. The consumption function (C) explained in the previous chapter begins the AE function with a given level of

Aggregate expenditures function (AE)

The total spending in an economy at different levels of real GDP.

EXHIBIT 2 Aggregate Expenditures and Keynesian Equilibrium

The aggregate expenditures function (AE) begins with the consumption function
(C). Then we add investment (I), government spending (G), and net exports
(X − M). Note that I, G, and (X − M) are assumed to be autonomous expenditures
and are therefore lines parallel to the C line. For the sake of simplicity, we assume
(X − M) is positive. The slope of the AE line is determined by the slope of the
consumption function, which equals the MPC ($\Delta C/\Delta Y$). At Y^* real GDP, aggregate
expenditures equals aggregate income/output (real GDP) along the 45-degree line
(AE = Y), and the economy is in equilibrium.

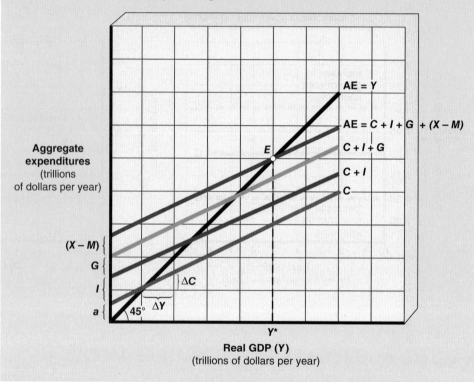

autonomous consumption spending (*a*). Next, recall that the consumption function is
determined by its slope, which equals the MPC. As shown in Exhibit 2, MPC is represented by the ratio of the change in consumption to the change in real GDP ($\Delta C/\Delta Y$).
Since consumption spending rises by less than real GDP, the MPC is less than 1. Note
that it is the slope of the consumption function that gives the entire AE function its
upward slope.

The next step in graphing a conceptual AE line is to add expenditures for *I*, *G*, and
(X − M). To do this, we assume businesses plan to spend a constant amount of investment at all levels of GDP. Therefore, autonomous investment (*I*) is added parallel to
consumption (C) at each level of real GDP. As a result, the AE line shifts vertically
upward and consists of C + I. Like consumption and investment, government spending

and net exports are also assumed to be autonomous spending that remains unchanged regardless of the level of real GDP. Adding government spending (*G*) results in a parallel upward shift in the AE line to $C + I + G$. The aggregate expenditures function is completed by adding net exports to the $C + I + G$ line, and the AE line shifts parallel upward, if we assume $(X - M)$ is positive, to $C + I + G + (X - M)$. Finally, macro equilibrium is established at point *E* where aggregate expenditures equal real GDP at Y^* along the 45-degree line.

> **CONCLUSION**
>
> At the equilibrium level of real GDP, the total value of goods and services produced [real GDP (Y)] is precisely equal to the total spending for these goods and services [aggregate expenditures (AE)].

9-2b Tabular Analysis of Keynesian Equilibrium

In this section, we will further explain macro equilibrium using hypothetical data. Exhibit 3 illustrates the relationship between employment, aggregate output and income (real GDP), and aggregate expenditures for our hypothetical economy. Real GDP (*Y*) is listed in column (1), consumption (*C*) is listed in column (2), and investment (*I*) in column (3) is an autonomous expenditure of $1 trillion from Exhibit 7(b) in the previous chapter. Government spending (*G*) in column (4) is also an autonomous expenditure of $1 trillion from Exhibit 1(a), and net exports (*X* − *M*) in column (5) are taken from

EXHIBIT 3 Equilibrium and Disequilibrium Levels of Employment, Output, and Income

(1) Aggregate Output and Income (real GDP) (*Y*)	(2) Consumption (*C*)	(3) Investment (*I*)	(4) Government (*G*)	(5) Net Exports (*X* − *M*)	(6) Aggregate Expenditures (AE)	(7) Unplanned Inventory Investment Depletion (−) or Accumulation (+)	(8) Direction of Real GDP and Employment
$0	$0.6	$1	$1	$−0.1	$2.5	$−2.5	Increase
1.0	1.1	1	1	−0.1	3.0	−2.0	Increase
2.0	1.6	1	1	−0.1	3.5	−1.5	Increase
3.0	2.1	1	1	−0.1	4.0	−1.0	Increase
4.0	2.6	1	1	−0.1	4.5	−0.5	Increase
5.0	3.1	1	1	−0.1	5.0	0	Equilibrium
6.0	3.6	1	1	−0.1	5.5	+0.5	Decrease
7.0	4.1	1	1	−0.1	6.0	+1.0	Decrease
8.0	4.6	1	1	−0.1	6.5	+1.5	Decrease

NOTE: All amounts are in trillions of dollars per year.

Exhibit 1(b) when we suppose net exports equals −0.1. The aggregate expenditures function (AE) in column (6) is the sum of the $C + I + G + (X - M)$ components of aggregate expenditures in columns (2) through (5).

Examination of the levels of real GDP in column (1) and the levels of aggregate expenditures in column (6) indicate that an equality exists only at the $5 trillion level of real GDP. All output levels other than $5 trillion are unsustainable macro disequilibrium levels. Consider what happens if businesses employ only enough workers to produce an output of $1 trillion real GDP. Business managers expect total spending to equal aggregate output at this level of production, but this does not happen. At the level of $1 trillion of output, aggregate expenditures of $3 trillion exceed aggregate output by an *unplanned inventory investment depletion* of $2 trillion, listed in column (7). Firms respond to this happy state of affairs by hiring more workers, expanding output, and generating additional aggregate income. As a result of this process, the economy moves toward the equilibrium of $5 trillion real GDP. Thus, the pressure of empty shelves and warehouses drives our hypothetical economy to create jobs and reduce the unemployment rate (not explicitly shown in the model).

The reverse is true for all levels of real GDP above the $5 trillion equilibrium level. Now suppose firms hire more workers and aggregate output is $7 trillion real GDP. At the real GDP disequilibrium level of $7 trillion, *unplanned inventory investment accumulation* occurs because aggregate expenditures of $6 trillion are insufficient to purchase $7 trillion of output. The result is that unwanted inventories worth $1 trillion remain unsold on the shelves and in the warehouses of business firms. Producers react to this undesirable condition by cutting the rate of output and employment. In this case, real GDP declines toward the equilibrium level of $5 trillion, jobs are lost, and unemployment rises.

CONCLUSION Aggregate expenditures in Keynesian economics pull aggregate output either higher or lower toward equilibrium in the economy, as opposed to the classical view that aggregate output generates an equal amount of aggregate spending.

9-2c Graphical Analysis of Keynesian Equilibrium

Aggregate expenditures model
The model that determines the equilibrium level of real GDP by the intersection of the aggregate expenditures and aggregate output and income (real GDP) curves.

Using the data from Exhibit 3, Exhibit 4 presents a graph measuring real aggregate expenditures on the y-axis and real GDP on the x-axis. Exhibit 4 illustrates the complete aggregate expenditures model. The **aggregate expenditures model** determines the equilibrium level of real GDP by the intersection of the aggregate expenditures and aggregate output and income (real GDP) curves. The aggregate expenditure model is sometimes called the *Keynesian Cross*. The 45-degree line now takes on a special significance. Each point along this line is equidistant from the horizontal and vertical axes. Therefore, each point reflects a *possible* equilibrium between real GDP aggregate output (Y) and aggregate expenditures (AE). Note that the AE line indicates aggregate expenditures along a line less steep than the 45-degree line. This is because the slope of the AE line is determined by the marginal propensity to consume (MPC), which is less than 1. Aggregate expenditures equal aggregate output at the $5 trillion real GDP level, and any other level of output is unstable.

EXHIBIT 4 The Keynesian Aggregate Expenditures Model

Aggregate expenditures (AE) equal aggregate output (Y) at the equilibrium level of $5 trillion real GDP. Below the equilibrium level of real GDP, an undesired inventory depletion causes businesses to expand production, which pushes the economy toward equilibrium output. Above the equilibrium level of real GDP, an unintended inventory accumulation causes businesses to reduce production, which pushes the economy toward equilibrium output. In Keynesian theory, the full-employment output of $6 trillion real GDP can be reached only by shifting the AE curve upward until the full-capacity output of $6 trillion real GDP is reached.

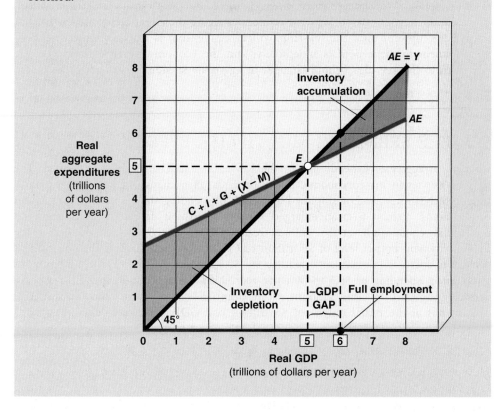

If businesses produce at some output level that is higher than equilibrium GDP, such as $7 trillion real GDP, the vertical distance between the 45-degree equilibrium line and the AE line measures an undesired inventory accumulation of $1 trillion. This leads businesses to reduce employment, and production drops downward until the economy reaches equilibrium at $5 trillion. You may have already recognized that the difference of $1 trillion between the equilibrium output (actual real GDP) at point E and the full-employment output (potential real GDP) is a negative *GDP gap*, discussed in the chapter on business cycles and unemployment (see Exhibit 9).

Now consider the case in which businesses hire only enough workers to produce aggregate output where the AE line is above the 45-degree equilibrium line. Since aggregate expenditures exceed aggregate output, businesses sell more than they currently produce, which depletes their inventories. Business managers react to this excess aggregate demand condition by hiring more workers and expanding production, causing movement upward along the AE function toward the equilibrium level of $5 trillion real GDP.

Now it's time to pause, take a breath, and appreciate what you have been studying so diligently. It's a powerful idea! Exhibit 4 illustrates the basic explanation offered by Keynes for the Great Depression: *Contrary to classical theory, once an equilibrium is established between aggregate expenditures and aggregate output, there is no tendency for the economy to change, even when equilibrium is well below full employment.* The solution Keynes offered Western economies facing the Great Depression is to shift the AE line upward until the full-employment equilibrium is reached. Otherwise, prolonged unemployment persists indefinitely, and the economy never self-corrects. We now turn to the key idea behind changes in aggregate spending to stabilize the macro economy.

9-3 THE SPENDING MULTIPLIER EFFECT

Changes in aggregate expenditures in the Keynesian model make things happen. The crux of Keynesian macroeconomic policy depends on a change in aggregate expenditures, which is multiplied or amplified by rounds of spending and respending throughout the economy. Exhibit 5 is an enlarged version of Exhibit 4. Our analysis begins at the initial equilibrium of $5 trillion real GDP (point E), which is below the full-employment output level of $6 trillion real GDP. Now let's assume the government decides to increase government spending by $0.5 trillion. An increase in autonomous government spending of $0.5 trillion per year shifts the aggregate expenditures curve *vertically* upward by this amount from point E on AE_1 to point a on AE_2. This means at the initial output of $5 trillion real GDP, aggregate demand expands by $0.5 trillion to $5.5 trillion. The initial expansion of spending causes inventories (not shown in the graph) to decline by $0.5 trillion because aggregate spending of $5.5 trillion exceeds aggregate output of $5.0 trillion real GDP. Firms respond by stepping up output by $0.5 trillion real GDP per year to replace inventories. The exhibit shows this by the move from point a to point b. Now the marginal propensity to consume enters the picture. Assuming the MPC is 0.50, the expansion of output from $5 trillion to $5.5 trillion puts an extra $500 billion of income into the pockets of workers. Given the MPC of 0.50, these workers increase spending on goods and services by $250 billion (movement from point b to point c; MPC $\times \Delta Y = 0.50 \times$ $500 billion $=$ $250 billion).

This expansion of consumer spending again causes inventories to decline and output, in turn, to expand by $250 billion, represented by the distance between point c and point d. This again puts extra income into workers' pockets, of which $125 billion (the distance between points d and e) is spent (MPC $\times \Delta Y = 0.50 \times$ $250 billion $=$ $125 billion)

EXHIBIT 5 The Spending Multiplier Effect of a Change in Government Spending

This graph is an enlargement of the spending multiplier process beginning at the point where the economy is in equilibrium at $5 trillion. Then an initial increase of $500 billion in government spending shifts the aggregate expenditures line up vertically from AE_1 to AE_2. After all spending–output–spending rounds are complete; a new equilibrium is restored at point E_1 with a full-employment output of $6 trillion. Thus, the $500 billion initial increase in government spending has caused a $1 trillion increase in real GDP, and the value of the multiplier is 2.

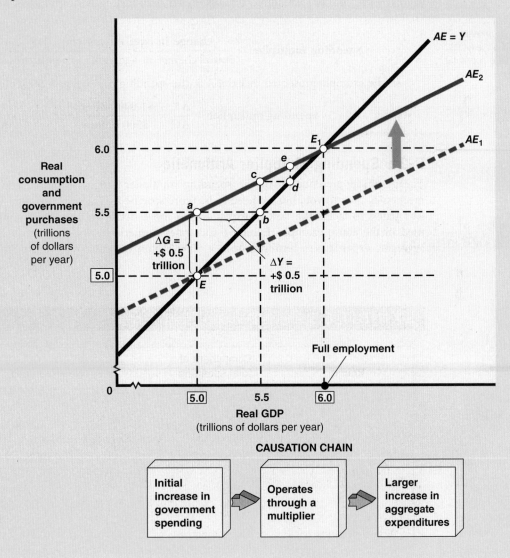

This process of spending-output-spending continues through an infinite number of rounds until output reaches the new equilibrium level of $6 trillion per year at point E_1. Thus, an initial expansion of government spending of $0.5 trillion expands equilibrium output by $1 trillion, which is twice the magnitude of the increase in government spending. Hence, the spending multiplier is 2. The **spending multiplier (SM)** is the ratio of the change in real GDP to the initial change in any component of aggregate expenditures, including consumption, investment, government spending, and net exports. The formula to compute the amount of change in government spending, or any other component of aggregate expenditures, required to shift equilibrium aggregate output measured by real GDP is

Spending multiplier (SM)

The ratio of the change in real GDP to an initial change in any component of aggregate expenditures, including consumption, investment, government spending, and net exports. As a formula, the spending multiplier equals 1/(1− MPC) or 1/MPS.

$$\text{Spending multiplier} = \frac{\textbf{change in equilibrium real GDP}}{\textbf{initial change in aggregate expenditures}}$$

In the example presented in Exhibit 5, the spending multiplier is computed as

$$\text{Spending multiplier} = \frac{\Delta Y}{\Delta G} = \frac{\$1,000 \text{ billion}}{\$500 \text{ billion}} = 2$$

9-3a Spending Multiplier Arithmetic

The graphical presentation of the spending multiplier process should make the basic mechanics clear to you, but we need to be more specific and derive a formula. Therefore, let's pause to tackle the task of explaining in more detail the spending multiplier of 2 used in the above example. Exhibit 6 illustrates numerically the cumulative increase in aggregate expenditures resulting from a $500 billion increase in government spending.

EXHIBIT 6 Spending Multiplier Effect

Round	Component of total spending	New spending
1	Government spending	$500
2	Consumption	250
3	Consumption	125
4	Consumption	62.5
.	.	.
.	.	.
.	.	.
All other rounds	Consumption	62.5
Total spending		$1,000

In the initial round, the government spends this amount for bridges, national defense, and so forth. Households receive this amount of income. In the second round, these households spend $250 billion (0.50 × $500 billion) on houses, cars, groceries, and other products. In the third round, the incomes of realtors, auto workers, grocers, and others are boosted by $250 billion, and they spend $125 billion (0.50 × $250 billion). These rounds of spending create income for respending in a downward spiral throughout the economy in smaller and smaller amounts until the total level of aggregate expenditures rises by an extra $1,000 billion.

Any initial change in spending by the government, households, firms, or foreigners creates a chain reaction of further spending, which causes a greater cumulative change in aggregate expenditures and real GDP.	**CONCLUSION**

You might recognize from algebra that the spending multiplier effect is a process based on an infinite geometric series. The formula for the sum of such a series of numbers is the initial number times $1/(1 - r)$, where r is the ratio that relates the numbers. Using this formula, the sum (total spending) is calculated as $500 billion $(\Delta G) \times [1/(1 - 0.50)] = $1,000$ billion. By simply defining r in the infinite series formula as MPC, the spending multiplier for aggregate demand is expressed as

$$\text{Spending multiplier} = \frac{1}{1 - \text{MPC}}$$

Applying this formula to our example:

$$\text{Spending multiplier} = \frac{1}{1 - 0.50} = \frac{1}{0.50} = 2$$

Recall from the previous chapter that MPC + MPS = 1; therefore, MPS = 1 − MPC. Hence, the above multiplier formula can be rewritten as

$$\text{Spending multiplier} = \frac{1}{\text{MPS}}$$

Applying the multiplier formula to our example:

$$\text{Spending multiplier} = \frac{1}{\text{MPS}} = \frac{1}{1 - 0.50} = 2$$

Since MPS and MPC are related, the size of the multiplier depends on the size of the MPC. What will the result be if people spend 80 percent or 33 percent of each dollar of income instead of 50 percent? If the MPC increases (decreases), consumers spend a larger (smaller) share of each additional dollar of output/income in each round, and the size of the multiplier increases (decreases). Exhibit 7 lists the multiplier for different values of MPC and MPS. Economists use real-world macroeconomic data to estimate a more complex multiplier than the simple spending multiplier formula developed in this chapter. Their estimates of the long-run real-world MPC range from 0.80 to 0.90. An MPC of 0.50 is used in the previous examples for simplicity.

EXHIBIT 7 Relationship between MPC, MPS, and the Spending Multiplier

(1) Marginal propensity to consume (MPC)	(2) Marginal propensity to save (MPS)	(3) Spending multiplier
0.90	0.10	10
0.80	0.20	5
0.75	0.25	4
0.67	0.33	3
0.50	0.50	2
0.33	0.67	1.5

9-4 RECESSIONARY AND INFLATIONARY GAPS

The multiplier is important in the Keynesian model because it means that the initial change in aggregate expenditures results in an amplified change in the equilibrium level of real GDP. Such inherent instability can mean bad or good news for an economy. The bad news occurs, for example, when the multiplier amplifies small declines in total spending from, say, consumer and business manager pessimism into much larger downturns in national output, income, and employment. The good news is that, in theory, macroeconomic policy can manage, or manipulate, the economy's performance by a relatively small initial change in aggregate expenditures. For example, in the previous situation, a $500 billion increase in government spending increased real GDP by $1,000 billion and stimulated the economy to full employment.

9-4a Recessionary Gap

Using Government Spending to Close a Recessionary Gap

Consider the aggregate expenditures function AE_1 in Exhibit 8. Beginning at point E_1, this hypothetical economy's initial equilibrium level is $4 trillion real GDP. The MPC is 0.50, and the spending multiplier is therefore 2. The full-employment output is $6 trillion real GDP, which means the economy faces a negative GDP gap of $2 trillion. Along the vertical line at the full-employment output level, look at the segment between point a on the initial AE_1 line and point E_2 on the AE_2 line, which is labeled a recessionary gap. A **recessionary gap** is the amount by which aggregate expenditures fall short of the amount required to achieve full-employment equilibrium. In our example, the recessionary gap is $1 trillion. What is the importance of the recessionary gap? The recessionary gap is the initial increase in autonomous spending required to trigger the multiplier, shift the aggregate expenditures function upward from AE_1 to AE_2, and eliminate the negative GDP gap. Stated as an expression,

Recessionary gap
The amount by which the aggregate expenditures fall short of the amount required to achieve full-employment equilibrium.

Initial increase in autonomous expenditures × spending multiplier

= increase in equilibrium output

EXHIBIT 8 A Recessionary Gap

The hypothetical economy begins in equilibrium at point E_1, with an equilibrium output of $4 trillion real GDP. With aggregate expenditures of AE_1, real GDP will not automatically increase to the $6 trillion full-employment output. The $1 trillion deficiency in total spending required to achieve full employment is the recessionary gap measured by the vertical distance between points a and E_2. Given a multiplier of 2, an initial increase in autonomous expenditures equal to the recessionary gap works through the spending multiplier and causes the economy to move from E_1 to E_2 and achieve full employment.

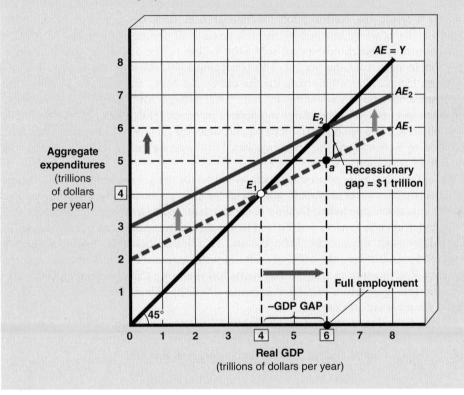

Using the data in our example,

$$\textbf{\$1 trillion} \times \textbf{2} = \textbf{\$2 trillion}$$

We now turn to the important question of how to inject an additional $1 trillion spending into the economy, cause AE_1 to shift upward to AE_2, and thereby increase the equilibrium output from $4 trillion to $6 trillion real GDP. Under Keynesian theory, when market forces do not automatically do the job, then the central government should take aggressive action and adopt policies that boost autonomous spending [C, I, G, or $(X-M)$] by an amount equal to the recessionary gap. One of those policy options is for government to simply increase its spending (G) by an amount equal to the recessionary gap to provide for full employment.

Using a Tax Cut to Close a Recessionary Gap

Instead of increasing government spending, let's assume the government decides to cut taxes to close the recessionary GDP gap in Exhibit 8. This is an option we have not yet discussed in the context of the aggregate expenditures model, and it requires special consideration. The government may consider changes in two types of taxes: autonomous taxes and income taxes. For simplicity, here the analysis is confined to the simpler concept of autonomous taxes, such as property taxes, which are independent of the levels of real output and income.

Suppose in Exhibit 8 the government reduces autonomous taxes by $800 billion. Would this tax cut be enough to stimulate the economy to full employment? Since real *disposable* income rises at every level of GDP, so does consumption at all levels of real GDP. As a result, the consumption function and, in turn, the aggregate expenditures function shifts upward, but not by the full amount of the tax cut. Since the MPC is 0.50, this means households spend only $400 billion of the additional $800 billion of disposable income from the tax cut. The remaining $400 billion of the tax cut is added to savings. Hence, after multiplying the tax cut by the MPC, the result of the tax cut is to increase consumption spending by only $400 billion. Multiplying this increase in total spending by the spending multiplier increases real GDP by $800 billion ($400 billion × 2 = $800 billion). Since equilibrium real GDP would increase only from $4 trillion to $4.8 trillion, the economy would still operate below the full-employment real GDP of $6 trillion.

An approach similar to a cut in taxes would be for the government to raise *transfer payments* (welfare, unemployment, and Social Security payments) by $800 billion. This increase in transfer payments, holding taxes constant, increases disposable income dollar for dollar at each level of real GDP. Hence, the consumption and aggregate expenditures lines shift upward by $400 billion. This initial boost in total spending is computed by multiplying the MPC of 0.50 times the increase of $800 billion in transfer payments. The increase in transfer payments has the same effect as an identical cut in taxes, and the equilibrium real GDP increases by $800 billion. Hence, a transfer payment is simply a cut in net taxes.

Another simpler method of calculating the impact of a change in taxes is to use a tax multiplier. The **tax multiplier** is the change in aggregate expenditures (total spending) resulting from an initial change in taxes. Expressed as a formula:

Tax multiplier = 1 − spending multiplier

After you calculate the tax multiplier, multiply your answer by the amount of the tax increase or decrease in order to determine the change in real GDP. Expressed as a formula:

Change in taxes (ΔT) × tax multiplier = change in real GDP

Returning to the example shown in Exhibit 8, suppose we wish to calculate the tax cut required to increase real GDP by $2 trillion from $4 trillion to $6 trillion and achieve full employment. Using the tax multiplier formula:

$$\textbf{Tax multiplier} = \textbf{1} - \textbf{2} = \textbf{−1}$$
$$\Delta T \times (\textbf{−1}) = \textbf{\$2 trillion}$$
$$\Delta T = \textbf{−\$2 trillion}$$

Therefore, in this hypothetical economy, a $2 trillion tax cut will increase real GDP by the $2 trillion required to achieve full employment.

Tax multiplier
The change in aggregate expenditures (total spending) resulting from an initial change in taxes. As a formula, the tax multiplier equals 1−spending multiplier.

Full-Employment Output, Where Are You?
Suppose the U.S. economy is in equilibrium at $15 trillion real GDP with a recessionary gap. Given an MPC of 0.50, the government estimates that a tax cut of $500 billion is just enough to restore full employment. What is the full-employment real GDP target?

CHECKPOINT

9-4b **Inflationary Gap**

Under other circumstances, an inflationary gap may burden an economy. An **inflationary gap** is the amount by which aggregate expenditures exceed the amount required to achieve full-employment equilibrium. In Exhibit 9, the inflationary gap of $1 trillion is

Inflationary gap
The amount by which the aggregate expenditures exceed the amount required to achieve full-employment equilibrium.

EXHIBIT 9 An Inflationary Gap

The hypothetical economy begins in equilibrium at point E_1 with an equilibrium output of $6 trillion real GDP. Given an initial aggregate expenditures function of AE_1, real GDP will not self-correct to the full-employment output of $4 trillion. The $1 trillion excess of total spending over the amount required at full employment is the inflationary gap measured by the vertical distance between points a and E_2. Given a multiplier of 2, an initial decrease in autonomous expenditures of $1 trillion causes the economy to move from point E_1 to E_2, achieve full employment, and cool the upward pressure on prices.

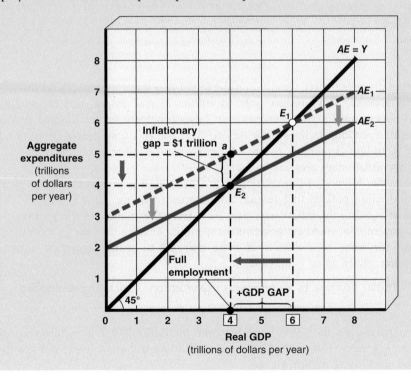

YOU'RE THE ECONOMIST

Applicable Concept: Aggregate Expenditures Model

Infrastructure Spending

Infrastructure spending has always been a politically popular form of government spending. Everyone enjoys good roads, bridges, tunnels, public transportation, and public parks. We appreciate well-functioning sewage and water treatment facilities, dams, airports, as well as many other publicly owned facilities. This infrastructure spending also creates lots of jobs. Moreover, it is a key ingredient for economic growth by enhancing the nation's productivity, which in turn raises our nation's average absolute standard of living over time.

But, how are we going to pay for this type of government spending? Perhaps history can be a guide.[1] Like so many American stories, the history of financing infrastructure best begins with George Washington. Washington was an avid supporter of infrastructure and used tolls to finance roads and canals. In addition to tolls, Thomas Jefferson's administration ushered in selling public lands in order to devote a portion of the proceeds to finance "…canals, roads, arts, manufactures, education, and other great objects within each state." In the mid-1800s, the federal government wanted to encourage private companies to build rail road tracks. To promote this infrastructure spending, the government transferred ownership of large tracts of publicly owned lands directly to railroad companies and offered them loan guarantees.

Then came the Great Depression and President Franklin Roosevelt's huge public works programs. The purpose of

infrastructure at this time was not to push the United States westward or to enhance the general well-being of society, but to create jobs, and lots of jobs fast. Roosevelt recognized the financing challenges he faced in being able to pay for these projects and the political risk his party took by backing large spending programs that added to the national debt. But, his primary concern was to create jobs. Later, infrastructure investments in the 1940s were largely for military purposes and

the vertical distance between point *a* on the initial AE_1 line and point E_2 on the AE_2 line. Since the economy can produce only $4 trillion in real output, this excess aggregate demand puts upward pressure on prices as buyers compete for this limited real output. If aggregate spending declines from AE_1 to AE_2, the economy moves from an equilibrium of $6 trillion at point E_1 to the full-employment equilibrium of $4 trillion at point E_2, and the inflationary pressure cools.

Again, the Keynesian prescription is for the central government to take aggressive action and adopt policies that reduce autonomous spending [C, I, G, or $(X - M)$] by an amount equal to the inflationary gap. Note from the analysis in the previous section that the government could cut government spending or use a tax hike or a cut in transfer payments (or some combination of these policies) to reduce aggregate autonomous expenditures. Stated as an expression,

Initial decrease in autonomous expenditures × spending multiplier

= decrease in equilibrium output

In our example, the MPC is 0.50, so the multiplier is 2. The actual real GDP of $6 trillion is greater than the potential real GDP of $4 trillion, so there is a positive real GDP gap equal to $2 trillion. Hence,

−$1 trillion × 2 = −$2 trillion.

were connected to U.S. involvement in WWII. These projects were financed by large deficits that added considerably to the national debt. In the 1950s, President Eisenhower was able to use tax revenues to pay for the interstate highway system.

In more recent times, President Obama, like Roosevelt before him, wanted to stimulate the economy, which was stuck in a severe recession. Obama championed "The American Recovery and Reinvestment Act of 2009," which poured hundreds of billions of dollars into infrastructure spending. Similar to Roosevelt's response to the Great Depression, these expenditures were largely financed by government borrowing, resulting in large deficits and a growing national debt.

Recently, President Trump has proposed new infrastructure spending. As reported in *U.S. News and World Report* in March, 2017:[2]

> In Trump's February address to Congress, he promised $1 trillion in new infrastructure spending. "Crumbling infrastructure will be replaced with new roads, bridges, tunnels, airports and railways gleaming across our beautiful land," Trump insisted. The plan, according to Trump, will create "millions of new jobs."

We will have to see how this or any other future government spending on infrastructure is paid for.

If history is our guide, infrastructure will remain in the headlines! The debate will likely continue to hinge on which public works projects should get priority. How should the government funds be distributed? Who should pay for these projects? Although it is true that infrastructure spending will stimulate an economy and promote economic growth over time, the relevant questions are by how much, and is this gain worth the cost?

ANALYZE THE ISSUE Assume $100 billion is spent on infrastructure this year, and this spending is entirely funded by raising taxes (which might include gas taxes, collecting tolls, imposing user fees, or other forms of taxation) of $100 billion. Use the Keynesian aggregate expenditures model to explain the impact on real GDP. Assume the MPC = 0.90, the economy is initially in equilibrium at $18 trillion, and there is a recessionary gap equal to $100 billion. What will the new equilibrium level of real GDP be equal to? Will this infrastructure spending, financed by raising taxes of an equal amount, be sufficient to close the recessionary gap?

---

1. Adam J. White, "Infrastructure Policy: Lessons from American History," The New Atlantis. A Journal of Technology and Science, Found at: http://www.thenewatlantis.com/publications/infrastructure-policy-lessons-from-american-history.

2. Tracy C. Miller and Michael Wilt. "Infrastructure Needs Innovation, The top-down federal approach is outdated and inefficient," U.S. News and World Report, March 27, 2017. Found at: https://www.usnews.com/opinion/economic-intelligence/articles/2017-03-27/donald-trumps-call-for-more-federal-infrastructure-spending-is-a-bad-deal.

How Much Spending Must Uncle Sam Cut?
Suppose the U.S. economy is troubled by inflation. The economy is in equilibrium at a real GDP of $15.5 trillion, the MPC is 0.90, and the full-employment output is $15 trillion. If the government decides to eliminate the inflationary gap by cutting government spending, what should be the size of the cut?

CHECKPOINT

Key Concepts

Aggregate expenditures function (AE)	Aggregate expenditures model	Spending multiplier (SM)	Tax multiplier
		Recessionary gap	Inflationary gap

Summary

- The Keynesian theory argues that the economy is inherently unstable and may require government intervention to control aggregate expenditures to achieve full employment. If we assume that real disposable income remains the same high proportion of real GDP, then we can substitute real GDP for real disposable income in the Keynesian model. Investment, government spending, and net exports can be treated as autonomous expenditures. Adding consumption (C), investment (I), government (G), and net exports (X − M) spending gives us the **aggregate expenditures function (AE)**.

Keynesian Equilibrium

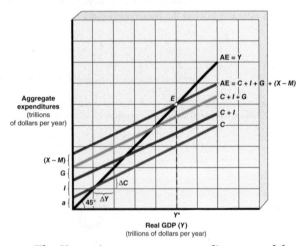

Aggregate expenditures (trillions of dollars per year)

Real GDP (Y)
(trillions of dollars per year)

- The **Keynesian aggregate expenditures model** determines the equilibrium level of real GDP by the intersection of the aggregate expenditures and the aggregate output and income curves. Each equilibrium level in the economy is associated with a level of employment and corresponding unemployment rate. Aggregate expenditures and real GDP are equal, graphically, where the $AE = C + I + G + (X − M)$ line intersects the 45-degree line. At any output greater or less than the equilibrium real GDP, unintended inventory investment pressures businesses to alter aggregate output and income until equilibrium real GDP is achieved. Equilibrium may occur at, below, or above full employment.

Keynesian Aggregate Expenditures Model

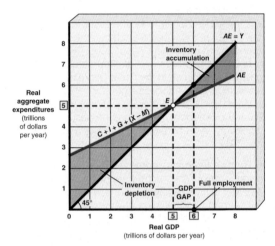

Real aggregate expenditures (trillions of dollars per year)

Real GDP
(trillions of dollars per year)

- The **spending multiplier** is the ratio of the change in equilibrium output to the initial change in any of the components of aggregate expenditures. Algebraically, the multiplier is the reciprocal of the marginal propensity to save. The multiplier effect causes the equilibrium level of real GDP to change by a multiple of the initial change in spending.

Spending Multiplier

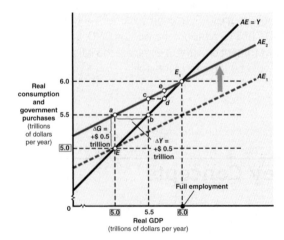

Real consumption and government purchases (trillions of dollars per year)

Real GDP
(trillions of dollars per year)

- A **recessionary gap** is the amount by which aggregate expenditures fall short of the amount necessary for the economy to operate at full-employment real GDP. To eliminate a negative GDP gap, the Keynesian solution is to increase autonomous spending by an amount equal to the recessionary gap and operate through the multiplier to increase equilibrium output and income to full employment.

- An **inflationary gap** is the amount by which aggregate expenditures exceed the amount necessary to establish full-employment equilibrium and indicates upward pressure on prices. To eliminate a positive GDP gap, the Keynesian solution is to decrease autonomous spending by an amount equal to the inflationary gap and operate through the multiplier to decrease equilibrium output and income to full employment.

Recessionary Gap

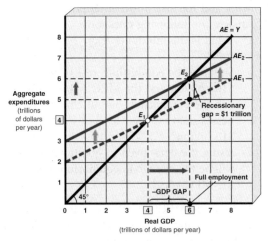

Inflationary Gap

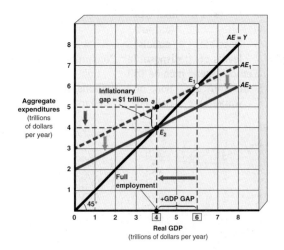

- The **tax multiplier** is the multiplier by which an initial change in taxes changes aggregate demand (total spending) after an infinite number of spending cycles. Expressed as a formula, the tax multiplier = 1 − spending multiplier.

Summary of Conclusion Statements

- At the equilibrium level of real GDP, the total value of goods and services produced (real GDP, or Y) is precisely equal to the total spending for these goods and services (aggregate expenditures, or AE).

- Aggregate expenditures in Keynesian economics pull aggregate output either higher or lower toward equilibrium in the economy, as opposed to the classical view that aggregate output generates an equal amount of aggregate spending.

- Any initial change in spending by the government, households, firms, or foreigners creates a chain reaction of further spending, which causes a greater cumulative change in aggregate expenditures and real GDP.

Study Questions and Problems

Please see Appendix A for answers to the odd-numbered questions. Your instructor has access to the answers for even-numbered questions.

1. Assume the level of autonomous investment is $100 billion and aggregate expenditures equal consumption and investment. Based on the following table, answer the following questions.

Employment, Output, Consumption, and Unplanned Inventory

Possible levels of employment (millions of workers)	Real GDP (output) equals disposable income (billions of dollars)	Consumption (billions of dollars)	Unplanned inventory (billions of dollars)
40	$325	$300	$____
45	375	325	____
50	425	350	____
55	475	375	____
60	525	400	____
65	575	425	____
70	625	450	____

a. Fill in the unplanned inventory column.
b. Determine the MPC and MPS.
c. If this economy employs a labor force of 40 million, what will happen to this level of employment? Explain and identify the equilibrium level of output.

2. Using the data given in question 1, what is the impact of adding net exports? Let imports equal $75 billion, and assume exports equal $50 billion. What is the equilibrium level of employment and output?

3. Explain the determination of equilibrium real GDP by drawing an abstract graph of the aggregate expenditures model. Label the aggregate expenditures line AE and the aggregate output line Y. Explain why the interaction of AE and Y determines the Keynesian equilibrium level of real GDP.

4. Use the aggregate expenditures model to demonstrate the multiplier effect.

5. How are changes in the MPC, changes in the MPS, and the size of the multiplier related? Answer the following questions:
   a. What is the multiplier if the MPC is 0? 0.33? 0.90?
   b. Suppose the equilibrium real GDP is $100 billion and the MPC is 4/5. How much will the equilibrium output change if businesses increase their level of investment by $10 billion?
   c. Using the data given in question 5(b), what will be the change in equilibrium real GDP if the MPC equals 2/3?

6. Assume the MPC is 0.90 and autonomous investment increases by $500 billion. What will be the impact on real GDP?

7. Suppose autonomous investment increases by $100 billion and the MPC is 0.75.
   a. Use the following table to compute four rounds of the spending multiplier effect:

Round	Components of total spending	New consumption spending (billions of dollars)
1	Investment	$____
2	Consumption	____
3	Consumption	____
4	Consumption	____
	Total spending	____

b. Use the spending multiplier formula to compute the final cumulative impact on aggregate spending.

8. First, use the data given in question 1, and assume the level of autonomous investment is $50 billion. If the full-employment level of output is $525 billion, what is the equilibrium level of output and employment? Does a recessionary gap or an inflationary gap exist? Second, assume the level of autonomous investment is $150 billion. What is the equilibrium level of output and employment? Does a recessionary gap or an inflationary gap exist? Explain the consequences of an inflationary gap using the aggregate expenditures model.

9. Assume an economy is in recession with a MPC of 0.75 and there is a GDP gap of $100 billion. How much must government spending increase to eliminate the gap? Instead of increasing government spending by the amount you calculate, what would be the effect of the government cutting taxes by this amount?

10. Suppose the government wishes to eliminate an inflationary gap of $100 billion and the MPC is 0.50. How much must the government cut its spending? Instead of decreasing government spending by the amount you calculate, what would be the effect of the government increasing taxes by this amount?

 CHECKPOINT ANSWERS

Full-Employment Output, Where Are You?

A tax cut of $500 billion boosts disposable income by this amount. Since the MPC is 0.50, consumers will spend $250 billion of the tax cut and save the remaining $250 billion. To compute the impact of the rise in consumption (ΔC) on real GDP (ΔY), use this formula:

$$\Delta C \times \text{multiplier} = \Delta Y$$

where

$$\text{Multiplier} = \frac{1}{\text{MPS}} = \frac{1}{1 - \text{MPC}} = \frac{1}{1 - 0.50} = 2$$

Thus, $250 billion × 2 = $500 billion. The increase in real GDP from the tax cut equals $500 billion, which is added to the initial equilibrium real GDP of $15 trillion to achieve full-employment output. If you said the full-employment real GDP is $15.5 trillion, **YOU ARE CORRECT**.

How Much Spending Must Uncle Sam Cut?

The GDP gap is $500 billion real GDP. To calculate the size of the government spending cut (ΔG) required to decrease real GDP (ΔY) by $500 billion, use this formula:

$$\Delta G \times \text{multiplier} = -\Delta Y$$

where

$$\text{Multiplier} = \frac{1}{\text{MPS}} = \frac{1}{1 - \text{MPC}} = \frac{1}{1 - 0.90} = 10$$

Thus,

$$\Delta G = \frac{-\Delta Y}{\text{multiplier}} = \frac{-\$500\,\text{billion}}{10} = -\$50\,\text{billion}$$

If you said the size of the cut in government spending should be $50 billion, **YOU ARE CORRECT**.

Sample Quiz

Please see Appendix B for answers to Sample Quiz questions.

1. Using C to represent consumption, I to represent investment, G to represent government spending, S to represent saving, X to represent exports, and M to represent imports, aggregate expenditures can be represented by
   a. $C + I + G + (X + M)$.
   b. $(C-S) + G + (X-M)$.
   c. $C + I + G + (X-M)$.
   d. $C + I + G + (X-M) - S$.

2. In the aggregate expenditures model, if aggregate expenditures (AE) are less than GDP, then
   a. inventory is depleted.
   b. inventory is unchanged.
   c. employment decreases.
   d. employment increases.

3. Which one of the following are the components of aggregate expenditures?
   a. Household consumption, business investment, government spending for goods and services, and net exports
   b. Household consumption, business investment, government transfer payments, and net exports
   c. Household consumption, business investment, government spending for goods and services, and exports
   d. Household consumption, business investment, government spending for goods and services, and saving

4. In the Keynesian model, investment, government spending, and net exports are treated as autonomous expenditures, which means they are independent of
   a. expectations.
   b. the price level.
   c. political processes.
   d. real GDP.

5. As shown in Exhibit 10, equilibrium GDP is
   a. $2 trillion.
   b. $6 trillion.
   c. $10 trillion.
   d. $12 trillion.

EXHIBIT 10 Keynesian Aggregate Expenditures Model

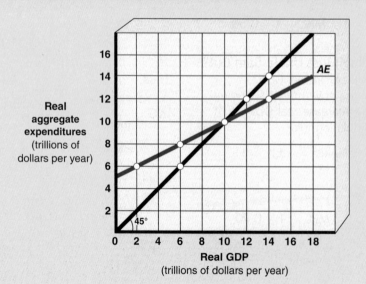

6. As shown in Exhibit 10, if GDP is $6 trillion, the economy experiences unplanned inventory
   a. depletion of $2 trillion.
   b. depletion of $6 trillion.
   c. accumulation of $2 trillion.
   d. accumulation of $6 trillion.

7. As shown in Exhibit 10, if GDP is $14 trillion, the economy experiences unplanned inventory
   a. accumulation of $12 trillion.
   b. depletion of $14 trillion.
   c. accumulation of $2 trillion.
   d. depletion of $4 trillion.

8. The ratio of the change in GDP to an initial change in aggregate expenditures (AE) is the
   a. spending multiplier.
   b. permanent income rate.
   c. marginal expenditure rate.
   d. marginal propensity to consume.

9. The formula to compute the spending multiplier is
   a. 1/(MPC + MPS).
   b. 1/(1 − MPC).
   c. 1/(1 − MPS).
   d. 1/(C + I).

10. If the marginal propensity to consume (MPC) is 0.80, the value of the spending multiplier is
    a. 2.
    b. 5.
    c. 8.
    d. 10.

11. When households' marginal propensity to consume (MPC) increases, the size of the spending multiplier
    a. also increases.
    b. decreases.
    c. remains unchanged.
    d. reacts unpredictably.

12. Mathematically, the value of the spending multiplier is given by the formula
    a. MPC − 1.
    b. (MPC − 1)/MPC.
    c. 1/MPC.
    d. 1/MPS.

13. Assume the economy is in recession, the MPC is 0.80, and an increase in real GDP of $200 billion is needed to reach full employment. The target can be reached if government spending is increased by
    a. $20 billion.
    b. $200 billion.
    c. $80 billion.
    d. $40 billion.

14. Using the aggregate expenditures model, assume the aggregate expenditures (AE) line is above the 45-degree line at full-employment GDP. This vertical distance is called a(an)
    a. inflationary gap.
    b. recessionary gap.
    c. negative GDP gap.
    d. marginal propensity to consume gap.

15. Assume that full-employment real GDP is $Y = \$1,200$ billion, the current equilibrium real GDP is $Y = \$1,600$ billion, and the MPC = 0.8. To bring the economy to a full-employment real GDP,
    a. a recessionary gap must be bridged by increasing aggregate expenditures by $80 billion.
    b. an inflationary gap must be bridged by cutting aggregate expenditures by $80 billion.
    c. nothing is needed to bring the economy into full-employment equilibrium.
    d. a recessionary gap must be bridged by increasing aggregate expenditures by $400 billion.
    e. an inflationary gap must be bridged by cutting aggregate expenditures by $400 billion.

16. If the MPC is 0.70, then the spending multiplier is equal to
    a. 0.70.
    b. 0.30.
    c. 0.14.
    d. 3.33.
    e. 5.

17. The equilibrium level of real GDP is $1,000, the target full-employment level of real GDP is

EXHIBIT 11 Keynesian Aggregate Expenditures Model

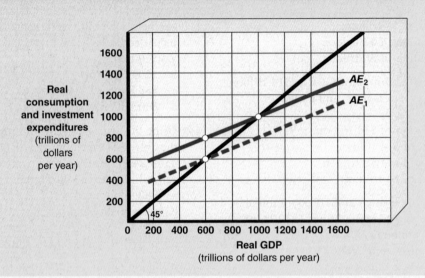

$1,500, and the marginal propensity to consume is 0.75. The target can be reached if government spending is
a. increased by $100 billion.
b. increased by $125 billion.
c. increased by $500 billion.
d. held constant.

18. In Exhibit 11, an increase in aggregate expenditures causes
a. a movement down the aggregate expenditures curve from equilibrium real GDP of $600 to equilibrium real GDP $1,000.
b. a movement up the aggregate expenditures curve from equilibrium real GDP of $1,200 to equilibrium real GDP $1,000.
c. a shift of the aggregate expenditures curve upward, causing equilibrium real GDP to increase from $600 to $1,000.

d. a shift of the aggregate expenditures curve downward the, causing equilibrium real GDP to decrease from $1,200 to $1,000.
e. no change in equilibrium real GDP.

19. In Exhibit 11, the value of the spending multiplier is
a. 3.
b. 4.
c. 5.
d. 2.
e. 6.

20. In Exhibit 11, assume the AE_2 line is aggregate expenditures and $1,000 is full-employment real GDP. If the economy operates at a real disposable income of $600, there will be
a. inventory accumulation of $100.
b. inventory accumulation of $200.
c. zero inventory.
d. inventory depletion of $200.

CHAPTER 10

Aggregate Demand and Supply

CHAPTER PREVIEW

Classical economic theory held that the economy would bounce back to full employment as long as prices and wages were flexible. As the unemployment rate soared and remained high during the Great Depression, British economist John Maynard Keynes formulated a new theory with new policy implications. Instead of taking a wait-and-see policy until markets self-correct the economy, Keynes argued that policymakers must take action to influence aggregate spending through changes in government spending and taxes. The prescription for the Great Depression was simple: Increase government spending and/or cut taxes and jobs will be created. Faced with the financial crisis of the Great Recession, Keynesian management of the economy was used to stabilize the U.S. and global economy. The opposition view today is based on the classical model that rejects the federal government

stimulus package concept because the economy will self-correct to full employment.

In this chapter, you will use aggregate demand and supply analysis to study the business cycle. The chapter opens with a presentation of the aggregate demand curve and then the aggregate supply curve. Once these concepts are developed, the analysis shows why modern macroeconomics teaches that shifts in aggregate supply or aggregate demand can influence the price level, the equilibrium level of real GDP, and employment. For example, although Keynes was not concerned with the problem of inflation, his theory has implications for fighting demand-pull inflation. In this case, the government must cut spending or increase taxes to reduce aggregate demand. You will probably return to this chapter often because it provides the basic tools with which to organize your thinking about the macro economy.

IN THIS CHAPTER, YOU WILL LEARN TO SOLVE THESE ECONOMICS PUZZLES:

- Why does the aggregate supply curve have three different segments?

- Would the greenhouse effect cause inflation, unemployment, or both?

- Was John Maynard Keynes's prescription for the Great Depression right?

10-1 THE AGGREGATE DEMAND CURVE

Aggregate demand curve (AD)

The curve that shows the level of real GDP purchased by households, businesses, government, and foreigners (net exports) at different possible price levels during a time period, ceteris paribus.

Here we view the collective demand for *all* goods and services, rather than the *market* demand for a particular good or service. Exhibit 1 shows the aggregate demand curve, which slopes downward and to the right for a given year. The **aggregate demand curve (AD)** curve shows the level of real GDP purchased by households, businesses, government, and foreigners (net exports) at different possible price levels during a time period, ceteris paribus. Stated differently, the aggregate demand curve shows us the total dollar amount of goods and services that will be demanded in the economy at various price levels. And just as there is an inverse relationship between the price and the quantity demanded for a specific product, it is also true that when there is a decrease in the economy-wide price level, there is a greater aggregate quantity demanded for all real goods and services in the broader economy, ceteris paribus. Similarly, when the overall price level rises, the aggregate quantity demanded decreases.

EXHIBIT 1 The Aggregate Demand Curve

The aggregate demand curve (AD) shows the relationship between the price level and the level of real GDP, other things being equal. The lower the price level, the larger the GDP demanded by households, businesses, government, and foreigners. If the price level is 300 at point *A*, a real GDP of $8 trillion is demanded. If the price level is 200 at point *B*, the real GDP demanded increases to $12 trillion.

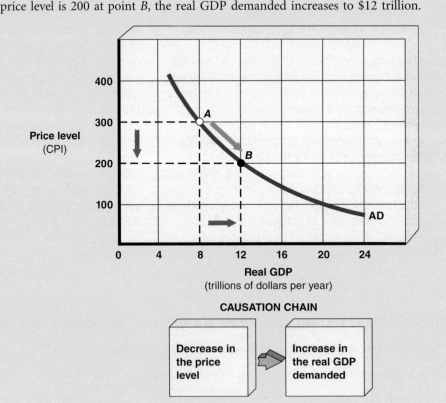

The downward slope of the aggregate demand curve shows that at a given level of aggregate income, people buy more goods and services at a lower average price level. While the horizontal axis in the market supply and demand model for a specific product measures *physical* units, such as bushels of wheat, the horizontal axis in the aggregate demand and supply model measures the value of *final* goods and services included in real GDP. Note that the horizontal axis represents the quantity of aggregate production demanded, measured in base-year dollars. The vertical axis is an *index* of the overall price level measured by the consumer price index (CPI), rather than the price per bushel of wheat. As shown in Exhibit 1, if the price level measured by the CPI is 300 at point *A*, a real GDP of $8 trillion is demanded in a given year. If the price level is 200 at point *B*, a real GDP of $12 trillion is demanded. Note that hypothetical data is used throughout this chapter and the next unless otherwise stated.

Although the aggregate demand curve looks like an individual market demand curve, these concepts are different. As we move along a market demand curve, the price of related goods is assumed to be constant. But when we deal with changes in the general or average price level in an economy, this assumption is meaningless because we are using a market basket measure for *all* goods and services.

> The aggregate demand curve and a specific market demand curve are not the same concept.

CONCLUSION

10-2 REASONS FOR THE AGGREGATE DEMAND CURVE'S SHAPE

The reasons for the downward slope of an aggregate demand curve include the *real balances effect*, the *interest-rate effect*, and the *net exports effect*.

10-2a Real Balances Effect

Recall from the discussion in the chapter on inflation that cash, checking deposits, savings accounts, and certificates of deposit are examples of financial assets whose real value changes with the price level. If prices are falling, the purchasing power of households rises, and they are more willing and able to spend. Suppose you have $1,000 in a checking account with which to buy 10 weeks' worth of groceries. If prices fall by 20 percent, $1,000 will now buy enough groceries for 12 weeks. This rise in your real wealth may make you more willing and able to purchase a new iPhone out of current income.

> Consumers spend more on goods and services when lower prices make their dollars more valuable. Therefore, the real value of money is measured by the quantity of goods and services each dollar buys.

CONCLUSION

On the other hand, inflation reduces the real value of fixed-value financial assets held by households. The result is lower consumption spending, and real GDP falls. The

Real balances effect
The impact on total spending (and therefore real GDP) caused by the inverse relationship between the price level and the real value of financial assets with fixed nominal value.

Interest-rate effect
The impact on total spending (and therefore real GDP) caused by the direct relationship between the price level and the interest rate.

effect of the change in the price level on real consumption spending is called the real balances effect. The **real balances effect** is the impact on total spending (and therefore real GDP) caused by the inverse relationship between the price level and the real value of financial assets with fixed nominal value.

10-2b Interest-Rate Effect

A second reason why the aggregate demand curve is downward sloping involves the interest-rate effect. The **interest-rate effect** is the impact on total spending (and therefore real GDP) caused by the direct relationship between the price level and the interest rate. A key assumption of the aggregate demand curve is that the supply of money available for borrowing remains fixed. A high price level means people must take more dollars from their wallets and checking accounts in order to purchase goods and services. At a higher price level, the demand for borrowed money to buy products also increases and results in a higher cost of borrowing, that is, higher interest rates. Rising interest rates discourage households from borrowing to purchase homes, cars, and other consumer products. Similarly, at higher interest rates, businesses cut investment projects because the higher cost of borrowing diminishes the profitability of these investments. Thus, assuming a fixed supply of credit (money), an increase in the price level increases the demand for money and interest rates rise. At this higher cost of borrowing, households and businesses borrow less as well as spend less, reducing the aggregate quantity demanded.

GLOBAL ECONOMICS

10-2c Net Exports Effect

Whether American-made goods have lower relative prices than foreign goods is another important factor in determining the aggregate demand curve. A higher domestic price level tends to make U.S. goods more expensive compared to foreign goods, and imports rise because consumers substitute imported goods for domestic goods. An increase in the price of U.S. goods in foreign markets also causes U.S. exports to decline. Consequently, a rise in the domestic price level of an economy tends to increase imports, decrease exports, and thereby reduce the net exports component of total spending which cause the quantity or real GDP purchased to fall. This condition is the net exports effect. The **net exports effect** is the impact on total spending (and, therefore, real GDP) caused by the inverse relationship between the price level and the net exports of an economy.

Net exports effect
The impact on total spending (and therefore real GDP) caused by the inverse relationship between the price level and the net exports of an economy.

Exhibit 2 summarizes the three effects that explain why the aggregate demand curve in Exhibit 1 is downward sloping.

10-3 NONPRICE-LEVEL DETERMINANTS OF AGGREGATE DEMAND

As was the case with individual demand curves, we must distinguish between *changes in real GDP demanded*, caused by changes in the price level, and *changes in aggregate demand*, caused by changes in one or more of the *nonprice-level determinants*. Once the ceteris paribus assumption is relaxed, changes in variables other than the price level cause a shift of the aggregate demand curve. Nonprice-level determinants include the consumption (*C*), investment (*I*), government spending (*G*), and net exports (*X*−*M*) components of aggregate expenditures explained in the chapter on GDP.

EXHIBIT 2 Why the Aggregate Demand Curve Is Downward Sloping

Effect	Causation chain
Real balances effect	Price level decreases → Purchasing power rises → Wealth rises → Consumers buy more goods → Real GDP demanded increases
Interest-rate effect	Price level decreases → Purchasing power rises → Demand for fixed supply of credit falls → Interest rates fall → Businesses and households borrow and buy more goods → Real GDP demanded increases
Net exports effect	Price level decreases → U.S. goods become less expensive than foreign goods → Americans and foreigners buy more U.S. goods → Exports rise and imports fall → Real GDP demanded increases

Any change in the individual components of aggregate expenditures shifts the aggregate demand curve.

CONCLUSION

A rightward shift of the AD curve reflects an increase in total spending. Exhibit 3 illustrates the link between an increase in aggregate expenditures and an increase in aggregate demand. Begin at point A on aggregate demand curve AD_1, with a price level of 200 and a real GDP purchased of $12 trillion. Assume the price level remains constant at 200 and the aggregate demand curve increases from AD_1 to AD_2. Consequently, the level of real GDP purchased rises from $12 trillion (point A) to $16 trillion (point B) at the price level of 200. This could have been caused by consumers becoming more optimistic about the future and therefore they increased their consumption expenditures (C). Another cause might be that a tax cut increased take-home income (disposable income) and consumer purchases increased at each possible price level. Or possibly an increase in business optimism has increased profit expectations, and the level of investment (I) has risen because businesses are spending more for plants and equipment. The same increase in aggregate demand could also have been caused by a boost in government spending (G) or a rise in net exports ($X-M$). On the other hand, movement toward more pessimistic expectations by consumers or firms will cause the aggregate demand curve to shift leftward. A leftward shift in the aggregate demand curve may also be caused by a tax increase or a decrease in government spending or net exports.

10-4 THE AGGREGATE SUPPLY CURVE

Just as we must distinguish between the aggregate demand and individual market demand curves, the theory for a specific market supply curve does not apply directly to the aggregate supply curve. Keeping this condition in mind, we can define the **aggregate supply curve (AS)** as the curve that shows the level of real GDP produced at different

Aggregate supply curve (AS)
The curve that shows the level of real GDP produced at different possible price levels during a time period, ceteris paribus.

EXHIBIT 3 A Shift in the Aggregate Demand Curve

At the price level of 200, the real GDP level is $12 trillion at point A on AD_1. An increase in one of the nonprice-level determinants of aggregate demand, which include consumption (C), investment (I), government spending (G), or net exports ($X - M$) causes the level of real GDP purchased to rise to $16 trillion at point B on AD_2. Because this effect occurs at any price level, an increase in aggregate expenditures (total spending) shifts the AD curve rightward. Conversely, a decrease in aggregate expenditures shifts the AD curve leftward.

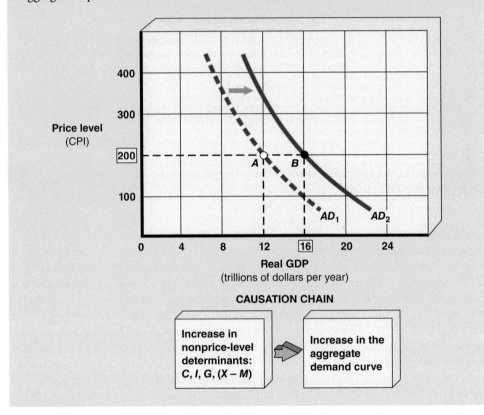

CAUSATION CHAIN

possible price levels during a time period, ceteris paribus. Stated simply, the aggregate supply curve shows us the total dollar amount of goods and services produced in an economy at various price levels. Given this general definition, we must pause to discuss two opposing views—the Keynesian horizontal aggregate supply curve and the classical vertical aggregate supply curve.

10-4a Keynesian View of Aggregate Supply

Keynes wrote in a time of great uncertainty and instability. In 1936, seven years after the beginning of the Great Depression and three years before the beginning of World War II, John Maynard Keynes published *The General Theory of Employment, Interest, and Money*. In this book, Keynes, a Cambridge University economist, argued that price and wage inflexibility during a recession means that unemployment can be a prolonged affair. Unless an economy trapped in a depression or severe recession is rescued by an increase in aggregate demand, full employment will not be achieved. This Keynesian prediction calls for government to intervene and actively manage aggregate demand to avoid a depression or recession.

Why do Keynesians assume that product prices and wages are fixed? Reasons for upward inflexibility include the following: First, during a deep recession, there are many idle resources in the economy. Consequently, producers are willing to sell at current prices because there are no shortages to put upward pressure on prices. Second, the supply of unemployed workers willing to work for the prevailing wage rate diminishes the power of workers to increase their wages. Reasons for downward inflexibility include: First, union contracts prevent businesses from lowering wage rates. Second, minimum wage laws prevent lower wages. Third, employers believe that cutting wages lowers worker morale and productivity. Therefore, during a recession employers prefer to freeze wages and lay off or reduce hours for some of their workers until the economy recovers. In fact, the CPI for the last month of each recession since 1948 was at or above the CPI for the first month of the recession. Given the Keynesian assumption of fixed or rigid product prices and wages, changes in the aggregate demand curve cause changes in real GDP along a horizontal aggregate supply curve. In short, Keynesian theory argues that only shifts in aggregate demand can revitalize a depressed economy.

Exhibit 4 portrays the core of Keynesian theory. We begin at equilibrium E_1, with a fixed price level of 200. Given aggregate demand schedule AD_1, the equilibrium level of real GDP supplied and demanded is $8 trillion. Now government spending (G) increases, causing aggregate demand to rise from AD_1 to AD_2 and equilibrium to shift from E_1 to E_2 along the horizontal aggregate supply curve (AS). At E_2, the economy moves to $12 trillion, which is closer to the full-employment GDP of $16 trillion.

When the aggregate supply curve is horizontal and an economy is in recession below full employment, the only effects of an increase in aggregate demand are increases in real GDP and employment, while the price level does not change. Stated simply, the Keynesian view is that "demand creates its own supply."

CONCLUSION

10-4b Classical View of Aggregate Supply

Prior to the Great Depression of the 1930s, a group of economists known as the *classical economists* dominated economic thinking.[1] The founder of the classical school of economics was Adam Smith (discussed in the chapter on economies in transition). Macroeconomics had not developed as a separate economic theory, and classical economics was therefore based primarily on microeconomic market equilibrium theory. The classical school of economics was mainstream economics from the 1770s to the Great Depression era. The classical economists believed in the *laissez-faire* "leave it alone" theory that the economy was self-regulating and would correct itself over time without government intervention. The classical economists believed, as you studied in Chapter 4, that the

---

[1]The classical economists included Adam Smith, J. B. Say, David Ricardo, John Stuart Mill, Thomas Malthus, Alfred Marshall, and others.

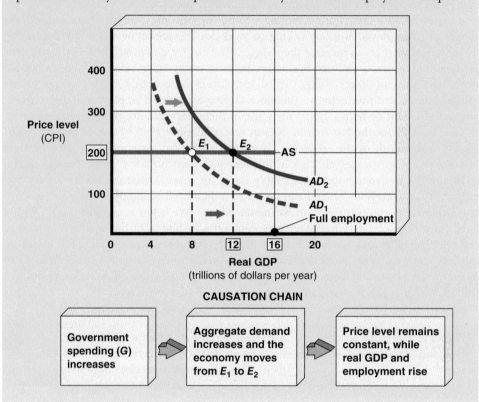

EXHIBIT 4 The Keynesian Horizontal Aggregate Supply Curve

The increase in aggregate demand from AD_1 to AD_2 causes a new equilibrium at E_2. Given the Keynesian assumption of a fixed price level, changes in aggregate demand cause changes in real GDP along the horizontal portion of the aggregate supply curve, AS. Keynesian theory argues that only shifts in aggregate demand possess the ability to restore a depressed economy to the full-employment output.

CAUSATION CHAIN

| Government spending (G) increases | ⇨ | Aggregate demand increases and the economy moves from E_1 to E_2 | ⇨ | Price level remains constant, while real GDP and employment rise |

forces of supply and demand naturally achieve an equilibrium price where the quantity supplied of products equals the quantity demanded. For the classicalists, a similar equilibrium in the macroeconomy would result in full employment because flexible prices (including wages and interest rates) in competitive markets bring all markets to equilibrium. After a temporary adjustment period, markets always clear because prices adjust to enable firms to sell all goods and services offered for sale. In short, recessions naturally cure themselves because the capitalistic price system automatically restores full employment.

Exhibit 5 uses the aggregate demand and supply model to illustrate the classical view that the aggregate supply curve, AS, is a vertical line at the full-employment output of $16 trillion. The vertical shape of the classical aggregate supply curve is based on two assumptions. First, the economy normally operates at its full-employment output level. Second, the price level of products and production costs change by the same percentage, that is, proportionally, in order to maintain a full-employment level of output. This

EXHIBIT 5 The Classical Vertical Aggregate Supply Curve

Classical theory argues that prices and wages adjust to keep the economy operating at its full-employment output of $16 trillion. A decline in aggregate demand from AD_1 to AD_2 will temporarily cause a surplus of $4 trillion, the distance from E' to E_1. Businesses respond by cutting the price level from 300 to 200. As a result, consumers increase their purchases because of the real balances effect. At the same time, wages adjust downward until full employment is achieved. Thus, classical economists predict the economy is self-correcting and will restore full employment at point E_2 but with a lower price level. E_1 and E_2 therefore represent points along a classical vertical aggregate supply curve, AS.

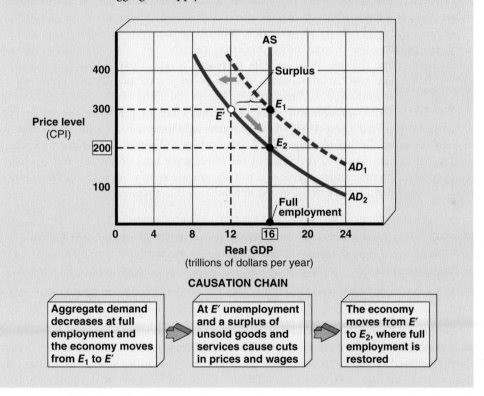

CAUSATION CHAIN

| Aggregate demand decreases at full employment and the economy moves from E_1 to E' | At E' unemployment and a surplus of unsold goods and services cause cuts in prices and wages | The economy moves from E' to E_2, where full employment is restored |

classical theory of flexible prices and wages is at odds with the Keynesian concept of sticky (inflexible) prices and wages.

Exhibit 5 also illustrates why classical economists believe a market economy over time automatically self-corrects to restore full employment without government intervention. Following the classical scenario, the economy is initially in equilibrium at E_1 where the aggregate quantity demanded equals the aggregate quantity supplied at the price level is 300. This equilibrium occurs at the full-employment level of real GDP of $16 trillion. Now suppose households and businesses become pessimistic about economic conditions and total spending falls. This causes AD_1 to shift leftward to AD_2. At a price level of 300, the immediate effect is that aggregate output exceeds aggregate spending by $4 trillion ($E_1$ to E'), and unexpected inventory accumulation (a surplus) occurs. To eliminate unsold inventories resulting from the decrease in aggregate demand, business firms temporarily cut back on production and reduce the price level from 300 to 200.

At E', the decline in aggregate output in response to the surplus also affects prices in the factor markets. As a result of the economy moving from point E_1 to E', there is a decrease in the demand for labor, natural resources, and other inputs used to produce products. This surplus condition in the factor markets means that some workers who are willing to work are laid off and compete with those who still have jobs by reducing their wage demands and wages fall. Owners of natural resources and capital likewise cut their prices.

How can the classical economists believe that prices and wages are completely flexible? The answer is contained in the *real balances effect*, explained earlier. When businesses reduce the price level from 300 to 200, the cost of living falls by the same proportion. When the price level falls by 33 percent, a nominal or money wage rate of, say, $21 per hour will purchase 33 percent more groceries after the fall in product prices than it would have before the fall. Workers will, therefore, accept a pay cut of 33 percent, or $7 per hour. Any worker who refuses the lower wage rate of $14 per hour will be replaced by an unemployed worker willing to accept the going rate.

Exhibit 5 shows an economy-wide proportional fall in prices and wages by the movement downward along AD_2 from E' to a new equilibrium at E_2. At E_2, the economy has self-corrected through downwardly flexible prices and wages to its full-employment level of $16 trillion worth of real GDP at the lower price level of 200. E_1 and E_2, therefore, represent points along a classical vertical aggregate supply curve, AS. (The classical model is explained in more detail in the appendix to this chapter.)

CONCLUSION   When the aggregate supply curve is vertical at the full-employment GDP, the only effect over time of a change in aggregate demand is a change in the price level. Stated simply, the classical view is that "supply creates its own demand."[2]

Although Keynes himself did not use the AD–AS model, we can use Exhibit 5 to distinguish between Keynes's view and the classical theory of flexible prices and wages. Keynes believed that once the aggregate demand curve has shifted from AD_1 to AD_2, the surplus (the distance from E' to E_1) will persist because he rejected price-wage downward flexibility. The economy therefore will remain at the less-than-full-employment output of $12 trillion until the aggregate demand curve shifts rightward and returns to its initial position at AD_1.

CONCLUSION   Keynesian theory rejects classical theory for an economy in recession because Keynesians argue that during a recession, prices and wages do not adjust downward to restore an economy to full-employment real GDP.

---

[2]This quotation is known as Say's Law, named after the French classical economist Jean-Baptiste Say (1767–1832).

10-4c Three Ranges of the Aggregate Supply Curve

Having studied the differing theories of the classical economists and Keynes, we will now discuss an eclectic or pragmatic view of how the shape of the aggregate supply curve varies as real GDP expands or contracts. The aggregate supply curve, AS, in Exhibit 6 has three distinct ranges or segments, labeled (1) *Keynesian range*, (2) *intermediate range*, and (3) *classical range.*

In Exhibit 6, below real GDP Y_K, the price level remains constant as the level of real GDP rises. This is the **Keynesian range**, or the horizontal segment of the aggregate supply curve, which represents an economy in a severe recession. Between Y_K and the full-employment output of Y_F, the price level rises as the real GDP level rises. This is the **intermediate range**, or the rising segment of the aggregate supply curve, which represents an economy approaching full-employment output. Finally, at Y_F, the level of real GDP remains constant, and only the price level rises as aggregate demand increases. This is the **classical range**, or the vertical segment of the aggregate supply curve, which represents an economy at full-employment output. We will now examine the rationale for each of these three quite distinct ranges.

Keynesian range
The horizontal segment of the aggregate supply curve, which represents an economy in a severe recession.

Intermediate range
The rising segment of the aggregate supply curve, which represents an economy as it approaches full employment output.

Classical range
The vertical segment of the aggregate supply curve, which represents an economy at full-employment output.

EXHIBIT 6 The Three Ranges of the Aggregate Supply Curve

The aggregate supply curve shows the relationship between the price level and the level of real GDP supplied. It consists of three distinct ranges: a Keynesian range between 0 and Y_K, wherein the price level is constant for an economy in severe recession; an intermediate range between Y_K and Y_F, where both the price level and the level of real GDP rises as an economy approaches full employment; and a classical range, where the price level can vary while the level of real GDP remains constant at the full-employment level of output, Y_F.

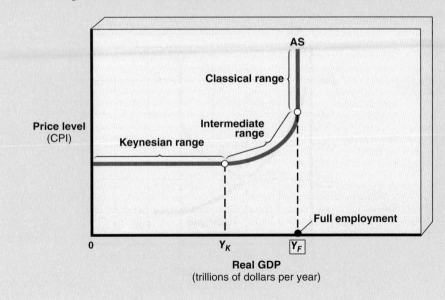

10-5 CHANGES IN AD–AS MACROECONOMIC EQUILIBRIUM

In Exhibit 7, the macroeconomic equilibrium level of real GDP is $8 trillion, and the equilibrium price level is 200, shown at point *E*. This is the unique combination of price level and output level that equates how much people want to buy with the amount businesses want to produce and sell. Because the entire real GDP value of final products is bought and sold at the price level of 200, there is no upward or downward pressure on the price level or production. Note that the economy shown in Exhibit 7 is operating on the edge of the Keynesian range, with a negative GDP gap of $8 trillion.

Suppose that in Exhibit 7, the level of output on the AS curve is below $8 trillion (for example, $4 trillion) and the AD curve remains fixed. At a price level of 200, the real GDP demanded ($8 trillion) exceeds the real GDP supplied ($4 trillion). Under such circumstances, businesses cannot fill orders quickly enough, and inventories are drawn down unexpectedly. Business managers react by hiring more workers and producing more output. Because the economy is operating in the Keynesian range, the price level remains constant at 200 as real GDP expands (to $8 trillion).

EXHIBIT 7   The Aggregate Demand and Aggregate Supply Model

Macroeconomic equilibrium occurs where the aggregate demand curve, AD, and the aggregate supply curve, AS, intersect. In this case, equilibrium, *E*, is located at the far end of the Keynesian range, where the price level is 200 and the equilibrium output is $8 trillion. In macroeconomic equilibrium, businesses neither overestimate (over produce) nor underestimate (under produce) the real GDP demanded at the prevailing price level.

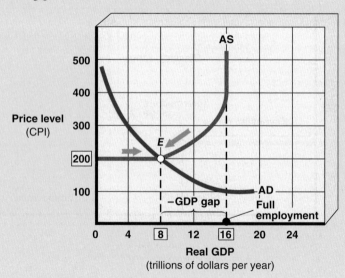

The opposite scenario occurs if the level of real GDP supplied on the AS curve exceeds the real GDP demanded on the AD curve. Consider this scenario in the context of the economy operating within the intermediate range, between $8 trillion and $16 trillion. In this output segment, the price level is between 200 and 400. Suppose the price level is 300. At a price level of 300, the aggregate quantity supplied would be $14 trillion, and the aggregate quantity demanded would be $4 trillion. Businesses face an unintended increase in their inventories of unsold goods equal to $10 trillion. Business would cut back on production, lay off workers, and reduce prices.

This adjustment process continues until the equilibrium price level and output level are reached at point E and there is no further downward pressure on the price level. Here the production decisions of sellers in the economy equal the total spending decisions of buyers during the given period of time.

| At macroeconomic equilibrium, sellers neither overestimate nor underestimate the real GDP demanded at the prevailing price level. | **CONCLUSION** |

One explanation of the business cycle is that the aggregate demand curve moves along a stationary aggregate supply curve. The next step in our analysis therefore is to *shift* the aggregate demand curve along the three ranges of the aggregate supply curve and observe the impact on real GDP and the price level. As the macroeconomic equilibrium changes, the economy experiences more or fewer problems with inflation and unemployment.

10-5a Keynesian Range

Keynes's macroeconomic theory offered a powerful solution to the Great Depression. Keynes perceived the economy as being driven by aggregate demand and Exhibit 8(a) demonstrates this theory with hypothetical data. The range of real GDP below $8 trillion is consistent with the Keynesian range of price and wage inflexibility. Assume the economy is in equilibrium at E_1, with a price level of 200 and a real GDP of $4 trillion. In this case, the economy is in recession far below the full-employment GDP of $16 trillion. The Keynesian prescription for a recession is to increase aggregate demand until the economy achieves full employment. Because the aggregate supply curve is horizontal in the Keynesian range, "demand creates its own supply." Suppose demand shifts rightward from AD_1 to AD_2 and a new equilibrium is established at E_2. Even at the higher real GDP level of $8 trillion, the price level remains at 200. Stated differently, aggregate output can expand throughout this range without raising prices. This is because in the Keynesian range, substantial idle production capacity (including property and unemployed workers competing for available jobs) can be put to work at existing prices.

| As aggregate demand increases in the Keynesian range, the price level remains constant as real GDP expands. | **CONCLUSION** |

EXHIBIT 8 Effects of Increases in Aggregate Demand

The effect of a rightward shift in the aggregate demand curve on the price and output levels depends on the range of the aggregate supply curve in which the shift occurs. In part (a), an increase in aggregate demand causing the equilibrium to change from E_1 to E_2 in the Keynesian range will increase real GDP from $4 trillion to $8 trillion, but the price level will remain unchanged at 200.

In part (b), an increase in aggregate demand causing the equilibrium to change from E_3 to E_4 in the intermediate range will increase real GDP from $8 trillion to $12 trillion, and the price level will rise from 200 to 250.

In part (c), an increase in aggregate demand causing the equilibrium to change from E_5 to E_6 in the classical range will increase the price level from 300 to 400, but real GDP will not increase beyond the full-employment level of $16 trillion.

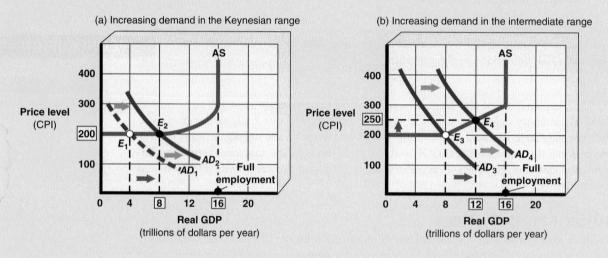

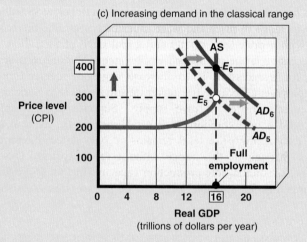

10-5b Intermediate Range

The intermediate range in Exhibit 8(b) is between $8 trillion and $16 trillion worth of real GDP. As output increases in this range of the aggregate supply curve near the full-employment level of output, the considerable slack in the economy experienced in the Keynesian range disappears. Assume an economy is initially in equilibrium at E_3 and aggregate demand increases from AD_3 to AD_4. As a result, the level of real GDP rises from $8 trillion to $12 trillion, and the price level rises from 200 to 250. In this output range, several factors contribute to inflation. First, *bottlenecks* (obstacles to output flow) develop when some firms have reached their productive capacity while other firms operate below full capacity. Suppose the steel industry is operating at full capacity and cannot fill all its orders for steel. An inadequate supply of one resource, such as steel, can hold up auto production even though the auto industry is operating well below capacity. Consequently, the bottleneck causes firms to compete for this steel, pushing up the price of steel and, in turn, the price of autos. Second, a shortage of certain labor skills while firms are earning higher profits causes businesses to expect that labor will exert its power to obtain sizable wage increases, so businesses raise prices. Wage demands are more difficult to reject when the economy is prospering because businesses fear workers will change jobs or strike. Besides, businesses believe higher prices can be passed on to consumers quite easily because consumers expect higher prices as output expands to near full capacity. Third, as the economy approaches full employment, firms must use less productive workers and less efficient machinery. This inefficiency creates higher production costs, which are passed on to consumers in the form of higher prices.

> In the intermediate range, increases in aggregate demand increase both the price level and the real GDP level.

CONCLUSION

10-5c Classical Range

While inflation resulting from an outward shift in aggregate demand was no problem in the Keynesian range and only a minor problem in the intermediate range, it becomes a serious problem in the classical or vertical range.

> Once the economy reaches full-employment output in the classical range, additional increases in aggregate demand merely cause inflation, rather than more real GDP.

CONCLUSION

Assume the economy shown in Exhibit 8(c) is in equilibrium at E_5, AD_5 intersects AS at the full-capacity output level of $16 trillion. Now suppose aggregate demand shifts rightward from AD_5 to AD_6. Because the aggregate supply curve AS is vertical at $16 trillion, this increase in the aggregate demand curve boosts the price level from 300 to 400, but it fails to expand real GDP. The explanation is that once the economy operates at capacity, further increases in spending enable businesses to raise their prices in order to ration fully employed resources to those willing to pay the highest prices.

In summary, the AD–AS model presented in this chapter is a combination of the conflicting assumptions of the Keynesian and classical theories separated by an intermediate range, which fits neither extreme precisely. Be forewarned that in later chapters, you will encounter a continuing great controversy over the shape of the aggregate supply curve. Modern-day classical economists believe the entire aggregate supply curve is steep, or vertical. In contrast, Keynesian economists contend that the aggregate supply curve is much flatter, or horizontal.

10-5d The AD–AS Model for 2008–2009 During the Great Recession

Exhibit 9 uses actual data to illustrate the AD–AS model. At E_1, the economy in the third quarter of 2008 was operating at a CPI of 219 and a real GDP of $14.9 trillion, which was below the full-employment real GDP of $15.5 trillion. In 2008, the combination of home prices falling sharply and a plunge in stock prices destroyed household wealth and consumption (C) fell. At the same time, new home construction fell rapidly, which decreased investment spending. Recall from the chapter on gross domestic

---

EXHIBIT 9 Effect of Decreases in Aggregate Demand During 2008–2009 of the Great Recession

Beginning in the third quarter of 2008 at E_1, the aggregate demand curve shifted leftward from E_1 to E_2 in the fourth quarter of 2008 along the intermediate range of the aggregate supply curve, AS. The CPI fell from 219 to 212, and real GDP fell from $14.9 trillion to $14.6 trillion. Next, the aggregate demand curve decreased from AD_2 at E_2 to AD_3 at E_3 in the second quarter of 2009 along the Keynesian range of the aggregate supply curve. Here the price level remained constant, and real GDP fell from $14.6 trillion to $14.3 trillion.

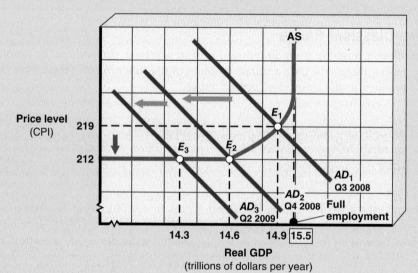

SOURCE: Bureau of Economic Analysis, *National Income Accounts*, http://www.bea.gov/iTable/index_nipa.cfm, Table 1.1.6 and Bureau of Labor Statistics, Consumer Price Index, http://data.bls.gov/cgi-bin/surveymost?cu.

product that new residential housing is included in investment spending (*I*). This recessionary condition is illustrated by a movement between E_1 and E_2 caused by the aggregate demand curve decreasing from AD_1 to AD_2 along the intermediate range of the aggregate supply curve AS. At E_2 in the fourth quarter of 2008, the CPI dropped to 212, and real GDP decreased from \$14.9 trillion to \$14.6 trillion. Next, the aggregate demand curve decreased again from AD_2 to AD_3 in the second quarter of 2009 along the flat Keynesian range between E_2 and E_3. Here the price level remained approximately constant at 212, while real GDP declined from \$14.6 trillion to \$14.3 trillion. Although not shown explicitly in the exhibit, the unemployment rate rose during this period from 4.7 percent to 9.5 percent.

10-6 NONPRICE-LEVEL DETERMINANTS OF AGGREGATE SUPPLY

Our discussion so far has explained changes in the quantity or real GDP supplied resulting from changes in the aggregate demand curve, given a stationary aggregate supply curve. Now we consider the situation when the aggregate demand curve is stationary and the aggregate supply curve shifts as a result of changes in one or more of the *nonprice-level determinants* of AS. The nonprice-level factors affecting aggregate supply include resource prices (domestic and imported), technological change, taxes, subsidies, and regulations. Note that each of these factors affects production costs. At a given price level, the profit businesses make at any level of real GDP depends on production costs. If costs change, firms respond by changing their output. Lower production costs shift the aggregate supply curve rightward; indicating greater real GDP is supplied at any price level. Conversely, higher production costs shift the aggregate supply curve leftward, meaning less real GDP is supplied at any price level.

Exhibit 10 represents a supply-side explanation of the business cycle, in contrast to the demand-side case presented in Exhibit 8. (Note that for simplicity the aggregate supply curve can be drawn using only the intermediate segment.) The economy begins in equilibrium at point E_1, with real GDP at \$10 trillion and the price level at 175. Then suppose labor unions become less powerful, and their weaker bargaining position causes the wage rate to fall. With lower labor costs per unit of output, businesses seek to increase profits by expanding production at any price level. Hence, the aggregate supply curve shifts rightward from AS_1 to AS_2, and equilibrium changes from E_1 to E_2. As a result, real GDP increases \$2 trillion, and the price level decreases from 175 to 150. Changes in other nonprice-level factors also cause an increase in aggregate supply. Lower oil prices, greater entrepreneurship, lower taxes, and reduced government regulation are other examples of conditions that lower production costs and therefore cause a rightward shift of the aggregate supply curve.

What kinds of events might raise production costs and shift the aggregate supply curve leftward? Perhaps there is war in the Persian Gulf or the Organization of the Petroleum Exporting Countries (OPEC) disrupts supplies of oil, and higher energy prices spread throughout the economy. Under such a "supply shock," businesses decrease their output at any price level in response to higher production costs per unit. Similarly, larger-than-expected wage increases, higher taxes to protect the environment (see Exhibit 8(a) in Chapter 4), greater government regulation, or firms having to pay higher health insurance premiums would increase production costs and therefore shift the

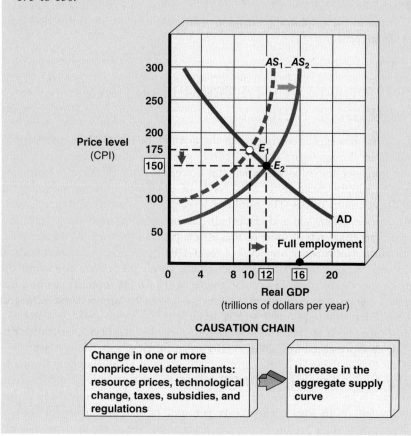

EXHIBIT 10 A Rightward Shift in the Aggregate Supply Curve

Holding the aggregate demand curve constant, the impact on the price level and real GDP depends on whether the aggregate supply curve shifts to the right or the left. A rightward shift of the aggregate supply curve from AS_1 to AS_2 will increase real GDP from $10 trillion to $12 trillion and reduce the price level from 175 to 150.

CAUSATION CHAIN

| Change in one or more nonprice-level determinants: resource prices, technological change, taxes, subsidies, and regulations | Increase in the aggregate supply curve |

aggregate supply curve leftward. A leftward shift in the aggregate supply curve is discussed further in the next section.

Exhibit 11 summarizes the nonprice-level determinants of aggregate demand and supply for further study and review. In the chapter on monetary policy, you will learn how changes in the supply of money in the economy can also shift the aggregate demand curve and influence macroeconomic performance.

10-6a Increase in Both Aggregate Demand and Aggregate Supply Curves

Let the trumpets blow! Aggregate demand and supply curves will now edify you by explaining the U.S. economy from the mid-1990s through 2000. Begin in Exhibit 12

EXHIBIT 11 Summary of the Nonprice-Level Determinants of Aggregate Demand and Aggregate Supply that Shift AD and AS

Nonprice-level determinants of aggregate demand (total spending)	Nonprice-level determinants of aggregate supply
1. Consumption (*C*)	1. Resource prices (domestic and imported)
2. Investment (*I*)	2. Taxes
3. Government spending (*G*)	3. Technological change
4. Net exports (*X − M*)	4. Subsidies
	5. Regulation

---

at E_1 with real GDP at \$10,164 billion and the CPI at 152. As shown in the AD–AS model for 1995, the economy operated below full employment (5.6 percent unemployment rate, not explicitly shown). Over the next five years, the U.S. economy moved to E_2 in 2000 and experienced strong growth in real GDP (from \$10,164 billion to \$12,565 billion) and mild inflation (the CPI increased from 152 to 172, which is 13.1 percent, or 2.6 percent per year).

The movement from E_1 (below full employment) to E_2 (full employment) was caused by an increase in AD_{95} to AD_{00} and an increase in AS_{95} to AS_{00}. The rightward shift in the AS curve was the result of technological advances, such as the Internet and electronic commerce, which produced larger-than-usual increases in productivity at each possible price level. And as shown earlier in Exhibit 9 of the chapter on business cycles and unemployment, the economy has been operating below its full-employment potential real GDP since the Great Recession of 2008 (but is projected to reach potential in 2018).

10-7 COST-PUSH AND DEMAND-PULL INFLATION REVISITED

We now apply the aggregate demand and aggregate supply model to the two types of inflation introduced in the chapter on inflation. This section begins with a historical example of *cost-push inflation* caused by a decrease in the aggregate supply curve. Next, another historical example illustrates *demand-pull inflation*, caused by an increase in the aggregate demand curve.

During the late 1970s and early 1980s, the U.S. economy experienced stagflation. **Stagflation** is the condition that occurs when an economy experiences the twin maladies of high unemployment and rapid inflation simultaneously. How could this happen? The dramatic increase in the price of imported oil in 1973–1974 was a villain explained by a *cost-push inflation* scenario. **Cost-push inflation**, defined in terms of our macro model, is a rise in the price level resulting from a decrease in the aggregate supply curve while the aggregate demand curve remains fixed. As a result of cost-push inflation, real output and employment decrease.

Stagflation
The condition that occurs when an economy experiences the twin maladies of high unemployment and rapid inflation simultaneously.

Cost-push inflation
An increase in the general price level resulting from an increase in the cost of production that causes the aggregate supply curve to shift leftward.

EXHIBIT **12** A Rightward Shift in the Aggregate Demand and Supply Curves

From late 1995 through 2000, the aggregate demand curve increased from AD_{95} to AD_{00}. Significant increases in productivity from technology advances shifted the aggregate supply curve from AS_{95} to AS_{00}. As a result, the U.S. economy experienced strong real GDP growth to full employment with mild inflation (the CPI increased from 152 to 172).

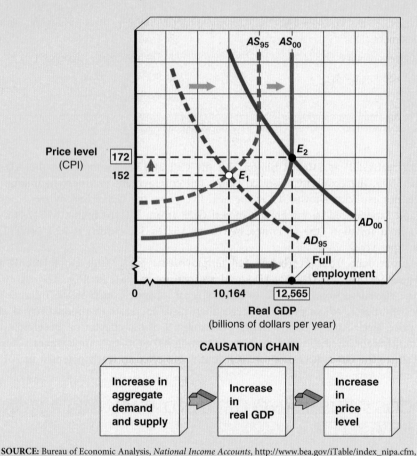

CAUSATION CHAIN

Increase in aggregate demand and supply ⟹ Increase in real GDP ⟹ Increase in price level

SOURCE: Bureau of Economic Analysis, *National Income Accounts*, http://www.bea.gov/iTable/index_nipa.cfm, Table 1.1.6 and Bureau of Labor Statistics, Consumer Price Index, http://data.bls.gov/cgi-bin/surveymost?cu.

Exhibit 13(a) uses actual data to show how a leftward shift in the supply curve can cause stagflation. In this exhibit, aggregate demand curve *AD* and aggregate supply curve AS_{73} represent the U.S. economy in 1973. Equilibrium was at point E_1, with the price level (CPI) at 44.4 and real GDP at \$5,418 billion. Then, in 1974, the impact of a major supply shock shifted the aggregate supply curve leftward from AS_{73} to AS_{74}. The explanation for this shock was the oil embargo instituted by OPEC in retaliation for U.S. support of Israel in its war with the Arabs. Assuming a stable aggregate demand curve between 1973 and 1974, the punch from the energy shock resulted in a new equilibrium at point E_2, with the 1974 CPI at 49.3. The inflation rate for 1973 was 6.2 percent and for 1974 was 11 percent [(49.3 − 44.4)/44.4] × 100. Real GDP fell from \$5,418 billion in

EXHIBIT **13** Cost-Push and Demand-Pull Inflation

Parts (a) and (b) illustrate the distinction between cost-push inflation and demand-pull inflation. Cost-push inflation is inflation that results from a decrease in the aggregate supply curve. In part (a), higher oil prices in 1973 caused the aggregate supply curve to shift leftward from AS_{73} to AS_{74}. As a result, real GDP fell from $5,418 billion to $5,390 billion, and the price level (CPI) rose from 44.4 to 49.3. This combination of higher price level and a lower real output level is called stagflation.

As shown in part (b), demand-pull inflation is inflation that results from an increase in aggregate demand beyond the Keynesian range of output. Government spending increased to fight the Vietnam War without a tax increase, causing the aggregate demand curve to shift rightward from AD_{65} to AD_{66}. Consequently, real GDP rose from $3,973 billion in 1965 to $4,235 billion in 1966, and the price level (CPI) rose from 31.5 to 32.4.

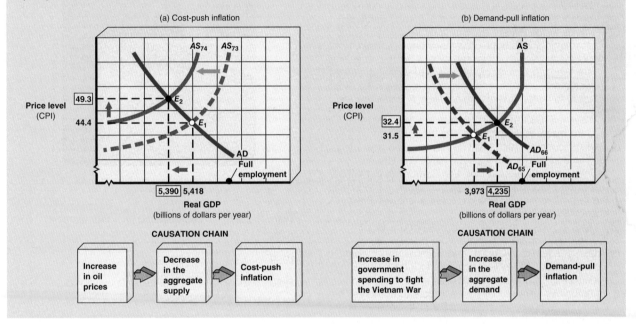

1973 to $5,390 billion in 1974, and the unemployment rate (not shown directly in the exhibit) climbed from 4.9 percent to 5.6 percent between these two years.[3]

In contrast, a rightward shift in the aggregate demand curve can result in *demand-pull inflation*. **Demand-pull inflation**, in terms of our macro model, is a rise in the price level resulting from an increase in the aggregate demand curve while the aggregate supply curve remains fixed. Again, we can use aggregate demand and supply analysis and actual data to explain demand-pull inflation. In 1965, when the unemployment rate of 4.5 percent was close to the 4 percent natural rate of unemployment of its time, government spending increased sharply to fight the Vietnam War without a tax increase (an income tax surcharge was later enacted in 1968). The inflation rate jumped sharply from 1.6 percent in 1965 to 2.9 percent in 1966.

Exhibit 13(b) illustrates what happened to the economy between 1965 and 1966. Suppose the economy was operating in 1965 at E_1, which is in the intermediate output range. The impact of the increase in military spending shifted the aggregate demand curve from

Demand-pull inflation
A rise in the general price level resulting from an excess of total spending (demand) caused by a rightward shift in the aggregate demand curve.

---

[3]*Economic Report of the President, 2012,* http://www.gpo.gov/fdsys/pkg/ERP-2012/content-detail.html, Tables B–11.

YOU'RE THE ECONOMIST

Applicable Concept: Aggregate Demand and Aggregate Supply Analysis

Was John Maynard Keynes Right?

In The General Theory of Employment, Interest, and Money, Keynes wrote:

> The ideas of economists and political philosophers, both when they are right and when they are wrong, are more powerful than is commonly understood. Indeed the world is ruled by little else. Practical men, who believe themselves to be quite exempt from any intellectual influences, are usually the slaves of some defunct economist. Madmen in authority, who hear voices in the air, are distilling their frenzy from some academic scribbler of a few years back.... There are not many who are influenced by new theories after they are twenty-five or thirty years of age, so that the ideas which civil servants and politicians and even agitators apply to current events are not likely to be the newest.[1]

Keynes (1883–1946) is regarded as the father of modern macroeconomics. He was the son of an eminent English economist, John Neville Keynes, who was a lecturer in economics and logic at Cambridge University. Keynes was educated at Eton and Cambridge in mathematics and probability theory, but ultimately he selected the field of economics and accepted a lectureship in economics at Cambridge.

Keynes was a many-faceted man who was an honored and supremely successful member of the British academic, financial, and political upper class. He amassed a $2 million personal fortune by speculating in stocks, international currencies, and commodities. (Use CPI index numbers to compute the equivalent amount in today's dollars.) In addition to making a huge fortune for himself, Keynes served as a trustee of King's College and increased its endowment over tenfold.

Keynes was a prolific scholar who is best remembered for The General Theory, published in 1936. This work made a convincing attack on the classical theory that capitalism would self-correct from a severe recession. Keynes based his model on the belief that increasing aggregate demand will achieve full employment, while prices and wages remain inflexible. Moreover, his bold policy prescription was for the government to raise its spending and/or reduce taxes in order to increase the economy's aggregate demand curve and put the unemployed back to work.

Hulton-Deutsch Collection/Historical/Corbis

Year	CPI	Real GDP (billions of 2009 dollars)	Unemployment rate (percent)
1933	13.0	778	24.9
1939	13.9	1,163	17.2
1940	14.0	1,265	14.6
1941	14.7	1,489	9.9

SOURCES: Bureau of Economic Analysis, National Income Accounts, http://www.bea.gov/iTable/index_nipa.cfm, Table 1.1.6, Bureau of Labor Statistics, Consumer Price Index, http://data.bls.gov/cgi-bin/surveymost?cu and Economic Report of the President, 2017, https://www.gpo.gov/fdsys/pkg/ERP-2017/content-detail.html, Table B–11.

ANALYZE THE ISSUE Was Keynes correct? Based on the data in the sidebar, use the aggregate demand and aggregate supply model to explain Keynes's theory that increases in aggregate demand propel an economy toward full employment.

---

1. J. M. Keynes, The General Theory of Employment, Interest, and Money (London: Macmillan, 1936), p. 383. J. M. Keynes, The General Theory of Employment, Interest, and Money (London: Macmillan, 1936), p. 383.

AD_{65} to AD_{66}, and the economy moved upward along the aggregate supply curve until it reached E_2. Holding the aggregate supply curve constant, the AD–AS model predicts that increasing aggregate demand at near full employment causes demand-pull inflation. As shown in Exhibit 13(b), real GDP increased from \$3,973 billion in 1965 to \$4,235 billion in 1966, and the CPI rose from 31.5 to 32.4. Thus, the inflation rate for 1966 was 2.9 percent ($[(32.4 - 31.5)/31.5] \times 100$). Corresponding to the rise in real output, the unemployment rate of 4.5 percent in 1965 fell to 3.8 percent in 1966.[4]

In summary, the aggregate supply and aggregate demand curves can shift in different directions for various reasons in a given time period. These shifts in the aggregate supply and aggregate demand curves cause upswings and downswings in real GDP—the business cycle. A leftward shift in the aggregate demand curve, for example, can cause a recession. Whereas, a rightward shift of the aggregate demand curve can cause real GDP and employment to rise, and the economy recovers. A leftward shift in the aggregate supply curve can cause a downswing, and a rightward shift will cause an upswing.

CONCLUSION

The business cycle is a result of shifts in the aggregate demand and aggregate supply curves.

Would Climate Change and the Greenhouse Effect Cause Inflation, Unemployment, or Both?

You are the chair of the president's Council of Economic Advisers. There has been an extremely hot and dry summer due to a climatic change known as the greenhouse effect. As a result, crop production has fallen drastically. The president calls you to the White House to discuss the impact on the economy. Would you explain to the president that a sharp drop in U.S. crop production would cause inflation, unemployment, or both?

CHECKPOINT

Key Concepts

Aggregate demand curve (AD)

Real balances effect

Interest-rate effect

Net exports effect

Aggregate supply curve (AS)

Keynesian range

Intermediate range

Classical range

Stagflation

Cost-push inflation

Demand-pull inflation

Summary

- The **aggregate demand curve** shows the level of real GDP purchased in the economy at different price levels during a period of time.

- Reasons why the aggregate demand curve is downward sloping include the following three effects:

---

[4]Ibid.

(1) The **real balances effect** is the impact on spending and therefore real GDP caused by the inverse relationship between the purchasing power of fixed-value financial assets and inflation, which causes a change in consumption spending,

(2) The **interest-rate effect** assumes a fixed money supply; therefore, inflation increases the demand for money. As the demand for money increases, the interest rate rises, causing consumption and investment spending to fall,

(3) The **net exports effect** is the impact on spending and, therefore, real GDP caused by the inverse relationship between net exports and inflation. An increase in the U.S. price level tends to reduce U.S. exports and increase imports, and vice versa.

Shift in the Aggregate Demand Curve. A rightward shift illustrates more spending at any price level

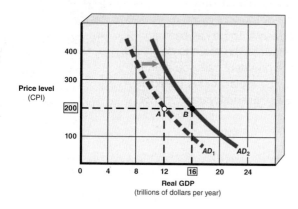

Real GDP
(trillions of dollars per year)

- The **aggregate supply curve** shows the level of real GDP that an economy will produce at different possible price levels. The shape of the aggregate supply curve depends on the flexibility of prices and wages as real GDP expands and contracts. The aggregate supply curve has three ranges:

  (1) The **Keynesian range** of the curve is horizontal because neither the price level nor production costs will increase or decrease as real GDP changes when there is substantial unemployment in the economy.

  (2) In the **intermediate range**, both prices and costs rise as real GDP rises toward full

employment. Prices and production costs rise because of bottlenecks, the stronger bargaining power of labor, and the utilization of less productive workers and capital.

  (3) The **classical range** is the vertical segment of the aggregate supply curve. It coincides with the full-employment output level. Because output is at its maximum, increases in aggregate demand will only create a higher price level.

Aggregate Supply Curve

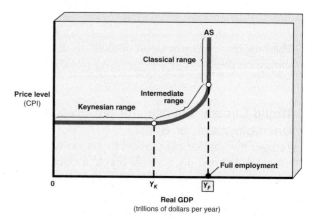

Real GDP
(trillions of dollars per year)

- **Aggregate demand and aggregate supply analysis** determines the equilibrium price level and the equilibrium real GDP by the intersection of the aggregate demand and aggregate supply curves. In macroeconomic equilibrium, businesses neither overestimate nor underestimate the real GDP demanded at the prevailing price level.

- **Stagflation** exists when an economy experiences inflation and unemployment simultaneously. Holding aggregate demand constant, a decrease in aggregate supply results in the unhealthy condition of a rise in the price level and a fall in real GDP and employment.

- **Cost-push inflation** is inflation that results from a decrease in the aggregate supply curve while the aggregate demand curve remains fixed. Cost-push inflation is undesirable because it is accompanied by declines in both real GDP and employment.

Cost-Push Inflation

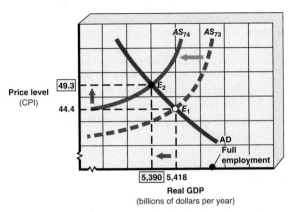

Real GDP
(billions of dollars per year)

of the aggregate supply curve, while the aggregate supply curve is fixed.

Demand-Pull Inflation

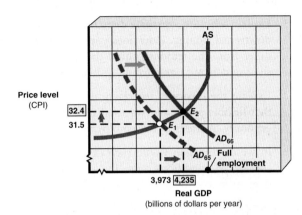

Real GDP
(billions of dollars per year)

* **Demand-pull inflation** is inflation that results from an increase in the aggregate demand curve in both the classical and the intermediate ranges

Summary of Conclusion Statements

* The aggregate demand curve and a specific market demand curve are not the same concept.

* Consumers spend more on goods and services when lower prices make their dollars more valuable. Therefore, the real value of money is measured by the quantity of goods and services each dollar buys.

* Any change in the individual components of aggregate expenditures shifts the aggregate demand curve.

* When the aggregate supply curve is horizontal and an economy is in recession below full employment, the only effects of an increase in aggregate demand are increases in real GDP and employment, while the price level does not change. Stated simply, the Keynesian view is that "demand creates its own supply."

* When the aggregate supply curve is vertical at the full-employment GDP, the only effect over time of a change in aggregate demand is a change in the price level. Stated simply, the classical view is that "supply creates its own demand."

* Keynesian theory rejects classical theory for an economy in recession because Keynesians argue that during a recession, prices and wages do not adjust downward to restore an economy to full-employment real GDP.

* At macroeconomic equilibrium, sellers neither overestimate nor underestimate the real GDP demanded at the prevailing price level.

* As aggregate demand increases in the Keynesian range, the price level remains constant as real GDP expands.

* In the intermediate range, increases in aggregate demand increase both the price level and the real GDP level.

* When the economy reaches full-employment output in the classical range, additional increases in aggregate demand merely cause inflation, rather than more real GDP.

* The business cycle is a result of shifts in the aggregate demand and aggregate supply curves.

Study Questions and Problems

Please see Appendix A for answers to the odd-numbered questions. Your instructor has access to the answers for even-numbered questions.

1. Explain why the aggregate demand curve is downward sloping. How does your explanation differ from the reasons behind the downward-sloping demand curve for an individual product?

2. Explain the theory of the classical economists that flexible prices and wages ensure that the economy operates at full employment.

3. In which direction would each of the following changes in conditions cause the aggregate demand curve to shift? Explain your answers.
   a. Consumers expect an economic downturn.
   b. A new U.S. president is elected, and the profit expectations of business executives rise.
   c. The federal government increases spending for highways, bridges, and other infrastructure.
   d. The United States increases exports of wheat and other crops to Russia, Ukraine, and other former Soviet republics.

4. Identify the three ranges of the aggregate supply curve. Explain the impact of an increase in the aggregate demand curve in each segment.

5. Consider this statement: "Equilibrium GDP is the same as full employment." Do you agree or disagree? Explain.

6. Assume the aggregate demand and aggregate supply curves intersect at a price level of 100. Explain the effect of a shift in the price level to 120 and to 50.

7. In which direction would each of the following changes in conditions cause the aggregate supply curve to shift? Explain your answers.
   a. The price of gasoline increases because of a catastrophic oil spill.
   b. Labor unions and all other workers agree to a cut in wages to stimulate the economy.

   c. Power companies switch to solar power, and the price of electricity falls.
   d. The federal government increases the excise tax on gasoline in order to finance a deficit.

8. Assume an economy operates in the intermediate range of its aggregate supply curve. State the direction of shift for the aggregate demand or aggregate supply curve for each of the following changes in conditions. What is the effect on the price level? On real GDP? On employment?
   a. The price of crude oil rises significantly.
   b. Spending on national defense doubles.
   c. The costs of imported goods increase.
   d. An improvement in technology raises labor productivity.

9. What shifts in aggregate supply or aggregate demand would cause each of the following conditions for an economy?
   a. The price level rises, and real GDP rises.
   b. The price level falls, and real GDP rises.
   c. The price level falls, and real GDP falls.
   d. The price level rises, and real GDP falls.
   e. The price level falls, and real GDP remains the same.
   f. The price level remains the same and real GDP rises.

10. Explain cost-push inflation verbally and graphically, using aggregate demand and aggregate supply analysis. Assess the impact on the price level, real GDP, and employment.

11. Explain demand-pull inflation graphically using aggregate demand and supply analysis. Assess the impact on the price level, real GDP, and employment.

✓ CHECKPOINT ANSWERS

Would Climate Change and the Greenhouse Effect Cause Inflation, Unemployment, or Both?

A drop in food production reduces aggregate supply. The decrease in aggregate supply causes the economy to contract, while prices rise. In addition to the OPEC oil embargo between 1972 and 1974, worldwide weather conditions destroyed crops and contributed to the supply shock that caused stagflation in the U.S. economy. If you said that a severe greenhouse effect would cause both higher unemployment and inflation, **YOU ARE CORRECT**.

Sample Quiz

Please see Appendix B for answers to Sample Quiz questions.

1. The aggregate demand curve shows how real GDP purchased varies with changes in
   a. unemployment.
   b. output.
   c. the price level.
   d. the interest rate.

2. Which of the following is *not* a component of the aggregate demand curve?
   a. Government spending (G)
   b. Investment (I)
   c. Consumption (C)
   d. Net exports ($X - M$)
   e. Saving

3. The real balances effect occurs because a higher price level will reduce the real value of people's
   a. financial assets.
   b. wages.
   c. unpaid debt.
   d. physical investments.

4. The real balance effect is the impact on real GDP caused by the _____ relationship between the price level and the real value of financial assets.
   a. direct
   b. inverse
   c. independent
   d. linear

5. The interest-rate effect is the impact on real GDP caused by the _____ relationship between the price level and the interest rate.
   a. direct
   b. independent
   c. linear
   d. inverse

6. The net exports effect is the _____ relationship between net exports and the price level of an economy.
   a. inverse
   b. independent
   c. direct
   d. linear

7. Which of the following would shift the aggregate demand curve to the left?
   a. An increase in exports
   b. An increase in investment
   c. An increase in government spending
   d. A decrease in government spending

8. Suppose workers become pessimistic about their future employment, which causes them to save more and spend less. If the economy is on the intermediate range of the aggregate supply curve, then
   a. both real GDP and the price level will fall.
   b. real GDP will fall, and the price level will rise.
   c. real GDP will rise, and the price level will fall.
   d. both real GDP and the price level will rise.

9. In Exhibit 14 resources are fully employed, and competition among producers for resources will lead to a higher price level in
   a. the segment labeled *ab*.
   b. the segment labeled *bc*.
   c. the segment labeled *cd*.
   d. segments *bc* and *cd*.

EXHIBIT 14 Aggregate Supply Curve

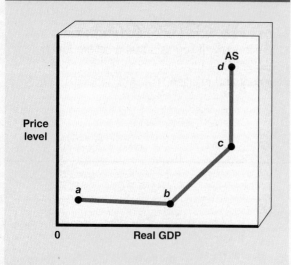

EXHIBIT 15 Aggregate Supply and Demand Curves

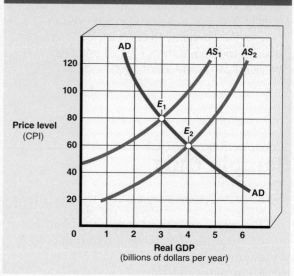

10. In Exhibit 14 as production increases, firms resort to offering higher wage rates to attract the dwindling supply of unemployed resources in
    a. the segment labeled *ab*.
    b. the segment labeled *bc*.
    c. the segment labeled *cd*.
    d. segments *bc* and *cd*.

11. An increase in oil prices will shift the aggregate
    a. demand curve leftward.
    b. demand curve rightward.
    c. supply curve leftward.
    d. supply curve rightward.

12. Stagflation is a period of time when the economy is experiencing
    a. inflation and low unemployment.
    b. high unemployment and low levels of inflation at the same time.
    c. high inflation and high unemployment at the same time.
    d. low inflation and low unemployment at the same time.

13. The shift from AS_2 to AS_1 in Exhibit 15 could be caused by a (an)
    a. sudden increase in the price of oil.
    b. increase in input prices for most firms.
    c. increase in workers' wages.
    d. All of the answers above are correct.

14. As the economy moves to the right in Exhibit 16 along the upward-sloping aggregate supply curve the
    a. unemployment rate rises.
    b. unemployment rate falls.
    c. inflation rate falls.
    d. None of the above occur.

EXHIBIT 16 Aggregate Supply and Demand Curves

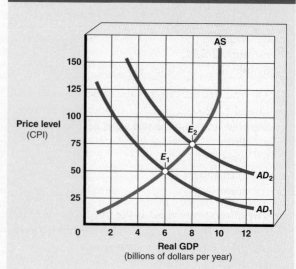

15. As the aggregate demand curve shifts from AD_1 to AD_2 in Exhibit 16 the economy experiences
    a. cost-push inflation.
    b. demand-pull inflation.
    c. wage-push inflation.
    d. hyperinflation.

16. The idea that higher prices reduce the purchasing power of financial assets and lead to less consumption and more saving is known as the
    a. real balances effect.
    b. foreign purchases effect.
    c. income effect.
    d. aggregate demand effect.

17. Which of the following is a belief of classical theory?
    a. Long-run full employment
    b. Inflexible wages
    c. Inflexible prices
    d. All of the above answers are correct

18. In Exhibit 17 if aggregate demand increases from AD_1 to AD_2,
    a. output and prices will increase.

    b. output and prices will decrease.
    c. output alone will increase.
    d. prices alone will decrease.
    e. prices alone will increase.

19. In Exhibit 17 the aggregate demand and supply curves reflect an economy in which
    a. full employment is at $1,000 billion GDP.
    b. excess aggregate supply is created when there is a shift from AD_1 to AD_2.
    c. excess aggregate demand forces prices up to P = 120.
    d. excess aggregate demand causes prices to stabilize at P = 110.
    e. a new equilibrium is found at point *b*.

20. In Exhibit 17 choosing to operate the economy at GDP = $1,200 billion and P = 110 would be opting for an economy of
    a. no unemployment with inflation.
    b. full employment without inflation.
    c. full employment with inflation.
    d. moderate cyclical unemployment without inflation.

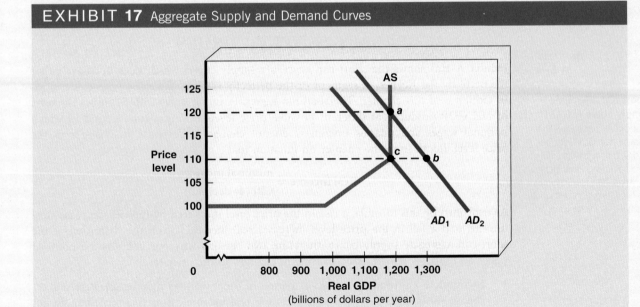

EXHIBIT 17 Aggregate Supply and Demand Curves

The Self-Correcting Aggregate Demand and Supply Model

It can be argued that the economy is self-regulating. This means that over time, the economy will move itself to full-employment equilibrium. Stated differently, this classical theory is based on the assumption that the economy might ebb and flow around it, but full employment is the normal condition for the economy regardless of gyrations in the price level. To understand this adjustment process, the AD–AS model presented in the chapter must be extended into a more complex model called the self-correcting AD–AS model. First, a distinction will be made between the short-run and long-run aggregate supply curves. Indeed, one of the most controversial areas of macroeconomics is the shape of the aggregate supply curve and the reasons for that shape. Second, we will explain long-run equilibrium using the self-correcting AD–AS model. Third, this appendix concludes by using the self-correcting AD–AS model to explain short-run and long-run adjustments to changes in aggregate demand.

10A-1 THE SHORT-RUN AND LONG-RUN AGGREGATE SUPPLY CURVES

Short-run aggregate supply curve (SRAS)

The curve that shows the level of real GDP produced at different possible price levels during a time period in which nominal incomes do not change in response to changes in the price level.

Exhibit A-1(a) shows the short-run aggregate supply curve, which does not have either the perfectly flat Keynesian segment or the perfectly vertical classical segment developed in Exhibit 6 of this chapter. The **short-run aggregate supply curve (SRAS)** shows the level of real GDP produced at different possible price levels during a time period in which nominal wages and salaries (incomes) do not change in response to changes in the price level. Recall from the chapter on inflation that

$$\text{Real income} = \frac{\text{nominal income}}{\text{CPI (as decimal)}}$$

As explained by this formula, a rise in the price level measured by the CPI decreases real income, and a fall in the price level increases real income. Given the definition of the short-run aggregate supply curve, there are two reasons why one can assume nominal wages and salaries remain fixed in spite of changes in the price level:

- **Incomplete knowledge.** In a short period of time, workers may be unaware that a change in the price level has changed their real incomes. Consequently, they do not adjust their wage and salary demands according to changes in their real incomes.

- **Fixed-wage contracts.** Unionized employees, for example, have nominal or money wages stated in their contracts. Also, many professionals receive set salaries for a

EXHIBIT **A-1** Aggregate Supply Curve

The short-run aggregate supply curve (SRAS) in part (a) is based on the assumption that nominal wages and salaries are fixed based on an expected price level of 100 and full-employment real GDP of $8 trillion. An increase in the price level from 100 to 150 increases profits, real GDP, and employment, moving the economy from point *A* to point *B*. A decrease in the price level from 100 to 50 decreases profits, real GDP, and employment, moving the economy from point *A* to point *C*.

The long-run aggregate supply curve (LRAS) in part (b) is vertical at full-employment real GDP. For example, if the price level rises from 100 at point *A* to 150 at point *B*, workers now have enough time to renegotiate higher nominal incomes by a percentage equal to the percentage increase in the price level. This flexible adjustment means that real incomes and profits remain unchanged, and the economy continues to operate at full-employment real GDP.

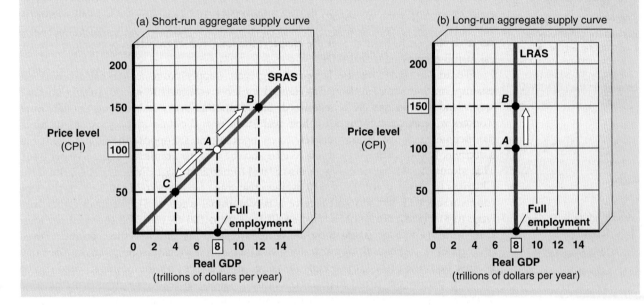

year. In these cases, nominal incomes remain constant, or "sticky," for a given time period regardless of changes in the price level.

Given the assumption that changes in the prices of goods and services measured by the CPI do not in a short period of time cause changes in nominal wages, let's examine Exhibit A-1(a) and explain the SRAS curve's upward-sloping shape. Begin at point *A* with a CPI of 100 and observe that the economy is operating at the full-employment real GDP of $8 trillion. Also assume that labor contracts are based on this expected price level. Now suppose the price level unexpectedly increases from 100 to 150 at point *B*. At higher prices for products, firms' revenues increase, and with nominal wages and salaries fixed, profits rise. In response, firms increase output from $8 trillion to $12 trillion, and the economy operates beyond its full-employment output. This occurs because firms increase work hours and train and hire homemakers, retirees, and unemployed workers who were not profitable at or below full-employment real GDP.

Now return to point *A* and assume the CPI falls to 50 at point *C*. In this case, the prices firms receive for their products drop while nominal wages and salaries remain fixed. As a result, firms' revenues and profits fall, and they reduce output from $8 trillion to $4 trillion real GDP. Correspondingly, employment (not shown explicitly in the model) falls below full employment.

CONCLUSION	The upward-sloping shape of the short-run aggregate supply curve (SRAS) is the result of fixed nominal wages and salaries as the price level changes.

10A-1a Why the Long-Run Aggregate Supply Curve Is Vertical

Long-run aggregate supply curve (LRAS)
The curve that shows the level of real GDP produced at different possible price levels during a time period in which nominal incomes change by the same percentage as the price level changes.

The long-run aggregate supply curve is presented in Exhibit A-1(b). The **long-run aggregate supply curve (LRAS)** shows the level of real GDP produced at different possible price levels during a time period in which nominal incomes change by the same percentage as the price level changes. Like the classical vertical segment of the aggregate supply curve developed in Exhibit 6 of the chapter, the long-run aggregate supply curve is vertical at full-employment real GDP.

To understand why the long-run aggregate supply curve is vertical requires the assumption that sufficient time has elapsed for labor contracts to expire, so that nominal wages and salaries can be renegotiated. Stated another way, over a long enough time, workers will calculate changes in their real incomes and obtain increases in their nominal incomes to adjust proportionately to changes in prices. Suppose the CPI is 100 (or as a decimal, 1.0) at point A in Exhibit A-1(b) and the average nominal wage is $10 per hour. This means the average real wage is also $10 ($10 nominal wage divided by 1.0). But if the CPI rises to 150 at point B, the $10 average real wage falls to $6.67 ($10/1.5). In the long run, workers will demand and receive a new nominal wage of $15, returning their real wage to $10 ($15/1.5). Thus, both the CPI (rise from 100 to 150) and the nominal wage (rise from $10 to $15) changed by the same rate of 50 percent, and the economy moved from point A to point B, upward along the long-run aggregate supply curve. Note that because both the prices of products measured by the CPI and the nominal wage rise by the same percentage, profit margins remain unchanged in real terms, and firms have no incentive to produce either more or less than the full-employment real GDP of $8 trillion. And because this same adjustment process occurs between any two price levels along LRAS, the curve is vertical, and potential real GDP is independent of the price level. Regardless of rises or falls in the CPI, potential real GDP remains the same.

CONCLUSION	The vertical shape of the long-run aggregate supply curve (LRAS) is the result of nominal wages and salaries eventually changing by the same percentage as the price level changes.

10A-1b Equilibrium in the Self-Correcting AD–AS Model

Exhibit A-2 combines aggregate demand with the short-run and long-run aggregate supply curves from the previous exhibit to form the self-correcting AD–AS model. Equilibrium in the model occurs at point E, where the economy's aggregate demand curve (AD) intersects the vertical long-run aggregate supply curve (LRAS) and the short-run

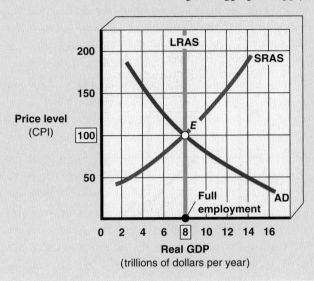

EXHIBIT A-2 Self-Correcting AD–AS Model

The short-run aggregate supply curve (SRAS) is based on an expected price level of 100. Point *E* shows that this equilibrium price level occurs at the intersection of the aggregate demand curve AD, SRAS, and the long-run aggregate supply curve (LRAS).

aggregate supply curve (SRAS). In long-run equilibrium, the economy's price level is 100, and full-employment real GDP is $8 trillion.

10A-1c The Impact of an Increase in Aggregate Demand

Now you're ready for some actions and reactions using the model. Suppose that beginning at point E_1 in Exhibit A-3, a change in a nonprice determinant of aggregate demand (summarized in Exhibit 11 at the end of the chapter) causes an increase in aggregate demand from AD_1 to AD_2. For example, the shift could be the result of an increase in consumption spending (*C*), government spending (*G*), or business investment (*I*), or greater demand for U.S. exports. Regardless of the cause, the short-run effect is for the economy to move upward along $SRAS_{100}$ to the intersection with AD_2 at the temporary or short-run equilibrium point E_2 with a price level of 150. Recall that nominal incomes are fixed in the short run. Faced with higher demand, firms raise prices for products, and because the price of labor remains unchanged, firms earn higher profits and increase employment by hiring workers who were not profitable at full employment. As a result, for a short period of time, real GDP increases above the full-employment real GDP of $8 trillion to $12 trillion. However, the economy cannot produce in excess of full employment forever. What forces are at work to bring real GDP back to full-employment real GDP?

Assume time passes and labor contracts expire. The next step in the transition process at E_2 is that workers begin demanding nominal income increases that will eventually bring their real incomes back to the same real incomes established initially at E_1.

EXHIBIT A-3 Adjustments to an Increase in Aggregate Demand

Beginning at long-run equilibrium E_1, the aggregate demand curve increases from AD_1 to AD_2. Since nominal incomes are fixed in the short run, firms raise product prices, earn higher profits, and expand output to short-run equilibrium point E_2. After enough time passes, workers increase their nominal incomes to restore their purchasing power, and the short-run supply curve shifts leftward along AD_2 to a transitional point such as E_3. As the economy moves from E_2 to E_4, profits fall, and firms cut output and employment. Eventually, long-run equilibrium is reached at E_4, with full employment restored by the self-correction process.

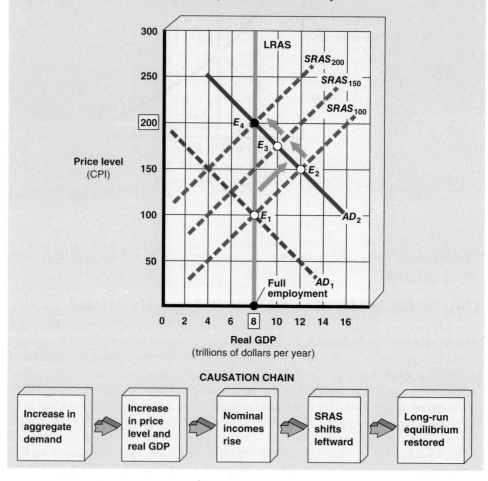

Since firms are anxious to maintain their output levels and they are competing for workers, firms meet the wage increase demands of labor. These higher wages and prices paid other resource owners increase costs of production, which shifts the short-run aggregate supply curve leftward. This causes an upward movement along AD_2. One of the successions of possible intermediate adjustment short-run supply curves along AD_2 is $SRAS_{150}$. This short-run intermediate adjustment is based on an expected price level of 150 determined by the intersection of $SRAS_{150}$ and LRAS. Although the short-run aggregate supply curve $SRAS_{150}$ intersects AD_2 at E_3, the adjustment to the increase in aggregate demand is not yet complete. Workers negotiated increases in nominal incomes based on an expected price level of 150, but the leftward shift of the short-run aggregate supply curve raised the price level to about 175 at E_3. Workers must therefore negotiate another round of higher nominal incomes to restore purchasing power. This process continues until long-run equilibrium is restored at E_4, where the adjustment process ends.

The long-run forecast for the price level at full employment is now 200 at point E_4. $SRAS_{100}$ has shifted leftward to $SRAS_{200}$, which intersects LRAS at point E_4. As a result of the shift in the short-run aggregate supply curve from E_2 to E_4 and the corresponding increase in nominal incomes, firms' profits are cut, and they react by raising product prices, reducing employment, and reducing output. At E_4, the economy has self-adjusted to both short-run and long-run equilibrium at a price level of 200 and full-employment real GDP of $8 trillion. If there are no further shifts in aggregate demand, the economy will remain at E_4 indefinitely. Note that nominal income is higher at point E_4 than it was originally at point E_1, but real wages and salaries remain unchanged, as explained in Exhibit A-1(b).

> **CONCLUSION**
>
> An increase in aggregate demand in the long run causes the short-run aggregate supply curve to shift leftward because nominal incomes rise and the economy self-corrects to a higher price level at full-employment real GDP.

10A-1d The Impact of a Decrease in Aggregate Demand

Point E_1 in Exhibit A-4 begins where the sequence of events described in the previous section ends. Now let's see what happens when the aggregate demand curve decreases from AD_1 to AD_2. The reason might be that a wave of pessimism from a stock market crash causes consumers to cut back on their spending and firms postpone buying new factories and equipment. As a result, firms find their sales and profits have declined, and they react by cutting product prices, output, and employment. Workers' nominal incomes remain fixed in the short run with contracts negotiated based on an expected price level of 200. The result of this situation is that the economy moves downward along $SRAS_{200}$ from point E_1 to short-run equilibrium point E_2. Here the price level falls from 200 to 150, and real GDP has fallen from $8 trillion to $4 trillion.

At E_2, the economy is in a serious recession, and after, say, a year, workers will accept lower nominal wages and salaries when their contracts are renewed in order to keep their jobs in a time of poor profits and competition from unemployed workers. This willingness to accept lower nominal incomes is made easier by the realization that lower prices for goods means it costs less to maintain the workers' standard of living. As workers make a series of downward adjustments in nominal incomes, costs of production fall, the short-run aggregate supply curve shifts to the right, and there is downward movement along AD_2 toward E_4. $SRAS_{150}$ illustrates one possible intermediate position corresponding to the long-run expected price level of 150 determined by the intersection of $SRAS_{150}$ and LRAS. However, like E_2, E_3 is not the point of long-run equilibrium.

EXHIBIT **A-4** Adjustments to a Decrease in Aggregate Demand

Assume the economy is initially at long-run equilibrium point E_1 and aggregate demand decreases from AD_1 to AD_1. Nominal incomes in the short run are fixed based on an expected price level of 200. In response to the fall in aggregate demand, firms' profits decline, and they cut output and employment. As a result, the economy moves downward along $SRAS_{200}$ to temporary equilibrium at E_2. When workers lower their nominal incomes because of competition from unemployed workers, the short-run aggregate supply curve shifts downward to an intermediate point, such as E_3. As workers decrease their nominal incomes based on the new long-run expected price level of 150 at point E_3, profits rise, and firms increase output and employment. In the long run, the short-run aggregate supply curve continues to automatically adjust downward along AD_2 until it again returns to long-run equilibrium at E_4.

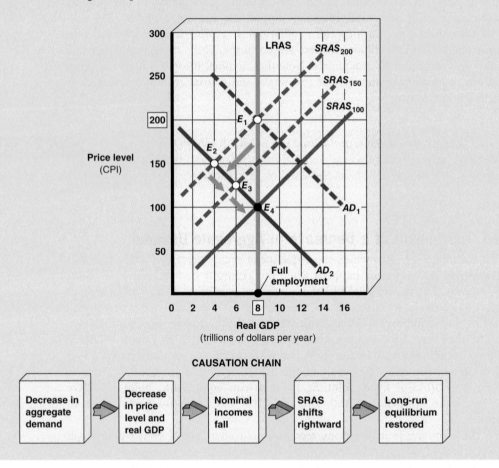

Workers negotiated decreases in nominal increases based on an expected price level of 150, but the rightward shift of the short-run aggregate supply curve has lowered the price level to about 125 at E_3. Under pressure from unemployed workers who will work for still lower real wages and salaries, workers will continue this process of adjusting their nominal incomes lower until $SRAS_{150}$ shifts rightward to point E_4.

Eventually, the long-run expected full-employment price level returns to 100 at point E_4, where the economy has self-corrected to long-run full-employment equilibrium. The result of this adjustment downward along AD_2 between E_2 and E_4 is that lower nominal incomes raise profits and firms respond by lowering prices of products, increasing employment, and increasing output so that real GDP increases from \$4 trillion to \$8 trillion. Unless aggregate demand changes, the economy will be stable at E_4 indefinitely. Finally, observe that average nominal income has decreased by the same percentage between points E_1 and E_4 as the percentage decline in the price level. Therefore, real incomes are unaffected as explained in Exhibit A-1(b).

CONCLUSION

A decrease in aggregate demand in the long run causes the short-run aggregate supply curve to shift rightward because nominal incomes fall and the economy self-corrects to a lower price level at full-employment real GDP.

10A-2 CHANGES IN POTENTIAL REAL GDP

Like the aggregate demand and short-run aggregate supply curves, the long-run aggregate supply curve can also shift. As explained in Chapter 2, changes in resources (land, labor, and capital) and technology shift the production possibilities curve outward. We now extend this concept of economic growth to the long-run aggregate supply curve as follows:

1. **Changes in resources.** An increase in land (natural resources) can increase potential real GDP. For example, the quantity of land can be increased by reclaiming land from the sea or revitalizing soil, or discovering new oil or mineral deposits. Over time, potential real GDP also increases if the full-employment number of workers increases, holding capital and technology constant. Such growth in the labor force can result from population growth. In addition, greater quantities of plants, production lines, computers, and other forms of capital also produce increases in potential real GDP. Capital includes *human capital*, which is the accumulation of education, training, experience, and health of workers.
2. **An advance in technology.** Technological change enables firms to produce more goods from any given amount of inputs. Even with fixed quantities of land, labor, and capital, the latest computer-age machinery increases potential GDP.

CONCLUSION

A rightward shift of the long-run aggregate supply curve represents economic growth in potential full-employment real GDP.

Over time, the U.S. economy typically adds resources and improves technology, and growth occurs in full-employment output. Exhibit A-5 uses basic aggregate demand and supply analysis to explain a hypothetical trend in the price level measured by the CPI between 2005, 2010, and 2015. The trend line connects the macro equilibrium points for each year. The following section uses real-world data to illustrate changes in the long-run aggregate supply curve over time.

EXHIBIT A-5 Trend of Macro Equilibrium Price Level over Time

Each hypothetical long-run equilibrium point shows the CPI and real GDP for a given year determined by the intersection of the aggregate demand curve, short-run aggregate supply curve, and long-run aggregate supply curve. Over time, these curves shift, and both the price level and real GDP increase.

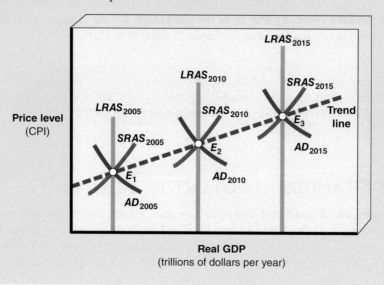

10A-2a Increase in the Aggregate Demand and Long-Run Aggregate Supply Curves

The self-correcting AD–AS model shown in Exhibit A-6 revisits Exhibit 12 in the chapter, which illustrated economic growth that occurred between 1995 and 2000 in the U.S. economy. Exhibit A-6, however, uses short-run and long-run aggregate supply curves to expand the analysis. (For simplicity, the real GDP amounts have been rounded.) In 1995, the economy operated at point E_1, with the CPI at 152 and a real GDP of $8.0 trillion. Since $LRAS_{95}$ at E_1 was estimated to be $8.3 trillion real GDP, the economy was operating below its full-employment potential with an unemployment rate of 5.6 percent (not explicitly shown in the model). Over the next 5 years, total spending increased and the U.S. economy moved to full employment at point E_3 in 2000 and experienced growth in real GDP from $8.0 trillion to $9.8 trillion. The CPI increased from 152 to 175 (mild inflation), and the unemployment rate fell to 4.0 percent.

During this time period, extraordinary technological change and capital accumulation, particularly in high-tech industries, caused economic growth in potential real GDP, represented by the rightward shift in the vertical long-run supply curve from $LRAS_{95}$ to $LRAS_{00}$. The movement from E_1 below full-employment real GDP was caused by an increase in AD_{95} to AD_{00} and a movement upward along short-run aggregate supply curve $SRAS_{95}$ to point E_2. Over time, the nominal or money wage rate increased, and $SRAS_{95}$ shifted leftward to $SRAS_{00}$. At point E_3, long-run equilibrium was established at the price level of 175 and equal to potential real GDP of $9.8 trillion.

EXHIBIT **A-6** A Rightward Shift in the Aggregate Demand and Long-Run Aggregate Supply Curves

In 1995, the U.S. economy was operating at $8.0 trillion below full-employment real GDP of $8.3 trillion at $LRAS_{95}$. Between 1995 and 2000, the aggregate demand curve increased from AD_{95} to AD_{00}, and the U.S. economy moved upward along the short-run aggregate supply curve $SRAS_{95}$ from point E_1 to point E_2. Nominal or money incomes of workers increased, and $SRAS_{95}$ shifted leftward to $SRAS_{00}$, establishing long-run full-employment equilibrium at E_3 on long-run aggregate supply curve $LRAS_{00}$. Technological changes and capital accumulation over these years caused the rightward shift from $LRAS_{95}$ to $LRAS_{00}$, and potential real GDP grew from $8.3 trillion to $9.8 trillion.

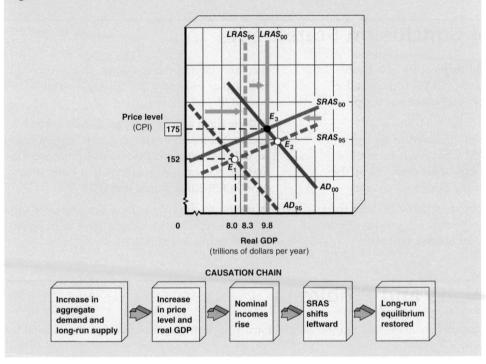

Key Concepts

Short-run aggregate supply curve (SRAS)

Long-run aggregate supply curve (LRAS)

Summary

- The **short-run aggregate supply curve (SRAS)** shows the level of real GDP produced at different possible price levels during a time period in which nominal wages and salaries (incomes) do not change in response to changes in the price level.

- In the long run, the **short-run aggregate supply curve (SRAS)** will shift leftward when inflation erodes workers' real incomes, and they respond by demanding higher wages and salaries. Higher wages and salaries increase costs of production and shift the SRAS leftward.

- In the long run, the **short-run aggregate supply curve (SRAS)** will shift rightward when unemployment pushes wages and salaries down. Lower wages and salaries decrease costs of production and shift the SRAS rightward.

- The **long-run aggregate supply curve (LRAS)** shows the level of real GDP produced at different possible price levels during a time period in which nominal incomes change

by the same percentage as the price level changes.

- The **long-run aggregate supply curve (LRAS)** is vertical at potential full-employment real GDP. It shows that, in the long run, changes in aggregate demand will change the price level, but will have no impact on potential full-employment real GDP.

- **Economic growth in potential real GDP** is represented by a rightward shift in the long-run aggregate supply curve (LRAS). Shifts in LRAS are caused by changes in resources and advances in technology.

Summary of Conclusion Statements

- The upward-sloping shape of the short-run aggregate supply curve (SRAS) is the result of fixed nominal wages and salaries as the price level changes.

- The vertical shape of the long-run aggregate supply curve (LRAS) is the result of nominal wages and salaries eventually changing by the same percentage as the price level changes.

- An increase in aggregate demand (AD) in the long run causes the short-run aggregate supply curve to shift leftward because nominal

incomes rise and the economy self-corrects to a higher price level at full-employment real GDP.

- A decrease in aggregate demand (AD) in the long run causes the short-run aggregate supply curve to shift rightward because nominal incomes fall and the economy self-corrects to a lower price level at full-employment real GDP.

- A rightward shift of the long-run aggregate supply curve represents economic growth in potential full-employment real GDP.

Study Questions and Problems

Please see Appendix A for answers to the odd-numbered questions. Your instructor has access to the answers for even-numbered questions.

1. The economy of Tuckerland has the following aggregate demand and supply schedules, reflecting real GDP in trillions of dollars:

Price level (CPI)	Aggregate demand	Short-run aggregate supply
250	$4	$16
200	8	12
150	12	8
100	16	4

a. Graph the aggregate demand curve and the short-run aggregate supply curve.
b. What are short-run equilibrium real GDP and the price level?
c. If Tuckerland's potential real GDP is $12 trillion, plot the long-run aggregate supply curve (LRAS) in the graph.

2. Using the graph from Question 1 and assuming long-run equilibrium at $12 trillion, explain the impact of a 10 percent increase in workers' income.

3. Use the graph drawn in Question 1 and assume the initial equilibrium is E_1. Next, assume

aggregate demand increases by $4 trillion. Draw the effect on short-run equilibrium.

4. Based on the assumptions of Question 3, explain verbally the impact of an increase of $4 trillion in aggregate demand on short-run equilibrium.

5. The economy shown in Exhibit A-7 is initially in equilibrium at point E_1, and the aggregate demand curve decreases from AD_1 to AD_2. Explain the long-run adjustment process.

6. In the first quarter of 2001, real GDP was $9.88 trillion, and the price level measured by the GDP chain price index was 101. Real GDP was approximately equal to potential GDP. In the third quarter, aggregate demand decreased to $9.83 trillion, and the price level rose to 103. Draw a graph of this recession.

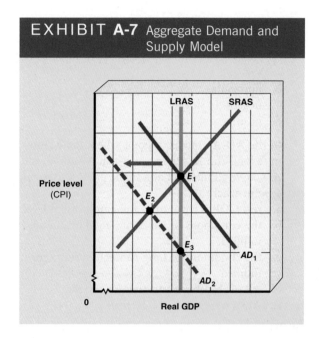

EXHIBIT A-7 Aggregate Demand and Supply Model

Sample Quiz

Please see Appendix B for answers to Sample Quiz questions.

1. One reason for the upward-sloping short-run aggregate supply curve (SRAS) is
   a. a fixed CPI market basket.
   b. perfect knowledge of workers.
   c. fixed-wage contracts.
   d. the upward-sloping production function.

2. The full-employment level of real GDP is the level that can be produced with
   a. given technology and productive resources.
   b. frictional and structural unemployment equal to zero.
   c. cyclical unemployment equal to zero.
   d. both a and b.
   e. both a and c.

3. Which of the following would cause a decrease in the short-run aggregate supply curve (SRAS)?
   a. An increase in oil prices
   b. An advance in technology

   c. An increase in the CPI
   d. An increase in the long-run aggregate supply curve (LRAS)

4. If nominal wages and salaries are fixed as firms change product prices, the short-run aggregate supply curve (SRAS) is
   a. vertical.
   b. horizontal.
   c. negatively sloped.
   d. positively sloped.

5. Which of the following explains why the short-run aggregate supply curve is upward sloping?
   a. The quantity of real output supplied is inversely related to the aggregate supply curve.
   b. Nominal incomes are fixed.
   c. The capital-output ratio becomes negative.
   d. An increase in price will increase the supply of money.

6. In an economy where nominal incomes adjust equally to changes in the price level, we would expect the long-run aggregate supply curve to be
   a. vertical.
   b. horizontal.
   c. negatively sloped.
   d. positively sloped.

7. In the AD-AS model, a point where the economy's long-run AS curve, short-run AS curve, and AD curve all intersect at a single point represents a point where
   a. real GDP is equal to its full-employment level.
   b. the conditions of short-run equilibrium are fulfilled.
   c. the conditions of long-run equilibrium are fulfilled.
   d. All of the above answers are correct.
   e. Answers a and c are correct.

8. The intersection between the long-run aggregate supply and aggregate demand curves determines the
   a. level of full-employment real GDP.
   b. average level of prices (CPI).
   c. marginal product.
   d. both a and b.

9. The adjustment of nominal incomes to changes in the price level (CPI) is fixed because of the
   a. volatility of investment spending.
   b. existence of long-term contracts.
   c. complete information possessed by workers.
   d. All of the above answers are correct.

10. In the self-correcting AD-AS model, the economy's short-run equilibrium position is indicated by the intersection of which two curves?
    a. Short-run aggregate supply and long-run aggregate supply
    b. Short-run aggregate supply and aggregate demand
    c. Long-run aggregate supply and aggregate demand
    d. Long-run aggregate demand and short-run personal consumption expenditures

11. Which of the following causes a leftward shift in the short-run aggregate supply curve?
    a. An increase of goods prices while nominal incomes are unchanged

b. An increase in nominal incomes
c. An increase of full-employment real GDP
d. An increase of personal consumption expenditures while the price level is unchanged

12. In part (a) of Exhibit A-8 the intersection of AD with SRAS indicates
    a. a short-run equilibrium.
    b. a long-run equilibrium.
    c. both short-run and long-run equilibrium.
    d. that the economy is at full employment.

EXHIBIT A-8 Macro AD-AS Models

(a)

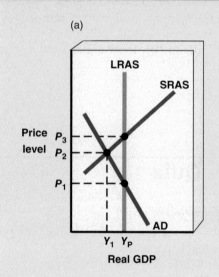

(b)

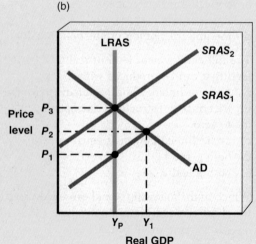

13. In part (a) of Exhibit A-8 suppose the initial equilibrium is at real GDP level Y_1 and price level P_2. At real GDP level Y_1 there is
    a. an inflationary gap.
    b. a recessionary gap.
    c. full employment.
    d. long-run equilibrium.

14. In part (b) of Exhibit A-8 the intersection of $SRAS_1$ with AD indicates
    a. an economy experiencing a recessionary gap.
    b. an economy experiencing an inflationary gap.
    c. that the economy is in long-run equilibrium.
    d. that the economy has an unemployment rate currently greater than the natural rate of unemployment.

15. In part (b) of Exhibit A-8 the intersection of $SRAS_2$ with LRAS indicates
    a. an economy experiencing a recessionary gap.
    b. an economy experiencing an inflationary gap.
    c. that the economy is in long-run equilibrium.
    d. that the economy has an unemployment rate currently less than the natural rate of unemployment.

16. As shown in Exhibit A-9 and assuming the aggregate demand curve shifts from AD_1 to AD_2 the full-employment level of real GDP is
    a. $10 billion.
    b. $4 billion.
    c. $100 billion.
    d. unable to be determined.

17. Beginning from a point of short-run equilibrium at point E_2 in Exhibit A-9 the economy's movement to a new position of long-run equilibrium from that point would best be described as
    a. a movement downward along the AD_2 curve with a shift in the $SRAS_1$ curve to $SRAS_2$.
    b. a movement along the $SRAS_2$ curve with a shift in the AD_2 curve.
    c. a shift in the LRAS curve to an intersection at E_3.
    d. no shift of any kind.

18. Based on Exhibit A-10 when the aggregate demand curve shifts to the position AD_2 and the economy is operating at point E_2 the economy's position of long-run equilibrium corresponds to point
    a. E_1.
    b. E_2.
    c. E_3.
    d. E_1 or E_3.

EXHIBIT A-9 Aggregate Demand and Supply Model

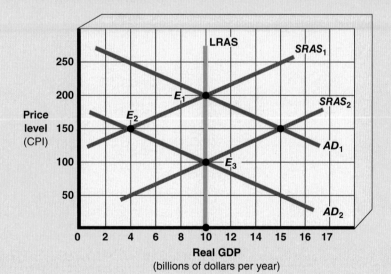

EXHIBIT A-10 Aggregate Demand and Supply Model

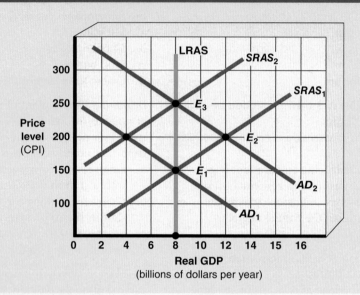

19. Beginning in Exhibit A-10 from long-run equilibrium at point E_1 the aggregate demand curve shifts to AD_2 The economy's path to a new long-run equilibrium is represented by a movement from
    a. E_3 to E_1 to E_2.
    b. E_1 to E_3 to E_2.
    c. E_2 to E_1 to E_2.
    d. E_1 to E_2 to E_3.

20. Economic growth would be represented in Exhibit A-10 by a(an)
    a. leftward shift in the long-run aggregate supply curve (LRAS).
    b. inward shift of the production possibilities curve.
    c. rightward shift in the long-run aggregate supply curve (LRAS).
    d. movement along the long-run aggregate supply curve (LRAS).

CHAPTER 11

Fiscal Policy

CHAPTER PREVIEW

In the early 1980s, under President Ronald Reagan, the federal government reduced personal income tax rates. The goal was to expand aggregate demand and boost real GDP output and employment in order to end the recession of 1980–1981. In the 1990s, a key part of President Bill Clinton's programs was to stimulate economic growth by boosting government spending on long-term investment, including highways, bridges, and education. In 2001, the United States experienced a recession, and during the next two years, President George W. Bush proposed and signed into law tax cuts to stimulate the economy. And in 2008, Americans received a $170 billion tax-rebate stimulus package, followed by another $787 billion federal stimulus package under the Obama administration in 2009 intended to jump-start the economy into recovery from the Great Recession. In 2013 after a government shutdown, government spending was cut and the debt ceiling was increased. Since then, annual deficits have fallen but continue to add to the national debt.

Fiscal policy is one of the major issues that touches everyone's life. **Fiscal policy** is the use of government spending and taxes to influence the nation's output, employment, and price level. Federal government spending policies affect Social Security, Medicare and Medicaid benefits, and employment in the defense industry. Tax policies can change the amount of your paycheck and, therefore, influence whether you purchase a car or attend college.

Using fiscal policy to influence the performance of the economy has been an important idea since the Keynesian revolution of the 1930s. This chapter removes the political veil and looks at fiscal policy from the viewpoint of two opposing economic theories. First, you will study Keynesian demand-side fiscal policies that "fine-tune" aggregate demand so that the economy grows and achieves full employment with a higher price level. Second, you will study supply-side fiscal policy, which gained prominence during the Reagan administration and has remained at the core of many conservative macroeconomic policies ever since. Supply-siders view aggregate supply as far more important than aggregate demand. Their fiscal policy prescription is to increase aggregate supply so that the economy grows and achieves full employment with a lower price level.

IN THIS CHAPTER, YOU WILL LEARN TO SOLVE THESE ECONOMICS PUZZLES:

- Does an increase in government spending or a tax cut of equal amount provide the greater stimulus to economic growth?

- Can Congress fight a recession without taking any action?

- How could one argue that the federal government can increase tax revenues by cutting taxes?

11-1 DISCRETIONARY FISCAL POLICY

Fiscal policy
The use of government spending and taxes to influence the nation's output, employment, and price level.

Discretionary fiscal policy
The deliberate use of changes in government spending or taxes to alter aggregate demand and stabilize the economy.

Here we begin where the previous chapter left off, that is, discussing the use of discretionary fiscal policy, as Keynes advocated, to influence the economy's performance. **Discretionary fiscal policy** is the deliberate use of changes in government spending or taxes to alter aggregate demand and stabilize the economy. Exhibit 1 lists three basic types of discretionary fiscal policies and the corresponding ways in which the government can pursue each of these options. The first column of the table shows that the government can choose to increase aggregate demand by following an *expansionary* fiscal policy. The second column lists *contractionary* fiscal policy options the government can use to restrain aggregate demand.

EXHIBIT 1 Discretionary Fiscal Policies

Expansionary fiscal policy	Contractionary fiscal policy
Increase government spending	Decrease government spending
Decrease taxes	Increase taxes
Increase government spending and taxes equally	Decrease government spending and taxes equally

11-1a Increasing Government Spending to Combat a Recession

Suppose the U.S. economy represented in Exhibit 2 has fallen into recession at equilibrium point E_1, where aggregate demand curve AD_1 intersects the aggregate supply curve, AS, in the near-full-employment range. The price level measured by the CPI is 210, and a real GDP gap of $1 trillion exists below the full-employment output of $14 trillion real GDP. As explained in the previous chapter (Exhibit 5), one approach the president and Congress can follow is provided by classical theory. The classical economists' prescription is to wait because the economy will self-correct to full employment in the long run by adjusting downward along AD_1. But election time is approaching, so there is political pressure to do something about the recession now. Besides, recall Keynes's famous statement, "In the long run, we are all dead." Hence, policymakers follow Keynesian economics and decide to shift the aggregate demand curve rightward from AD_1 to AD_2 and thereby cure the recession.

How can the federal government do this? In theory, any increase in consumption (C), investment (I), or net exports (X − M) can spur aggregate demand. But these spending boosts are not directly under the government's control as is government spending (G). After all, there is always a long wish list of spending proposals for federal highways, health care, education, environmental programs, and so forth. Rather than crossing their fingers and waiting for things to happen in the long run, suppose members of Congress gladly increase government spending to boost employment now.

But just how much new government spending is required? Note that the economy is operating $1 trillion below its full-employment output, but the horizontal distance between AD_1 and AD_2 is $2 trillion. This gap between AD_1 and AD_2 is indicated by

EXHIBIT 2 Using Government Spending to Combat a Recession

The economy in this exhibit is in recession at equilibrium point E_1 on the intermediate range of the aggregate supply curve, AS. The price level is 210, with an
output level of $13 trillion real GDP. To reach the full-employment output of
$14 trillion in real GDP, the aggregate demand curve must be shifted to the right
by $2 trillion real GDP, measured by the horizontal distance between point E_1 on
curve AD_1 and point X on curve AD_2. The necessary increase in aggregate demand
from AD_1 to AD_2 can be accomplished by increased government spending. Given a
spending multiplier of 2, a $1 trillion increase in government spending brings about
the required $2 trillion rightward shift in the aggregate demand curve, and equi-
librium in the economy changes from E_1 to E_2. Note that the equilibrium real GDP
changes by $1 trillion and not by the full amount by which the aggregate demand
curve shifts horizontally.

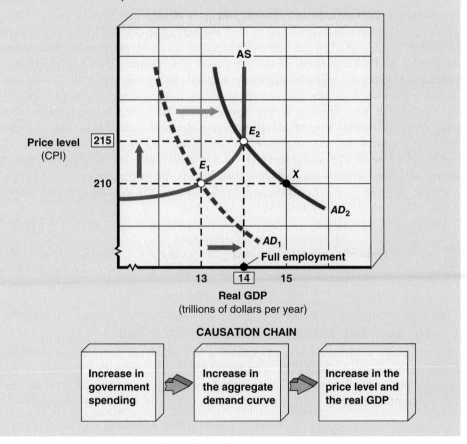

the dotted line between points E_1 and X ($15 trillion − $13 trillion). This means that
the aggregate demand curve must be shifted to the right by $2 trillion. But it is not
necessary to increase government spending by this amount. The following formula
can be used to compute the amount of additional government spending required to

shift the aggregate demand curve rightward and establish a new full-employment real GDP equilibrium:

Initial change in government spending (ΔG) $\times$ spending multiplier

$=$ change in aggregate demand (total spending)

The *spending multiplier* in the formula amplifies the amount of new government spending. The **spending multiplier (SM)** is the change in aggregate demand (total spending) resulting from an initial change in any component of aggregate demand, including consumption, investment, government spending, and net exports. Assume the value for the spending multiplier in our example is 2. The next section explains the algebra behind the spending multiplier so that the example can be solved:

$\Delta G \times 2 = \$2$ trillion

$\Delta G = \$1$ trillion

Note that the Greek letter Δ (delta) means "a change in." Thus, it takes $1 trillion worth of new government spending to shift the aggregate demand curve to the right by $2 trillion. As described in the previous chapter (Exhibit 6), bottlenecks occur throughout the upward-sloping range of the AS curve. This means prices rise as production increases in response to greater aggregate demand. Returning to Exhibit 2, you can see that $1 trillion worth of new government spending shifts aggregate demand from AD_1 to AD_2. As a result, firms increase output upward along the aggregate supply curve, AS, and total spending moves upward along aggregate demand curve AD_2. This adjustment mechanism moves the economy to a new equilibrium at E_2, with full employment, a higher price level of 215, and a real GDP of $14 trillion per year. At point E_2, the economy experiences *demand-pull inflation*. And here is the important point: Although the aggregate demand curve has increased by $2 trillion, the equilibrium real GDP has increased by only $1 trillion from $13 to $14 trillion.

Spending multiplier (SM)

The change in aggregate demand (total spending) resulting from initial change in any component of aggregate expenditures, including consumption, investment, government spending, and net exports. As a formula, spending multiplier equals $1/(1 - \text{MPC})$ or $1/\text{MPS}$.

CONCLUSION   In the intermediate segment of the aggregate supply curve, the equilibrium real GDP changes by less than the change in government spending times the spending multiplier.

11-1b Spending Multiplier Arithmetic Revisited[1]

Now let's pause to tackle the task of explaining in more detail the spending multiplier of 2 used in the above example. The spending multiplier begins with a concept called the marginal propensity to consume. The **marginal propensity to consume (MPC)** is the change in consumption spending resulting from a given change in income. Algebraically,

Marginal propensity to consume (MPC)

The change in consumption spending resulting from a given change in income.

$$\text{MPC} = \frac{\text{change in consumption spending}}{\text{change in income}}$$

Exhibit 3 illustrates numerically the cumulative increase in aggregate demand resulting from a $1 trillion increase in government spending. In the initial round, the

---

[1]This section duplicates material presented earlier in the chapters titled "The Keynesian Model" and "The Keynesian Model in Action." The reason for repeating this material is that an instructor may choose to skip the Keynesian model presented in these two chapters.

EXHIBIT 3 The Spending Multiplier Effect

Round	Component of total spending	New spending (billions of dollars)
1	Government spending	$1,000
2	Consumption	500
3	Consumption	250
4	Consumption	125
.	.	.
.	.	.
.	.	.
All other rounds	Consumption	125
	Total spending	$2,000

government spends this amount for bridges, national defense, and so forth. Households receive this amount of income. In the second round, these households spend $500 billion (0.50 × $1 trillion, or equivalently 0.50 × $1,000 billion) on houses, cars, groceries, and other products. In the third round, the incomes of realtors, autoworkers, grocers, and others are boosted by $500 billion, and they spend $250 billion (0.50 × $500 billion). Each round of spending creates income for consumption respending in a downward spiral throughout the economy in smaller and smaller amounts until the total level of aggregate demand rises by an extra $2,000 billion ($2 trillion).

> Any initial change in spending by the government, households, firms, or foreigners on our exports creates a chain reaction of further spending, which causes a greater cumulative change in aggregate demand.

CONCLUSION

You might recognize from algebra that the spending multiplier effect is a process based on an *infinite geometric series*. The formula for the sum of such a series of numbers is the initial number times $1/(1 - r)$, where r is the ratio that relates the numbers. Using this formula, the sum (total spending) is calculated as $1 trillion $(\Delta G) \times [1/(1 - 0.50)]$ = $2 trillion. By simply defining r in the infinite series formula as MPC, the spending multiplier for aggregate demand is expressed as follows:

$$\text{Spending multiplier} = \frac{1}{1 - \text{MPC}}$$

Applying this formula to our example:

$$\text{Spending multiplier} = \frac{1}{1 - 0.50} = \frac{1}{0.50} = 2$$

Marginal propensity to save (MPS)
The change in saving resulting from a given change in income.

If households spend a portion of each extra dollar of income, then the remaining portion of each dollar is saved. The **marginal propensity to save (MPS)** is the change in saving resulting from a given change in income. Therefore,

$$MPC + MPS = 1$$

rewritten as

$$MPS = 1 - MPC$$

Hence, the above spending multiplier formula can be rewritten as

$$Spending \ multiplier = \frac{1}{MPS}$$

Since MPS and MPC are related, the size of the multiplier depends on the size of the MPC. What will the result be if people spend 80 percent or 33 percent of each dollar of income instead of 50 percent? If the MPC increases (decreases), consumers spend a larger (smaller) share of each additional dollar of output/income in each round, and the size of the multiplier increases (decreases). Exhibit 4 lists the multiplier for different values of MPC and MPS.

CHECKPOINT

What Is the MPC for Uncle Sam's Stimulus Package?

Assume the economy is in a recession, and a stimulus package of $800 billion is passed by the federal government. The administration predicts that this measure will provide a $3,200 billion boost to GDP this year because consumers will spend their extra cash on HD televisions, cars and other items. For this amount of stimulus, what is the established value of MPC used in this forecast?

11-1c Cutting Taxes to Combat a Recession

Another expansionary fiscal policy intended to increase aggregate demand and to achieve full employment calls for the government to cut taxes. Let's return to point E_1 in

---

EXHIBIT 4 Relationship between MPC, MPS, and the Spending Multiplier

(1) Marginal propensity to consume (MPC)	(2) Marginal propensity to save (MPS)	(3) Spending multiplier
0.90	0.10	10
0.80	0.20	5
0.75	0.25	4
0.67	0.33	3
0.50	0.50	2
0.33	0.67	1.5

Exhibit 2. As before, the problem is to shift the aggregate demand curve to the right by $2 trillion. But this time, instead of a $1 trillion increase in government spending, assume Congress votes for a $1 trillion tax cut. How does this cut in taxes affect aggregate demand? First, *disposable personal income* (take-home pay) increases by $1 trillion —the amount of the tax reduction. Second, once again assuming the MPC is 0.50, the increase in disposable personal income induces new consumption spending of $500 billion (0.50 × $1 trillion). Thus, a cut in taxes triggers a multiplier process similar to, but smaller than, the same dollar increase in government spending.

Exhibit 5 demonstrates that a tax reduction adds less to aggregate demand than does an equal increase in government spending. Column 1 reproduces the effect of increasing government spending by $1 trillion, and column 2 gives for comparison the effect of lowering taxes by $1 trillion. Note that the only difference between increasing government spending and cutting taxes by the same amount is the impact in the initial round. The reason is that a tax cut injects zero new spending into the economy because the government has purchased no new goods and services. The effect of a tax reduction in round 2 is that people spend a portion (determined by the size of the MPC) of the $1 trillion boost in after-tax income from the tax cut introduced in round 1. Subsequent rounds in the tax multiplier chain generate a cumulative increase in consumption expenditures that totals $1 trillion. Comparing the total changes in aggregate demand in columns (1) and (2) of Exhibit 4 leads to the following:

A tax cut has a smaller multiplier effect on aggregate demand than an equal increase in government spending.

CONCLUSION

EXHIBIT 5 Comparison of the Spending and Tax Multipliers

| | | Increase in aggregate demand from a | |
| | Component of total | (1) $1 trillion increase in government | (2) $1 trillion cut in taxes |
Round	spending	spending $(+\Delta G)$	$(-\Delta T)$
1	Government spending	$1,000	$0
2	Consumption	500	500
3	Consumption	250	250
4	Consumption	125	125
.	.	.	.
.	.	.	.
.	.	.	.
All other rounds	Consumption	125	125
	Total spending	$2,000	$1,000

Tax multiplier (TM)
The change in aggregate demand (total spending) resulting from an initial change in taxes. As a formula, tax multiplier equals 1 − spending multiplier.

The tax multiplier can be computed by using a formula and the information from column 2 of Exhibit 5. The **tax multiplier (TM)** is the change in aggregate demand (total spending) resulting from an initial change in taxes. Mathematically, the tax multiplier is given by this formula:

$$\text{Tax multiplier} = 1 - \text{spending multiplier}$$

Returning to Exhibit 2, the tax multiplier formula can be used to calculate the cumulative increase in the aggregate demand from a $1 trillion tax cut. Applying the formula given above and a spending multiplier of 2 yields a tax multiplier of −1. Note that the sign of the tax multiplier is always negative. Thus, a $1 trillion tax cut shifts the aggregate demand curve rightward by only $1 trillion and fails to restore full-employment equilibrium at point E_2. Mathematically,

$$\text{Change in taxes } (\Delta T) \times \text{tax multiplier } (TM) = \text{change in aggregate demand } (AD)$$

$$-\$1 \text{ trillion} \times -1 = \$1 \text{ trillion}$$

The key to the amount of real GDP growth achieved from a stimulus package depends on the size of the MPC. What proportion of the government spending increase or tax cut is spent for consumption? The answer means the difference between a deeper or milder recession as well as the speed of recovery. What are estimates of real-world multipliers? In Congressional testimony given in July 2008, Mark Zandi, chief economist for Moody's Economy.com, provided estimates for the one-year multiplier effect for several fiscal policy options. The spending multiplier varied from 1.36 to 1.73 for different federal government spending programs, such as food stamps, extended unemployment insurance benefits, aid to state governments, or bridges and highways. The tax multiplier also varied from 0.27 to 1.29 for different temporary tax cut plans. Recent studies confirm these estimates and point to the fact that a more complex multiplier is at play, which takes into account a marginal propensity of taxation as well as a marginal propensity to import foreign goods that we do not take into consideration here.

11-1d Using Fiscal Policy to Combat Inflation

So far, Keynesian expansionary fiscal policy, born of the Great Depression, has been presented as the cure for an economic downturn. Contractionary fiscal policy, on the other hand, can serve in the fight against inflation. Exhibit 6 shows an economy operating at point E_1 on the classical range of the aggregate supply curve, AS. Hence, this economy is producing the full-employment output of $14 trillion real GDP, and the price level is 220. In this situation, any increase in aggregate demand only causes inflation, while real GDP remains unchanged.

Suppose Congress and the president decide to use fiscal policy to reduce the CPI from 220 to 215 because they fear the wrath of voters suffering from the consequences of inflation. Although a fall in consumption, investment, or net exports might do the job, Congress and the president may be unwilling to wait, and they prefer taking direct action by cutting government spending. Given a marginal propensity to consume of 0.50, the spending multiplier is 2. As shown by the horizontal distance between point E_1 on AD_1 and point E' on AD_2 in Exhibit 6, aggregate demand must be decreased by $1 trillion in

EXHIBIT 6 Using Fiscal Policy to Combat Inflation

The economy in this exhibit is in equilibrium at point E_1 on the classical range of the aggregate supply curve, AS. The price level is 220, and the economy is operating at the full-employment output of $14 trillion real GDP. To reduce the price level to 215, the aggregate demand curve must be shifted to the left by $1 trillion, measured by the horizontal distance between point E_1 on curve AD_1 and point E' on curve AD_2. One way this can be done is by decreasing government spending. With MPC equal to 0.50, and therefore a spending multiplier of 2, a $500 billion decrease in government spending results in the needed $1,000 billion (or $1 trillion) leftward shift in the aggregate demand curve. As a result, the economy reaches equilibrium at point E_2, and the price level falls from 220 to 215, while real output remains unchanged at full capacity.

An identical decrease in the aggregate demand curve can be obtained by a hike in taxes. A $1 trillion tax increase works through a tax multiplier of -1 and provides the needed $1 trillion decrease in the aggregate demand curve from AD_1 to AD_2.

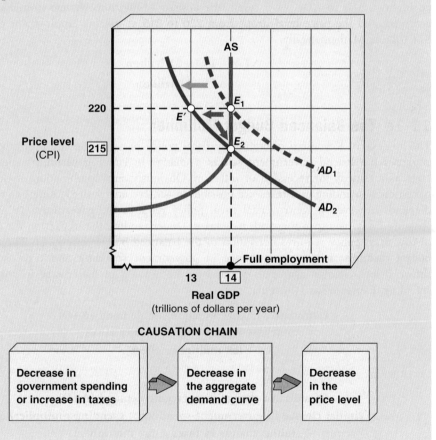

order to shift the aggregate demand curve from AD_1 to AD_2 and establish equilibrium at E_2, with a price level of 215. Mathematically,

$$\Delta G \times 2 = -\$1 \text{ trillion}$$
$$\Delta G = -\$500 \text{ billion}$$

Using the above formula, a $500 billion cut in real government spending would cause a $1 trillion decrease in the aggregate demand curve from AD_1 to AD_2. The result is a temporary excess aggregate supply of $1 trillion, measured by the distance from E' to E_1. As explained in Exhibit 5 of the previous chapter, the economy follows classical theory and moves downward along AD_2 to a new equilibrium at E_2. Consequently, inflation cools with no change in the full-employment real GDP.

Another approach to the inflation problem would be for Congress and the president to raise taxes. Although tax increases are often considered political suicide, let's suppose Congress calculates just the correct amount of a tax hike required to reduce aggregate demand by $1 trillion.

Assuming a spending multiplier of 2, the tax multiplier is -1. Therefore, a $1 trillion tax increase provides the necessary $1 trillion leftward shift in the aggregate demand curve from AD_1 to AD_2. As a result, the desired equilibrium change from E_1 to E_2 is achieved, and the price level drops from 220 to 215 at the full-employment output of $14 trillion. Mathematically,

$$\Delta T \times -1 = -\$1 \text{ trillion}$$
$$\Delta T = \$1 \text{ trillion}$$

11-1e The Balanced Budget Multiplier

The analysis of Keynesian discretionary fiscal policy presented in the previous sections supposes the federal government selects a change in *either* government spending or taxes as a remedy for recession or inflation. Obviously, any combination of changes in government spending and taxes are possible to achieve any desired change in aggregate demand. However, a controversial fiscal policy requires the government to match, or "balance," any new spending with new taxes. Understanding the impact on the economy of this fiscal policy requires derivation of the balanced budget multiplier. The **balanced budget multiplier** is an equal change in government spending and taxes, which, as shown below, changes aggregate demand by the amount of the change in government spending. Expressed as a formula,

Balanced budget multiplier
An equal change in government spending and taxes, which changes aggregate demand by the amount of the change in government spending.

Cumulative change in aggregate demand (ΔAD)
= government spending multiplier effect
+ tax multiplier effect

rewritten as

Cumulative change in aggregate demand (ΔAD)
= (initial change in government spending $\times$ spending multiplier)
+ (initial change in taxes $\times$ tax multiplier)

To see how the balanced budget multiplier works, suppose Congress enacts a $1 billion increase in government spending for highways and it finances these purchases with a $1 billion increase in gasoline taxes. Mathematically,

$$\Delta AD = \left(\$1 \text{ billion} \times \frac{1}{1 - \text{MPC}} \right) + \left(\$1 \text{ billion} \times 1 - \frac{1}{1 - \text{MPC}} \right)$$

$$= \left(\$1 \text{ billion} \times \frac{1}{1 - 0.50} \right) + \left(\$1 \text{ billion} \times 1 - \frac{1}{1 - 0.50} \right)$$

$$= \left(\$1 \text{ billion} \times 2 \right) + \left(\$1 \text{ billion} \times -1 \right)$$

$$= \$2 \text{ billion} - \$1 \text{ billion}$$

$$= \$1 \text{ billion}$$

Hence, the balanced budget multiplier is always equal to 1, and the cumulative change in aggregate demand is $1 billion—*the amount of the initial change in government spending*!

> **CONCLUSION**
>
> Regardless of the MPC, the net effect on the economy of an equal initial increase (decrease) in government spending and taxes is an increase (decrease) in aggregate demand equal to the initial increase (decrease) in government spending.

CHECKPOINT

Walking the Balanced Budget Tightrope

Suppose the president proposes an $800 billion economic stimulus package intended to create jobs. A major criticism of this new spending proposal is that it is not matched by a tax increase. Assume the U.S. economy is below full employment, and Congress has passed a law requiring that any increase in spending be matched or balanced by an equal increase in taxes. The MPC is 0.75, and aggregate demand must be increased by $1,000 billion to reach full employment. Will the economy reach full employment if Congress increases spending by $800 billion and increases taxes by the same amount?

11-2 AUTOMATIC STABILIZERS

Unlike discretionary fiscal policy, automatic stabilizers are policy tools built into the federal budget that help fight unemployment and inflation, while spending and tax laws remain unchanged. **Automatic stabilizers** are federal expenditures and tax revenues that automatically change levels in order to stabilize an economic expansion or contraction. Automatic stabilizers are sometimes referred to as *nondiscretionary fiscal policy*. Exhibit 7 illustrates the influence of automatic stabilizers on the economy. The downward-sloping line, *G*, represents federal government expenditures, including such *transfer payments* as unemployment compensation, Medicaid, and welfare. This line falls as real GDP rises. When the economy expands, unemployment falls, and government spending for unemployment compensation, welfare, and other transfer payments decreases. During a downturn, people lose their jobs, and government spending automatically increases because unemployed individuals become eligible for unemployment compensation and other transfer payments.

Automatic stabilizers
Federal expenditures and tax revenues that automatically change levels in order to stabilize an economic expansion or contraction; sometimes referred to as *nondiscretionary fiscal policy*.

EXHIBIT 7 Automatic Stabilizers

Federal government spending varies inversely with real GDP and is represented by the downward-sloping line, G. Taxes, in contrast, vary directly with real GDP and are represented by the upward-sloping line, T. This means government spending for welfare and other transfer payments rises and tax collections fall as real GDP falls. Thus, if real GDP falls below $14 trillion, the budget deficit rises automatically. The size of the budget deficit is shown by the vertical distance between lines G and T. This budget deficit assists in offsetting a recession because it stimulates aggregate demand. Conversely, when real GDP rises above $14 trillion, federal budget surplus increases automatically and assists in offsetting inflation.

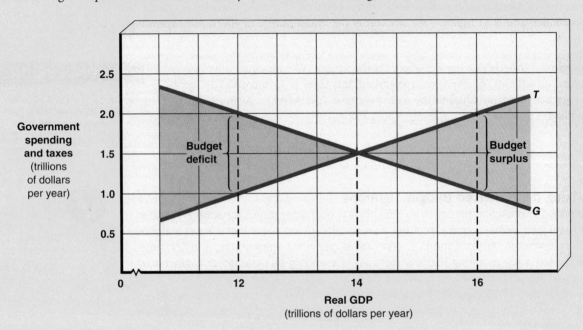

CAUSATION CHAIN

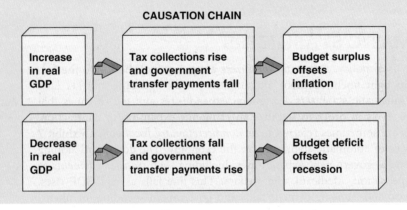

The direct relationship between tax revenues and real GDP is shown by the upward-sloping line, *T*. During an expansion, jobs are created, unemployment falls, and workers earn more income and therefore pay more taxes. Thus, income tax collections automatically vary directly with increases in real GDP.

We begin the analysis of automatic stabilizers with a balanced federal budget at full employment. Federal spending, *G*, is equal to tax collections, *T*, and the economy is in equilibrium at the full-employment $14 trillion real GDP level. Now assume consumer optimism soars and a spending spree increases the consumption component (*C*) of total spending. As a result, the economy moves to a new equilibrium at $16 trillion real GDP. The rise in real GDP creates more jobs and higher tax collections. Consequently, taxes rise to $2 trillion on line *T*. Also, government expenditures fall to $1 trillion because fewer people are collecting transfer payments, such as unemployment compensation and welfare. As a result, the vertical distance between lines *T* and *G* represents a federal budget surplus of $1 trillion. A **budget surplus** occurs when government revenues exceed government expenditures in a given time period.

Now begin again with the economy at full employment equilibrium of $14 trillion in Exhibit 7, and let's change the scenario. Assume that business managers lower their profit expectations. Their revised outlook causes business executives to become pessimistic, so they cut investment spending (*I*), causing aggregate demand to decline. The corresponding decline in real GDP from $14 trillion to $12 trillion causes tax revenues to fall from $1.5 trillion to $1 trillion on line *T*. The combined effect of the rise in government spending and the fall in taxes creates a budget deficit. A **budget deficit** occurs when government expenditures exceed government revenues in a given time period. The vertical distance between lines *G* and *T* at $12 trillion real GDP illustrates a federal budget deficit of $1 trillion.

The key feature of automatic stabilization is that it "leans against the prevailing wind." In short, changes in federal spending and taxes moderate changes in aggregate demand. Stated differently, built-in stabilizers diminish or reduce swings in real GDP. When the economy expands, the fall in government spending for transfer payments and the rise in the level of taxes result in a budget surplus. As the budget surplus grows, people send more money to Washington, which applies braking power against further increases in real GDP. When the economy contracts, the rise in government spending for transfer payments and the fall in the level of taxes yield a budget deficit. As the budget deficit grows, people receive more money from Washington to spend, which slows further decreases in real GDP.

Budget surplus
A budget in which government revenues exceed government expenditures in a given time period.

Budget deficit
A budget in which government expenditures exceed government revenues in a given time period.

> Automatic stabilizers assist in offsetting a recession when real GDP falls and in offsetting inflation when real GDP expands.

CONCLUSION

11-3 SUPPLY-SIDE FISCAL POLICY

The focus so far has been on fiscal policy that affects the macro economy solely through the impact of government spending and taxation on aggregate demand. Supply-side economists, whose intellectual roots are in classical economics, argue that *stagflation* in the 1970s was the result of the federal government's failure to follow the theories of supply-side fiscal policy. **Supply-side fiscal policy** emphasizes government policies that

Supply-side fiscal policy
A fiscal policy that emphasizes government policies that increase aggregate supply in order to achieve long-run growth in real output, full employment, and a lower price level.

increase aggregate supply in order to achieve long-run growth in real output, full employment, and a lower price level. Supply-side policies became an active economic idea with the election of Ronald Reagan as president in 1980. As discussed in the previous chapter, the U.S. economy in the 1970s experienced high rates of both inflation and unemployment. This stagflation aroused concern about the ability of the U.S. economy to generate long-term advances in the standard of living. This set the stage for a new macroeconomic policy.

Suppose the economy is initially at E_1 in Exhibit 8(a), with a CPI of 150 and an output of $8 trillion real GDP. The economy is experiencing high unemployment, so the goal is to achieve full employment by increasing real GDP to $12 trillion. As described earlier in this chapter, the federal government might follow Keynesian expansionary fiscal policy and shift the aggregate demand curve rightward from AD_1 to AD_2. Higher government spending or lower taxes operate through the multiplier effect and cause this increase in aggregate demand. The good news from such a demand-side fiscal policy prescription is that the economy moves to full employment, but the bad news is that the price level rises. In this case, *demand-pull inflation* would cause the price level to rise from 150 to 200.

Exhibit 8(b) represents the supply-siders' alternative to Keynesian fiscal policy. Again, suppose the economy is initially in equilibrium at E_1. Supply-side economists argue that the federal government should adopt policies that shift the aggregate supply curve rightward from AS_1 to AS_2. An increase in aggregate supply would move the economy to E_2 and achieve the full-employment level of real GDP. Under supply-side theory, there is an additional bonus to full employment. Instead of rising as in Exhibit 8(a), the price level in Exhibit 8(b) falls from 150 to 100. Comparing the two graphs in Exhibit 8, you can see that the supply-siders have a better theoretical case than proponents of demand-side fiscal policy when both inflation and unemployment are concerns.

Note the causation chain under each graph in Exhibit 8. The demand-side fiscal policy options are from column 1 of Exhibit 1 in this chapter, and the supply-side policy alternatives are similar to Exhibit 10 in the previous chapter. For supply-side economics to be effective, the government must implement policies that increase the total output that firms produce at each possible price level. An increase in aggregate supply can be accomplished by some combination of cuts in resource prices, technological advances, subsidies, and reductions in government taxes and government regulations.

Although a laundry list of supply-side policies was advocated during the Reagan administration, the most familiar policy action taken was the tax cuts implemented in 1981. By reducing tax rates on wages and profits, the Reagan administration sought to increase the aggregate supply of goods and services at any price level. However, tax cuts are a Keynesian policy intended to increase aggregate demand, so supply-siders must have a different view of the impact of tax cuts on the economy. To explain these different views of tax cuts, let's begin by stating that both Keynesians and supply-siders agree that tax cuts increase disposable personal income. In Keynesian economics, this boost in disposable personal income works through the *tax multiplier* to increase aggregate demand, as shown earlier in Exhibit 5. Supply-side economists argue instead that changes in disposable income affect the incentive for people to work, to save, and to invest.

Consider how a supply-side tax cut influences the labor market. Suppose supply and demand in the labor market are initially in equilibrium at point E_1 in Exhibit 9. Before a cut in personal income tax rates, the equilibrium hourly wage rate is W_1, and workers

EXHIBIT 8 Keynesian Demand-Side versus Supply-Side Effects

In part (a), assume an economy begins in equilibrium at point E_1, with a price level of 150 and a real GDP of $8 trillion. To boost real output and employment, Keynesian economists prescribe that the federal government raise government spending or cut taxes. By following such demand-side policies, this changes total spending and works through the multiplier effect, shifting the aggregate demand curve from AD_1 to AD_2. As a result, the equilibrium changes to E_2, where real GDP rises to $12 trillion, but the price level also rises to 200. Hence, full employment has been achieved at the expense of higher inflation.

The initial situation for the economy at point E_1 in part (b) is identical to that shown in part (a). However, supply-siders offer a different fiscal policy prescription than the Keynesians. Using some combination of cuts in resource prices, technological advances, tax cuts, subsidies, and regulation reduction, supply-side fiscal policy attempts to shift the aggregate supply curve from AS_1 to AS_2. As a result, the equilibrium in the economy changes to E_2, and real GDP increases to $12 trillion, just as in part (a). The advantage of the supply-side stimulus over the demand-side stimulus is that the price level falls to 100, rather than rising to 200.

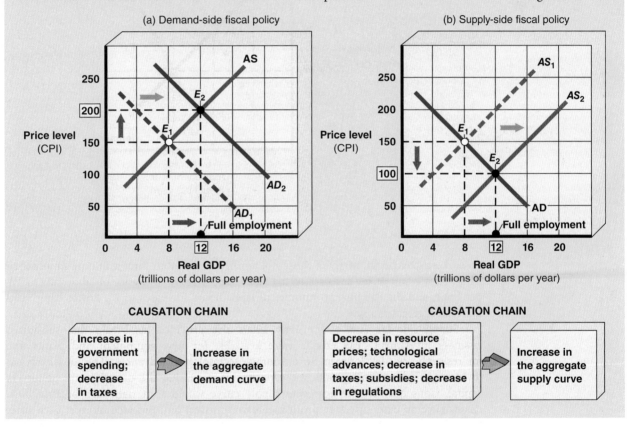

supply L_1 hours of labor per year at this wage rate. When the tax rates are cut, supply-side theory predicts the labor supply curve will shift rightward and establish a new equilibrium at E_2. The rationale is that an increase in the after-tax wage rate gives workers the incentive to work more hours per year. Those in the labor force will want to work longer hours and take fewer vacations. And because Uncle Sam takes a smaller bite out

EXHIBIT 9 How Supply-Side Fiscal Policies Affect Labor Markets

Begin with equilibrium in the labor market at point E_1. Here the intersection of the labor supply and demand curves determines a wage rate of W_1 and L_1 hours of labor per year. By lowering tax rates, supply-side fiscal policies increase net after-tax earnings. This extra incentive causes workers to provide additional hours of labor per year. As a result, the labor supply curve increases and establishes a new equilibrium at point E_2. The new wage rate paid by employers falls to W_2, and they use more labor hours per year, L_2.

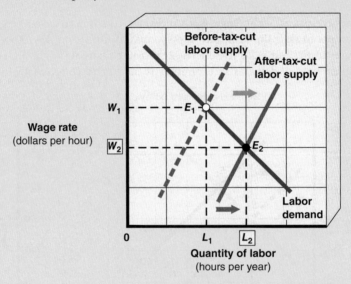

of workers' paychecks, many of those not already in the labor force will now supply their labor. As a result of the increase in the labor supply curve, the price of labor falls to W_2 per hour, and the equilibrium number of labor hours increases to L_2. Lower labor costs increase aggregate supply.

Supply-side tax cuts of the early 1980s also provided tax breaks that subsidized business investment. Tax credits were available for new equipment and plants and for research and development to encourage technological advances. The idea here was to increase the nation's productive capacity by increasing the quantity and quality of capital. Consequently, the aggregate supply curve would shift rightward because businesses have an extra after-tax profit incentive to invest and produce more at each price level.

The idea of using tax cuts to shift the aggregate supply curve outward is controversial, and you may have heard the critics refer to supply-side economics as "trickle-down economics." Despite its logic, the Keynesians argue that the magnitude of any rightward shift in aggregate supply is likely to be small and occur only in the long run. They point out that it takes many years before tax cuts for business generate any change in actual plants and equipment or technological advances. Moreover, individuals can accept tax cuts with a "thank you, Uncle Sam" and not work longer or harder. Meanwhile, unless a reduction in government spending offsets the tax cuts, the effect will be a Keynesian increase in the aggregate demand curve and a higher price level. Exhibit 10 summarizes the important distinction between the supply-side and Keynesian theories on tax cut policy.

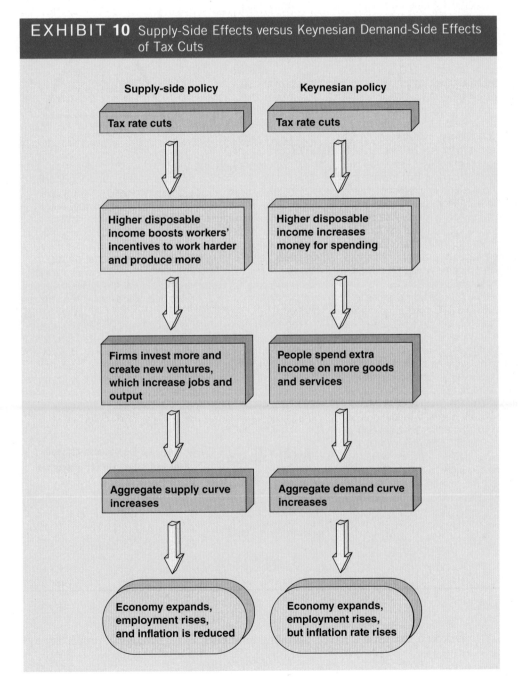

EXHIBIT 10 Supply-Side Effects versus Keynesian Demand-Side Effects of Tax Cuts

Supply-side policy

Tax rate cuts

↓

Higher disposable income boosts workers' incentives to work harder and produce more

↓

Firms invest more and create new ventures, which increase jobs and output

↓

Aggregate supply curve increases

↓

Economy expands, employment rises, and inflation is reduced

Keynesian policy

Tax rate cuts

↓

Higher disposable income increases money for spending

↓

People spend extra income on more goods and services

↓

Aggregate demand curve increases

↓

Economy expands, employment rises, but inflation rate rises

Laffer curve
A graph depicting the relationship between tax rates and total tax revenues.

The Laffer Curve

Supply-side economics became popular during the presidential campaign of 1980. This fiscal policy prescription gained prominence after supply-side economist Arthur Laffer, using his pen to draw on a paper napkin, explained what has come to be known as the Laffer curve to an editor of *The Wall Street Journal* at a restaurant in Washington, D.C., in 1974. The **Laffer curve** is a graph depicting the relationship between tax rates and total tax revenues. As shown in the figure, the hypothetical Laffer curve can be drawn with the federal tax rate on the horizontal axis and tax revenue on the vertical axis. The idea behind this curve is that the federal tax rate affects the incentive for people to work, save, invest, and produce, which in turn influences tax revenue. As the tax rate climbs, Laffer and other supply-siders argue that the erosion of incentives shrinks national income and total tax collections. The editor kept the napkin and published the curve in an editorial in *The Wall Street Journal.* And a theory was born.

Here is how the Laffer curve works. Suppose the federal government sets the federal income tax rate at zero (point *A*). At a zero income tax rate, people have the maximum incentive to produce, and optimum national income would be earned, but there is zero tax revenue for Uncle Sam. Now assume the federal government sets the income tax rate at the opposite extreme of 100 percent (point *D*). At a 100 percent confiscating income tax rate, people have no reason to work, take business risks, produce, and earn income. People seek ways to reduce their tax liabilities by engaging in unreported or underground transactions or by not working at all. As a result, no tax revenue is collected by the Internal Revenue Service. Laffer compared this situation to Robin Hood and his band of merry men (the government) who robbed rich people (taxpayers) traveling through Sherwood Forest to give to the poor. Laffer posed this question, "Do you think that travelers continued to go through Sherwood Forest?" The answer is "no," and Robin Hood's "revenue" would fall.

Because the federal government does not want to collect zero tax revenue, Congress sets the federal income tax rate between zero and 100 percent. Assuming that the income tax rate is related to tax revenue as depicted in the figure, maximum tax revenue, R_{max}, is collected at a tax rate of T_{max} (point *B*).

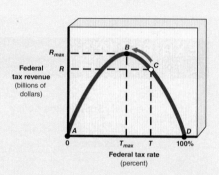

Laffer argued that the federal income tax rate of *T* (point *C*) in 1981 exceeded T_{max} and the result would be tax revenue of *R*, which is below R_{max}. In Laffer's view, reducing the federal income tax rate leads to an increase in tax revenue because people increase their work effort, saving, and investment and reduce their attempts to avoid paying taxes. Thus, Laffer argued that a cut in federal income tax rates would unleash economic activity and boost tax revenues needed to reduce the federal budget deficit. President Reagan's belief in the Laffer curve was a major reason why he thought that the federal government could cut personal income tax rates and still balance the federal budget.

The Laffer curve remains a controversial part of supply-side economics. There is still considerable uncertainty about the shape of the Laffer curve and at what point, *B*, *C*, or otherwise, along the curve the U.S. economy is operating. There is also no certainty for what tax rate yields maximum tax revenue. And note that below T_{max}, tax rate increases do increase total revenue. Thus, the existence and the usefulness of the Laffer curve are a matter of dispute.

ANALYZE THE ISSUE   Compare the common perception of how a tax rate cut affects tax revenues with economist Laffer's theory.

Key Concepts

| Fiscal policy | Discretionary fiscal policy | Spending multiplier (SM) | Marginal propensity to consume (MPC) |

Marginal propensity to save (MPS)

Tax multiplier (TM)

Balanced budget multiplier

Automatic stabilizers

Budget surplus

Budget deficit

Supply-side fiscal policy

Laffer curve

Summary

- **Fiscal policy** is the use of government spending and taxes to stabilize the economy.

- **Discretionary fiscal policy** follows the Keynesian argument that the federal government should manipulate aggregate demand in order to influence the output, employment, and price levels in the economy. Discretionary fiscal policy requires new legislation to change either government spending or taxes in order to stabilize the economy.

Discretionary Fiscal Policies

Expansionary fiscal policy	Contractionary fiscal policy
Increase government spending	Decrease government spending
Decrease taxes	Increase taxes
Increase government spending and taxes equally	Decrease government spending and taxes equally

- The **spending multiplier (SM)** is the multiplier by which an initial change in one component of aggregate demand, for example, government spending, alters aggregate demand (total spending) after an infinite number of spending cycles. Expressed as a formula, the spending multiplier = 1/(1 − MPC).

- **Expansionary fiscal policy** is a deliberate increase in government spending, a deliberate decrease in taxes, or some combination of these two options.

- **Contractionary fiscal policy** is a deliberate decrease in government spending, a deliberate increase in taxes, or some combination of these two options. Using either expansionary or contractionary fiscal policy, the government can shift the aggregate demand curve in order to combat

recession, cool inflation, or achieve other macroeconomic goals.

- The **marginal propensity to consume (MPC)** is the change in consumption spending divided by the change in income.

- The **marginal propensity to save (MPS)** is the change in savings divided by the change in income.

- The **tax multiplier** is the change in aggregate demand (total spending) that results from an initial change in taxes after an infinite number of spending cycles. Expressed as a formula, the tax multiplier (TM) = 1 − spending multiplier.

- **Combating recession and inflation** can be accomplished by changing government spending or taxes. The total change in aggregate demand from a change in government spending is equal to the change in government spending times the spending multiplier.

- The total change in aggregate demand from a change in taxes is equal to the change in taxes times the tax multiplier.

Combating Recession

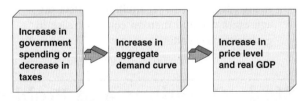

Combating Inflation

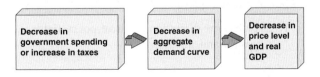

- The **balanced budget multiplier** is not neutral. A dollar of government spending increases real GDP more than a dollar cut in taxes. Thus, even though the government does not spend more than it collects in taxes, it is still stimulating the economy.

- A **budget surplus** occurs when government revenues exceed government expenditures. A **budget deficit** occurs when government expenditures exceed government revenues.

- **Automatic stabilizers** are changes in taxes and government spending that occur automatically in response to changes in the level of real GDP. Also known as non-discretionary fiscal policies, they add stability to the business cycle. A *budget surplus* slows an expanding economy; a *budget deficit* stimulates a contracting economy.

Automatic Stabilizers

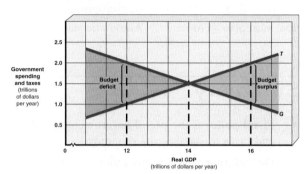

- According to **supply-side fiscal policy**, lower taxes encourage work, saving, and investment, which shift the aggregate supply curve rightward. As a result, output and employment increase and inflation is reduced.

- The **Laffer curve** represents the relationship between the income tax rate and the amount of income tax revenue collected by the government.

Summary of Conclusion Statements

- In the intermediate segment of the aggregate supply curve, the equilibrium real GDP changes by less than the change in government spending times the spending multiplier.

- Any initial change in spending by the government, households, firms, or foreigners on our exports creates a chain reaction of further spending, which causes a greater cumulative change in aggregate demand.

- A tax cut has a smaller multiplier effect on aggregate demand than an equal increase in government spending.

- Regardless of the MPC, the net effect on the economy of an equal initial increase (decrease) in government spending and taxes is an increase (decrease) in aggregate demand equal to the initial increase (decrease) in government spending.

- Automatic stabilizers assist in offsetting a recession when real GDP falls and in offsetting inflation when real GDP expands.

Study Questions and Problems

Please see Appendix A for answers to the odd-numbered questions. Your instructor has access to the answers for even-numbered questions.

1. Explain how discretionary fiscal policy fights recession and inflation.

2. How does each of the following affect the aggregate demand curve?
   a. Government spending increases.
   b. The amount of taxes collected decreases.

3. In each of the following cases, explain whether the fiscal policy is expansionary, contractionary, or neutral.
   a. The government decreases government spending.
   b. The government increases taxes.
   c. The government increases spending and taxes by an equal amount.

4. Why does a reduction in taxes have a smaller multiplier effect than an increase in government spending of an equal amount?

5. Suppose you are an economic adviser to the president and the economy needs a real GDP increase of $500 billion to reach full-employment equilibrium. If the marginal propensity to consume (MPC) is 0.75 and you are a Keynesian, by how much do you believe Congress must increase government spending to restore the economy to full employment?

6. Consider an economy that is operating at the full-employment level of real GDP. Assuming the MPC is 0.90, predict the effect on the economy of a $50 billion increase in government spending balanced by a $50 billion increase in taxes.

7. Why is a $100 billion increase in government spending for goods and services more expansionary than a $100 billion decrease in taxes?

8. What is the difference between discretionary fiscal policy and automatic stabilizers? How are federal budget surpluses and deficits affected by the business cycle?

9. Assume you are a supply-side economist who is an adviser to the president. If the economy is in recession, what would your fiscal policy prescription be?

10. Suppose Congress enacts a tax reform law and the average federal tax rate drops from 30 percent to 20 percent. Researchers investigate the impact of the tax cut and find that the income subject to the tax increases from $600 billion to $800 billion. The theoretical explanation is that workers have increased their work effort in response to the incentive of lower taxes. Is this a movement along the downward-sloping or the upward-sloping portion of the Laffer curve?

11. Indicate how each of the following would change either the aggregate demand curve or the aggregate supply curve.
    a. Expansionary fiscal policy
    b. Contractionary fiscal policy
    c. Supply-side economics
    d. Demand-pull inflation
    e. Cost-push inflation

 CHECKPOINT ANSWERS

What Is the MPC for Uncle Sam's Stimulus Package?

To calculate the value of the MPC required to increase real GDP (ΔY) by $3,200 billion from an increase in government spending (ΔG) of $800 billion, use this formula:

$$\Delta G \times \text{multiplier} = \Delta Y,$$

Where

$$\$800 \text{ billion} \times \text{multiplier} = \$3,200$$

Thus,

$$\text{Multiplier} = \frac{\$3,200}{\$800 \text{ billion}} = 4$$

Using Exhibit 4, if you said that the MPC is 0.75, **YOU ARE CORRECT**.

Walking the Balanced Budget Tightrope

An $800 billion increase in government spending increases aggregate demand by $3,200 billion [government spending increase × spending multiplier, where the spending multiplier $= 1/(1 - MPC) = 1/0.25 = 4$]. On the other hand, an $800 billion increase in taxes reduces aggregate demand by $2,400 billion (tax cut × tax multiplier, where the tax multiplier $= 1 -$ spending multiplier $= 1 - 4 = -3$). Thus, the net effect of the spending multiplier and the tax multiplier is an increase in aggregate demand of $800 billion. If you said Congress has missed its goal of a $1,000 billion boost in aggregate demand by $200 billion and has not restored full employment, **YOU ARE CORRECT**.

Sample Quiz

Please see Appendix B for answers to Sample Quiz questions.

1. Which of the following is an example of expansionary fiscal policy?
   a. An increase in taxes
   b. A decrease in government spending
   c. An increase in government spending
   d. An increase in taxes and a decrease in government spending equally

2. In the _____ range of the aggregate supply curve, expansionary fiscal policy causes aggregate _____ to increase, which results in a higher price level and a higher equilibrium level of real GDP.
   a. Keynesian, supply
   b. Classical, demand
   c. Intermediate, demand
   d. Intermediate, supply

3. An expansionary fiscal policy may include
   a. increases in government spending.
   b. discretionary increases in transfer payments.
   c. reductions in taxes.
   d. All of the answers above are correct.

4. Suppose the economy in Exhibit 11 is in equilibrium at point E_1 and the marginal propensity to consume (MPC) is 0.80. Following Keynesian economics, to restore full employment, the government should increase its spending by
   a. $200 billion.
   b. $250 billion.
   c. $500 billion.
   d. $1 trillion.

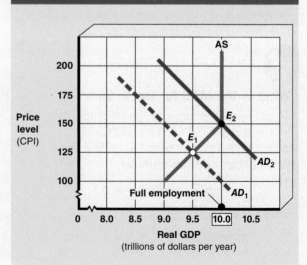

EXHIBIT 11 Aggregate Demand and Supply Model

5. Beginning at equilibrium E_1 in Exhibit 11, when the government increases spending or cuts taxes, the economy will experience
   a. an inflationary recession.
   b. stagflation.
   c. cost-push inflation.
   d. demand-pull inflation.

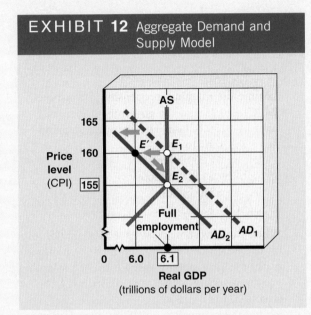

EXHIBIT 12 Aggregate Demand and Supply Model

Price level (CPI)

165
160
155

AS
E'
E_1
E_2
Full employment
AD_2 AD_1

0   6.0   6.1

Real GDP
(trillions of dollars per year)

6. Suppose the economy in Exhibit 12 is in equilibrium at point E_1 and the marginal propensity to consume (MPC) is 0.75. Following Keynesian economics, the federal government can move the economy to point E_2 and reduce inflation by
   a. decreasing government spending by $750 billion.
   b. decreasing government spending by $100 billion.
   c. increasing government spending by $25 billion.
   d. decreasing government spending by $25 billion.

7. Mathematically, the value of the tax multiplier in terms of the marginal propensity to consume (MPC) is given by the formula
   a. MPC − 1.
   b. (MPC − 1)/MPC.
   c. 1/MPC.
   d. 1 − [1/(1 − MPC)].

8. A tax multiplier equal to −4.30 would imply that a $100 tax increase would lead to a
   a. $430 decline in real GDP.
   b. $430 increase in real GDP.
   c. 4.3 percent increase in real GDP.
   d. 4.3 percent decrease in real GDP.
   e. 43 percent decrease in real GDP.

9. Equal increases in government spending and taxes will
   a. cancel each other out so that the equilibrium level of real GDP remains unchanged.
   b. lead to an equal decrease in the equilibrium level of real GDP.
   c. lead to an equal increase in the equilibrium level of real GDP.
   d. lead to an increase in the equilibrium level of real GDP output that is larger than the initial change in government spending and taxes.

10. When the economy enters a recession, automatic stabilizers create
    a. higher taxes.
    b. more discretionary spending.
    c. budget deficits.
    d. budget surpluses.

11. Automatic stabilizers "lean against the prevailing wind" of the business cycle because
    a. wages are controlled by the minimum wage law.
    b. federal expenditures and tax revenues change as the level of real GDP changes.
    c. the spending and tax multipliers are constant.
    d. they include the power of special interests.

12. Unemployment compensation payments
    a. rise during a recession and thus reduce the severity of the recession.
    b. rise during a recession and thus increase the severity of the recession.
    c. rise during inflationary episodes and thus reduce the severity of the inflation.
    d. fall during a recession and thus increase the severity of the recession.

13. According to supply-side fiscal policy, reducing tax rates on wages and profits will
    a. create demand-pull inflation.
    b. lower the price level but may trigger a recession.
    c. result in stagflation.
    d. reduce both unemployment and inflation.

14. Supply-side economics calls for
    a. lower taxes on businesses and individuals.
    b. regulatory reforms to increase productivity.
    c. government subsidies to promote technological advance.
    d. All of the above answers are correct.

EXHIBIT **13** Aggregate Demand and Supply Model

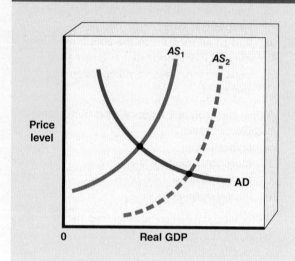

15. In Exhibit 13, supply-siders claim that a shift from AS_1 to AS_2 would occur if the government
    a. increased tax rates and increased the amount of government regulation.
    b. increased tax rates and decreased the amount of government regulation.
    c. decreased tax rates and increased the amount of government regulation.
    d. decreased tax rates and decreased the amount of government regulation.

16. The Laffer curve belongs to which of the following schools of economic thought?
    a. Keynesian
    b. Supply-side
    c. Demand management
    d. Classical

17. According to the Laffer curve, when the tax rate is 100 percent, tax revenue will be
    a. 0.
    b. at the maximum value.
    c. the same as it would be at a 50 percent tax rate.
    d. greater than it would be at a 50 percent tax rate.
    e. the same as it would be at a 20 percent tax rate.

18. Assume the marginal propensity to consume (MPC) is 0.75 and the government increases taxes by $250 billion. The aggregate demand curve will shift to the
    a. left by $1,000 billion.
    b. right by $1,000 billion.
    c. left by $750 billion.
    d. right by $750 billion.

19. When the government levies a $100 million tax on people's income and puts the $100 million back into the economy in the form of a spending program, such as new interstate highway construction, the
    a. tax then generates a $100 million decline in real GDP.
    b. level of real GDP expands by $100 million.
    c. effect on real GDP is uncertain.
    d. tax multiplier overpowers the spending multiplier, triggering a rollback in real GDP.

20. Assume the economy is in recession and real GDP is below full employment. The marginal propensity to consume (MPC) is 0.75, and the government follows Keynesian economics by using expansionary fiscal policy to increase aggregate demand (total spending). If an increase of $1,000 billion aggregate demand can restore full employment, the government should
    a. increase spending by $250 billion.
    b. decrease spending by $750 billion.
    c. increase spending by $1,000 billion.
    d. increase spending by $750 billion.

CHAPTER 12

The Public Sector

CHAPTER PREVIEW

In the early 1980s, President Ronald Reagan adopted the Laffer curve theory that the federal government could cut tax rates and increase tax revenues. Critics said the result would be lower tax revenues. During the 2000 campaign for the Republican presidential nomination, Steve Forbes continued his attempt to win support for a flat tax, and George W. Bush advocated cutting individual marginal tax rates. However, President Bill Clinton said cutting taxes was not a good idea because ensuring the integrity of Social Security should come first. Between 2001 and 2004, President George W. Bush signed laws that provided for phased-in cuts in the marginal tax rates and increased spending for the war in Iraq and homeland defense. Critics argued that changing the tax structure while increasing spending would worsen the long-term federal budget outlook. And in 2011, grassroots "Tea Parties" were conducted across the nation to protest a too-large federal government that is spending large amounts on economic stimulus packages to deal with the Great Recession. In 2013, a highly partisan dispute between Republicans and Democrats over spending on Obamacare led to a government shutdown. In more recent years the deficit has fallen, and focus has shifted once again to tax reform.

These events illustrate the persistent real-world controversy surrounding fiscal policy. The previous chapter presented the theory behind fiscal policy. In this chapter, you will examine the practice of fiscal policy. Here the facts of taxation and government expenditures are clearly presented and placed in perspective. You can check, for example, the trend in federal taxes and expenditures during the Obama administration and compare these figures to those of other countries. And you will discover why the government uses different types of taxes and tax rates.

The final section of the chapter challenges the economic role of the public sector. Here you will learn a theory called *public choice*, which examines public sector decisions of politicians, government bureaucrats, voters, and special-interest groups.

IN THIS CHAPTER, YOU WILL LEARN TO SOLVE THESE ECONOMICS PUZZLES:

- How does the tax burden in the United States compare to other countries?

- How does the Social Security tax favor the upper-income worker?

- Is a flat tax fair?

- Should we replace the income tax with a national sales tax or a flat tax?

12-1 GOVERNMENT SIZE AND GROWTH

Government expenditures
Federal, state, and local government outlays for goods and services, including transfer payments.

How big is the public sector in the United States? If we look at Exhibit 1, we see total **government expenditures** or outlays—including those of federal, state, and local governments—as a percentage of GDP for the 1929–2016 period. When we refer to *government expenditures*, we refer to more than the *government consumption expenditures and investment* (G) account used by national income accountants to calculate GDP (see Exhibit 2 in the chapter on GDP). Government expenditures, or outlays, equal government purchases plus *transfer payments*. Recall from the chapter on GDP that the government national income account (G) includes federal government spending for defense, highways, and education. Transfer payments, not in (G), include payments to persons entitled to welfare, Social Security, and unemployment benefits.

EXHIBIT 1 The Growth of Government Expenditures as a Percentage of GDP in the United States, 1929–2016

The graph shows the growth of the federal, state, and local governments as measured by government expenditures as a percentage of GDP since 1929. Expenditures rose dramatically during World War II and fell dramatically after the war, but not to previous peacetime levels. Taking account of all government outlays, including transfer payments, the government sector has grown from about one-quarter of GDP in 1950 to about one-third of GDP beginning in 1975 and remained at this level until total government expenditures increased sharply following the Great Recession to 40 percent of GDP in 2009. Total government expenditures fell after 2009, reaching 37 percent in 2016.

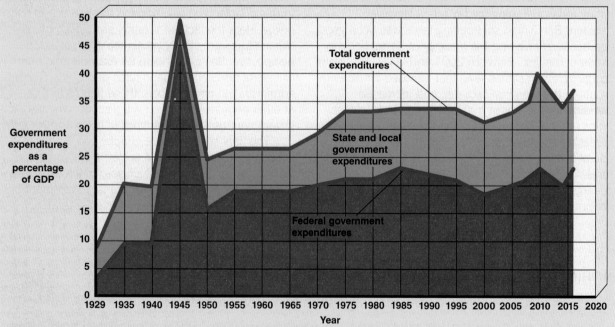

SOURCE: *Economic Report of the President, 2017,* https://www.govinfo.gov/features/ERP-2017, Table B–20, and Bureau of Economic Analysis, National Income Accounts, http://www.bea.gov/iTable/index_nipa.cfm, Tables 3.2 and 3.3.

As shown in Exhibit 1, total government expenditures skyrocketed as a percentage of GDP during World War II and then took a sharp plunge, but not to previous peacetime levels. Since 1950, total government expenditures grew from about one-quarter of GDP to about one-third beginning in 1975 and remained at this level until total expenditures increased sharply following the Great Recession to 40 percent of GDP in 2009. In 2016, total government expenditures fell to 37 percent of GDP. The other side of the coin is that today the private sector's share of national output is 63 percent of GDP. The exhibit also shows that federal government expenditures decreased slightly from a high of 24 percent of GDP in 2009 to 20 percent in 2014 but increased to 23 percent in 2016. Issues concerning federal government spending and financing its debt are discussed in the next chapter.

12-1a **Government Expenditures Patterns**

Exhibit 2 shows program categories for federal government expenditures for 1970 and 2016. The largest category by far in the federal budget for 2016 was the 54 percent of the budget spent for a category called *income security*. "Security" means these payments provide income to the elderly or disadvantaged, including Social Security, Medicare, unemployment compensation, public assistance (welfare), federal retirement, and disability benefits. These entitlements are transfer payments in the form of either direct cash payments or in-kind transfers that redistribute income among persons. In 2016, 44 percent of income security expenditures was spent for Social Security and 29 percent for Medicare.

The third largest category of federal government expenditures in 2016 was national defense. Note that the percentage of the federal budget spent for defense declined from

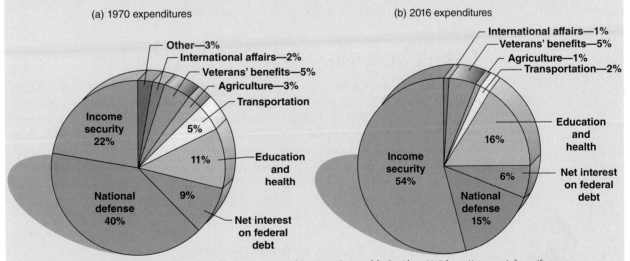

EXHIBIT 2 Federal Government Expenditures, 1970 and 2016

Between 1970 and 2016, income security became the largest category of federal expenditures. During the same period, national defense declined from the largest spending category to the third largest. Income security and national defense combined accounted for 69 percent of federal outlays in 2016.

(a) 1970 expenditures

Other—3%
International affairs—2%
Veterans' benefits—5%
Agriculture—3%
Transportation
5%
Income security 22%
11%
Education and health
National defense 40%
9%
Net interest on federal debt

(b) 2016 expenditures

International affairs—1%
Veterans' benefits—5%
Agriculture—1%
Transportation—2%
16%
Education and health
Income security 54%
6%
Net interest on federal debt
National defense 15%

SOURCE: *Economic Report of the President, 1975*, Table C–65, p. 325; and *Economic Report of the President, 2017*, https://www.govinfo.gov/features /ERP-2017, Table B–20.

40 percent in 1970 to 15 percent in 2016, while income security ("safety net") expenditures grew from 22 percent in 1970 to 54 percent in 2016. Hence, the dominant trend in federal government spending between 1970 and 2016 was an increase in the redistribution-of-income role of the federal government and a decrease in the portion of the budget spent for defense.

Federal expenditures for education and health were in second place in 2016, and net interest on the federal debt was in fourth place. Net interest paid is the interest on federal government borrowings minus the interest earned on federal government loans, and in 2016, this category of the budget was 6 percent. Thus, the federal government spent about the same proportion of the budget on financing its debt as on international affairs, veterans' benefits, and agriculture combined.

Finally, you need to be aware that the size and growth of government are measured several ways. We could study *absolute* government spending rather than percentages or compare the growth of spending after adjusting for inflation. Still another technique is to measure the proportion of the population that the public sector employs. Using any of these measurements confirms the following conclusion reached from Exhibits 1 and 2:

CONCLUSION

The government's share of total economic activity has generally increased since World War II ended in 1945. Most of the growth in combined government expenditures as a percentage of GDP reflects rapidly growing federal government transfer programs.

12-1b Government Expenditures in Other Countries

In 2015, U.S. government spending for all levels as a percentage of GDP was lower than other advanced industrial countries. As shown in Exhibit 3, the governments of France, Norway, Germany, and other countries spent a higher percentage of their GDPs than the federal, state, and local governments of the United States.

12-2 FINANCING GOVERNMENT BUDGETS

Where does the federal government obtain the funds to finance its outlays? Exhibit 4 tells the story. We find that the largest revenue source in 2016 was individual income taxes (47 percent), followed closely by social insurance taxes (34 percent), which include payroll taxes paid by employers and employees for Social Security, workers' compensation, and unemployment insurance. The third best revenue collector was corporate income taxes (9 percent). An excise tax is a sales tax on the purchase of a particular good or service. Excise taxes contributed 3 percent of total tax receipts. The "Other" category includes receipts from such taxes as customs duties, estate taxes, and gift taxes.

12-2a The Tax Burden in Other Countries

Before turning our attention in the next section to the criteria for selecting which tax to impose, we must ask how burdensome overall taxation in the United States

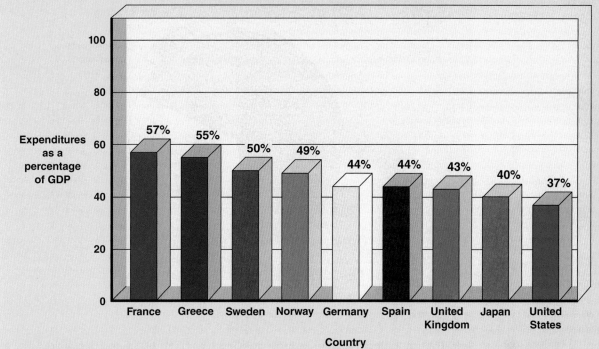

EXHIBIT 3 Government Expenditures in Other Countries, 2015

In 2015, the U.S. government was less of a spender than other advanced industrial countries. The governments of all of the countries depicted in the exhibit spent a higher percentage of their GDPs than the combined spending of the federal, state, and local governments of the United States.

SOURCE: OECD data, https://data.oecd.org/gga/general-government-spending.htm; OECD (2017),*Government at a Glance 2017*, OECD Publishing, Paris. http://dx.doi.org/10.1787/gov_glance-2017-en; and OECD (2017) *National Accounts of OECD Countries, General Government Accounts 2016,* OECD Publishing, http://www.oecd-ilibrary.org/economics/national-accounts-of-oecd-countries-general-government-accounts-2016_na_gga-2017-en.

is. It may surprise you to learn that by international standards, U.S. citizens are among the most lightly taxed people in the industrialized world. Exhibit 5 reveals that in 2015, the tax collector was clearly much more heavy-handed in most other advanced industrial countries based on the fraction of GDP paid in taxes. The Norwegians, French, Swedes, Greeks, and Germans for example, pay far higher taxes as a percentage of GDP than Americans. It should be noted that countries that tax more heavily also are expected to provide more public services than the United States provides.

Another way to study the burden of taxation in the United States is to observe how it has changed over time. Exhibit 6 charts the growth of taxes as a percentage of GDP in the United States since 1929. Total government taxes, including federal, state, and local taxes, climbed from 11 percent of GDP in 1929 to their highest level of 33 percent in 2000 and then fell and rose again to 32 percent in 2016. The exhibit also shows that in 2000, federal taxes as a percentage of GDP rose to a post–World War II high of 20 percent before falling and rising again to about 19 percent in 2016.

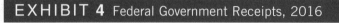

EXHIBIT 4 Federal Government Receipts, 2016

In 2016, the largest source of revenue for the federal government was individual income taxes, and the second largest source was social insurance taxes.

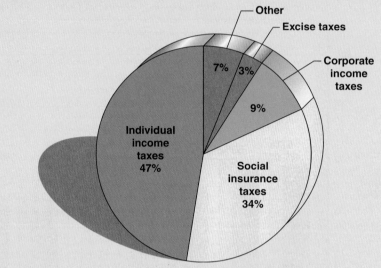

SOURCE: *Economic Report of the President, 2017*, https://www.govinfo.gov/features/ERP-2017. Table B–20.

12-3 THE ART OF TAXATION

Jean-Baptiste Colbert, finance minister to King Louis XIV of France, once said, "The art of taxation consists of so plucking the goose as to obtain the largest amount of feathers while promoting the smallest amount of hissing." Each year with great zeal, members of Congress and other policymakers debate various ways of raising revenue without causing too much "hissing." As you will learn, the task is difficult because each kind of tax has a different characteristic. Government must decide which tax is "appropriate" based on two basic philosophies of fairness—benefits received and ability to pay.

12-3a The Benefits-Received Principle

Benefits-received principle
The concept that those who benefit from government expenditures should pay the taxes that finance their benefits.

What standard or guideline can we use to be sure everyone pays his or her "fair" share of taxes? One possibility is the **benefits-received principle** of taxation, which is the concept that those who benefit from government expenditures should pay the taxes that finance their benefits. The gasoline tax is an example of a tax that follows the *benefits-received principle*. The number of gallons of gasoline bought is a measure of the amount of highway services used, and the more gallons purchased, the greater the tax paid. Applying benefit-cost analysis, voters will approve additional highways only if the benefits they receive exceed the costs in gasoline taxes they must pay for highway construction and repairs.

Although the benefits-received principle of taxation is applicable to a private good such as gasoline, the nature of *public goods* often makes it impossible to apply this principle. Recall from Chapter 4 that national defense is a public good, which users

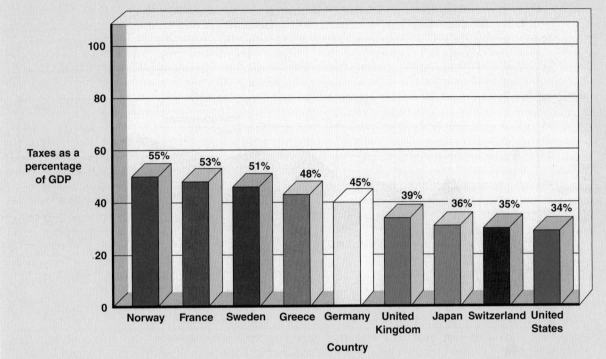

EXHIBIT 5 The Tax Burden in Selected Countries, 2015

Americans were more lightly taxed in 2015 than the citizens of other advanced industrial countries. For example, the Norwegians French, Swedes, Greeks, and Germans, pay higher taxes as a percentage of GDP.

SOURCE: OECD data, https://data.oecd.org/gga/general-government-spending.htm; OECD (2017), *Government at a Glance 2017*, OECD Publishing, Paris, http://dx.doi.org/10.1787/gov_glance-2017-en; and OECD (2017) *National Accounts of OECD Countries, General Government Accounts 2016*, OECD Publishing, http://www.oecd-ilibrary.org/economics/national-accounts-of-oecd-countries-general-government-accounts-2016_na_gga-2017-en.

collectively consume. So how can we separate those who benefit from national defense and make them pay? We cannot, and there are other goods and services for which the benefits-received principle is inconsistent with societal goals. It would be foolish, for example, to ask families receiving food stamps to pay all the taxes required to finance their welfare benefits.

12-3b The Ability-to-Pay Principle

A second popular principle of fairness in taxation sharply contrasts with the benefits-received principle. The **ability-to-pay principle** of taxation is the concept that those who have higher incomes can afford to pay a greater proportion of their income in taxes, regardless of benefits received. Under this tax philosophy, the rich may send their children to private schools or use private hospitals, but they should bear a heavier tax burden because they are better able to pay. How could there possibly be a problem with such an approach? An individual who earns $200,000 per year should pay X more taxes than an individual who earns only $10,000 per year. The difficulty lies in

Ability-to-pay principle
The concept that those who have higher incomes can afford to pay a greater proportion of their income in taxes, regardless of benefits received.

EXHIBIT 6 The Growth of Taxes as a Percentage of GDP in the United States, 1929–2016

The graph shows the growth in federal, state, and local government taxes as a percentage of GDP since 1929. Total government taxes climbed from about 11 percent of GDP in 1929 to their highest level of 33 percent in 2000 before falling and rising again to 32 percent in 2016. In 2000, federal taxes as a percentage of GDP reached a post–World War II high of 21 percent before falling and rising again to 19 percent in 2016.

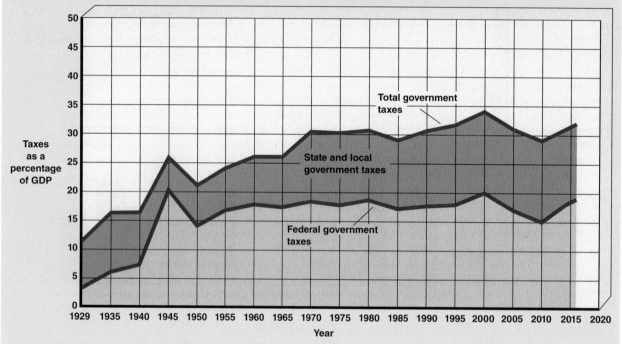

SOURCE: *Economic Report of the President, 2017,* https://www.govinfo.gov/features/ERP-2017, Table B–20, and Bureau of Economic Analysis, National Income Accounts, http://www.bea.gov/iTable/index_nipa.cfm, Tables 3.2 and 3.3.

determining exactly how much more the higher-income individual *should* pay in taxes to ensure he or she is paying a "fair" amount. Unfortunately, no scientific method can measure precisely what one's "ability" to pay taxes means in dollars or percentage of income. Nevertheless, in the U.S. economy, the ability-to-pay principle dominates the benefits-received principle.

12-3c Progressive, Regressive, and Proportional Taxes

As we have seen, governments raise revenues from various taxes, such as income taxes, sales taxes, excise taxes, and property taxes. For purposes of analysis, economists classify each of these taxes into three types of taxation—*progressive*, *regressive*, and *proportional*. The focus of these three classifications is the relationship between changes in the tax rates and increases or decreases in income. Income is the tax base because people pay taxes out of income, even though a tax is levied on property, such as land, buildings, automobiles, and furniture.

Progressive Taxes

Following the ability-to-pay principle, individual and corporate income taxes are progressive taxes. A **progressive tax** is a tax that charges a higher percentage of income as income rises. For example, if a person earning $10,000 a year pays $1,500 in taxes, the *average* tax rate is 15 percent. If another person earns $100,000 a year and pays $28,000 in taxes, the average tax rate is 28 percent. This tax rate progressivity is the principle behind the federal and state income tax systems. Exhibit 7 illustrates the progressive nature of the federal income tax for a single person filing a 2017 tax return.

Column (1) of Exhibit 7 lists the *taxable income* tax brackets. Taxable income is gross income minus the personal exemption and the standard deduction. The personal exemption and the standard deduction are adjusted each year so inflation does not push taxpayers into higher tax brackets. Column (2) shows the tax bill that a taxpayer at the upper income of each of the six lowest taxable income brackets must pay, and the figures in column (3) are the corresponding average tax rates. The **average tax rate** is the tax divided by the income:

$$\text{Average tax rate} = \frac{\text{total tax due}}{\text{total taxable income}}$$

Thus, at a taxable income of $37,950, the average tax rate is 14 percent ($5,226.25 divided by $37,950), and at $91,900, it is 20 percent ($18,713.75 divided by $91,900). A taxable income of over $418,400 is included to represent the upper-income bracket. As these figures indicate, our federal individual income tax is a progressive tax because the average tax rate rises as income increases.

Another key tax rate measure is the **marginal tax rate**, which is the fraction of additional income paid in taxes. The marginal tax rate formula is expressed as

$$\text{Marginal tax rate} = \frac{\text{change in taxes due}}{\text{change in taxable income}}$$

Progressive tax
A tax that charges a higher percentage of income as income rises.

Average tax rate
The tax divided by the income.

Marginal tax rate
The fraction of additional income paid in taxes.

EXHIBIT 7 Federal Individual Income Tax Rate Schedule for a Single Taxpayer, 2017

(1) Taxable income		(2)	(3) Average tax rate [(2)/(1)]	(4) Change in taxable income	(5) Change in tax	(6) Marginal tax rate [(5)/(4)]
Over	But not over	Tax*				
$0	$9,325	$932.50	10%	$9,325	$932.50	10.0%
9,325	37,950	5,226.25	14	28,625	4,293.75	15.0
37,950	91,900	18,713.75	20	53,950	13,487.50	25.0
91,900	191,650	46,643.75	24	99,750	27,930.00	28.0
191,650	416,700	120,910.25	29	225,050	74,266.50	33.0
416,700	418,400	121,505.25	29	1,700	595	35.0
418,400	...	...	...	...	...	39.6

*Tax calculated at the top of the taxable income brackets.

SOURCE: Internal Revenue Service, 2017 tax tables, https://www.efile.com/tax-rate/federal-income-tax-rates/#2017.

Column (6) in Exhibit 7 computes the marginal tax rate for each federal tax bracket in the table. You can comprehend the marginal tax rate by observing in column (1) that when taxable income rises from $9,325 to $37,950 in the second lowest tax bracket, the tax rises from $932.50 to $5,226.25 in column (2). Column (4) reports this change in taxable income, and column (5) shows the change in the tax. The marginal tax rate in column (6) is therefore 15 percent ($4293.75 divided by $28,625). Apply the same analysis when taxable income increases by $53,950 from $37,950 to $91,900 in the next bracket. An additional $13,487.50 is added to the $5,226.25 tax bill, so the marginal tax rate on this extra income is 25 percent ($13,487.50 divided by $53,950). Similar computations provide the marginal tax rates for the remaining taxable income brackets. The marginal tax rate is important because it determines how much a taxpayer's tax bill changes as his or her income rises or falls within each tax bracket.

Regressive Taxes

Regressive tax
A tax that charges a lower percentage of income as income rises.

A tax can also be a regressive tax. A **regressive tax** charges a lower percentage of income as income rises. Suppose Mutt, who is earning $10,000 a year, pays a tax of $5,000, and Jeff, who earns $100,000 a year, pays $10,000 in taxes. Although Jeff pays twice the absolute amount, this would be regressive taxation because richer Jeff pays an average tax rate of 10 percent and poorer Mutt suffers a 50 percent tax bite. Such a tax runs afoul of the ability-to-pay principle of taxation.

We will now demonstrate that sales and excise taxes are regressive taxes. Assume that there is a 5 percent sales tax on all purchases and that the Jones family earned $80,000 during the last year, while the Jefferson family earned $20,000. A sales tax is regressive because the richer Jones family will spend a smaller portion of their income to buy food, clothing, and other consumption items. The Joneses, with an $80,000 income, can afford to spend $40,000 on groceries and clothes and save the rest, while the Jeffersons, with a $20,000 income, spend their entire income to feed and clothe their family. Because each family pays a 5 percent sales tax, the lower-income Jeffersons pay sales taxes of $1,000 (0.05 × $20,000). This $1,000 sales tax is 5 percent of their income ($1,000/$20,000). The higher-income Joneses, on the other hand, pay sales taxes of $2,000 (0.05 × $40,000). This $2,000 sales tax is only 2.5 percent of their income ($2,000/$80,000). Although the richer Jones family pays twice the amount of sales tax to the tax collector, the sales tax is regressive because their average tax rate is lower than the Jefferson family's tax rate.

In practice, an example of a regressive tax is the Social Security payroll tax, FICA. The payroll tax is a fixed percentage (currently 6.2 percent) levied on each worker's earnings and deducted from the worker's paycheck by the employer. Payroll taxes are regressive for two reasons. First, only wages and salaries are subject to this tax, while other sources of income, such as interest and dividends, are not. Because wealthy individuals typically receive a larger portion of their income from sources other than wages and salaries than do lower-income individuals, the wealthy pay a smaller fraction of their total income in payroll taxes. Second, earnings above a certain level are exempt from the Social Security tax. Thus, the *marginal tax rate* above a given threshold level is zero. In 2017, this level was $127,200 for wage and salary income subject to Social Security tax. Hence, any additional dollars earned above this figure add no additional taxes, and the average tax rate falls. On the other hand, there is no wage base limit for the Medicare tax. It is noteworthy that one idea for reforming Social Security is to adjust or remove the limit on income subject to Social Security tax.

Finally, property taxes are also considered regressive for two reasons. First, property owners add this tax to the rent paid by tenants who generally are lower-income persons.

Second, property taxes are a higher percentage of income for poor families than rich families because the poor spend a much greater proportion of their incomes for housing.

Proportional Taxes

There continues to be considerable interest in simplifying the federal progressive income tax by substituting a *proportional tax*, also called a *flat tax*. A **proportional tax** charges the same percentage of income, regardless of the size of income. For example, one way to reform the federal progressive income tax rate system would be to eliminate all deductions, exemptions, and loopholes and simply apply the same tax rate, say, 17 percent of income to everyone. Such a reform is illustrated in Exhibit 8. This might avoid the hissing from taxpayers who would no longer require legions of accountants and lawyers to file their tax returns. Actually, most flat-tax proposals are not truly proportional because they exempt income below some level and are, therefore, somewhat progressive. Also, it is debatable that a 17 percent flat tax would raise enough revenue.

Let's look at whether the flat tax satisfies the benefits-received principle and the ability-to-pay principle. First, the flat tax does not necessarily relate to the benefits received from any particular government good or service. Second, consider a 17 percent tax that collects $17,000 from Ms. "Rich," who is earning $100,000 a year, and $1,700

Proportional tax
A tax that charges the same percentage of income, regardless of the size of income. Also called a *flat tax rate* or simply a *flat tax*.

EXHIBIT 8 The Progressive Income Tax versus a Flat Tax

The taxable income tax brackets for 2016 are drawn from Exhibit 7. In contrast to the stair-step tax rates, a flat tax would charge a single rate of, say, 17 percent. This reform proposal is controversial and is discussed in the You're the Economist, "Is It Time to Trash the 1040s?"

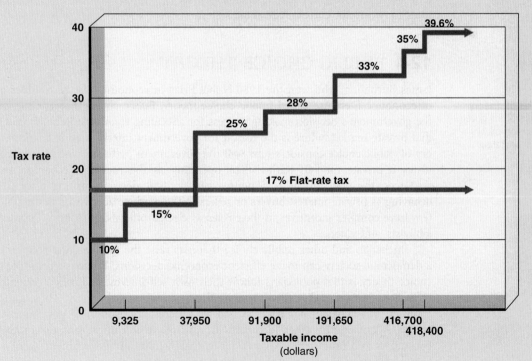

from Mr. "Poor," who is earning $10,000 a year. Both taxpayers pay the same proportional 17 percent of their incomes, but the $1,700 tax is thought to represent a much greater sacrifice to Mr. Poor than does the $17,000 tax paid by Ms. Rich. After paying her taxes, Ms. Rich can still live comfortably, but Mr. Poor complains that he desperately needed the $1,700 to buy groceries for his family. To be fair, one can argue that the $17,000 paid by Ms. Rich is not enough based on the ability-to-pay principle.

12-3d Reforming the Tax System

The Supreme Court declared the personal income tax unconstitutional in 1895. This changed in 1913 when the states ratified the Sixteenth Amendment to the Constitution, granting Congress the power to levy taxes on income. The federal income tax was an inconsequential source of revenue until World War II, but since then, it has remained a major source. Over the years, Congress has enacted various reforms of the federal tax system. The Tax Reform Act of 1986, for example, marked the first time Congress has completely rewritten the Federal Tax Code since 1954. This law removed millions of households from the tax rolls by roughly doubling the personal exemption allowed for each taxpayer and his or her dependents. Before the tax law changed, there were 15 marginal tax brackets for individuals, ranging from 11 to 50 percent. The Tax Reform Act of 1986 reduced the number of tax brackets to only four. Most taxpayers are in the lower brackets, so the loss in tax revenue that resulted from lowering the individual tax rates was in part offset by raising taxes on corporations and closing numerous tax loopholes. Consistent with the two key taxation objectives, the intention of this major revision of the federal income tax law was to improve efficiency and make the system fairer by shifting more of the tax burden to corporations. As shown in Exhibits 7 and 8, there are currently seven tax brackets, and critics argue that another tax reform act is long overdue. The You're the Economist titled "Is It Time to Trash the 1040s?" discusses ideas to reform the current federal tax system.

12-4 PUBLIC CHOICE THEORY

Public choice theory
The analysis of the government's decision-making process for allocating resources.

James Buchanan, who won the 1986 Nobel Prize in economics, is the founder of a body of economic literature called public choice theory. **Public choice theory** is the analysis of the government's decision-making process for allocating resources. Recall from Chapter 4 that private-market failure is the reason for government intervention in markets. The theory of public choice considers how well the government performs when it replaces or regulates a private market. Rather than operating as the market mechanism to allocate resources, the government is a nonmarket, political decision-making force. Instead of behaving as private-interest buyers or sellers in the marketplace, actors in the political system have complex incentives in their roles as elected officials, bureaucrats, special-interest lobbyists, and voters.

Buchanan and other public choice theorists raise the fundamental issue of how well a democratic society can make efficient economic decisions. The basic principle of public choice theory is that politicians follow their own self-interest and seek to maximize their reelection chances, rather than promote the best interests of society. Thus, a major contribution of Buchanan has been to link self-interest motivation to government officials just as Adam Smith earlier identified the pursuit of self-interest as the motivation for consumers and producers. In short, individuals within any government agency or institution will act analogously to their private-sector counterparts; they will give first priority

YOU'RE THE ECONOMIST

Applicable Concepts: Flat Tax, National Sales Tax, and Value Added Tax (VAT)

Is It Time to Trash the 1040s?

Two controversial fundamental tax reform ideas are often hot news topics. One proposal is the flat tax discussed earlier in this chapter, and the other is a national sales tax. The flat tax would grant a personal exemption of say, $36,000, for a typical family and then tax income above this amount at 17 percent with no deductions. As stated by Senator John McCain as a presidential candidate, the argument for a flat tax is that it would allow people to file their tax returns on a postcard and reduce the number of tax cheats. McCain proposed that the flat tax be optional to the current tax system.

The flat-tax plan described earlier creates serious political problems by eliminating taxes on income from dividends, interest, capital gains, and inheritances. Also, eliminating deductions and credits would face strong opposition from the public. For example, eliminating the mortgage interest deduction and exemptions for health care and charity would be a difficult political battle. And there is the fairness question. People at the lower end of the current system of seven progressive rates could face a tax increase while upper-income people would get the biggest tax break. The counterargument is that under the current tax system, many millionaires pay nothing because they shelter their income. Under a flat-tax scheme, they would lose deductions and credits.

A national retail sales tax is another tax reform proposal. In 2014, Mike Huckabee, Republican candidate for president, made this idea, called the Fair Tax, central to his campaign. A consumption tax could eliminate all federal income taxes entirely (personal, corporate, and Social Security) and tax only consumer purchases at a given percentage. Like the flat tax, loopholes would be eliminated, and tax collection would become so simple that the federal government could save billions of dollars by cutting or eliminating the IRS. Taxpayers could save because they would no longer need to hire tax preparers and lawyers to prepare their complicated 1040 tax returns. Also, the tax base would broaden because, while not everyone earns income, almost everyone makes purchases.

Critics of a national sales tax argue that retail businesses would have the added burden of being tax collectors for the federal government, and the IRS would still be required to ensure that taxes are collected on billions of sales transactions. Moreover, huge price increases from the national sales tax would lead to "black market" transactions. The counterargument is that this problem would be no worse than current income tax evasion, and a sales tax indirectly taxes

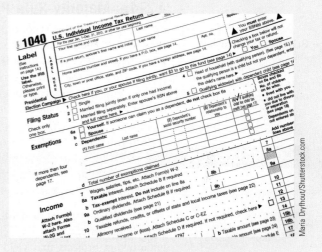

participants in illegal markets when they spend their income in legal markets. Also, a sales tax is regressive because the poor spend a greater share of their income on food, housing, and other necessities. To offset this problem, sales tax advocates propose subsidy checks paid up to some level of income. Critics also point out that retired people who pay little or no federal income tax will not welcome paying a national sales tax.

There are also debates on using a value-added tax (VAT) that is popular in Europe and many other countries. VAT is a consumption tax levied at each stage of production. Suppose a vendor buys apples from a farmer to sell at a market. The vendor's VAT is based on a percentage of the difference (value added) between the cost the vendor paid and the sales price customers pay. Customers who buy the apples bear the VAT cost built in the price of the apples they purchase.

ANALYZE THE ISSUE

Assume the federal government replaces the federal income tax with a national sales tax on all consumption expenditures. Analyze the impact of this tax change on taxation efficiency and equity. Note that the federal government already collects a nationwide consumption tax through excise taxes on gasoline, liquor, and tobacco.

to improving their own earnings, working conditions, and status, rather than to being altruistic.

Given this introduction to the subject, let's consider a few public choice theories that explain why the public sector, like the private sector, may also "fail."

12-4a Majority-Rule Problem

Benefit-cost analysis
The comparison of the additional rewards and costs of an economic alternative.

To evaluate choices, economists often use a technique called benefit-cost analysis. **Benefit-cost analysis** is the comparison of the additional rewards and costs of an economic alternative. If a firm is considering producing a new product, its benefit ("carrots") will be the extra revenue earned from selling the product. The firm's cost ("sticks") is the opportunity cost of using resources to make the product. How many units of the product should the firm manufacture?

CONCLUSION   Rationally, a profit-maximizing firm follows the marginal rule and produces additional units so long as the marginal benefit exceeds the marginal cost.

The basic rule of benefit-cost analysis is that undertaking a program whose cost exceeds its benefit is an inefficient waste of resources. In the competitive market system, undertaking projects that yield benefits greater than costs is a sure bet. In the long run, any firm that does not follow the benefit-cost rule will either go out of business or switch to producing products that yield benefits equal to or greater than their costs. Majority-rule voting, however, can result in the approval of projects whose costs outweigh their benefits. Exhibit 9 illustrates how an inefficient economic decision can result from the ballot box.

As shown in Exhibit 9, suppose Bob, Juan, and Theresa are the only voters in a mini-society that is considering whether to add two publicly financed park projects, A and B. The total cost to taxpayers of either park project is $300, and the marginal cost of park A or park B to each taxpayer is an additional tax of $100 [columns (2) and (5)]. Next, assume each taxpayer determines his or her additional dollar value derived from the benefits of park projects A and B [columns (3) and (6)]. Assuming each person applies marginal analysis, each will follow the *marginal rule* and vote for a project only if his or her benefit exceeds the cost of the $100 tax. Consider park

EXHIBIT 9 Majority-Rule Benefit-Cost Analysis of Two Park Projects

| (1) Voter | Park Project A | | | Park Project B | | |
	(2) Marginal cost (taxes)	(3) Marginal benefit	(4) Vote	(5) Marginal cost (taxes)	(6) Marginal benefit	(7) Vote
Bob	$100	$0	No	$100	$90	No
Juan	100	101	Yes	100	90	No
Theresa	100	101	Yes	100	301	Yes
Total	$300	$202	Passes	$300	$481	Fails

project *A*. This project is worth $0 to Bob, $101 to Juan, and $101 to Theresa, and this means two Yes votes and one No vote: the majority votes for park *A* [column (4)]. This decision would not happen in the business world. The Walt Disney Company, for example, would rationally reject such a project because the total of all consumers' marginal benefits is only $202, which is less than its $300 marginal cost.

The important point here is that majority-rule voting can make the correct benefit-cost marginal analysis, but it can also lead to a rejection of projects with marginal total benefits that exceed marginal costs. Suppose park project *B* costs $300 as well, and Bob's benefits are $90, Juan's $90, and Theresa's $301 [column (6)]. The total of all marginal benefits from constructing park *B* is $481, and this project would be undertaken in a private-sector market. But because only Theresa's benefits exceed the marginal $100 tax, park project *B* in the political arena receives only one Yes vote against two No votes and fails.

Why is there a distinction between political majority voting and benefit-cost analysis? The reason is that dollars can measure the intensity of voter preferences and "one-person, one-vote" does not. A count of ballots can determine whether a proposal passes or fails, but this count may not be proportional to the dollar strength of benefits among the individual voters.

12-4b Special-Interest Group Effect

In addition to benefit-cost errors from majority voting, special-interest groups can create government support for programs with costs outweighing their benefits. The *special-interest effect* occurs when the government approves programs that benefit only a small group within society, but society as a whole pays the costs. The influence of special-interest groups is indeed a constant problem for effective government because the benefits of government programs to certain small groups are great and the costs are relatively insignificant to each taxpayer. For example, let's assume the benefits of support prices for dairy farmers are $100 million. Because of the size of these benefits to dairy farmers, this special-interest group can well afford to hire professional lobbyists and donate a million dollars or so to the reelection campaigns of politicians voting for dairy price supports.

In addition to the incentive of financial support from special interests, politicians can also engage in *logrolling*. Logrolling is the political practice of trading votes of support for legislated programs. Politician A says to politician B, "You vote for my dairy price support bill, and I will vote for your tobacco price support bill."

But who pays for these large benefits to special-interest groups? Taxpayers do, of course, but the extra tax burden per taxpayer is very low. Although Congress may enact a $200 million program to favor, say, a few defense contractors, this expenditure costs 100 million taxpayers only $2 per taxpayer. Because in a free society it is relatively easy to organize special-interest constituencies and lobby politicians to spread the cost, it is little wonder that spending programs are popular. Moreover, the small cost of each pet program per taxpayer means there is little reward for a single voter to learn the details of the many special-interest legislation proposals.

12-4c Rational Voter Ignorance

Politicians, appointed officials, and bureaucrats constitute the supply side of the political marketplace. The demand side of the political market consists of special-interest groups and voters who are subject to what economists call rational ignorance. **Rational ignorance** is a voter's decision that the benefit of becoming informed about an issue is not worth the cost. A frequent charge in elections is that the candidates are not talking about the issues. One explanation is that the candidates realize that a sizable portion of the voters

Rational ignorance
The voter's choice to remain uninformed because the marginal cost of obtaining information is higher than the marginal benefit from knowing it.

will make a calculated decision not to judge the candidates based on in-depth knowledge of their positions on a wide range of issues. Instead of going to the trouble of reading position papers and doing research, many voters choose their candidates based simply on party affiliation or on how the candidate appears on television. This approach is rational if the perceived extra effort required to be better informed exceeds the marginal benefit of knowing more about the candidate.

The principle of rational ignorance also explains why eligible voters fail to vote on election day. A popular explanation is that low voter participation results from apathy among potential voters, but the decision can be an exercise in practical benefit-cost analysis. Nonvoters presumably perceive that the opportunity cost of going to the polls outweighs the benefit gained from any of the candidates or issues on the ballot. Moreover, nonvoters perceive that one extra vote is unlikely to change the outcome.

Public choice theorists argue that one reason benefits are difficult to measure is that the voter confronts an *indivisible* public service. In a grocery store, the consumer can decide to spend so much on apples, oranges, and other *divisible* items, but voting involves candidates who take stands on many issues. The point is that voting does not allow the voter to pick and choose among the candidate's good and bad positions. Most voters, in short, must "buy" a confusing mixture of "wants" and "unwants" that are difficult to interpret as a benefit.

12-4d Bureaucratic Inefficiency

The bureaucracy is the body of nonelected officials and administrators who operate government agencies. As government grows, one of the concerns is that the bureaucracy may become more powerful than the executive, legislative, and judicial branches. Public choice theory also considers how bureaucratic behavior affects economic decision making. One principle is that the government bureaucracy tends to be inefficient because of the absence of the profit motive.

What happens when a government agency performs poorly? First, there is no competition from other producers to take away market share. There are no shareholders demanding reform when profits are falling because taxpayers are a poor substitute for stockholder pressure. Second, the typical government response each year is to request a larger budget. Without profits as a measure of performance, the tendency is to use the size of an agency's budget and staff as an indicator of success. In brief, the basic incentive structure of government agencies encourages inefficient management because, unlike the market system, there is a lack of incentive to be cost-conscious or creative. Instead, the hallmark of the bureaucrat is to be extremely cautious and make all decisions "by the book." Such behavior may maximize prestige and security, but it usually fails to minimize costs.

12-4e Shortsightedness Effect

Finally, it can be argued that democracy has a bias toward programs offering clear benefits and hidden costs. The reason is that political officeholders must run for reelection after a relatively short period of two to six years. Given this reality, politicians tend to favor proposals providing immediate benefits, with future generations paying most of the costs. Conversely, they reject programs that have easily identifiable short-run high costs, but offer benefits only after a decade. Hence, the essence of the hidden costs bias, or *shortsightedness effect*, is that both voters and politicians suffer from a short time horizon. Such a myopic view of either future costs or future benefits can cause an irrational acceptance of a program, even though long-run costs exceed short-run benefits, or an irrational rejection of a program with long-run benefits that outweigh short-run costs.

What Does Public Choice Say about a Budget Deficit?

In 2002, the situation switched from a few years in which the federal government spent less than it collected in taxes to spending more than tax revenues (discussed in the next chapter). James Buchanan predicted over 30 years ago that growing government deficits would be inevitable. He maintained that government officials would increase spending for their constituents in order to gain votes. Furthermore, politicians would shy away from tax increases for fear of alienating voters. The net effect would be deficits. Was Buchanan's prediction based on the rational ignorance effect, government inefficiency, or the shortsightedness effect?

CHECKPOINT

Key Concepts

Government expenditures

Benefits-received principle

Ability-to-pay principle

Progressive tax

Average tax rate

Marginal tax rate

Regressive tax

Proportional or flat tax

Public choice theory

Benefit-cost analysis

Rational ignorance

Summary

- **Government expenditures**, including transfer payments, have grown from about one-quarter of GDP in 1950 to about 37 percent of GDP today.

Federal Tax Revenues

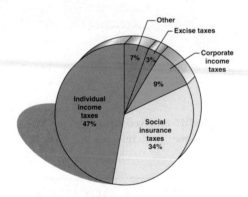

Government Expenditures

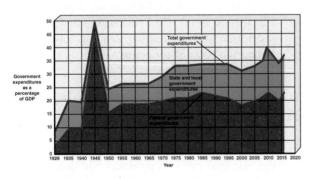

- *Federal tax revenues* are collected primarily from individual income taxes and social insurance taxes.

- The *taxation burden*, measured by taxes as a percentage of GDP, is lighter in the United States than in many other advanced industrial countries.

Taxation Burden

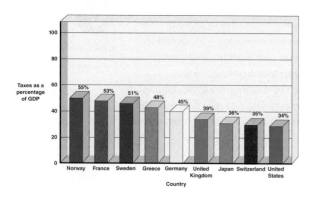

Taxes as a percentage of GDP

- *Total tax revenues* amounted to about 11 percent of GDP in 1929 and reached the highest level of close to 33 percent in 2000 before falling and rising again to 32 percent in 2016. Federal taxes take a larger share of GDP than state and local governments.

Total Tax Revenues

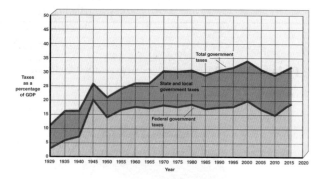

- The **benefits-received principle** and the **ability-to-pay principle** are two basic

philosophies of taxation fairness. The gasoline tax is a classic example of the benefits-received principle because users of the highways pay the gasoline tax.

- **Progressive income taxes** follow the ability-to-pay principle because there is a direct relationship between the average tax rate and income size. Sales, excise, property, and **flat-rate taxes** violate this principle because each results in a greater burden on the poor than on the rich. These types of taxes can be a **regressive tax**, which is a tax that charges a lower percentage of income as income rises.

- An **average tax rate** is calculated by dividing the tax paid by income. The **marginal tax rate** is the fraction of additional income paid as taxes. When the marginal tax rate rises as income rises, the tax is a *progressive tax*. When the marginal tax rate falls as income rises, the tax is a *regressive tax*. When the marginal tax rate remains constant as income rises, the tax is a *proportional* or *flat tax*.

- **Public choice theory** reveals the government's decision-making process. For example, government failure can occur for any of the following reasons: (1) The majority voting may not follow benefit-cost analysis. (2) Special-interest groups can obtain large benefits and spread their costs over many taxpayers. (3) Rational voter ignorance means a sizable portion of the voters will decide not to make informed judgments. (4) Bureaucratic behavior may not lead to cost-effective decisions. (5) Politicians suffer from a short time horizon, leading to a bias toward hiding the costs of programs.

Summary of Conclusion Statements

- The government's share of total economic activity has generally increased since World War II ended in 1945. Most of the growth in combined government expenditures as a percentage of GDP reflects rapidly growing federal government transfer programs.

- Rationally, a profit-maximizing firm follows the marginal rule and produces additional units so long as the marginal benefit exceeds the marginal cost.

Study Questions and Problems

Please see Appendix A for answers to the odd-numbered questions. Your instructor has access to the answers for even-numbered questions.

1. Explain why federal, state, and local expenditures account for about 40 percent of GDP, but total government spending (*G* in GDP) is only about 20 percent of GDP.

2. What are the four largest categories of expenditures of the federal government?

3. Describe the changes in the composition of the major federal government expenditures since 1970.

4. Which of the following taxes satisfy the benefits-received principle, and which satisfy the ability-to-pay principle?
   a. Gasoline tax
   b. Federal income tax
   c. Tax on Social Security benefits

5. What is the difference between the marginal tax rate and the average tax rate?

6. Explain why a 5 percent sales tax on gasoline is regressive.

7. Ms. Jones has a taxable income of $30,000, and she must pay $3,000 in taxes. Mr. Smith has a taxable income of $60,000. How much tax must Mr. Smith pay for the tax system to be
   a. progressive?
   b. regressive?
   c. proportional?

8. Explain why each of the following taxes is progressive or regressive.
   a. A $1 per pack federal excise tax on cigarettes.
   b. The federal individual income tax.
   c. The federal payroll tax.

9. Complete the following table, which describes the sales tax paid by individuals at various income levels. Indicate whether the tax is progressive, proportional, or regressive.

Income	Total spending	Sales tax paid	Sales tax paid as a percentage of income
$ 1,000	$ 1,000	$ 100	_____%
5,000	3,500	350	_____
10,000	6,000	600	_____
100,000	40,000	4,000	_____

10. Calculate the average and marginal tax rates in the following table, and indicate whether the tax is progressive, proportional, or regressive. What observation can you make concerning the relationship between marginal and average tax rates?

Income	Tax paid	Average tax rate	Marginal tax rate
$ 0	$ 0	0%	0%
100	10	_____	_____
200	30	_____	_____
300	60	_____	_____
400	100	_____	_____
500	150	_____	_____

11. Compare "dollar voting" in private markets with "majority voting" in the political decision-making system.

CHECKPOINT ANSWERS

What Does Public Choice Say about a Budget Deficit?

The government uses the deficit to finance clear short-term benefits with little attention to long-term consequences. If you said public choice predicts that government officials will emphasize near-term benefits to gain votes (the shortsightedness effect), **YOU ARE CORRECT**.

Sample Quiz

Please see Appendix B for answers to Sample Quiz questions.

1. Currently, total government expenditures in the United States is approximately
   a. 37 percent of GDP.
   b. 50 percent of GDP.
   c. 75 percent of GDP.
   d. 80 percent of GDP.

2. Which of the following categories accounted for the largest percentage of total federal government expenditures in recent years?
   a. Income security
   b. National defense
   c. Education and health
   d. Interest on the national debt

3. Which of the following taxes contributed the greatest percentage of total federal government tax revenues in recent years?
   a. Individual income taxes
   b. Corporate income taxes
   c. Social Security taxes
   d. Excise taxes

4. How do total taxes as a percentage of GDP in the United States compare to those of Western European countries, such as the United Kingdom, Germany, and Sweden?
   a. U.S. taxation is smaller.
   b. U.S. taxation is about the same.
   c. U.S. taxation is slightly larger.
   d. U.S. taxation is substantially larger.

5. The benefits-received principle of taxation is *most* evident in
   a. progressive tax rates.
   b. excise taxes on gasoline.
   c. the personal income tax.
   d. the corporate income tax.

6. A tax is regressive if it collects a
   a. larger amount as income rises.
   b. constant amount as income rises.
   c. smaller fraction of income as income falls.
   d. smaller fraction of income as income rises.

7. Which of the following is an example of a progressive tax?
   a. The excise tax on cigarettes
   b. The federal tax on gasoline
   c. The federal personal income tax
   d. All of the above answers are correct

8. A tax structured so that people with the same income pay the same percentage of their income in taxes is called a(an)
   a. flat tax.
   b. regressive tax.
   c. progressive tax.
   d. excise tax.

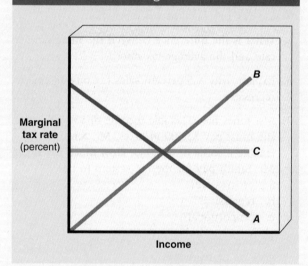

EXHIBIT 10 Marginal Tax Rate Lines

9. In Exhibit 10, line *A* represents a(an)
   a. regressive tax.
   b. progressive tax.
   c. proportional tax.
   d. ability-to-pay tax.

10. In Exhibit 10, line *B* represents a
    a. regressive tax.
    b. progressive tax.
    c. proportional tax.
    d. flat tax.

11. In Exhibit 10, line *C* represents a(an)
    a. regressive tax.
    b. progressive tax.
    c. proportional tax.
    d. ability-to-pay tax.

12. In Exhibit 10, if *A* represents state and local taxes and *B* represents federal income taxes, what is the result of imposing both types of taxes?
    a. A regressive tax
    b. A progressive tax
    c. A proportional tax
    d. An ability-to-pay tax

13. The study of the decision-making process of government is the study of
    a. Keynesian economics.
    b. public choice theory.
    c. rational expectations theory.
    d. social economics.

14. People who often create benefits for the minority and impose the cost on the majority are called
    a. fair-interest groups.
    b. encounter groups.
    c. laissez-faire groups.
    d. special-interest groups.

15. Voters may choose to remain uninformed about an issue because of
    a. the special-interest effect.
    b. rational ignorance.
    c. bureaucratic inefficiency.
    d. the shortsightedness effect.

16. Which of the following categories accounted for the lowest percentage of total federal government expenditures in recent years?

    a. Income security
    b. National defense
    c. Education and health
    d. Interest on the national debt

17. Since 1929, total government taxes as a percentage of GDP
    a. climbed from about 10 percent to about 30 percent.
    b. remained close to 30 percent.
    c. climbed from about 30 percent to about 50 percent.
    d. climbed from about 15 percent to about 50 percent.

18. "It would be an undue hardship to require people whose income is below $15,000 per year to pay income taxes." This statement reflects which of the following principles for a tax?
    a. Benefits-received
    b. Inexpensive-to-collect
    c. Ability-to-pay
    d. Fairness of contribution

19. If a person is taxed $100 on an income of $1,000, taxed $180 on an income of $2,000, and taxed $220 on an income of $3,000, this person is paying a
    a. progressive tax.
    b. poll tax.
    c. proportional tax.
    d. regressive tax.

20. According to the shortsightedness effect, politicians tend to favor projects with
    a. short-run benefits and short-run costs.
    b. short-run benefits and long-run costs.
    c. long-run benefits and short-run costs.
    d. long-run benefits and long-run costs.

CHAPTER 13

Federal Deficits, Surpluses, and the National Debt

CHAPTER PREVIEW

The U.S. government has been in the red almost continuously since the Revolutionary War forced the Continental Congress to borrow money. The only exception was a brief interlude more than a century and a half ago when our government was debt-free. In December 1834, President Andrew Jackson proudly reported to Congress what he considered to be a major accomplishment of his administration. By New Year's Day 1835, the federal government would succeed in paying off the national debt. It was Jackson's second term as president. Since the close of the War of 1812, the country had experienced tremendous growth, and revenues flowed into the U.S. Treasury from import tariffs and the sale of public land. By early 1836, the nation had been out of debt for two years, and there was a budget surplus of $37 million. The dilemma in those days was how to use the surplus. In 1836, Congress simply decided to divide all but $5 million of the surplus among the states. Then the financial panic of 1837 caused the government to plunge into debt again, where it remains today and for the foreseeable future.

Unlike Andrew Jackson, Abraham Lincoln in his 1864 Annual Message to Congress, expressed no concern for paying off the national debt. Lincoln stated:

> The great advantage of citizens being creditors as well as debtors, with relation to the public debt, is obvious. Men can readily perceive that they cannot be much oppressed by a debt which they owe to themselves.

As this text is written in 2017, federal government borrowing to cover its budget deficits had accumulated a national debt of about $20 trillion. To the average citizen, this is an incomprehensible amount of money for even the government to owe. Perhaps the best way to picture this sea of red ink is that your individual share is over $61,000 and rising.

IN THIS CHAPTER, YOU WILL LEARN TO SOLVE THESE ECONOMICS PUZZLES:

- Can Uncle Sam go bankrupt?

- How does the national debt of the United States compare to the debt of other countries?

- Are we passing the debt burden to our children?

- Who owns the national debt?

13-1 THE FEDERAL BUDGET BALANCING ACT

What will happen next? Like a high-wire performer swinging one way and then another while the crowd below gazes transfixed, the public in the late 1990s and early 2000s watched the federal budget sway back and forth between deficits and surpluses. As you learned in the preceding chapter on fiscal policy, a federal budget deficit occurs whenever the government spends more than it collects in taxes. The accumulation of these budget deficits over the years is the origin of the national debt. When the federal government has a surplus in its budget, some or all of the surplus can be used to retire the national debt, and it decreases. Here you will take a closer look at the actual budgetary process that creates and finances our national debt.

13-1a The Federal Budgetary Process

In theory, Keynesian discretionary fiscal policy requires that legislation be enacted to change government spending or taxes in order to shift the aggregate demand curve represented in the AD-AS model. In practice, the federal budgetary process, which determines the level of spending and taxation, is not so orderly. The annual "battle of the budget" on Capitol Hill involves political decisions on how much the government plans to spend and where the money will come from to finance these outlays. Wrangling takes place between all sorts of camps: the president versus Congress, Republicans versus Democrats, national security versus economic equality, price stability versus full employment, health care versus tax cuts, and so on. Given the complexities of world events, special-interest groups, volatile public opinion, and political ambitions that complicate the budget process, it is no wonder actual fiscal policy often ignores textbook macroeconomics.

The following brief look at the federal budgetary process shows how Congress and the president make federal spending and tax decisions each year:

Stage 1: Presidential Budget Submission

The president must submit the budget to Congress on or before the first Monday in February of each year. The official title is *The Budget of the United States*. This unveiling of the administration's budget is always big news. Does the president recommend that less money be spent for defense and more for education? Is there an increase in the Social Security payroll tax or the income tax? And how large is the national debt? Is there a budget deficit or a budget surplus?

Stage 2: Budget Resolution

After the president submits the budget in January, Congress takes the lead in the budgetary process. The president's budget now becomes the starting point for congressional consideration. The Congressional Budget Office (CBO) employs a professional staff who advise Congress on the budget much the way the Office of Management and Budget (OMB) advises the president. The CBO analyzes the budget by February and reports its evaluation at budget committee hearings in both the House of Representatives and the Senate. After debate in May, Congress approves an overall budget outline called the *budget resolution*, which sets target levels for spending, tax revenues, and the budget deficit or surplus.

Stage 3: Budget Passed

Throughout the summer and supposedly ending by October 1, Congress and the president debate while congressional committees and subcommittees prepare specific spending and

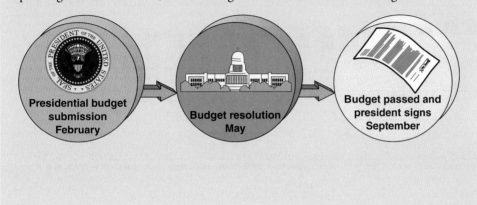

EXHIBIT 1 Major Steps in the Federal Budgetary Process

The first step is the president's transmittal of the administration's budget to Congress. In the second step, Congress passes a budget resolution that sets targets for spending, taxes, and the deficit or surplus. In the third step, Congress passes the budget consisting of specific spending and tax bills. When the president signs the spending and revenue bills, the federal government has its actual budget.

Presidential budget submission February

Budget resolution May

Budget passed and president signs September

tax law bills. The budget resolution is supposed to guide the spending and revenue decisions of these committees. After Congress passes and the president signs the spending and revenue bills, the federal government has its actual budget for spending and tax collection.

As summarized in Exhibit 1, the budgetary process seems orderly enough, but in practice it does not work so smoothly. The process can, and often does, go astray. One problem is that Congress does not necessarily follow its own rules. The budget bills are not always passed on time, and when that happens, the fiscal year starts without a budget. Then federal agencies must operate on the basis of *continuing resolutions*, which means each agency operates as it did the previous year until spending bills are approved. In some years, Congress even fails to pass a continuing resolution, and the federal government must shut down and government workers stay home until Congress approves the necessary funds.

13-1b Financing the National Debt

Over the years, the federal government budget experiences imbalances. A budget deficit occurs when federal expenditures, including spending for final goods plus transfer payments, exceed tax revenues collected. A surplus occurs when the government collects more in taxes than it spends. For example, for four years between 1998 and 2001, budget surpluses existed, as discussed in the next You're the Economist feature. As shown in Exhibit 2, deficits returned after the 2001 recession, and following the Great Recession of 2007–2009, deficits reached record highs. In 2009, a record-breaking federal deficit was $1.4 trillion. By 2016 the deficit was only about one-third as high as it was in 2009.

What happens when the government overspends, and the U.S. Treasury must borrow to finance the difference between expenditures and revenues? The answer to that

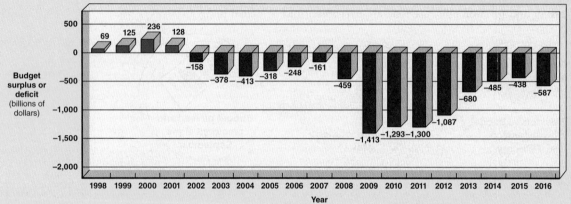

EXHIBIT 2 U.S. Federal Budget Surpluses and Deficits, 1998–2016

During 1998 through 2001, the annual federal government budget was in surplus each year. After the recession of 2001, these surpluses disappeared and deficits appeared, exploding to $1.4 trillion in 2009, and shrinking back to $587 billion by 2016.

SOURCE: *Economic Report of the President, 2017*, https://www.gpo.gov/fdsys/pkg/ERP-2017/pdf/ERP-2017-table19.pdf, Table B-19.

National debt
The total amount owed by the federal government to owners of government securities.

Net public debt
National debt minus all government interagency borrowing.

question is the U.S. Treasury borrows by selling Treasury bills (T-bills), notes, and bonds promising to make specified interest payments and to repay the borrowed funds on a given date. These government securities are IOUs of the federal government. They are considered a safe haven for idle funds and are purchased by Federal Reserve banks, government agencies, private banks, corporations, individual U.S. citizens, and foreigners. If you own a U.S. government savings bond, for example, you have loaned your funds to the federal government. The stock of these federal government IOUs accumulated over the years is called the *gross public debt*, *federal debt*, or *national debt*. The **national debt** is the total amount owed by the federal government to owners of government securities. There are national debt clocks on the Internet and in several cities around the United States that display the amount of money owed by the federal government.

Note that the national debt does not include state and local governments' debt. Also, as mentioned above, the national debt does include U.S. Treasury securities purchased by various federal agencies, such as the Social Security trust fund. When the Social Security trust fund collects more in taxes than it pays out in retirement benefits, it lends the extra money to the federal government for spending. This means federal budget deficits would be significantly higher, or budget surpluses would be significantly lower, without federal government borrowing from this trust fund. If we subtract the portion of the national debt held by all government agencies (what the federal government owes to itself), we can compute the **net public debt**. Beware! Confusion sometimes occurs when the media use the term *public debt* without specifying whether the reference is to "gross" or "net" public debt.

Before proceeding, let's pause and explain the Social Security trust fund in a little more detail. A misconception is that the Social Security Administration (SSA) collects the annual Social Security surpluses and stacks the cash with reserve cash from previous surpluses in a vault, or special checking account. When the trust fund is in deficit as the

YOU'RE THE ECONOMIST

Applicable Concept: Federal Budget Surplus

The Great Federal Budget Surplus Debate

As unprecedented deficit figures flowed during the Great Recession, it is hard to believe that for four years the federal budget was in surplus. After a one-year small budget surplus in 1969, it took 29 contentious years to eliminate federal budget deficits. And then surpluses occurred between 1998 and 2001, as shown in Exhibits 2 and 3, before becoming today what seems to be a historic relic. These federal budget surpluses aroused as much controversy in their time as deficits do in their years. In short, the hotly contested debate involved whether the surplus should be saved, spent, or devoted to tax cuts. The case for tax cuts and smaller government is based on the view that a surplus is the result of excess tax collections. Proponents of tax cuts pointed out that in 2000, federal tax revenues as a percentage of GDP were the highest since during World War II. Moreover, tax rate cuts would spur the economy and result in higher future tax revenues. The argument for spending a surplus is based on "unmet needs." Instead of tax cuts, the surplus could be used to finance spending for defense, public infrastructure, research and development, and social programs such as education or health care. Also, a large proportion of American households pay no income taxes. Tax cuts therefore do not benefit people who are not prosperous enough to pay taxes.

An alternative to tax cuts and spending increases is paying down the national debt. Former Federal Reserve chairman Alan Greenspan supported this approach. He said Congress faced the quandary of trying to establish fiscal policy based on long-range forecasts that may prove inaccurate. He stated that if Congress cuts taxes, it also has to be prepared to cut spending significantly in the event that the forecasts on which the cuts were based are proved wrong. On the other hand, using the budget surplus to fund "irrevocable spending programs" would be "the worst of all outcomes." Testifying before the Senate Budget Committee in 2001, Greenspan suggested that the proposed tax cut bill include provisions that would limit the tax cuts if specified future targets for the budget surpluses or debt reduction were not met. These provisions were not included in the 2001 tax bill.

The outcome of the "Great Federal Budget Surplus Debate" was that President George W. Bush signed a $1.35 trillion tax cut bill in 2001 spread over ten years. It was the largest and most widespread tax cut since the 1980s, during Ronald Reagan's presidency. And in spite of the tax cuts, the outlook for surpluses in the future was optimistic. In August 2001, the Office of Management and Budget (OMB)

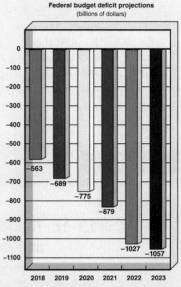

Federal budget deficit projections
(billions of dollars)

−563
−689
−775
−879
−1027
−1057

2018   2019   2020   2021   2022   2023

SOURCE: Congressional Budget Office, *10-Tear Budget Projections, June, 2017. CBO's Baseline Budget Projections, by Category,* https://www.cbo.gov/about/products/budget-economic-data#3; http://www.whitehouse.gov/OMB/budget/overview, Summary Table 5.1.

projected continuously growing budget surpluses that would peak at about $400 billion in 2007. The actual federal budget in 2007 was a $161 billion deficit. The graph in this section shows the OMB's deficit projections for several years. As actual deficit figures become available, check the accuracy of OMB estimates reported here.

ANALYZE THE ISSUE

1. Refer to Exhibit 1 in the chapter on fiscal policy. Using demand-side and supply-side fiscal policy theories, explain how a tax cut could either increase or decrease the price level.

2. Using the Laffer curve discussed in the You're the Economist box in the chapter on fiscal policy, explain how proponents could claim that the tax cut would increase tax revenues.

baby boomers retire and the ratio of workers paying into the system to people drawing benefits shrinks, the SSA will open the vault and/or write a check to draw on trust fund reserves to pay its obligations.

Here is what really happens to Social Security tax dollars. When excess Social Security taxes are collected by the SSA, these surplus funds must, by law, be immediately withdrawn and given to the Treasury, which, in turn, issues "nonmarketable" interest-bearing Treasury bonds to the SSA. The Treasury then spends this money on welfare, roads, tax cuts, defense, or whatever the federal government decides. On the other hand, if the trust fund cannot pay for retirees' needs, then the SSA will ask the Treasury to redeem its bonds for cash to pay benefits. In this situation, where will the Treasury get the money to repay the SSA? It will either print it, borrow it, levy additional taxes, or cut spending elsewhere. In short, the full faith and credit of the U.S. federal government promises to pay itself enough money when needed to pay for Social Security.

CONCLUSION	The national debt includes the Social Security trust fund, and as a result, federal budget deficits are reduced or budget surpluses are raised.

13-1c The Rise and Fall of Federal Budget Surpluses and Deficits

Here we will examine in more detail recent federal budget surpluses and deficits. Spending caps combined with tax increases and a growing high-employment economy driven by technological advances, such as the Internet, transformed federal budget deficits into surpluses during the late 1990s. Exhibit 3(a) shows federal expenditures and tax revenues expressed as a percentage of GDP. The difference between these two curves represents the federal deficit or surplus, also expressed as a percentage of GDP. Between 1991 and 2000, federal government expenditures as a percentage of GDP declined from 22 percent to 18 percent of GDP, and federal government tax revenues as a percentage of GDP crept steadily upward from 18 percent to 21 percent of GDP. The result of these changes in tax and spending percentages of GDP was four years of federal surpluses from 1998 to 2001. Since 2002, the federal budget has returned to red ink deficits.

After the Great Recession of 2007–2009, the deficit surged to historic highs when in 2009 federal expenditures climbed sharply to 25 percent of GDP, while tax revenues plummeted to a record low of only 15 percent of GDP. Recall from the automatic stabilizers explained in the previous chapter that during a recession government expenditures rise for transfer payments when people lose jobs and tax revenues decline from individuals and companies making less money. Moreover, these unprecedented deficit figures flowed from the Wall Street bailout and an economic stimulus bill, which sharply increased federal government spending relative to tax collections.

Exhibit 3(b) provides an alternate graph of the federal budget deficit or surplus as a percentage of GDP. During President Reagan's first term in the early 1980s and following the 1990–1991 recession, the deficit as a percentage of GDP reached close to 6 percent and 5 percent, respectively. However, during the Great Recession in 2009, the federal deficit soared to a record high since World War II of 10 percent of GDP. It is interesting to note that during the Great Depression, federal deficits were unimpressive by Great Recession standards. As a share of GDP, Roosevelt's New Deal deficits

EXHIBIT 3   Federal Expenditures, Revenues, and Deficits as a Percentage of GDP, 1985–2016

Part (a) shows that after the 1990–1991 recession, federal government expenditures as a percentage of GDP declined until 2000, while federal government tax revenues rose steadily. The results were federal surpluses between 1998 and 2001. After the Great Recession beginning in 2007, the deficit reached a record high when expenditures rose to 25 percent of GDP in 2009, and tax revenues plummeted to only 15 percent of GDP. In 2016, expenditures were 20.7 percent of GDP and taxes were 17.5 percent.

Part (b) focuses on the federal deficit or surplus as a percentage of GDP. In 1992, the federal deficit as a percentage of GDP was about 5 percent. After reaching a budget surplus peak of 2.4 percent in 2000, the federal budget deficit soared to a historic high of 10 percent of GDP in 2009 and fell back to 3.2 percent of GDP in 2016.

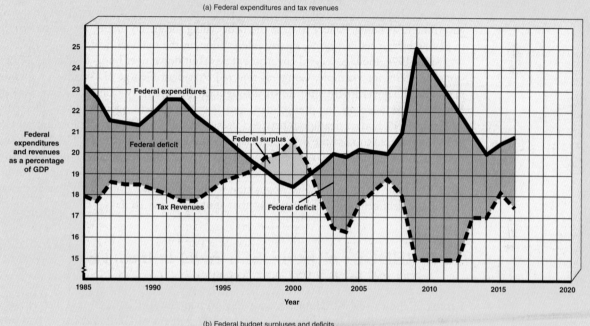

(a) Federal expenditures and tax revenues

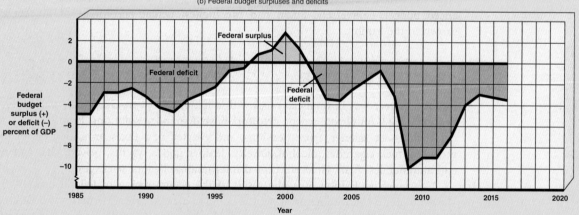

(b) Federal budget surpluses and deficits

SOURCE: *Economic Report of the President, 2017,* https://www.gpo.gov/fdsys/pkg/ERP-2017/pdf/ERP-2017-table19.pdf, Table B-19; Federal Reserve Bank of St. Louis, https://fred.stlouisfed.org/series/FYFSGDA188S.

(stimulus package) peaked at 5.4 percent of GDP in 1934. On the other hand, during World War II, deficits reached their all-time high of almost 27 percent of GDP in 1943. In 2016, the deficit was 3.2 percent of GDP.

13-1d Debt Ceiling

Debt ceiling
A legislated legal limit on the national debt.

The debt ceiling is a method for curbing the national debt. A **debt ceiling** is a legislated legal limit on the national debt. This means that the federal government cannot legally allow a budget deficit to raise the national debt beyond the ceiling. It works like the credit limit on your charge card. When you reach the limit, you cannot charge any more and you must pay cash. When the federal government hits the debt limit, it cannot borrow any more to supplement its cash from taxes and other sources. What usually happens when the budget pushes against the debt ceiling is that the federal government raises its own ceiling to accommodate the budget deficit. Raising the debt ceiling often provokes a fiery political debate over government spending. Failure to raise the debt ceiling means no money for the government to pay its bills, meet its payroll, or pay interest due on the national debt.

Since 1976, the U.S. federal government has shut down over budget issues on 18 occasions. In 1990, for example, Congress rejected President George H. W. Bush's spending plan, and the government shut down throughout the three-day Columbus Day weekend. Most workers were off for the holiday, and few government agencies were affected. In 1995 and 1996, budget deadlocks between President Bill Clinton and the Republican Congress that refused to raise the debt limit lasted 5 and 21 days respectively. The 21-day shutdown is the longest to date. A dispute occurred between the Republican-controlled House of Representatives and the Democrat-controlled Senate supported by President Obama in 2013. The issue was Republicans' opposition to the Affordable Care Act (Obamacare) and raising the debt ceiling. The duration of that shutdown was 16 days.

13-2 BUDGET SURPLUSES AND DEFICITS IN OTHER COUNTRIES

Exhibit 4 shows several countries with government budget deficits as a percentage of GDP in 2016. Iceland had a budget surplus of 17 percent of GDP and Latvia had a balanced budget. Conversely, Spain had the highest deficit percentage of the countries shown in the exhibit.

13-3 WHY WORRY OVER THE NATIONAL DEBT?

In 2011, Greece was in financial crisis with a national debt-to-GDP ratio of 170 percent. Fearing default on Greece's debt, creditors have demanded solutions. In response, Greece cut civil service salaries, froze pensions, and enacted new taxes on a long list of items, including fuel, cigarettes, alcohol, jewelry, leather goods, yachts, private jets, and high-end automobiles. Also, Greece accepted international bailout packages.

As shown in Exhibit 5(a), the result of the accumulation of federal deficits in the United States is that the national debt is rising at a rapid rate. The national debt crossed $1 trillion in 1982. And it took 14 years before another $4 trillion was added, reaching the $5 trillion mark in 1996. Fourteen years later in 2010, the national debt accelerated by $8 trillion to over $14 trillion. In 2016, the national debt rose to almost $20 trillion.

EXHIBIT 4 A Global Comparison of Government Surpluses and Deficits as a Percentage of GDP, 2016

In 2016, Iceland had a budget surplus of 17 percent of GDP and Latvia had a balanced budget. Conversely, Spain had the highest deficit percentage of the countries shown in the exhibit.

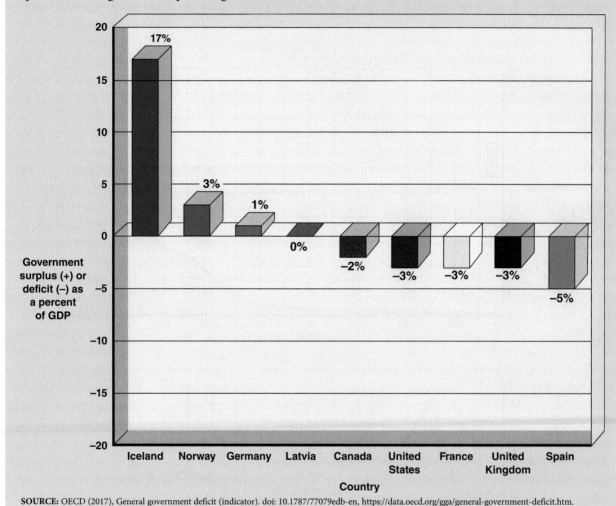

SOURCE: OECD (2017), General government deficit (indicator). doi: 10.1787/77079edb-en, https://data.oecd.org/gga/general-government-deficit.htm.

What are some major causes of the rising national debt? Observe in Exhibit 5(a) the increase in the debt during World War II. In wartime, the government must increase military expenditures sharply and escalate the national debt. Recessions also cause the national debt to rise dramatically. Cyclical downturns such as the 1930s, 1974–1975, 1981–1982, 1990–1991, 2001, and the 2007–2009 "Great Recession," caused the debt to rise rapidly because a decline in real GDP automatically increases the budget deficit due to lower tax collections and greater spending for unemployment compensation and welfare. For example, during the Great Recession, the federal government financed the

EXHIBIT 5 The National Debt, 1930–2016

In part (a), we see that the federal debt has skyrocketed since 1980. A concern is that sooner or later the U.S. government will be bankrupt. The counterargument is shown in part (b). The national debt as a percentage of GDP declined since the end of World War II, when it reached a peak of about 120 percent. After 1980, the federal debt as a percentage of GDP increased and has risen sharply to a high of about 105 percent in 2016.

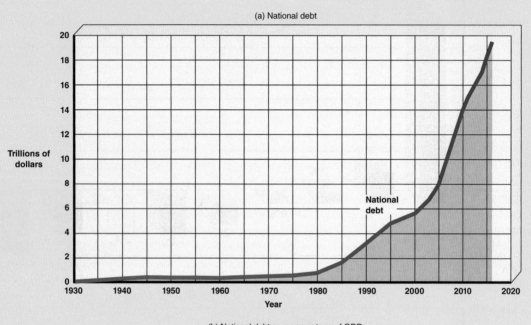

(a) National debt

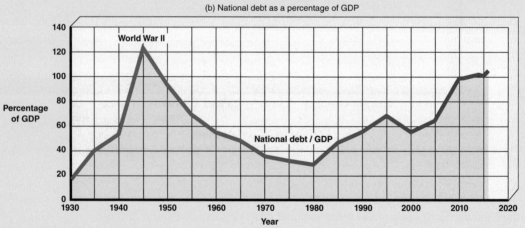

(b) National debt as a percentage of GDP

SOURCE: *Economic Report of the President, 2017,* https://www.gpo.gov/fdsys/pkg/ERP-2017/pdf/ERP-2017-table17.pdf, Table B-17; Federal Reserve Bank of St. Louis, https://fred.stlouisfed.org/series/GFDEGDQ188S#0.

bailouts and stimulus spending to boost troubled credit markets by borrowing. That borrowing caused the federal deficit, debt ceiling, and national debt to increase considerably.

Politicians and nonpoliticians alike often speak of the gloom and doom of the national debt. Should we lose sleep over it? To find out, we'll consider three controversial questions:

13-3a Can Uncle Sam Go Bankrupt?

Reasons to Worry

If households and firms persistently operate in the red, as the federal government does, they will go bankrupt sooner or later. How long can a national debt continue to rise before the U.S. government is broke? Those who view government debt as being similar to privately held debt are concerned that government debt may be fast approaching a level that could result in government being unable to repay its debt.

Reasons Not to Worry

Whether private or public debt is the issue, debt must be judged relative to the debtor's ability to repay the principal and interest on the debt. Exhibit 5(b) shows that the national debt as a percentage of GDP is lower today than at the end of World War II. In 1946, public debt was about 120 percent of GDP, and by 1980, the ratio of debt to GDP had fallen to 33 percent. This means the debt grew considerably slower than GDP between 1945 and 1980. Since 1980, however, the trend reversed, and the debt has grown faster than GDP. Between 1980 and 2016, the national debt grew from 33 percent to 105 percent of GDP. Still, the United States was not bankrupt in 1946 when the ratio was higher than in 2016. In the future, it can be argued that the debt will again grow slower than the GDP and the ratio will fall again.

There is an even more important point: Uncle Sam never has to pay off the national debt. At the maturity date on a government security, the U.S. Treasury has the constitutional authority to collect taxes levied by Congress, print money, or refinance its obligations. Suppose the government decides not to raise taxes or cause inflation by simply printing money, so it refinances the debt. When a $1 million government bond comes due, as described earlier in this chapter, the U.S. Treasury can simply "roll over" the debt. This financial trade expression means a borrower (here the federal government) pays off its $1 million bond that reaches maturity by issuing a new $1 million bond. In short, the federal government refinances its debt by replacing old bonds with new bonds. This means the federal government never has to pay off the national debt. These debts can be rolled over forever, provided bond buyers have faith in Uncle Sam.

Global Perspective on National Debt

Exhibit 6 provides a global perspective on the national debt. This figure shows the ratio of national debt to GDP for several industrialized nations. Greece and Portugal have a higher debt in relation to GDP than the United States. The United States, on the other hand, has a national debt-to-GDP ratio almost 2.5 times as large as Norway's ratio.

GLOBAL **ECONOMICS**

EXHIBIT 6 A Global Comparison of National Debt Ratios, 2016

This exhibit shows estimated ratios of national debt to GDP in 2016 for selected industrialized countries. Compared to the United States, Greece and Portugal have higher national debt-to-GDP ratios. On the other hand, the United States has a debt ratio almost 2.5 times as large as Norway's.

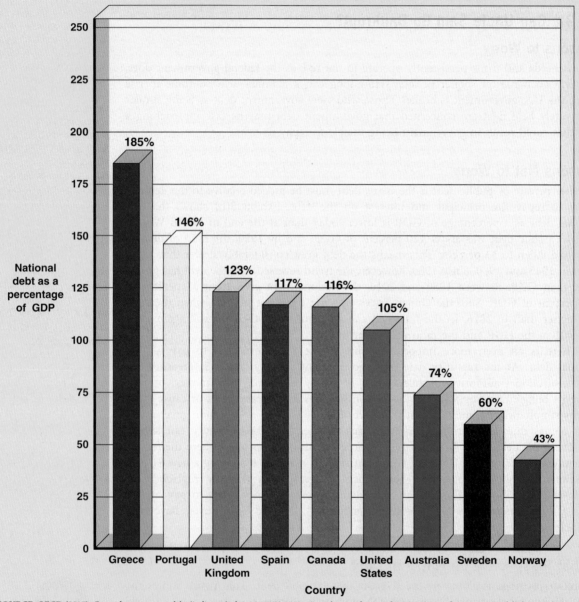

SOURCE: OECD (2017), General government debt (indicator). doi: 10.1787/a0528cc2-en. https://data.oecd.org/gga/general-government-debt.htm#indicator -chart; *Economic Report of the President, 2017,* https://www.gpo.gov/fdsys/pkg/ERP-2017/pdf/ERP-2017-table19.pdf, Table B-19.

What's behind the National Debt?

Suppose the federal government has a balanced budget this year, but the entire national debt has come due. How could the federal government pay off the national debt without refinancing, raising taxes, or printing money?

CHECKPOINT

13-3b Are We Passing the Debt Burden to Our Children?

Reasons to Worry

The fear is that interest payments to finance the national debt will swallow an enormous helping of the federal government's budget pie. This means future generations will pay more of their tax dollars to the government's creditors and have less to spend for highways, health care, defense, and other public-sector programs. Exhibit 7 shows net interest payments as a percentage of GDP. The net interest payment was only 1.7 percent of GDP right after World War II in 1950, but it increased dramatically after the mid-1970s to more than 3 percent in 1995. Since 1995, the interest payment burden declined to 1.3 percent of GDP in 2016.

EXHIBIT 7 Federal Net Interest as a Percentage of GDP, 1940–2016

Some fear that interest payments on the national debt will swallow an enormous portion of the federal budget. The exhibit shows that the net interest payment as a proportion of GDP was only about 1.7 percent right after World War II in 1950. In the 1980s and early 1990s, however, the interest-rate burden increased dramatically to more than 3 percent in 1995, but then it declined to 1.3 percent in 2016.

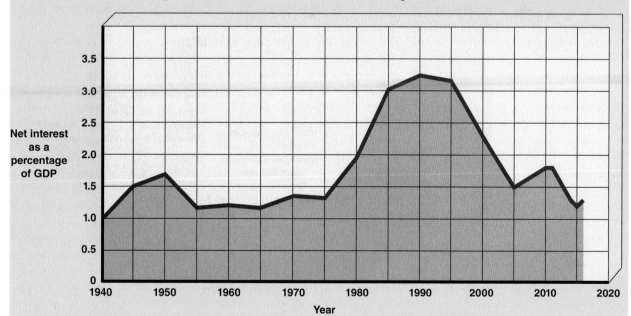

SOURCE: *Economic Report of the President, 2017,* https://www.gpo.gov/fdsys/pkg/ERP-2017/pdf/ERP-2017-table19.pdf, Table B-19.

Reasons Not to Worry

The burden of the national debt on present and future generations depends on who owns the accumulated national debt. Stated more precisely, the burden of the debt depends on whether it is held internally or externally. The bulk of the public debt is internal national debt. **Internal national debt** is the portion of the national debt owed to a nation's own citizens. Internal debt financing is viewed as "we owe it to ourselves." One U.S. citizen buys a government security and lends Uncle Sam the money to pay the interest and principal on a maturing government security held by another U.S. citizen. Although this redistribution of income and wealth does indeed favor bondholders, who are typically upper-income individuals, transferring dollars between U.S. citizens does not alter the overall purchasing power in the U.S. economy.

Those on the "not to worry" side of this issue also concede that an external national debt is a concern. **External national debt** is the portion of the national debt owed to foreign citizens. Financing the external national debt means interest and principal payments are transfers of money from U.S. citizens to other nations. If foreign governments, banks, corporations, and individual investors hold part of the national debt, the "we owe it to ourselves" argument is weakened. Exhibit 8 shows who owns the securities the U.S. Treasury has issued. In 2016, foreigners owned 32 percent of the total national debt. The largest foreign holders of the debt were China and Japan with 11 percent each of the total national

Internal national debt
The portion of the national debt owed to a nation's own citizens.

External national debt
The portion of the national debt owed to foreign citizens.

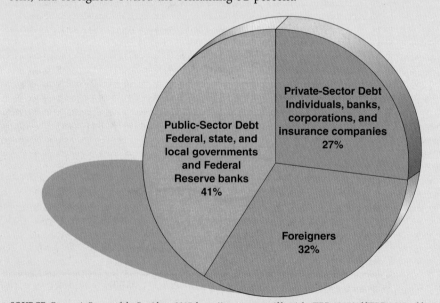

EXHIBIT 8 Ownership of the National Debt, 2016

In 2016, 41 percent of the national debt was held by the public sector, including federal, state, and local governments and Federal Reserve banks. The private sector, including individuals, banks, corporations, and insurance companies, held 27 percent, and foreigners owned the remaining 32 percent.

Private-Sector Debt
Individuals, banks,
corporations, and
insurance companies
27%

Public-Sector Debt
Federal, state, and
local governments
and Federal
Reserve banks
41%

Foreigners
32%

SOURCE: *Economic Report of the President, 2017,* https://www.gpo.gov/fdsys/pkg/ERP-2017/pdf/ERP-2017-table19.pdf, Table B-24.

debt. Forty-one percent was held by the federal, state, and local governments, primarily by federal agencies such as the U.S. Treasury, the Social Security Administration, and Federal Reserve banks. The Federal Reserve is an independent government agency, as explained in the next chapter. The private sector, consisting of individuals, banks, corporations, and insurance companies, held 27 percent of the national debt. The debt held by the private sector and government entities constitutes the internal national debt.

Although 68 percent of the national debt was internal, the 32 percent of total U.S. debt that is external debt is not necessarily undesirable. Foreign investment in the United States supplements domestic saving. Borrowing from abroad can prevent the higher interest rates that would exist if the U.S. Treasury relied only on domestic savers to purchase federal government securities. A lower interest rate increases U.S. investment and consumer spending, causing the aggregate demand curve to shift rightward.

If we do not need to worry about shifting the burden to future generations, can the current generation escape the debt burden? The answer is *No*. During World War II, for example, the United States operated at full employment along its *production possibilities curve*. As illustrated earlier in Exhibit 2 of Chapter 2, the people at that time in history were forced to trade off consumer goods production for military goods production. Because massive amounts of resources were diverted to fight World War II, people at that time were forced to give up private consumption of houses, cars, refrigerators, and so on. After the war was over, resources were again devoted to producing more consumer goods and fewer military goods. The same analysis can be used today. At full employment, the burden of the national debt on the current generation is the opportunity cost of private-sector goods and services forgone because land, labor, and capital are used to produce public-sector goods and services.

In other words, the burden of the national debt is incurred when production takes place; it is not postponed until the debt is paid by future generations. When the debt comes due in the future, the government can simply refinance the debt and redistribute money from one group of citizens to another. This redistribution of income does not cause a reallocation of resources away from consumer goods and services in favor of government programs.

13-3c Does Government Borrowing Crowd Out Private-Sector Spending?

Reasons to Worry

Critics of Keynesian fiscal policy believe that government spending or tax cuts financed by borrowing designed to boost aggregate demand has little, if any, effect on growth of real GDP. The reason is that the *crowding-out effect* dampens the stimulus to aggregate demand from increased federal government spending or cuts in taxes. The **crowding-out effect** is a reduction in private-sector spending as a result of higher interest rates caused by U.S. Treasury borrowing (selling securities) to finance government deficits. For example, suppose the federal government spends and borrows, rather than collecting taxes, to finance new health care programs. In this case, the size of the national debt rises, and interest rates are pushed up in loan markets. Interest rates rise because the federal government competes with private borrowers for available savings, and less credit is available to consumers and business borrowers. The result of this crowding-out effect is lower consumption $(-\Delta C)$ and business investment $(-\Delta I)$, which offset the boost in aggregate demand $(+\Delta AD)$ from increased government spending $(+\Delta G)$ operating through the spending multiplier. It is important to note that the same crowding-out effect could occur if government reduced taxes and did not pay

Crowding-out effect
A reduction in private-sector spending as a result of federal budget deficits financed by U.S. Treasury borrowing. When federal government borrowing increases interest rates, the result is lower consumption spending by households and lower investment spending by businesses.

for the tax cuts by reducing its spending. Again, the resulting deficit would have to be financed by government borrowing.

The crowding-out effect contradicts the theory, explained in the previous Reasons Not to Worry section, that future generations do not bear some of today's debt burden. Recall from Chapter 2 that current investment spending is an ingredient for economic growth that increases living standards in the future by shifting the production possibilities curve outward (Exhibit 5 in Chapter 2). If federal borrowing crowds out private investment in plants and equipment, future generations will have a smaller possible productive capacity.

The AD-AS model will help you understand the crowding-out concept. Exhibit 9 reproduces the situation in which government spending or tax cuts are used to combat a recession, depicted earlier in Exhibit 2 of the chapter on fiscal policy. Begin at E_1, with

---

EXHIBIT 9 Zero, Partial, and Complete Crowding Out

Beginning at equilibrium E_1, the federal government borrows to finance a deficit created by expansionary fiscal policy. Keynesian theory predicts zero crowding out, which means that an increase in government spending operates through the spending multiplier to shift aggregate demand from AD_1 to AD_2. If crowding out is zero, consumption and investment spending are unaffected by the increase in government spending financed by borrowing. Partial crowding out occurs when a decrease in private spending partially offsets the multiplier effect from an increase in deficit-financed government spending. Partial crowding out results in a shift only from AD_1 to AD'_2 and an equilibrium at E'_2, rather than E_2. If crowding out is complete, a decrease in private spending completely offsets the increase in government deficit spending financed by debt. In this case, the aggregate demand curve remains at AD_1, and the economy remains at E_1.

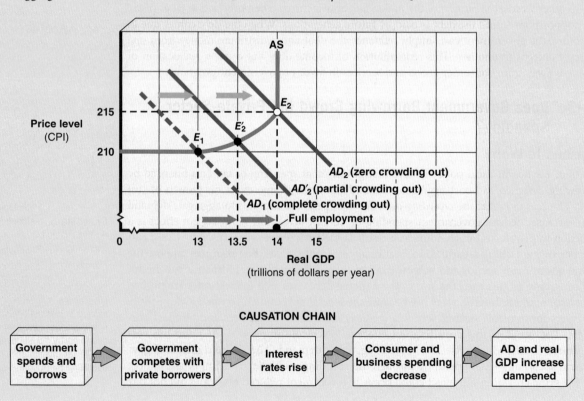

YOU'RE THE ECONOMIST

Applicable Concepts: National Debt and Federal Deficit

How Real Is Uncle Sam's Debt?

Perhaps the national debt and federal budget deficits are really not so large and threatening. For example, it can be argued that we should use real rather than nominal values to report the national debt—similar to using real GDP to report economic growth. For example, if you have a debt of $100 at the beginning of the year, and the inflation rate is 3 percent a year, then the value of the debt at the end of the year is effectively $97 in today's dollars. Notice that each year inflation wipes out a portion of the real value of the debt. In fact, the national debt could increase by 3 percent every year, and if inflation is 3 percent annually, then the real growth in the national debt would be zero.

Critics also warn that federal accounting rules are an economic policy disaster. Private businesses, as well as state and local governments, use two budgets. One is the *operating budget*, which includes salaries, interest payments, and other current expenses. The second type of budget, called a *capital budget*, includes spending for investment items, such as machines, buildings, and roads. Expenditures on the capital budget yield benefits over time and may be paid for by long-term borrowing. The federal government does not use a capital budget. Capital budgeting allows spreading the cost of long-lasting assets over future years. For example, the federal budget makes no distinction between the rental cost of a federal office building and the cost of constructing a new federal office building to replace rented office space. However, payments on borrowing for a new building provide the benefit of a long-lasting asset that offsets rent payments. If a capital budgeting system were used, the public would see that most federal borrowing really finances assets yielding long-term benefits. In short, proponents of a capital budget believe the operating budget should be the public's main focus. The operating budget may give a truer picture of the federal deficit because this budget could reflect asset expenditures that may not be beneficial to society as a whole. Opponents of changing the accounting rules argue that controversial expenditures would be placed in the capital budget in order to manipulate the size of the deficit or surplus for political reasons.

Finally, some economists argue for other numerical adjustments that show the federal deficit or surplus is really not as it seems. They say it is not the federal deficit or surplus that really matters, but the combined deficits or surpluses of federal, state, and local governments. When state and local governments run budget surpluses, these surpluses are a source of savings in financial markets that add to federal surpluses or offset federal borrowing to finance its deficit.

Tetra Images/Alamy Stock Photo

ANALYZE THE ISSUE

1. Do households make a distinction between spending for current expenses and spending for capital expenses? Compare borrowing $5,000 to take a vacation in Hawaii to borrowing $125,000 to buy a condominium and move out of your rented apartment.

2. Critics of "new accounting" for federal borrowing argue that it does not matter what the government spends the money for. What matters is the total amount that the government spends minus taxes collected. Explain this viewpoint.

an equilibrium GDP of $13 trillion, and assume the government increases its spending and uses the spending multiplier to shift the aggregate demand curve rightward from AD_1 to AD_2. Following Keynesian theory, there is zero crowding out, and the economy achieves full employment at equilibrium point E_2, corresponding to real GDP of $14 trillion. Critics of Keynesian theory, however, argue that crowding out occurs. The result of expansionary fiscal policy is not E_2, but some equilibrium point along the AS line between E_1 and E_2. For example, a fall in private expenditures might partially offset the government spending or tax cut stimulus. With incomplete crowding out, the aggregate demand curve increases only to AD'_2 because of the decline in consumption and investment spending. The economy, therefore, moves to E'_2 at a real GDP of $13.5 trillion and does not achieve full employment at E_2. Or crowding out can completely offset the multiplier effect of increased government spending. The fall in private expenditures by consumers and businesses can result in no change in aggregate demand curve AD_1. In this case, the economy remains at E_1, with unemployment unaffected by expansionary fiscal policy. Meanwhile, the deficit required to finance extra government spending or reduced taxes increases the national debt.

Reasons Not to Worry

Crowding-in effect
An increase in private-sector spending as a result of federal budget deficits financed by U.S. Treasury borrowing. At less than full employment, consumers hold more Treasury securities and this additional wealth causes them to spend more. Business investment spending increases because of optimistic profit expectations.

The crowding-out effect is controversial. Keynesian economists counter critics by saying that any crowding-out effect is small or nonexistent. Instead, at below full-employment real GDP, their counterargument is the **crowding-in effect**. For example, government capital spending for highways, dams, universities, and infrastructure financed by borrowing might offset any decline in private investment. Another Keynesian argument is that consumers and businesspersons may believe that federal spending is "just what the doctor ordered" for an ailing economy. Federal borrowing incurred to finance the new spending would boost consumption and therefore increase aggregate demand. The reason is because holders of Treasury bills, notes, and bonds feel richer. As a result of their greater wealth, consumers spend more now and plan to spend more in the future. Such a blush of optimism may also raise the profit expectations of business managers, and they may increase investment spending. The effect of increased private-sector spending could nullify some or all of the crowding-out effect, which would otherwise offset the boost in aggregate demand from increased government spending or tax cuts. Hence, as explained in the graphical analysis in Exhibit 9, the spending multiplier shifts the aggregate demand curve from AD_1 to AD_2, with zero crowding out.

Finally, both sides of the debate agree that complete crowding out occurs in one situation. Suppose the economy is operating at full employment (point E_2). This is comparable to being on the economy's production possibilities curve. If the government shifts the aggregate demand curve rightward by increasing spending or cutting taxes, the result will be higher prices and a replacement of private-sector output with public-sector output.

CONCLUSION Crowding out is complete if the economy is at full employment, but it is debatable at less than full employment.

Key Concepts

National debt	Debt ceiling	External national debt	Crowding-in effect
Net public debt	Internal national debt	Crowding-out effect	

Summary

- The **national debt** is the dollar amount that the federal government owes holders of government securities. It is the cumulative sum of past deficits. The U.S. Treasury issues government securities to finance the deficits. The debt has increased sharply since 1980.

National Debt

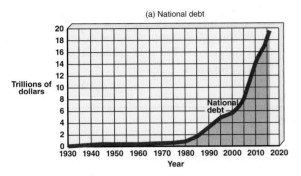

(a) National debt

<table>
<tr><td>Trillions of dollars</td><td></td></tr>
</table>

- The **net public debt** is the national debt minus all government interagency borrowing (the debt that the federal government owes to itself).

- A **debt ceiling** is a method used to restrict the growth of the national debt.

- **Internal national debt** is the percentage of the national debt a nation owes to its own citizens, including individuals, banks, corporations, insurance companies, and government entities. The "we owe it to ourselves" argument over the debt is that U.S. citizens own the bulk of the U.S. national debt. **External national debt** is a burden because it is the portion of the national debt a nation owes to foreigners. The interest paid on external debt transfers purchasing power to other nations.

Internal and External National Debt

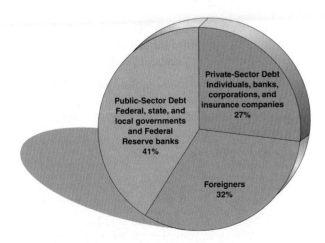

Public-Sector Debt
Federal, state, and
local governments
and Federal
Reserve banks
41%

Private-Sector Debt
Individuals, banks,
corporations, and
insurance companies
27%

Foreigners
32%

- The **burden of the debt debate** involves controversial questions:

1. **Can Uncle Sam Go Bankrupt?** The U.S. government will not go bankrupt because it never has to pay off its debt. When government securities mature, the U.S. Treasury can refinance, or roll over, the debt by issuing new securities.

2. **Are We Passing the Debt Burden to Our Children?** One side of this argument is that the burden of the debt falls only on the current generation when the trade-off between public-sector goods and private-sector goods along the production possibilities curve occurs. In short, when resources are used to make missiles today, citizens are forced to give up, say, airplane production in the current period and not later. The counterargument is that there is a sizable external national debt that transfers purchasing power to foreigners.

3. **Does Government Borrowing Crowd Out Private-Sector Spending?** The **crowding-out effect** is a burden of the national debt that occurs when the government borrows to finance its deficit, causing the interest rate to rise. As the interest rate rises, consumption and business investment spending fall. If crowding out occurs, reduced private spending completely or partially offsets the multiplier effect of increased government spending or reductions in taxes. As a result, the expected magnitude of the rightward shift in the aggregate demand curve is partially or completely offset.

   Opponents believe in the **crowding-in effect**. In this view, government capital spending for highways, dams, universities, and infrastructure offsets any decline in business investment from crowding out.

Zero, Partial, and Complete Crowding Out

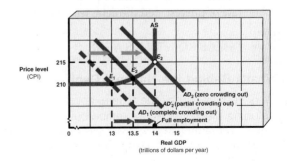

Summary of Conclusion Statements

- The national debt includes the Social Security trust fund and as a result, federal budget deficits are reduced or budget surpluses are raised.

- Crowding out is complete if the economy is at full employment, but it is debatable at less than full employment.

Study Questions and Problems

Please see Appendix A for answers to the odd-numbered questions. Your instructor has access to the answers for even-numbered questions.

1. Explain the relationship between budget deficits and the national debt.

2. Discuss various ways of measuring the size of the national debt.

3. Explain this statement: "The national debt is like taking money out of your left pocket and putting it into your right pocket."

4. Explain this statement: "The most unlikely problem of the national debt is that the government will go bankrupt."

5. Suppose the percentage of the federal debt owned by foreigners increases sharply. Would this trend concern you? Why or why not?

6. Explain the theory that crowding out can weaken or nullify the effect of expansionary fiscal policy financed by federal government borrowing.

7. Suppose the federal government has no national debt and spends $100 billion, while raising only $50 billion in taxes.
   a. What amount of government bonds will the U.S. Treasury issue to finance the deficit?
   b. Next year, assume tax revenues remain at $50 billion. If the government pays a 10 percent rate of interest, add the debt-servicing interest payment to the government's $100 billion expenditure for goods and services the second year.
   c. For the second year, compute the deficit, the amount of new debt issued, and the new national debt.

8. Suppose the media report that the federal deficit this year is $200 billion. The national debt was $5,000 billion last year, and it is $5,200 billion this year. The price level this year is 3 percent higher than it was last year. What is the real deficit?

9. During the presidential campaign of 1932 in the depth of the Great Depression, candidates Herbert Hoover and Franklin D. Roosevelt both advocated reducing the budget deficit using tax hikes and/or expenditure reductions. Evaluate this fiscal policy.

10. Consider this statement: "Our grandchildren may not suffer the entire burden of a federal deficit." Do you agree or disagree? Explain.

11. Suppose you are the economic policy adviser to the president and are asked what should be done to eliminate a federal deficit. What would you recommend?

 CHECKPOINT ANSWERS

What's Behind the National Debt?

Every item owned by the federal government, including the White House, office buildings, tanks, and computers, is an asset standing behind the national debt. If you said the assets of the federal government could be sold to pay off the national debt, **YOU ARE CORRECT**.

Sample Quiz

Please see Appendix B for answers to Sample Quiz questions.

1. Each year, the president must submit a budget proposal to Congress by
   a. February.
   b. April.
   c. July.
   d. October.

2. If the fiscal year begins without a budget and Congress fails to pass continuing resolution, then
   a. the president has the right to raise the debt ceiling.
   b. federal agencies operate on the basis of the previous year's budget.
   c. the interest rate paid on the national debt automatically increases.
   d. the federal government shuts down.

3. Between 1998 and 2001, the federal budget was
   a. never in surplus.
   b. in surplus about as often as it was in deficit.
   c. in surplus.
   d. never in deficit.

4. The sum of past federal budget deficits is the
   a. GDP debt.
   b. trade debt plus GDP.
   c. national debt.
   d. Congressional debt.

5. To finance a federal budget deficit, the U.S. Treasury borrows by selling
   a. Treasury bills.
   b. Treasury notes.
   c. Treasury bonds.
   d. All of the above answers are correct.

6. Most of the U.S. national debt is owed to _____. Thus, a rising national debt implies that there will be a future redistribution of income and wealth in favor of _____.
   a. foreigners, foreigners
   b. other U.S. citizens, bondholders
   c. foreigners, those needing government services
   d. other U.S. citizens, those needing government services

7. Which of the following statements is *false*?
   a. The size of the national debt decreased steadily after World War II.
   b. The national debt increases in size whenever the federal government has a surplus budget.
   c. Currently, the size of the national debt is about the same size as it was during World War II.
   d. All of the answers above are false.

8. Which of the following statements is *true*?
   a. Currently, the size of the national debt is about the same size as it was during World War II.
   b. The national debt increases in size whenever the federal government has a surplus budget.
   c. The size of the national debt decreased steadily after 1980.
   d. The current U.S. national debt is over $19 trillion.

9. Compared to the United Kingdom, the national debt as a percentage of GDP in the United States is
   a. substantially larger.
   b. the same.
   c. slightly larger.
   d. smaller.

10. The national debt is unlikely to cause national bankruptcy because the federal government can
    a. raise taxes.
    b. print money.
    c. refinance its debt.
    d. do all of the above.

11. In recent years, net interest on the national debt paid by the federal government as a percentage of GDP was equal to approximately
    a. 1 percent.
    b. 6 percent.
    c. 16 percent.
    d. 25 percent.

12. Which of the following U.S. Treasury securities represents ownership of the national debt?

a. Bonds owned by the banks and insurance companies
b. Bonds owned by the Social Security Administration
c. Bonds owned by private individuals
d. All of the above answers are correct.

13. "Crowding out" refers to the situation in which
a. borrowing by the federal government raises interest rates and causes firms to invest less.
b. foreigners sell their bonds and purchase U.S. goods and services.
c. borrowing by the federal government causes state and local governments to lower their taxes.
d. increased federal taxes to balance the budget cause interest rates to increase and consumer credit to decrease.

14. The crowding-out effect can be
a. zero.
b. partial.
c. complete.
d. any of the answers are correct.

15. "Crowding in" refers to federal government deficits that
a. are used for public infrastructure will offset any decline in business investment.
b. reduce private business and consumption spending.
c. reduce future rates of economic growth.
d. all of the answers are correct.

16. If Congress fails to pass a budget before the fiscal year starts, then federal agencies may continue to operate only if Congress has passed a
a. balanced budget amendment.
b. deficit reduction plan.

c. conference resolution.
d. continuing resolution.

17. With regard to the national debt, to whom does the federal government owe money?
a. Taxpayers
b. Federal government workers
c. The Federal Reserve system
d. Investors who buy U.S. Treasury bills, bonds, and notes

18. When measured as a percentage of GDP, the U.S. national debt reached its highest levels as a result of
a. World War II.
b. the Vietnam War.
c. the Reagan defense buildup and tax cut.
d. the Obama economic recovery program.

19. The national debt is unlikely to cause national bankruptcy because the
a. national debt can be refinanced by issuing new bonds.
b. interest on the public debt equals GDP.
c. national debt cannot be shifted to future generations for repayment.
d. federal government cannot refinance the outstanding national debt.

20. An increase in our federal government's budget deficit will likely
a. increase the national debt.
b. increase interest rates.
c. decrease borrowing by households and businesses.
d. be less effective in stimulating the economy than the spending multiplier implies because of crowding out.
e. do all of the above.

PART 4
Macroeconomics Theory and Policy

This road map feature helps you tie together material in the part as you travel the Economic Way of Thinking Highway. The following are review questions listed by chapter from the previous part. The key concept in each question is given for emphasis, and each question or set of questions concludes with an interactive game to reinforce the concepts. The correct answers to the multiple choice questions are given in Appendix C. If your instructor has included MindTap in your course, visit MindTap to play the interactive Causation Chain Game.

Chapter 8: The Keynesian Model

1. Key Concept: Consumption function

The consumption function will shift for all of the following reasons except

a. a change in a household's real assets.
b. a change in interest rates.
c. expectations of price changes.
d. changes in a household's disposable incomes.
e. changes in taxation policy.

CAUSATION CHAIN GAME
Movement Along and Shifts in the Consumption Function—Exhibit 4

2. Key Concept: Investment demand curve

Which of the following will increase investment spending?

a. More optimistic business expectations
b. An increase in interest rates
c. An increase in business taxes
d. A decrease in capacity utilization
e. All of the answers above are correct.

CAUSATION CHAIN GAME
Movement Along and Shifts in a Firm's Investment Demand—Exhibit 6

Chapter 9: The Keynesian Model in Action

3. Key Concept: Spending multiplier

The ratio of the change in GDP to an initial change in aggregate expenditures (AE) is the

a. spending multiplier.
b. permanent income rate.
c. marginal expenditure rate.
d. marginal propensity to consume.

CAUSATION CHAIN GAME
The Multiplier Effect and Government Spending—Exhibit 5

Chapter 10: Aggregate Demand and Supply

4. Key Concept: Aggregate demand curve

Which of the following could *not* be expected to shift the aggregate demand curve?

a. Net exports fall
b. Consumption spending decreases
c. An increase in government spending
d. A change in real GDP.

CAUSATION CHAIN GAME
A Shift in the Aggregate Demand Curve—Exhibit 3

5. Key Concept: Aggregate supply curve

The horizontal segment of the aggregate supply curve

a. shows that real GDP can increase only by affecting the economy's price level.
b. shows that real GDP can increase without affecting the economy's price level.
c. depicts a positive relationship between real GDP and the price level.
d. depicts a negative relationship between real GDP and the price level.
e. marks the full-employment level of real GDP.

CAUSATION CHAIN GAME
The Keynesian Horizontal Aggregate Supply Curve—Exhibit 4

6. Key Concept: Aggregate supply curve

According to classical theory, if the aggregate demand curve decreased and the economy experienced unemployment, then

a. the economy would remain in this condition indefinitely.
b. the government must increase spending to restore full employment.
c. prices and wages would fall quickly to restore full employment.
d. the supply of money would increase until the economy returned to full employment.

CAUSATION CHAIN GAME
The Classical Vertical Aggregate Supply Curve—Exhibit 5

7. Key Concept: Aggregate supply curve

If a new method for obtaining oil from dry oil fields is found, then we will see

a. the AS curve shifting to the left.
b. a movement to the left along the AD curve.
c. the AD curve shifting to the left.
d. the AD curve shifting to the right.
e. the AS curve shifting to the right.

CAUSATION CHAIN GAME
A Rightward Shift in the Aggregate Demand and Supply Curves—Exhibit 12

8. Key Concept: Cost-push inflation

Cost-push inflation occurs when the

a. aggregate demand curve shifts leftward while the aggregate supply curve is fixed.
b. aggregate supply curve shifts leftward while the aggregate demand curve is fixed.
c. aggregate demand curve shifts rightward while the aggregate supply curve is fixed.
d. aggregate supply curve shifts rightward.

CAUSATION CHAIN GAME
Cost-Push and Demand-Pull Inflation—Exhibit 13

9. Key Concept: Demand-pull inflation

Demand-pull inflation is caused by an

a. increase in aggregate demand.
b. decrease in aggregate demand.
c. increase in aggregate supply.
d. decrease in aggregate supply.

CAUSATION CHAIN GAME
Cost-Push and Demand-Pull Inflation—Exhibit 13

Chapter 11: Fiscal Policy

10. Key Concept: Fiscal policy

Which of the following is an appropriate discretionary fiscal policy to use when the economy is in a recession?

a. Increased government spending
b. Higher taxes
c. A balanced-budget reduction in both spending and taxes
d. An expansion in the money supply

CAUSATION CHAIN GAME
Using Government Spending to Combat a Recession—Exhibit 2

11. Key Concept: Fiscal policy

Suppose the economy is currently at full employment and the aggregate demand curve increases and shifts to the right by $900 billion at any level of prices. Assuming the marginal propensity to consume is 0.90, this increase in aggregate demand could be prevented by

a. increasing government spending by $500 billion.
b. increasing government spending by $140 billion.
c. decreasing taxes by $40 billion.
d. increasing taxes by $100 billion.

CAUSATION CHAIN GAME
Using Fiscal Policy to Combat Inflation—Exhibit 6

12. Key Concept: Automatic stabilizers

Automatic stabilizers "lean against the prevailing wind" of the business cycle because

a. wages are controlled by the minimum wage law.
b. federal expenditures and tax revenues change as the level of real GDP changes.
c. the spending and tax multipliers are constant.
d. they include the power of special interests.

CAUSATION CHAIN GAME
Automatic Stabilizers—Exhibit 7

13. Key Concept: Supply-side economics

An advocate of supply-side fiscal policy would advocate which of the following?

a. Subsidies to produce technological advances
b. Reduction in regulation
c. Reduction in resource prices
d. Reduction in taxes
e. All of the answers above are correct.

CAUSATION CHAIN GAME
Keynesian Demand-Side versus Supply-Side Effects—Exhibit 8

Chapter 12: The Public Sector

14. Key Concept: The Art of Taxation

If a person is taxed $100 on an income of $1,000, taxed $180 on an income of $2,000, and taxed $220 on an income of $3,000, this person is paying a

a. progressive tax.
b. poll tax.
c. proportional tax.
d. regressive tax.

CAUSATION CHAIN GAME
Major Steps in the Federal Budgetary Process—Exhibit 1

Chapter 13: Federal Deficits, Surpluses, and the National Debt

15. Key Concept: Federal budget process

If Congress fails to pass a budget before the fiscal year starts, then federal agencies may continue to operate only if Congress has passed a

a. balanced budget amendment.
b. deficit reduction plan.
c. conference resolution.
d. continuing resolution.

CAUSATION CHAIN GAME
Major Steps in the Federal Budgetary Process—Exhibit 1

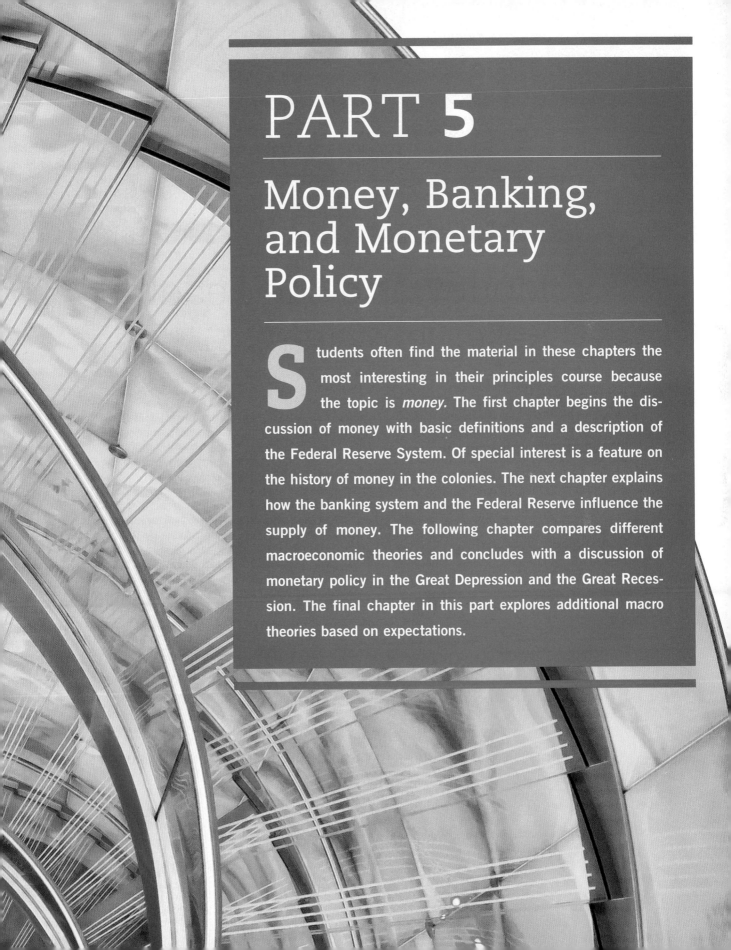

PART 5

Money, Banking, and Monetary Policy

Students often find the material in these chapters the most interesting in their principles course because the topic is *money.* The first chapter begins the discussion of money with basic definitions and a description of the Federal Reserve System. Of special interest is a feature on the history of money in the colonies. The next chapter explains how the banking system and the Federal Reserve influence the supply of money. The following chapter compares different macroeconomic theories and concludes with a discussion of monetary policy in the Great Depression and the Great Recession. The final chapter in this part explores additional macro theories based on expectations.

CHAPTER **14**

Money and the Federal Reserve System

CHAPTER PREVIEW

As the lyrics of the old song go, "Money makes the world go round, the world go round, the world go round." Recall the circular flow model presented in the chapter on GDP. Households exchange *money* for goods and services in the product markets, and firms exchange *money* for resources in the factor markets. In short, money affects the way an economy works. In the chapter on aggregate demand and supply and the chapter on fiscal policy presented earlier in the text, the AD-AS model was developed without explicitly discussing money. In this chapter, and throughout this part, money takes center stage.

Exactly what is money? The answer may surprise you. Imagine yourself on the small South Pacific island of Yap. You are surrounded by exotic fowl, crystal-clear lagoons, delicious fruits, and sunny skies. Now suppose while leisurely strolling along the beach one evening, you suddenly discover a beautiful bamboo hut for sale. As you will discover in this chapter, to pay for your dream hut, you must roll a 5-foot-diameter stone to the area of the island designated as the "bank."

We begin our discussion of money with the three functions money serves. Next, we identify the components of three different definitions of the money supply used in the United States. The remainder of the chapter describes the organization and services of the Federal Reserve System, our nation's central bank. Also, we discuss the Monetary Control Act of 1980 and its relationship to the savings and loan crisis of the 1980s and early 1990s that predated the banking crisis and Great Recession of 2007–2009. Beginning in this chapter and in the next three chapters, you will learn how the Federal Reserve System controls the stock of money in the economy. Then, using the AD-AS model, you will learn how variations in the stock of money in the economy affect total spending, unemployment, and prices.

IN THIS CHAPTER, YOU WILL LEARN TO SOLVE THESE ECONOMICS PUZZLES:

- Why do nations use money?

- Is "plastic money" really money?

- What does the Federal Reserve System do?

14-1 WHAT MAKES MONEY?

Can exchange occur in an economy without money? It certainly can, using a trading system called barter. **Barter** is the direct exchange of one good or service for another good or service, rather than for money. The problem with barter is that it requires a *coincidence of wants*. Imagine for a moment that dollars and coins are worthless. Farmer Brown needs shoes, so he takes his bushels of wheat to the shoe store and offers to barter wheat for shoes. Unfortunately, the store owner refuses to barter because she wants to trade shoes for pencils, toothpaste, and coffee. Undaunted, Farmer Brown spends more time and effort to find Mr. Jones, who has pencils, toothpaste, and coffee he will trade for bushels of wheat. Although Farmer Brown's luck has improved, he and Mr. Jones must agree on the terms of exchange. Exactly how many pounds of coffee, for example, is a bushel of wheat worth? Assuming this exchange is worked out, Farmer Brown must spend more time returning to the shoe store and negotiating the terms of an exchange of pencils, coffee, and toothpaste for shoes.

Barter
The direct exchange of one good or service for another good or service, rather than for money.

> The use of money simplifies and therefore increases market transactions. Money also prevents wasting time that can be devoted to production, thereby promoting economic growth by increasing a nation's production possibilities.

CONCLUSION

14-1a The Three Functions of Money

Suppose citizens of the planet of Starcom want to replace their barter system and must decide what to use for money. Assuming this planet is fortunate enough to have economists, they would explain that anything, regardless of its intrinsic value, can serve as money if it conforms to the following definition. **Money** is anything that serves as a medium of exchange, unit of account, and store of value. Money is not limited to dimes, quarters, and dollar bills. Notice that "anything" meeting the three tests is a candidate to serve as money. This explains why precious metals, beaver skins, wampum (shells strung in belts), and cigarettes have all served as money. Let's discuss each of the three functions money serves.

Money
Anything that serves as a medium of exchange, unit of account, and store of value.

Money as a Medium of Exchange

In a simple society, barter is a way for participants to exchange goods and services in order to satisfy wants. Barter, however, requires wasting time in the process of exchange that people could use for productive work. If the goal is to increase the volume of transactions and live in a modern economy, the most important function of money is to serve as a medium of exchange. **Medium of exchange** is the primary function of money to be widely accepted in exchange for goods and services. Money removes the problem of coincidence of wants because everyone is willing to accept money in payment, rather than haggling over goods and services. You give up two $20 bills in exchange for a ticket to a rock concert. Because money serves as generalized purchasing power, all in society know that no one will refuse to trade their products for money. In short, money increases trade by providing a much more convenient method of exchange than a cumbersome barter system.

Medium of exchange
The primary function of money to be widely accepted in exchange for goods and services.

A fascinating question is whether people will find digital cash a more convenient means of payment. Each year more people avoid using checks, paper currency, or coins by transferring funds electronically from their accounts via various Internet-based and other systems. In fact, it is possible that widespread adoption of privately issued digital cash will ultimately replace government-issued currency. Vending and copy machines on many college campuses already accept plastic stored-value cards. Someday vending machines everywhere are likely to have smart card readers that accept electronic money.

Money as a Unit of Account

Unit of account
The function of money to provide a common measurement of the relative value of goods and services.

How does a wheat farmer know whether a bushel of wheat is worth one, two, or more pairs of shoes? How does a family compare its income to expenses or a business know whether it is making a profit? Government must be able to measure tax revenues collected and program expenditures made. And GDP is the *money* value of final goods and services used to compare the national output of the United States to, say, Japan's output. In each of these examples, money serves as a unit of account. **Unit of account** is the function of money to provide a common measurement of the relative value of goods and services. Without dollars, there is no common denominator. We must therefore decide if one pizza equals a box of pencils, 20 oranges equals one quart of milk, and so forth. Now let's compare the value of two items using money. If the price of one pizza is $20 and the price of a movie ticket is $10, then the value of one pizza equals two movie tickets. In the United States, the monetary unit is the dollar; in Japan, it is the yen; Mexico has its peso; and so on.

Money as a Store of Value

Store of value
The ability of money to hold value over time.

Can you put shrimp under your mattress for months and then exchange them for some product? No! Money, on the other hand, serves as a store of value in exchange for some item in the future. **Store of value** is the ability of money to hold value over time. You can bury money in your backyard or store it under your mattress for months or years and not worry about it spoiling. This also means you can save money and be confident that you can spend it in the future. However, recall from the chapter on inflation that hyperinflation can destroy money's store-of-value function and, in turn, its medium-of-exchange function.

CONCLUSION   Money is a useful mechanism for transforming income in the present into future purchases.

The key property of money is that it is completely *liquid*. This means that money is immediately available to spend in exchange for goods and services without any additional expense. Money is more liquid than real assets (real estate or gold) or paper assets (stocks or bonds). These assets also serve as stores of value, but liquidating (selling) them often involves expenses, such as brokerage fees, and time delays.

CONCLUSION   Money is the most liquid form of wealth because it can be spent directly in the marketplace.

14-1b Are Credit Cards Money?

Credit cards, such as Visa, MasterCard, and American Express, are often called "plastic money," but are these cards really money? Let's test credit cards for the three functions of money. First, because credit cards are widely accepted, they serve as a means of payment in an exchange for goods or services.

Second, the credit card statement, and not the card itself, serves as a unit of account. One of the advantages of credit cards is that you receive a statement listing the exact price in dollars paid for each item you charged. Your credit card statement clearly records the dollar amount you spent for gasoline, a dinner, or a trip.

But credit cards clearly fail to meet the store-of-value criterion and are therefore *not* money. The word *credit* means receiving money today to buy products in return for a promise to pay in the future. A credit card represents only a prearranged short-term loan up to a certain limit. If the credit card company goes out of business or for any reason decides not to honor your card, it is worthless. Hence, credit cards do not store value and are *not* money.

CHECKPOINT

> **Are Debit Cards Money?**
> Debit cards are used to pay for purchases, and the money is automatically deducted from the user's bank account. Are debit cards money?

14-1c Other Desirable Properties of Money

Once something has passed the three basic requirements to serve as money, there are additional hurdles to clear. First, an important consideration is *scarcity*. Money must be scarce, but not too scarce. Sand, for example, could theoretically serve as money, but sand is a poor choice because people can easily gather a bucketful to pay their bills. A Picasso painting would also be undesirable as money. Because there are so few for circulation, people would have to resort to barter.

Counterfeiting threatens the scarcity of money. Advances in computer graphics, scanners, and color copiers were allowing counterfeiters to win their ongoing battle with the U.S. Secret Service. In response, new bills were issued with a polymer security thread running through them. The larger off-center portraits on the bills allow for a watermark next to the portrait that is visible from both sides against a light.

CONCLUSION

> The supply of money must be great enough to meet ordinary transaction needs, but not be so plentiful that it becomes worthless.

Second, money should be *portable* and *divisible*. That is, people should be able to reach into their pockets and make change to buy items at various prices. Statues of George Washington might be attractive money, but they would be difficult to carry and make change. Finally, money must be *uniform*. An ounce of gold is an ounce of gold. The quality differences of beaver skins and seashells, on the other hand, complicate using these items for money. Each exchange would involve the extra trouble of buyers and sellers arguing over which skins or shells are better or worse.

GLOBAL ECONOMICS

Why a Loan in Yap Is Hard to Roll Over

Applicable Concept: Functions of Money

On the tiny South Pacific island of Yap, life is easy, but the currency is hard as a rock. For nearly 2,000 years, the Yapese have used large stone wheels to pay for major purchases, such as land, canoes, and permission to marry. The people of Yap have been using stone money ever since a Yapese warrior named Anagumang used canoes to bring the huge stones over the sea in ancient times from limestone caverns on neighboring Palau. Inspired by the moon, he fashioned the stones into large circles, and the rest is history. The stone's value remained high because of the difficulty and hazards involved in obtaining them over the rough seas.

Yap is a U.S. trust territory, and the dollar is used in grocery stores and gas stations, but reliance on stone money continues. Buying property with stones is "much easier than buying it with U.S. dollars," says John Chodad, who purchased a building lot with a 30-inch stone wheel. "We don't know the value of the U.S. dollar." However, stone wheels don't make good pocket money, so Yapese use other forms of currency, such as beer for small transactions. Besides stone wheels and beer, the Yapese sometimes spend gaw, consisting of necklaces of stone beads strung together around a whale's tooth. They also buy things with yar, a currency made from large seashells, but these are small change.

Stone disks may change ownership during marriage, transfer of land title, or other exchanges. Yapese lean the stone wheels against their houses or prop up rows of them in village "banks." Most of the stones are smaller in diameter, but some are as much as 12 feet in diameter. Each has a hole in the center so that it can be slipped onto the trunk of a fallen betel nut tree and carried. It takes 20 men to lift some wheels. Rather than risk a broken stone—or their backs—Yapese leave the larger stones where they are and make a mental accounting that the ownership has

O.D. Vande Veer/Alamy Stock Photo

been transferred. There are some decided advantages to using massive stones for money. They are in short supply, difficult to steal, pose formidable obstacles to counterfeiting, and serve as a tourist attraction.

ANALYZE THE ISSUE

1. Explain how Yap's large stones pass the three tests in the definition of money.
2. Briefly discuss Yap's large stones in terms of other desirable properties of money.

14-1d What Stands Behind Our Money?

Commodity money
Anything that serves as money while having market value based on the material from which it is made.

Historically, early forms of money played two roles. If, for example, a ruler declared beans as money, you could spend them or sell them in the marketplace. Precious metals, tobacco, cows, and other tangible goods are examples of commodity money. **Commodity money** is anything that serves as money while having market value based on the material from which it is made. This means that this money itself has intrinsic worth (the market value of the material). For example, money can be pure gold or silver, both of which are valuable for nonmoney uses, such as making jewelry and serving other industrial purposes.

Today, U.S. paper money and coins are no longer backed by gold or silver. Our paper money was exchangeable for gold or silver until 1934. As a result of the Great Depression, people rapidly tried to get rid of their paper money. The U.S. Treasury's stock of gold dropped so low that Congress passed a law in 1934 that prevented anyone from exchanging gold for $5 and larger bills. Later, in 1963, Congress removed the right to exchange $1 bills for silver. And in the mid-1960s, zinc, copper, and nickel replaced silver in coins.

The important consideration for money is acceptability. The acceptability of a dollar is due in no small degree to the fact that Uncle Sam decrees it to be fiat money. **Fiat money** is money accepted by law, and not because of its redeemability or intrinsic value. A dollar bill contains only about 3 cents worth of paper, printing inks, and other materials. A quarter contains maybe 10 cents worth of nickel and copper. Pull out a dollar bill and look at it closely. In the upper left corner on the front side is small print that proclaims, "THIS NOTE IS LEGAL TENDER FOR ALL DEBTS, PUBLIC AND PRIVATE." This means that your paper money is fiat money. Also notice that nowhere on the note is there any promise to redeem it for gold, silver, or anything else.

So, what stands behind our fiat money? That is, why are people still willing to accept it as payment even though it has no intrinsic value? Because they are confident in the government's ability to keep inflation under control and, therefore, to maintain its purchasing power over time. If that confidence erodes, then that fiat money may cease to serve the functions of money and may become worthless.

Fiat money
Money accepted by law and not because of its redeemability or tangible value.

An item's ability to serve as money does not depend on its own market value or the backing of precious metal.

CONCLUSION

Are Bitcoins Money?
Bitcoins are a relatively new innovative virtual currency used for electronic payment. Bitcoins are not issued by any government, nor do they possess any intrinsic value. Are bitcoins really money?

CHECKPOINT

14-2 MONEY SUPPLY DEFINITIONS

Now that you understand the basic definition of money, we turn to exactly what constitutes the money supply of the U.S. economy. The following sections examine the two basic methods used to measure the money supply, officially called M1 and M2.

14-2a M1: The Most Narrowly Defined Money Supply

M1 is the narrowest definition of the money supply. This money definition measures purchasing power immediately available to the public without borrowing or having to

HISTORY OF MONEY IN THE COLONIES

The early colonists left behind their well-developed money system in Europe. North American Indians accepted wampum as money, which are beads of polished shells strung in belts. Soon, a group of settlers learned to counterfeit wampum, and it lost its value. As a result, the main method of trading with the Indians was to barter. Later, trade developed with the West Indies, and Spanish coins called "pieces of eight" were circulated widely. Colonists often cut these coins into pieces to make change. Half of a coin became known as "four bits." A quarter part of the coin was referred to as "two bits." The first English colony to mint its own coins was Massachusetts in 1652. A striking pine tree was engraved on these coins called shillings. Other coins such as a six-pence and three-pence were also produced at a mint in Boston. Several other colonies followed by authorizing their own coin issues.

The first national coin of the United States was issued in 1787 when Congress approved a one-cent copper coin. One side was decorated with a chain of 13 links encircling the

---

M1
The narrowest definition of the money supply. It includes currency and checkable deposits.

give notice. Specifically, **M1** measures the currency and checkable deposits held by the public at a given time, such as a given day, month, or year. Expressed as a formula:

$$M1 = currency + checkable\ deposits$$

Exhibit 1 shows the components of M1 and M2 money supply definitions based on weekly averages in 2017.

Currency

Currency
Money, including coins and paper money.

Currency includes coins and paper money, officially called Federal Reserve notes, that the public holds for immediate spending. The purpose of currency is to enable us to make small purchases. Currency represents 42 percent of M1.

Checkable Deposits

Checkable deposits
The total money in financial institutions that can be withdrawn by writing a check.

Most "big ticket" purchases are paid for with checks or credit cards (which are not money), rather than currency. Checks eliminate trips to the bank, and they are safer than cash. If lost or stolen, checks and credit cards can be replaced at little cost—money cannot. Exhibit 1 shows that a major share of M1 consists of checkable deposits. **Checkable deposits** are the total money in financial institutions that can be withdrawn "on demand" by writing a check. A checking account balance is a bookkeeping entry, often called a *demand deposit* because it can be converted into cash "on demand." Before the 1980s, only commercial banks could legally provide demand deposits. However, the law changed with the passage of the Depository Institutions Deregulation and Monetary Control Act of 1980. (This act will be discussed later in the chapter.) Today, checking accounts are available from many different financial institutions, such as savings and loan associations, credit unions, and mutual savings banks. For example, many people

words "We Are One." The other side had a sundial, the noonday sun, and the Latin word *fugo*, meaning "time flies." Later, this coin became known as the Franklin cent, although there is no evidence that Benjamin Franklin played any role in its design.

In 1792, Congress established a mint in Philadelphia. It manufactured copper cents and half-cents about the size of today's quarters and nickels. In 1794, silver half-dimes and half-dollars increased the variety of available coins. The next year gold eagles ($10) and half-eagles ($5) appeared. The motto "E Pluribus Unum" ("out of many, one") was first used on the half-eagle in 1795. The next year America's first quarters and dimes were issued.

The first paper money in the Americas was printed in 1690. Massachusetts soldiers returned to the colony from fighting the French in Quebec, where they had unsuccessfully laid siege to the city. The colony had no precious metal to pay the soldiers. Hundreds of soldiers threatened mutiny, and the colony decided it must issue bills of credit, which were simply pieces of paper promising to pay the soldiers. Other colonies followed this example and printed their own paper money. Soon paper money was being widely circulated.

In 1775, the need to finance the American Revolution forced the Continental Congress to issue paper money called "continentals," but so much was issued that it rapidly lost its value. George Washington complained, "A wagon load of money will scarcely purchase a wagon load of provisions." This statement is today shortened to the phrase "not worth a continental."

hold deposits in negotiable order of withdrawal (NOW) accounts or automatic transfer of savings (ATS) accounts, which serve as interest-bearing checking accounts. NOW and ATS accounts permit depositors to spend their deposits without a trip to the bank to withdraw funds. In 2017, 58 percent of M1 was checkable deposits.

14-2b M2: Adding Near Monies to M1

M2 is a broader measure of the money supply because it equals M1 plus *near monies*. Many economists consider M1 to be too narrow a measure because it does not include near money accounts that can be used to purchase goods and services. These include passbook savings accounts, money market accounts, mutual fund accounts, and time deposits of less than $100,000. Near monies are interest-bearing deposits easily converted into spendable funds. Written as a formula:

$$\textbf{M2} = \textbf{M1} + \textbf{near monies}$$

rewritten as

$$\textbf{M2} = \textbf{M1} + \textbf{savings deposits} + \textbf{small time deposits of less than \$100,000}$$

M2
The definition of the money supply that equals M1 plus near monies, such as savings deposits and small time deposits of less than $100,000.

Savings Deposits

As shown in Exhibit 1, M1 was 26 percent of M2 in 2017, with savings deposits and small time deposits constituting the remainder of M2. Savings deposits are interest-bearing accounts that can be easily withdrawn. These deposits include passbook savings accounts, money market accounts, mutual fund accounts, and other types of interest-bearing deposits with commercial banks, mutual savings banks, savings and loan associations, and credit unions.

Each of the two pie charts represents the money supply in 2017. M1, the most narrowly defined money supply, is equal to currency (coins and paper money) in circulation plus checkable deposits in financial institutions. M2 is a more broadly defined money supply, and it is equal to M1 plus savings deposits and small time deposits of less than $100,000.

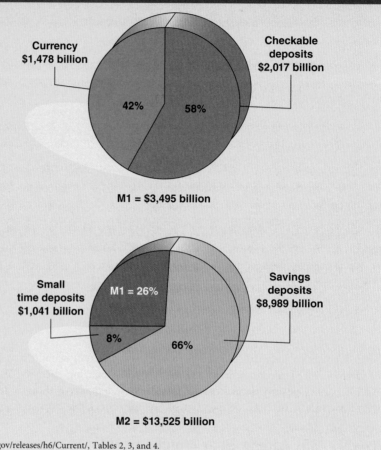

Currency
$1,478 billion

Checkable deposits
$2,017 billion

42%   58%

M1 = $3,495 billion

Small time deposits
$1,041 billion

M1 = 26%

Savings deposits
$8,989 billion

8%   66%

M2 = $13,525 billion

SOURCE: *Federal Reserve Board*, http://www.federalreserve.gov/releases/h6/Current/, Tables 2, 3, and 4.

Small Time Deposits

There is a distinction between a *checkable deposit* and a *time deposit*. A time deposit is an interest-bearing account in a financial institution with guaranteed interest for a specified period of time. Certificates of deposit (CDs), for example, are deposits for a specified time, with a penalty charged for early withdrawal. Where is the line drawn between a small and a large time deposit? The answer is that time deposits of less than $100,000 are "small" and therefore are included in M2. In 2017, 8 percent of M2 was small time deposits.

CONCLUSION   M1 is more liquid than M2.

To simplify the discussion throughout the remainder of this text, we will be referring to M1 when we discuss the money supply. However, one can argue that M2, or another measurement of the money supply, may be the best definition. Actually, the boundary lines for any definition of money are somewhat arbitrary.

14-3 THE FEDERAL RESERVE SYSTEM

What controls the money supply in the United States? The answer is the *Federal Reserve System*, popularly called the "Fed." The **Federal Reserve System (Fed)** is the central bank of the United States, and provides banking services to commercial banks, other financial institutions, and the federal government. The Fed regulates, supervises, and is responsible for policies concerning money. Congress and the president consult with the Fed to control the size of the money supply and thereby influence the economy's performance.

Other major nations have central banks as well, such as the Bank of England, the Bank of Japan, and the European Central Bank. The movement in the United States to establish a central banking system gained strength early in the twentieth century as a series of bank failures resulted in The Panic of 1907. In that year, stock prices fell, many businesses and banks failed, and millions of depositors lost their savings. The prescription for preventing financial panic was for the government to establish more centralized control over banks. This desire for more safety in banking led to the creation of the Federal Reserve System by the Federal Reserve Act of 1913 during the administration of President Woodrow Wilson. No longer would the supply of money in the economy be determined by individual banks.

14-3a The Fed's Organizational Chart

The *Federal Reserve System* is an independent agency of the federal government. Congress is responsible for overseeing the Fed, but does not interfere with its day-to-day decisions. The chairman of the Fed reports to Congress twice each year and often coordinates its actions with the U.S. Treasury and the president. Although the Fed enjoys independent status, its independence can be revoked. If the Fed were to pursue policies contrary to the interests of the nation, Congress could abolish the Fed.

The Federal Reserve System consists of 12 central banks that service banks and other financial institutions within each of the Federal Reserve districts. Each Federal Reserve Bank serves as a central banker for the private banks in its region. The United States is the only nation in the world to have 12 separate regional banks instead of a single central bank. In fact, the Fed's structure is the result of a compromise between the traditionalists, who favored a single central bank, and the populists, who distrusted concentration of financial power in the hands of a few. In addition, 25 Federal Reserve branch banks are located throughout the country. The map in Exhibit 2 shows the 12 Federal Reserve districts.

The organizational chart of the Federal Reserve System, given in Exhibit 3, shows that the Board of Governors, located in Washington, D.C., administers the system. The **Board of Governors** is made up of seven members, appointed by the president and confirmed by the U.S. Senate, who serve for one nonrenewable 14-year term. Their responsibility is to supervise and control the money supply and the banking system of the United States. Fourteen-year terms for Fed governors create autonomy and insulate the Fed from short-term politics. These terms are staggered so that one term expires every two years. This staggering of terms prevents a president from stacking

Federal Reserve System (Fed)
The 12 Federal Reserve District Banks that service banks and other financial institutions within each of the Federal Reserve districts; popularly called the Fed.

Board of Governors
The seven members appointed by the president and confirmed by the U.S. Senate who serve for one nonrenewable 14-year term. Their responsibility is to supervise and control the money supply and the banking system of the United States.

EXHIBIT 2 The Twelve Federal Reserve Districts

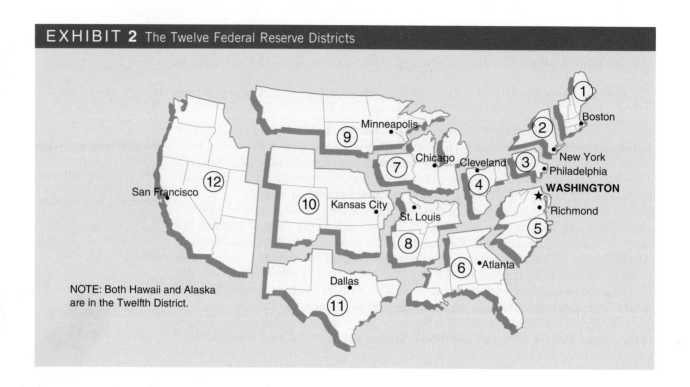

NOTE: Both Hawaii and Alaska are in the Twelfth District.

EXHIBIT 3 The Organization of the Federal Reserve System

The Federal Open Market Committee (FOMC) and the Federal Advisory Council assist the Federal Reserve System's Board of Governors. The 12 regional Federal Reserve District Banks and their 25 branches implement broad policies affecting the money supply.

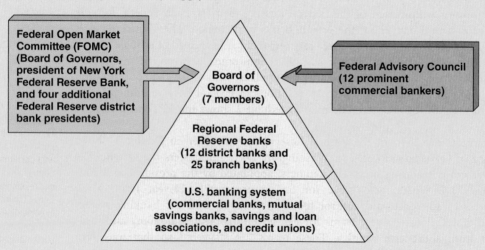

the board with members favoring the incumbent party's political interests. A president usually makes two appointments in a one-term presidency and four appointments in a two-term presidency. The president designates one member of the Board of Governors to serve as chair for a four-year term. The chair is the principal spokesperson for the Fed and has considerable power over policy decisions. In fact, it is often argued that the Fed's chairman is the most powerful individual in the United States next to the president. Janet Yellen was appointed Chair by President Obama and her term expires February 3, 2018.

The Federal Reserve System receives no funding from Congress. This creates financial autonomy for the Fed by removing the fear of congressional review of its budget. Then where does the Fed get funds to operate? Recall from Exhibit 8 of the previous chapter that the Fed holds government securities issued by the U.S. Treasury. The Fed earns interest income from the government securities it holds and the loans it makes to depository institutions. Because the Fed returns any profits to the Treasury, it is motivated to adopt policies to promote the economy's well-being, rather than earning a profit. Moreover, the Board of Governors does not take orders from the president or any other politician. Thus, the Board of Governors is the independent, self-supporting authority of the Federal Reserve System.

On the left side of the organizational chart in Exhibit 3 is the very important Federal Open Market Committee. The **Federal Open Market Committee (FOMC)** directs the buying and selling of U.S. government securities, which are major instruments for controlling the money supply. The FOMC consists of the 7 members of the Board of Governors, the president of the New York Federal Reserve Bank, and the presidents of 4 other Federal Reserve District Banks. The FOMC meets eight times per year to discuss trends in inflation, unemployment, growth rates, and other macro data. FOMC members express their opinions on implementing various monetary policies and then issue policy statements known as *FOMC directives*. A directive, for example, might set the operation of the Fed to stimulate or restrain M1 in order to influence the economy. The next 2 chapters explain the tools of monetary policy in more detail.

As shown on the right side of the chart, the *Federal Advisory Council* consists of 12 prominent commercial bankers. Each of the 12 Federal Reserve District Banks selects one member each year. The council meets periodically to advise the Board of Governors, but has no policy-making authority.

Finally, at the bottom of the organizational chart is the remainder of the Federal Reserve System, consisting of only about 3,000 member banks of the approximately 8,000 commercial banks in the United States. Although these 3,000 Fed member banks represent only about 38 percent of U.S. banks, they have about 70 percent of all U.S. bank deposits. A sure sign of Fed membership is the word *National* in a bank's name. The U.S. comptroller of the currency charters national banks, and they are required to be Fed members. Banks that do not have "National" in their title can also be Fed members. States can also charter banks, and these state banks have the option of joining the Federal Reserve. Less than 20 percent of state banks choose to join the Fed. Exhibit 4 shows the top 10 U.S. banks based on their assets.

Nonmember depository institutions, including many commercial banks, savings and loan associations (S&Ls), savings banks, and credit unions, are not official members of the Fed team. They are, however, influenced by and depend on the Fed for a variety of services, which we will now discuss.

Federal Open Market Committee (FOMC)
The Federal Reserve's committee that directs the buying and selling of U.S. government securities, which are major instruments for controlling the money supply. The FOMC consists of the seven members of the Federal Reserve's Board of Governors, the president of the New York Federal Reserve Bank, and the presidents of four other Federal Reserve District Banks.

EXHIBIT 4 Top 10 Banks in the United States, 2017

The top 10 banks in the United States include JPMorgan Chase, Bank of America, and Wells Fargo.

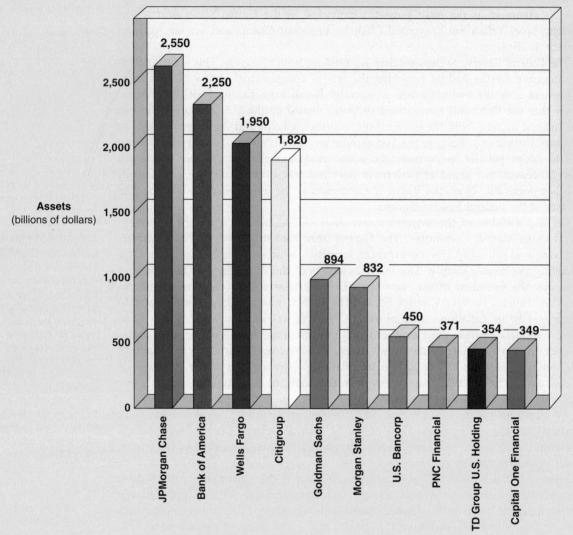

SOURCE: National Information Center, http://www.ffiec.gov/. Bankrate, http://www.bankrate.com/banking/americas-top-10-biggest-banks/#slide=1. Banks around the World, https://www.relbanks.com/top-us-banks/assets.

14-4 WHAT A FEDERAL RESERVE BANK DOES

The typical bank customer never enters the doors of a Federal Reserve District Bank or one of its branch banks. The reason is that the Fed does not offer the public checking accounts, savings accounts, or any of the services provided by commercial banks. Instead, the Federal Reserve serves as a "banker's bank." Following are brief descriptions of some of the principal functions of the Federal Reserve.

14-4a Controlling the Money Supply

The primary role of the Fed is to control the nation's money supply. The mechanics of Fed control over the money supply are explained in the next two chapters. To most people, this is a wondrously mysterious process. So that you do not suffer in complete suspense, here is a sneak preview: The Fed has three policy tools, or levers, it can use to change the stock of money in the banking system. The potential macro outcome of changes in the money supply is to affect total spending and, therefore, real GDP, employment, and the price level.

14-4b Clearing Checks

Because people and businesses use checks to pay for goods and services, check clearing is an important function. Suppose you live in Virginia and have a checking account with a bank in that state. While on vacation in California, you purchase tickets to Disneyland with a check for $200. Disneyland accepts your check and then deposits it in its business checking account in a California bank. This bank must collect payment for your check and does so by sending an electronic copy of your check to the Federal Reserve Bank in San Francisco. From there, your check is sent to the Federal Reserve Bank in Richmond. At each stop along its journey, the check earns a black stamp mark on the back. Finally, the process ends when $200 is subtracted from your personal checking account. Banks in which checks are deposited have their Fed accounts credited, and banks on which checks are written have their accounts debited. The Fed clearinghouse process is much speedier than depending on the movement of a check between commercial banks.

14-4c Supervising and Regulating Banks

The Fed examines banks' books, sets limits for loans, approves bank mergers, and works with the Federal Deposit Insurance Corporation. The **Federal Deposit Insurance Corporation (FDIC)** is a government agency established in 1933 that insures commercial bank deposits up to a limit if a bank fails. Congress created the FDIC in response to the huge number of bank failures during the Great Depression and set the insurance limit at $25,000. If the government provides a safety net, people are less likely to panic and withdraw their funds from banks during a period of economic uncertainty. When deposits are insured and a bank fails, the government stands ready to pay depositors or transfer their deposits to a solvent bank. Banks that are members of the Fed are members of the FDIC. State agencies supervise state-chartered banks that are not members of either the Federal Reserve System or the FDIC. To shore up confidence in the U.S. banking system in the wake of bank failures in 2008, the $700 billion U.S. financial industry rescue law (entitled: Troubled Assets Relief Program, or TARP) raised the FDIC coverage of bank deposits to $250,000 per customer from $100,000.

Federal Deposit Insurance Corporation (FDIC)
A government agency established in 1933 to insure customer deposits up to a limit if a bank fails.

14-4d Maintaining and Circulating Currency

Recall that the M1 money supply consists of currency (coins and Federal Reserve notes) and checkable deposits. Note that the Fed does *not* print currency—it *maintains* and *circulates* money. All Federal Reserve notes are printed at the U.S. Bureau of Engraving and Printing's facilities in Washington, D.C., and Fort Worth, Texas. The Treasury mints and issues all coins. Coins are made at U.S. mints located in Philadelphia and Denver. The bureau and the mints ship new notes and coins to the Federal Reserve Banks for circulation. Much of this money is printed or minted simply to replace worn-out bills and

YOU'RE THE ECONOMIST

Applicable Concept: The Federal Reserve System

Should the Fed Be Independent?

The Federal Reserve is perhaps the most independent government agency in the United States. Periodically, there is a resurgence of interest in curtailing its independence. Should the Fed be independent of partisan politics, or would we be better off with a central bank under the control of Congress and the president?

The Case for an Independent Fed

Those in favor of an independent Federal Reserve argue politicians in charge of the nation's money supply might use that power to achieve short-term political objectives that could create longer-term economic problems. For example, prior to an election incumbents may be tempted to increase the money supply. This would push interest rates down, encourage borrowing and spending that would stimulate the economy and reduce unemployment. The problem is that too much money in circulation creates higher rates of inflation and higher interest rates over time, long after the election is over. Moreover, putting the Fed under control of the president might be dangerous because deficit spending requires the Treasury to issue more government debt (U.S. Treasury bills, notes, and bonds) that tends to push interest rates up. However, expanding the money supply would tend to keep interest rates low. Unfortunately, if the Fed attempts to monetize the deficit and the national debt, it will again result in

Mesut Dogan/Shutterstock.com

higher rates of inflation over time. Perhaps an independent Fed may accommodate these kinds of political objectives, but the advocates of an independent Fed argue this is less likely because of reduced political pressures.

Another argument for an independent Fed is that politicians lack the expertise to manage the money supply, they are short-sighted, and are rarely capable of making informed decisions in a timely manner, all of

coins. Another use of new currency is to meet public demand. Suppose it is the holiday season and banks need more paper money and coins to meet their customers' shopping needs. The Federal Reserve must be ready to ship extra money from its large vaults by armored truck.

14-4e Protecting Consumers

Since 1968, the Federal Reserve has played a role in protecting consumers by enforcing statutes enacted by Congress. Perhaps the most important is the *Equal Credit Opportunity Act*, which prohibits discrimination based on race, color, gender, marital status, religion, or national origin in the extension of credit. It also gives married women the right to establish credit histories in their own names. The Federal Reserve receives and tries to resolve consumer complaints against banks.

In 2010, the **Consumer Financial Protection Bureau (CFPB)** was established. This is an independent bureau within the Federal Reserve that helps consumers make financial decisions. The goal of the CFPB is to promote fairness and make mortgages, credit cards, and other consumer financial services understandable. The objective is to let consumers see clearly the costs and features of loans. As a result, consumers will not be caught by hidden fees or sign loans they cannot afford.

Consumer Financial Protection Bureau (CFPB)
An independent bureau within the Federal Reserve that helps consumers make financial decisions.

which would contribute to poorer long-term economic performance. Moreover, an independent Fed is free to pursue politically unpopular policies, like pushing inter- est rates up to fight inflation that serves the long-term public interest. Indeed, some politicians may be pri- vately grateful the Fed is independent because pursuing politically unpopular economic policies rarely gets them re-elected.

Advocates for an independent Fed also point to the hyperinflation in Germany from 1914–1923 to show how political control over a central bank can lead to disastrous results. To finance its efforts in WWI, Germany chose not to increase taxes. That would have been politically unpopular. Instead its government issued huge amounts of debt that was bought up by its central bank under its control. After WWI, faced with huge war reparations, the German gov- ernment essentially "got out the printing press" to pay that debt. Its money supply increased so much, driving prices up so fast, that by 1923 it would literally take a wheel bar- row full of German marks to buy a single loaf of bread.

The Case against an Independent Fed

Critics of an independent Fed argue that it is unconsti- tutional for Congress to delegate its constitutional obli- gation to "coin money [and] regulate the value thereof" to an independent agency. Opponents of Fed indepen- dence also suggest that it is undemocratic to have an unelected Board of Governors who are unaccountable to the voting public to be dictating monetary policy that may well be the most important factor determining our economic well-being. In addition, elected officials

already control fiscal policy and they should also have control over monetary policy to ensure these two policies are working in tandem to maximize the performance of the economy, and are not working against each other.

Critics also argue that an independent Fed has not always exercised its discretion successfully. It failed mis- erably in managing the money supply and preventing bank failures during the Great Depression, and it increased the money supply too much during the 1970s contributing to the rapid inflation of that decade. More recently, many hold the Fed responsible for the global financial crisis of 2007–2008.

Is an independent Fed a good thing or a bad thing? Although the debate has existed for a long time and will likely continue, there has been growing consensus around the world that more independent central banks are better at realizing lower rates of inflation over time, and are at least as good at stabilizing their economies and minimizing unemployment as less independent central banks.

ANALYZE THE ISSUE What is the most important function of the Fed? Make an argument why an independent Fed would do a better job at performing its number one role. Make an argument why a Fed under the control of Congress and the president would do a better job at performing its most important function.

14-4f Maintaining Federal Government Checking Accounts and Gold

The Fed is also Uncle Sam's bank. The U.S. Treasury has the Fed handle its checking account. From this account, the federal government pays for such expenses as federal employees' salaries, Social Security, tax refunds, veterans' benefits, defense, and highways.

Finally, it is interesting to note that the New York Federal Reserve District Bank holds one of the oldest forms of money—*gold*. This gold belongs mainly to foreign gov- ernments and is one of the largest accumulations of this precious metal in the world. Viewing a Federal Reserve Bank's vault is not something that most tourists typically have on their list of things to do, but I strongly recommend this tour.

The gold vault at the New York Federal Reserve Bank is nearly half the length of a football field and filled with steel and concrete walls several yards thick. Most cells contain the gold of only one nation, and only a few bank employees know the identities of the owners. When trade occurs between two countries, payment between the parties can be made by transferring gold bars from one compartment to another. Note that the Fed and the monetary system of the Yapese have a similarity. Recall from the Global Economics box that in Yap large stone wheels are not moved; they just change ownership.

14-4g Lender of Last Resort

The Fed acts as the lender of last resort to prevent a banking crisis. For example, after the terrorist attacks in 2001, the Fed issued billions in loans to banks throughout the United States. And in 2008, several large banks collapsed and others were on the verge. The Fed lent banks enough required reserve balances to meet their obligation to depositors.

14-5 THE U.S. BANKING REVOLUTION

Prior to the 1980s, the U.S. banking system was simpler. It consisted of many commercial banks authorized by law to offer checking accounts. Then there were the other financial institutions, the so-called thrifts, which included S&Ls, mutual savings banks, and credit unions. The thrifts by law were permitted to accept only savings deposits with no checking privileges. The commercial banks, on the other hand, could not pay interest on checkable deposits. Moreover, a "maximum interest rate allowed by law" limited competition among commercial banks and other financial institutions. As will be explained momentarily, this relatively tranquil U.S. banking structure changed dramatically, and the stage was set for a fascinating banking "horror story."

14-5a The Monetary Control Act of 1980

Monetary Control Act
A law, formally titled the Depository Institutions Deregulation and Monetary Control Act of 1980, that gave the Federal Reserve System greater control over nonmember banks and made all financial institutions more competitive.

A significant law affecting the U.S. banking system is the Depository Institutions Deregulation and Monetary Control Act of 1980, commonly called the **Monetary Control Act**. This law gave the Federal Reserve System greater control over nonmember banks and made all financial institutions more competitive. The act's four major provisions are the following:

1. *The authority of the Fed over nonmember depository institutions was increased.* Before the Monetary Control Act, less than half the banks in the United States were members of the Fed and subject to its direct control. Under the act's provisions, the Federal Reserve sets uniform reserve requirements for *all* commercial banks, including state and national banks, S&Ls, and credit unions with checking accounts.
2. *All depository institutions are able to borrow loan reserves from Federal Reserve banks.* This practice, called *discounting*, will be explained in the next chapter. Banks also have access to check clearing and other services of the Fed.
3. *The act allows commercial banks, thrifts, money market mutual funds, stock brokerage firms, and retailers to offer a wide variety of banking services.* For example, commercial banks and other financial institutions can pay unrestricted interest rates on checking accounts. Also, S&Ls and other financial institutions can offer checking accounts. Federal credit unions are authorized to make residential real estate loans, and other major corporations can offer traditional banking services.
4. *The act eliminated all interest rate ceilings.* Before this act, S&Ls were allowed to pay depositors a slightly higher interest rate on passbook savings deposits than those paid by commercial banks. The Monetary Control Act removed this advantage of S&Ls over other financial institutions competing for depositors.

Finally, the movement toward deregulation, which blurred the distinctions between financial institutions, continued in 1999 when the *Financial Services Modernization Act* was signed into law. This sweeping measure lifted Depression-era barriers and allows banks, securities firms, and insurance companies to merge and sell each other's products.

YOU'RE THE ECONOMIST   Applicable Concept: Deposit Insurance

The Wreck of Lincoln Savings and Loan

The case of Lincoln Savings and Loan is a classic example of what went wrong during one of the worst financial crises in U.S. history prior to the banking crisis and Great Recession of 2007–2009. In 1984, the Securities and Exchange Commission charged Charles Keating, Jr., with fraud in an Ohio loan scam, but regulators later allowed him to buy Lincoln Savings and Loan in California. Keating hired a staff to carry out his wishes and paid them and his relatives millions. Keating was also generous with politicians in Washington, D.C. Allegedly, five U.S. senators received $1.5 million in campaign contributions from Keating to influence regulators.

Where did Keating's money come from? It came from Lincoln Savings depositors and, ultimately, from taxpayers because the federal government insures deposits of failed S&Ls. When Keating took over Lincoln, it was a healthy S&L with assets of $1.1 billion. But because of deregulation mandated by the Monetary Control Act and other legislation and the lack of enforcement of regulations under the new laws, many S&Ls plunged into high-risk, but potentially highly profitable, ventures. Keating therefore took Lincoln out of sound home mortgage loans and into speculation in Arizona hotels costing $500,000 per room to build, real estate for golf courses, shopping centers, and even junk bonds, and currency futures.

In 1987, after it was already too late, California regulators became alarmed at the way Lincoln operated and asked the FBI and the FSLIC to take over Lincoln. Keating responded by contacting his friends in Washington, and the regulatory process moved at a snail's pace. Years passed before the government finally closed Lincoln and informed the public that their deposits were not safe in this S&L. During the time regulators were deciding what action to take, it is estimated that Lincoln cost taxpayers another $1 billion. Ultimately, the collapse of Lincoln cost U.S. taxpayers about $3 billion, making it the most expensive S&L failure of all.

Keating and other S&L entrepreneurs say they did nothing wrong. After all, Congress and federal regulators encouraged, or did not discourage, S&Ls to compete by borrowing funds at high interest rates and making risky, but potentially highly profitable,

investments. If oil prices and land values fall unexpectedly and loans fail, this is simply the way a market economy works and not the fault of risk-prone wheeler-dealers like Keating.

In 1993, a federal judge sentenced Keating to 12 1/2 years in prison for swindling small investors. The sentence ran concurrently with a 10-year state prison sentence. The judge also ordered Keating to pay $122.4 million in restitution to the government for losses caused by sham property sales. However, the government has been unable to locate any significant assets. Keating served 4 years and 9 months.

ANALYZE THE ISSUE   Critics of federal banking policy argue that deposit insurance is a key reason for banking failures. The banks enjoy a "heads I win, tails the government loses" proposition. Several possible reforms of deposit insurance have been suggested. For example, the limit on insured deposits can be raised, reduced, or eliminated. Do you think a change in deposit insurance would prevent bank failures?

14-5b The Savings and Loan Crisis

In 2013, Cyprus experienced a financial crisis and closed its banks. After the banks re-opened, depositors stood in long lines day after day hoping to be able to withdraw a limited amount from their accounts. Could this happen in the United States? In fact it has happened. Before the Great Recession financial crisis discussed in the chapter on monetary policy, the savings and loan crisis of the 1980s and early 1990s was one of the worst U.S. financial crises since the Great Depression and a classic case of the unintended consequences of legislation. After the Monetary Control Act removed interest rate ceilings on deposits, competition for customers forced S&Ls to pay higher interest rates on short-term deposits. Unlike the banks, however, S&Ls were earning their income from long-term mortgages at fixed interest rates below the rate required to keep or attract new deposits. The resulting losses enticed the S&Ls to forsake home mortgage loans, which they knew best, and seek high-interest, but riskier, commercial and consumer loans. Unfortunately, these risky higher-interest loans resulted in defaults and more losses. If conditions were not bad enough, lower oil prices depressed the oil-based state economies in Texas, Louisiana, and Oklahoma.

The Federal Savings and Loan Insurance Corporation (FSLIC) was the agency that insured deposits in S&Ls, similar to how the FDIC insures bank deposits. The magnitude of the losses exceeded the insurance fund's ability to pay depositors, and Congress placed the FSLIC's deposit-insurance fund under the FDIC's control. To close or sell ailing S&Ls and protect depositors, Congress enacted the Thrift Bailout Bill in 1989. One provision of this act created the Resolution Trust Corporation (RTC) to carry out a massive federal bailout of failed institutions. The RTC bought the assets and deposits of failed S&Ls and sold them to offset the cost borne by taxpayers. The RTC closed in 1995, and the ultimate cost to taxpayers totaled $125 billion!

Key Concepts

Barter

Money

Medium of exchange

Unit of account

Store of value

Commodity money

Fiat money

M1, M2

Currency

Checkable deposits

Federal Reserve System

Board of Governors of the Federal Reserve System

Federal Open Market Committee (FOMC)

Federal Deposit Insurance Corporation (FDIC)

Consumer Financial Protection Bureau (CFPB)

Monetary Control Act

Summary

- **Barter** is the direct exchange of one good or service for another good or service, rather than for money. The problem with barter is that it requires a *coincidence of wants*.

- **Money** can be anything that meets these three tests. Money must serve as (1) a medium of exchange, (2) a unit of account, and (3) a store of value.

Money facilitates more efficient exchange than barter. Other desirable properties of money include scarcity, portability, divisibility, and uniformity.

- **Medium of exchange** is the most important function of money. This means that money is widely accepted in payment for goods and services.

- **Unit of account** is another important function of money. Money is used to measure relative values by serving as a common yardstick for valuing goods and services.

- **Store of value** is the ability of money to hold its value over time. Money is said to be highly *liquid*, which means it is readily usable in exchange.

- **Credit cards** are not money. Credit cards represent a short-term loan and, therefore, fail to satisfy the store of value function of money.

- **Commodity money** is money that has a marketable value, such as gold and silver. Today, the United States uses *fiat money*, which has no intrinsic value and must be accepted by law, but is not convertible into gold, silver, or any commodity.

- **M1** is the narrowest definition of the money supply, which equals currency plus checkable deposits. **Currency** includes coins and paper currency. **Checkable deposits** is the total money in financial institutions that can be withdrawn by writing a check. **M2** is a broader definition of the money supply, which equals M1 plus *near monies*, such as savings deposits and small time deposits.

- The **Federal Reserve System**, our central bank, was established in 1913. The Fed consists of 12 Federal Reserve District Banks with 25 branches. The **Board of Governors** is the Fed's governing body. The **Federal Open Market Committee (FOMC)** directs the buying and selling of U.S. government securities, which is a key method of controlling the money supply.

- **Basic Federal Reserve Bank functions** are (1) controlling the money supply, (2) clearing checks, (3) supervising and regulating banking, (4) maintaining and circulating currency, (5) protecting consumers, (6) maintaining the

federal government's checking accounts and gold, and (7) lender of last resort

Definitions of Money Supply (M1 and M2):

M1 = currency + checkable deposits
M2 = M1 + savings deposits + small time deposits of less than $100,000

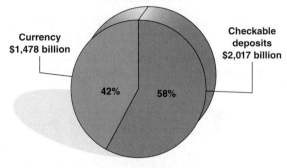

M1 = $3,495 billion

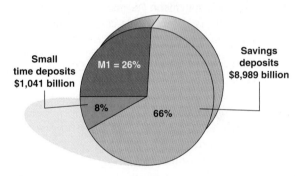

M2 = $13,525 billion

- The **Federal Deposit Insurance Corporation (FDIC)** is a government agency established in 1933 that insures commercial bank deposits up to a limit if a bank fails.

- In 2010, the **Consumer Financial Protection Bureau (CFPB)** was established. This is an independent bureau within the Federal Reserve that helps consumers make financial decisions.

- The **Monetary Control Act of 1980** revolutionized U.S. banking by expanding the authority of the Federal Reserve System to all financial institutions. In addition, this law increased competition by blurring the distinctions between commercial banks, thrift institutions, and even nonfinancial institutions.

Summary of Conclusion Statements

- The use of money simplifies and therefore increases market transactions. Money also prevents wasting time that can be devoted to production, thereby promoting economic growth by increasing a nation's production possibilities.

- Money is a useful mechanism for transforming income in the present into future purchases.

- Money is the most liquid form of wealth because it can be spent directly in the marketplace.

- The supply of money must be great enough to meet ordinary transaction needs, but not be so plentiful that it becomes worthless.

- An item's ability to serve as money does not depend on its own market value or the backing of precious metal.

- M1 is more liquid than M2.

Study Questions and Problems

Please see Appendix A for answers to the odd-numbered questions. Your instructor has access to the answers for even-numbered questions.

1. Discuss this statement: "A man with a million dollars who is lost in the desert learns the meaning of money."

2. Could each of the following items potentially serve as money? Consider each as a medium of exchange, a unit of account, or a store of value.
   a. Visa credit card.
   b. Federal Reserve note.
   c. Debit card
   d. Picasso painting

3. Consider each of the items in Question 2 in terms of scarcity, portability, divisibility, and uniformity.

4. What backs the U.S. dollar? Include the distinction between commodity money and fiat money in your answer.

5. What are the components of the most narrowly defined money supply in the United States?

6. Distinguish between M1 and M2. What are near monies?

7. What is the major purpose of the Federal Reserve System? What is the major responsibility of the Board of Governors and the Federal Open Market Committee?

8. Should the Fed be independent or a government agency subordinate to Congress and the president?

9. Which banks must be insured by the FDIC? Which banks can choose not to be insured by the FDIC?

10. Briefly discuss the importance of the Depository Institutions Deregulation and Monetary Control Act of 1980.

 CHECKPOINT ANSWERS

Are Debit Cards Money?

Debit cards satisfy the medium of exchange function of money because they serve as a means of payment, and debit card statements serve as a unit of account. Finally, unlike credit cards, debit cards serve as a store of value because they are a means of accessing checkable deposits and not an extension of credit. If you said debit cards are money because they serve all three functions required for money, **YOU ARE CORRECT**.

Are Bitcoins Money?

Bitcoins are increasingly becoming accepted as a means of payment around the world. They also serve as a unit of account because the price of various goods and services are denominated in bitcoins. One can also store value or purchasing power in bitcoins. In addition, bitcoins are scarce (after they are "mined" no more bitcoins will be created), portable, divisible, and uniform. If you said bitcoins are money because they serve all three functions required, even though they are not issued by any government, and enjoy the other desirable properties of money, **YOU ARE CORRECT.**

Sample Quiz

Please see Appendix B for answers to Sample Quiz questions.

1. Buying a cup of coffee with a dollar bill represents the use of money as a
   a. medium of exchange.
   b. unit of account.
   c. store of value.
   d. All of the answers are correct.

2. Comparing how many dollars it takes to attend college each year to annual earnings on a job represents the use of money as a
   a. medium of exchange.
   b. unit of account.
   c. store of value.
   d. store of coincidence.

3. Which of the following items does *not* provide a store of value?
   a. Currency
   b. Checkable deposits
   c. Credit cards
   d. All of the answers are correct.

4. Anything can be money if it acts as a
   a. unit of account.
   b. store of value.
   c. medium of exchange.
   d. All of the answers are correct.

5. The ease with which an asset can be converted into a medium of exchange is known as
   a. volatility.
   b. liquidity.
   c. currency.
   d. speculative exchange.

6. Which of the following items is included when computing M1?
   a. Coins in circulation
   b. Currency in circulation
   c. Checking accounting entries
   d. All of the answers are correct.

7. Which of the following statements is *true?*
   a. Money must be relatively "scarce" if it is to have value.
   b. Money must be divisible and portable.
   c. M1 is the narrowest definition of money.
   d. All of the answers are correct.

8. M1 money includes all but which of the following?
   a. Checkable deposits
   b. Savings accounts
   c. Paper money
   d. Coins

9. Which of the following is counted as part of M2?
   a. Currency
   b. Checkable deposits at commercial banks
   c. Money market funds
   d. All of the answers are correct.

10. Which definition of the money supply includes credit cards?
    a. M1
    b. M2
    c. Both answers include credit card balances.
    d. Neither answer includes credit card balances.

11. With respect to controlling the money supply, the law requires the Fed to take orders from
    a. the president.
    b. the Speaker of the House.
    c. the Secretary of the Treasury.
    d. no one—the Fed is an independent agency.

12. Which of the following is *not* part of the Federal Reserve System?
    a. Council of Economic Advisors
    b. Board of Governors
    c. Federal Open Market Committee
    d. 12 Federal Reserve District Banks

13. The Fed's principal decision-making body, which directs buying and selling U.S. government securities, is known as the
    a. Federal Deposit Insurance Corporation.
    b. District Board of Governors.
    c. Federal Open Market Committee.
    d. Reserve Requirement Regulation Conference.

14. The major protection against a sudden mass attempt to withdraw cash from banks is the
    a. Federal Reserve.
    b. Consumer Protection Act.
    c. deposit insurance provided by the FDIC.
    d. gold and silver backing the dollar.

15. The Monetary Control Act of 1980
    a. created less competition among various financial institutions.
    b. allowed fewer institutions to offer checking account services.
    c. restricted savings and loan associations to long-term loans.
    d. did none of these choices.

16. Which of the following is a store of value?
    a. Federal reserve notes
    b. Debit card
    c. Passbook savings deposit
    d. Each of the above answers is a store of value.

17. The difference between M1 and M2 is given by which of the following?
    a. M1 includes currency, coins, gold, and silver, whereas M2 does not contain gold and silver.
    b. M1 is made up of currency and checkable deposits, whereas M2 contains M1 plus savings deposits and small time deposits.
    c. M1 is limited to checkable deposits, whereas M2 contains currency.
    d. M1 includes only currency, whereas M2 contains M1 plus checkable deposits.

18. Which of the following is a desirable property of money?
    a. Scarcity
    b. Portability
    c. Divisibility
    d. All of the answers are correct.

19. The Federal Reserve System was founded in
    a. 1913.
    b. 1929.
    c. 1933.
    d. 1935.

20. The Monetary Control Act of 1980 extended the Fed's authority to
    a. impose required reserve ratios on all depository institutions.
    b. control the discount rate.
    c. control the federal funds rate.
    d. All of the answers are correct.

CHAPTER 15

Money Creation

CHAPTER PREVIEW

It has been said that the most important person in Washington, D.C., is the chair of the Federal Reserve because he or she can influence the money supply and therefore the performance of the economy. This chapter builds on your knowledge of money and the Federal Reserve System gained in the previous chapter. You will discover that the Federal Reserve (the Fed) and the banks work together to determine the money supply. The chapter begins with a brief history of the evolution of banking. Then we examine the mechanics of how banks create money in a simplified system during a normal economy. This remarkable process depends on the ability of banks to amplify checkable deposits by generating a spiral of new loans and, in turn, deposits for new spending in the economy. Finally, the Fed's toolkit swings open, and we discuss the three tools used by the Fed to change the money supply.

A common misconception is that banks (including savings and loans and other depository institutions) accept deposits and make loans, and that's about the end of the story. But there is another very important chapter to tell. Banking transactions expand or contract the money supply. Without minting coins or using the printing presses to make paper money, your local bank and other banks can "create" money; that is, banks can increase the money supply (M1).

The reason people do not understand money creation is that they think the federal government controls the money supply by turning the printing presses on and off. As explained in the previous chapter, this notion is only partly true because money consists largely of bookkeeping entries (checkable deposits). Consequently, writing checks, using an automatic teller machine, and getting a loan affect the size of the checkable deposits component of the money supply.

IN THIS CHAPTER, YOU WILL LEARN TO SOLVE THESE ECONOMICS PUZZLES:

- Exactly how is money created in the economy? That is, how does the money supply increase?

- What are the major tools the Federal Reserve uses to control the supply of money?

- Why is there nothing "federal" about the federal funds rate?

15-1 MONEY CREATION BEGINS

In the Middle Ages, gold was the money of choice in most European nations. One of the problems with gold is that it is a heavy commodity, which makes it difficult to use in transactions or to hide from thieves. The medieval solution was to keep it safely deposited with the people who worked with gold, called *goldsmiths*. This demand for their services inspired goldsmith entrepreneurs to become the founders of modern-day banking.

The goldsmiths sat on their benches with ledgers close by and recorded the amounts of gold placed in their vaults. In fact, the word *bank* is derived from the Italian word for bench, which is *banco*. After assessing the purity of the gold, a goldsmith issued a receipt to the customer for the amount of gold deposited. In return, the goldsmith collected a service charge, just as you pay today for services at your bank. Anyone who possessed the receipt and presented it to the goldsmith could make a withdrawal for the amount of gold written on the receipt.

With these gold receipts in circulation, people began paying their debts with these pieces of paper, rather than actually exchanging gold. Thus, goldsmith receipts became paper money. At first, the goldsmiths were very conservative and issued receipts exactly equal to the amount of gold stored in their vaults. However, some shrewd goldsmiths observed that net withdrawals in any period were only a *fraction* of all the gold "on reserve." This observation produced a powerful idea. Goldsmiths discovered that they could make loans for more gold than they actually held in their vaults. As a result, goldsmiths made extra profit from interest on these loans, and borrowers had more money for spending in their hands.

The medieval goldsmiths were the first to practice fractional reserve banking. Modern **fractional reserve banking** is a system in which banks keep only a percentage of their deposits on reserve as vault cash and deposits at the Fed. In a 100 percent reserve banking system, banks would be unable to create money by making loans. However, as you will learn momentarily, holding less than 100 percent on reserve allows banks to make loans, and in turn, these loans create money in the economy.

Fractional reserve banking
A system in which banks keep only a percentage of their deposits on reserve as vault cash and deposits at the Fed.

15-1a Banker Bookkeeping

We begin our exploration of how the fractional reserve banking system operates in the United States by looking at the balance sheet of a single bank, Typical Bank. A balance sheet is a statement of the assets and liabilities of a bank at a given point in time. Balance sheets are called *T-accounts*. The hypothetical T-account of Typical Bank in Balance Sheet 1 lists only major categories and omits details to keep things simple.

On the right side of the balance sheet are the bank's *liabilities*. Liabilities are the amounts the bank owes to others. In our example, the only liabilities are *checkable deposits*, or demand deposits. Note that checkable deposits are assets on the customers' personal balance sheets, but they are debt obligations of Typical Bank. If a depositor writes a check against his or her checking account, the bank must pay this amount. Therefore, checkable deposits are liabilities to the bank.

On the left side of the balance sheet, we see Typical Bank's *assets*. Assets are amounts the bank owns. In our example, these assets consist of *required reserves, excess reserves*, and *loans*. **Required reserves** are the minimum balance of reserves that the Fed requires a bank to hold in vault cash or on deposit with the Fed. Typical Bank will maximize profits by trying to keep only the minimum amount possible in required reserves.

Required reserves
The minimum balance that the Fed requires a bank to hold in vault cash or on deposit with the Fed.

TYPICAL BANK			
Balance Sheet 1			
Assets		**Liabilities**	
Required reserves	$ 5 million	Checkable deposits	$50 million
Excess reserves	0		
Loans	45 million		
Total	$50 million	Total	$50 million

The Fed requires the bank to keep 10 percent of its checkable deposits in reserves. Holding $5 million in required reserves, the bank has zero excess reserves and $45 million in loans to earn profit.

The required reserve ratio determines the minimum required reserves. The **required reserve ratio** is the *percentage* of deposits that the Fed requires a bank to hold in vault cash or on deposit with the Fed rather than being loaned. Here we assume that the Fed's required reserve ratio is 10 percent. Thus, the bank must have required reserves of $5 million (10 percent of $50 million). This leaves Typical Bank with $45 million in loans that provide profit to the bank.

Exhibit 1 shows that the actual required reserve ratio depends on the level of a bank's checkable deposits. Note that the Fed requires a lower percentage for a smaller bank. In the real world, Typical Bank's required reserve ratio would be 3 percent if its checkable deposits were between $15.5 million and $115.1 million.

Typical Bank has zero excess reserves so far in our analysis. **Excess reserves** are potential loan balances of reserves held in vault cash or on deposit with the Fed in excess of required reserves. We will see shortly that excess reserves play a starring role in the banking system's ability to change the money supply. The relationship between reserves accounts can be expressed as follows:

Required reserve ratio
The percentage of deposits that the Fed requires a bank to hold in vault cash or on deposit with the Fed.

Excess reserves
Potential loan balances held in vault cash or on deposit with the Fed in excess of required reserves.

$$\textbf{Total reserves} = \textbf{required reserves} + \textbf{excess reserves}$$

or

$$\textbf{Excess reserves} = \textbf{total reserves} - \textbf{required reserves}$$

EXHIBIT 1 Required Reserve Ratio of the Federal Reserve	
Type of deposit	**Required reserve ratio**
Checkable deposits	
$15.5–$115.1 million	3%
Over $115.1 million	10

SOURCE: Federal Reserve Bank, *Reserve Requirements*, http://www.federalreserve.gov/monetarypolicy/reservereq.htm.

The final entry on the asset side of Typical Bank's balance sheet is loans, which are interest-earning assets of the bank. Loans are bank assets because they represent outstanding credit payable to the bank. In a fractional reserve banking system, the bank uses balances not held in reserves to earn income. In our example, loan officers have written loans totaling $45 million. Finally, note that Typical Bank's assets equal its liabilities. As you will see momentarily, any change on one side of the T-account must be accompanied by an equal amount of change on the other side of the balance sheet.

15-1b Step One: Accepting a New Deposit

You are now prepared to see how a bank creates money. Assume the required reserve ratio is 10 percent and one of Best National Bank's depositors, Brad Rich, takes $100,000 in cash from under his mattress and deposits it in his checking account. Balance Sheet 2 records this change by increasing the bank's checkable deposits on the liability side by $100,000. Brad's deposit is a liability of the bank because Brad could change his mind and withdraw his money. On the asset side, Brad's deposit increases assets because the bank has an extra $90,000 to lend after setting aside the proper amount of required reserves. Balance Sheet 2 shows that total reserves are divided between required reserves of $10,000 (10 percent of the deposit) and excess reserves of $90,000 (90 percent of the deposit). Thus, the bank's assets and liabilities remain equal when Brad makes his deposit.

Before proceeding, we must pause to make an important point. Depositing coins or paper currency in a bank has no initial effect on the money supply (M1). Recall from the previous chapter that M1 includes currency in circulation. Therefore, the transfer of $100,000 in cash from the mattress to the bank creates no money because M1 already counts this amount. Moreover, the money supply would *not* have increased had Brad Rich's initial $100,000 deposit been a check written on another bank. In this case, an increase in the assets and liabilities of Best National Bank by $100,000 would simply decrease the assets and liabilities of the other bank by $100,000. Recall that M1 also includes checkable deposits.

BEST NATIONAL BANK				
Balance Sheet 2				
Assets		**Liabilities**		**Change in M1**
Required reserves	+$ 10,000	Brad Rich account	+$100,000	0
Excess reserves	+ 90,000			
Total	$100,000	Total	$100,000	

Step 1: Brad Rich deposits $100,000 in cash, which increases checkable deposits. The Fed requires the bank to keep 10 percent of its new deposit in required reserves, so this account is credited with $10,000. The remaining 90 percent is excess reserves of $90,000. There is no effect on the money supply.

| Transferring currency to a bank and moving deposits from one bank to another do not affect the money supply (M1). | **CONCLUSION** |

15-1c Step Two: Making a Loan

So far, M1 has not changed, as shown in Balance Sheet 2, because Brad has simply taken $100,000 in currency and transferred it to a checkable deposit. Stated differently, the public holds the same $100,000 for spending, and only the form has changed from cash to a checkable deposit. In step two, the actual money creation process occurs. The profit motive provides the incentive for bank officials not to let $90,000 from a new deposit sit languishing in excess reserves. Instead, Best National Bank is eager to make loans and earn a profit by charging interest. Suppose, coincidentally, that Connie Jones walks in with a big smile, asking for a $90,000 loan to purchase equipment for her health spa. Connie has a fine credit record, so the bank accepts Connie's note (IOU) agreeing to repay the loan. Then the bank gives Connie a check for $90,000, which she deposits in her account with the bank. This increases the bank's liabilities by $90,000 to $190,000.

As shown in Balance Sheet 3, three entries on the assets side have changed. First, the loan to Connie Jones boosts the loans account to $90,000. Second, the bank must increase required reserves by $9,000 because of the $90,000 increase in checkable deposits on the liabilities side. (Recall that required reserves are 10 percent of checkable deposits.) Required reserves are now $19,000. Third, transferring $9,000 from excess reserves to required reserves reduces the bank's excess reserves from $90,000 to $81,000. Total reserves remain at $100,000 in both Balance Sheet 2 and Balance Sheet 3.

The corresponding entry on the liabilities side of the balance sheet is the bread and butter of money creation. Checkable deposits have increased by $90,000 to $190,000. The reason is that the bank issued a check in Connie's name drawn on a checking account in the bank. Thus, Best National Bank has performed money magic with this transaction. Look what happened to the $100,000 deposited by Brad Rich. It has generated a new $90,000 *loan*, which was added to checkable deposits and therefore increased the money supply by $90,000.

BEST NATIONAL BANK				
Balance Sheet 3				
Assets		**Liabilities**		**Change in M1**
Required reserves	$ 19,000	Brad Rich account	$100,000	
Excess reserves	81,000	Connie Jones account	+90,000	+$90,000
Loans	+90,000			
Total	$190,000	Total	$190,000	

Step 2: The bank loans Connie Jones $90,000 by crediting her checking account with this amount. A corresponding $90,000 balance is added to the loan account. The result is an increase of $90,000 in the money supply.

CONCLUSION	When a bank makes a loan, it creates deposits, and the money supply increases by the amount of the loan because the money supply includes checkable deposits.

Before proceeding further, you need to pause and take particular notice of the impact of these transactions on the money supply. In step one, Brad's initial deposit did not change M1. But in step two, M1 increased by $90,000 when Best National Bank created money out of thin air by making the loan to Connie Jones. Now Connie has more money in her checking account than she did before, and no one else has less. Connie can now use this money to buy goods and services.

15-1d Step Three: Clearing the Loan Check

Now Connie Jones can use her new money to purchase equipment for her spa. Suppose Connie buys equipment for her business from Better Health Spa and writes a check for $90,000 drawn on Best National Bank. The owner of Better Health Spa then deposits the check in the firm's account at Yazoo National Bank. Yazoo National will send the check to its Federal Reserve district bank for collection. Recall that each bank maintains required reserves at the Fed. The Fed clears the check by debiting the reserve account of Best National Bank and crediting the reserve account of Yazoo National Bank. The Fed then returns the check to Best National Bank, and this bank reduces Connie Jones's checking account by $90,000. As shown in Balance Sheet 4, Connie Jones's checking account falls to zero, and Best National Bank's liabilities are reduced by $90,000. On the asset side of the balance sheet, required reserves decrease by $9,000, and excess reserves return to zero. Now that all the dust has settled, Best National Bank has required reserves of $10,000 and an IOU for $90,000. Note that this check-clearing process in step three has no effect on M1. The $90,000 increase in M1 created by Best

BEST NATIONAL BANK				
Balance Sheet 4				
Assets		**Liabilities**		**Change in M1**
Required reserves	$ 10,000	Brad Rich account	$100,000	0
Excess reserves	0	Connie Jones account	0	
Loans	90,000			
Total	$100,000	Total	$100,000	

Step 3: Connie Jones pays Better Health Spa with a $90,000 check drawn on Best National Bank. Better Health Spa deposits the check in Yazoo National Bank, which collects from Best National Bank. The result is a debit to Connie's account and to her bank's reserves accounts.

National Bank's loan to Connie remains on deposit at Yazoo National Bank in Better Health Spa's checking account.

Finally, if Brad Rich withdraws $100,000 in cash from Best National Bank, the process described above operates in reverse. The result is a $90,000 decline (destruction) in the money supply.

15-2 MULTIPLIER EXPANSION OF MONEY BY THE BANKING SYSTEM

The process of money creation (loans) does not stop at the doors of Best National Bank. Just like the spending multiplier from the chapter on fiscal policy, there is a money multiplier process. Let's continue our story by following the effect on Yazoo National after Better Health Spa deposits $90,000 from Connie Jones. As shown in Balance Sheet 5, Yazoo National's checkable deposits increase by $90,000. Given a required reserve ratio of 10 percent, Yazoo National Bank must keep $9,000 in required reserves, and the remaining $81,000 goes into excess reserves.

Yazoo National's loan officer now has $81,000 in additional excess reserves to lend and thus create additional checkable deposits, excess reserves, and eventually loans in other banks. Exhibit 2 presents the expansion of the money supply created when Brad Rich makes his initial $100,000 deposit, and then banks make loans that are deposited in other banks.

In Exhibit 2, we see that, lo and behold, an initial deposit of $100,000 in Best National Bank can eventually create a $900,000 increase in the money supply (M1). This is because Brad Rich's initial $100,000 deposit eventually creates total excess reserves of $900,000 in the banking system as a whole. This was created by new loans and, in turn, new deposits in different banks. As this process continues, each bank accepts smaller and smaller increases in checkable deposits because 10 percent of each deposit is held as required reserves. Note that the initial $100,000 was from cash already counted in M1, and so it is not counted in the expansion of the money supply.

YAZOO NATIONAL BANK			
Balance Sheet 5			
Assets		**Liabilities**	
Required reserves	+$ 9,000	Better Health Spa account	+$90,000
Excess reserves	+ 81,000		
Total	$90,000	Total	$90,000

Given a required reserve ratio of 10 percent, Better Health Spa's deposit of $90,000 from Connie Jones creates $81,000 in additional excess reserves that the bank can lend and thus create additional checkable deposits.

EXHIBIT 2 Expansion of the Money Supply

Round	Bank	Increase in checkable deposits	Increase in required reserves	Increase in excess reserves
1	Best National Bank	$ 100,000	$ 10,000	$ 90,000
2	Yazoo National Bank	90,000	9,000	81,000
3	Bank A	81,000	8,100	72,900
4	Bank B	72,900	7,290	65,610
5	Bank C	65,610	6,561	59,049
6	Bank D	59,049	5,905	53,144
7	Bank E	53,144	5,314	47,830
.	.	.	.	.
.	.	.	.	.
.	.	.	.	.
Total all other banks		478,297	47,830	430,467
Total increase		$1,000,000	$100,000	$900,000 ($\Delta$M1)

NOTE: A $100,000 cash deposit in Best National Bank creates $900,000 in new deposits in other banks. Each round creates excess reserves, which are loaned to a customer who deposits the loan check in another bank in the next round.

15-2a The Money Multiplier

Money multiplier
The maximum change in the money supply (checkable deposits) due to an initial change in the excess reserves banks hold. The money multiplier is equal to 1 divided by the required reserve ratio.

Fortunately, we do not need to calculate all the individual bank transactions listed in Exhibit 2 in order to derive the change in the money supply initiated by a deposit or withdrawal. Instead, we can use the *money multiplier*, or *deposit multiplier*. The **money multiplier** gives the *maximum* change in the money supply (checkable deposits) due to an initial change in the excess reserves held by banks.[1] The money multiplier is equal to 1 divided by the required reserve ratio. Expressed as a formula:

$$\text{Money multiplier (MM)} = \frac{1}{\text{required reserve ratio (RRR)}} = \frac{1}{1/10} = 10$$

The actual change in the money supply is computed by the following formula:

$$\text{Actual money supply change } (\Delta M1) = \text{initial change in excess reserves (ER)} \times \text{money multiplier (MM)}$$

Symbolically, using the data in Exhibit 2,

$$\Delta M1 = \Delta ER \times MM$$
$$\$900,000 = \$90,000 \times 10$$

---

[1]The money multiplier (MM) is the sum of the infinite geometric progression $1 + (1 - r) + (1 - r)^2 + (1 - r)^3 + \ldots + (1 - r)^\infty$, where r equals the required reserve ratio.

15-2b The Real-World Money Multiplier

In reality, for several reasons, the size of the money multiplier can be considerably smaller than our handy little formula indicates. First, Connie Jones, or any other customer along the money creation process, can decide to put a portion of the loan in her pocket, rather than writing a check to Better Health Spa for the full amount of the loan. Money outside the banking system in someone's wallet or purse or underneath the mattress is a cash leakage, which reduces the value of the money multiplier.

Second, the size of the money multiplier falls when banks do not use all their excess reserves to make loans. Perhaps a financial crisis causes many people to lose confidence in the banking system, and they make large deposit account withdrawals. As a result, banks hold their excess reserves. Or some banks can hold excess reserves because they lack enough "worthy" loan applications. This is the situation under the recent credit crunch described in the You're the Economist feature in the next chapter. In short, banks are very cautious to make new loans when they are suffering from holding bad mortgage loans.

> When banks decide to retain excess reserves, the money multiplier will be smaller.

CONCLUSION

15-3 HOW MONETARY POLICY CREATES MONEY

The previous chapter explained that the principal function of the Fed is to control the money supply using three policy tools, or levers. The Fed's use of these tools to influence the economy is more precisely called *monetary policy*. **Monetary policy** is the Federal Reserve's use of open market operations, changes in the discount rate, and changes in the required reserve ratio to change the money supply (M1). Using these three tools, or levers, of monetary policy, the Fed can limit or expand deposit creation by the banks and thereby change the money supply.

Monetary policy
The Federal Reserve's use of open market operations, changes in the discount rate, and changes in the required reserve ratio to change the money supply (M1).

15-3a Open Market Operations

You have seen how decisions of the public—including those of Brad Rich, Connie Jones, and Better Health Spa—worked through the banking system and increased M1. In this section, you will build on this foundation by learning how the Fed can expand or contract the money supply. We begin with the aggregated Balance Sheet 6 of the 12 Federal Reserve Banks of the Federal Reserve System. Total assets of the Fed on August 3, 2017 were $4,512 billion. The majority of these assets ($2,465 billion) were held in U.S. Treasury securities in the form of Treasury bills, Treasury notes, and Treasury bonds. This contrasts with commercial banks, which hold most of their assets in loans. Finally, assets of the Fed include high-grade mortgage-backed securities ($1,769 billion) purchased from banks in order to help stabilize the banking system during the Great Recession. Other assets include Federal Reserve loans to banks.

A major liability of the Fed was $1,563 billion worth of Federal Reserve notes—paper currency. This is in contrast to the major liability of commercial banks, which is checkable deposits. As explained in the previous chapter, the Fed issues, but does not

FEDERAL RESERVE SYSTEM

Balance Sheet 6
August 3, 2017 (billions of dollars)

Assets		Liabilities	
U.S. Treasury securities	$2,465	Federal Reserve notes	$1,563
Mortgagee-backed securities	1,769	Deposits	2,271
Other assets	278	Other liabilities and net worth	678
Total assets	$4,512	Total liabilities and net worth	$4,512

SOURCE: Federal Reserve Board, *Factors Affecting Reserve Balances*, http://www.federalreserve.gov/releases/h41/Current/.

actually print, Federal Reserve notes. Instead, the Fed decides how much to issue and then calls the Bureau of Engraving and Printing to order new batches of $10, $20, $50, and $100 bills, which the Fed sends to the banks in armored trucks.

Another important liability of the Fed is the deposits of banks and the U.S. Treasury totaling $2,271 billion. The Fed therefore serves as a bank for these banks and the Treasury. Note that these bank deposits include the required reserve deposits discussed at the beginning of the chapter. Finally, total liabilities and net worth equaled total assets of $4,512 billion. Details of the balance sheet are omitted for simplicity.

Recall the Federal Open Market Committee (FOMC) introduced in the previous chapter. The FOMC, as its name implies, determines the money supply through *open market operations*. **Open market operations** are the buying and selling of government securities by the Federal Reserve System. The New York Federal Reserve Bank's trading desk executes these orders. Suppose the FOMC (Federal Open Market Committee; remember from the previous chapter this is part of the Fed) decides to increase the money supply and instructs the New York Fed trading desk to *buy* $100,000 worth of 90-day U.S. Treasury bills (called T-bills).[2] The Fed contacts securities dealers in the private sector for competitive bids. Suppose the Fed accepts the lowest bid, buys $100,000 worth of T-bills, and pays the dealer with a check drawn against itself. As shown in Balance Sheet 7, the Fed's assets increase by $100,000 worth of U.S. government IOUs. Once the securities dealer deposits the Fed's check in the firm's account at Best National Bank, the bank will send the $100,000 check back to the Fed. When the Fed receives the check, it will increase Best National's reserves account at the Fed by this amount. The Fed therefore increases its liabilities by $100,000, and M1 increases immediately by $100,000 because the security dealer's checking account increases at Best National Bank. Like a magician waving a magic wand, the Fed has created new money: the initial $100,000 checkable deposit *and* the additional excess reserves that will result from the numerous loans working through the money multiplier process. Given a 10 percent reserve requirement, the money multiplier equals 10. Best National Banks' required

Open market operations
The buying and selling of government securities by the Federal Reserve System.

[2]The U.S. Treasury issues T-bills in minimum denominations of $10,000. These marketable obligations of the federal government mature in three months, six months, or one year and are used to finance the budget deficit, as explained in the chapter entitled "Federal Deficits, Surpluses, and the National Debt." The Treasury sells three-month bills at weekly auctions and six-month and one-year bills less often.

reserves increase by $10,000, and its excess reserves increase by $90,000. Therefore, the money supply will potentially increase by $1 million (the $100,000 initial increase in M1 when the Fed buys the security, *plus* the change in excess reserves multiplied by the money multiplier of 10). Note that unlike the example shown previously in Exhibit 2 involving an initial $100,000 cash deposit already counted in M1, here the initial deposit was created by the Fed and therefore not already counted in M1. Expressed as a formula:

Actual money supply change = **initial checkable deposit (CD)**
+ (**initial change in excess reserves**
× **money multiplier**)
$$\Delta M1 = \Delta CD + (\Delta ER \times MM)$$
$$\$1,000,000 = \$100,000 + (\$90,000 \times 10)$$

The process goes into reverse if the FOMC directs the New York Fed trading desk to *sell* U.S. government securities for the Fed's portfolio. As shown in Balance Sheet 8, the goal of the Fed is to decrease the money supply by selling, say, $100,000 in Treasury bonds from the asset side of its balance sheet. In this case, the Fed accepts the best offer from a securities dealer. Again, assume the securities dealer's $100,000 check payable to the Fed is written on the firm's account with Best National Bank. When the Fed accepts the check, it reduces the reserves recorded on the liabilities side of Balance Sheet 8, and Best National Bank reduces the checkable deposits account of the securities dealer. By subtracting $100,000 from Best National Bank's reserves, the Fed decreases M1 initially by $100,000. Again, the Fed has waved its magic wand and extinguished money in the banking system. Given a 10 percent reserve requirement, the money supply can potentially fall by $1 million (the $100,000 initial decrease in M1 when the Fed sells the security *plus* the change in excess reserves multiplied by the money multiplier of 10).

Another way to study open market operations is to look at a typical day at the trading desk located at the Federal Reserve Bank of New York. The manager of the trading desk starts the day by studying estimates of excess reserves in the banking system. If excess reserves are low, few banks have funds to lend. High excess reserves mean many banks can make loans. After collecting this information and other data, the manager looks at the directive from the FOMC and formulates the day's "game plan." Then the manager makes conference calls to several members of the FOMC for approval. With

FEDERAL RESERVE BANK		
Balance Sheet 7		
Assets	**Liabilities**	**Initial change in M1**
U.S. government securities +$100,000	Reserves of Best National Bank +$100,000	+$100,000

To increase the money supply, the Fed conducted open market operations by purchasing $100,000 in government securities. The Fed pays a securities dealer with a Fed check, which the dealer deposits in its bank. The initial change in the money supply is an increase of $100,000.

FEDERAL RESERVE BANK		
Balance Sheet 8		
Assets	**Liabilities**	**Initial change in M1**
U.S. government securities −$100,000	Reserves of Best National Bank −$100,000	−$100,000

To decrease the money supply, the Fed conducted open market operations by selling $100,000 in government securities. The Fed accepts a securities dealer's check drawn on the dealer's bank. The initial change in the money supply is a decrease of $100,000.

their blessing, the manager has traders in the trading room call dealers who trade in government securities for price quotations. The open market operation has two alternative objectives: purchase or sell government securities.

CONCLUSION A purchase of government securities by the Fed injects reserves into the banking system and increases the money supply. A sale of government securities by the Fed reduces reserves in the banking system and decreases the money supply.

Exhibit 3 illustrates the Federal Reserve's open market operations.

CHECKPOINT

Who Has More Dollar Creation Power?
You find a $1,000 bill hidden beneath the floorboards in your house and decide to deposit it in your checking account. On the same day, the Fed decides to buy $1,000 in government securities from your bank. Assuming a 10 percent reserve requirement, which of these actions creates more money in the economy?

15-3b The Discount Rate

So far, money creation in the banking system depends on excess reserves acquired from new checkable deposits. Actually, the Fed itself provides another option for banks to obtain reserves through its *discount window*. This is a department within each of the Federal Reserve District Banks and not an actual window. Suppose Best National Bank has no excess reserves and Brad Rich does not walk in with a deposit. Also assume the Fed does not purchase government securities and pay a dealer with a check deposited in Best National Bank. Now enter Connie Jones, who asks for a loan. In this situation, the bank has no money to lend, but it can borrow reserves from the Fed for a short period and pay the *discount rate*. The **discount rate** is the interest rate the Fed charges on loans of reserves to banks. All banks and other depository institutions have the privilege of occasionally borrowing at the Fed to cover reserve deficiencies. Changes in the discount rate often signal the Fed's monetary policy direction and therefore can affect the public's

Discount rate
The interest rate the Fed charges on loans of reserves to banks.

EXHIBIT 3 Open Market Operations

When the Fed buys government securities from dealers, it increases the reserves of the banks. Banks can use these reserves to make loans, which operate through the money multiplier to expand the money supply. When the Fed sells government securities to dealers, it decreases the reserves of the banks. Thus, the banks' capacity to lend diminishes, and as a consequence, the money supply decreases.

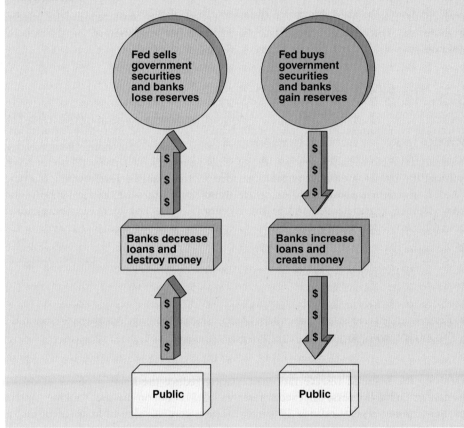

expectations about the economy. A lower discount rate encourages banks to borrow reserves and make loans. A higher discount rate discourages banks from borrowing reserves and making loans.

If the Fed wants to expand the money supply, it reduces the discount rate. If the objective is to contract the money supply, the Fed raises the discount rate.

CONCLUSION

Banks wanting to expand their reserves in order to seek profitable loan opportunities can also turn to the federal funds market. The **federal funds market** is a private market in which banks lend reserves to each other for less than 24 hours. The word *federal*

Federal funds market
A private market in which banks lend reserves to each other for less than 24 hours.

does not mean it is a government market. It simply means this is an economy-wide or national market. In this market, a bank short of reserves can borrow some reserves from another bank. Using the interbank loan market, Best National Bank can borrow excess reserves from Yazoo National and pay the federal funds rate. The **federal funds rate** is the interest rate banks charge for overnight loans of reserves to other banks. Reserves borrowed in the federal funds market have no effect on the money supply because such borrowing simply moves reserves from one bank to another. Note that most banks borrow money to meet their reserve requirements primarily through the federal funds market and not the discount window. Also, the federal funds rate is a primary barometer of Fed policy reported in the media. The following You're the Economist provides further explanation of the federal funds rate.

Federal funds rate
The interest rate banks charge for overnight loans of reserves to other banks.

15-3c The Required Reserve Ratio

Under the Monetary Control Act of 1980, discussed in the preceding chapter, the Fed can set reserve requirements by law for all banks, savings and loan associations, and credit unions. By changing the required reserve ratio, the Fed can change banks' excess reserves and, therefore, banks' lending ability. This is potentially a powerful policy lever. Recall that the money multiplier equals 1 divided by the required reserve ratio. Suppose the Fed is concerned about inflation, so it wants to restrain the money supply and thereby dampen aggregate demand in the economy. If the Fed increases the required reserve ratio, the effect is to reduce excess reserves *and* generate a smaller change in the money supply because the money supply multiplier is smaller. For example, a required reserve ratio of 10 percent yields a money multiplier of 10 (1/0.10). If the Fed increases the ratio to 20 percent, the money multiplier falls to 5 (1/0.20).

CONCLUSION
There is an inverse relationship between the size of the required reserve ratio and the money multiplier.

Raising the required reserve ratio can sharply reduce the lending power of banks. Consider an initial increase in excess reserves of $10 billion in the banking system when the required reserve ratio is 10 percent. The potential value of loans (deposits) is $100 billion ($10 billion of excess reserves × 10). Now assume the Fed raises the required reserve ratio to 20 percent. The potential value of loans (deposits) falls to $50 billion ($10 billion of excess reserves × 5).

CONCLUSION
If the Fed wants to increase the money supply, it decreases the required reserve ratio. If the objective is to decrease the money supply, the Fed increases the required reserve ratio. In reality, changing the required reserve ratio is considered a heavy-handed approach that is an infrequently used tool of monetary policy.

The Fed used all three of its monetary policy tools to increase the money supply and battle the 1990–1991 recession. In the fall of 1990, the Fed recognized the economy was slipping into a recession, so it purchased federal government securities to inject new reserves into the banking system. The discount rate was lowered eight times between the end of 1990 and early 1992. In early 1992, the reserve requirement on demand deposits was also lowered from 12 percent to 10 percent. In 2002, the Fed responded to the 2001 recession by using open market purchases of securities to increase the money supply, and it decreased the discount rate numerous times. These responses by the Fed eased the negative effects of the terrorist attacks and the recession.

During the Great Recession of 2007–2009, the Fed again followed expansionary monetary policy and used open market purchases to sharply increase the money supply and decrease interest rates by dropping the federal funds rate to a historic low of about zero percent. Moreover, the Fed reduced its reserve requirement and dramatically expanded its scope in response to the loss in confidence among lenders and panic sweeping financial markets that resulted in the flow of credit falling sharply. Using Depression-era emergency powers, the Fed took the radical step of becoming a "lender of last resort" source of short-term loans for a wide range of institutions other than banks. For example, the Fed provided funds to bail out Fannie Mae (the Federal National Mortgage Association) and Freddie Mac (the Federal Home Mortgage Corporation), which backed about half of the nation's mortgage loans, and the Fed provided loans for AIG, the huge insurance firm, because it was simply too large to fail. For more details on monetary policy, read the You're the Economist titled "How Does the FOMC Really Work?"

Exhibit 4 presents a summary of the impact of monetary policy tools.

What Could the Fed Do to Reduce Unemployment?

Suppose we are in a recession. Unemployment is high, and the economy is growing below the desired 3 to 3.5 percent growth rate. How could the Fed utilize its monetary policy tools to stimulate the economy and put the country back to work?

CHECKPOINT

EXHIBIT 4 The Effect of Monetary Policy Tools on the Money Supply

Type of monetary policy	Monetary policy action	Mechanism	Change in the money supply
Expansionary	Open market operations purchase	Reserves increase	Increases
Contractionary	Open market operations sale	Reserves decrease	Decreases
Expansionary	Discount rate decreases	Borrowing reserves becomes cheaper	Increases
Contractionary	Discount rate increases	Borrowing reserves becomes costlier	Decreases
Expansionary	Required reserve ratio decreases	Money multiplier increases	Increases
Contractionary	Required reserve ratio increases	Money multiplier decreases	Decreases

YOU'RE THE ECONOMIST

Applicable Concept: Monetary Policy

How Does the FOMC Really Work?

The Federal Open Market Committee (FOMC), which is the Fed's most powerful monetary policy-making group, and meets eight times a year at the Federal Reserve in Washington, D.C. Often it seems that the whole world is watching for the results. Before the meeting, board members are given three books prepared by the Fed's staff. The "Green Book" forecasts aggregate demand and various prices based on a variety of equations and the assumptions that monetary policy does or does not change. The "Blue Book" might discuss as many as three monetary policy options, the rationale for each option, and the impact of each option on the economy. There is also a "Beige Book," published eight times per year, that gathers anecdotal information on current economic conditions obtained from interviews with key businesspersons, economists, bankers, and other sources.

Federal Reserve/Alamy Stock Photo

The meeting begins at precisely 9 a.m. with a discussion of foreign currency operations and domestic open market operations illustrated with colorful graphics. Next, the staff presents their analysis of recent developments and forecasts for the economy laid out in the Green Book. Then each board member around the impressive 27-foot oval mahogany table expresses his or her views about the analyses, except for the chair, who may choose not to participate in this round. Now it's coffee time and everyone relaxes beneath a 23-foot ceiling with a 1,000-pound chandelier.

After the coffee break, the staff discusses each policy option from the "Blue Book" without recommending a particular option. Generally, three options are presented.

15-4 MONETARY POLICY SHORTCOMINGS

Monetary policy, like fiscal policy, has its limitations. The Fed's control over the money supply is imperfect for the following reasons.

15-4a Money Multiplier Inaccuracy

If the Fed is to manage the money supply, it must know the size of the money multiplier so that it can forecast the change in the money supply resulting from a change in excess reserves. The value of the money multiplier, however, can be uncertain and subject to decisions independent of the Fed. As explained earlier in the chapter, the public's decision to hold cash and the willingness of banks to make loans affect the total expansion or contraction of the money supply from an initial change in excess reserves. These decisions vary with conditions of prosperity and recession. When the business cycle is in an upturn, banks are very willing to use their excess reserves for making loans, and the money multiplier becomes larger and, therefore, any additional loans increase the money supply rather dramatically. During a downturn, bankers are less willing to use their excess reserves for making loans, the money multiplier becomes smaller and the money supply tends to contract.

Option A is always a decline in interest rates, Option B is always no change in interest rates, and Option C is always an increase. After the staff presentation, board members politely discuss the policy options, but with an important difference. In this policy round, the chair goes first. He or she leads the discussion and advocates a policy decision. After other board members express their views, the chair summarizes the consensus and reads a draft of the Directive to be voted on. The Directive gives instructions to the Fed's staff on how to conduct open market operations until the next FOMC meeting. For example, the New York Fed's trading desk may be instructed to increase the money supply in the range of 1 to 5 percent and lower interest rates by buying 90-day U.S. Treasury bills. After discussion, board members vote on the Directive, with the chair voting first and the decision going to the majority. The chair is always expected to be on the winning side. The Directive is sent to the New York Fed's trading desk, and soon about four dozen bond dealers receive the Fed's call. If there is a change in policy, it will be announced at 2:15 that afternoon.

The Fed communicates its changes in monetary policy by announcing changes in its targets for the federal funds rate. Recall that the Fed does not set this interest rate, but it can influence the rate through open market operations. If the Fed buys bonds, the supply of excess reserves in the banking system increases, and the rate falls. If the Fed sells bonds, the supply of excess reserves in the banking system decreases, and

the rate increases. As a result, interest rates in general are influenced. The next chapter explains in more detail the link between changes in the interest rate and changes in other key macro measures. Between 2001 and 2003, for example, the Fed cut the federal funds rate target 13 times to support economic recovery. Then from 2004 to 2006, the Fed became concerned about inflation and increased the federal funds rate 17 times. When measuring inflation, the Fed pays closest attention to the core CPI—the CPI excluding food and fuel because it is less volatile than the total CPI inflation rate. In 2007, the Fed changed its focus again because it became concerned that a housing slump and credit crunch would slow the economy, and it cut this key rate for the first time in four years. Beginning in 2008, the Fed followed a policy called "quantitative easing (QE)" that used a sharp rise in purchases of Treasury and mortgage-backed securities to continuously increase the money supply and lower interest rates. In fact, the Fed continued cutting the federal funds rate until it reached a record low of almost zero in 2011. The annual rate for 2016 was also close to zero at about 0.4 percent.

ANALYZE THE ISSUE   **What happened at the last FOMC meeting? Visit** http://www.federalreserve.gov/fomc/default.htm.

15-4b Which Money Definition Should the Fed Control?

As discussed in the previous chapter, there are different definitions of the money supply. What if the Fed masterfully controls M1, but the public transfers more of its deposits to M2? For example, banks can pay higher interest and attract more customers to invest in certificates of deposit. Consequently, the Fed might respond by focusing on M2 instead of M1. In fact, in recent years, the Fed has focused more on M2 than M1 because M2 more closely correlates with changes in GDP.

15-4c Lags in Monetary Policy versus Fiscal Policy

Fiscal policy does not happen instantaneously, and neither does monetary policy. Like fiscal policy, monetary policy is subject to time lags. First, an *inside lag* exists between the time a policy change is needed and the time the Fed identifies the problem and decides which policy tool to use. The inside lag is fairly short because financial data are available daily, data on inflation and unemployment monthly, and data on real GDP within three months. When the Fed has the data, it can quickly decide which policy changes are needed and make appropriate adjustments. The inside lag for monetary policy is shorter than for fiscal policy because fiscal policy is usually the result of a long political budget process.

Second, there is an *outside lag* between the time a policy decision is made and the time the policy change has its effect on the economy. This lag refers to the length of time it takes the money multiplier and the spending multiplier to have its full effect on aggregate demand and, in turn, employment, the price level, and real GDP.

Now it's time to answer an important question: Who is the hare and who is the tortoise in the race to the finish line of stabilizing the economy? In the popular version of this story, the hare is much faster, but goofs off along the way and eventually loses to the tortoise at the finish line. In our economics story, however, the Fed is the hare and wins easily over fiscal policy (the tortoise). Although computer model estimates differ widely, the total lag (inside plus outside lags) for monetary policy can be 3 to 12 months. In contrast, the total lag for fiscal policy is not less than a year, and a total lag of 3 years is quite possible.

Key Concepts

Fractional reserve banking

Required reserves

Required reserve ratio

Excess reserves

Money multiplier

Monetary policy

Open market operations

Discount rate

Federal funds market

Federal funds rate

Summary

- **Fractional reserve banking**, the basis of banking today, originated with the goldsmiths in the Middle Ages. Because depository institutions (banks) are not required to keep all their deposits in vault cash or with the Federal Reserve, banks create money by making loans.

- **Required reserves** are the minimum balance that the Fed requires a bank to hold in vault cash or on deposit with the Fed. The percentage of deposits that must be held as required reserves is called the **required reserve ratio**.

- **Excess reserves** exist when a bank has more reserves than required. Excess reserves allow a bank to create money by exchanging loans for deposits. The money supply is reduced when excess reserves are reduced and loans are repaid.

- The **money multiplier** is used to calculate the maximum change (positive or negative) in

checkable deposits (money supply) due to a change in excess reserves. As a formula:

$$\text{Money multiplier} = \frac{1}{\text{required reserve ratio}}$$

The actual change in the money supply is computed as

Money multiplier
× initial change in excess reserves =
money supply change

- **Monetary policy** is action taken by the Fed to change the money supply. The Fed uses three basic tools: open market operations, changes in the discount rate, and changes in the required reserve ratio.

- **Open market operations** are the buying and selling of government securities by the Fed through its trading desk at the New York

Federal Reserve Bank. *Buying government securities* creates extra bank reserves and loans, thereby *expanding* the money supply. *Selling government securities* reduces bank reserves and loans, thereby *contracting* the money supply.

- Changes in the **discount rate** occur when the Fed changes the rate of interest it charges on loans of reserves to banks. Lowering the discount rate makes it easier for banks to borrow reserves from the Fed and expands the money supply. Raising the discount rate discourages banks from borrowing reserves from the Fed and contracts the money supply.

- Banks wanting to expand their reserves in order to seek profitable loan opportunities can also turn to the federal funds market. The **federal funds market** is a private market in which banks lend reserves to each other for less than 24 hours. The **federal funds rate** is the interest rate banks charge for overnight loans of reserves to other banks. Reserves borrowed in the federal funds market have no effect on the money supply.

- Changes in the **required reserve ratio** and the size of the money multiplier are *inversely* related. Thus, if the Fed decreases the required reserve ratio, the money multiplier and money supply increase.

If the Fed increases the required reserve ratio, the money multiplier and money supply decrease.

Open Market Operations

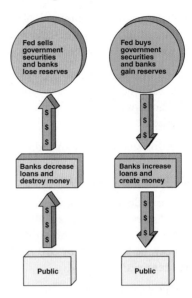

- *Monetary policy limitations* include the following: The size or value of the money multiplier can vary; the Fed might control M1, but the public can shift funds to the M2 money supply definition; time lags occur.

Summary of Conclusion Statements

- Transferring currency to a bank and moving deposits from one bank to another do not affect the money supply (M1).

- When a bank makes a loan, it creates deposits, and the money supply increases by the amount of the loan because the money supply includes checkable deposits.

- When banks decide to retain excess reserves, the money multiplier will be smaller.

- A purchase of government securities by the Fed injects reserves into the banking system and increases the money supply. A sale of government securities by the Fed reduces reserves in the banking system and decreases the money supply.

- If the Fed wants to expand the money supply, it reduces the discount rate. If the objective is to contract the money supply, the Fed raises the discount rate.

- There is an inverse relationship between the size of the required reserve ratio and the money multiplier.

- If the Fed wants to increase the money supply, it decreases the required reserve ratio. If the objective is to decrease the money supply, the Fed increases the required reserve ratio. In reality, changing the required reserve ratio is considered a heavy-handed approach, so it is an infrequently used tool of monetary policy.

Study Questions and Problems

Please see Appendix A for answers to the odd-numbered questions. Your instructor has access to the answers for even-numbered questions.

1. Relate Shakespeare's admonition "Neither a borrower nor a lender be" to the goldsmiths' evolutionary use of fractional reserve banking.

2. If you deposit a $20 bill into a checking account and your bank has a 10 percent reserve requirement, by how much will the bank's excess reserves rise?

3. Consider this statement: "Banks do not create money because this is the Fed's responsibility." Do you agree or disagree? Explain.

4. In what form does a bank hold its required reserves? Assume the Fed has a 20 percent required reserve ratio. What amount of checkable deposits can be supported by $10 million in required reserves?

5. Suppose you deposit your paycheck drawn on another bank. Explain the impact on the money supply.

6. Suppose you remove $1,000 from under your mattress and deposit it in First National Bank. Using a balance sheet, show the impact of your deposit on the bank's assets and liabilities. If the required reserve ratio is 10 percent, what is the maximum amount the bank can loan from this deposit?

7. Suppose it is the holiday season and you withdraw $1,000 from your account at First National Bank to purchase presents. Using a balance sheet, show the impact on this bank's assets and liabilities. If the required reserve ratio is 20 percent, what is the impact on the bank's loans?

8. Suppose the Federal Reserve's trading desk buys $500,000 in T-bills from a securities dealer who then deposits the Fed's check in Best National Bank. Use a balance sheet to show the impact on the bank's loans. Consider the money multiplier and assume the required reserve ratio is 10 percent. What is the maximum increase in the money supply that can result from this open market transaction?

9. Assume the required reserve ratio is 10 percent and a bank's excess reserves are $50 million. Explain why checkable deposits resulting from new loans based on excess reserves are not likely to generate the maximum of $500 million.

10. Briefly describe the effect on the money supply of the following monetary policies:
    a. The Fed purchases $20 million worth of U.S. Treasury bonds.
    b. The Fed increases the discount rate.
    c. The Fed decreases the discount rate.
    d. The Fed sells $40 million worth of U.S. T-bills.
    e. The Fed decreases the required reserve ratio.

11. What are some problems faced by the Fed in controlling the money supply?

 CHECKPOINT ANSWERS

Who Has More Dollar Creation Power?

Your action adds $1,000 to your bank's liabilities. Also, assets in the form of required reserves increase by $100 (0.10 × $1,000). This means excess reserves increase by $900, allowing the bank to make this amount of new loans. When the Fed buys $1,000 in government securities, the bank again receives $1,000 in reserves. But the Fed's transaction does not change the bank's liabilities; therefore, the full $1,000 can go into loans. Comparing the effect on the total money supply, the money multiplier effect shows a $9,000 addition to the money supply from your action and a $10,000 addition from the Fed's action. If you said the Fed's action creates more money, **YOU ARE CORRECT**.

What Could the Fed Do to Reduce Unemployment?

A high rate of unemployment and slow growth rate means that aggregate demand (total spending) is too low to provide for full employment. The Fed needs to push interest rates down to stimulate borrowing and spending. To reduce interest rates the Fed will need to increase the money supply. If you said the Fed could buy U.S. government securities, reduce the discount rate, and/or decrease the required reserve ratio to reduce unemployment, **YOU ARE CORRECT**.

Sample Quiz

Please see Appendix B for answers to Sample Quiz questions.

1. European banks began with which of the following?
   a. Monarchs were the first bankers, lending out cash to help the poor learn a craft.
   b. Churches were the first bankers, lending out cash to help the poor learn a craft.
   c. Goldsmiths were the first bankers, and the paper receipts they issued for gold held on deposit became valued as money.
   d. Fishermen were the first bankers, and the paper receipts they issued for fish they stored in the hulls of their ships became valued as money.

2. Which of the following does *not* appear on the asset side of a bank's balance sheet?
   a. Required reserves
   b. Checkable deposits
   c. Loans
   d. Excess reserves

3. Which of the following is *not* an interest bearing asset of commercial banks?
   a. Required reserves
   b. Securities
   c. Loans
   d. All of the above are interest bearing assets of commercial banks.

4. Banks would be expected to minimize holding excess reserves because this practice is
   a. illegal.
   b. not profitable.
   c. technically difficult.
   d. subject to a stiff excess reserves tax.

5. Which of the following appears on the asset side of a bank's balance sheet?
   a. Excess reserves
   b. Loans
   c. Required reserves
   d. None of the above answers are correct.
   e. All of the above answers are correct.

6. Assume a simplified banking system in which all banks are subject to a uniform reserve requirement of 20 percent and checkable deposits are the only form of money. A bank that received a new checkable deposit of $10,000 would be able to extend new loans up to a maximum of
   a. $2,000.
   b. $8,000.
   c. $9,000.
   d. $10,000.

7. If the required reserve ratio is a uniform 25 percent on all deposits, the money multiplier will be
   a. 4.00.
   b. 2.50.
   c. 0.40.
   d. 0.25.

8. Assume a simplified banking system subject to a 20 percent required reserve ratio. If there is an initial increase in excess reserves of $100,000, the money supply
   a. increases $100,000.
   b. increases $500,000.
   c. increases $600,000.
   d. decreases $500,000.

9. If the required reserve ratio decreases, the
   a. money multiplier increases.
   b. money multiplier decreases.

c. amount of excess reserves the bank has decreases.

d. money multiplier stays the same.

10. Decisions regarding purchases and sales of government securities by the Fed are made by the
    a. Federal Deposit Insurance Commission (FDIC).
    b. Discount Committee (DC).
    c. Federal Open Market Committee (FOMC).
    d. Federal Funds Committee (FFC).

11. The cost to a member bank of borrowing from the Federal Reserve is the
    a. reserve requirement.
    b. price of securities in the open market.
    c. discount rate.
    d. yield on government bonds.

12. Which of the following policy actions by the Fed would cause the money supply to decrease?
    a. An open market purchase of government securities
    b. A decrease in required reserve ratios
    c. An increase in the discount rate
    d. A decrease in the discount rate

13. The rate of interest charged by the Federal Reserve to member banks for reserves borrowed from the Fed is the
    a. federal funds rate.
    b. discount rate.
    c. repurchase rate.
    d. Q ceiling rate.

14. Which of the following actions by the Fed would increase the money supply?
    a. Reducing the required reserve ratio
    b. Selling government bonds in the open market
    c. Increasing the discount rate
    d. None of the above answers are correct.

EXHIBIT 5 Lower Walloon National Bank

Assets		Liabilities	
Reserves	$10,000	Checkable deposits	$10,000

15. In Exhibit 5 if the required reserve ratio is 20 percent for all banks and every bank in the banking system loans out all of its excess reserves, then a $10,000 deposit from Mr. Brown in checkable deposits could create for the entire banking system

a. $8,000 worth of new money.
b. $2,000 worth of new money.
c. $10,000 worth of new money.
d. $40,000 worth of new money.

16. The required reserve ratio for a bank is set by
    a. Congress.
    b. the bank itself.
    c. the Treasury Department.
    d. the banking system.
    e. the Federal Reserve.

17. Assume we have a simplified banking system in balance-sheet equilibrium. Also assume that all banks are subject to a uniform 10 percent reserve requirement and demand deposits are the only form of money. A commercial bank receiving a new demand deposit of $100 would be able to extend new loans in the amount of
    a. $10.
    b. $90.
    c. $100.
    d. $1,000.

18. A bank faces a required reserve ratio of 5 percent. If the bank has $200 million of checkable deposits and $15 million of total reserves, then how large are the bank's excess reserves?
    a. $0
    b. $5 million
    c. $10 million
    d. $15 million

19. A bank currently has checkable deposits of $100,000, reserves of $30,000, and loans of $70,000. If the required reserve ratio is lowered from 20 percent to 15 percent, this bank can increase its loans by
    a. $10,000.
    b. $15,000.
    c. $75,000.
    d. $5,000.
    e. $0.

20. When the Fed purchases government securities, it
    a. increases banks' reserves and makes possible an increase in the money supply.
    b. decreases banks' reserves and makes possible a decrease in the money supply.
    c. automatically raises the discount rate.
    d. uses discounting operations to influence margin requirements.
    e. has no effect on either the money supply or the discount rate.

CHAPTER 16

Monetary Policy

CHAPTER PREVIEW

Vladimir Lenin, the first communist leader of the Soviet Union, once said the best way to destroy a nation is to destroy its money. Adolf Hitler had the same idea. During World War II, he planned to counterfeit British currency and drop it from planes flying over England. Both cases illustrate that the amount of money in circulation matters. A sudden increase in the quantity of money can render a nation's money valueless. As a consequence, people must resort to barter and waste time making direct exchanges of goods and services, rather than being productive.

The previous two chapters provided the prerequisites for understanding the market for money. You have learned two definitions for the money supply, how the banking system creates money, and how the Fed can control the money supply. Here you will begin by studying the demand for and the supply of money and how they interact to determine the rate of interest.

Then we add to this story by linking changes in the money supply to the aggregate demand and aggregate supply model. Using this tool of analysis, you will understand how changes in the demand for money affect interest rates and, in turn, real GDP, employment, and prices.

The first half of this chapter explores how Keynesian economists view the relationship between monetary policy and the economy. The second half of the chapter presents the opposing view of the monetarists. This debate is a clash between two radically different perspectives over the channels through which monetary policy influences the economy. This ideologically charged confrontation is important to the United States' future and is still far from resolved. The chapter concludes with two You're the Economist features that allow you to analyze the Keynesian and monetarist views applied to the Great Recession and the Great Depression.

IN THIS CHAPTER, YOU WILL LEARN TO SOLVE THESE ECONOMICS PUZZLES:

- Why do people want to hold money balances?

- What is a monetary policy transmission mechanism?

- Why would a Nobel laureate economist suggest replacing the Federal Reserve with an intelligent horse?

16-1 HOW ARE INTEREST RATES DETERMINED?

16-1a The Demand for Money

Why do people hold (demand) currency and checkable deposits (M1), rather than put their money to work in stocks, bonds, real estate, or other nonmoney forms of wealth? Because money yields no direct return, people (including businesses) who hold cash or checking account balances incur an *opportunity cost* of forgone interest or profits on the amount of money held. So what are the benefits of holding money? Why would people hold money and thereby forgo earning interest payments? There are three important motives for doing so: transactions demand, precautionary demand, and speculative demand.

Transactions Demand for Money

Transactions demand for money
The stock of money people hold to pay everyday predictable expenses.

The first motive to hold money is the transactions demand. The **transactions demand for money** is the stock of money people hold to pay everyday predictable expenses. The desire to have "walking around money" to make quick and easy purchases is the principal reason for holding money. Students, for example, have a good idea of how much money they will spend on rent, groceries, utilities, gasoline, and other routine purchases. A business can also predict its payroll, utility bills, supply bills, and other routine expenses. Without enough cash, the public must suffer forgone interest and possibly withdrawal penalties as a result of converting their stocks, bonds, or certificates of deposit into currency or checkable deposits in order to make transactions.

Precautionary Demand for Money

Precautionary demand for money
The stock of money people hold to pay unpredictable expenses.

In addition to holding money for ordinary expected purchases, people have a second motive to hold money, called the precautionary demand. The **precautionary demand for money** is the stock of money people hold to pay unpredictable expenses. This is the "mattress money" people hold to guard against those proverbial rainy days. For example, your car might break down, or your income may drop unexpectedly. Similarly, a business might experience unexpected repair expenses or lower-than-anticipated cash receipts from sales. Because of unforeseen events that could prevent people from paying their bills on time, people hold precautionary balances. This affords the peace of mind that unexpected payments can be made without having to cash in interest-bearing financial assets or to borrow.

Speculative Demand for Money

Speculative demand for money
The stock of money people hold to take advantage of expected future changes in the price of bonds, stocks, or other nonmoney financial assets.

The third motive for holding money is the speculative demand. The **speculative demand for money** is the stock of money people hold to take advantage of expected future changes in the price of bonds, stocks, or other nonmoney financial assets. In addition to the transactions and precautionary motives, individuals and businesses demand "betting money" to speculate, or guess, whether the prices of alternative assets will rise or fall. This desire to take advantage of profit-making opportunities when the prices of nonmoney assets fall is the driving force behind the speculative demand. When the interest rate is high, people buy, say, Microsoft 30-year bonds because the opportunity cost of holding money is the high forgone interest earned on these nonmoney assets. When the interest rate is low, people hold more money because there is less opportunity cost in forgone interest earned on investing in bonds. Suppose the interest rate on Microsoft

30-year bonds is low. If so, people decide to hold more of their money in the bank and *speculate* that soon the interest rate will climb higher.

> As the interest rate falls, the opportunity cost of holding money falls, and people increase their speculative balances.

CONCLUSION

The Demand for Money Curve

The three motives for holding money combine to create a **demand for money curve**, which represents the quantity of money people hold at different possible interest rates, ceteris paribus. As shown in Exhibit 1, people increase their money balances when interest rates fall. The reason is that many people move their money out of, for example, money market mutual funds and into checkable deposits (M1).

Demand for money curve
A curve representing the quantity of money that people hold at different possible interest rates, ceteris paribus.

> There is an inverse relationship between the quantity of money demanded and the interest rate.

CONCLUSION

What determines the shape of the demand for money curve? Let's start with the transactions and the precautionary demands for money. These money balances are computed as a given proportion of real GDP. Suppose real GDP is $5,000 billion and people wish to hold, say, 10 percent for transactions and precautionary purposes. This means the first $500 billion read along the horizontal axis in Exhibit 1 are held to make purchases and handle unforeseen events.

Now consider the impact of changes in the interest rate on the speculative demand for money. As the interest rate falls, people add larger speculative balances to their transactions and precautionary balances. For example, when the rate is 4 percent per year, the total quantity of money demanded at point *A* is $1,000 billion, of which $500 billion are speculative balances. If the interest rate is 2 percent, the total quantity of money demanded increases to $1,500 billion at point *B*, of which $1,000 billion are speculative balances. Therefore, the demand for money curve, labeled MD, looks much like any other demand curve.

> The speculative demand for money at possible interest rates gives the demand for money curve its downward slope.

CONCLUSION

16-1b The Equilibrium Interest Rate

We are now ready to form the money market and determine the equilibrium interest rate by putting the demand for money and the supply of money together. In Exhibit 2, the money demand curve (MD) is identical to that in Exhibit 1. The supply of money curve (MS) is a vertical line because the $1,000 billion quantity of money supplied does not respond to changes in the interest rate. The reason is that our model assumes the Fed has used its tools to set the money supply at this quantity of money regardless of the interest rate.

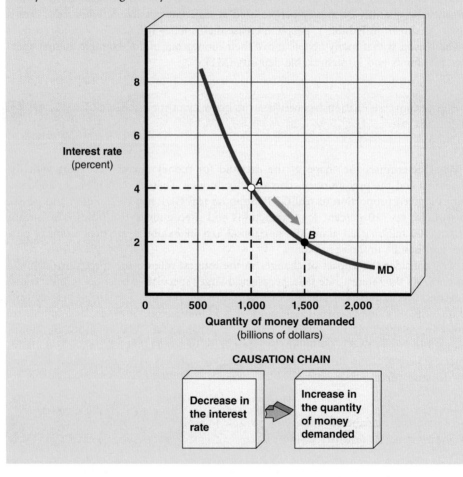

EXHIBIT 1 The Demand for Money Curve

Assume the level of real GDP is $5,000 billion. Also assume households and businesses demand to hold 10 percent of real GDP ($500 billion) for transactions and precautionary balances. The speculative demand for money varies inversely with the interest rate. At an interest rate of 4 percent, the quantity of money demanded (M1) is $1,000 billion (point *A*), calculated as the sum of transactions and precautionary demand ($500 billion) and speculative demand ($500 billion). At a lower interest rate, a greater total quantity of money is demanded because the opportunity cost of holding money is lower.

CAUSATION CHAIN

Decrease in the interest rate → Increase in the quantity of money demanded

At point *E*, the equilibrium interest rate is 4 percent, determined by the intersection of the demand for money curve and the vertical supply of money curve. People wish to hold exactly the amount of money in circulation, therefore, there is neither upward nor downward pressure on the interest rate.

Excess Quantity of Money Demanded

Suppose the interest rate in Exhibit 2 is 2 percent instead of 4 percent. Such a low opportunity cost of money means that people desire to hold a greater quantity of money than

EXHIBIT 2 The Equilibrium Interest Rate

The money market consists of the demand for and the supply of money. The market demand curve represents the quantity of money people are willing to hold at various interest rates. The money supply curve is a vertical line at $1,000 billion, based on the assumption that this is the quantity of money supplied by the Fed. The equilibrium interest rate is 4 percent and occurs at the intersection of the money demand and money supply curves (point *E*). At any other interest rate, for example, 6 percent or 2 percent, the quantity of money people desire to hold does not equal the quantity available.

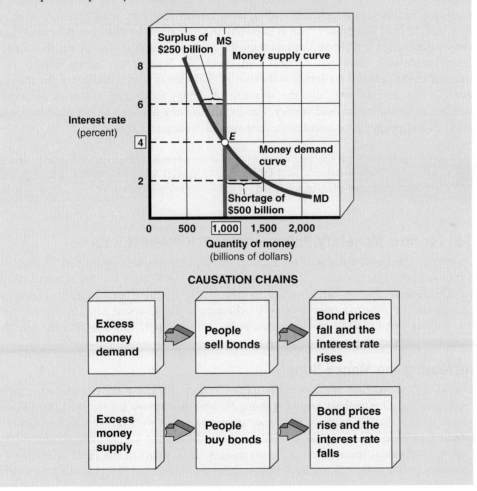

the quantity supplied. To eliminate this shortage of $500 billion, individuals and businesses adjust their asset portfolios. They seek more money by selling their bonds or other nonmoney assets. When many sell or try to sell their bonds, there is an increase in the supply of bonds for sale. Consequently, the price of bonds falls, and the interest rate rises. This rise in the interest rate ceases at the equilibrium interest rate of 4 percent because people are content with their portfolio of money and bonds at point *E*.

Here we need to pause and look at an example to understand what is happening. Suppose Apple pays 2 percent on its $1,000 30-year bonds. This means Apple pays a bondholder $20 in interest each year and promises to repay the original $1,000 price (face amount) at the end of 30 years. However, a holder of these bonds can sell them before maturity at a market-determined price. If bondholders desire to hold more money than is supplied, they will sell more of these bonds. Then the increase in the supply of bonds causes the price of bonds to fall to, say, $500. As a result, the interest rate rises to 4 percent ($20/$500).

Excess Quantity of Money Supplied

The story reverses for any rate of interest above 4 percent. Let's say the interest rate is 6 percent. In this case, people are holding more money than they wish. Stated differently, they wish to hold less money than is currently in circulation. In this case, the quantity of money demanded is $250 billion less than the quantity supplied. To correct this imbalance, people will move out of cash and checkable deposits by buying bonds. This increase in the demand for bonds will drive up the price of bonds and lower the interest rate. As the interest rate falls, the quantity of money demanded increases as people become more willing to hold money. Finally, the money market reaches equilibrium at point E, and people are content with their mix of money and bonds.

CONCLUSION There is an inverse relationship between bond prices and the interest rate that enables the money market to achieve equilibrium.

16-1c How Monetary Policy Affects the Interest Rate

Assuming a stationary demand for money, the equilibrium rate of interest changes in response to changes in monetary policy. As we learned in Exhibit 4 of the previous chapter, the Federal Reserve can alter the money supply through open market operations, changes in the required reserve ratio, or changes in the discount rate. In this section, you will see that the Fed's power to change the money supply can also alter the equilibrium rate of interest.

Increasing the Money Supply

Exhibit 3(a) shows how increasing the money supply will cause the equilibrium rate of interest to fall. Our analysis begins at point E_1, with the money supply at $1,000 billion, which is equal to the quantity of money demanded, and with the equilibrium interest rate at 6 percent. Now suppose the Fed increases the money supply to $1,500 billion by buying government securities in the open market. The impact of the Fed's expansionary monetary policy is to create a $500 billion surplus of money at the prevailing 6 percent interest rate.

How will people react to this excess money in their pockets or checking accounts? Money becomes a "hot potato," and people buy bonds. The rush to purchase bonds drives the price of bonds higher and the interest rate lower. As the interest rate falls, people are *willing* to hold larger money balances. Or, stated differently, the quantity of money demanded increases until the new equilibrium at E_2 is reached. At the lower interest rate of 4 percent, the opportunity cost of holding money is also lower, and the imbalance between the money demand and money supply curves disappears.

EXHIBIT 3 The Effect of Changes in the Money Supply

In part (a), the Federal Reserve increases the money supply from $1,000 billion ($MS_1$) to $1,500 billion ($MS_2$). At the initial interest rate of 6 percent (point E_1), there is an excess of $500 billion beyond the amount people wish to hold. They react by buying bonds, and the interest rate falls until it reaches a new lower equilibrium interest rate at 4 percent (point E_2).

The reverse happens in part (b). The Fed decreases the money supply from $1,500 billion ($MS_1$) to $1,000 billion ($MS_2$). Beginning at 4 percent (point E_1), people want to hold $500 billion more than is available. This shortage disappears when people sell their bonds. As the price of bonds falls, the interest rate rises to the new higher equilibrium interest rate of 6 percent at point E_2.

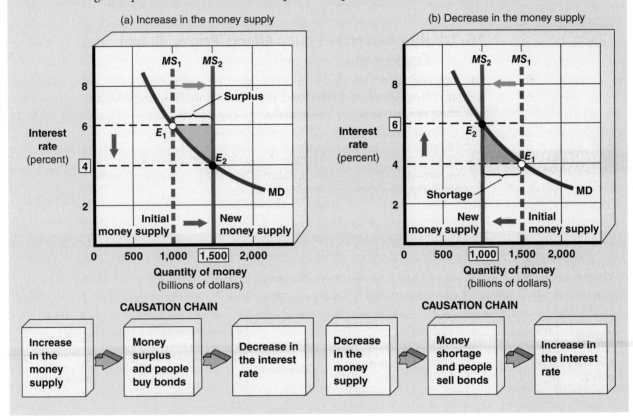

Decreasing the Money Supply

Exhibit 3(b) illustrates how the Fed can put upward pressure on the interest rate with contractionary monetary policy. Beginning at point E_1, the money market is in equilibrium at an interest rate of 4 percent. This time the Fed shrinks the money supply by selling government securities through its trading desk, raising the required reserve ratio, or raising the discount rate. As a result, the money supply decreases from $1,500 billion to $1,000 billion. At the initial equilibrium interest rate of 4 percent, this decrease in the money supply causes a shortage of $500 billion.

Individuals and businesses wish to hold more money than is available. How can the public put more money in their pockets and checking accounts? They can sell their bonds for cash. This selling pressure lowers bond prices, causing the rate of interest to rise. At point E_2, the upward pressure on the interest rate stops. Once the equilibrium interest rate reaches 6 percent, people willingly hold the $1,000 billion money supply.

CHECKPOINT

What Could the Fed Do If It Wanted to Push Interest Rates Down?
Suppose the Fed has a policy of adjusting the money supply to achieve interest rate targets. For example, the Fed might set a 4 percent target federal funds rate. If an increase in the demand for money boosts the federal funds rate above 4 percent, what could the Fed do to push interest rates back down?

16-1d How Monetary Policy Affects Prices, Output, and Employment

The next step in our journey is to understand how monetary policy alters the macro economy. Here you should pause and study Exhibit 4. This exhibit illustrates the causation chain linking monetary policy and economic performance.

CONCLUSION   In the Keynesian model, changes in the supply of money affect interest rates. In turn, interest rates affect investment spending, aggregate demand, and, finally, real GDP, employment, and prices.

EXHIBIT 4 The Keynesian Monetary Policy Transmission Mechanism

Keynesians focus on how changes in the money supply affect interest rates and investment spending. In turn, aggregate demand shifts and affects prices, real GDP, and employment.

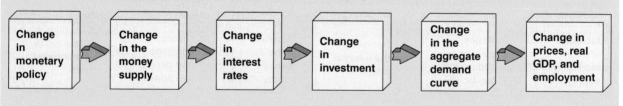

The Impact of Monetary Policy Using the AD–AS Model

How do changes in the rate of interest affect aggregate demand? Begin with Exhibit 5(a), which is identical to Exhibit 3(a) and represents the money market. As explained earlier, we assume that the Fed increases the money supply from $1,000 billion ($MS_1$) to $1,500 billion ($MS_2$) and the equilibrium interest rate falls from 6 percent to 4 percent. In part (b), we can see that the falling rate of interest causes an increase in the quantity of investment spending from $800 billion to $850 billion per year. Stated another way, there is a movement downward along the *investment demand curve* (*I*), which you recall from the chapter on GDP is a component of total spending or aggregate demand. The investment demand curve shows the amount businesses spend for investment goods at different possible interest rates.

EXHIBIT 5 The Effect of Expansionary Monetary Policy on Aggregate Demand

In part (a), the money supply is initially MS_1, and the equilibrium rate of interest is 6 percent. The equilibrium point in the money market changes from E_1 to E_2 when the Fed increases the money supply to MS_2. This causes the quantity of money people want to hold to increase from $1,000 billion to $1,500 billion, and a new lower equilibrium interest rate is established at 4 percent.

The fall in the rate of interest shown in part (b) causes a movement downward along the investment demand curve from point A to point B. Thus, the quantity of investment spending per year increases from $800 billion to $850 billion.

In part (c), the investment component of the aggregate demand curve increases, causing this curve to shift outward from AD_1 to AD_2. As a result, the aggregate demand and supply equilibrium in the product market changes from E_1 to E_2, and the real GDP gap is eliminated. The price level also increases from 210 to 215.

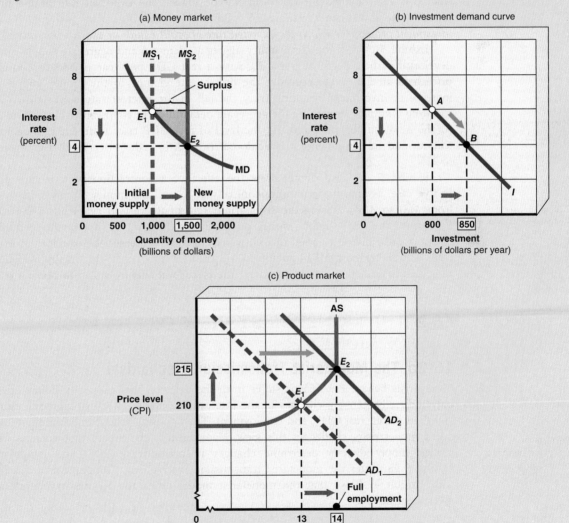

The classical economists believed that the interest rate alone determines the level of investment spending. Keynes disputed this idea. Instead, Keynes argued that the expectation of future profits is the primary factor determining investment and the interest rate is the financing cost of any investment proposal. Using a micro example to illustrate the investment decision–making process, suppose a consulting firm plans to purchase a new computer program for $1,000 that will be obsolete in a year. The firm anticipates the new software will increase its revenue by $1,100. Thus, assuming no taxes and other expenses, the expected rate of return or profit is 10 percent.

Now consider the impact of the cost of borrowing funds to finance the software investment. If the interest rate is less than 10 percent, the business will earn a profit, and it will make the investment expenditure to obtain the computer program. On the other hand, a rate of interest higher than 10 percent means the software investment will be a loss, so this purchase will not be made. The expected rate of the profit–interest rate–investment relationship follows this rule: *Businesses will undertake all investment projects for which the expected rate of profit equals or exceeds the interest rate.*

Exhibit 5(c) uses the fiscal policy aggregate demand and aggregate supply analysis developed earlier. Begin at point E_1, with a real GDP per year of $13 trillion and a price level of 210. Now consider the link to the change in the money supply. The increase in investment resulting from the fall in the interest rate works through the *spending multiplier* and shifts the aggregate demand curve rightward from AD_1 to AD_2. At the new equilibrium point, E_2, the level of real GDP rises from $13 trillion to $14 trillion, and full employment is achieved. In addition, the price level rises from 210 to 215.

Exhibit 5 can also demonstrate the effect of a contractionary monetary policy. In this case, assume the economy is initially at E_2 and the money supply shifts inward from MS_2 to MS_1, causing the equilibrium rate of interest to rise from 4 percent to 6 percent. The Fed's "tight" money policy causes the level of investment spending to fall from $850 billion to $800 billion, which, in turn, decreases the equilibrium level of real GDP per year from $14 trillion to $13 trillion. As a result, the unemployment rate rises, and the inflation rate falls because the price level falls from 215 to 210.

16-2 THE MONETARIST VIEW OF THE ROLE OF MONEY

16-2a The Monetarist Transmission Mechanism

Monetarism

The theory that changes in the money supply directly determine changes in prices, real GDP, and employment.

Monetarists believe Keynesians suffer from the delusion that monetary policy operates only indirectly, causing changes in the interest rate before affecting aggregate demand and then prices, real GDP, and employment. The opposing school of economic thought, called monetarism, challenges this view. **Monetarism** is the theory that changes in the money supply directly determine changes in prices, real GDP, and employment. Exhibit 6 illustrates the monetarist transmission mechanism. Comparison of this figure with Exhibit 4 shows that the monetarist model omits the Keynesian interest rate–investment linkage.

The Equation of Exchange

Monetarists put the spotlight on the money supply. They argue that to predict the condition of the economy, you simply look at the money supply. If it expands too much,

EXHIBIT **6** The Monetarist Monetary Policy Transmission Mechanism

Monetarists believe that changes in the money supply directly cause changes in the aggregate demand curve and thereby changes in prices, real GDP, and employment.

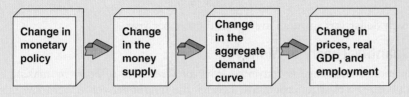

higher rates of inflation will be the forecast. If it contracts too much, unemployment lines will lengthen. Monetarism has its intellectual roots in classical economics, introduced in the chapter on aggregate demand and supply. Monetarists proudly wear *laissez faire* on their sleeves and believe the price system is the macro economy's best friend. To understand monetarism, we begin with the equation of exchange developed by the classical economists in the 19th century. The **equation of exchange** is an accounting identity that states the money supply times the velocity of money equals total spending. Expressed as a formula, the equation of exchange is written as

$$MV = PQ$$

Let's begin with the left side of the equation ($M \times V$). M is the money supply (more precisely M1) in circulation, and V represents the velocity of money. The **velocity of money** is the average number of times per year a dollar of the money supply is spent on final goods and services. Assume you have one crisp $20 bill and this is the only money in an ultrasimple economy. Suppose you spend this money on a pizza and soda at Zeno's Pizza Hut. Once Mr. Zeno puts your money in his pocket, he decides to buy an economics book and learn how the views of Keynesians and monetarists differ. And so, Mr. Zeno buys the book at the Wise Professor Book Store for exactly $20. At this point, both Mr. Zeno and Ms. Wise have sold $20 worth of goods. Thus, a single $20 bill has financed $40 worth of total spending. And as long as this $20 bill passes from hand to hand during, say, one year, the value of sales will increase. For example, assume the $20 travels from hand to hand 5 times. This means the velocity of money is 5, and the equation of exchange is expressed as

$$\$20 \times 5 = \$100$$

The equation of exchange is an *identity*—true by definition—that expresses the fact that the value of what people spend is equal to, or exchanged for, what they buy. What people buy is nominal GDP, or ($P \times Q$). Recall that nominal, or money, GDP is equal to the average selling price during the year (P) multiplied by the quantity of actual output of final goods and services (Q). In our simple economy, total spending equals $100. Note that the identity between MV and PQ does not say what happens to either P or Q if MV increases. Although we know by how much the total value of output (PQ) increases, we do not know whether the price level (P) or the quantity of output (Q) or both increase.

Consider a more realistic example. Suppose that nominal GDP last year was $5 trillion and M1 was $1 trillion. How many times did each dollar of the money supply have

Equation of exchange
An accounting identity that states the money supply times the velocity of money equals total spending.

Velocity of money
The average number of times per year a dollar of the money supply is spent on final goods and services.

to be spent to generate this level of total spending in the economy? Using the equation of exchange,

$$M \times V = P \times Q$$
$$\textbf{\$1 trillion} \times V = \textbf{\$5 trillion}$$
$$V = 5$$

Thus, each dollar was spent an average of 5 times per year.

The Quantity Theory of Money

The equation of exchange is converted from an *identity* to a *theory* by making certain assumptions. The classical economists became the forerunners of modern-day monetarists by arguing that the velocity of money (*V*) and real output (*Q*) are fairly constant. The classical economists viewed *V* as constant because people's habits of holding a certain quantity of money, and therefore the number of times a dollar is spent, are slow to change. Recall from the chapter on aggregate demand and supply that classical economists believed in price and wage flexibility. Hence, they believed the economy would automatically adjust to long-run full-employment output (*Q*).

Quantity theory of money
The theory that changes in the money supply are directly related to changes in the price level.

Because *V* and *Q* are constant by assumption, we have one of the oldest theories of inflation, called the quantity theory of money. The **quantity theory of money** states that changes in the money supply are directly related to changes in the price level. Monetary policy based on the quantity theory of money therefore directly affects the price level. To illustrate, we will modify the equation of exchange by putting a bar (–) over *V* and *Q* to indicate they are fixed or constant in value:

$$M \times \overline{V} = P \times \overline{Q}$$

What if the money supply doubles? The price level also doubles. Or if the Fed cuts the money supply in half, then the price level is also cut in half. Meanwhile, real output of goods and services, *Q*, remains unchanged.

CONCLUSION   According to the quantity theory of money, any change in the money supply must lead to a proportional change in the price level.

In short, monetarists say the cause of inflation is "too much money chasing too few goods." The quantity theory of money denies any role for nonmonetary factors, such as supply shocks from a hike in oil prices, which cause cost-push inflation [see Exhibit 13(a) in the chapter on aggregate demand and supply]. Moreover, this theory ignores the impact of fiscal policy changes in taxation and spending on the price level.

What do the data reveal about the link between changes in the money supply and changes in the rate of inflation? Although the relationship does not exist for all years, the evidence supports the general conclusion that sustained levels of higher growth in the money supply correspond to increases in the inflation rate. For example, when the money supply growth rate was low and averaged 1.5 percent between 1953 and 1962, the inflation rate averaged 1.3 percent. During 1973–1982, the money supply grew at a higher average rate of 6.7 percent, and the average inflation rate rose to 8.8 percent. More recently, between 1994 and 2007, the money supply increased at a lower average rate of 1.6 percent, and the average inflation rate dropped to 2.7 percent. After the Great Recession beginning in 2007, the money supply growth rate soared to 16.7 percent in

2008 and was around 8.6 percent in 2016. If high growth rates of the money supply are sustained, the concern is that the inflation rate will rise.

Modern Monetarism

Today's monetarists have changed the assumptions of the classical quantity theory of money. The evidence indicates that velocity is not constant and the economy does not always operate at full employment. Although *M* and *P* are correlated, they do not change proportionally. *Monetarists argue that although velocity is not unchanging, it is nevertheless predictable.* Suppose the predicted velocity of money is 5 and the money supply increases by $100 billion this year. Monetarists would predict that nominal GDP will increase by about $500 billion $(\Delta M \times V)$. [The circumflex ($\wedge$) indicates velocity is predicted.] If the economy is far below full employment, most of the rise in total spending will be in real output. If the economy is near full employment, much of the increase will be in rising prices.

Monetarists refute the Keynesian view that the rate of interest is so important. Instead, the monetarist view is often expressed in the famous single-minded statement that "money does matter." Instead of working through the rate of interest to affect investment and, in turn, the economy, changes in the money supply directly determine economic performance.

> To avoid inflation and unemployment, the monetarists' prescription is to be sure that the money supply is at the proper level.

CONCLUSION

Fixed Money Target

Monetarism gained credibility in the late 1950s and 1960s, led by Professor Milton Friedman at the University of Chicago. The monetarists have an answer for how to make sure the economy grows at the right rate: Instead of risking policy errors, forget about the rate of interest and follow a steady, predictable monetary policy. Recall from the chapter on money creation that there are limitations on the Fed's ability to control the money supply because of the independent actions of households, firms, banks, and the U.S. Treasury. Monetarists would stop the Fed from tinkering with the money supply, missing the target, and making the economy worse, rather than better. Instead, they say the money supply should expand at the same rate as the potential growth rate in real GDP. That is, it should increase somewhere between 3 percent and 5 percent per year. The Fed should therefore pick a rate and stick to it, even if unexpected changes in velocity cause short periods of inflation or unemployment. This is called following a *monetary rule*. Monetarists argue that their "straitjacket" approach would reduce the intensity and duration of unemployment and inflation by eliminating the monetarists' public enemy number one—the Fed's discretion to change the money supply. A Keynesian once summarized the fixed money supply approach as "Don't do something, just stand there."

> Monetarists advocate that the Federal Reserve increase the money supply by a constant percentage each year equal to the potential annual growth rate in real GDP.

CONCLUSION

How Stable Is Velocity?

How stable, or predictable, is the velocity of money? This is a critical question in the Keynesian–monetarist debate. Keynesians do not accept the monetarists' argument that over long periods of time velocity is stable and predictable. Hence, a change in the money supply can lead to a much larger or smaller change in GDP than the monetarists would predict. As shown in Exhibit 7, Keynesians are quick to point out the turbulent variations in velocity. Velocity gyrated up and down during the 1980s, early 1990s, and years after 2001. Monetarists counter by pointing to the evidence that during the periods of 1960–1981 and 1993–2000 velocity generally rose along a quite predictable or steady annual rate trend line. Since 2007, velocity has declined steadily.

EXHIBIT 7 The Velocity of Money, 1960–2016

The velocity of money (V) equals GDP divided by the supply of money (M1). Keynesians argue that velocity is not stable. During the 1980s, early 1990s, and years after 2001, velocity became quite unpredictable. Monetarists believe velocity is stable and predictable over the long term.

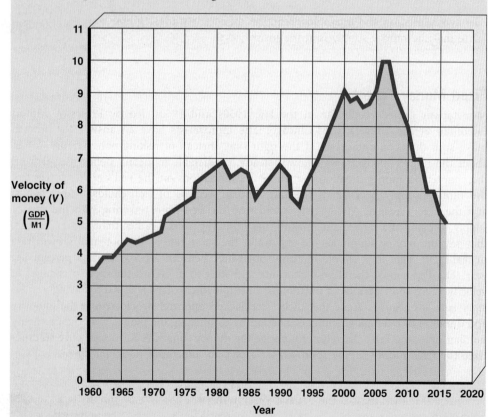

SOURCE: *Economic Report of the President, 2017,* Tables B-2 and B-26, https://www.gpo.gov/fdsys/browse/collection.action?collectionCode=ERP.

Keynesians focus on short-run variations in V that accompany any long-run velocity growth rate. They therefore argue that following a monetary rule is folly. Suppose the money supply increases at a constant rate, but velocity is greater than expected. This means that total spending (aggregate demand) will be greater than predicted, causing inflation. Lower-than-predicted velocity results in unemployment because total spending is less than expected, which causes the economy to expand too little. The Keynesians believe that the Federal Reserve must be free to change the money supply to offset unexpected changes in velocity. Monetarists counter that the Fed *cannot* predict short-run variations in V, so its "quick-fix" changes in the money supply will often be wrong. This is why monetarists advocate that the Fed follow a monetary rule. Keynesians are willing to accept occasional policy errors and reject this idea in favor of maintaining Fed flexibility to change the money supply in order to affect interest rates, aggregate demand, and the economy.

A Horse of Which Color?

A famous economist once proposed replacing the Fed with an intelligent horse. Each New Year's Day, the horse would stand in front of Fed headquarters to answer monetary policy questions. Reporters would ask, "What is going to happen to the money supply this year?" The horse would tap its hoof four times, and the next day headlines would read "Fed to Once Again Increase the Money Supply 4 Percent." Is this famous economist a Keynesian or a monetarist?

CHECKPOINT

16-3 A COMPARISON OF MACROECONOMIC VIEWS

By now, your head is probably spinning with dueling schools of economic thought. The debate among the classicals, Keynesians, and monetarists can be quite confusing. This chapter has presented differences in monetary policy between these schools. To refresh your memory and complete the discussion, this section presents a brief review of key differences in fiscal policy introduced in earlier chapters. Exhibit 8 gives a thumbnail summary of the key differences between the three camps. Note the similarity between the classical and the monetarist schools.

16-3a Classical Economics

As discussed in the chapter on aggregate demand and supply, the dominant school of economic thought before the Great Depression was classical economics. **Classical economics** is the theory that free markets will restore full employment without government intervention. The basic theory of the classical economists, introduced by Adam Smith in *The Wealth of Nations* and followed by the eighteenth- and nineteenth-century economists, was that a market-directed economy will automatically correct itself to full employment. Consequently, there is no need for fiscal policy designed to restore full employment.

Classical economics
The theory that free markets will restore full employment without government intervention.

YOU'RE THE ECONOMIST

Applicable Concept: Monetarism

Did the Fed Cause the Great Recession?

The story of the worst collapse of the housing market and the most serious financial crisis since the Great Depression is filled with villains and no action hero to sweep down from the sky and save the day. It is an Alice in Wonderland story with plenty of blame to go around: homeowners who bought a Trojan horse, rampant speculation, predatory lenders, slick Wall Street operators, greedy CEOs, lax regulators, and debatable Fed policy. Perhaps a phrase by Alan Greenspan, former Fed chairman, called "The Maestro," best described the bust of the housing market bubble when he said, "How do we know when irrational exuberance has unduly escalated asset values?"

The stage was set for the housing crisis by the Fed's response to the recession of 2001. The annual change in the money supply jumped sharply upward from −3.1 percent in 2000 to an 8.7 percent increase in 2001. And, as shown in the accompanying graph within this "You're the Economist," the Fed decreased interest rates sharply after 2001 and kept them historically low in order to boost aggregate demand and prevent another recession. Then in 2004, Greenspan addressed the Credit Union Association and said, "American consumers might benefit if lenders provided greater mortgage product alternatives to the traditional fixed rate mortgage." And as if following the Fed chairman's advice, adjustable-rate mortgages (ARMs) became the loan of choice for **subprime mortgage loan** borrowers who had poor or less than ideal credit scores. Mailboxes were stuffed with offers to borrow 100 percent or more of a home's value with zero down. Television shows advertised the idea that anyone could make it rich in real estate, and housing became a speculative game.

Payments and "teaser" interest rates were held artificially low for the first few years of the loan and then would jump sharply upward. Forget worrying about not affording the home, your income would not be checked, following a "no document" lending practice. In fact, some loans were made to people who were no longer living. Thus, using risky ARMs, banks lent billions of dollars to home buyers who could not pay the bank when the payments and interest rates rose.

Faced with accumulating portfolios of risky debt, banks and mortgage companies sold these risky mortgages to New York investment firms such as Bear Stearns (acquired by JPMorgan Chase with financial backing from the Fed) and Merrill Lynch, who pooled them with other securities. These packages, often called collateralized debt obligations, or CDOs, were sold to customers around the world—a process called "securitization." And this securitization

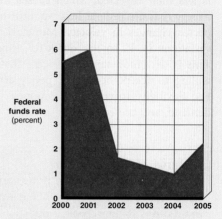

SOURCE: FRB Federal Open Market Committee, http://www.federalreserve.gov/fomc/fundsrate.htm.

Subprime mortgage loan
A home loan made to borrowers with an above-average risk of default.

Recall that a key assumption of classical theory is that, given time to adjust, prices and wages will decrease to ensure the economy operates at full employment. A decrease in the aggregate demand curve causes a temporary surplus, which, in turn, causes businesses to cut prices, and, in turn, causes more goods to be purchased because of the real balances effect. As a result, wages adjust downward, and employment rises. Classical economists therefore view the economy as operating in the long run along a vertical aggregate supply curve originating at the full-employment real GDP.

16-3b Keynesian Economics

The Great Depression challenged the classical prescription to wait until markets adjust and full employment is automatically restored. As the unemployment rate rose to

occurred with the blessing of ratings agencies such as Standard & Poor's, which actually did not know how to evaluate the risk of these securities. With each of these transactions, large fees were collected, and in short, consummation of the deal was the criterion and not validity of the assessment of risk.

Expansion of the housing market bubble was based on an assumption by all the players that the party would never end and real estate prices would always go up. However, beginning in the summer of 2005, subprime foreclosures rose and home prices dropped as people's payments rose under their ARMs. Also, once the value of homes fell below the loan value, people could not refinance loans to get lower payments. When people walked away from their mortgages, Wall Street and foreign investors were stuck with bad loans in their CDOs to write off, CEOs were fired, and many real estate executives were indicted for mortgage fraud. As a result, lenders greatly tightened their lending standards to avoid further risky loans, and a credit crunch made home financing difficult to obtain. The housing bubble burst in October 2007 culminating into a full-blown global financial crisis that erupted in the fall of 2008 which became the worst banking crisis since the Great Depression.

In response to the financial collapse in 2008, the Fed announced that it would allow Wall Street investment firms to receive emergency loans and exchange risky investments for Treasury securities. Also, the Housing and Economic Recovery Act of 2008 was passed that allowed some borrowers to refinance their mortgages with new fixed-rate loans backed by a federal guarantee, and it provided grants for state and local governments in the hardest-hit communities to buy foreclosed property. It also included a tax credit for first-time home buyers who buy housing that is unoccupied. And the Treasury Department was given authority to bail out or take over Fannie Mae and Freddie Mac, the troubled government-created firms that fund the vast majority of mortgage loans in the United States.

In addition, a massive $700 billion bailout plan was enacted in 2008 that gave the Treasury the authority to implement TARP (Troubled Assets Recovery Program) to buy and resell bad mortgage debt from financial institutions. But TARP changed its original purpose because it was very difficult to determine the price that the government should pay for the risky assets. Consequently, TARP changed its plan and spent over half of its funds to invest government capital into banks by buying preferred stock with a 5 percent rate of return, which is the equivalent of a loan to the bank. In 2010 Congress passed Dodd-Frank which is a controversial and extensive act intended to increase accountability and regulation of financial institutions. This act gives more oversight authority to the Fed over products that financial institutions provide. In 2013 the Volcker Rule, named after the former Federal Reserve chairman, was approved. This rule limits banks investment in complex financial instruments. And in 2014, Bank of America admitted that it took part in faulty mortgage-backed securities practices and agreed to a $16.5 billion settlement with the U.S. government. Other litigation concerning settlements with the U.S. Department of Justice has also emerged.

ANALYZE THE ISSUE In support of the Fed's monetary policy prior to the deflation of the home prices bubble, one can argue that the reality is that increasing the money supply and low-interest rates were required to sustain expansion. Based on the monetarist school of thought, criticize the Fed's policy.

24.9 percent in 1933, people asked how long it would take for the market mechanism to adjust. John Maynard Keynes responded with his famous saying "In the long run we are all dead." Keynes, in his book *The General Theory*, attacked classical theory and in the process revolutionized macroeconomic thought.

As explained in the chapter on fiscal policy, using fiscal policy to affect aggregate demand is a cornerstone of Keynesian economics. **Keynesian economics** is the theory, first advanced by John Maynard Keynes, that the role of the federal government is to increase or decrease aggregate demand to achieve economic goals. While Keynesians believe monetary policy is often not very powerful, especially during a downturn, they regard fiscal policy as their "top banana." However, Keynesians recognize that one of the potential problems of fiscal policy is the *crowding-out effect*. As shown earlier in

Keynesian economics
The theory, first advanced by John Maynard Keynes, that the role of the federal government is to increase or decrease aggregate demand to achieve economic goals.

EXHIBIT 8 Comparison of Macroeconomic Theories

Issue	Classical	Keynesian	Monetarist
	Library of Congress Prints and Photographs Division [LC-US262-17407] **Adam Smith**	*Walter Stoneman/Samuel Bourne/Hulton Archive/ Getty Images* **John Maynard Keynes**	*Bachrach/Archive Photos/Getty Images* **Milton Friedman**
Stability of economy	Stable in long run at full employment	Inherently unstable at less than full employment	Stable in long run at full employment
Price-wage flexibility	Yes	No	Yes
Velocity of money	Stable	Unstable	Predictable
Cause of inflation	Excess money supply	Excess aggregate demand	Excess money supply
Causes of unemployment	Short-run price and wage adjustment	Inadequate aggregate demand	Short-run price and wage adjustment
Effect of monetary policy	Changes aggregate demand and prices	Changes interest rate, which changes investment and real GDP	Changes aggregate demand and prices
Effect of fiscal policy	Not necessary	Spending multiplier changes aggregate demand	No effect because of crowding-out effect

Exhibit 9 of the chapter on federal deficits and the national debt, financing a federal deficit by borrowing competes with private borrowers for funds. Given a fixed money supply, the extra demand for money from the federal government to finance its deficit causes the interest rate to rise. As a result, businesses cut back on investment spending and offset at least some of the expected increase in aggregate demand. The Keynesian view, however, is that the investment demand curve is not very sensitive to changes in the interest rate, and therefore, only a relatively small amount of investment spending will be crowded out. Thus, the decline in investment only slightly counteracts or offsets an increase in aggregate demand created by a deficit.

CONCLUSION Keynesians view the shape of the investment demand curve as rather steep or vertical, so the crowding-out effect is insignificant.

YOU'RE THE **ECONOMIST**

Monetary Policy During the Great Depression

Monetarists and Keynesians still debate the causes of the Great Depression. Monetarists Milton Friedman and Anna Schwartz, in their book *A Monetary History of the United States*, argued that the Great Depression was caused by the decline in the money supply, as shown in Exhibit 9(a).

During the 1920s, the money supply expanded steadily, and prices were generally stable. In response to the great stock market crash of 1929, bank failures, falling real GDP, and rising unemployment, the Fed changed its monetary policy. Through the Great Depression years from 1929 to 1933, M1 declined by 27 percent. Assuming velocity is relatively constant, how will a sharp reduction in the quantity of money in circulation affect the economy? Monetarists predict a reduction in prices, output, and employment. Between 1929 and 1933, the price level declined by 24 percent. In addition to deflation, real GDP was 27 percent lower in 1933 than in 1929. Unemployment rose from 3.2 percent in 1929 to 24.9 percent in 1933. Friedman and Schwartz argued that the ineptness of the Fed's monetary policy during the Great Depression caused the trough in the business cycle to be more severe and sustained.

The Great Depression was indeed not the Fed's finest hour. What should the Fed have done? Friedman and Schwartz argued that the Fed should have used open market operations to increase the money supply. Thus, they concluded that the Fed was to blame for not pursuing an expansionary policy, which would have reduced the severity and duration of the contraction. As shown in part (b), this was not the case for the Great Recession of 2007–2009. From the beginning, the Fed followed an expansionary policy and sharply increased the money supply.

Finally, although the emphasis here is monetary policy, parts (c) and (d) contrast fiscal policy during the two periods using the federal deficit as a percentage of GDP. During the Great Depression, there was a slight budget surplus until 1931 when the budget turned into a slight budget deficit

before reaching a deficit of 5.9 percent of GDP in 1934. In contrast, fiscal policy was more expansionary by running deficits from the beginning of the recession in 2007 to an estimated 10 percent of GDP in 2009.

ANALYZE THE ISSUE

1. Explain why monetarists believe the Fed should have expanded the money supply during the Great Depression.
2. The Keynesians challenge the Friedman–Schwartz monetarists' monetary policy cure for the Great Depression. Use the AD-AS model to explain the Keynesian view. (Hint: Your answer must include the investment demand curve.)

SOURCE: Milton Friedman and Anna J. Schwartz, A Monetary History of the United States, 1867–1960 (Princeton, N.J.: Princeton University Press, 1963).

16-3c Monetarism

Monetarists are iconoclasts because they attack the belief in the ability of either the Fed or the federal government to stabilize the economy. They argue that fiscal policy is an essentially useless tool that has little or no impact on output or employment because of a *total* crowding-out effect. Suppose the money supply remains fixed and the federal government borrows to finance its deficit. The intended goal is to increase aggregate demand and restore full employment. According to the monetarists, financing the deficit

EXHIBIT **9** The Great Depression Economic Data, 1929–1934 Compared to the Great Recession of 2007–2009

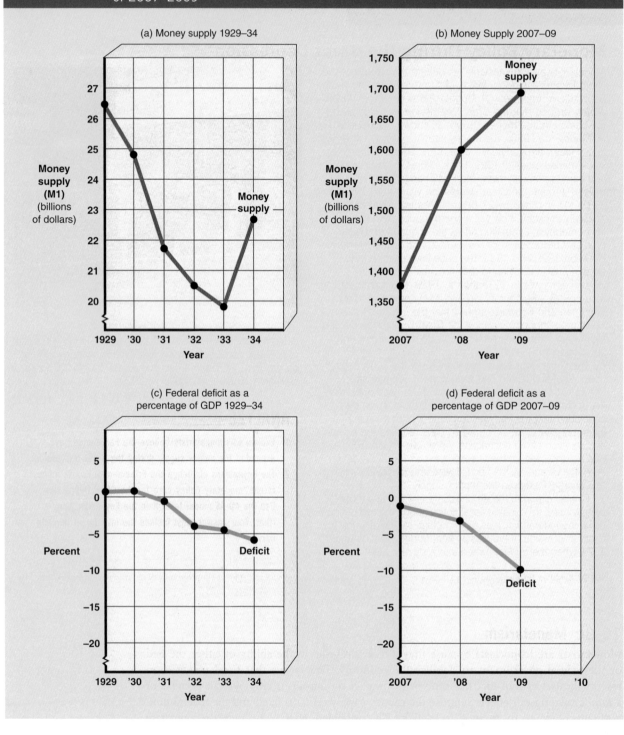

will drive up the interest rate and crowd out a substantial, not a small, amount of investment spending. The reason is that the monetarists view the investment demand curve as sensitive to changes in the interest rate; therefore, greater amounts of investment spending will be crowded out. In fact, according to the monetarists, the decline in investment would totally offset any increase in deficit spending. As a result, the net effect is no increase in aggregate demand and no reduction in unemployment.

> **CONCLUSION**
>
> Monetarists view the shape of the investment demand curve as less steep or relatively flat, so the crowding-out effect is significant.

Although the monetarists do not trust the Federal Reserve to use discretionary monetary policy, they are quick to point out that only money is important. Changes in the money supply, the basic lever of monetary policy, have a powerful impact. Instead of ineffectual government deficit spending to cure unemployment, an increase in the money supply would definitely stimulate the economy based on the quantity theory of money. In short, changes in the money supply directly result in changes in real GDP.

Key Concepts

Transactions demand for money

Precautionary demand for money

Speculative demand for money

Demand for money curve

Monetarism

Equation of exchange

Velocity of money

Quantity theory of money

Classical economics

Subprime mortgage loan

Keynesian economics

Summary

- The *demand for money* in the Keynesian view consists of three reasons why people hold money: (1) **Transactions demand** is money held to pay for everyday predictable expenses. (2) **Precautionary demand** is money held to pay unpredictable expenses. (3) **Speculative demand** is money held to take advantage of price changes in nonmoney assets.

- The **demand for money curve** shows the quantity of money people wish to hold at various rates of interest. As the interest rate rises, the quantity of money demanded is less than when the interest rate is lower.

Demand for Money Curve

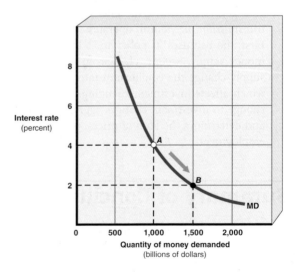

- The *equilibrium interest rate* is determined in the money market by the intersection of the demand for money and the supply of money curves. The money supply (M1), which is determined by the Fed, is represented by a vertical line.

The Equilibrium Interest Rate

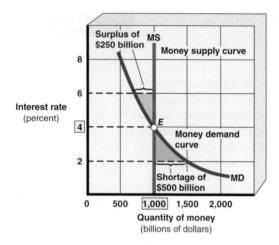

- An *excess quantity of money demanded* causes households and businesses to increase their money balances by selling bonds. This causes the price of bonds to fall, thus driving up the interest rate.

- An *excess quantity of money supplied* causes households and businesses to reduce their money balances by purchasing bonds. The effect is to cause the price of bonds to rise, and thereby, the rate of interest falls.

- The *Keynesian view of the monetary policy transmission mechanism* operates as follows: First, the Fed uses its policy tools to change the money supply. Second, changes in the money supply change the equilibrium interest rate, which affects investment spending. Finally, a change in investment changes aggregate demand and determines the level of prices, real GDP, and employment.

- **Monetarism** is the simpler view that changes in monetary policy directly change aggregate demand, and thereby prices, real GDP, and employment. Thus, monetarists focus on the money supply, rather than on the rate of interest.

- The **equation of exchange** is an accounting identity that is the foundation of monetarism. The equation ($MV = PQ$) states that the money supply multiplied by the velocity of money is equal to the price level multiplied by real output. The **velocity of money** is the number of times each dollar is spent during a year. Keynesians view velocity as volatile, but monetarists disagree.

- The **quantity theory of money** is a monetarist argument that the velocity of money (V) and output (Q) variables in the equation of exchange are relatively constant. Given this assumption, changes in the money supply yield proportional changes in the price level. The monetarist solution to inept Fed tinkering with the money supply that causes inflation or recession is to have the Fed simply pick a rate of growth in the money supply that is consistent with real GDP growth and stick to it.

- *Keynesians' and monetarists' views on fiscal policy* are also different. Keynesians believe the investment demand curve is relatively vertical, and monetarists view it as relatively flat. Monetarists assert that the *crowding-out effect* is large and, therefore, fiscal policy is ineffective. Keynesians argue that the crowding-out effect is small and that fiscal policy is effective.

- **Classical economics** is the theory that free markets will restore full employment without government intervention.

- A **sub-prime mortgage** is a loan made to borrowers with an above-average risk of default.

- **Keynesian economics** is the theory, first advanced by John Maynard Keynes, that the role of the federal government is to increase or decrease aggregate demand to achieve economic goals.

Summary of Conclusion Statements

- As the interest rate falls, the opportunity cost of holding money falls, and people increase their speculative balances.

- There is an inverse relationship between the quantity of money demanded and the interest rate.

- The speculative demand for money at possible interest rates gives the demand for money curve its downward slope.

- There is an inverse relationship between bond prices and the interest rate that enables the money market to achieve equilibrium.

- In the Keynesian model, changes in the supply of money affect interest rates. In turn, interest rates affect investment spending, aggregate demand, and, finally, real GDP, employment, and prices.

- According to the quantity theory of money, any change in the money supply must lead to a proportional change in the price level.

- To avoid inflation and unemployment, the monetarists' prescription is to be sure that the money supply is at the proper level.

- Monetarists advocate that the Federal Reserve increase the money supply by a constant percentage each year equal to the potential annual growth rate in real GDP.

- Keynesians view the shape of the investment demand curve as rather steep or vertical, so the crowding-out effect is insignificant.

- Monetarists view the shape of the investment demand curve as less steep or relatively flat, so the crowding-out effect is significant.

Study Questions and Problems

Please see Appendix A for answers to the odd-numbered questions. Your instructor has access to the answers for even-numbered questions.

1. How much money do you keep in cash or checkable deposits on a typical day? Under the following conditions, would you increase or decrease your demand for money? Also identify whether the condition affects your transactions demand, precautionary demand, or speculative demand.
   a. Your salary doubles.
   b. The rate of interest on bonds and other assets falls.
   c. An automated teller machine (ATM) is installed next door, and you have an ATM card.
   d. Bond prices are expected to rise.
   e. You are paid each week instead of monthly.

2. What are the basic motives for the transactions demand, precautionary demand, and speculative demand? Explain how these three demands are combined in a graph to show the total demand for money.

3. Suppose a bond pays annual interest of $80. Compute the interest rate per year that a bondholder can earn if the bond has a face value of $800, $1,000, and $2,000. State the conclusion drawn from your calculations.

4. Using the demand and supply schedule for money shown in Exhibit 10, do the following:

EXHIBIT 10 Money Market

Interest rate (percent)	Demand for money (billions of dollars)	Supply of money (billions of dollars)
8%	$100	$200
6	200	200
4	300	200
2	400	200

   a. Graph the demand for money and the supply of money curves.
   b. Determine the equilibrium interest rate.
   c. Suppose the Fed increases the money supply by $100 billion. Show the effect in your graph, and describe the money market adjustment process to a new equilibrium rate. What is the new equilibrium rate of interest?

5. Assume you are the chair of the Federal Reserve Board of Governors and the condition of the economy is shown in Exhibit 5. Assume you are a Keynesian, and start at point E_1 in the money

market and the product market. State the likely direction of change in the price level, real GDP, and employment caused by each of the following monetary policies:

a. The Fed makes an open market sale of government bonds.

b. The Fed reduces the required reserve ratio.

c. The Fed increases the discount rate.

6. "A monetarist investigator might say that the sewer flow of 6,000 gallons an hour consisted of an average of 200 gallons in the sewer at any one time with a complete turnover of the water 30 times every hour."[1] Interpret this statement using the equation of exchange.

7. What is the quantity theory of money, and what does each term in the equation represent?

8. Exhibit 6 shows the monetarist monetary policy transmission mechanism. Assume the

economy is in a recession. At each arrow, identify a reason why the transmission process could fail.

9. Explain the difference between the Keynesian and the monetarist views on how an increase in the money supply causes inflation.

10. Based on the quantity theory of money, what would be the impact of increasing the money supply by 25 percent?

11. Suppose the investment demand curve is a vertical line. Would the Keynesian or the monetarist view of the impact of monetary policy on investment spending be correct?

12. Why is the shape of the aggregate supply curve important to the Keynesian-monetarist controversy? (Hint: Review Exhibit 6 in the chapter on aggregate demand and supply.)

 ## CHECKPOINT ANSWERS

What Could the Fed Do If It Wanted to Push Interest Rates Down?

To decrease interest rates, the Fed would have to increase the money supply. An increase in the money supply can be accomplished by the Federal Reserve's use of open market operations, changes in the required reserve ratio, or changes in the discount rate. If you said the Fed should buy government securities in the open market, decrease the required reserve ratio, or decrease the discount rate to push interest rates down, **YOU ARE CORRECT**.

A Horse of Which Color?

The famous economist is Milton Friedman, who favored a monetary rule for the Fed. The horse is a sarcastic way of rejecting Keynesian activist policies that could destabilize the economy. Friedman even argued that the Board of Governors of the Federal Reserve System should announce the growth rate for the money supply each year and must resign if the target is missed. If you said the economist is a monetarist, **YOU ARE CORRECT**.

[1]Werner Sichel and Peter Eckstein, *Basic Economic Concepts* (Chicago: Rand McNally, 1974), p. 344.

Sample Quiz

Please see Appendix B for answers to Sample Quiz questions.

1. The demand for money that households keep for emergency purposes is known as the
   a. precautionary demand.
   b. emergency demand.
   c. speculative demand.
   d. temporary demand.

2. The quantity of money held in response to interest rates is the
   a. transactions motive for holding money.
   b. precautionary motive for holding money.
   c. speculative motive for holding money.
   d. unit-of-account motive for holding money.

3. The speculative demand for money
   a. varies inversely with income.
   b. is only concerned with active money.
   c. involves holding money for unexpected problems.
   d. varies directly with the transactions demand for money.
   e. varies inversely with the interest rate.

4. Other things being equal, the quantity of money that people want to hold can be expected to
   a. increase as the interest rate increases.
   b. decrease as the interest rate increases.
   c. decrease as real GDP increases.
   d. None of the answers are correct.

5. A decrease in the interest rate, other things being equal, causes a (an)
   a. upward movement along the demand curve for money.
   b. downward movement along the demand curve for money.
   c. rightward shift of the demand curve for money.
   d. leftward shift of the demand curve for money.

6. Which of the following statements is *true*?
   a. The speculative demand for money at possible interest rates gives the demand for money curve its upward slope.
   b. There is an inverse relationship between the quantity of money demanded and the interest rate.

   c. According to the quantity theory of money, any change in the money supply will have no effect on the price level.
   d. All of the answers are correct.

7. In Exhibit 11, assume an equilibrium with an interest rate of 6 percent and the money supply at $400 billion. The Fed uses its policy tools to move the economy to a new equilibrium at E_2 with money supply of $600 billion and an interest rate of 4 percent. This change could be the result of a(an)
   a. open market sale of securities by the Fed.
   b. higher discount rate set by the Fed.
   c. higher required reserve ratio set by the Fed.
   d. open market purchase of securities by the Fed.

8. According to Keynesians, an increase in the money supply will
   a. decrease the interest rate, and increase investment, aggregate demand, prices, real GDP, and employment.
   b. decrease the interest rate, and decrease investment, aggregate demand, prices, real GDP, and employment.

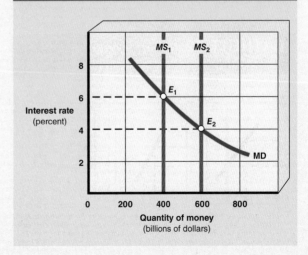

EXHIBIT 11 Money Market Demand and Supply Curves

c. increase the interest rate and decrease investment, aggregate demand, prices, real GDP, and employment.

d. only increase prices.

9. While the classicists believed that both velocity and output are stable, Keynesians believe
    a. velocity is stable, and output is variable.
    b. velocity and output are both variable.
    c. output is stable, and velocity is variable
    d. the same as the classical economists that both output and velocity are stable.

10. In Exhibit 12, when the money supply increases from MS_1 to MS_2 the equilibrium interest rate
    a. remains unchanged.
    b. increases from i_2 to i_1, increasing investment spending from I_1 to I_1.
    c. increases from i_2 to i_1, decreasing investment spending from I_2 to I_1.
    d. decreases from i_1 to i_2, increasing investment spending from I_1 to I_2.

11. In Exhibit 12, if the interest rate falls from i_1 to i_2 investment spending will
    a. increase, and aggregate demand will shift from AD_1 to AD_2.
    b. decrease, and aggregate demand will shift from AD_2 to AD_1.
    c. remain the same, and aggregate demand will shift from AD_2 to AD_3.
    d. increase, and aggregate demand will shift from AD_2 to AD_1.

12. In Exhibit 12, a shift in aggregate demand from AD_1 to AD_2
    a. cannot raise real GDP because the economy is at full employment.
    b. cannot raise real GDP because the aggregate supply curve is upward sloping at GDP_2.
    c. will raise real GDP because the economy is operating below the full-employment level.
    d. will cause the interest rate to decrease from i_1 to i_2.

13. The monetarist transmission mechanism through which monetary policy affects the price level, real GDP, and employment depends on the
    a. indirect impact of changes on the interest rate.
    b. indirect impact of changes on profit expectations.
    c. direct impact of changes in fiscal policy on aggregate demand.
    d. direct impact of changes in the money supply on aggregate demand.

14. The equation of exchange states
    a. $MV = PQ$.
    b. $MP = VQ$.
    c. $MP = V/Q$.
    d. $V = M/PQ$.

15. The quantity theory of money assumes that the velocity of money
    a. is constant.
    b. will rise if the money supply rises and fall if the money supply falls.
    c. will rise if the money supply rises, but will not change if the money supply falls.
    d. will fall if the money supply rises, and will rise if the money supply falls.

16. The transactions demand for money is the demand for money by households for
    a. rainy day spending.
    b. predictable spending purposes.
    c. emergency purposes.
    d. investing purposes.

17. People react to an excess supply of money by
    a. selling bonds, thus driving up the interest rate.

EXHIBIT 12 Money, Investment, and Product Markets

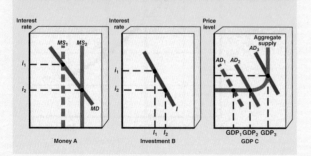

b. selling bonds, thus driving down the interest rate.

c. buying bonds, thus driving up the interest rate.

d. buying bonds, thus driving down the interest rate.

18. The belief that the velocity of money is *not* constant but is highly predictable is associated with the
    a. classical school.
    b. Keynesian school.
    c. supply-side school.
    d. rational expectations school.
    e. monetarist school.

19. The monetary rule is the view of the
    a. Keynesians that monetary policy is most important.
    b. monetarists that monetary policy is least important.
    c. classical economists that monetary policy is most important.
    d. monetarists that the Fed should expand the money supply at a constant rate.

20. Which of the following statements is *true*?
    a. Keynesians advocate increasing the money supply during economic recessions but decreasing the money supply during economic expansions.
    b. Monetarists advocate increasing the money supply by a constant rate year after year.
    c. Keynesians argue that the crowding-out effect is rather insignificant.
    d. Monetarists argue that the crowding-out effect is rather large.
    e. All of the answers are correct.

Policy Disputes Using the Self-Correcting Aggregate Demand and Supply Model

In the appendix to the chapter on aggregate demand and supply, the classical self-correcting aggregate demand and supply model was explained without disagreement. Expansionary and contractionary fiscal policy was discussed in the chapter on fiscal policy, and this chapter explained monetary policy. In this appendix, we combine these topics and examine contrasting fiscal and monetary policies using the self-correcting model.

16A-1 THE CLASSICAL VERSUS KEYNESIAN VIEWS OF EXPANSIONARY POLICY

The Keynesian activist approach rejects classical nonintervention policy to stabilize the economy in favor of using discretionary fiscal and monetary policies. Exhibit A-1 illustrates these opposing theories for restoring an economy in recession to full employment. In both parts (a) and (b), the economy starts with a real GDP of $8 trillion and a price level of 150 at macro equilibrium E_1. Since full-employment real GDP is $12 trillion, there is a recessionary gap. In part (a), the economy closes the gap through the self-correction process. The key classical assumption is that nominal wages are flexible and fall as a result of competition among unemployed workers for jobs. Over time, the result is that the short-term aggregate supply curve ($SRAS_1$) shifts rightward to $SRAS_2$ and the economy automatically adjusts to long-run macro full-employment equilibrium at E_2 with a price level of 100.

Part (b) illustrates the opposing Keynesian theory. This view argues that nominal wages are fixed in the short run. In contrast to the self-correction classical model, Keynesians advocate using discretionary fiscal policy in which the federal government manages the aggregate demand curve (AD) by increasing government spending or cutting taxes. Both of these policy options work through the multiplier process and increase AD_1 to AD_2. The result is that the economy achieves full employment at macro equilibrium point E_2 where the price level is 200.

Keynesians also argue that activist monetary policy can stabilize the economy. The Federal Reserve can increase the money supply, which lowers the interest rate, and in response, business investment spending increases. As a result, AD_1 shifts to AD_2 in part (b) of Exhibit A-1, and full employment is restored at E_2.

Note that both the classical and Keynesian approaches in parts (a) and (b) restore full-employment real GDP; however, the impact on the price level is quite different. If classical theory is correct, the price level falls from 150 to 100. In contrast, if Keynesian theory is correct, the price level rises from 150 to 200, resulting in a higher inflation rate.

EXHIBIT A-1 Opposing Anti-Recession Theories

Part (a) illustrates classical theory, which advocates noninterventionist fiscal and monetary policy. The classical assumption is that nominal wages are flexible. At point E_1, unemployed workers compete for jobs, and the wage rate falls causing the short-run aggregate supply curve to shift from SRAS$_1$ to SRAS$_2$. Full employment is therefore automatically restored over time at point E_2.

In part (b), Keynesian policy advocates interventionist fiscal and monetary policy. Discretionary fiscal policy increases government spending or cuts taxes to increase the aggregate demand curve from AD$_1$ to AD$_2$. Discretionary monetary policy would increase the money supply to increase AD$_1$ to AD$_2$.

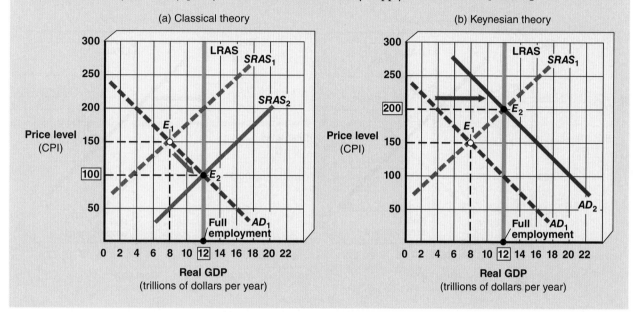

The classical approach to a recession is to let market forces shift the short-run aggregate supply curve rightward and restore the economy to full employment. The opposing Keynesian approach to cure a recession is to use discretionary fiscal and monetary policy to increase aggregate demand and achieve full-employment real GDP.

CONCLUSION

16A-2 CLASSICAL VERSUS KEYNESIAN VIEWS OF CONTRACTIONARY POLICY

Exhibit A-2 shows alternative theories for closing an inflationary gap. The classical non-intervention policy relies on competition between firms in response to a shortage of labor. In parts (a) and (b), the economy is at macro equilibrium at point E_1 where the price level is 150 and real GDP is $16 trillion. There is an inflationary gap because current GDP is greater than the potential real GDP of $12 trillion. In part (a), classical

EXHIBIT A-2 Opposing Anti-Inflation Theories

In part (a), the classical assumption is that at point E_1, firms face a labor shortage and their competition for available workers drives up the nominal wage rate. Under a noninterventionist policy, the short-run aggregate supply curve shifts leftward from SRAS$_1$ to SRAS$_2$, and the economy is automatically restored to full employment at E_2.

Part (b) shows the effect of Keynesian contractionary policy. Discretionary fiscal policy decreases government spending or increases taxes to shift the aggregate demand curve leftward from AD_1 to AD_2. Discretionary monetary policy would decrease the money supply to decrease AD_1 to AD_2.

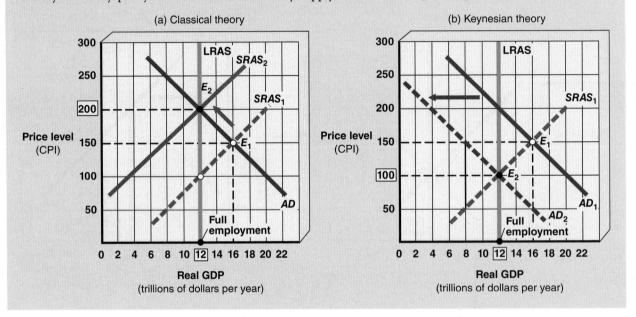

theory assumes flexible wages, so nominal wages rise, causing the SRAS$_1$ to shift upward to SRAS$_2$, and the economy reaches full-employment real GDP at point E_2 with a price level of 200.

In part (b), Keynesian contractionary fiscal policy aims at decreasing AD_1 to AD_2 using cuts in government spending or tax hikes. Working through the multiplier process, the inflationary gap is eliminated, and the economy moves from point E_1 to E_2 where the price level falls from 150 to 100 and full-employment real GDP of $12 trillion is achieved.

According to Keynesians, monetary policy can also be used to shift the aggregate demand curve leftward. In this case, the Federal Reserve could follow a contractionary policy and decrease the money supply, resulting in a higher interest rate, and firms respond by decreasing their investment spending. Consequently, AD_1 decreases to AD_2, and full-employment real GDP is reached at E_2.

As shown in the previous exhibit, opposing theories have different impacts on the price level. In part (a) of Exhibit A-2, the classical approach leads to an increase in the price level from 150 to 200. In contrast, the Keynesian approach yields a decrease in the price level from 150 to 100.

> The classical approach to an inflationary gap is to let market forces shift the short-run aggregate supply curve leftward and restore the economy to full employment. The opposing Keynesian approach to cure inflation uses discretionary fiscal and monetary policy to decrease aggregate demand and achieve full-employment real GDP.

CONCLUSION

Summary

- The *Keynesian prescription for a recession* rejects the classical assumption that wages are flexible and will fall, causing the short-run aggregate supply curve to shift downward and restore full-employment GDP. Instead, Keynesians support expansionary fiscal and monetary policy to increase aggregate demand and return the economy to the natural rate of unemployment.

- The *Keynesian cure for inflation* also rejects the classical assumption that wages are flexible and will rise, causing the short-run aggregate supply curve to shift upward and restore full-employment GDP. In contrast, Keynesian theory advocates contractionary fiscal and monetary policy to decrease aggregate demand and achieve full-employment macro equilibrium.

Summary of Conclusion Statements

- The classical approach to a recession is to let market forces shift the short-run aggregate supply curve rightward and restore the economy to full employment. The opposing Keynesian approach to cure a recession is to use discretionary fiscal and monetary policy to increase aggregate demand and achieve full-employment real GDP.

- The classical approach to an inflationary gap is to let market forces shift the short-run aggregate supply curve leftward and restore the economy to full employment. The opposing Keynesian approach to cure inflation uses discretionary fiscal and monetary policy to decrease aggregate demand and achieve full-employment real GDP.

Study Questions and Problems

Please see Appendix A for answers to the odd-numbered questions. Your instructor has access to the answers for even-numbered questions.

1. Consider an economy in equilibrium with a recessionary gap. Draw a graph where the equilibrium real GDP is $8 trillion and the price level of 150. Label this equilibrium E_1 where the aggregate demand, AD_1, intersects the short-run aggregate supply curve ($SRAS_1$). Include in your graph a long-run aggregate supply curve (LRAS) at the full-employment Real GDP level of, say, $12 trillion.

   a. From a classical perspective, which assumes flexible wages and prices, what happens to wages over time as a result of this recessionary unemployment? How is this change in wage rates reflected in terms of the short-run aggregate supply curve over time? Illustrate this in your graph.

   b. Illustrate long-run equilibrium on your graph as E_2. What has happened to real GDP and the price level in this classical long-run adjustment to full employment?

2. Consider an economy in equilibrium with a recessionary gap. Draw a graph where the equilibrium real GDP is $8 trillion and the price level of 150. Label this equilibrium E_1 where the aggregate demand, AD_1, intersects the short-run aggregate supply curve ($SRAS_1$). Include in your graph a long-run aggregate supply curve (LRAS) at the full-employment Real GDP level of, say, $12 trillion.

   a. From a Keynesian perspective, what should government do with its fiscal and monetary policies to achieve full employment? How is this expansionary policy reflected in terms of the aggregate demand curve? Illustrate this in your graph.

   b. Illustrate long-run equilibrium on your graph as E_2. What has happened to real GDP and the price level as a result of Keynesian policy to achieve full employment in the long run?

3. Consider an economy in equilibrium with an inflationary gap. Draw a graph where the equilibrium real GDP is $16 trillion and the price level of 150. Label this equilibrium E_1 where the aggregate demand, AD_1, intersects the short-run aggregate supply curve ($SRAS_1$). Include in your graph a long-run aggregate supply curve (LRAS) at the full-employment Real GDP level of, say, $12 trillion.

a. From a Keynesian perspective, what should government do with its fiscal and monetary policy to combat inflation and to achieve full employment? How is this contractionary policy reflected in terms of the aggregate demand curve? Illustrate this in your graph.

b. Illustrate long-run equilibrium on your graph as E_2. What has happened to real GDP and the price level as a result of Keynesian policy to achieve full employment in the long run?

4. Consider an economy in equilibrium with an inflationary gap. Draw a graph where the equilibrium real GDP is $16 trillion and the price level of 150. Label this equilibrium E_1 where the aggregate demand, AD_1, intersects the short-run aggregate supply curve ($SRAS_1$). Include in your graph a long-run aggregate supply curve (LRAS) at the full-employment Real GDP level of, say, $12 trillion.

   a. From a classical perspective, which assumes flexible wages and prices, what happens to wages over time as a result of this inflationary gap? How is this change in wage rates reflected in terms of the short-run aggregate supply curve over time? Illustrate this in your graph.

   b. Illustrate long-run equilibrium on your graph as E_2. What has happened to real GDP and the price level in this classical long-run adjustment to full employment?

Sample Quiz

Please see Appendix B for answers to Sample Quiz questions.

1. Classical theory advocates _____ policy, and Keynesian theory advocates _____ policy.
   a. Nonintervention; intervention
   b. Active; nonstabilization
   c. Fixed wages; flexible wages
   d. Active; passive

2. If the economy is in short-run disequilibrium, an economist following classical theory would advocate that the Federal Reserve make appropriate changes in the

   a. money supply.
   b. reserve requirement.
   c. federal funds rate.
   d. None of the answers are correct.

3. Assuming the economy is experiencing a recessionary gap, classical economists predict that
   a. wages will remain fixed.
   b. monetary policy should intervene.

c. higher wages will shift the short-run aggregate supply curve leftward.

d. lower wages will shift the short-run aggregate supply curve rightward.

4. Assume the economy is operating at a real GDP above full-employment real GDP. Keynesian economists would prescribe which of the following policies?
   a. Nonintervention
   b. Passive monetary policy
   c. Contractionary
   d. Expansionary

5. Assume the economy is experiencing an inflationary gap, Keynesian economists believe that
   a. flexible wages will restore full employment.
   b. the federal government should decrease spending to shift the aggregate demand curve leftward.
   c. the Federal Reserve should lower the interest rate.
   d. the federal government should increase spending to shift the aggregate demand curve rightward.

6. Assume the economy is in short-run equilibrium at a real GDP below its potential real GDP. According to Keynesian theory, which of the following policies should be followed?
   a. The Federal Reserve should decrease the money supply.
   b. The federal government should increase spending.
   c. The federal government should do nothing because the economy will self-correct to potential real GDP.
   d. All of the answers are correct.

7. A policy to do nothing and allow the economy to self-correct or adjust without interference from the federal government is also called a (an) _____ policy.
   a. Nonintervention
   b. Active
   c. Stabilization
   d. Fixed rule

8. Assume the economy is experiencing a recessionary gap. Keynesian economists would support which of the following policies?

a. Nonstabilization
b. Expansionary
c. Nonintervention
d. Fixed wage

9. Assuming the economy is in a recession, Keynesian economists predict that
   a. wages will remain fixed.
   b. monetary policy will sell government securities.
   c. higher wages will shift the short-run aggregate supply curve leftward.
   d. lower wages will shift the short-run aggregate supply curve rightward.

10. Assume the economy is in short-run equilibrium at a real GDP above its potential real GDP. According to classical theory, which of the following policies should be followed?
    a. The Federal Reserve should use open market operations and buy U.S. government securities.
    b. The Federal Reserve should not follow a fixed rule.
    c. The federal government should cut taxes.
    d. Fiscal policy and monetary policy should *not* be activist.

11. Assume the economy is experiencing an inflationary gap, classical economists believe that
    a. flexible wages will restore full employment.
    b. the federal government should decrease spending to shift the aggregate demand curve leftward.
    c. the Federal Reserve should lower the interest rate.
    d. the federal government should increase spending to shift the aggregate demand curve rightward.

12. In part (a) of Exhibit A-3, the economy is initially in short-run equilibrium at real GDP level Y_1 and price level P_2. Classical theory argues
    a. the federal government must shift AD_1 to AD_2 as shown in part (b).
    b. the federal government must shift $SRAS_2$ to $SRAS_1$.
    c. $SRAS_1$ will shift to $SRAS_2$ without government intervention.
    d. AD_1 will shift to AD_2 as shown in part (b), without government intervention.

EXHIBIT A-3 Policy Alternatives

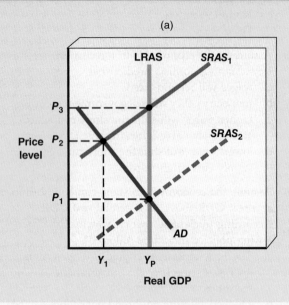

(a)

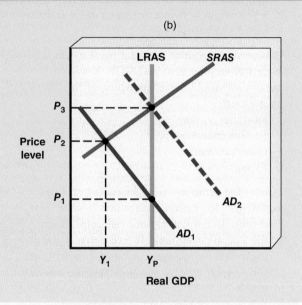

(b)

13. Assume that the economy depicted in part (a) of Exhibit A-3 is in short-run equilibrium with AD and $SRAS_1$. If the economy is left to correct itself according to classical theory
    a. wages will fall as long as real GDP is above Y_p.
    b. lower wages will result in a shift from $SRAS_1$ to $SRAS_2$.
    c. long-run equilibrium will be established at Y_p and P_3.
    d. All of these events will take place.

14. In part (b) of Exhibit A-3, the economy is initially in short-run equilibrium at real GDP level Y_1 and price level P_2. If the government decides to intervene, it would
    a. increase taxes.
    b. decrease the money supply.

c. increase the level of government spending for goods and services.
d. decrease the level of government spending for goods and services.

15. Assume that the economy depicted in part (b) of Exhibit A-3 is in short-run equilibrium with AD_1 and $SRAS$. Keynesian theory argues
    a. nominal wages will fall as long as employment remains above the natural level of unemployment.
    b. lower wages will result in a shift from $SRAS_1$ to $SRAS_2$ as shown in part (a).
    c. long-run equilibrium will be established at Y_p and P_1.
    d. Government intervention must shift AD_1 to AD_2.

CHAPTER 17

The Phillips Curve and Expectations Theory

CHAPTER PREVIEW

This chapter explores the Phillips curve, expectations theory, and incomes policies (wage and price controls). The Phillips curve traces the relationship between two of the greatest problems of economies everywhere—inflation and unemployment. One of the most fascinating puzzles in economics is whether a stable trade-off exists between these two economic evils. If true, policymakers face a dilemma described by the old saying "Inside each solution there is another problem looking to work its way out." If policymakers reduce the unemployment rate, the inflation rate worsens. Or if they reduce the inflation rate, the unemployment rate rises. In the 1960s, most economists and policymakers thought the way to achieve a particular inflation-unemployment point on the Phillips curve menu was to use Keynesian demand-management policies.

Just as the reality of the Great Depression refuted classical theory, the Great Stagflations of the 1970s and early 1980s challenged the Phillips curve and Keynesian policies. To understand how varying rates of inflation can occur at the same rate of unemployment, we explore two competing ways of thinking called *adaptive expectations* and *rational expectations*. Both of these theories are attacks on the Keynesians who urge the government to intervene in the market economy in order to achieve full employment.

The chapter begins with a discussion of the Phillips curve that explains why both expectations camps believe there is no permanent inflation-unemployment tradeoff. In the last part of this chapter, you will see what happens when policymakers fight inflation using policies to control wages and prices (called "incomes policies"), rather than monetary and fiscal policies.

IN THIS CHAPTER, YOU WILL LEARN TO SOLVE THESE ECONOMICS PUZZLES:

- Why might expansionary fiscal and monetary policies be useless in the long run?

- If the Fed is independent, why would the money supply increase before a presidential election?

- Can economic theory explain pop quizzes?

- Can wearing a button reduce inflation?

17-1 THE PHILLIPS CURVE

In a celebrated article published in 1958, Australian economist A. W. Phillips of the London School of Economics plotted data on unemployment rates and the rate of change in wage rates between 1861 and 1957 in the United Kingdom.[1] Phillips showed there was a remarkably stable inverse relationship between changes in money wages and the unemployment rate. Economists have since extended this concept to the following definition of the Phillips curve. The **Phillips curve** is a curve showing an inverse relationship between the inflation rate and the unemployment rate. The reason it is acceptable to use the inflation rate, rather than the change in wages, is that wages are the main component of prices. At low rates of unemployment, labor has the market power to push up wages and, in turn, prices. When many workers are pounding the pavement eager for jobs, labor lacks bargaining power to ask for raises. As a result, the upward pressure on prices eases.

Phillips curve
A curve showing an inverse relationship between the inflation rate and the unemployment rate.

17-1a The Phillips Curve in Theory

Exhibit 1 shows the relationship between the AD-AS model developed earlier and the Phillips curve. In part (a), we assume that the aggregate supply curve, AS, is stationary. Thus, points *A−D* represent possible equilibrium points depending on the location of

EXHIBIT 1 The Theoretical Relationship between Changes in Aggregate Demand and the Phillips Curve

In part (a), the aggregate demand curve shifts upward, while the aggregate supply curve remains stationary. The result is a series of equilibrium points *A−D*. As aggregate demand rises along the *AS* curve, the price level (CPI), real GDP, and employment increase. Points *A−D* in parts (a) and (b) correspond. An increase in aggregate demand from AD_1 to AD_4 causes the unemployment rate to fall, but the inflation rate rises. Thus, the increase in aggregate demand results in a movement upward along the Phillips curve.

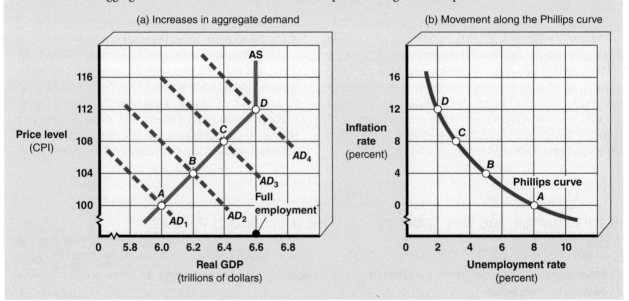

[1]A. W. Phillips, "The Relation between Unemployment and the Rate of Change in Money Wage Rates in the United Kingdom, 1861–1957," *Economica* 25 (November 1958): 283–299.

the aggregate demand curve. As the aggregate demand curve increases from AD_1 to AD_4, real GDP rises from \$6.0 trillion to \$6.6 trillion, more workers are employed, and the price level (CPI) rises from 100 to 112. The astute reader will recognize from the chapter on aggregate demand and supply that this illustrates *demand-pull inflation*.

The inverse relationship between the price level and unemployment in part (a) determines the shape of the Phillips curve in part (a). Points $A-D$ in both figures correspond. If the economy operates at point A, the annual rate of inflation is zero, and the unemployment rate is 8 percent. If the economy is at point B, the annual rate of inflation is 4 percent, and the unemployment rate is 5 percent. Similarly, points C and D correspond in both graphs. Note that below point A the price level is below 100 and the economy experiences deflation.

> Changes in aggregate demand cause a movement along a stationary Phillips curve.

CONCLUSION

17-1b The Phillips Curve in Practice

So far so good. If the world works this way, policymakers must choose from a menu of inflation rate and unemployment rate combinations along the Phillips curve. Do we want X percent less unemployment with an opportunity cost of Y percent more inflation? Early studies verified the Phillips curve for the U.S. economy in the 1960s. As shown in Exhibit 2, the data fit the Phillips curve very well. Based on this evidence, most economists, including Nobel laureates Paul Samuelson and Robert Solow of MIT, believed the Phillips curve was stable. Policymakers might choose low inflation and high unemployment, as in 1961. Or they may prefer higher inflation and lower unemployment, as, for example, in 1969. And the most popular way in the 1960s to reach a particular point on the Phillips curve was to fine-tune the economy using Keynesian demand-management policies.

Then, just as policymakers and economists became comfortable with the Phillips curve, the dream turned into a nightmare. As shown in Exhibit 3, the points for 1970–1990 show the Phillips curve in chaos. The pattern disappeared, and many points moved far above and to the right of the 1960s data. At higher unemployment rates, the corresponding inflation rate was much higher than the Phillips curve predicted. For example, look at 1975, 1979, 1980, and 1981. These data reflect bouts with stagflation—the simultaneous increase in unemployment *and* inflation, which occurred in the 1970s and early 1980s. Recall from Exhibit 13(a) in the chapter on aggregate demand and supply that *cost-push inflation* is the result of a leftward shift of the aggregate supply curve. In the Great Stagflations of 1973–1974 and 1979–1980, the influence of such "supply shocks" as soaring oil prices pushed up production costs and shifted the economy's aggregate supply curve inward. Thus, the Phillips curve theory was in shambles as the nation simultaneously experienced both high inflation and high unemployment. Policymakers therefore turned their focus from the Phillips curve, based on trade-offs, to a "misery index," which added the inflation and unemployment rates.

17-2 THE LONG-RUN PHILLIPS CURVE

The simple idea of a stable trade-off between unemployment and inflation was an overnight sensation in the 1960s. By the early 1970s, the Phillips curve was becoming a has-been. Because Keynesian demand-management policies generate the curve, it will come

EXHIBIT 2 The Phillips Curve for the United States in the 1960s

The figure plots the inflation rate and unemployment rate combinations for the period 1960–1969. A freehand curve drawn through the points conforms very well to the Phillips curve.

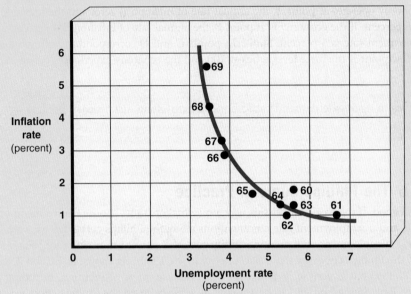

SOURCE: *Historical Inflation Rate,* http://www.inflation.eu/inflation-rates/united-states/historic-inflation/cpi-inflation-united-states.aspx and *Economic Report of the President 1980,* http://www.presidency.ucsb.edu/economic_reports/1980.pdf and Table B–52, and Bureau of Labor Statistics https://data.bls.gov/pdq/SurveyOutputServlet.

as no surprise that monetarists such as Milton Friedman and Edmund S. Phelps always believed the Phillips curve was just a transitory, short-run relationship. In the mid-1960s, they suggested that the unemployment rate and the rate of inflation are unrelated in the long run. As shown in Exhibit 4, the challengers argued that after a few years the Phillips curve is a vertical line. As explained in the following, this monetarist view is also debatable.

17-2a Natural Rate Hypothesis

If the Phillips curve is vertical in the long run, there are profound implications for macroeconomic policy. Expansionary monetary and fiscal policies can at best produce a short-lived lowering of unemployment. This is the so-called natural rate hypothesis. The **natural rate hypothesis** argues that the economy will self-correct to the natural rate of unemployment. The long-run Phillips curve is therefore a vertical line at the natural rate of unemployment. Recall from the chapter on business cycles and unemployment that the natural rate of unemployment, or the full-employment unemployment rate, is equal to the sum of the frictional and structural unemployment rates. In Exhibit 4, let's assume the natural rate of unemployment is 6 percent. Two versions of expectations theory explain the natural rate model. We begin our analysis using *adaptive expectations theory* and then turn to the more recent *rational expectations theory.*

Natural rate hypothesis
The concept that argues that the economy will self-correct to the natural rate of unemployment. The long-run Phillips curve is therefore a vertical line at the natural rate of unemployment.

EXHIBIT 3 Inflation and Unemployment Rates for the United States, 1970–1990

By 1990, the Phillips curve became unstable. Clearly, many points have been established upward and to the right. The inflation rate therefore can be much higher at any unemployment rate than the Phillips curve of the 1960s predicted.

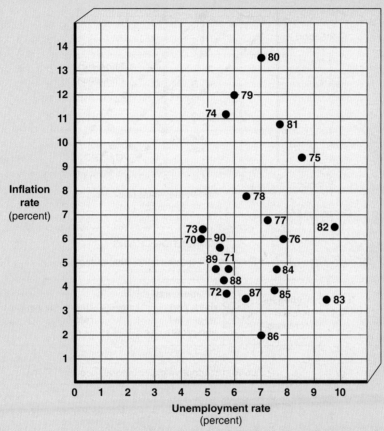

SOURCE: *Historical Inflation Rate*, http://www.inflation.eu/inflation-rates/united-states/historic-inflation/cpi-inflation-united-states.aspx and *Economic Report of the President 2017*, https://www.govinfo.gov/content/pkg/ERP-2017/pdf/ERP-2017.pdf, Tables B-10 and B-12.

17-2b Adaptive Expectations Theory

To explain the reasoning behind the natural rate hypothesis, let us begin in Exhibit 4 with the economy operating at point *A*, with a 3 percent inflation rate and a 6 percent unemployment rate. Assume the inflation rate has been 3 percent in recent years and this trend is expected to continue. Based on this recent 3 percent rise in the CPI, collective bargaining agreements call for hourly nominal or money wages of $10.00 this year and $10.30 next year. Now suppose an election is approaching and the president and Congress strive to make voters happy by reducing the unemployment rate to 4 percent. Or perhaps policymakers "incorrectly" believe 4 percent is the natural rate of unemployment. Regardless of the reason for setting this goal, suppose the new expansionary fiscal

EXHIBIT 4 The Short-Run and Long-Run Phillips Curves

Beginning at point *A*, the economy is operating at the 6 percent natural rate of unemployment. The actual and anticipated inflation rates are 3 percent. An increase in aggregate demand temporarily causes the inflation rate to rise to 6 percent. Under adaptive expectations theory, real wages fall, profits rise, and more workers are employed. The unemployment rate falls to 4 percent, and the economy moves along the short-run Phillips curve PC_1 to point *B*. Over time, workers demand and get nominal wage rate hikes, and profits fall. Workers lose their jobs, and the unemployment rate returns to 6 percent at point *C* on the short-run Phillips curve PC_2. This process will repeat each time expansionary policy attempts to reduce unemployment below the natural rate. The long-run Phillips curve is therefore a vertical line at the natural rate of unemployment. This suggests that Keynesian expansionary policies create only inflation over time.

Under rational expectations theory, workers do not rely only on recent experience. They adjust their nominal wages quickly in proportion to changes in prices. Expansionary policy will move the economy directly upward along the long-run Phillips curve.

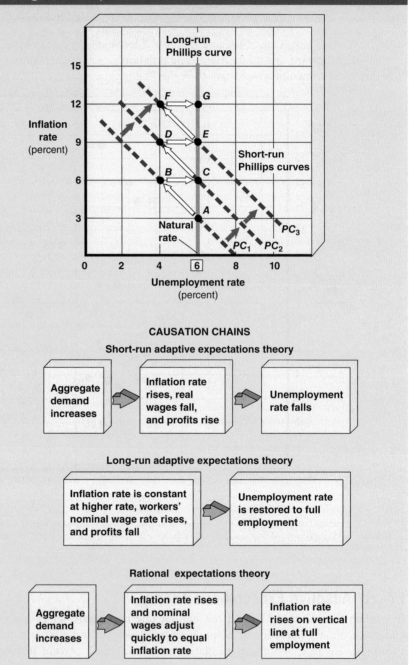

policy shifts the aggregate demand curve upward along the aggregate supply curve and the economy moves unexpectedly from point *A* this year to point *B* the next year.

Keynesians declare "mission accomplished" when the economy moves up the short-run Phillips curve PC_1 from point *A* to point *B*. This unexpected change brings good news to businesses. Based on an expected inflation rate of 3 percent, employers agreed to pay real wages of $10.00 at point *B*. However, if the inflation rate rises unexpectedly to 6 percent, real wages fall to $9.72 as prices rise.[2] With cheaper labor costs in real terms, profits increase, more workers are hired, real GDP expands, and the unemployment rate drops to 4 percent.

So far, Keynesians and monetarists agree that policymakers and businesses are running the race as though they are the hare and the workers are acting like the tortoise. But monetarists do not believe workers are caught flatfooted as time passes. Workers soon realize that higher prices have eroded their purchasing power. Consequently, they demand an extra 3 percent raise in the nominal wage rate so that their real wages can be restored to the level prior to the unexpected rise in the inflation rate from 3 to 6 percent. When workers get their raise to offset the higher cost of living, business profits decline, and some workers are laid off until the unemployment rate returns to 6 percent at point *C*. At point *C*, the unemployment rate is right back where it began before the government unsystematically changed its fiscal policy, but the inflation rate has risen from 3 to 6 percent. Keynesians, on the other hand, believe nominal wages are fixed because workers do not demand and get an extra 3 percent rise in nominal wages. In the Keynesian view, demand stimulus reduced unemployment in exchange for the higher inflation rate, and the economy remains at point *B* and does not automatically move in time to point *C*.

Our story describes a *wage-price spiral*, defined in the chapter on inflation, and we need a theory to explain how people form their inflationary expectations. The reason the economy moved from point *A* to point *B* is based on adaptive expectations theory. **Adaptive expectations theory** is the concept that people believe the best indicator of the future is recent information. As a result, people persistently underestimate inflation when it is accelerating and overestimate it while it is slowing down. Adaptive expectations theory assumes ignorance of future events, including changes in fiscal and monetary policies. People learn from recent experience and gradually adjust their anticipated inflation rate to the actual inflation rate. This means that at point *C* workers expect a higher rate of inflation at any unemployment rate because last year the actual rate of inflation was 6 percent. Unions therefore expect a 6 percent rate of inflation and are no longer satisfied with a contract with less than a 6 percent increase in the nominal wage rate; since anything less would mean a cut in real wages. Thus, workers *adapt* their expectations to 6 percent instead of 3 percent, and the short-run Phillips curve shifts outward from PC_1 to PC_2 in Exhibit 4. In other words, the economy moves from point *A* to point *C* on the vertical long-run Phillips curve. If policymakers follow a contractionary policy, adaptive expectations operate in reverse, and the inflation rate declines (see You're the Economist: The Political Business Cycle).

Suppose policymakers figure expansionary policy worked last time, so why not try it again? So they take another stab at creating jobs by stimulating aggregate demand. This time the economy will ride up the new short-run Phillips curve PC_2 from point *C* to point *D*, and the whole process will repeat. When the actual inflation rate rises from 6 to 9 percent, nominal wage increases will be a step slow in catching up with price hikes. In time, workers will demand and get a nominal wage hike, which restores their real wage rate, and the economy will reach point *E*. Faced with the new short-run Phillips curve PC_3, the government will cause an inflation rate of 12 percent at point *F* if it persists in trying to achieve 4 percent

Adaptive expectations theory

The concept that people believe the best indicator of the future is recent information. As a result, people persistently underestimate inflation when it is accelerating and overestimate it while it is slowing down.

---

[2]Assume the price level at point *A* is 100 and the price level rises to 106 at point *B*. The real wage is computed as the nominal wage multiplied by the initial price level divided by the new price level. Thus, the real wage rate at point *B* is equal to $10.30 × (100/106) = $9.72. If the price level had risen to 103, as expected, the real wage at point *B* would have equaled $10.30 × (100/103) = $10.00.

unemployment. Eventually, nominal wages will rise (reducing profits), some workers will lose their jobs, and the economy will move from point *F* to point *G*.

CONCLUSION According to adaptive expectations theory, expansionary monetary and fiscal policies to reduce the unemployment rate are useless in the long run. After a short-run reduction in unemployment, the economy will self-correct to the natural rate of unemployment, but at a higher inflation rate. Thus, there is no long-run trade-off between inflation and unemployment.

17-2c The Long-Run Phillips Curve and the Labor Market

We can now give one explanation for the tendency of the inflation-unemployment points shown earlier in Exhibit 3 to shift upward to the right in the 1970s and early 1980s. Demand stimulus policies in the 1960s caught people by surprise, and there was a movement upward along a short-run Phillips curve. As inflation worsened during the 1970s and the early 1980s, adaptive expectations caused the short-run Phillips curves to shift outward. As the inflation rate dropped sharply during the late 1980s, people's inflationary expectations adapted in the downward direction, and the short-run Phillips curve shifted inward. Moreover, as discussed in the chapter on business cycles and unemployment, economists estimated that the *natural rate of unemployment* increased from the 1960s to the 1980s. Recall that the natural rate of unemployment is the full-employment unemployment rate at which the economy operates at capacity (potential GDP). This means the vertical long-run Phillips curve intersecting each short-run Phillips curve shifted to the right. The explanation, in part, is because women and teenagers became a larger percentage of the labor force, and these groups of workers often experience higher rates of unemployment. It is also argued that the following measures might reduce the natural rate of unemployment: revising unemployment compensation, changing the minimum wage law, providing better education and training, improving information on available jobs, removing discrimination, and reducing the monopoly power of unions and businesses.

17-3 THE THEORY OF RATIONAL EXPECTATIONS

Rational expectations theory
The belief that people use all available information to predict the future, including the future impact of predictable expansionary monetary and fiscal policies. Predictable expansionary macroeconomic policies can therefore be negated by immediately flexible wages and prices when businesses and workers anticipate the effects of these policies on the economy.

Whether expectations are formed "adaptively" or "rationally" is a hotly contested debate among economists. In the mid-1970s, Robert Lucas of the University of Chicago (1995 Nobel Laureate) is generally credited with introducing rational expectations theory, which is the competing view that adaptive expectations theory is too simplistic. **Rational expectations theory** is the belief that people use all available information to predict the future, including future monetary and fiscal policies. Hands-on discretionary macroeconomic policies intended to stabilize the economy can therefore be negated when businesses and workers anticipate the effects of these policies on the economy. According to the rational expectations hypothesis, people do not simply think inflation will be about the same next year as last year. Although everyone's crystal ball is clouded, people are intelligent and informed on how the economy works. They not only consider past price changes, but also consider how changes in the federal deficit or money supply will affect inflation next year. Suppose businesses and workers predict that a surge in the money supply or a tax cut will raise the actual inflation rate to, say, 6 percent. They

YOU'RE THE **ECONOMIST**

Applicable Concept: Adaptive Expectations

The Political Business Cycle

The basic ideal of Keynesian economics is that the government uses monetary and fiscal policies to stabilize the economy. On the other hand, the government may be diabolical and deliberately cause business cycles. The **political business cycle** is therefore Keynesianism in reverse. A political business cycle is a business cycle caused by policymakers to improve politicians' reelection chances.

A basic assumption of the political business cycle model is that democratic government causes business cycles. This theory views politics as by nature a short-run game. The rational self-interest goal of politicians is to maximize votes today and worry about tomorrow when tomorrow comes. This means a politician who faces an election must act now and not later. Voters are also short-sighted and want good news now, rather than promises of long-term solutions. If people want jobs, for example, the politicians who seek reelection will use expansionary policies to create jobs. The political process will therefore gladly force a lower unemployment rate now in exchange for a higher inflation rate in the future. The politician who commits the sin of truth and tells the voters a "quick fix" is harmful will probably taste defeat.

Given the realities of politics, politicians may find it easier to let the Fed stimulate the economy. Expansionary fiscal policy requires Congress to approve tax cuts or spending increases. Since members of Congress belong to opposing parties, each side has an incentive to prevent the other party from taking credit for legislation. Even if a bill eventually passes, it may be too late for the election. Fiscal policy takes considerable time to implement and actually affect the economy and, in turn, the voters.

If the Fed is independent, why would the Fed be willing to create political business cycles? Recall that the president appoints the Fed chair and members of the Board of Governors. Thus, the Fed is a semiseparate branch of government that often wishes to avoid conflict with Congress or the president. If the Fed is willing to stimulate aggregate demand before an election, incumbent politicians will benefit at the expense of their opponents. Once the election is over, the Fed will slow down the economy to reduce

Pool/Hulton Archive/Newsmakers/Getty Images

the inflation rate. Then the concern becomes recession until the next election looms and the Fed stimulates the economy again. Meanwhile, politicians can blame the Fed for driving up prices or starting the downturn.

Exhibit 5 reveals that the money supply has generally been on the rise before presidential elections. In 1964, 1968, 1972, 1976, 1980 (slight), 1988, 1992, 2008, and 2012, the money supply rose before the presidential election and then fell afterward (it rose before the 2016 election, too, and time will tell whether it falls much after that). The 1984, 1996, 2000, and 2004 elections were exceptions.

ANALYZE THE ISSUE   Based on adaptive expectations theory, assume an expansionary monetary policy has moved the economy to point *C* in Exhibit 4. Now suppose the election is over and inflation concerns policymakers, so the Fed applies the brakes to monetary policy. Use this diagram to explain the short-run and long-run effects of a contractionary monetary policy.

will immediately raise their expectations of the inflation rate to 6 percent even though the most recent rate of inflation was 3 percent. In short, rational expectationists believe that both nominal wages and prices are flexible.

Let's reconsider the case in which the government is trying to reduce the unemployment rate. Begin at point *A* in Exhibit 4 and suppose policymakers strive to reduce unemployment using new expansionary policies to stimulate demand. Under rational

Political business cycle
A business cycle caused by policymakers to improve politicians' reelection chances.

EXHIBIT 5 Money Supply Growth and Presidential Elections, 1960–2016

Since 1960, the money supply has often increased prior to presidential elections. The 1984, 1996, 2000, and 2004 elections were exceptions.

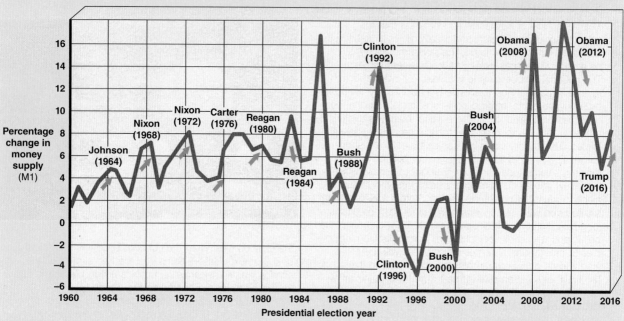

SOURCE: *Economic Report of the President 2017*, https://www.govinfo.gov/features/ERP-2017, Table B–26.

expectations theory, workers are not caught napping. Workers will not simply wait until the actual inflation rate exceeds the expected inflation rate at point *B* and then ask for a raise. Although they may lack formal training in forecasting, workers are quite sophisticated in understanding the macro economy. They watch news on television; check economic data on the Internet, and read *The Wall Street Journal*, *Time*, the local newspapers, and AFL-CIO publications for information on government policies and future changes in prices. When new information becomes available, workers revise their expectations.

Because workers wisely use all relevant information to predict future changes, they anticipate that the aggregate demand curve is going to shift rightward, causing a rise in the price level and a fall in real wages. They know that unless they get wage hikes to match the price increases, they will be losers. Consequently, workers rationally raise their nominal wage demands without a time lag so that no gap between the actual and expected rates of inflation occurs. In fact, many collective bargaining agreements contain escalator clauses or cost-of-living-adjustments (COLAs), providing automatic nominal wage increases as the price level rises. Assuming that workers correctly anticipate the inflation rate, real wages remain unchanged because nominal wages and prices rise proportionately. This means the temporary increase in profits, real GDP, and employment does *not* happen as predicted by adaptive expectationists. In short, rational expectationists refute the short-run Phillips curves drawn in Exhibit 4. There would be, for example, no decrease in unemployment from 6 percent (point *A*) to 4 percent (point *B*). Instead, the only movement in the inflation rate is directly from 3 percent (point *A*) to 6 percent (point *C*). This means higher anticipated inflation is added without delay to current nominal wages and prices, which generates a vertical Phillips curve along such points as *A*, *C*, *E*, and *G*.

> **CONCLUSION**
>
> According to rational expectations theory, expansionary monetary and fiscal policies used to reduce unemployment are not only useless, but they are also harmful because the only result is higher inflation.

On the brighter side, rational expectations theory argues that a credible "stay the course" contractionary fiscal and monetary policy can quickly cool inflation without increasing unemployment. Suppose the economy is at the natural rate of unemployment and the Fed decreases the money supply to lower the rate of inflation. Workers analyze available information on the future impact of the Fed's action from AFL-CIO economists and other sources. They are convinced that policymakers are committed to decreasing aggregate demand until the price level recedes. Armed with this analysis, workers are not surprised, and they reduce their nominal wages as prices fall. In this case, there is no short-run Phillips curve. Contrary to adaptive expectations, inflation can be cured without recession because workers are not caught off guard.

Keynesians reject rational expectations theory because they argue that prices and wages are "sticky" downward (see Exhibit 4 of the chapter on aggregate demand and supply). On the other hand, the classical economists believed that the economy automatically adjusts after short-run delays to full employment in the long run. But in the rational expectations model, not so! There is no short run. Nevertheless, because the theory of rational expectations is similar to the self-correction model of the classical economists, rational expectationists are called *new classical* economists.

> **CONCLUSION**
>
> According to rational expectations theory, flexible wages and prices adjust immediately to negate predictable monetary and fiscal policy changes, so the economy's self-correction mechanism will very quickly restore the natural rate of unemployment. Therefore, discretionary policies should be abandoned and fixed-rule, stable policies to achieve constant money supply growth and a balanced federal budget are therefore the best way to lower the inflation rate.

Does Rational Expectations Theory Work in the Classroom?

An economics professor is considering improving class attendance and preparation by giving pop quizzes. Two approaches are being considered: If rational expectations theory operates in the classroom, should the professor give pop quizzes on days when homework is due, or keep the pop quizzes a secret and give them randomly?

CHECKPOINT

17-4 APPLYING THE AD-AS MODEL TO THE GREAT EXPECTATIONS DEBATE

The distinction between adaptive expectations and rational expectations can be analyzed using the aggregate demand-aggregate supply model presented in Exhibit 6. Assume the economy is currently in equilibrium at point E_1, with a full-employment output of $6 trillion. Now suppose the Fed pursues an expansionary monetary policy designed to create jobs and further reduce unemployment. Hence, the aggregate demand curve shifts rightward from AD_1 to AD_2 along the short-run aggregate supply curve $SRAS_1$. Based on adaptive expectations theory, a monetarist urges the Fed to leave the economy alone. The monetarist's prediction is that the economy will move from equilibrium at E_1 to E_2, causing real GDP to rise from the potential GDP of $6 trillion to the GDP of $6.5 trillion. Recall from Exhibit 9 of the chapter on business cycles and unemployment that this condition in the economy is a positive GDP gap of $0.5 trillion. In addition, the price level (CPI) increases from 100 to 105. Eventually, at equilibrium E_2, with unemployment below the natural rate, workers are no longer "caught off guard" and demand higher nominal wages to offset the rise in prices. As a result, production costs rise, causing the short-run aggregate supply curve to shift leftward from $SRAS_1$ to $SRAS_2$; therefore, a new equilibrium is established at E_3. This response drives up the unemployment rate to the natural rate as real output returns to the initial level of $6 trillion. However, Fed activism has not had a neutral effect on the price level because it has risen from the initial level of 100 to 110. The monetarist's prediction is therefore higher inflation and no impact on employment and real GDP in the long run.

A rational expectationist sees events differently. Most people are not "fooled." They are able to rationally predict the consequences of expansionary monetary policies. People anticipate that the economy will move from point E_1 to point E_3, the price level will rise from 100 to 110, and real GDP will not change. Consequently, businesses and workers do not stumble around in the dark, unable to see what the actual inflation rate is going to be. They know, or *anticipate*, that the inflation rate is going to rise 10 percent, and they react immediately by raising prices and wages 10 percent. Because prices and wages increase quickly and proportionately, rational expectations theory predicts a direct path of change in the economy's equilibrium from E_1 to E_3. Stated differently, if firms and workers formulate expectations rationally, any impact of stimulative monetary policy is nullified. Under rational expectations theory, only *unanticipated* or *surprise* policies can influence output and employment. But monetary and fiscal policies based on surprises are not practical.

If workers foresee inflation and prevent erosion of their real wages by demanding and receiving nominal wage raises in advance, aggregate supply is the vertical curve, LRAS. When real wages remain unchanged, there is no incentive for businesses to alter production as prices rise. If rational expectations theory is correct, the economy does not enjoy the short-lived pleasure of lower unemployment at point E_2, as predicted by adaptive expectations theory.

EXHIBIT 6 Adaptive Expectations versus Rational Expectations

Suppose policymakers use expansionary policies to increase the aggregate demand curve from AD_1 to AD_2. Adaptive expectations theory argues that labor adjusts nominal wages sluggishly. As a result, the path of the economy is E_1 to E_2 to E_3 with a temporary increase in real GDP to $6.5 trillion and lower unemployment at point E_2. The theory of rational expectations is the competing view that the expansionary policy used to increase the aggregate demand curve from AD_1 to AD_2 is anticipated. Workers anticipate that the price level (CPI) will rise to 110, so they increase their nominal wages without a period of adjustment. As a result, the aggregate supply curve shifts from $SRAS_1$ to $SRAS_2$, causing the economy to move directly from equilibrium point E_1 to point E_3. The result of Keynesian expansionary policies under both theories is that inflation becomes worse and there is no effect on real GDP or employment.

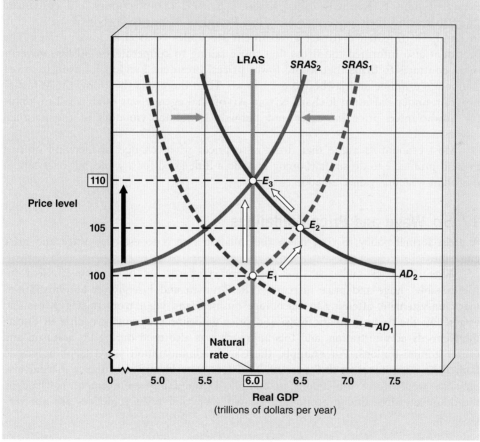

17-5 INCOMES POLICY

Suppose we accept the power of unions and businesses to raise wages and prices as inevitable. Let's also assume Milton Friedman is correct that discretionary monetary and fiscal policies are useless or counterproductive. Then what approach is left to fight inflation? There is another way, used in the past, which is a collection of regulatory policies called incomes policies. **Incomes policies** are federal government policies designed to affect the real incomes of workers by controlling nominal wages and prices. Such policies include presidential jawboning, wage-price guidelines, and wage-price controls.

17-5a Presidential Jawboning

The mildest form of incomes policies is jawboning. **Jawboning** is oratory intended to pressure unions and businesses to reduce wage and price increases. The government attempts to prevent or roll back wage and price hikes by appealing to labor and business leaders. The most spectacular success with this technique occurred in 1962. President John F. Kennedy called major U.S. steel manufacturers and convinced them to rescind their price increases. But President Kennedy jawboned with a club in hand. He threatened to sell government stockpiles of steel at lower prices. The president also informed the firms that those failing to cooperate would lose government contracts to firms that would lower prices. President Lyndon Johnson followed Kennedy's example and jawboned even more. Then there was the "Blow the Whistle" program under President Richard Nixon. An official agency was established to monitor unwarranted price increases and publicly announce violators of the national interest.

Most economists argue that firms raise prices when changes in demand or cost make it profitable to do so. Jawboning may do a little good for a while, but over time it is a blunt weapon against inflation.

17-5b Wage and Price Guidelines

A more formal policy to cool down the inflation rate is to establish wage and price guidelines.

Wage and price guidelines are voluntary standards set by the government for "permissible" wage and price increases. The Truman and Eisenhower administrations made unsystematic attempts to discourage business and labor from raising prices and wages. But the first systematic wage and price guideline program was initiated during the Kennedy administration, and this approach was also used during the Johnson and Carter administrations. For example, the Carter administration asked labor unions to limit their wage increases to 7 percent. Violators were identified in hopes that adverse publicity would force the unions to comply. Without any enforcement mechanism, the dominant view among economists is that wage and price guidelines are not very effective.

17-5c Wage and Price Controls

When guidelines have the force of law, the economy moves to a mandatory system of wage and price controls. **Wage and price controls** are legal restrictions on wage and price increases. Violations can result in fines and imprisonment. After people believe

Incomes policies
Federal government policies designed to affect the real incomes of workers by controlling nominal wages and prices. Such policies include presidential jawboning, wage-price guidelines, and wage-price controls.

Jawboning
Oratory intended to pressure unions and businesses to reduce wage and price increases.

Wage and price guidelines
Voluntary standards set by the government for "permissible" wage and price increases.

Wage and price controls
Legal restrictions on wage and price increases. Violations can result in fines and imprisonment.

wages and prices are under control by law, the good news is that they expect lower prices. The bad news is that controls are government interference with market supply and demand.

As discussed in Chapter 4, a ceiling price established below the equilibrium price will cause shortages in markets (see Exhibit 5 in Chapter 4). This usually means rationing of such scarce items as gasoline. When price is not allowed to serve as the rationing device, consumers must incur higher opportunity costs by waiting in long lines for gasoline. This happened in 1979, when the government imposed a price ceiling on gasoline. Another rationing device is government ration coupons that give the right to buy a good. Ration coupons were used for many goods during World War II. Shortages also lead to *black markets*, which are illegal markets for goods at unregulated prices. To enforce the system requires a government bureaucracy at taxpayers' expense.

Long lines for products, ration coupons, and black markets are not popular. This explains why wage and price controls appear primarily during war and rarely in peacetime. The United States imposed wage and price controls during World War II; the Korean War and the Nixon administration hoped to combat high inflationary expectations built up during the Vietnam War. The inflation rate from 1969 to 1971 averaged 5.2 percent, an alarming rate in those days. The plan was to control inflation and then fight unemployment, which averaged 4.8 percent over the same period. The first phase of the attack was a 90-day freeze on wages and prices in August 1971. A 15-member Pay Board and a 7-member Price Commission administered the controls. For three months, businesses could not raise prices, wages were frozen, and landlords could not charge higher rents. The intent was to give inflationary expectations a shock treatment. Then the freeze lifted, and wage and price controls were established to limit increases between 1971 and 1974. The bottom line is that in 1971 the inflation rate was 4.4 percent. In 1973, the inflation rate climbed to 6.2 percent. When the experiment with controls ended in 1974, the inflation rate rose to 11 percent. During the same period, the unemployment rate remained between 5 and 6 percent. Obviously, controls did not slay the inflation dragon, although some economists have argued that controls made the dragon less fierce.

In 1968, the Council of Economic Advisors eloquently stated the opinion of most economists on wage and price controls:

> *While such controls may be necessary under conditions of an all-out war, it would be folly to consider them as a solution to inflationary pressures that accompany high employment under any other circumstance.... Although such controls may be unfortunately popular when they are in effect, the appeal quickly disappears once people live under them.*[3]

The majority view is that controls destroy the efficient allocation of resources provided by the price system and intrude on economic freedom. Defenders of controls believe this is a small price to pay.

---

[3]*Annual Report of the Council of Economic Advisors* (Washington, D.C.: Government Printing Office, 1968), p. 119.

CHECKPOINT

Can Wage and Price Controls Cure Stagflation?

Suppose war in the Persian Gulf destroys much of the world's oil reserves. As a result, the U.S. economy is experiencing a bout of stagflation. You are a member of Congress, and a bill is introduced to fight the problems of high inflation and high unemployment by imposing wage and price controls. Using the AD-AS model, will you vote in favor of controls to cure stagflation by freezing the price level? [Hint: Look at Exhibit 5 of Chapter 4 and Exhibit 13(a) in the chapter on aggregate demand and supply.]

17-6 HOW DIFFERENT MACROECONOMIC THEORIES ATTACK INFLATION

If incomes policies do not cure an overheated economy during peacetime, policymakers must decide which macroeconomic school "hat" to wear. Exhibit 7 gives a brief description of how four basic macroeconomic models deal with inflation. Recall the monetarist view presented in the previous chapter and supply-side economics explained in the chapter on fiscal policy.

EXHIBIT 7   How Different Macroeconomic Models Cure Inflation

School of thought Monetarism

Inflation prescription

Monetarists see the cause of inflation as "too much money chasing too few goods," based on the quantity of money theory (MV = PQ). To cure inflation, they would cut the money supply and force the Fed to stick to a fixed money supply growth rate. In the short run, the unemployment rate will rise, but in the long run, it self-corrects to the natural rate.

School of thought Keynesianism

Inflation prescription

Keynesians believe in using contractionary fiscal and monetary policies to cool an overheated economy. To decrease aggregate demand, they advocate that the government use tax hikes and/or spending cuts. The Fed should reduce the money supply and cause the rate of interest to rise. The opportunity cost of reducing inflation is greater unemployment. Keynesians also believe that incomes policies are effective.

School of thought Supply-side economics

Inflation prescription

Supply-siders view the cause of inflation as "not enough goods." Their approach is to increase aggregate supply through cuts in marginal tax rates, government regulations, and import barriers. The effect provides incentives to work, invest, and expand production capacity. Thus, both the inflation rate and the unemployment rate fall.

School of thought New classical school

Inflation prescription

The theory of rational expectations asserts that the public must be convinced that policymakers will stick to restrictive and persistent fiscal and monetary policies. If policymakers have credibility, the inflation rate will be anticipated and will quickly fall without a rise in unemployment.

YOU'RE THE ECONOMIST

Applicable Concept: Incomes Policies

Ford's Whip Inflation Now (WIN) Button

The most interesting historical artifact of the fight against inflation is gathering dust in the White House attic. In October 1974, President Gerald Ford proposed the "WIN" button to a joint session of Congress. The idea was that Americans would wear their "Whip Inflation Now" buttons, and this would break the wage-price spiral. The WIN button represented an appeal to patriotism that would discourage businesses and labor from raising prices and wages.

The logical question is, What circumstances drove the president of the United States to use a button against inflation? We will begin the story in 1971, when the Nixon administration approved wage and price controls to cool inflationary expectations. Beginning in 1972, bad crops caused food prices to soar, and the OPEC oil embargo boosted the price of crude oil. These supply shocks boosted the inflation rate from 3.2 percent in 1972 to 6.2 percent in 1973. Clearly, the wage and price control program was falling apart before controls ended in 1974.

Following the demand-management prescription against inflation, the Fed raised the discount rate in late 1973. Federal Reserve Chair Arthur Burns stated that the Fed must follow a contractionary monetary policy for years to come. Despite the Fed's restrictive policy, the inflation rate rose to an annual rate of about 14 percent in early 1974. By late 1974, the unemployment rate had risen to 6 percent, but policymakers remained committed to anti-inflation policies. The Fed raised the discount rate again in the fall of 1974, and President Ford called an economic summit meeting. The outcome of the summit was a resolve to stick to the battle plan and beat inflation before turning to the worsening unemployment problem. Aiming for public support, President Ford unveiled the WIN button, accompanied by a tax surcharge and federal spending ceiling proposals. While the fight against inflation preoccupied policymakers, the unemployment rate rose from 5.6 percent in 1974 to 8.5 percent in 1975. The percentage change in real GDP between 1974 and 1975 was −0.6 percent, and recession suddenly replaced inflation as the number one enemy. In response, Congress approved a $22.8 billion tax cut bill in 1975, and the Fed

Gerald R. Ford Presidential Museum/U.S. National Archives and Records Administration (NARA)

increased the money supply. In 1974, the inflation rate was 11.0 percent, and in 1975, the inflation rate was still at the high rate of 9.1 percent.

What caused this puzzling twist in stabilization policy to deal with stagflation? Many economists explain this turn of events by the absence of a conceptual framework to understand the effects of supply shocks on the aggregate supply curve. Instead, policymakers tried to shift the aggregate demand curve back and forth while asking people to wear a WIN button.

ANALYZE THE ISSUE Assume the economy is in equilibrium at full employment and the public anticipates restrictive monetary and fiscal policies, including WIN buttons, which decrease aggregate demand in order to combat inflation. Use the AD-AS model depicted in Exhibit 6 to explain the new classical predictions of the impact on the price level, real GDP, and the unemployment rate.

Key Concepts

Phillips curve

Natural rate hypothesis

Adaptive expectations theory

Rational expectations theory

Political business cycle

Incomes policies

Jawboning

Wage and price guidelines

Wage and price controls

Summary

- The **Phillips curve** shows a stable inverse relationship between the inflation rate and the unemployment rate. If policymakers reduce inflation, unemployment increases, and vice versa. During the 1960s, the curve closely fit the inflation and unemployment rates in the United States. Since 1970, the Phillips curve has not conformed to the stable inflation-unemployment trade-off pattern of the 1960s.

The Phillips Curve for the United States in the 1960s

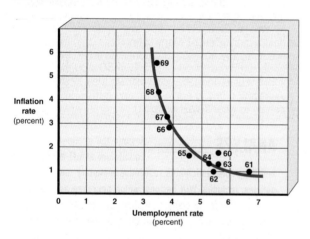

- The **natural rate hypothesis** argues that the economy self-corrects to the natural rate of unemployment. Over time, changes in the rate of inflation are fully anticipated, and prices and wages rise or fall proportionately. As a result, the long-run Phillips curve is a vertical line at the natural rate of unemployment. Thus, Keynesian demand-management policies ultimately cause

only higher or lower inflation, and the natural rate of unemployment remains unchanged.

- **Adaptive expectations theory** is the proposition that people base their economic forecasts on recent past information, rather than future information. Once the government causes the inflation rate to rise or fall, people adapt their inflationary expectations to the current inflation rate. The result is a short-run Phillips curve that intersects the vertical long-run Phillips curve. Over time, the economy self-corrects to the natural rate of unemployment.

- **Rational expectations theory** argues that it is naive to believe that people change their inflationary expectations based only on the current inflation rate. Rational expectationists belong to the new classical school. Assuming the impact of government policy is predictable; people immediately anticipate higher or lower inflation. Workers quickly change their nominal wages as businesses change prices. Consequently, inflation worsens or improves, and unemployment remains unchanged at the natural rate. Thus, there is no short-run Phillips curve, and the vertical long-run Phillips curve is identical to adaptive expectations theory.

- The **political business cycle** is created by the incentive for politicians to manipulate the economy to get re-elected. Using expansionary policies, officeholders can stimulate the economy before an election. Unemployment falls, and the price level rises. After the election, the strategy is to contract the economy to fight inflation, and unemployment rises.

- **Incomes policies** are a variety of federal government programs aimed at directly controlling wages and prices. Incomes policies include jawboning, wage-price guidelines, and wage-price controls. Over time, incomes policies tend to be ineffective.

- **Jawboning** is oratory intended to pressure unions and businesses to reduce wage and price increases.

- **Wage and price guidelines** are voluntary standards, set by the government for "permissible" wage and price increases.

- **Wage and price controls** are legal restrictions on wages and prices. Most economists do not favor wage and price controls in peacetime. Such controls are expensive to administer, destroy efficiency, and intrude on economic freedom.

Summary of Conclusion Statements

- Changes in aggregate demand cause a movement along a stationary Phillips curve.

- According to adaptive expectations theory, expansionary monetary and fiscal policies to reduce the unemployment rate are useless in the long run. After a short-run reduction in unemployment, the economy will self-correct to the natural rate of unemployment, but at a higher inflation rate. Thus, there is no long-run trade-off between inflation and unemployment.

- According to rational expectations theory, expansionary monetary and fiscal policies used to reduce unemployment are not only useless, but they are also harmful because the only result is higher inflation.

- According to rational expectations theory, flexible wages and prices adjust immediately to negate predictable monetary and fiscal policy changes, so the economy's self-correction mechanism will very quickly restore the natural rate of unemployment. Therefore, discretionary policies should be abandoned, and fixed-rule, stable policies to achieve constant money supply growth and a balanced federal budget are the best way to lower the inflation rate.

Study Questions and Problems

Please see Appendix A for answers to the odd-numbered questions. Your instructor has access to the answers for even-numbered questions.

1. What is a short-run Phillips curve? Assuming the economy's short-run aggregate supply curve is stable, how would an increase in aggregate demand affect the unemployment rate and the inflation rate?

2. What were the inflation rate and the unemployment rate last year? Do these rates lie on a Phillips curve?

3. What happened in the 1970s and early 1980s to cast doubt on the Phillips curve?

4. Suppose you flipped an honest coin ten times and heads came up eight times. You are about to toss the coin another ten times. Using adaptive expectations, how many heads do you expect?

Based on rational expectations, how many heads do you expect?

5. According to adaptive expectations, what happens to the inflation rate and the unemployment rate in the following situations?
   a. Initially, the economy is operating at the natural rate of 6 percent unemployment. The anticipated rate of inflation is 6 percent, and the actual rate is also 6 percent.
   b. In the next period, there is an unexpected rise in the inflation rate to 10 percent.
   c. In the next period, there is an unexpected rise in the inflation rate to 12 percent.

6. Explain what happens under adaptive expectations theory when monetary and fiscal policymakers use expansionary policy to achieve an unemployment rate below the natural rate.

7. Keynesians believe monetary and fiscal policymakers should stabilize the business cycle. Compare the political business cycle to Keynesian policy objectives.

8. Use Exhibit 8 to answer the questions that follow.
   a. Which points represent the natural unemployment rate?
   b. Which points represent an unemployment rate below the natural unemployment rate?
   c. Which points represent an unemployment rate above the natural unemployment rate?
   d. Explain points A and D on the graph.
   e. Explain points B and C on the graph.
   f. Explain points E and F on the graph.
   g. Why is curve PC_2 to the right of curve PC_1?

9. Based on rational expectations theory, what happens to the inflation rate and the unemployment rate in the following situations?
   a. Initially, the economy is operating at the natural unemployment rate of 4 percent, and the inflation rate is also 4 percent. People correctly anticipate that an increase in the money supply will increase the inflation rate to 6 percent next year.

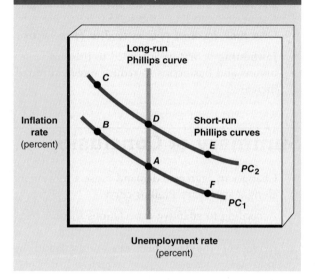

EXHIBIT 8 Long-Run and Short-Run Phillips Curve

b. In the next period, people correctly forecast that a tax cut will cause the inflation rate to rise to 8 percent.

c. In the next period, people correctly anticipate that the Fed's hike in the discount rate will cause the inflation rate to fall to 4 percent.

 CHECKPOINT ANSWERS

Does Rational Expectations Theory Work in the Classroom?

Under rational expectations, if the students know what is going to happen, they will use this information to negate the policy. If pop quizzes are given on the same day homework is due, the rational students will be certain to attend class on those days and take cuts on other days. If quizzes are random, quiz dates are unknown, so there is always a chance that missing a class may mean missing a quiz. If you said the professor will keep pop quizzes a secret and give them randomly, **YOU ARE CORRECT**.

Can Wage and Price Controls Cure Stagflation?

Assume the economy begins in equilibrium at E_1 in Exhibit 9 and an oil shock causes the economy to move to a new equilibrium at E_2. Without wage and price controls, the price level increases from 150 to 200, and real GDP decreases from $4 trillion to $3 trillion. Now assume laws keep the price level frozen at 150. This means firms cannot raise prices to meet higher costs, so under controls they are forced to lay off more workers and cut production even further. The economy's equilibrium moves from E_2 to E_3, and real GDP is $2 trillion, rather than $3 trillion, causing unemployment to climb even higher.

Using wage and price controls to fight inflation would cause an even more severe decrease in real GDP; therefore, unemployment is greater than would otherwise be the case. If you voted *no* on the wage and price controls bill because it causes greater shortages and a deeper recession, **YOU ARE CORRECT**.

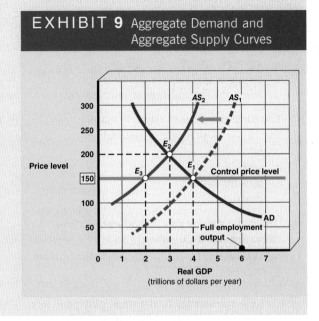

EXHIBIT 9 Aggregate Demand and Aggregate Supply Curves

Sample Quiz

Please see Appendix B for answers to Sample Quiz questions.

1. The Phillips curve relates the inflation rate to
   a. the unemployment rate.
   b. GDP.
   c. disposable personal income.
   d. the interest rate.

2. On a Phillips curve diagram, an increase in the rate of inflation and a decrease in the rate of unemployment, is represented by a(an)
   a. upward movement along the Phillips curve.
   b. downward movement along the Phillips curve.
   c. upward shift of the Phillips curve.
   d. downward shift of the Phillips curve.

3. Economists began to lose confidence in the Phillips curve during the
   a. 1930s.
   b. 1960s.
   c. 1970s.
   d. 1980s.

4. The Phillips curve
   a. was relatively well-defined during the 1960s.
   b. demonstrates how to achieve stable economic growth.
   c. shows the trade-off between deficits and inflation.
   d. helps to stimulate entrepreneurial profits.

5. If the long-run Phillips curve is vertical, then any government policy designed to lower
   a. unemployment will not change the unemployment rate and only increase the inflation rate.
   b. unemployment will work, leaving the inflation rate unchanged.
   c. inflation will cause employment to rise.
   d. unemployment will work, causing the inflation rate to fall.

6. The natural rate hypothesis argues that the economy will

   a. self-correct to the natural rate of inflation.
   b. require expansionary fiscal policy to reach the natural rate of unemployment.
   c. self-correct to the natural rate of unemployment.
   d. require expansionary monetary policy to reach the natural rate of unemployment.

7. The long-run Phillips curve is a(an) _____ line at the natural rate of unemployment.
   a. horizontal
   b. vertical
   c. upward-sloping
   d. downward-sloping

8. Under the natural rate hypothesis, expansionary monetary and fiscal policies can at *best* produce a
   a. permanent change in the long-run Phillips curve.
   b. short-run change in the unemployment rate.
   c. long-run change in the unemployment rate.
   d. permanent change in the unemployment rate.

9. The hypothesis that people believe that the *best* indicator of the future is the recent past is
   a. rational expectations.
   b. adaptive expectations.
   c. lagged expectations.
   d. trend expectations.

10. Under adaptive expectations theory, people expect the rate of inflation this year to be
   a. zero, regardless of the rate last year.
   b. the same as last year.
   c. the rate based on predictable fiscal policies.
   d. All of the answers are correct.

11. According to adaptive expectations theory, expansionary monetary and fiscal policies to reduce the unemployment rate are
   a. useless in the long run.
   b. useless in the short run.
   c. ineffective in impacting the price level.
   d. None of the answers are correct.

12. "Preannounced, stable policies to achieve a low and constant money supply growth and a balanced federal budget are therefore the *best* way to lower the inflation rate." This statement best illustrates
   a. Keynesian theory.
   b. rational expectations theory.

   c. incomes policy.
   d. supply-side theory.

13. Suppose the economy in Exhibit 10 is at point E_1, and the Fed increases the money supply. If people have adaptive expectations, then the economy will move
   a. to point A in the short run and point B in the long run.
   b. directly to point B.
   c. to point C in the short run and point D in the long run.
   d. directly to point D.

14. Suppose the economy in Exhibit 10 is at point E_1, and the Fed increases the money supply. If people have rational expectations, then the economy will move
   a. to point A in the short run and point B in the long run.
   b. directly to point B.
   c. to point C in the short run and point D in the long run.
   d. directly to point D.

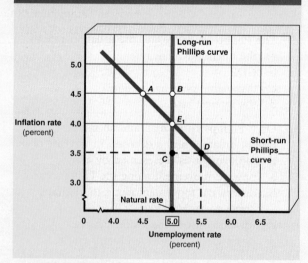

EXHIBIT 10 Short-Run and Long-Run Phillips Curves

15. Which of the following is an example of an incomes policy?
   a. Presidential jawboning
   b. Wage and price guidelines
   c. Wage and price controls
   d. All of the above answers are correct.

16. As shown in Exhibit 11, if people behave according to adaptive expectations theory, an increase in the aggregate demand curve from AD_1 to AD_2 will cause the economy to move
    a. directly from E_1 to E_3 and then remain at E_3.
    b. directly from E_1 to E_2 and then remain at E_2.
    c. from E_1 to E_2 initially and then eventually back to E_1.
    d. from E_1 to E_2 initially and then eventually to E_3.

17. As shown in Exhibit 11, if people behave according to adaptive expectations theory, an increase in the aggregate demand curve from AD_1 to AD_2 will cause the price level to move
    a. directly from 100 to 110 and then remain at 110.
    b. directly from 100 to 105 and then remain at 105.
    c. from 100 to 105 initially and then eventually back to 100.
    d. from 100 to 105 initially and then eventually to 110.

18. As shown in Exhibit 11, if people behave according to adaptive expectations theory, an increase in the aggregate demand curve from AD_1 to AD_2 will cause
    a. labor to adjust nominal wages sluggishly.
    b. the aggregate supply curve to shift from $SRAS_1$ to $SRAS_2$.
    c. the price level to eventually rise from 100 to 110.
    d. All of the above answers are correct.

19. As shown in Exhibit 11, if people behave according to rational expectations theory, an increase in the aggregate demand curve from AD_1 to AD_2 will cause the price level to move
    a. directly from 100 to 105 and then remain at 105.

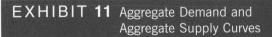

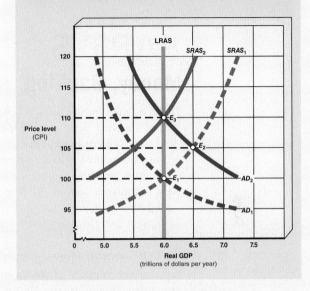

EXHIBIT 11 Aggregate Demand and Aggregate Supply Curves

    b. directly from 100 to 110 and then remain at 110.
    c. from 100 to 105 initially and then eventually back to 100.
    d. from 100 to 105 initially and then eventually to 110.

20. As shown in Exhibit 11, if people behave according to rational expectations theory, an increase in the aggregate demand curve from AD_1 to AD_2 will cause the economy to move
    a. directly from E_1 to E_3 and then remain at E_3.
    b. directly from E_1 to E_2 and then remain at E_2.
    c. from E_1 to E_2 initially and then eventually back to E_1.
    d. from E_1 to E_2 initially and then eventually to E_3.

PART 5
Money, Banking, and Monetary Policy

This road map feature helps you tie together material in the part as you travel the Economic Way of Thinking Highway. The following are review questions listed by chapter from the previous part. The key concept in each question is given for emphasis, and each question or set of questions concludes with an interactive game to reinforce the concepts. The correct answers to the multiple choice questions are given in Appendix C. If your instructor has included MindTap in your course, visit MindTap to play the interactive Causation Chain Game.

Chapter 14: Money and the Federal Reserve System

1. Key Concept: Money supply definitions

Suppose you transfer $1,000 from your checking account to your savings account. How does this action affect the M1 and M2 money supplies?

a. M1 and M2 are both unchanged.
b. M1 falls by $1,000, and M2 rises by $1,000.
c. M1 is unchanged, and M2 rises by $1,000.
d. M1 falls by $1,000, and M2 is unchanged.

2. Key Concept: Federal Reserve System

Which of the following groups administers the Federal Reserve System?

a. House of Representatives
b. President's Council of Economic Advisors
c. U.S. Treasury Department
d. None of the above because the Fed is an independent agency

3. Key Concept: Monetary Control Act

The Monetary Control Act of 1980

a. allowed savings and loan associations to offer checking accounts.
b. allowed more institutions to offer checking account services.
c. created greater competition among various financial institutions.
d. did all of the above.
e. did none of the above.

Chapter 15: Money Creation

4. Key Concept: Open market operations

When the Fed sells government securities, it

a. lowers the cost of borrowing from the Fed, encouraging banks to make loans to the general public.

b. raises the cost of borrowing from the Fed, discouraging banks from making loans to the general public.

c. increases the amount of excess reserves that banks hold, encouraging them to make loans to the general public.

d. increases the amount of excess reserves that banks hold, discouraging them from making loans to the general public.

e. decreases the amount of excess reserves that banks hold, discouraging them from making loans to the general public.

5. Key Concept: Open market operations

When the Fed buys government securities, it

a. lowers the cost of borrowing from the Fed, encouraging banks to make loans to the general public.

b. raises the cost of borrowing from the Fed, discouraging banks from making loans to the general public.

c. increases the amount of excess reserves that banks hold, encouraging them to make loans to the general public.

d. increases the amount of excess reserves that banks hold, discouraging them from making loans to the general public.

e. decreases the amount of excess reserves that banks hold, discouraging them from making loans to the general public.

Chapter 16: Monetary Policy

6. Key Concept: Money demand curve

In a two-asset economy with money and T-bills, the quantity of money that people will want to hold, other things being equal, can be expected to

a. decrease as real GDP increases.

b. increase as the interest rate decreases.

c. increase as the interest rate increases.

d. do all of the above.

 CAUSATION CHAIN GAME
Causation Game: The Demand for Money Curve—Exhibit 1

7. Key Concept: Equilibrium interest rate

Assume the current interest rate is 2 percent and is below the equilibrium interest rate of 4 percent. In response, people will

a. sell bonds, thus driving up the interest rate.

b. buy bonds, thus driving down the interest rate.

c. buy bonds, thus driving up the interest rate.

d. sell bonds, thus driving down the interest rate.

8. Key Concept: Equilibrium interest rate

If the quantity supplied of money exceeds the quantity demanded, people will

a. sell bonds, thus driving up the interest rate.

b. sell bonds, thus driving down the interest rate.
c. buy bonds, thus driving up the interest rate.
d. buy bonds, thus driving down the interest rate.

CAUSATION CHAIN GAME

Causation Chain Game: The Equilibrium Interest Rate—Exhibit 2

9. Key Concept: Change in money supply

Assume the demand for money curve is stationary and the Fed increases the money supply. The result is that people

a. increase the supply of bonds, thus driving up the interest rate.
b. increase the supply of bonds, thus driving down the interest rate.
c. increase the demand for bonds, thus driving up the interest rate.
d. increase the demand for bonds, thus driving down the interest rate.

10. Key Concept: Change in money supply

Assume a fixed demand for money curve and the Fed decreases the money supply. In response, people will

a. sell bonds, thus driving up the interest rate.
b. sell bonds, thus driving down the interest rate.
c. buy bonds, thus driving up the interest rate.
d. buy bonds, thus driving down the interest rate.

CAUSATION CHAIN GAME

Causation Chain Game: The Effect of Changes in the Money Supply—Exhibit 3

11. Key Concept: Keynesian transmission mechanism

The Keynesian cause-and-effect sequence predicts that a decrease in the money supply will cause interest rates to

a. fall, boosting investment and shifting the AD curve rightward, leading to an increase in real GDP.
b. fall, boosting investment and shifting the AD curve rightward, leading to a decrease in real GDP.
c. rise, cutting investment and shifting the AD curve rightward, leading to an increase in real GDP.
d. rise, boosting investment and shifting the AD curve rightward, leading to an increase in real GDP.
e. rise, cutting investment and shifting the AD curve leftward, leading to a decrease in real GDP.

CAUSATION CHAIN GAME

Causation Chain Game: The Keynesian Monetary Policy Transmission Mechanism—Exhibit 4

12. **Key Concept: Monetarists transmission mechanism**

Most monetarists favor

a. frequent changes in the growth rate of the money supply to avoid inflation.
b. placing the Federal Reserve under the Treasury.
c. a steady, gradual shrinkage of the money supply.
d. a constant increase in the money supply year after year equal to the potential annual growth rate in real GDP.

CAUSATION CHAIN GAME
Causation Chain Game: The Monetarist Policy Transmission Mechanism—Exhibit 6

Chapter 17: The Phillips Curve and Expectations Theory

13. **Key Concept: Adaptive expectations**

According to adaptive expectations theory, expansionary monetary and fiscal policies to reduce the unemployment rate are

a. useless in the long run.
b. useless in the short run.
c. ineffective in impacting the price level.
d. None of the answers above are correct.

14. **Key Concept: Rational expectations**

The belief that the government can do absolutely nothing in either the short run or the long run to reduce the unemployment rate, because people will anticipate the government's actions, is held by the

a. rational expectations school.
b. neo-Keynesian school.
c. classical school.
d. supply-side school.
e. Keynesian school.

CAUSATION CHAIN GAME
Causation Chain Game: The Short-Run and Long-Run Phillips Curve—Exhibit 4

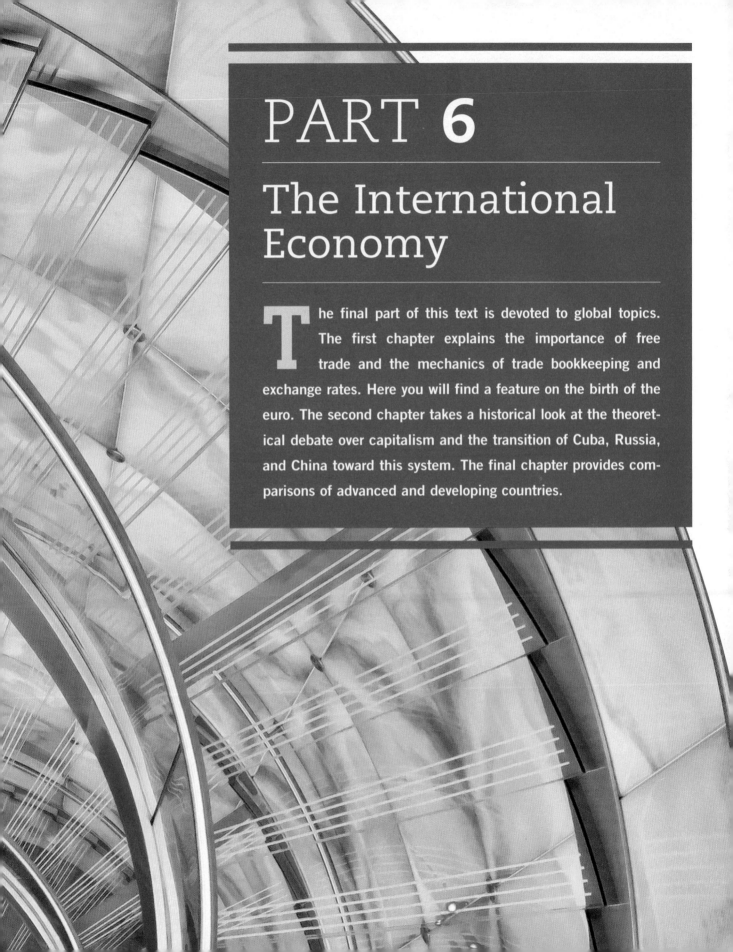

PART 6

The International Economy

The final part of this text is devoted to global topics. The first chapter explains the importance of free trade and the mechanics of trade bookkeeping and exchange rates. Here you will find a feature on the birth of the euro. The second chapter takes a historical look at the theoretical debate over capitalism and the transition of Cuba, Russia, and China toward this system. The final chapter provides comparisons of advanced and developing countries.

CHAPTER 18

International Trade and Finance

CHAPTER PREVIEW

Just imagine your life without world trade. For openers, you could not eat bananas from Honduras or chocolate from Nigerian cocoa beans. Nor could you sip French wine, Colombian coffee, or Indian tea. Also, forget about driving a Japanese motorcycle or automobile. In addition, you could not buy Italian shoes and most DVDs, televisions, fax machines, and personal computers because they are foreign-made. Taking your vacation in London would also be ruled out if there were no world trade. And the list goes on and on, so the point is clear. World trade is important because it gives consumers more power by expanding their choices. Today, the speed of transportation and communication means producers must compete on a global basis for the favor of consumers.

Trade is often highly controversial. Regardless of whether it is a World Trade Organization (WTO) meeting or a G8 summit meeting, trade talks face protesters in the streets complaining that globalization has triggered a crisis in the world, such as global warming, poverty, soaring oil prices, or food shortages. And in the United States, outsourcing jobs to lower-paid workers overseas continues to be a hotly debated issue.

The first part of this chapter explains the theoretical reason why countries should specialize in producing certain goods and then trade them for imports. Also, you will study arguments for and against the United States protecting itself from "unfair" trade practices by other countries. In the second part of the chapter, you will learn how nations pay each other for world trade. Here you will explore international bookkeeping and discover how supply and demand forces determine that, for example, 1 dollar is worth 100 Japanese yen.

IN THIS CHAPTER, YOU WILL LEARN TO SOLVE THESE ECONOMICS PUZZLES:

- How does Babe Ruth's decision not to remain a pitcher illustrate an important principle in global trade?

- Is there a valid argument for trade protectionism?

- Should the United States return to the gold standard?

18-1 WHY NATIONS NEED TRADE

The United States leads the world in imports while also being one of the top exporters in the world. Exhibit 1 reveals which regions are our major trading partners (exports plus imports). Leading the list of nations is China, our largest trading partner, followed by Canada, Mexico, and Japan. Leading U.S. exports are chemicals, machinery, agricultural products, computers, automobiles, and airplanes. Major imports include petroleum, cars, trucks, clothing, and electronics. Why does a nation even bother to trade with the rest of the world? Does it seem strange for the United States to import goods it could produce for itself? Indeed, why doesn't the United States become self-sufficient by growing all its own food, including bananas, sugar, and coffee, making all its own cars, and prohibiting sales of all foreign goods? This section explains why specialization and trade are a nation's keys to a higher standard of living.

18-1a The Production Possibilities Curve Revisited

Consider a world with only two countries—the United States and Japan. To keep the illustration simple, also assume both countries produce only two goods—grain and steel. Accordingly, we can construct in Exhibit 2 a *production possibilities curve* for each

---

EXHIBIT 1 U.S. Trading Partners, 2016

In 2016, Canada, China, Mexico, and Japan accounted for over 40 percent of U.S. trade (exports plus imports).

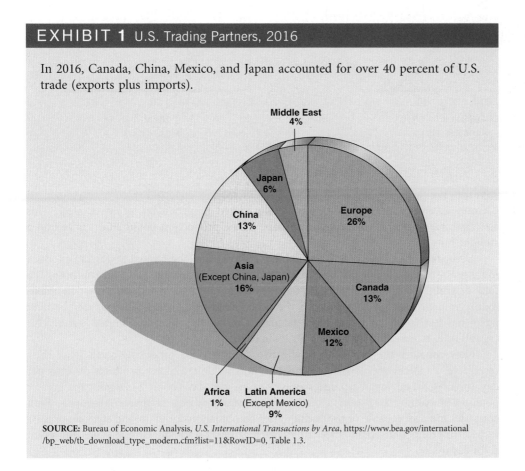

SOURCE: Bureau of Economic Analysis, *U.S. International Transactions by Area*, https://www.bea.gov/international/bp_web/tb_download_type_modern.cfm?list=11&RowID=0, Table 1.3.

EXHIBIT 2 The Benefits of Specialization and Trade

As shown in part (a), assume the United States chooses point *B* on its production possibilities curve, *PPC*$_{U.S.}$ Without trade, the United States produces and consumes 60 tons of grain and 20 tons of steel. In part (b), assume Japan also operates along its production possibilities curve, *PPC*$_{Japan}$, at point *E*. Without trade, Japan produces and consumes 30 tons of grain and 10 tons of steel.

Now assume the United States specializes in producing grain at point *A* and imports 20 tons of Japanese steel in exchange for 30 tons of grain. Through specialization and trade, the United States moves to consumption possibility point *B′*, outside its production possibilities curve. Japan also moves to a higher standard of living at consumption possibility point *E′*, outside its production possibilities curve.

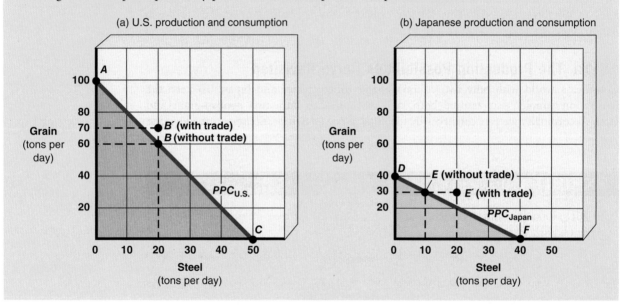

country. We will also set aside the *law of increasing opportunity costs*, explained in Chapter 2, and assume workers are equally suited to producing grain or steel. This assumption transforms the bowed-out shape of the production possibilities curve into a straight line.

Comparing parts (a) and (b) of Exhibit 2 shows that the United States can produce more grain than Japan. If the United States devotes all its resources to this purpose, 100 tons of grain are produced per day, represented by point *A* in Exhibit 2(a). The maximum grain production of Japan, on the other hand, is only 40 tons per day because Japan has less labor, land, and other factors of production than the United States. This capability is represented by point *D* in Exhibit 2(b).

Now consider the capacities of the two countries for producing steel. If all their respective resources are devoted to this output, the United States produces 50 tons per day (point *C*), and Japan produces only 40 tons per day (point *F*). Again, the greater potential maximum steel output of the United States reflects its greater resources. Both countries are also capable of producing other combinations of grain and steel along their respective production possibilities curves, such as point *B* for the United States and point *E* for Japan.

18-1b Specialization without Trade

Assuming no world trade, the production possibilities curve for each country also defines its *consumption possibilities*. Stated another way, we assume that both countries are *self-sufficient* because without imports they must consume only the combination chosen along their production possibilities curve. Under the assumption of self-sufficiency, suppose the United States prefers to produce and consume 60 tons of grain and 20 tons of steel per day (point *B*). Also assume Japan chooses to produce and consume 30 tons of grain and 10 tons of steel (point *E*). Exhibit 3 lists data corresponding to points *B* and *E* and shows that the total world output is 90 tons of grain and 30 tons of steel.

Now suppose the United States specializes by producing and consuming at point *A*, rather than point *B*. Suppose also that Japan specializes by producing and consuming at point *F*, rather than point *E*. As shown in Exhibit 3, specialization in each country increases total world output per day by 10 tons of grain and 10 tons of steel. Because this extra world output has the potential for making both countries better off, why wouldn't the United States and Japan specialize and produce at points *A* and *F*, respectively? The reason is that although production at these points is clearly possible, neither country wants to consume these combinations of output. The United States prefers to consume less grain and more steel at point *B* compared to point *A*. Japan, on the other hand, prefers to consume more grain and less steel at point *E*, rather than point *F*.

When countries specialize, total world output increases, and therefore, the potential for greater total world consumption also increases.

CONCLUSION

18-1c Specialization with Trade

Now let's return to Exhibit 2 and demonstrate how world trade benefits countries. Suppose the United States agrees to specialize in grain production at point *A* and to import 20 tons of Japanese steel in exchange for 30 tons of its grain output. Does the United

---

EXHIBIT 3   Effect of Specialization without Trade on World Output

	Grain production (tons per day)	Steel production (tons per day)
Before specialization		
United States (at point *B*)	60	20
Japan (at point *E*)	30	10
Total world output	90	30
After specialization		
United States (at point *A*)	100	0
Japan (at point *F*)	0	40
Total world output	100	40

States gain from trade? The answer is Yes. At point *A*, the United States produces 100 tons of grain per day. Subtracting the 30 tons of grain traded to Japan leaves the United States with 70 tons of its own grain production to consume. In return for grain, Japan unloads 20 tons of steel on U.S. shores. Hence, specialization and trade allow the United States to move from point *A* to point *B'*, which is a consumption possibility *outside* its production possibilities curve in Exhibit 2(a). At point *B'*, the United States consumes the same amount of steel and 10 more tons of grain compared to point *B* (without trade).

Japan also has an incentive to specialize by moving its production mix from point *E* to point *F*. With trade, Japan's consumption will be at point *E'*. At point *E'*, Japan has as much grain to consume as it had at point *E* (30 tons), plus 10 more tons of steel (now having 20 tons). Thus, point *E'* is a consumption possibility that lies *outside* Japan's production possibilities curve.

CONCLUSION	Global trade allows a country to consume a combination of goods that exceeds its production possibilities curve.

18-2 ABSOLUTE AND COMPARATIVE ADVANTAGE

Why did the United States decide to produce and export grain instead of steel? Why did Japan choose to produce and export steel rather than grain? Here you study the economic principles that determine specialization and trade. These concepts are absolute advantage and comparative advantage. **Absolute advantage** is the ability of a country to produce more of a good using the same or fewer resources as another country. **Comparative advantage** is the ability of a country to produce a good at a lower opportunity cost than another country.

Absolute advantage
The ability of a country to produce a good using the same or fewer resources than another country.

Comparative advantage
The ability of a country to produce a good at a lower opportunity cost than another country.

Perhaps a noneconomic example will clarify the difference between absolute advantage and comparative advantage. When Babe Ruth played for the New York Yankees, he was the best hitter and the best pitcher not only on the team, but also in all of Major League Baseball. In fact, before Ruth was traded to the Yankees and switched to the outfield, he was the best left-handed pitcher in the American League for a few seasons with the Boston Red Sox. His final record was 94–46. In other words, he had an *absolute advantage* in both hitting and throwing the baseball. Stated differently, Babe Ruth could produce the same home runs as any other teammate with fewer times at bat. The problem was that if he pitched, he would bat fewer times because pitchers need rest after pitching. The coaches decided that the Babe had a *comparative advantage* in hitting. A few pitchers on the team could pitch almost as well as the Babe, but no one could touch his hitting. In terms of opportunity costs, the Yankees would lose fewer games if the Babe specialized in hitting.

18-2a Absolute Advantage

So far in our grain versus steel example, a country's production and trade decisions have not considered how much labor, land, or capital either the United States or Japan uses to produce a ton of grain or steel. For example, Japan might have an absolute advantage in producing *both* grain and steel. In our example, compared to the United States, Japan might use fewer resources per ton to produce grain and steel. Maybe the Japanese work harder or are more skilled. In short, the Japanese may be more productive producers, but their absolute advantage does not matter in specialization and world trade decisions. If Japan has a comparative advantage in steel, it should specialize in steel even if, compared to the United States, it can produce both grain and steel with fewer resources.

> Specialization and trade are based on opportunity costs (comparative advantage) and not on absolute advantage.

CONCLUSION

18-2b Comparative Advantage

Engaging in world trade permits countries to consume more than they ever could without trade. The decision of the United States to specialize in and export grain and the decision of Japan to specialize in and export steel are based on comparative advantage. Continuing our example from Exhibit 2, we can calculate opportunity costs for the two countries and use comparative advantage to determine which country should specialize in grain and which should specialize in steel. For the United States, the opportunity cost of producing 50 tons of steel is 100 tons of grain not produced, so 1 ton of steel costs 2 tons of grain ($100/50 = 2$). For Japan, the opportunity cost of producing 40 tons of steel is 40 tons of grain, so 1 ton of steel costs 1 ton of grain ($40/40 = 1$). Japan's steel is therefore cheaper in terms of grain forgone. This means Japan has a comparative advantage in steel production because it must give up less grain to produce steel than the United States. Stated differently, the opportunity cost of steel production is lower in Japan than in the United States.

The other side of the coin is to measure the opportunity cost of grain in terms of steel. For the United States, the opportunity cost of producing 100 tons of grain is 50 tons of steel not produced. This means 1 ton of grain costs 1/2 ton of steel ($50/100 = \frac{1}{2}$). For Japan, the opportunity cost of producing 40 tons of grain is 40 tons of steel so 1 ton of grain costs 1 ton of steel ($40/40 = 1$). The United States has a comparative advantage in grain because its opportunity cost in terms of steel forgone is lower. Thus, the United States should specialize in grain because it is more efficient in grain production. Japan, on the other hand, is relatively more efficient at producing steel and should specialize in this product.

> Comparative advantage refers to the relative opportunity costs between different countries of producing the same goods. World output and consumption are maximized when each country specializes in producing and trading goods for which it has a comparative advantage.

CONCLUSION

Do Nations with an Advantage Always Trade?
Comparing labor productivity, suppose the United States has an absolute advantage over Costa Rica in the production of calculators and towels. In the United States, a worker can produce 4 calculators or 400 towels in 10 hours. In Costa Rica, a worker can produce 1 calculator or 100 towels in the same amount of time. Under these conditions, would Costa Rica specialize in calculators and trade for towels? Would Costa Rica specialize in towels and trade for calculators?

CHECKPOINT

18-3 FREE TRADE VERSUS PROTECTIONISM

Free trade
The flow of goods between countries without restrictions or special taxes.

In theory, global trade should be based on comparative advantage and free trade. **Free trade** is the flow of goods between countries without restrictions or special taxes. In practice, despite the advice of economists, to some degree, every nation protects its own domestic producers from foreign competition. Behind these barriers to trade are special interest groups whose members feel that their jobs and incomes are threatened, so they clamor to the government for protectionism. **Protectionism** is the government's use of embargoes, tariffs, quotas, and other trade restrictions to protect domestic producers from foreign competition.

Protectionism
The government's use of embargoes, tariffs, quotas, and other restrictions to protect domestic producers from foreign competition.

18-3a Embargo

Embargo
A law that bars trade with another country.

Embargoes are the strongest limit on trade. An **embargo** is a law that bars trade with another country. For example, the communist government in Cuba seized a U.S.-owned oil refinery, prompting the United States to impose an embargo in the 1960s. Although the embargo is still enforced, many travel restrictions have been lifted during the last decade. The United States also maintains embargoes against North Korea, Sudan, and Syria.

18-3b Tariff

Tariff
A tax on an import.

Tariffs are the most popular and visible measures used to discourage trade. A **tariff** is a tax on an import. Tariffs are also called customs duties. Suppose the United States imposes a tariff of 2.9 percent on autos. If a foreign car costs $40,000, the amount of the tariff equals $1,160 ($40,000 $\times$ 0.029), and the U.S. price, including the tariff, is $41,160. The current U.S. tariff code specifies tariffs on over 6,000 imports. A tariff can be based on weight, volume, or number of units, or it can be *ad valorem* (figured as a percentage of the price). The average U.S. tariff is less than 5 percent, but individual tariffs vary widely, and 22 agricultural products even have tariffs over 100 percent. Tariffs are imposed to reduce imports by raising import prices and to generate revenues for the U.S. Treasury. Exhibit 4 shows the trend of the average tariff rate since 1930.

During the worldwide depression of the 1930s, when one nation raised its tariffs to protect its industries against foreign competition, other nations retaliated by raising their tariffs. Under the Smoot–Hawley tariffs of the 1930s, the average tariff in the United States reached a peak of 20 percent. Durable imports, which were one-third of imports, were subject to an unbelievable tariff rate of 60 percent. In 1947, most of the world's industrialized nations mutually agreed to end the tariff wars by signing the *General Agreement on Tariffs and Trade* (GATT). Since then, GATT nations have met periodically to negotiate lower tariff rates. GATT agreements have significantly reduced tariffs over the years among member nations. In the 1994 *Uruguay Round*, member nations signed a GATT agreement that decreased tariffs and reduced other trade barriers. The most divisive element of this agreement was the creation in 1995 of the Geneva-based **World Trade Organization (WTO)** to enforce rulings in global trade disputes. The WTO currently has 164 members and a standing appellate body to render final decisions regarding disputes between WTO members. Critics fear that the WTO might be far more likely to rule in favor of other countries in their trade disputes with the United States. Some people argue that the WTO is unaccountable, and these critics reject free trade and discount the gains from globalization.

World Trade Organization (WTO)
An international organization of member countries that oversees international trade agreements and rules on trade disputes.

EXHIBIT 4 The Average Tariff Rate, 1930–2015

Under the Smoot–Hawley Act of 1930, the average tariff rate peaked at 20 percent. Since the *General Agreement on Tariffs and Trade (GATT)* in 1947 and other trade agreements, tariffs have declined to less than 5 percent.

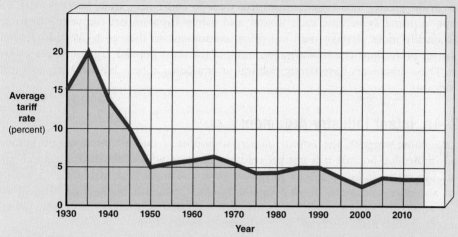

SOURCE: Economic Report of the President 1989, http://www.imf.org/external/index.htm, p. 151 and WTO Country Profiles, http://stat.wto.org/CountryProfiles/US_e.htm.

To illustrate an interesting case, the United States imposed tariffs in 2002 on steel imports to protect jobs in the struggling U.S. steel industry against foreign competition. The WTO ruled these tariffs were illegal, and countries in Europe and Asia prepared a list of retaliatory tariffs. These levies targeted products such as citrus fruit grown in Florida and apparel produced in southern states crucial to President Bush's reelection. Meanwhile, U.S. automakers and other steel-consuming industries complained because the tariffs increased their costs. Facing these complaints and an upcoming Presidential reelection bid in 2004, the United States removed the tariffs on steel imports in 2003.

18-3c Quota

Another way to limit foreign competition is to impose a quota. A **quota** is a limit on the quantity of a good that may be imported in a given time period. For example, the United States may allow 10 million tons of sugar to be imported over a one-year period. After this quantity is reached, no more sugar can be imported for the year. There are import quotas on sugar, dairy products, textiles, steel, and even ice cream. Quotas can limit imports from all foreign suppliers or from specific countries. Critics argue that, like all barriers to trade, quotas invite nations to retaliate with their own measures to restrict trade, and consumers are harmed by higher prices because of the lack of competition from lower-priced imports. In addition to embargoes, tariffs, and quotas, some nations use subtler measures to discourage trade, such as setting up an overwhelming number of bureaucratic steps that must be taken in order to import a product.

Quota
A limit on the quantity of a good that may be imported in a given time period.

18-4 ARGUMENTS FOR PROTECTION

Free trade provides consumers with lower prices and larger quantities of goods from which to choose. Thus, removing import barriers might save each family a few hundred dollars a year. The problem, however, is that imports could cost some workers their jobs and thousands of dollars per year from lost income. Hence, it is no wonder that in spite of the greater total benefits from free trade to consumers, trade barriers exist. The reason is primarily because each worker and owner from import-competing firms has substantially more at stake than individual consumers, so they go to Washington and lobby for protection. The following are some of the most popular arguments for protection. These arguments have strong political or emotional appeal, but weak support from economists.

18-4a Infant Industry Argument

As the name suggests, the *infant industry argument* is that a new domestic industry needs protection because it is not yet ready to compete with established foreign competitors. An infant industry is in a formative stage and must bear high start-up costs to train an entire workforce, develop new technology, establish marketing channels, and reach economies of scale. With time to grow and with protection, an infant industry can reduce costs and "catch up" with established foreign firms.

Economists ask where one draws the arbitrary line between an "infant" and a "grown-up" industry. It is also difficult to make a convincing case for protecting an infant industry in a developed country, such as the United States, where industries are well established. The infant industry argument, however, may have some validity for less-developed countries. Yet, even for these countries, there is a danger. When protection is granted, the new industry will not experience the competitive pressures necessary to encourage reasonably quick growth and participation in world trade. Also, after an industry is given protection, it is difficult to take it away.

18-4b National Security Argument

Another common argument is that defense-related industries must be protected with embargoes, tariffs, and quotas to ensure national security. By protecting critical defense industries, a nation will not be dependent on foreign countries for the essential defense-related goods it needs to defend itself in wartime. The *national defense argument* has been used to protect a long list of industries, including petrochemicals, munitions, steel, and rubber.

This argument gained validity during the War of 1812. Great Britain, the main trading partner of the United States, became an enemy that blockaded our coast. Today, this argument makes less sense for the United States. The government stockpiles missiles, sophisticated electronics, petroleum, and most goods needed in wartime.

18-4c Employment Argument

The *employment argument* suggests that restricting imports increases domestic jobs in protected industries. According to this protectionist argument, the sale of an imported good comes at the expense of its domestically produced counterpart. Lower domestic output therefore leads to higher domestic unemployment than would otherwise be the case.

It is true that protectionism can increase output and save jobs in some industries at home. Ignored, however, are the higher prices paid by consumers because protectionism reduces competition between domestic goods and imported goods. In addition, there are employment reduction effects to consider. For example, suppose a strict quota is imposed on steel imported into our nation. Reduced foreign competition allows U.S. steelmakers to charge higher prices for their steel. As a result, prices rise and sales fall for cars and other products using steel, causing production and employment to fall in these industries. Thus, the import quota on steel may save jobs in the steel industry, but at the expense of more jobs lost in the steel-consuming industries. Also, by selling U.S. imports, foreigners earn dollars that they can use to buy U.S. exports. Import quotas cause foreigners to have fewer dollars to spend on U.S. exports, resulting in a decrease in employment in U.S. export industries. In short, protectionism may cause a net reduction in the nation's total employment.

18-4d Cheap Foreign Labor Argument

Another often-heard popular claim is the *cheap labor argument*. It goes something like this: "How can we compete with such unfair competition? Labor costs $15 an hour in the United States (a hypothetical example), and firms in many developing countries pay only $1 an hour. Without protection against outsourcing our jobs, U.S. wages will be driven down, and our standard of living will fall."

A major flaw in this argument is that it neglects the reason for the difference in the wage rates between countries. A U.S. worker has more education, training, capital, and access to advanced technology. Therefore, if U.S. workers produce more output per hour than workers in another country, U.S. workers will justifiably earn higher wages without a competitive disadvantage. Suppose textile workers in the United States are paid $15 per hour. If a U.S. worker takes 1 hour to produce a rug, the labor cost per rug is $15. Now suppose a worker in India earns $1 per hour, but requires 20 hours to produce a rug on a handloom. In this case, the labor cost per rug is $20. Although the wage rate is 15 times higher in the United States, U.S. productivity is 20 times higher because a U.S. worker can produce 20 rugs in 20 hours, while the worker in India produces only 1 rug in the same amount of time.

Sometimes U.S. companies move their operations to foreign countries where labor is cheaper. Such moves are not always successful because the savings from paying foreign workers a lower wage rate are offset by lower productivity. Other disadvantages of foreign operations include greater transportation costs to U.S. markets and greater uncertainty due to political instability.

18-4e Free-Trade Agreements

The trend in recent years has been for nations to negotiate a reduction in trade barriers. In 1993, Congress approved the *North American Free Trade Agreement (NAFTA)*, which linked the United States to its second- and third-largest trading partners, Canada and Mexico. Under NAFTA, which became effective January 1, 1994, tariffs were phased out, and other impediments to trade and investment were eliminated among the three nations. For example, elimination of trade restrictions allows the United States to supply Mexico with more U.S. goods and to boost U.S. jobs. On the other hand, NAFTA was expected to raise Mexico's wages and standard of living by increasing Mexican exports to the United States. Note that NAFTA made no changes in restrictions on labor

GLOBAL ECONOMICS

World Trade Slips on Banana Peel

Applicable Concept: Protectionism

Growing bananas for European markets was a multibillion-dollar bright spot for Latin America's struggling economies. In fact, about half of this region's banana exports traditionally were sold to Europe. Then, in 1993, the European Union (EU) adopted a package of quotas and tariffs aimed at cutting Europe's banana imports from Latin America. The purpose of these restrictions was to give trade preference to 66 banana-growing former colonies of European nations in Africa, the Caribbean, and the Pacific. Ignored was the fact that growers in Latin America grow higher-quality bananas at half the cost of EU-favored growers because of their low labor costs and flat tropical land near port cities.

In 1999, the World Trade Organization (WTO) ruled that the EU was discriminating in favor of European companies importing the fruit and the WTO imposed $191.4 million per year in punitive tariffs on European goods. This was the first time in the four years the WTO had been in existence that such retaliation had

Jean-Daniel Sudres/Encyclopedia/Corbis

been approved and only the second time going back to its predecessor, the General Agreement on Tariffs and Trade. When the EU failed to comply with the WTO findings, the United States enforced its WTO rights by imposing increased duties on EU imports, including goods ranging from cashmere sweaters and Italian handbags to sheep's milk cheese, British biscuits, and German coffeemakers.

movement, and workers must enter the United States under a limited immigration quota or illegally. The success of NAFTA remains controversial. At the conclusion of this chapter, we will use data to examine its impact. In 2005, the *Central American Free Trade Agreement (CAFTA)* was signed by six additional Central American countries and extended the NAFTA free-trade zone to include Costa Rica, Guatemala, El Salvador, Honduras, Nicaragua, and Dominican Republic.

The United States and other countries are considering other free-trade agreements. In Europe, 27 nations are members of the *European Union (EU)*, which is dedicated to removing all trade barriers within Europe, thereby creating a single European economy almost as large as the U.S. economy. See the Birth of the Euro boxed feature in this chapter.

The *Asia-Pacific Economic Cooperation (APEC)* was formed in 1989 and today has 21 member nations, including China, Hong Kong, Russia, Japan, and Mexico. This organization is based on a nonbinding agreement to reduce trade barriers between member nations. Eleven of APEC's nations negotiated the Trans-Pacific Partnership (TPP) agreement to lower trade tariffs and reduce trade barriers. In 2017, before the agreement went into effect, President Trump withdrew the United States from this deal.

The effect of the U.S. sanctions was to double the wholesale prices of these items. Denmark and the Netherlands were exempt from the U.S. tariffs because they were the only nations that voted against the EU banana rules.

Critics charged that the United States was pushing the case for political reasons. American companies, including Chiquita Brands International and Dole Food Company, grow most of their bananas in Latin America. With America's trade deficit running at a record level, U.S. trade experts also argued that the United States had little choice but to act against the EU for failing to abide by the WTO's ruling. Moreover, with increasing voices in the United States questioning the wisdom of globalization, it was important that the WTO prove that it could arbitrate these disputes.

In 2001, it appeared that the banana dispute might be resolved. The EU agreed to increase market access for U.S. banana distributors, and the United States lifted its retaliatory duties on EU products. The agreement also provided that the United States could reimpose the duties if the EU did not complete its phased-in reductions in restrictions on Latin American banana imports.

But the banana story just kept "slipping along." European Union anti-fraud officials say that illegal banana trafficking is proving more lucrative than that in cocaine. An exposed scheme saw Italian banana importers use false licenses to pay greatly reduced customs duties on non-quota fruit. The fraud netted smugglers hundreds of millions of euros over a two-year period.

In 2004, Latin American growers again complained that the EU was discriminating against their bananas in favor of producers from African, Caribbean, and Pacific countries. Under the 2001 WTO ruling, the EU was compelled to replace its complex quota and tariff system on bananas with a tariff-only regime. So the EU placed a 176-euro tariff per ton on Latin American suppliers to get into the EU market, while bananas from African and Caribbean countries could export up to 775,000 tons duty-free. The banana war continued in 2008 when a WTO dispute panel ruled for the third time that the EU tariff/quota banana regime was unfair. Finally, in 2012 the EU and 11 Latin American countries ended the longest running trade dispute since the 1990s. They reached an agreement to gradually reduce the EU's tariffs on Latin American bananas.

ANALYZE THE ISSUE Make an argument in favor of the European import restrictions. Make an argument against this plan.

Critics are concerned that regional free-trade accords will make global agreements increasingly difficult to achieve. Some fear that trading blocs may erect new barriers, creating "Fortress North America," "Fortress Europe," and similar impediments to the worldwide reduction of trade barriers.

18-5 THE BALANCE OF PAYMENTS

When trade occurs between the United States and other nations, many types of financial transactions are recorded in a summary called the **balance of payments**. The **balance of payments** is a bookkeeping record of all the international transactions between a country and other countries during a given period of time. This summary is the best way to understand interactions between economies because it records the value of a nation's spending inflows and outflows made by individuals, firms, and governments. Exhibit 5 presents a simplified U.S. balance of payments for 2016.

Note the pluses and minuses in the table. A transaction that is a payment to the United States is entered as a positive amount. A payment by the United States to another country is entered with a minus sign. As our discussion unfolds, you will learn that the balance of payments provides much useful information.

Balance of payments
A bookkeeping record of all the international transactions between a country and other countries during a given period of time.

BIRTH OF THE EURO

In 1958, several European nations formed a Common Market to eliminate trade restrictions among member countries. The Common Market called for gradual removal of tariffs and import quotas on goods traded among member nations. Later the name was changed to the *European Economic Community (EEC)*, and it is now called the *European Union (EU)*. This organization established a common system of tariffs for imports from nonmember nations and created common policies for economic matters of joint concern, such as agriculture and transportation. The EU now comprises the 27 nations listed in the following table.

In 1999, 11 European countries, joined later by Greece, followed the United States as an example and united in the *European Economic and Monetary Union (EMU)*. In the United States, 50 states are linked with a common currency, and the Federal Reserve serves as the central bank by conducting monetary policy for the nation. Among the states, trade, labor, and investment enjoy freedom of movement. In 2002, many of the EMU members replaced their national currencies with a single currency, the euro. The objective was to remove exchange rate fluctuations that impede cross-border transactions. This is why the U.S. Congress created a

national currency in 1863 to replace state and private bank currencies.

The EU faces many unanswered questions. Unlike the states of the United States, the EU's member nations do not share a common language or a common government. This makes maintaining common macro policies difficult, and in recent years, Greece and several other members have experienced financial crises. France, for example, might seek to use fiscal or budgetary policies to control inflation, whereas Germany has reducing unemployment as its highest fiscal priority. Coordinating monetary policy among EU

18-5a Current Account

The first section of the balance of payments is the *current account*, which includes trade in goods and services and income receipts and payments. The most widely reported part of the current account is the balance of trade, also called the trade balance. The **balance of trade** is the value of a nation's imports subtracted from its exports, and it can be expressed in terms of goods, services, or goods and services. The balance of trade most often reported is in terms of goods and services. As shown in lines 1–4, the United States had a *balance of trade deficit* of −$501 billion in 2016. A trade deficit occurs when the value of a country's imports exceeds the value of its exports. When a nation has a trade deficit, it is called an *unfavorable balance of trade* because more is spent for imports than is earned from exports. Recall that net exports $(X - M)$ can have a positive (favorable) or negative (unfavorable) effect on $GDP = C + I + G + (X - M)$.

Exhibit 6 charts the annual balance of trade for the United States from 1975 through 2016. Observe that the United States experienced a *balance of trade surplus* in 1975. A trade surplus arises when the value of a country's exports is greater than the value of its imports. This is called a *favorable balance of trade* because the United States earned more from exports than it spent for imports. Since 1975, however, sizable trade deficits have occurred. These trade deficits have attracted much attention because in part they reflect the popularity of foreign goods and the lack of competitiveness of goods "Made in

Balance of trade
The value of a nation's imports subtracted from its exports. Balance of trade can be expressed in terms of goods, services, or goods and services.

nations is also difficult. Although the EU has established the *European Central Bank* headquartered in Frankfurt, Germany, with sole authority over the supply of euros, the central banks of member nations still function. But these national central banks operate similar to the district banks of the Federal Reserve System in the United States. Only time will tell whether EU nations will perform better with a single currency than with separate national currencies. Currently, 19 EU countries have adopted the euro as their national currency.

European Union (EU) members		
Austria	Germany	Poland
Belgium	Greece	Portugal
Bulgaria	Hungary	Romania
Croatia	Ireland	Slovakia
Cyprus	Italy	Slovenia
Czech Republic	Latvia	Spain
Denmark	Lithuania	Sweden
Estonia	Luxembourg	
Finland	Malta	
France	Netherlands	

U.S.A." Between 2005 and 2008, the U.S. trade deficits reached record-breaking levels of about $700 billion due in part to the rising price of oil imports. During this period, the price per barrel grew steadily until it reached a peak in 2008, and the U.S. trade deficit with OPEC countries doubled while our trade deficit with China tripled. After 2008, oil import prices decreased from a high of $125 per barrel in 2008 to $38 per barrel in 2016. As a result, U.S. trade deficits with OPEC countries fell, contributing to the fall in the U.S. balance of trade deficits after 2008.

Lines 3–5 of the current account in Exhibit 5 list ways other than trade of goods that move dollars back and forth between the United States and other countries. Services include insurance, banking, transportation, and tourism. For example, a Japanese tourist who pays a hotel bill in Hawaii buys an export of services, which is a plus, or credit, to our current account (line 3). Similarly, an American visitor to foreign lands buys an import of services, which is a minus, or debit, to our services and therefore a minus to our current account (line 4). As shown on line 5, income flowing back from U.S. investments abroad, such as plants, real estate, and securities, is a payment for use of the services of U.S. capital. Foreign countries also receive income receipts flowing from the services of their capital owned in the United States. This category also includes gifts made by our government, charitable organizations, or private individuals to other governments or private parties elsewhere in the world. For example, this item includes U.S. foreign aid to other nations. Similar unilateral transfers into the United States must be

EXHIBIT 5 U.S. Balance of Payments, 2016 (billions of dollars)

Type of transaction	
Current account	
1. Goods exports	$ + 1,460
2. Goods imports	− 2,210
3. Service exports	+ 752
4. Service imports	− 503
Trade balance (lines 1–4)	− 501
5. Income (net)	+ 19
Current account balance (lines 1–5)	− 482
Capital account	
6. U.S. capital inflow	+ 759
7. U.S. capital outflow	− 331
Capital account balance (lines 6–7)	+ 428
8. Statistical discrepancy	−54
Net balance (lines 1–8)	0

SOURCE: Bureau of Economic Analysis, U.S. International Transactions, https://www.bea.gov/international/bp_web /tb_download_type_modern.cfm?list=1&RowID=1, Table 1.1.

subtracted to determine net income transfers. In 2016, line 5 of the table reports a net income flow of $19 billion to the United States.

Adding lines 1–5 gives the current account balance deficit of −$482 billion in 2016. This deficit means that foreigners sent us more goods, services, and income than we sent to them. Because the current account balance includes more than goods and services, it is a broader measure than the trade balance. Since 1982, the trend in the current account balance has followed the swing into the red shown by the trade balance in Exhibit 6.

18-5b Capital Account

The second section of the balance of payments is the *capital account*, which records payment flows for financial capital, such as real estate, corporate stocks, bonds, government securities, and other debt instruments. For example, when Chinese investors buy U.S. Treasury bills or Japanese investors purchase farmland in Hawaii, there is an inflow of dollars into the United States. As Exhibit 5 shows, foreigners made payments of $759 billion to our capital account (line 6). This exceeded the −$331 billion outflow (line 7) from the United States to purchase foreign-owned financial capital.

An important feature of the capital account is that the United States finances any deficit in its current account through this account. The capital account balance in 2016 was $428 billion. This surplus indicates that there was more foreign investment in U.S. assets than U.S. investment in foreign assets during this year.

EXHIBIT 6 U.S. Balance of Trade, 1975–2016 (billions of dollars)

Since 1975, the United States has experienced trade deficits in which the value of goods and services imported has exceeded the value of goods and services exported. These trade deficits attract much attention because, in part, they reflect the popularity of foreign goods in the United States. During the recession in 2001, the U.S. trade deficit narrowed briefly before continuing an upward trend. The deficit grew to an all-time high of about $700 billion between 2005 and 2008 before declining to $501 billion in 2016.

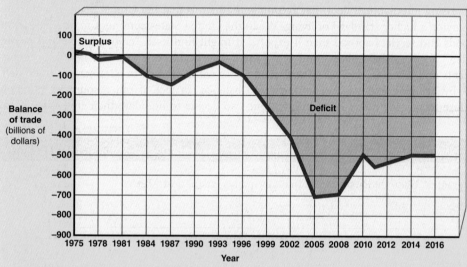

SOURCE: Bureau of Economic Analysis, *U.S. International Transactions*, http://www.bea.gov/international/index.htm, Tables 1.1 and 12.

A current account deficit is financed by a capital account surplus.

CONCLUSION

The current account deficit should equal the capital account surplus, but line 8 in the exhibit reveals that the balance of payments is not perfect. The capital account balance does not exactly offset the current account balance. Hence, a credit or debit amount is simply recorded as a statistical discrepancy; therefore, the balance of payments always balances, or equals zero.

18-5c The International Debt of the United States

If each nation's balance of payments is always zero, why is there so much talk about a U.S. balance-of-payments problem? The problem is with the *composition* of the balance of payments. Suppose the United States runs a $500 billion deficit in its current account. This means that the current account deficit must be financed by a net annual capital inflow in the capital account of $500 billion. That is, foreign lenders, such as banks and businesses, must purchase U.S. assets and grant loans to the United States that on balance equal $500 billion. For example, a Chinese bank could buy U.S. Treasury bonds.

Recall from Exhibit 8 in the chapter on federal deficits and the national debt that the portion of the national debt owed to lenders outside the United States is called *external debt.*

In 1984, the United States became a net debtor for the first time in about 70 years. This means that investments in the United States accumulated by foreigners—stocks, bonds, real estate, and so forth—exceeded the stock of foreign assets owned by the United States. In fact, during the decade of the 1980s, the United States moved from being the world's largest creditor nation to being the largest debtor nation.

Exhibit 7 shows that the United States has its largest trade deficits with China, Germany, Mexico, and Japan, respectively. The concern over continuing trade deficits and the rising international debt that accompanies them is that the United States is artificially enjoying a higher standard of living. When the United States continues to purchase more goods and services abroad than it exports, it might find itself "enjoying now and paying later." Suppose the Chinese and other foreigners decide not to make new U.S. investments and loans. In this case, the United States will be forced to eliminate its trade deficit by bringing exports and imports into balance. In fact, if other countries not only refuse to provide new capital inflows, but also decide to liquidate their investments, the

EXHIBIT 7 U.S. Balance of Trade with Selected Countries, 2016 (billions of dollars)

The United States has its greatest trade deficits with China, Germany, Japan, and Mexico.

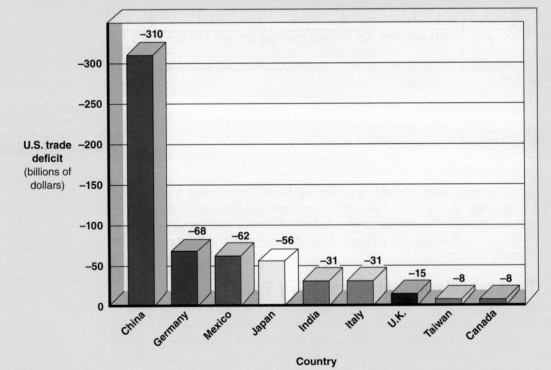

SOURCE: Bureau of Economic Analysis, *U.S. International Transactions by Area,* https://www.bea.gov/international/bp_web/tb_download_type_modern .cfm?list=11&RowID=0, Table 1.3.

United States would be forced to run a trade surplus. Stated differently, we would be forced to tighten our belts and accept a lower standard of living. How a change in foreign willingness to purchase U.S. assets also affects the international value of the dollar is the topic to which we now turn.

Should Everyone Keep a Balance of Payments?

Nations keep balances of payments and calculate accounts such as their trade deficit or surplus. If nations need these accounts, the 50 states should also maintain balances of payments to manage their economies. Or should they? What about cities?

CHECKPOINT

18-6 EXCHANGE RATES

Each transaction recorded in the balance of payments requires an exchange of one country's currency for that of another. Suppose you buy a Japanese car made in Japan, say, a Mazda. Mazda wants to be paid in yen and not dollars, so dollars must be traded for yen. On the other hand, suppose Pink Panther Airline Company in France purchases an airplane from Boeing in the United States. Pink Panther has euros to pay the bill, but Boeing wants dollars. Consequently, euros must be exchanged for dollars.

The critical question for Mazda, Pink Panther, Boeing, and everyone involved in world trade is, "What is the exchange rate?" The **exchange rate** is the number of units of one nation's currency that equals one unit of another nation's currency. For example, assume 1.30 dollars can be exchanged for 1 British pound. This means the exchange rate is 1.30 dollars = 1 pound. Alternatively, the exchange rate can be expressed as a reciprocal. Dividing 1 British pound by 1.30 dollars gives 0.769 pounds per dollar. Now suppose you are visiting England and want to buy a T-shirt with a price tag of 10 pounds. Knowing the exchange rate tells you the T-shirt costs $ 13.00 (10 pounds × $1.30/pound).

Exchange rate
The number of units of one nation's currency that equals one unit of another nation's currency.

An exchange rate can be expressed as a reciprocal.

CONCLUSION

18-6a Supply and Demand for Foreign Exchange

The exchange rate for dollars, or any nation's currency floats, which means it is determined by global forces of supply and demand. For example, consider the exchange rate of yen to dollars, shown in Exhibit 8. Like the price and the quantity of any good traded in markets, the quantity of dollars exchanged is measured on the horizontal axis, and the price per unit is measured on the vertical axis. In this case, the price per unit is the value of the U.S. dollar expressed as the number of yen per dollar.

The demand for dollars in the world currency market comes from Japanese individuals, corporations, and governments that want to buy U.S. exports. Because the Japanese buyers must pay for U.S. exports with dollars, they *demand* to exchange their yen for dollars. As expected, the demand curve for dollars or any foreign currency is downward sloping. A decline in the number of yen per dollar means that one yen buys a larger portion of a dollar. This means U.S. goods and investment opportunities are less expensive to Japanese buyers because they must pay fewer yen for each dollar. Thus, as

EXHIBIT 8 The Supply of and Demand for Dollars

The number of Japanese yen per dollar in the foreign exchange market is determined by the demand for dollars by Japanese citizens and the supply of dollars by U.S. citizens. The equilibrium exchange rate is 100 yen per dollar, and the equilibrium quantity is $300 million per day.

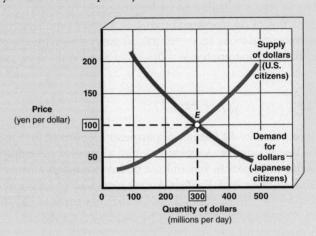

the yen price of dollars decreases, the quantity of dollars demanded by the Japanese to purchase Fords, stocks, land, and other U.S. products and investments increases. For example, suppose a CD recording of the hottest rock group has a $20 price tag. If the exchange rate were 200 yen to the dollar, a Japanese importer would pay 4,000 yen. If the price of dollars to Japanese buyers falls to 100 yen each, the same $20 CD will cost Japanese importers only 2,000 yen. This lower price causes Japanese buyers to increase their orders, which, in turn, increases the quantity of dollars demanded.

The supply curve of dollars is upward sloping. This curve shows the amount of dollars offered for exchange at various yen prices per dollar in the world currency exchange market. Similar to the demand for dollars, the supply of dollars in this market flows from individuals, corporations, and governments in the United States that want to buy Mazdas, stocks, land, and other products and investments from Japan. Because U.S. citizens must pay for the Japanese goods and services in yen, they must exchange dollars for yen. An example will illustrate why the supply curve of dollars slopes upward. Suppose a Nikon camera sells for 100,000 yen in Tokyo and the exchange rate is 100 yen per dollar or 0.01 dollar per yen ($1/100 yen). Therefore, the camera costs an American tourist $1,000. Now assume the exchange rate rises to 250 yen per dollar or 0.004 dollar per yen ($1/250 yen). The camera will now cost the American buyer only $400. Because the prices of the Nikon camera and other Japanese products fall when the number of yen per dollar rises, Americans respond by purchasing more Japanese imports, which, in turn, increases the quantity of dollars supplied.

The foreign exchange market in Exhibit 8 is in equilibrium at an exchange rate of 100 yen for $1. As you learned in Chapter 3, if the exchange rate is above equilibrium, there will be a surplus of dollars in the world currency market. Citizens of the United States are supplying more dollars than the Japanese demand, and the exchange rate falls. On the other hand, below equilibrium, there will be a shortage of dollars in the world currency market. In this case, the Japanese are demanding more dollars than Americans supply, and the exchange rate rises.

18-6b Shifts in Supply and Demand for Foreign Exchange

For most of the years between World War II and 1971, currency exchange rates were *fixed*. Exchange rates were based primarily on gold. For example, the German mark was fixed at about 25 cents. The dollar was worth 1/35 of an ounce of gold, and 4 German marks were worth 1/35 of an ounce of gold. Therefore, 1 dollar equaled 4 marks, or 25 cents equaled 1 mark. In 1971, Western nations agreed to stop fixing their exchange rates and to allow their currencies to *float* according to the forces of supply and demand. Exhibit 9 illustrates that these rates can fluctuate widely. For example, in 1980, 1 dollar was worth about 230 Japanese yen. After gyrating up and down over the years, the exchange rate hit a postwar low of 80 yen per dollar in 2011. In 2016, the rate rose to 109 yen per dollar.

Recall from Chapter 3 that the equilibrium price for products changes in response to shifts in the supply and demand curves. The same supply and demand analysis applies to equilibrium exchange rates for foreign currency. There are four important sources of shifts in the supply and demand curves for foreign exchange. Let's consider each in turn.

Tastes and Preferences

Exhibit 10(a) illustrates one important factor that causes the demand for foreign currencies to shift. Suppose the Japanese lose their "taste" for tobacco, U.S. government bonds, and other U.S. products and investment opportunities. This decline in the popularity of U.S. products in Japan decreases the demand for dollars at each possible exchange rate, and the demand curve shifts leftward from D_1 to D_2. This change causes the equilibrium

---

EXHIBIT 9 Changes in the Yen-per-Dollar Exchange Rate, 1980–2016

Today, most economies are on a system of flexible exchange rates. As the demand and supply curves for currencies change, exchange rates change. In 1980, 1 dollar was worth about 230 Japanese yen. By 2011, the exchange rate had dropped to a postwar low of 80 yen per dollar. In 2016, the rate rose to 109 yen per dollar.

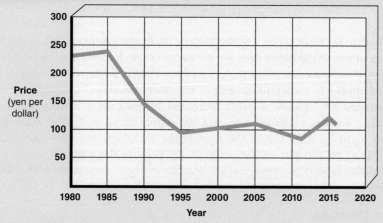

SOURCE: Foreign Exchange Rates, http://www.federalreserve.gov/releases/G5A/current/. Japan/U.S. Foreign Exchange, Fred, Federal Reserve Bank of St. Louis.

EXHIBIT **10**   Changes in the Supply and Demand Curves for Dollars

In part (a), U.S. exports become less popular in Japan. This change in tastes for U.S. products and investments decreases the demand for dollars, and the demand curve shifts leftward from D_1 to D_2. As a result, the equilibrium exchange rate falls from 150 yen to the dollar at E_1 to 100 yen to the dollar at E_2.

Part (b) assumes U.S. citizens are influenced by the "Buy American" idea. In this case, our demand for Japanese imports decreases, and U.S. citizens supply fewer dollars to the foreign currency market. The result is that the supply curve shifts leftward from S_1, and the equilibrium exchange rate rises from 100 yen per dollar at E_1 to 150 yen per dollar at E_2.

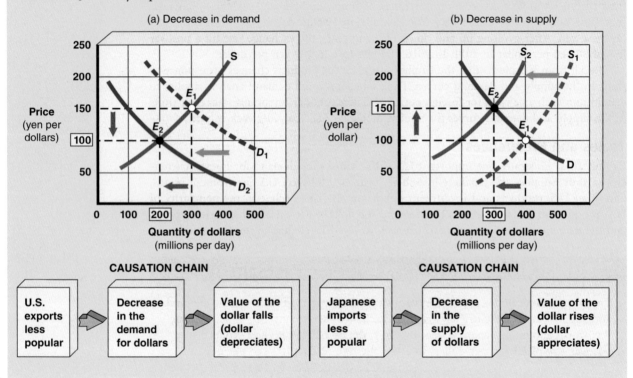

exchange rate to fall from 150 yen to the dollar at E_1 to 100 yen to the dollar at E_2. Because the number of yen to the dollar declines, the dollar is said to *depreciate* or become *weaker*. **Depreciation of currency** is a fall in the price of one currency relative to another.

Depreciation of currency
A fall in the price of one currency relative to another.

What happens to the exchange rate if the "Buy American" idea changes our tastes and the demand for Japanese imports decreases? In this case, U.S. citizens supply fewer dollars at any possible exchange rate, and the supply curve in Exhibit 10(b) shifts leftward from S_1 to S_2. As a result, the equilibrium exchange rate rises from 100 yen to the dollar at E_1 to 150 yen to the dollar at E_2. Because the number of yen per dollar rises, the dollar is said to *appreciate* or become *stronger*. **Appreciation of currency** is a rise in the price of one currency relative to another.

Appreciation of currency
A rise in the price of one currency relative to another.

Relative Incomes

Assume income in the United States rises, while income in Japan remains unchanged. As a result, U.S. citizens buy not only more domestic products and but more Japanese imports as well. The results are a rightward shift in the supply curve for dollars and a decrease in the equilibrium exchange rate. Paradoxically, growth of U.S. income leads to the dollar depreciating, or becoming weaker, against the Japanese yen.

> An expansion in relative U.S. income causes a depreciation of the dollar.
>
> **CONCLUSION**

Relative Price Levels

Now we consider a more complex case in which a change in a factor causes a change in both the supply and demand curves for dollars. Assume the foreign exchange rate begins in equilibrium at 100 yen per dollar, as shown at point E_1 in Exhibit 11. Now assume the

EXHIBIT 11 The Impact of Relative Price Level Changes on Exchange Rates

Begin at E_1, with the exchange rate equal to 100 yen per dollar. Assume prices in Japan rise relative to those in the United States. As a result, the demand for dollars increases, and the supply of dollars decreases. The new equilibrium is at E_2 when the dollar appreciates (rises in value) to 200 yen per dollar.

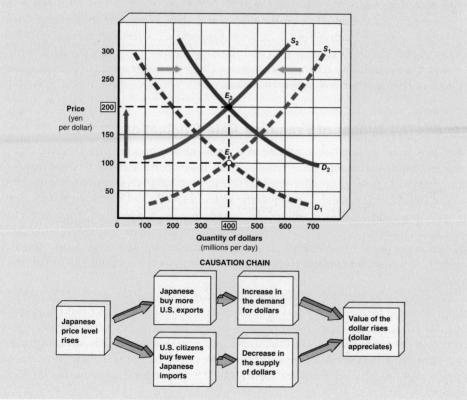

price level increases in Japan, but remains constant in the United States. The Japanese therefore want to buy more U.S. exports because they have become cheaper relative to Japanese products. This willingness of the Japanese to buy U.S. goods and services shifts the demand curve for dollars rightward from D_1 to D_2. In addition, U.S. products are cheaper for U.S. citizens compared to Japanese imports. As a result, the willingness to import from Japan is reduced at each exchange rate, which means the supply curve of dollars decreases from S_1 to S_2. The result of the shifts in both the demand and supply curves for dollars is to establish a new equilibrium at point E_2, and the exchange rate reaches 200 yen per dollar.

CONCLUSION   A rise in a trading partner's relative price level causes the dollar to appreciate.

Relative Real Interest Rates

Changes in relative real (inflation-adjusted) interest rates can have an important effect on the exchange rate. Suppose real interest rates in the United States rise, while those in Japan remain constant. To take advantage of more attractive yields, Japanese investors buy an increased amount of bonds and other interest-bearing securities issued by private and government borrowers in the United States. This change increases the demand for dollars, which increases the equilibrium exchange rate of yen to the dollar, causing the dollar to appreciate (or the yen to depreciate).

There can also be an effect on the supply of dollars. When real interest rates rise in the United States, our citizens purchase fewer Japanese securities. Hence, they offer fewer dollars at each possible exchange rate, and the supply curve for dollars shifts leftward. As a result, the equilibrium exchange rate increases, and the dollar appreciates from changes in both the demand for and supply of dollars.

18-6c The Impact of Exchange Rate Fluctuations

Now it is time to stop for a minute and draw some important conclusions. As you have just learned, exchange rates between most major currencies are flexible. Instead of being pegged to gold or another fixed standard, their value floats as determined by the laws of supply and demand. Consequently, shifts in supply and demand create a weaker or a stronger dollar. But it should be noted that exchange rates do not fluctuate with total freedom. Governments often buy and sell currencies to prevent wide swings in exchange rates. Governments attempt to manipulate exchange rates since the strength, weakness, and volatility of any nation's currency have a profound impact on its economy.

A weak dollar is a "mixed blessing." Ironically, a weak dollar makes U.S. producers happy. Because foreigners pay less of their currency for dollars, this means U.S. producers can sell their less expensive exports to foreign buyers. As export sales rise, jobs are created in the United States. On the other hand, a weak dollar makes foreign producers and domestic consumers unhappy because the prices of imports, like Japanese cars, French wine, and Italian shoes are higher. As U.S. imports fall, jobs are lost in foreign countries.

When the dollar is weak, or depreciates, U.S. goods and services cost foreign consumers less, so they buy more U.S. exports. At the same time, a weak dollar means foreign goods and services cost U.S. consumers more, so they buy fewer imports.

CONCLUSION

A strong dollar is also a "mixed blessing." A strong dollar makes our major trading partners happy. U.S. buyers pay fewer dollars for foreign currency which means the prices of Japanese cars, French wine, and Italian shoes are lower. A strong dollar, contrary to the implication of the term, makes U.S. producers unhappy because their exports are more expensive and related jobs decline. Conversely, a strong dollar makes foreign producers happy because the prices of their goods and services are lower, causing U.S. imports to rise. Exhibit 12 summarizes the weak versus strong dollar effects.

When the dollar is strong, or appreciates, U.S. goods and services cost foreign consumers more, so they buy fewer U.S. exports. At the same time, a strong dollar means foreign goods and services cost U.S. consumers less, so they buy more foreign imports.

CONCLUSION

EXHIBIT 12 Effects of a Strong or Weak Dollar on U.S. Trade

A strong dollar leads to a decrease in exports and an increase in imports. A weak dollar leads to an increase in exports and a decrease in imports.

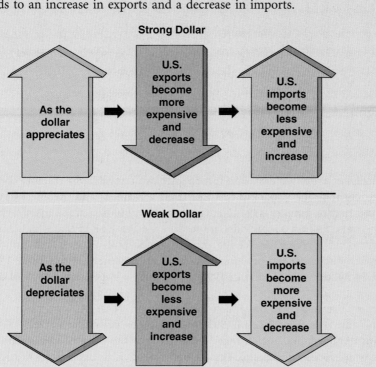

GLOBAL ECONOMICS

Return to the Yellow Brick Road?

Applicable Concept: Exchange Rates

Gold is always a fascinating story. *The Wonderful Wizard of Oz* was first published in 1900, and this children's tale has been interpreted as an allegory for political and economic events of the 1890s. For example, the Yellow Brick Road represents the gold standard, Oz in the title is an abbreviation for ounce, Dorothy is the naive public, Emerald City symbolizes Washington, D.C., the Tin Woodman represents the industrial worker, the Scarecrow is the farmer, and the Cyclone is a metaphor for a political revolution. In the end, Dorothy discovers magical powers in her *silver* shoes (changed to ruby in the 1939 film) to find her way home and not the fallacy of the Yellow Brick Road. Although the author of the story, L. Frank Baum, never stated it was his intention, it can be argued that the issue of the story concerns the election of 1896. Democratic presidential nominee William Jennings Bryan (the Cowardly Lion) supported fixing the value of the dollar to both gold and silver (bimetallism), but Republican William McKinley (the Wicked Witch) advocated using only the gold standard. Since McKinley won, the United States remained on the Yellow Brick Road.[1]

The United States adopted the gold standard in 1873, and until the 1930s, most industrial countries were on the gold standard. The gold standard served as an international monetary system in which currencies were defined or pegged in terms of gold. Under the gold standard, a nation with a balance of payments deficit was required to ship gold to other nations to finance the deficit. Hence, a large excess of imports over exports meant a corresponding outflow of gold from a nation. As a result, that nation's money supply decreased, which, in turn, reduced the aggregate demand for goods and services. Lower domestic demand led to falling prices, lower production, and fewer jobs. In contrast, a nation with a balance of payments surplus would experience an inflow of gold and the opposite effects. In this case, the nation's money supply increased, and its aggregate demand for goods and services rose. Higher aggregate spending, in turn, boosted employment and the price level. In short, the gold standard meant that governments could not control their money supplies to conduct monetary policy.

The gold standard worked fairly well as a fixed exchange rate system so long as nations did not face sudden or severe swings in flows from their stocks of gold. The Great Depression marked the beginning of the end of the gold standard. Nations faced with trade deficits and high unemployment began going off the gold standard, rather than contracting their money supplies by following the gold standard.

In 1933, President Franklin D. Roosevelt took the United States off the gold standard and ordered all 1933 gold

Finally, as promised earlier in this chapter, we return to the discussion of NAFTA in order to illustrate the impact of this free-trade agreement and the effect of a strong dollar. Recall that in January 1994, NAFTA began a gradual phase-out of tariffs and other trade barriers. Exhibit 13 provides trade data for the United States and Mexico for the years surrounding NAFTA. As the exhibit shows, both exports and imports of goods and services increased sharply after NAFTA. On the other hand, a small U.S. trade surplus of $4 billion with Mexico in 1993 turned into a huge trade deficit of $62 billion in 2016.

Before blaming this trade deficit entirely on NAFTA, you must note that the exchange rate rose from 3.12 in 1993 to 18.67 pesos per dollar in 2016. Since 1995, the peso was devalued, and the stronger dollar has put the price of U.S. goods out of reach for many Mexican consumers. This is one reason U.S. exports to Mexico have been lower than they would have been otherwise. At the same time, Mexican goods became less expensive for U.S. consumers, so U.S. imports from Mexico have risen.

double eagle coins already manufactured to be melted down and not circulated. Through a long twisted story worthy of a Sherlock Holmes mystery novel involving the Smithsonian Institution, the former king of Egypt, the Treasury Department, the Justice Department, the U.S. Mint, and a long list of intriguing supporting characters, one 1933 double eagle surfaced and was sold for $7.59 million in 2002. This was double the previous record for a coin.

Once the Allies felt certain they would win World War II, the finance ministers of Western nations met in 1944 at Bretton Woods, New Hampshire, to establish a new international monetary system. The new system was based on fixed exchange rates and an international central bank called the *International Monetary Fund (IMF)*. The IMF makes loans to countries faced with short-term balance-of-payments problems. Under this system, nations were expected to maintain fixed exchange rates within a narrow range. In the 1960s and early 1970s, the Bretton Woods system became strained as conditions changed. In the 1960s, inflation rates in the United States rose relative to those in other countries, causing U.S. exports to become more expensive and U.S. imports to become less expensive. This situation increased the supply of dollars abroad and caused an increasing surplus of dollars, thus putting downward pressure on the exchange rate. Monetary authorities in the United States worried that central banks would demand gold for their dollars, the U.S. gold stock would diminish sharply, and the declining money supply would adversely affect the economy.

Something had to give, and it did. In August 1971, President Richard Nixon announced that the United States would no longer honor its obligation to sell gold at $35 an ounce. By 1973, the gold standard was dead, and most of our trading partners were letting the forces of supply and demand determine exchange rates.

Today, some people advocate returning to the gold standard. These gold buffs do not trust the government to control the money supply without the discipline of a gold standard. They argue that if governments have the freedom to print money, political pressures will sooner or later cause them to increase the money supply too much and let inflation rage.

One argument against the gold standard is that no one can control the supply of gold. Big gold discoveries can cause inflation and have done so in the past. On the other hand, slow growth in the stock of mined gold can lead to slow economic growth and a loss of jobs. Governments, therefore, are unlikely to return to the gold standard because it would mean turning monetary policy over to uncontrollable swings in the stock of gold.

ANALYZE THE ISSUE Return to Exhibit 8, and assume the equilibrium exchange rate is 150 yen per dollar and the equilibrium quantity is $300 million. Redraw this figure, and place a horizontal line through the equilibrium exchange rate to represent a fixed exchange rate. Now use this figure to explain why a country would abandon the gold standard.

---

1. Bradley A. Hansen, "The Fable of the Allegory," *Journal of Economic Education*, Summer 2002, pp. 254–264.

EXHIBIT 13 U.S. Trade Balances with Mexico, Selected Years

Year	U.S. exports to Mexico (billions of dollars)	U.S. imports from Mexico (billions of dollars)	Exchange rate (pesos per dollar)	U.S. trade surplus (+) or deficit (−) (billions of dollars)
1993	$52	$48	3.12	$4
1995	55	71	6.45	−16
2000	127	148	9.46	−21
2005	143	188	10.89	−45
2010	188	247	12.62	−59
2016	262	324	18.67	−62

SOURCES: Bureau of Economic Analysis, *U.S. International Transactions by Area*, http://www.bea.gov/international/index.htm, Table 1.3, and Mexico/U.S. Foreign Exchange Rate, FRED, Federal Reserve Bank of St. Louis.

Key Concepts

Absolute advantage	Embargo	Quota	Depreciation of currency
Comparative advantage	Tariff	Balance of payments	Appreciation of currency
Free trade	World Trade	Balance of trade	
Protectionism	Organization (WTO)	Exchange rate	

Summary

- **Absolute Advantage** is the ability of a country to produce more of a good using the same or fewer resources as another country.

- **Comparative advantage** is a principle that allows nations to gain from trade. Comparative advantage means that each nation *specializes* in a product for which its opportunity cost is lower in terms of the production of another product, and then nations trade. When nations follow this principle, they gain. The reason is that world output increases, and each nation ends up with a higher standard of living by consuming more goods and services than would be possible without specialization and trade.

Comparative Advantage

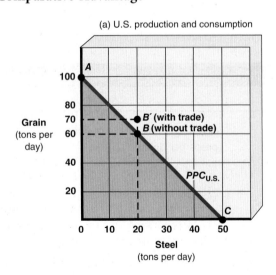

(a) U.S. production and consumption

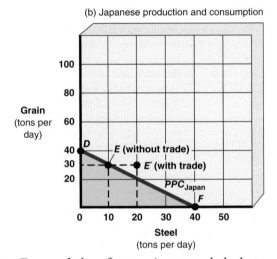

(b) Japanese production and consumption

- **Free trade** benefits a nation as a whole, but individuals may lose jobs and incomes because of the competition from foreign goods and services.

- **Protectionism** is a government's use of embargoes, tariffs, quotas, and other methods to impose barriers intended to both reduce imports and protect particular domestic industries. *Embargoes* prohibit the import or export of particular goods. *Tariffs* discourage imports by making them more expensive. *Quotas* limit the quantity of imports or exports of certain goods. These trade barriers often result primarily from domestic groups that exert political pressure on government in order to gain from these barriers.

- The **balance of payments** is a summary bookkeeping record of all the international transactions a country makes during a year. It is divided into different accounts, including the *current account*, the *capital account*, and the *statistical discrepancy*. The current account summarizes all transactions in currently produced goods and services. The overall balance of payments is always zero after an adjustment for the statistical discrepancy.

- The **balance of trade** is the value of a nation's imports subtracted from its exports. A balance of trade can be in deficit or in surplus. The balance of trade is the most widely reported and largest part of the current account. Since 1975, the United States has experienced balance of trade deficits.

Balance of Trade

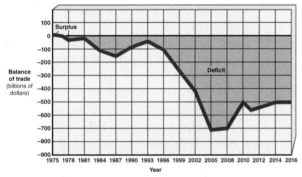

- An **exchange rate** is the price of one nation's currency in terms of another nation's currency. Foreigners who wish to purchase U.S. goods, services, and financial assets demand dollars. The supply of dollars reflects the desire of U.S. citizens to purchase foreign goods, services, and financial assets. The intersection of the supply

and demand curves for dollars determines the number of units of a foreign currency per dollar.

Exchange Rate

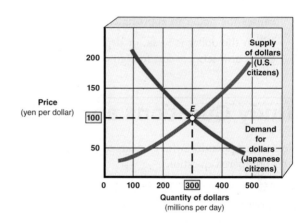

- **Shifts in supply and demand for foreign exchange** result from changes in such factors as tastes, relative price levels, relative real interest rates, and relative income levels.

- **Depreciation of currency** occurs when one currency becomes worth fewer units of another currency. If a currency depreciates, it becomes weaker. Depreciation of a nation's currency increases its exports and decreases its imports.

- **Appreciation of currency** occurs when one currency becomes worth more units of another currency. If a currency appreciates, it becomes stronger. Appreciation of a nation's currency decreases its exports and increases its imports.

Summary of Conclusion Statements

- When countries specialize, total world output increases, and therefore, the potential for greater total world consumption also increases.

- Global trade allows a country to consume a combination of goods that exceeds its production possibilities curve.

- Specialization and trade are based on opportunity costs (comparative advantage) and not on absolute advantage.

- Comparative advantage refers to the relative opportunity costs between different countries of producing the same goods. World output and consumption are maximized when each country specializes in producing and trading goods for which it has a comparative advantage.

- A current account deficit is financed by a capital account surplus.

- An exchange rate can be expressed as a reciprocal.
- An expansion in relative U.S. income causes a depreciation of the dollar.
- A rise in a trading partner's relative price level causes the dollar to appreciate.
- When the dollar is weak, or depreciates, U.S. goods and services cost foreign consumers less, so they buy more U.S. exports. At the same time, a weak dollar means foreign goods and services cost U.S. consumers more, so they buy fewer imports.
- When the dollar is strong, or appreciates, U.S. goods and services cost foreign consumers more, so they buy fewer U.S. exports. At the same time, a strong dollar means foreign goods and services cost U.S. consumers less, so they buy more foreign imports.

Study Questions and Problems

Please see Appendix A for answers to the odd-numbered questions. Your instructor has access to the answers for even-numbered questions.

1. The countries of Alpha and Beta produce diamonds and pearls. The following production possibilities schedule describes their potential output in tons per year:

Points on production possibilities curve	Alpha		Beta	
	Diamonds	Pearls	Diamonds	Pearls
A	150	0	90	0
B	100	25	60	60
C	50	50	30	120
D	0	75	0	180

Using the data in the table, answer the following questions:
   a. What is the opportunity cost of diamonds for each country?
   b. What is the opportunity cost of pearls for each country?
   c. In which good does Alpha have a comparative advantage?
   d. In which good does Beta have a comparative advantage?
   e. Suppose Alpha is producing and consuming at point B on its production possibilities curve and Beta is producing and consuming at point C on its production possibilities curve. Use a table such as Exhibit 3 to explain why both nations would benefit if they specialized.
   f. Draw a graph, and use it to explain how Alpha and Beta benefit if they specialize and Alpha agrees to trade 50 tons of diamonds to Beta and Alpha receives 50 tons of pearls in exchange.

2. Bill can paint either two walls or one window frame in 1 hour. In the same time, Frank can paint either three walls or two window frames. To minimize the time spent painting, who should specialize in painting walls, and who should specialize in painting window frames?

3. Consider this statement: "The principles of specialization and trade according to comparative advantage among nations also apply to states in the United States." Do you agree or disagree? Explain.

4. Would the U.S. government gain any advantage from using tariffs or quotas to restrict imports?

5. Suppose the United States passed a law stating that we would not purchase imports from any country that imposed any trade restrictions on our exports. Who would benefit and who would lose from such retaliation?

6. Now consider Question 5 in terms of the law's impact on domestic producers that export goods. Does this policy adversely affect domestic producers that export goods?

7. Consider this statement: "Unrestricted foreign trade costs domestic jobs." Do you agree or disagree? Explain.

8. Do you support a constitutional amendment to prohibit the federal government from imposing any trade barriers, such as tariffs and quotas, except in case of war or national emergency? Why or why not?

9. Discuss this statement: "Because each nation's balance of payments equals zero, it follows that there is actually no significance to a balance of payments deficit or surplus."

10. For each of the following situations, indicate the direction of the shift in the supply curve or the demand curve for dollars, the factor causing the change, and the resulting movement of the equilibrium exchange rate for the dollar in terms of foreign currency:
    a. American-made cars become more popular overseas.
    b. The United States experiences a recession, while other nations enjoy economic growth.
    c. Inflation rates accelerate in the United States, while inflation rates remain constant in other nations.
    d. Real interest rates in the United States rise, while real interest rates abroad remain constant.
    e. The Japanese put quotas and high tariffs on all imports from the United States.
    f. Tourism from the United States increases sharply because of a fare war among airlines.

11. The following table summarizes the supply and the demand for euros:

	U.S. Dollars per Euro				
	$0.05	$0.10	$0.15	$0.20	$0.25
Quantity demanded (per day)	500	400	300	200	100
Quantity supplied (per day)	100	200	300	400	500

Using the previous table:
    a. Graph the supply and demand curves for euros.
    b. Determine the equilibrium exchange rate.
    c. Determine what the effect of a fixed exchange rate at $0.10 per euro would be.

 CHECKPOINT ANSWERS

Checkpoint: Do Nations with an Advantage Always Trade?

In the United States, the opportunity cost of producing 1 calculator is 100 towels. In Costa Rica, the opportunity cost of producing 1 calculator is 100 towels. If you said because the opportunity cost is the same for each nation, specialization and trade would not boost total output and therefore these countries would not trade these products, **YOU ARE CORRECT**.

Checkpoint: Should Everyone Keep a Balance of Payments?

The principal purpose of the balance of payments is to keep track of payments of national currencies. Because states and cities within the same nation use the same national currency, payments for goods and services traded between these parties do not represent a loss (outflow) or gain (inflow). If you said only nations need to use the balance of payments to account for flows of foreign currency across national boundaries, **YOU ARE CORRECT**.

Sample Quiz

Please see Appendix B for answers to Sample Quiz questions.

1. The theory of comparative advantage suggests that a (an)
   a. industrialized country should not import.
   b. country that is not competitive should import everything.
   c. country specialize in producing goods or services for which it has a lower opportunity cost.
   d. None of the above answers are correct.

2. Assume the United States can use a given amount of its resources to produce either 20 airplanes or 8 automobiles and Japan can employ the same amount of its resources to produce either 20 airplanes or 10 automobiles. The United States should specialize in
   a. airplanes.
   b. automobiles.
   c. both goods.
   d. neither good.

EXHIBIT 14 Potatoes and Wheat Output (tons per hour)

Country	Potatoes	Wheat
United States	4	2
Ireland	3	1

3. In Exhibit 14, the United States has an absolute advantage in producing
   a. potatoes.
   b. wheat.
   c. both potatoes and wheat.
   d. neither potatoes nor wheat.

4. In Exhibit 14, Ireland's opportunity cost of producing one unit of wheat is
   a. 1/3 ton of potatoes.
   b. 3 tons of potatoes.
   c. either a or b.
   d. neither a nor b.

5. In Exhibit 14, the United States has a comparative advantage in producing
   a. potatoes.
   b. wheat.
   c. both potatoes and wheat.
   d. neither potatoes nor wheat.

6. If each nation in Exhibit 14, specializes in producing the good for which it has a comparative advantage, then
   a. Ireland would produce neither potatoes nor wheat.
   b. the United States would produce both potatoes and wheat.
   c. the United States would produce potatoes.
   d. Ireland would produce potatoes.

7. A tariff is a
   a. tax on an exported product.
   b. limit on the number of goods that can be exported.
   c. limit on the number of goods that can be imported.
   d. tax on an imported product.
   e. subsidy on an imported product.

8. The principal objective of the WTO is to
   a. reduce the level of all tariffs.
   b. establish fair prices for all goods traded internationally.
   c. prevent the trading of services across nations' borders.
   d. encourage countries to establish quotas.

9. Which of the following is *not* an argument used in favor of protectionism?
   a. to protect an "infant" industry
   b. to protect domestic jobs
   c. to preserve national security
   d. to protect against "unfair" competition because of cheap foreign labor
   e. to reduce prices paid by domestic consumers

10. The main explanation for why the cheap foreign labor argument is a poor reason for restricting international trade is that
   a. workers who get paid less tend to have lower productivity than those who get paid more.

b. all firms and workers gain when there are no restrictions on international trade.

c. infant industries such as steel and automobiles need to be protected.

d. specialization and free trade usually raise the prices of all the traded goods, so that the workers can get paid more.

11. The account that records a nation's foreign economic transactions is called the
  a. trade account.
  b. T account.
  c. exchange market.
  d. balance of payments.

12. Expenditures for services such as tourism, income for foreign investment, and foreign gifts are tabulated in the
  a. current account.
  b. capital account.
  c. official reserve account.
  d. goods account.

13. Suppose a German bank purchases a U.S. Treasury bond. This transaction would be recorded in the
  a. capital account.
  b. current account.
  c. goods trade balance.
  d. unilateral transfers.

EXHIBIT **15** Foreign Exchange Market for U.S. Dollars and British Pounds

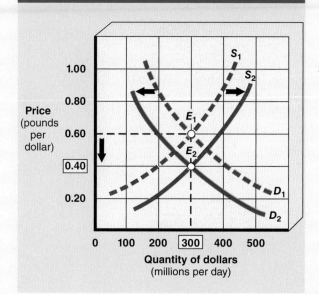

14. Exhibit 15 shows a situation in which
  a. both the dollar and the pound have depreciated.
  b. both the dollar and the pound have appreciated.
  c. the dollar has depreciated and the pound has appreciated.
  d. the dollar has appreciated and the pound has depreciated.

15. Which of the following could cause the dollar-pound exchange rate to change as shown in Exhibit 15?
  a. American goods become more popular in Great Britain.
  b. British incomes rise, while U.S. incomes remain unchanged.
  c. The U.S. price level rises, while the British price level remains unchanged.
  d. The U.S. real interest rate rises, while the British real interest rate remains unchanged.

16. A country that has a lower opportunity cost of producing a good
  a. has a comparative advantage.
  b. can produce the good using fewer resources than another country.
  c. requires fewer labor hours to produce the good.
  d. All of the above answers are correct.

17. If one country can produce a good with fewer resources than another country, this is called
  a. specialization.
  b. geographic advantage.
  c. comparative advantage.
  d. absolute advantage.

18. One big difference between tariffs and quotas is that tariffs
  a. raise the price of a good while quotas lower it.
  b. generate tax revenues while quotas do not.
  c. stimulate international trade while quotas inhibit it.
  d. hurt domestic producers while quotas help them.

19. Which of the following is *not* included in the current account?
    a. exports of goods
    b. imports of goods
    c. U.S. capital inflow and outflow
    d. unilateral transfers

20. A shift of the U.S. demand curve for Mexican pesos to the left and a decrease in the peso price per dollar would result from

    a. an increase in the U.S. inflation rate relative to the rate in Mexico.
    b. a change in U.S. consumers' tastes away from Mexican products and toward products made in South Korea, India, and Taiwan.
    c. U.S. buyers perceiving that domestically - produced products are of a lower quality than products made in Mexico.
    d. all of the above answers are correct.

CHAPTER 19

Economies in Transition

CHAPTER PREVIEW

The inherent vice of capitalism is the unequal sharing of blessings. The inherent virtue of communism is the equal sharing of miseries.

—Winston Churchill

The emergence of the market system in Russia, China, and other countries continues while leaders of these countries who were devoted followers of Marxist ideology now say they believe that capitalism, private property, and profit are ideas superior to the communist system. The failure of communism and the transformation toward a market system is personified by the success of McDonald's in Russia and Walmart in China. Today, Russia and other countries continue to experience economic problems during their restructuring, but the commitment to free-market reforms remains. In contrast, in 2009, the media reported the news

that the United States was nationalizing banks and General Motors. And in 2011 and 2012, a protest movement called Occupy Wall Street spread across the United States. The anticapitalist slogan of the protests was "We are the 99 percent." The main issues protested were inequity between the wealthiest 1 percent and the rest of the population and corrupt influence of corporations on government. What caused these astonishing turn of events?

To understand how the pieces of the global economic puzzle fit together, this chapter begins with a discussion of the three basic types of economies. Then you will examine the pros and cons of the "isms"—capitalism, socialism, and communism. Here you will explore the worldwide clash between the ideas of Adam Smith and Karl Marx and study their current influence on economic systems. Finally, you will examine economic reforms in Cuba, Russia, and China.

IN THIS CHAPTER, YOU WILL LEARN TO SOLVE THESE ECONOMICS PUZZLES:

- Why did drivers in the former Soviet Union remove the windshield wipers and side mirrors whenever they parked their cars?

- What did Adam Smith mean when he said that an "invisible hand" promotes the public interest?

- If the Soviet Union was foolish to run its economy on five-year plans, why do universities, businesses, and governments in a capitalistic economy bother to plan?

19-1 BASIC TYPES OF ECONOMIC SYSTEMS

Economic system
The organizations and methods used to determine what goods and services are produced, how they are produced, and for whom they are produced.

North Korea and South Korea share the same language and historical background. However, South Korea today is a modern economy and people starve in North Korea. This difference relates to their differing economic systems. An **economic system** consists of the organizations and methods used to determine what goods and services are produced, how they are produced, and for whom they are produced. As explained earlier in Chapter 2, scarcity forces each economic system to decide what combination of goods to produce, how to produce such goods, and who gets the output once it is produced. The decision-making process involves interaction among many aspects of a nation's culture, such as its laws, form of government, ethics, religions, and customs. Each economic system can be classified into one of three basic types: (1) Traditional, (2) Command, or (3) Market.

19-1a The Traditional Economy

Traditional economy
An economic system that answers the What, How, and For Whom questions the way they have always have been answered.

Why does England have a king or queen? Tradition is the answer. Historically, the traditional economy has been a common system for making economic decisions. The **traditional economy** is a system that answers the What, How, and For Whom questions the way they have always been answered. People in this type of society learn that copying the previous generation allows them to feel accepted. Anyone who changes ways of doing things asks for trouble from others. This is because people in such a society believe that what was good yesterday, and years ago, must still be a good idea today.

Although most traditional economies have changed to keep pace with modern economic trends, traditional systems are used today, for example, by the Ainu of Canada, the native people of Brazil's rain forest, and the Amish of Pennsylvania. In these societies, the way past generations decided what crops are planted, how they are harvested, and to whom they are distributed remains unchanged over time. People perform their jobs in the manner established by their ancestors. The Amish are well known for rejecting tractors and using horse-drawn plows. Interestingly, the Amish reject Social Security because their society voluntarily redistributes wealth to members who are needy.

19-1b The Traditional Economy's Strengths and Weaknesses

The benefit of the traditional approach is that it minimizes friction among members because relatively little is disputed. Consequently, people in this system may cooperate more freely with one another. In today's industrial world, the Amish and other traditional economies appear very satisfied with their relatively uncomplicated systems. However, critics argue that the traditional system restricts individual initiative and therefore does not lead to the production of advanced goods, new technology, and economic growth.

19-1c The Command Economy

Command economy
An economic system that answers the What, How, and For Whom questions by a dictator or central authority.

In a **command economy**, a dictator or group of central planners makes economic decisions for society. In this system, the What, How, and For Whom questions are answered by a dictator or planners with central authority. The former Soviet Union in the past and Cuba and North Korea today are examples of nations with command economies using national economic plans implemented through powerful government committees.

Politically selected committees decide on everything, including the number, color, size, quality, and price of autos, brooms, sweaters, and tanks. The state owns the factors of production and dictates answers to the three basic economic questions. The authorities might decide to produce modern weapons instead of schools, or they might decide to devote resources to building huge monuments like the pyramids, built by the rulers of ancient Egypt to honor their dead kings and queens.

In the old Soviet economy, for example, the three basic economic questions were answered by a central planning agency called the *Gosplan*. Following the policies of the political authority (the Politburo), the Gosplan set production quotas and prices for farms, factories, mines, housing construction, medical care, and other producing units. What should the cows be fed? If it is hay, how much land can be used to grow it? How much milk should the cows give? How many people will be dairy farmers? What wages should a dairy farmer earn? Should milk be given to everyone, to a few, or to people chosen by the leaders? If there was a shortage of goods in the shops, then goods would be rationed through queuing. The Gosplan tried to make all these decisions. Today, in Russia and the other former Soviet republics, the Gosplan is a distant memory of the discarded Soviet command system.

The pyramid shown in Exhibit 1 represents the command economy. At the top of the pyramid is a supremely powerful group of central planners, such as the old Soviet Gosplan. That agency established production targets and prices for goods and services.

EXHIBIT 1 The Command Economy Pyramid

The principal feature of a command economy is the central planning board at the top, which transmits economic decisions down to the various producing and consuming units below. This process begins with an overall plan from a supreme planning board, such as the old Soviet Gosplan. The Gosplan established production targets and was the ultimate authority over a layer of specialized planning agencies, which authorized capital expansion, raw material purchases, prices, wages, and all other production decisions for individual producing units. Finally, the factories, farms, mines, and other producers distributed the specified output to consumers according to the approved master plan.

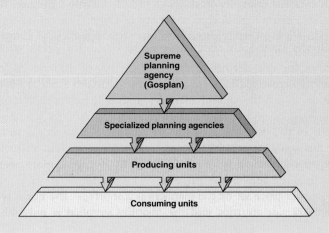

Then the Gosplan transmitted this information to a second layer of specialized state planning agencies. One of these specialized government bureaucracies purchased raw materials, another agency established fashion trends, another set prices, and another government bureaucracy made decisions based on employment and wages.

Production objectives were transmitted from the upper authority layers to the individual producing units, represented by the third layer of the pyramid in Exhibit 1. These producers supplied goods and services to the consumers, as commanded by the central authorities. The bottom portion of the pyramid illustrates the distribution, according to the master plan, of output to consuming units of individuals and households.

19-1d The Command Economy's Strengths and Weaknesses

Believe it or not, the command system can be defended. Proponents argue that economic change occurs much faster in a command system than in a traditional economy. This is one reason those dissatisfied with a traditional society might advocate establishment of a command system. The central authorities can ignore custom and order new ways of doing things. Another reason for adopting a command economy is the controversial belief that the government will provide economic security and equity. It is alleged that central authorities ensure that everyone is provided food, clothing, shelter, and medical care regardless of their ability to contribute to society.

The absolute power of central authorities to make right decisions is also the power to be absolutely wrong. Often the planners do not set production goals accurately, and either shortages or surpluses of goods and services are the result. For example, at one point, the planners miscalculated and produced too few windshield wipers and side mirrors for Soviet cars. Faced with shortages of these parts, Soviet drivers removed windshield wipers and side mirrors whenever they parked their cars to prevent theft. On the other hand, the Gosplan allocated some collective farms far more fertilizer than they could use. To receive the same amount of fertilizer again the next year, farmers simply burned the excess fertilizer. As a result of such decision-making errors, people waited in long lines or stole goods. How does any decision-making group really know how many windshield wipers to produce each year and how much workers making them should earn?

Because profit is not the motive of producers in a command economy, quality and variety of goods also suffer. If the Gosplan ordered a state enterprise to produce 400,000 side mirrors for cars, for example, producers had little incentive to make the extra effort required to create a quality product in a variety of styles. The easiest way to meet the goal was to produce a low-quality product in one style regardless of consumer demand.

Exhibit 2 illustrates how the pricing policy of central planners causes shortages. The demand curve for side mirrors conforms to the law of demand. At lower prices in rubles, the quantity demanded increases. The supply curve is fixed at 400,000 side mirrors because it is set by the central planners and is therefore unresponsive to price variations.

Suppose one of the principal goals of the command economy is to keep the price low. To reach this goal, the central planners set the price of side mirrors at 20 rubles, which is below the equilibrium price of 40 rubles. At 20 rubles, more people can afford a side mirror than at the equilibrium price set by an uncontrolled marketplace. The consequence of this lower price set by the planners is a shortage. The quantity demanded at 20 rubles is 800,000 side mirrors, and the quantity supplied is only 400,000 mirrors.

EXHIBIT 2 Central Planners Fixing Prices

The central planners' goal is to keep prices low, so they set the price of a side mirror for a car at 20 rubles, which is below the market-determined equilibrium price of 40 rubles. At the set price, however, the quantity demanded is 800,000 side mirrors per year. Also set by the planners, the quantity supplied is 400,000 per year. Thus, the shortage at the government-established price is 400,000 side mirrors per year. As a result, long lines form to buy side mirrors, and black markets appear.

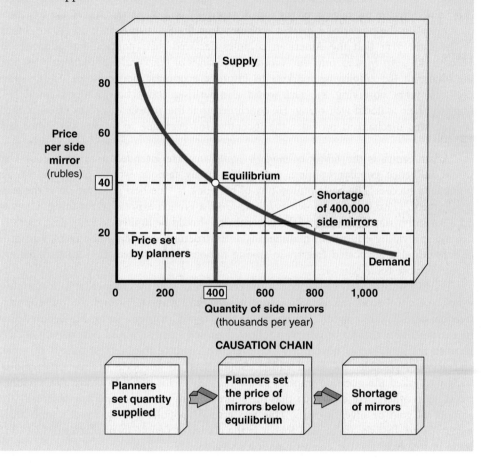

Thus, the model explains why side mirrors disappeared from stores long before many willing buyers could purchase them.

The same graphical analysis applies to centrally planned rental prices for apartments. The central planners in the former Soviet Union set rents below the equilibrium rental prices for apartments. As the model predicts, low rents resulted in a shortage of housing. Meanwhile, the planners promised that improvements in housing would come in time.

CONCLUSION   When central planners set prices below equilibrium for goods and services, they create shortages, which mean long lines, empty shelves, and black markets.[1]

19-1e The Market Economy and the Ideas of Adam Smith

In a market economy, neither customs nor a single person or group of central planners answers the three basic economic questions facing society. **The market economy** is an economic system that answers the What, How, and For Whom questions using prices determined by the interaction of the forces of supply and demand. One of the first people to explain the power of a market economy was the Scottish economist Adam Smith. In the same year that the American colonies declared their political independence in 1776, Smith's *An Inquiry into the Nature and Causes of the Wealth of Nations* presented the blueprint for employing markets to improve economic performance. Smith spent over ten years observing the real world and writing about how nations could best improve their material well-being. He concluded that the answer was to use free markets because this mechanism provides the incentive for everyone to follow his or her *self-interest*.

Adam Smith is the *father of modern economics*. He intended to write a book that would influence popular opinion, and unlike many famous works, his book was an immediate success. The basic philosophy of his book is "the best government is the least government." This belief is known as *laissez-faire*, a French expression meaning "allow to act." As Smith stated, the role of the government should be limited to providing national defense, providing education, maintaining infrastructure, enforcing contracts, and little else. Smith also advocated free trade among nations and rejected the idea that nations should impose trade barriers.

During Smith's lifetime, European nations such as England, France, and Spain intervened to control economic activities. In *The Wealth of Nations*, he argued that economic freedoms are "natural rights" necessary for the dignity of humankind. He believed that free competition among people who follow their self-interest would best benefit society because markets free of government interference produce the greatest output of goods and services possible. As noted earlier, Smith was an advocate of free international trade and asked the question implied in the full title of his book: Why are some nations richer than others? He explained that the source of any nation's wealth is not really the amount of gold or silver it owns. This was an idea popular during Smith's time called *mercantilism*. Instead, he argued that it is the ability of people to produce products and trade in free markets that creates a nation's wealth.

The importance of markets is that they harness the power of self-interest to answer the What, How, and For Whom questions. Without central planning, markets coordinate the actions of millions of consumers and producers. Smith said that the market economy seemed to be controlled by an *invisible hand*. The **invisible hand** is a phrase that expresses the belief that the best interests of a society are served when individual consumers and producers compete to achieve their own private interests. Guided by an invisible hand, producers must compete with one another to win consumers' money. The

Market economy
An economic system that answers the What, How, and For Whom questions using prices determined by the interaction of the forces of supply and demand.

Invisible hand
A phrase that expresses the belief that the best interests of a society are served when individual consumers and producers compete to achieve their own private interests.

---

[1]Recall from Exhibit 5 in Chapter 4 that a black market is an illegal market that emerges when a price ceiling is imposed in a free market.

profit motive in a competitive marketplace provides profits as a reward for efficient producers, while losses punish inefficient producers. Smith saw profit as the necessary driving force in an individualistic market system. The profit motive leads the butcher, the baker, and other producers to answer the What, How, and For Whom questions at the lowest prices. Consumers also compete with one another to purchase the best goods at the lowest price. Competition automatically regulates the economy and provides more goods and services than a system in which government attempts to accomplish the same task in the *public interest*. In Smith's own words:

> *Every individual necessarily labours to render the annual revenue of the society as great as he can. He generally, indeed, neither intends to promote the public interest, nor knows how much he is promoting it. By … directing that industry in such a manner as its produce may be of the greatest value, he intends only his own gain, and he is in this, as in many other cases, led by an invisible hand to promote an end which was no part of his intention. Nor is it always the worse for the society that it was no part of it. By pursuing his own interest he frequently promotes that of the society more effectually than when he really intends to promote it.[2]*

19-1f The Market Economy's Strengths and Weaknesses

In a market system, if consumers want Sudoku puzzles, they can buy them because sellers seek to profit from the sale of Sudoku puzzles. No single person or central planning board makes a formal decision to shift resources and tells firms how to produce what many might view as a frivolous product. Because no central body or set of customs interferes, the market system provides a wide variety of goods and services that buyers and sellers exchange at the lowest prices.

A market economy answers the What to produce and How to produce questions very effectively.	**CONCLUSION**

Those who attack the market economy point out the market failure problems of lack of competition, externalities, lack of public goods, and income inequality, discussed in Chapter 4. For example, critics contend that competition among buyers and sellers results in people who are very wealthy and people who are very poor. In a market economy, output is divided in favor of people who earn higher incomes and own property. Some people will dine on caviar in fine restaurants, while others will wander the streets and beg for food and shelter. Supporters of the market system argue that this inequality of income must exist to give people incentives or rewards for the value of their contributions to others.

19-1g The Mixed Economy

In the real world, no nation is a pure traditional, command, or market economy. Even primitive tribes employ a few markets in their system. For example, members of a tribe may exchange shells for animal skins. In China, the government allows many private shops and farms to operate in free markets. Although the United States is best described

---

[2]Adam Smith, An Inquiry into the Nature and Causes of the Wealth of Nations (1776; reprint, New York: Random House, 1937), p. 423.

as a market economy, it is also a blend of the other two systems. As mentioned earlier, the Amish operate a well-known traditional economy in our nation. The draft during wartime is an example of a command economy in which the government obtains involuntary labor. In addition, taxes "commanded" from taxpayers fund government programs, such as national defense and Social Security. If the economic systems of most nations do not perfectly fit one of the basic definitions, what term best describes their economies? A more appropriate description is that most countries employ a blend of the basic types of economic systems, broadly called a mixed economy. A **mixed economy** is a system that answers the What, How, and For Whom questions through a mixture of traditional, command, and market systems.

Mixed economy
An economic system that answers the What, How, and For Whom questions through a mixture of traditional, command, and market systems.

The traditional, command, and market economies can exist in a wide variety of political situations. For instance, the United States and Japan are politically "free" societies in which the market system flourishes. But China uses the market system to a limited degree in spite of its lack of political freedom. Moreover, some of the Western democracies engage in central economic planning. French officials representing government, business, and labor meet annually to discuss economic goals for industry for the next five-year period, but compliance is voluntary. In Japan, a government agency called the *Ministry of Economy, Trade and Industry (METI)* engages in long-term planning. One of the goals of the METI is to encourage exports so that Japan can earn the foreign currencies it needs to pay for oil and other resources.

19-2 THE "ISMS"

What type of economic system will a society choose to answer the What, How, and For Whom questions? We could call most economies "mixed," but this would be too imprecise. In the real world, economic systems are labeled with various forms of the popular "isms"—capitalism, socialism, and communism, which are based on the basic types of systems.

19-2a Capitalism

Capitalism
An economic system characterized by private ownership of resources and markets.

The popular term for the market economy discussed previously is capitalism. **Capitalism** is an economic system characterized by private ownership of resources and markets. *Capitalism* is also called the *free enterprise system*. Regardless of its political system, a capitalist economic system must possess two characteristics: private ownership of resources, and decentralized decision making using markets.

Private Ownership

Ownership of resources determines to a great degree who makes the What, How, and For Whom decisions. In a capitalist system, resources are primarily *privately* owned and controlled by individuals and firms, rather than having property rights be *publicly* held by government on behalf of society. In the United States, most capital resources are privately owned, but the term *capitalism* is somewhat confusing because it stresses private ownership of factories, raw materials, farms, and other forms of *capital* even though public ownership of land exists as well.

Decentralized Decision Making

This characteristic of capitalism allows buyers and sellers to exchange goods in markets without government involvement. A capitalist system operates on the principle of consumer sovereignty. **Consumer sovereignty** is the freedom of consumers to cast their dollar votes to buy, or not to buy, at prices determined in competitive markets. As a result, consumer spending determines what goods and services firms produce. In a capitalist system, most allocative decisions are coordinated by consumers and producers interacting through markets and making their own decisions guided by Adam Smith's "invisible hand." Friedrich Hayek, an Austrian economist who was a 1974 recipient of the Nobel Prize and author of *The Road to Serfdom*, argued that political and economic freedoms are inseparable.

In the real world, many U.S. markets are not perfectly open or free markets with the consumer as sovereign. For example, consumers cannot buy illegal drugs or body organs. In Chapter 4, you learned that the U.S. government has set minimum prices (support prices) for wheat, milk, cheese, and other products. These markets are free only if the market price is above the support price. Similarly, the minimum wage law forces employers to pay a wage above some dollar amount per hour regardless of market conditions.

Consumer sovereignty
The freedom of consumers to cast their dollar votes to buy, or not to buy, at prices determined in competitive markets.

> No nation in the world precisely fits the two criteria for capitalism; however, the United States comes close.

CONCLUSION

19-2b Capitalism's Strengths and Weaknesses

One of the major strengths of capitalism is its capacity to achieve *economic efficiency* because competition and the profit motive force production at the lowest cost. Another strength of pure capitalism is *economic freedom* because economic power is widely dispersed. Individual consumers, producers, and workers are free to make decisions based on their own self-interest. Economist Milton Friedman makes a related point: Private ownership limits the power of government to deny goods, services, or jobs to its adversaries.

Critics of capitalism cite several shortcomings. First, capitalism tends toward an unequal distribution of income. This inequality of income among citizens results for several reasons. Private ownership of capital and the other factors of production can cause these factors to become concentrated in the hands of a few individuals or firms. Also, people do not have equal labor skills, and the marketplace rewards those with greater skills. These inequalities may be perpetuated because the rich can provide better education, legal aid, political platforms, and wealth to their heirs. Second, private markets can fail to provide an adequate amount of public goods, like roads and national defense. Third, some critics believe capitalism inevitably leads to macroeconomic instability that can result in severe recessions or even depressions. Finally, pure capitalism is criticized for its failure to protect the environment. The pursuit of profit and self-interest can take precedence over damage or pollution to the air, rivers, lakes, and streams. Recall the graphical model used in Chapter 4 to illustrate the socially unacceptable impact of producers who pollute the environment.

19-2c Socialism

The idea of socialism has existed for thousands of years. Its basis is the command system. **Socialism** is an economic system characterized by government ownership of resources and centralized decision making. Socialism is also called *command socialism*. Under a socialist economy, a command system owns and controls in the *public interest* the major industries, such as steel, electricity, and agriculture. However, some free markets can exist in farming, retail trade, and certain service areas. Just as no pure capitalist system

Socialism
An economic system characterized by government ownership of resources and centralized decision making.

exists in the real world, none of the socialist countries in the world today practices pure socialism. In fact, there are as many variants of socialism as there are countries called socialist. Even in the United States, there are some elements of socialism. For example, the federal government owns and operates the Tennessee Valley Authority (TVA), the National Aeronautics and Space Administration (NASA), and the U.S. Postal Service, while at the same time allowing private utilities and mail service firms to operate.

Advocates of socialism believe that the market failures in a capitalist system create so much economic hardship that a country is better off using socialism to organize its production; however, because it is impossible to objectively measure the extent to which these market failures exist, reasonable people often disagree over the degree to which the government should intervene to try to correct for these problems. On the other side of the issue, critics of socialism argue that the government may fail to improve on these market outcomes. Or worse yet, government intervention may make matters worse. These critics believe that socialism produces poor economic results mostly because some government officials are corrupt, ignorant, or succumb to special-interest-group political pressure.

Before discussing socialism further, you must realize that socialism is an economic system, and political systems should not be confused with economic systems. Socialist economies may be controlled by any number of political systems ranging from a dictatorship to a democracy. Generally, socialist economies run by non-democratic governments are referred to as *communist* nations today. On the other hand, *democratic socialism* exists when the government is a freely and fairly elected democracy. The degree of socialism, or government influence over economic affairs, can vary dramatically among nations. And, it is difficult to say when a country has become a "socialist" state. Nevertheless, there are elements of socialism in every nation. For example, Great Britain, France, Italy, and the Scandinavian nations of Norway, Sweden, and Denmark all have representative democracies, but many of their major industries (such as railroads and coal mining) are or have been nationalized.

19-2d The Ideas of Karl Marx

Despite the transition toward more capitalist systems in Russia and Eastern Europe, China, Cuba, and many less-developed countries are still primarily socialist. The theory for socialism and *communism* can be traced to Karl Marx. Marx was a nineteenth-century German philosopher, revolutionary, and economist. Unlike other economists of the time who followed Adam Smith, Marx rejected the concept of a society operating through private interest and profit.

Karl Marx (1818–1883) His criticism of capitalism advanced communism. He wrote *The Communist Manifesto and Das Kapital.*

Karl Marx was born in Germany, the son of a lawyer. In 1841, after receiving a doctorate in philosophy from Berlin University, he turned to journalism and became interested in radical politics. In 1843, Marx married the daughter of a wealthy family and moved to Paris, but his political activities forced him to leave Paris for England. From the age of 31, he lived and wrote his books in London. In London, Marx lived an impoverished life while he and his lifelong friend Friedrich Engels wrote *The Communist Manifesto* published in 1848. A massive work followed, titled *Das Kapital*, which was published in three volumes between 1867 and 1894. These two works made Karl Marx the most influential economist in the history of socialism. In fact, he devoted his entire life to a revolt against capitalism. As Marx read *The Wealth of Nations*, he saw profits as unjust payments to owners of firms—the capitalists. Marx predicted that the market system would destroy itself because wealthy owners would go too far and exploit workers because unrelenting greed for profits would lead the owners to pay starvation wages. Moreover, the owners would force laborers to work in unsafe conditions, and many would not have a job at all.

Marx believed that private ownership and exploitation would produce a nation driven by a class struggle between a few "haves" and many "have-nots." As he stated in *The Communist Manifesto*, "The history of all existing society is the history of class struggle. Freeman and slave, patrician and plebeian, lord and serf, guildmaster and journeyman, in a word, oppressor and oppressed."[3] In Marx's vision, capitalists were the modern-day oppressors, and the workers were the oppressed proletariat. Someday, Marx predicted, the workers would rise up in a spontaneous bloody revolution against a system benefiting only the owners of capital. Marx believed communism to be the ideal system, which would evolve in stages from capitalism through socialism. **Communism** is a stateless, classless economic system in which all the factors of production are owned by the workers and people share in production according to their needs. This is the highest form of socialism toward which the revolution should strive.

Under communism, no private property exists to encourage self-interest. There is no struggle between classes of people, and everyone cooperates. In fact, there is no reason to commit crime, and police, lawyers, and courts are unnecessary. Strangely, Marx surpassed Adam Smith in advocating a system with little central government. Marx believed that those who work hard, or are more skilled, will be public spirited. Any "haves" will give voluntarily to "have-nots." In Marx's own words, people would be motivated by the principle "from each according to his ability, to each according to his need." World peace would evolve as nation after nation accepted cooperation and rejected profits and competition. Under the idealized society of communism, there would be no state. No central authority would be necessary to pursue the interests of the people.

Today, we call the economic systems that existed in the former Soviet Union and Eastern Europe, and still exist in Cuba and other countries, *communist*. However, the definition of *socialism* given in this chapter more accurately describes their real-world economic systems. Actually, no nation has achieved the ideal communist society described by Marx, nor has capitalism self-destructed as he predicted. The 1917 communist revolution in Russia did not fit Marx's theory. At that time, Russia was an underdeveloped country, rather than an industrial country filled with greedy capitalists who exploited workers.

Communism
A stateless, classless economic system in which all the factors of production are owned by the workers and people share in production according to their needs. In Marx's view, this is the highest form of socialism toward which the revolution should strive.

19-2e Characteristics of Socialism

Regardless of a society's political system, a socialist economy has two basic characteristics: public ownership, and centralized decision making.

Public Ownership

Under socialism, the government owns most of the factors of production, including factories, farms, mines, and natural resources. Agriculture in the old Soviet Union illustrates how even this real-world socialist country deviated from total public ownership. In the Soviet Union, there were three rather distinct forms of agriculture: state farms, collective farms, and private plots. In both the state farm and collective farm sectors, central planning authorities determined prices and outputs. In contrast, the government allowed those holding small private plots on peasant farms to operate primarily in free markets that determined price and output levels. Reforms allowed farmers to buy land, tractors, trucks, and other resources from the state, and dramatically end the collectivization of agriculture begun under Josef Stalin.

Centralized Decision Making

Instead of the pursuit of *private interest*, the motivation of pure socialism is the *public interest* of the whole society. For instance, a factory manager cannot decide to raise or

---

[3]Karl Marx and Friedrich Engels, The Communist Manifesto (New York: International Press, 1848), p. 31.

lower prices to obtain maximum profits for the factory. Regardless of inventory levels or the opportunity to raise prices, the planners will not permit this action. Instead of exploiting the ups and downs of the market, the goal of the socialist system is to make centralized decisions that protect workers and consumers from decentralized market decisions. Critics argue that the main objective of this centralization is to perpetuate the personal dictatorships of leaders such as Stalin in the old Soviet Union and Raul Castro in Cuba.

Before the open market reforms, Soviet planners altered earnings to attract workers into certain occupations and achieve planned goals. For example, if space projects needed more engineers, then the state raised the earnings of engineers until the target number of people entered the engineering profession. As shown earlier in Exhibit 2, central planners in the Soviet Union also manipulated consumer prices. If consumers desired more cars than were available, the authorities increased the price of cars. If people wished to purchase less of an item than was available, planners lowered prices. The problem was that this decision process took time. And while the market awaited its orders from the Soviet planners, excess inventories of some items accumulated, and consumers stood in line for cheap products that never seemed to be available. There was an old Soviet saying, "If you see a line, get in it. Whatever it is, it's scarce, and you will not see it tomorrow."

The Soviet factory system did not adhere completely to the command system. The government rewarded successful managers with bonuses that could be substantial. Better apartments, nice vacations, and medals were incentives for outstanding performance. Under economic reforms, plant managers now make decisions based on profitability instead of centralized controls.

CHECKPOINT

To Plan or Not to Plan—That Is the Question

You make plans. You planned to go to college. You plan which career to follow. You plan to get married, and so on. Businesses plan to hire employees, expand their plants, increase profits, and so forth. Because individuals and businesses plan in a market economy, there is really no difference between our system and a command economy. Or is there?

19-2f Socialism's Strengths and Weaknesses

Proponents of the socialism model argue that this system is superior in achieving an equitable distribution of income. This is because government ownership of capital and other resources prevents a few individuals or groups from acquiring a disproportionate share of the nation's wealth. Also, supporters argue that rapid economic growth is achieved when planners have the power to direct more resources to producing capital goods and fewer resources to producing consumer goods (see Exhibit 5 in Chapter 2).

National goals may seem to be easily formulated and pursued under state directives, but there are problems. For example, proponents of such an economy can claim there is no unemployment because the government assigns all workers a job and allocates resources to complete their production goals. However, economic inefficiency results because the government often uses many workers to perform work requiring only one or two workers. Critics also point out that the absence of the profit motive discourages entrepreneurship and innovation and thus suppresses economic growth.

Socialism is particularly vulnerable to the charge that it ignores the goal of economic freedom and instead creates a privileged class of government bureaucrats who assume the role of "capitalists." Central planners are the key translators of information about consumer preferences and production capabilities flowing to millions of economic units. This complex and cumbersome process is subject to errors and is unresponsive to the wants of the majority of the population. Critics also question whether the distribution of income under socialism is more equitable than under capitalism. In the socialist system, "perks" for government officials, nepotism, and the illegal use of markets create disparities in income.

19-2g Comparing Economic Systems

In reality, all nations operate economic systems that blend capitalism and socialism. Exhibit 3 presents a continuum that attempts to place countries between the two extremes of pure socialism on the left and pure capitalism on the right. Economies characterized by a high degree of both private ownership and market allocation are closest to pure capitalism. Hong Kong, Japan, the United States, and Canada fall at the capitalism end of the line. Conversely, economies characterized by much government ownership of resources and central planning are closest to pure socialism. North Korea and Cuba fall close to the pure socialism end of the spectrum, with China and Russia further away from pure socialism.

19-3 ECONOMIES IN TRANSITION

By the early 1990s, the centrally planned economies in the old Soviet Union and Eastern Europe had collapsed. After more than 70 years in the Soviet Union and over 40 years in Eastern Europe and China, the failed communist economies made a startling switch to embrace capitalism. Faced with severe shortages of food, housing, cars, and other consumer goods, communism could no longer claim better living standards for its citizens. The following is a brief discussion of reforms aimed at introducing market power into the economic systems of Cuba, Russia, and China.

19-3a Cuba

Cuba is a landscape of crumbling once-elegant buildings that often experiences daily power blackouts, fuel shortages, housing shortages, food shortages, and other economic hardships. But regardless of its economic woes, Cuba remains wedded to the communist

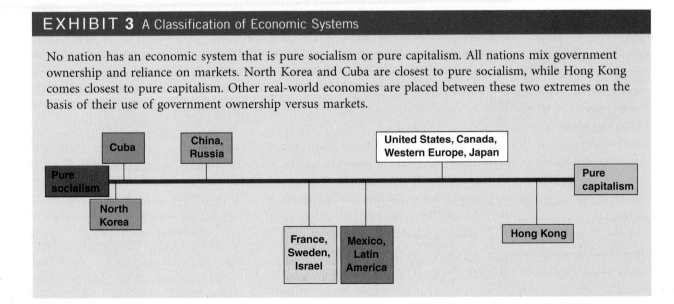

EXHIBIT 3 A Classification of Economic Systems

No nation has an economic system that is pure socialism or pure capitalism. All nations mix government ownership and reliance on markets. North Korea and Cuba are closest to pure socialism, while Hong Kong comes closest to pure capitalism. Other real-world economies are placed between these two extremes on the basis of their use of government ownership versus markets.

YOU'RE THE ECONOMIST

Applicable Concept: Socialism

The Unrealistic Path to Communism

Marx believed that capitalism would create a class of rich business owners and a class of poor workers, which would wage class warfare when workers realized that they were being exploited. Marx also believed that the working class would win this struggle because, as he put it, capitalism will "sow the seeds of its own destruction." In Marx's view, wealth would become increasingly concentrated in a capitalist society, adding to the number of people in the working class, eliminating the middle class, and reducing the ranks of the rich class. As the working class became larger, they would become more successful in the struggle between the classes and eventually win, eliminating the classes in society. In the early 1900s, many European intellectuals felt that the injustices of their day could be traced to capitalism, and they grew impatient for change. The intellectuals wanted to move things along. In Russia, Vladimir Lenin led a revolution that established a socialist government, with its ability to make rapid decisions informed by experts. Lenin believed that socialism would enable Russia to industrialize rapidly, allowing the country to more quickly transition to communism. Lenin also believed his government was a "vanguard state," and necessary only for a short period of time until "the state could wither away" and the communist ideal of a classless society could be attained. In Lenin's vision, the state's rulers had the purest of motives, and they did what they thought was best for the people.[1]

Vladimir Lenin and James Buchanan

Library of Congress Prints and Photographs Division Washington, D.C. 20540 USA http://hdl.loc.gov/loc.pnp/pp.print/LC-DIG-ds-04387

MIKE THEILER/AFP/Getty Images

Lenin's vision of the path to a utopian communist state has come under attack from several different quarters, one being from academia. For example, Nobel Laureate James Buchanan and his co-author Gordon Tullock argued that it was unrealistic to believe that people, who are motivated by self-interest in a market setting, would act benevolently when they made decisions in their capacity as government officials. They believed that human action can best be

system. Nevertheless, the collapse of Soviet bloc aid, coupled with the effects of the U.S. trade embargo forced the late Fidel Castro and the country's new leader, Raul Castro, die-hard Marxists, to reluctantly adopt limited free market reforms. To earn foreign exchange, the dollar has been legalized, and the Cuban government has poured capital into tourism by building several new state-owned hotels and restoring historic sections of Havana. Interestingly, Cuba operates special medical tourist hospitals that treat foreigners and diplomats while excluding Cubans. Cuba has also set up quasi-state enterprises that accept only hard currency. Because few Cubans have dollars or other hard currency, many are earning it by turning to illegal schemes, such as driving gypsy cabs, engaging in prostitution, or selling Cuba's famous cigars and coffee on the black market. Other Cubans have abandoned state jobs and opened small businesses under these new rules. For example, spare rooms in houses can be rented, and artisans can sell their work to tourists. In addition, state farm enterprises have been organized into worker-owned units, and the government allows farmers to sell produce left over after they have met the state's quota. As a result of this free market, some farmers have become venture capitalists, and more food, and a greater variety of food have become available. In 2008, a series of changes opened access to cell phones, computers, and DVD players. Cubans are now also allowed to patronize tourist hotels; however, such luxuries are prohibitive for most Cubans. And in 2009, to improve its woeful transportation system, Cuban

explained by assuming people are motivated by their own self-interests regardless of the environment in which they find themselves.[2]

Another major criticism of Lenin's vision came from a socialist leader who helped lead one of these vanguard governments. Milovan Djilas, who was second in charge of Yugoslavia, a country in the old Soviet bloc, leveled a devastating criticism against the vanguard state. Djilas wrote in a time when the governments of the Soviet Union (Russia) and many of the Eastern European countries were ruled by vanguard states that claimed to be moving their countries toward the ideal stateless communist society. These governments claimed that they had eliminated all classes, so that there were not rich people and poor people. Basically, these governments asserted that they were forcing a classless society on their citizens until the people were willing to form them on their own. Djilas started his critique by agreeing with Marx's argument that in capitalist societies, capital owners form a rich class and workers form a poorer class. However, Djilas did not believe that the vanguard states in Eastern Europe had eliminated classes. Djilas argued these governments just changed who were in the classes. In these countries, the government officials were rich and made up one class, while everyone else was poor and made up the other class. Djilas revealed that government officials used their positions to benefit themselves. They spent resources enhancing their own lifestyles rather than using these resources to help the workers.[3]

Djilas, Buchanan, and Tullock all point to the pitfalls of trusting leaders of a socialist government to act for society's benefit rather than their own. Even within a primarily capitalist country like the United States, a similar lesson applies. The founding fathers realized that we were a nation governed by men and not by angels. Consequently, they set up democratic institutions that could produce good results even though our leaders are self-interested rather than angelic. Our democratic government's system of checks and balances is an attempt to create a system that works for how people are really motivated, rather than how we wish they were motivated.

ANALYZE THE ISSUE

1. Aside from the government, what other institutions have leaders who claim that they do not act in their own self-interest?

2. In the institutions that you named in the previous question, do you think the leaders are self-interested as Buchanan and Tullock might predict, or do they have a different motivation? Explain.

---

1. V.I. Lenin, State and Revolution (New York: International Publishers, 1943).
2. James Buchanan and Gordon Tullock, The Calculus of Consent: Logical Foundations of Constitutional Democracy (Ann Arbor: University of Michigan Press, 1962).
3. Milovan Djilas, The New Class: An Analysis of the Communist System (New York: Praeger, 1957).

owners of classic American cars were recruited by the government to apply for taxi licenses and set their own fares subject to price floors. And in 2014, a new law allows Cubans to buy cars from the government. However, few were able to buy the cars because of heavy taxes designed to redistribute money from the very rich. A joke is that "if you buy a car, the next day the police show up and ask where you got the money."

In spite of the private enterprise reforms, Cuba remains essentially a communist system. Workers receive free education, housing, health care, low state salaries in pesos, and rations of staples, such as a monthly allowance of rice, beans, and milk. Profits from hotels and shops go directly into the central bank and help finance Castro's government. The state also discourages private enterprises by taxing them heavily on expected earnings, rather than on actual sales. In addition, there are highly restrictive regulations. For example, restaurants in Havana are limited to 12 seats and cannot expand regardless of demand. And Cuba has halted new licenses for some types of self-employment, including jewelers, mousetrap makers, and magicians or clowns.

In 2014 the United States announced sweeping changes. Diplomatic relations with Cuba were restored and an embassy was set up. The United States also loosen restrictions on travel and trade with Cuba. For example, the export of certain goods, such as telecommunications equipment and medicine, is now permitted. However, these moves stop short of lifting the economic embargo against Cuba.

GLOBAL ECONOMICS

Shining Light on a Debate

Applicable Concept: Comparative Economic Systems

For a long time, economists have argued whether socialism or capitalism is better equipped to produce rapid rates of economic growth. This issue is not as easy to resolve as you might imagine. It is not enough to say a country like Great Britain is capitalist and rich and another country like Sudan is socialist and poor, so capitalism is a better economic system. Great Britain may be rich for reasons that have nothing to do with its economic system. It may have abundant natural resources, or a hard-working educated workforce. Sudan may be poor for reasons that have nothing to do with its economic system. It may have suffered the hardships of long wars that put investments at such risk that people failed to build new plants and equipment.

The best way to determine which economic system is most effective is to have two identical areas that differ only in their economic systems. This type of controlled experiment is commonplace in a chemistry lab, but not an option open to economists. The closest economists can come to the laboratory setting is when a natural experiment occurs (a real world event that approximates the controls available in a laboratory). The Korean experience may approximate such a natural experiment.

After World War II, the Soviet Union and the United States split up Korea. The Soviet Union and China extended their influences into North Korea, and South Korea became aligned with the United States. At the time of the split, these two Koreas were similar. They had people with similar work habits and education. They had similar access to natural resources and roughly the same amount of per-capita income. Actually, in the 1950s North Korea was a bit richer than South Korea.[1] Although a natural experiment is never perfect, the story of the two Koreas remains enlightening.

In the first few years after the split, it would have been hard to determine which economic system was better at creating wealth. However, 80 years after Korea was divided, the differences are dramatic. South Korea has

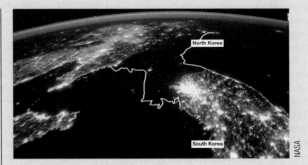

NASA

become a nation as rich as some European countries. North Korea has remained poor. Perhaps the old adage "a picture is worth a 1,000 words" can shed some light on the huge impact an economic system can make to a country's standard of living. See the satellite picture of the Korean Peninsula at night. Notice that South Korea is lit up with bright lights. The socialist North Korea, on the other hand, is dark. Not enough of its residents can turn on lights for the light to show up in pictures. Lights, which we take for granted in most capitalist countries, are not widely available to North Koreans.

ANALYZE THE ISSUE

1. Beyond the amount of light that can be visible from a satellite at night, what might be some other relatively easy ways to measure the differences in the standards of living between the two Koreas?

2. Suppose that North Korea eventually decided to join South Korea and live under South Korea's political and economic system. After this union, what would happen to the distribution of light in the night-time satellite picture?

---

1. Key Points in Developments in East Asia: 20th Century, Asia for Educators Columbia University, http://afe.easia.columbia.edu/main_pop/kpct/kp_korea1945.htm.

19-3b Russia

In 1991, communist rule ended in Russia. To function efficiently, markets must offer incentives, so workers, the public, and even foreign investors were permitted to buy state property. This meant individuals could own the factors of production and earn profits. Such market incentives were a dagger thrust into the heart of a system previously devoted to rejecting capitalism. A key reform for Russia was to allow supply and demand to set higher prices for basic consumer goods. As shown earlier in Exhibit 2, without central planners, when prices rise to their equilibrium level, the quantity supplied increases and the quantity demanded decreases. At the beginning of 1992, the Russian government removed direct government price controls on most market goods. As the model predicts, average prices rose, leaping 1,735 percent in 1992, and a greater variety of goods started appearing on the shelves. Although workers had to pay more for basic consumer goods, they could at least find goods to buy.

Since 1992, Russia has established an independent central bank and implemented anti-inflationary monetary policies. Cities throughout Russia now have restaurants, megamalls, decent hotels, and streets choked with foreign cars. Russian entrepreneurial spirit and acceptance of it in society is in an embryonic stage, and corruption, including in the legal system, is a frequent way of life. Although Russia is far from a successful market economy, the nation is struggling to achieve an amazing economic transition. Russian privatization plans have been implemented, and steps are continuing to create an economy embracing capitalism. And *Forbes* magazine reports that 77 billionaires reside in Russia.

19-3c The People's Republic of China

Unlike Russia, China has sought economic reform under the direction of its Communist Party. Fundamental economic reforms began in China after the death of Mao Zedong in 1976. Much of this reform was due to the leadership of Deng Xiaoping. Mao was devoted to the egalitarian ideal of communist ideology. Under his rule, thoughts of self-interest were counterrevolutionary, and photographs of Marx, Lenin, and Mao hung on every street corner and in every office and factory. Deng shifted priorities by increasing production of consumer goods and steering China toward becoming a global economic power. And the results have been dramatic. International trade expanded from less than 1 percent of U.S. trade in 1975 to 15 percent in 2016, and the label "Made in China" is common throughout the world. China joined the WTO in 2001 and agreed to open some markets closed to foreigners. China's real GDP growth rate averaged 9.5 percent between 2005 and 2016, making it the world's fastest-growing economy.

To make China an industrial power in the twenty-first century, Chinese planners introduced a two-tier system for industry and agriculture in 1978. Each farm and state enterprise was given a contract to produce a quota. Any amount produced over the quota could be sold in an open market. The Chinese government also encouraged the formation of nonstate enterprises owned jointly by managers and their workforces and special economic zones open to foreign investment. In other words, a blend of capitalism and socialism would provide the incentives needed to increase output. As Deng Xiaoping explained, "It doesn't matter whether the cat is black or white as long as it catches mice." These reforms worked, leading to huge increases in farm and industrial output in the 1980s. In fact, some peasant farmers became the wealthiest people in China. After Deng's death in the mid-1990s, leadership of China passed to leaders who continued the policy of free market reforms. Today, forests of glossy skyscrapers, expressways, upscale apartments, and enormous shopping malls in Beijing, Shanghai, and other cities attest to the market-oriented reforms begun years ago. And life in China's fast lane now includes the opportunity of dining at Kentucky

Fried Chicken and McDonald's restaurants located in cities throughout the country. Disney opened its theme park in 2016, and China is estimated to overtake the United States in total theme park visits by 2020. Also, despite government censorship, China has the largest number of Internet users in the world. Today, China is a huge nation transforming itself swiftly into a powerful player in the global economy. U.S. exporters are overjoyed at the prospect of selling products to over a billion Chinese consumers. For example, swarms of bicyclists once synonymous with urban China are being pushed off the road by consumers who now can afford cars and trucks. Rolls-Royce and Bentley, the ultra-luxury cars, have expanded into China, and it is estimated that by 2030, China will have more cars on the road than the United States. Also, more Chinese are traveling by air. Consequently, the Chinese are buying more Boeing airplanes and American-made cars. The other side of the coin is the threat of what goods the industrious Chinese workers, with increasing training and foreign investment, might produce and sell abroad. For example, China manufactures most of the world's copiers, microwave ovens, Blu-ray players, and shoes. A ballooning U.S. trade deficit with China is often cited as evidence that China is not playing fair, and the political rhetoric has intensified on both sides of the issue. Other countries fear that China will eliminate their export business with the United States. Moreover, there is concern that lowering trade barriers under free trade agreements will increase Chinese imports into domestic markets and eliminate jobs. In 2007, one Chinese-made product after another was removed from U.S. shelves, for example, lethal pet food, toxic toothpaste, and other contaminated products. This prompted calls for more stringent safety regulations for imports.

China's economic growth has caused some problems. There is discontent over labor issues, pollution, and income inequality. While some people dig through trash bins, there are now wealthy private business owners. Despite the unease, China remains a market of great profit and promise and a target for protectionists as it continues its transition from a communist command economy to capitalism. And the debate continues over whether China, a socialist economy, is a strategic trading partner or an emerging economic colossus that will dominate the world economy.

19-3d Privatization versus Nationalization

Privatization
The process of turning a government enterprise into a private enterprise.

Nationalization
The act of transforming a private enterprise's assets into a government enterprise.

The previous discussions of Cuba, Russia, and China provide examples of privatization. **Privatization** is the process of turning a government enterprise into a private enterprise. It is the opposite of **nationalization**, which is the act of transforming a private enterprise's assets into government ownership. The motives for nationalization are political as well as economic. Proponents believe that government ownership enables the state on behalf of the people to exercise more effective control and equitable redistribution of wealth and income. Critics argue that government ownership suppresses incentives, entrepreneurship, and private investment that are essential for an enterprise to prosper. During a financial crisis, the argument in favor of nationalization is that a brief period of nationalization is needed to prevent the largest corporations and banks from a downward spiral that affects the entire economy. This is the "too big to fail" argument.

The United States has a history of nationalization—most of which was temporary. But one that has endured: Amtrak is a government-owned corporation created in 1971 after railroads had petitioned repeatedly to abandon unprofitable passenger service. As discussed at the conclusion of the chapter on money and the Federal Reserve System, the Resolution Trust Corporation (RTC) was established in 1989 to take over more than 1,000 failed savings and loans institutions (S&Ls) with bad loans and foreclosed homes. After fulfilling its mission to sell the assets of these S&Ls, the RTC was closed in 1995. The financial crisis of the Great Recession generated several nationalizations and General Motors (GM) provides a prime case. With GM facing bankruptcy in 2009, the U.S. government replaced the CEO and took a 60 percent controlling share, with Canada taking a 12.5 percent share, the United Auto Workers (UAW) taking a 17.5 percent share, and bondholders ending up with the remaining 10 percent. Existing stockholders were given zero shares. However, by 2015 the U.S. and Canadian governments had sold all of their shares of GM stock, and by 2017 the UAW had sold about half of their shares.

Key Concepts

Economic system	Market economy	Capitalism	Communism
Traditional economy	Invisible hand	Consumer sovereignty	Privatization
Command economy	Mixed economy	Socialism	Nationalization

Summary

- An **economic system** is the set of established procedures by which a society answers the What, How, and For Whom to produce questions.

- **Three basic types of economic systems** are the traditional, command, and market systems. The **traditional system** makes decisions according to custom, and the **command system**, shown in the figure below, answers the three economic questions through some powerful central authority. In contrast, the **market system** uses the impersonal mechanism of the interaction of buyers and sellers in markets to answer the What, How, and For Whom questions.

Command Economy

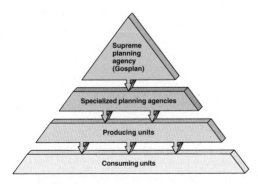

- **Capitalism** is an economic system in which the factors of production are privately owned and economic choices are made by consumers and firms in markets. As prescribed by Adam Smith, government plays an extremely limited role, and self-interest is the driving force, held in check, or regulated, by competition.

- **Consumer sovereignty** is the freedom of consumers to determine the types and quantities of products that are produced in an economy by choosing to buy or not to buy.

- **Socialism** is an economic system in which the government owns the factors of production. The central authorities make the myriad of society's economic decisions according to a national plan. The collective good, or public interest, is the intended guiding force behind the central planners' decisions.

- **Communism** is an economic system envisioned by Karl Marx to be an ideal society in which the workers own all the factors of production. Marx believed that workers who work hard will be public spirited and voluntarily redistribute income to those who are less productive. Such a communist nation described by Marx has never existed.

- **Privatization** is the process of turning a government enterprise into a private enterprise. It is the opposite of **nationalization**, which is the act of transforming a private enterprise's assets into government ownership.

Summary of Conclusion Statements

- When central planners set prices below equilibrium for goods and services, they create shortages, which mean long lines, empty shelves, and black markets.

- A market economy answers the What to produce and How to produce questions very effectively.

- No nation in the world precisely fits the two criteria for capitalism; however, the United States comes close.

Study Questions and Problems

Please see Appendix A for answers to the odd-numbered questions. Your instructor has access to the answers for even-numbered questions.

1. Give an example of how a nation's culture affects its economic system.

2. Explain the advantages and disadvantages of any two of the three basic types of economic systems.

3. Suppose a national program of free housing for the elderly is paid for by a sizable increase in income taxes. Explain a trade-off that might occur between economic security and efficiency.

4. "The schools are not in the business of pleasing parents and students, and they cannot be allowed to set their own agendas. Their agendas are set by politicians, administrators, and various constituencies that hold the keys to political power. The public system is built to see to it that the schools do what their government wants them to do—that they conform to the higher-order values their governors seek to impose."[4] Relate this statement to Exhibit 1.

5. Suppose you are a farmer. Explain why you would be motivated to work in traditional, command, and market economies.

6. Karl Marx believed the market system was doomed. Why do you think he was right or wrong?

7. If all real-world economies are mixed economies, why is the U.S. economy described as capitalist, while the Cuban economy is described as communist?

8. Suppose you are a factory manager. Describe how you might reach production goals under a system of pure capitalism and under a system of pure socialism.

 CHECKPOINT ANSWERS

To Plan or Not to Plan—That Is the Question

When an individual or a business plans in a market economy, other individuals are free to make and follow their own plans. Suppose Hewlett-Packard decides to produce X number of laser printers and sell them at a certain price. The decision does not prohibit IBM from producing Y number of laser printers and selling them for less than Hewlett-Packard's printers. If either firm makes a mistake, only that firm suffers, and other industries are for the most part unaffected. Under a command system, a central economic plan would be made for all laser printer manufacturers. If the central planners order the wrong quantity or quality, there could be major harm to other industries and society. If you said there is a major difference between individual planning and central planning for all society, **YOU ARE CORRECT**.

[4]John Chubb and Terry More, Politics, Markets, and the Nation's Public Schools (Washington, D.C.: Brookings Institution, 1990), p. 38.

Sample Quiz

Please see Appendix B for answers to Sample Quiz questions.

1. An economic system is the organizations and methods used to determine
   a. what goods and services are produced.
   b. how goods and services are produced.
   c. for whom goods and services are produced.
   d. All of the above answers are correct.

2. In a command economy, the basic economic questions are answered by
   a. central authority.
   b. individual buyers and sellers.
   c. traditional methods.
   d. None of the above answers are correct.

3. Adam Smith was an advocate of
   a. mercantilism.
   b. a nation maximizing its stock of gold.
   c. unrestricted or free trade.
   d. the "visible hand" of public interest.

4. In Adam Smith's competitive market economy, the question of what goods to produce is determined by the
   a. "invisible hand" of the price system.
   b. "invisible hand" of government.
   c. "invisible hand" of public interest.
   d. "visible hand" of laws and regulations.

5. Adam Smith wrote that the
   a. economic problems of eighteenth-century England were caused by free markets.
   b. government should control the economy.
   c. pursuit of private self-interest promotes the public interest in a market economy.
   d. public or collective interest is not promoted by people pursuing their self-interest.

6. Which of the following is a criticism of capitalism?
   a. Unequal distribution of income
   b. Failure to protect the environment
   c. Exploitation of workers
   d. All of the above answers are correct.

7. Which of the following statements is true?
   a. The doctrine of *laissez-faire* advocates an economic system with extensive government intervention and little individual decision making.
   b. In capitalism, income is distributed on the basis of need.
   c. Adam Smith was the father of socialism.
   d. Most real-world economies are mixed economic systems.

8. Which of the following is a strength of a command-based economic system?
   a. Goods can be allocated based on need rather than willingness and ability to pay.
   b. Producers have strong incentives to innovate because successful innovators are rewarded with higher profit.
   c. Consumers can transmit their preference for product quality and variety by way of their "dollar votes" cast in the marketplace.
   d. Because price is freely set based on supply and demand, there are few shortages or surpluses.

9. The term *socialism* refers to which of the following?
   a. A religion centered on community interaction
   b. An economic system characterized by private ownership of resources and decentralized market-price allocation
   c. An economic system characterized by government ownership of resources and centralized allocation
   d. An economic system characterized by voluntary allocation

10. Karl Marx was a (an)
    a. nineteenth-century German philosopher.
    b. eighteenth-century Russian economist.
    c. fourteenth-century Polish banker.
    d. nineteenth-century Russian journalist.

11. Karl Marx published
    a. *Das Kapital.*
    b. *General Theory of Communism.*
    c. *The Wealth of Nations.*
    d. *The Capitalist Manifesto.*

12. In Marx's ideal communist society, the state
    a. actively promotes income incentives.
    b. follows the doctrine of *laissez-faire*.
    c. owns resources and conducts planning.
    d. does not exist.

13. According to Adam Smith, the "invisible hand" refers to which of the following?
    a. The "best interests of society" (public interest) will occur as an outcome of the market process coordinating the self-interested interactions of buyers and sellers (private interest).
    b. Government interference in markets to prevent greed.
    c. Bribes and graft that interfere with the market process.
    d. The "best interest of society" (public interest) will occur as an outcome of careful guidance by government authorities in allocating scarce good and services according to private interest.

14. A principal feature of a command economy is that _____.
    a. production decisions are made by profit-maximizing firms.
    b. there is a central planning board at the top, which transmits economic decisions down to the various producing and consuming units below.
    c. consumers are allowed to determine that is produced based on their demand for goods and services.
    d. regulatory agencies constrain the most egregious forms of market power in a market system of allocation.

15. Which nation achieved the ideal communist society as described by Marx?
    a. Castro's Cuba
    b. Mao's China
    c. Stalin's Soviet Union
    d. No nation has achieved Marx's vision of a communist society.

16. Adam Smith's book, *Wealth of Nations* was published at the time of the
    a. War of 1812.
    b. U.S. Declaration of Independence.
    c. U.S. Civil War.
    d. Great Depression.

17. Which of the following economies is an example of a mixed system?
    a. United States
    b. United Kingdom
    c. Sweden
    d. All of the above answers are correct.

18. Property rights allowing individuals to own goods, services, and factors of production are *most* important in
    a. socialistic economies.
    b. planned economies.
    c. capitalist economies.
    d. command economies.

19. Which of the following is a correct characterization of socialism?
    a. Tradition answers the basic economic questions.
    b. Markets are used exclusively to answer the basic economic questions.
    c. Central planning is used to answer the basic economic questions.
    d. Government ownership of many resources and centralized decision-making answers the basic economic questions.

20. Which of the following statements is *true*?
    a. The United States today comes closer to the socialist form of economic organization than it does to capitalism.
    b. When central planners set prices above equilibrium for goods and services, they create shortages.
    c. According to Karl Marx, under capitalism, workers would be exploited and would revolt against the owners of capital.
    d. Adam Smith argued that government's role in society would be to do absolutely nothing.

CHAPTER **20**

Growth and the Less-Developed Countries

CHAPTER PREVIEW

How would your life be different if you lived in Rwanda or Haiti instead of the United States? It is unlikely that anyone in your family would have a telephone or a car. You surely would not own a personal computer or an iPad. You would not have new clothes or be enrolled in a college or university studying economics. You would not be going out to restaurants or movies. You would be fortunate to have shoes and one full meal each day. You would receive little or no medical care and live in unsanitary surroundings. Hunger, disease, and squalor would engulf you. In fact, the World Bank estimates that hundreds of millions of people survive on at or below $1.90 per day. It is exceedingly difficult for Americans to grasp that one-fifth of the world's population lives at such a meager subsistence level. This chapter's important task is unraveling the secrets of economic growth and development. Why do some countries prosper while others decline?

At different times in history, Egypt, China, Italy, and Greece were highly developed by the standards of their time. On the other hand, at one time the United States was a struggling, relatively poor country on the path to becoming a rich country. Its growth came in three stages: First, was the agricultural stage. Then came the manufacturing stage when industries such as railroads, steel, and automobiles were driving forces toward economic growth. And, finally, there has been a shift toward service industries. This is the U.S. success story, but it is not the only road countries can follow to lift themselves from the misery of poverty.

IN THIS CHAPTER, YOU WILL LEARN TO SOLVE THESE ECONOMICS PUZZLES:

• Is there a difference between economic growth and economic development?

• Why are some countries rich and others poor?

• Is trade a better "engine of growth" than foreign aid and loans?

20-1 COMPARING DEVELOPED AND LESS-DEVELOPED COUNTRIES

Income disparity exists not only among families within the United States, but also among nations. In this section, the great inequality of income between the families of nations will be used to classify nations as rich or poor.

20-1a Classifying Countries by GDP per Capita

GDP per capita

The value of final goods produced (GDP) divided by the total population.

Industrially advanced countries (IACs)

High-income nations that have market economies based on large stocks of technologically advanced capital and well-educated labor. The United States, Canada, Australia, New Zealand, Japan, and most of the countries of Western Europe are IACs.

Less-developed countries (LDCs)

Nations without large stocks of technologically advanced capital and without well educated labor. LDCs are economies based on agriculture, such as most countries of Africa, Asia, and Latin America.

There are about 195 countries in the world. Exhibit 1 shows a ranking of selected countries from high to low GDP per capita. **GDP per capita** is the value of final goods produced (GDP) divided by the total population. Although any system of defining rich versus poor countries is arbitrary, GDP per capita or average GDP is a fundamental measure of a country's economic well-being. At the top of the income ladder are 39 developed countries called the industrially advanced countries. **Industrially advanced countries (IACs)** are high-income nations that have market economies based on large stocks of technologically advanced capital and well-educated labor. The United States, Canada, Australia, New Zealand, Japan, and most of the countries of Western Europe are IACs. Excluded from the IACs are countries with high incomes whose economies are based on oil under the sand, and not on widespread industrial development. The United Arab Emirates is an example of such a country.

Countries of the world other than IACs are classified as underdeveloped or less-developed countries. **Less-developed countries (LDCs)** are nations without large stocks of technologically advanced capital and without well-educated labor. Their economies are based on agriculture, as in most countries of Africa, Asia, and Latin America. Most of the world's population live in LDCs and share widespread poverty.

A closer examination of Exhibit 1 reveals that the differences in living standards between the IACs and LDCs are enormous. For example, the GDP per capita in the United States was $57,436, which is much greater than the average income of $795 in Ethiopia. Stated differently, the 2016 average income in the United States was about 72 times larger than the average income in Ethiopia. What a difference! Imagine trying to live on only $795 a year in the United States. You probably would not survive.

Exhibit 2 compares GDP per capita for IACs to LDCs by regions of the world for 2016. The average citizen in the IACs enjoyed an income of $47,383, which was 12 times that of the average citizen in Sub-Saharan Africa. Sub-Saharan Africa includes countries such as Nigeria, Angola, Congo, Sudan, and Zimbabwe. The exhibit also reveals that the greatest concentrations of world poverty are located in the rural areas of Sub-Saharan Africa and Asia. These regions have many countries characterized by bleak and pervasive poverty, but there are notable exceptions, nicknamed the "Four Tigers" of East Asia—Hong Kong, Singapore, South Korea, and Taiwan. These Pacific Rim countries are newly industrialized economies.

20-1b Problems with GDP per Capita Comparisons

Several problems are associated with using GDP per capita to compare rich versus poor countries. First, there is a measurement problem because countries tabulate GDP with differing degrees of accuracy. LDCs in general do not use sophisticated methods of gathering and processing GDP and population data. For example, in countries whose economies are based largely on agriculture, a family is more likely to produce goods and services outside

EXHIBIT 1 Annual GDP per Capita for Selected Countries, 2016

Country	GDP per capita	Country	GDP per capita
Industrially Advanced Countries (IACs)			
Luxembourg	$103,199	Germany	41,902
Switzerland	79,242	Belgium	41,283
Norway	70,392	United Kingdom	40,096
Ireland	62,562	Japan	38,917
United States	57,436	New Zealand	38,345
Denmark	53,744	France	38,128
Singapore	52,961	Israel	37,262
Australia	51,850	Italy	30,507
Sweden	51,165	South Korea	27,539
Netherlands	45,283	Spain	26,609
Austria	44,498	Taiwan	22,453
Hong Kong	43,528	Portugal	19,832
Finland	43,169	Greece	17,901
Canada	42,210		
Less-Developed Countries (LDCs)			
Panama	13,654	Georgia	3,842
Chile	13,576	Egypt	3,685
Turkey	10,743	Indonesia	3,604
Romania	9,465	Ukraine	2,194
Venezuela	9,258	Vietnam	2,173
Russia	8,929	India	1,723
Brazil	8,727	Pakistan	1,468
Mexico	8,555	Bangladesh	1,411
China	8,113	Ethiopia	795
Thailand	5,899	Haiti	761
South Africa	5,261	Rwanda	729
Iran	4,683	Mozambique	392
Iraq	4,631		

SOURCE: International Monetary Fund, World Economic Outlook Database April 2017, http://www.imf.org
/externalpubs/ft/weo/2017/01.

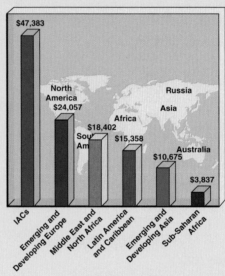

EXHIBIT 2 Average GDP per Capita for IACs and LDCs by Region, 2016

This exhibit shows average GDP per capita by regions of the world for 2016. The differences between the rich, industrially advanced countries (IACs) and the poor, less-developed countries (LDCs) in the various regions of the world are enormous. For example, the average citizen in the IACs had an income 12 times that of the average citizen in the LDCs of Sub-Saharan Africa.

SOURCE: IMF, Selected Country Groups, World Economic Outlook

the price system. In LDCs, families often grow their own food, make their own clothes, and build their own homes. Estimating the value of this output at market prices is difficult.

CONCLUSION LDCs' GDP per capita is subject to greater measurement errors than data for IACs.

Second, GDP per capita comparisons among countries can be misleading because they ignore the relative income distribution. Some countries have very high per capita incomes, yet most of the income goes to just a few wealthy families. The United Arab Emirates' GDP per capita is higher than that of several IACs. However, the UAE earns its income from oil exports, and its income is actually distributed disproportionately to a relatively small number of wealthy families.

CONCLUSION GDP per capita comparisons among nations can be misleading because GDP per capita does not measure income distribution.

Third, GDP per capita comparisons between nations are subject to conversion problems. Making these data comparisons requires converting one nation's currency, say,

Japan's yen, into a common currency, the U.S. dollar. Because, as explained in the chapter on international trade and finance, the value of a country's currency can rise or fall for many reasons, the true value of a nation's output can be distorted. For example, during a given year, one government might maintain an artificially high exchange rate and another government might not.

A conversion problem may widen or narrow the GDP per capita gap between nations because the fluctuations in exchange rates do not reflect actual differences in the value of goods and services produced.

CONCLUSION

20-1c Quality-of-Life Measures of Development

GDP per capita measures market transactions, but this measure does not give a complete picture of differences in living standards among nations. Exhibit 3 presents other selected socioeconomic indicators of the quality of life. These are variables such as life expectancy at birth, infant mortality rate, literacy rate, per capita electricity consumption, and economic freedom ranking. Take a close look at the statistics in Exhibit 3. These data reflect the dimensions of poverty in many of the LDCs. For example, a person born in Japan has a life expectancy that is much longer than a person born in Mozambique, and the infant mortality rate is dramatically higher in Mozambique. Per capita electricity consumption measures the use of nonhuman energy to perform work. In IACs, most work is done by machines, and in LDCs, virtually all work is done by people. For example, the average American uses 12,973 kilowatts of electricity per year, while the average person

EXHIBIT 3 Quality-of-Life Indicators for Selected Countries, 2015

Country	(1) GDP per capita	(2) Life expectancy at birth (years)	(3) Infant mortality rate[1]	(4) Literacy rate[2]	(5) Per capita electricity consumption[3]	(6) Economic freedom rank[4]
United States	$57,436	79	6	99%	12,973	17
Japan	38,917	84	2	99	7,829	40
Mexico	8,555	77	11	95	2,071	70
China	8,113	76	9	96	3,927	111
India	1,723	68	38	72	805	143
Bangladesh	1,411	72	31	61	311	128
Mozambique	392	55	57	59	463	158

[1] Per 1,000 live births

[2] Percentage age 15 and over who can read and write

[3] Kilowatts per capita

[4] The Heritage Foundation

SOURCES: World Bank, http://www.worldbank.org/en/country and The Heritage Foundation, http://www.heritage.org/index/. Per capita GDP is for 2016, electricity consumption is for 2014, the remaining data is from 2015.

in Mozambique uses only 463 kilowatts. Finally, it is interesting to note that GDP per capita and other quality-of-life indicators are related to the ranking in economic freedom.

How good an indicator of the quality of life is GDP per capita? Exhibit 3 reflects the principle that GDP per capita is highly correlated with alternative measures of the quality of life.

CONCLUSION	In general, GDP per capita is highly correlated with alternative measures of quality of life.

20-2 ECONOMIC GROWTH AND DEVELOPMENT AROUND THE WORLD

Economic growth and development are major goals of IACs and LDCs. People all over the world strive for a higher quality of life for their generation and future generations. However, growth is closer to a life-or-death situation for many LDCs, such as Bangladesh and Mozambique.

Economic growth and economic development are somewhat different, but related, concepts. As shown in Exhibit 4, recall from Chapter 2 that economic growth is the ability of an economy to produce greater levels of output, represented by an outward shift of its production possibilities curve (PPC). Thus, economic growth is defined on a *quantitative* basis using the percentage change in GDP per capita. When a nation's GDP rises more rapidly than its population, GDP per capita rises, and the nation experiences a higher average absolute standard of living. Conversely, if GDP expands less than the population of a nation, GDP per capita falls, and the nation experiences a lower average standard of living.

Economic development is a broader concept that is more *qualitative* in nature. Economic development encompasses improvement in the quality of life, including economic growth in the production of goods and services. In short, continuous economic growth is necessary for economic development, but economic growth is not the only consideration. For example, as explained earlier, GDP per capita does not measure the distribution of income or the political environment that provides the legal, monetary, education, and transportation structures necessary for economic development, which can impact the quality of life.

Economic growth and development involve a complex process that is determined by several interrelated factors. Like the performance of an NBA basketball team, success depends on the joint effort of team players, and one or two weak players can greatly reduce overall performance. However, there is no precise formula for winning. If your team has a player like NBA great LeBron James, it can win even with a few weak players. The remainder of this section examines the key factors, or players, that operate together to produce a nation's economic well-being.

20-2a Endowment of Natural Resources

Most of the LDCs have comparatively limited bases of natural resources, including mineral deposits and arable land resources. In these countries, most of the available land is

EXHIBIT 4 Economic Growth

The economy begins with the capacity to produce combinations along production possibilities curve PPC_1. Growth in the resource base or a technological advance shifts the production possibilities curve outward from PPC_1 to PPC_2. Points along PPC_2 represent new production possibilities that were previously impossible. The distance that the curve shifts represents an increase in the nation's productive capacity.

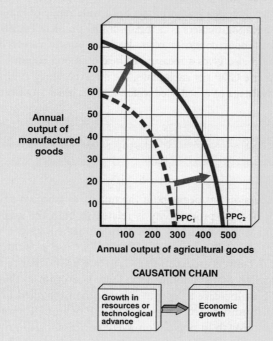

CAUSATION CHAIN

Growth in resources or technological advance → Economic growth

used for agricultural production, and clearing tropical forests to obtain more land can cause soil erosion. Also, tropical climates prevail in Central and South America, Africa, the Indian subcontinent, and Southeast Asia. The hot, humid climate in these regions is conducive to weed and insect infestations that plague agriculture.

Although a narrow base of resources does pose a barrier to economic growth and development, no single conclusion can be drawn. For example, how have Hong Kong, Japan, and Israel achieved high standards of living in spite of limited natural resource bases? Each has practically no minerals, little fertile land, and no domestic sources of energy. Nonetheless, these economies have become prosperous. In contrast, Argentina and Venezuela have abundant fertile land and minerals. Yet these and other countries have been growing slowly or not at all. Venezuela, for example, is one of the most oil-rich countries in the world. Ghana, Kenya, and Bolivia are also resource-rich countries that are poor, with little or no economic growth.

Natural resource endowment can promote economic growth, but a country can develop without a large natural resource base.

CONCLUSION

20-2b Investment in Human Resources

A low level of human capital can also present a barrier to economic growth and development. Recall that human capital is the education, training, experience, and health that improve the knowledge and skills of workers to produce goods and services. In most of the LDCs, investment in human capital is much less than in the IACs. Look back at column (4) in Exhibit 3. Consider how low the literacy rate is for the poorer countries. A country with a lower literacy rate has less ability to educate its labor force and create a basic foundation for economic growth. In fact, often the skills of workers in the poor countries are suited primarily to agriculture, rather than being appropriate for a wide range of industries and economic growth. Further complicating matters is a "brain drain" problem because the best educated and trained workers of poor countries often leave to pursue careers in richer countries. Column (2) of Exhibit 3 also gives a measure of health among countries with varying levels of GDP per capita. As the GDP per capita falls, the life expectancy at birth falls. Thus, richer countries have the advantage of a better educated and healthier workforce.

CONCLUSION   Investment in human capital generally results in increases in GDP per capita.

Thus far, the discussion has been about the quality of labor. We must also talk about the quantity of labor because productivity is related to both the quality and quantity of labor. Overpopulation is a problem for LDCs. In a nutshell, here is why: Other factors held constant, population (labor force) growth can increase a country's GDP. Yet rapid population growth can convert an expanding GDP into a GDP per capita that is stagnant, slow growing, or negative. Stated another way, there is no gain to the output available to the average person if an increase in output is more than matched by an increase in the number of mouths that must be fed. Suppose the GDP of an LDC grows at, say, 3 percent per year. If there is no growth in population, GDP per capita also grows at 3 percent per year. But what if the population also grows at 3 percent per year? The result is that GDP per capita remains unchanged. If population growth is instead only 1 percent per year, GDP per capita rises 2 percent per year. Obstacles to population control are great and include strong religious and sociocultural arguments against birth control programs.

CONCLUSION   Rapid population growth combined with low human capital investment explains why many countries are LDCs.

CHECKPOINT

Does Rapid Growth Mean a Country Is Catching Up?
Suppose country Alpha has a production possibilities curve closer to the origin than the curve for country Beta. Now assume Alpha experiences a 3 percent growth rate in GDP for ten years and Beta experiences a 6 percent growth rate in GDP for ten years. At the end of five years, which of the following is the best prediction for the standard of living? (1) Alpha's residents are better off. (2) Beta's residents are better off. (3) Which country's residents are better off cannot be determined.

20-2c Accumulation of Capital

It did not take long for Robinson Crusoe stranded on a deserted island to invest in a net in order to catch more fish than he could catch with his hands. Similarly, farmers working with modern tractors can cultivate more acres than farmers working with horse-drawn plows. Recall from Chapter 1 that capital in economics means factories, tractors, trucks, roads, computers, irrigation systems, electricity-generating facilities, and other human-made goods used to produce goods and services.

LDCs suffer from a critical shortage of capital. A family in Somalia owns little in the way of tools except a wooden plow. To make matters worse, roads are terrible, there are few plants generating electricity, and telephone lines are scarce. As shown in Exhibit 5, recall from Chapter 2 that a high-investment country can shift its production possibilities curve outward, but investment in capital goods is not a "free lunch." When more resources are used to produce more factories and machines, there is an opportunity cost of fewer resources available for the production of current consumer goods. This means that LDCs are often caught in a vicious circle of poverty. A **vicious circle of poverty** is the trap in which countries are poor and cannot afford to save. And low savings translate into low investment. Low investment results in low productivity, which, in turn, keeps incomes low. Any savings that do exist among higher-income persons in poor LDCs are often invested in IACs. This phenomenon is often called "capital flight." These wealthy individuals are afraid to save in their own countries because they fear that their governments may be overthrown and their savings could be lost.

Vicious circle of poverty The trap in which countries are poor because they cannot afford to save and invest, but they cannot save and invest because they are poor.

EXHIBIT 5 Alpha's and Beta's Present and Future Production Possibilities Curves

In part (a), each year Alpha produces only enough capital (K_a) to replace existing capital that is worn out. Without greater capital and assuming other resources remain fixed, Alpha is unable to shift its production possibilities curve outward. In part (b), each year Beta produces K_a capital, which is more than the amount required to replenish its depreciated capital. In 2018, this expanded capital provides Beta with the extra production capacity to shift its production possibilities curve to the right. If Beta chooses point B on its curve, it has the production capacity to increase the amount of consumer goods from C_b to C_c without producing fewer capital goods.

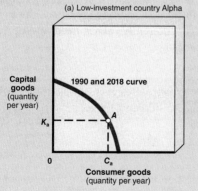

(a) Low-investment country Alpha

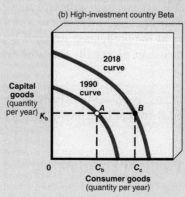

(b) High-investment country Beta

The United States and other nations have attempted to provide LDCs with foreign aid so that they might grow. These countries desperately need more factories and infrastructure. **Infrastructure** is capital goods usually provided by the government, including highways, bridges, waste and water systems, and airports. Unfortunately, the amount of foreign aid provided to the LDCs for capital improvements is relatively small, and as explained earlier, workers in the LDCs lack the skills necessary to use the most modern forms of capital. More specifically, LDCs face a major obstacle to capital accumulation because of the lack of entrepreneurs to assume the risks of capital formation.

| CONCLUSION | There is a significant positive relationship between investment and economic growth and development. |

Infrastructure
Capital goods usually provided by the government, including highways, bridges, waste and water systems, and airports.

20-2d Technological Progress

As explained earlier in Chapter 2, holding natural resources, labor, and capital constant, advancing the body of knowledge applied to production shifts the production possibilities curve of a country. In fact, technological advances have been at the heart of economic growth and development in recent history. During the last 250 years, brainpower has invented new power-driven machines, advanced communication devices, new energy sources, and countless ways to produce more output with the same resources. How have innovative products improved your productivity? Consider, to name just a few products, the impact of personal computers, word processing software, cell phone photography, the iPhone, and the Internet. In contrast, in many poor countries, waterwheels still bring water to the surface, cloth is woven on handlooms, and oxcarts are the major means of transportation. Consequently, large inputs of human effort are used relative to capital resources.

The United States and other IACs have provided the world with an abundant accumulation of technological knowledge that might be adopted by those LDCs without the resources to undertake the required cost of research and development. However, the results of this transfer process have been mixed. For example, countries such as China, Hong Kong, Singapore, Taiwan, South Korea, and Japan have surely achieved rapid growth in part from the benefit of technological borrowing. The other side of the coin is that much available technology is not well-suited to LDCs. The old saying "You need to learn to walk before you can run" often applies to the LDCs. For example, small farms of most LDCs are not well-suited for much of the agricultural technology developed for IACs' large farms. And how many factories in the LDCs are ready to use the most modern robotics in the production process? Stated differently, LDCs need appropriate technology, rather than necessarily the latest technology.

| CONCLUSION | Many LDCs continue to experience low growth rates even though IACs have developed advanced technologies that the world can utilize. |

20-2e Political Environment

The preceding discussion leads to the generalization that in order for LDCs to achieve economic growth and development, they must wisely use natural resources, invest in human and physical capital, and adopt advanced technology. This list of policies is not complete. LDC governments must also create a political environment favorable to economic growth. All too often a large part of the problem in poor countries is that resources are wasted as a result of war and political instability. Political leaders must not be corrupt and/or incompetent. Instead of following policies that favor a small elite ruling class, LDC governments must adopt appropriate domestic and international economic policies, discussed under the following three headings of law and order, infrastructure, and international trade.

Law and Order

A basic governmental function is to establish domestic law and order. This function includes many areas, such as a stable legal system, stable money and prices, competitive markets, and private ownership of property. In particular, expropriation of private property rights among LDCs is a barrier to growth. Well-defined private property rights have fostered economic growth in the IACs because this institutional policy has encouraged an entrepreneurial class. Private ownership provides individuals with the incentive to save money and invest in businesses. A stable political environment that ensures private ownership of profits also provides an incentive for individuals in other countries to invest in developing poor countries.

Infrastructure

Assuming an LDC government maintains law and order and the price system is used to allocate goods and services, it is vital that wise decisions be made concerning infrastructure. Indeed, inadequate infrastructure is one of the greatest problems of LDCs. Without such public goods as roads, schools, bridges, and public health and sanitation services, poor countries are unable to generate the substantial external benefits that are an important ingredient in economic growth and development. From the viewpoint of individual firms, government must provide infrastructure because these public goods projects are too costly for a firm to undertake.

International Trade

In general, LDCs can benefit from an expanding volume of trade. This is the theory behind the North American Free Trade Agreement (NAFTA), the General Agreement on Tariffs and Trade (GATT), and the World Trade Organization (WTO) discussed in the chapter on international trade and finance. As explained earlier in this chapter, policies such as tariffs and quotas restrain international trade and thereby inhibit economic growth and development. These trade policies are antigrowth because they restrict the ability of people in one country to trade with people in other countries. Similarly, a country that fixes the exchange rate of its own currency above the market-determined exchange rate makes that country's exports less attractive to foreigners. This means, in turn, that domestic citizens sell less of their goods to foreigners and earn less foreign currency with which to buy imports.

By fixing its exchange rates and by imposing trade barriers, a country will lower its economic growth rate.	**CONCLUSION**

Exhibit 6 summarizes the key factors explained earlier that determine the economic growth and development of countries. Analysis of this exhibit reveals that economic growth and development are the result of a multidimensional process. This means that

GLOBAL ECONOMICS

India and China's Economic Growth: An Updated Version of Aesop's Tale

Applicable Concept: Sustaining Growth

The most famous footrace ever held occurred in the pages of a book and is a fictional tale involving two animals. As the story unfolds, a rabbit gets off to a fast start, but he does not keep up this pace, and instead takes a nap, halting his progress. A tortoise, on the other hand, starts slow but maintains his pace, eventually overtaking the rabbit to win the race. Some economists have argued that India and China are in an economic development race that shares many characteristics of the race between the tortoise and the hare.

Before the race began in 1978, China and India were both very poor. When the starting gun fired, China, playing the role of the rabbit in our analogy, began running with dazzling speed as a result of a series of reforms that allowed it to use its factors of production more productively. First, China reformed its agricultural sector. Before the reforms, 70 percent of the Chinese labor force worked in agriculture, and yet the country was still unable to provide its people with even the United Nations' minimum recommended daily intake of 2,300 calories a day.[1] China's new leader Deng Xiaoping inherited a system where farmers had to meet production quotas and sell all their output to the government at official prices, which were so low that farmers had no incentive to produce beyond their quotas. Under Deng's reforms, farmers were still required to produce their quotas and to sell this amount of grain to the government at the mandated prices; however, Deng allowed farmers to sell any extra output they produced beyond their

Boris15/Shutterstock.com

mandated quotas and receive market prices in return. Market prices were high enough to encourage more production, and to encourage farmers to discover more efficient ways to grow their crops. In just six years agricultural output in China increased by 47 percent.

Farm workers became more productive, so fewer workers were needed to produce crops. Over the next 30 years, the share of the labor force in agriculture dropped to 26 percent—less than half of what it had been. With fewer workers needed on farms, these workers could move to cities and work in industry. In cities, workers were exposed to advanced capital-intensive production processes, which elevated their productivity. In 1978 nonfarm workers were six times more productive than farm workers, so simply getting workers off the farm, where they are relatively unproductive, and into cities, where they are much more

it is difficult for countries to break the poverty barrier because they must improve many factors in order to increase their economic well-being. But it is important to remember that lack of one or more key factors, such as natural resources, does not necessarily keep an LDC in the trap of underdevelopment.

CONCLUSION   There is no single strategy for economic growth and development.

productive, enabled very robust economic growth in China.

In the 1990s, China initiated another round of reforms. It began to allow government-owned enterprises to shrink and even to fail. Between 1995 and 2001, the state-run sector of the economy went from employing 17 percent to employing 12 percent of the workforce. These newly mobile workers needed some place to go, and China's next policy found such a place. China allowed foreign countries to build factories within its borders. This foreign investment allowed China to move even more of its labor force into its productive manufacturing sector.

Whereas China got off to a quick start, India did not even leave the starting blocks until 1991, when it opened up its economy in three important ways.[2] First, India reduced trade barriers, slashing tariffs in half within 4 years. The increased foreign competition forced Indian firms to become more efficient. Second, India removed a requirement that had prevented foreigners from owning a majority ownership stake in Indian firms. As a result, large amounts of foreign investment flowed into India, giving Indian workers access to better technology and enabling them to work in firms that were larger and more efficient. Finally, the country moved away from a reliance on inefficient bureaucratic government planning and toward a greater reliance on market forces to direct the economy. All three reforms increased India's economic growth by encouraging self-interested market participants to use resources more efficiently.

Both countries are still growing rapidly; however, economist Jagdish Bhagwati contends that India is more likely than China to sustain its high growth rates.[3]

He believes India's democracy gives it an important advantage over China. In a democracy, when people are displeased, they can channel their energies into an election, making them feel that they have some influence over government policy. Democratic governments are also good at coming up with compromises that no one loves, but that everyone can live with. In short, democracies provide a pressure release valve that prevents unrest from creating enough political uncertainty to derail economic growth. China, on the other hand, does not possess democratic institutions; therefore, if the Chinese people are unhappy, they may challenge the government directly, causing enough political unrest to threaten the government's survival. The accompanying uncertainty will discourage investments and cause Chinese economic growth to come to a screeching halt. If Professor Bhagwati is correct, India is like the tortoise in the famous race. India got off to a slow start, but because it is more likely to sustain its economic growth, it may eventually become a richer country than China.

ANALYZE THE ISSUE

1. What have been the ingredients for economic growth and development that China and India share? What have been their differences?

2. How important do you think democracy is for economic growth and development? What political reforms would you recommend for China? How likely are these recommendations to be implemented in China?

---

1. The data about and the discussion of China in this passage come from the following source. Xiaodong Zhu, "Understanding China's Growth: Past, Present, and Future," *Journal of Economic Perspectives* 26, 4 (Fall 2012), pp. 103–124.
2. The discussion on India's economic growth is derived from the following source. Montek S. Ahluwalia, "Economic reforms in India Since 1991: Has Gradualism Worked," *Journal of Economic Perspectives* 16, 3 (Summer 2002): pp. 67–88.
3. Jagdish Bhagwati, "Indian Lessons," *Wall Street Journal*, February 28, 2006, p. A16.

20-3 THE HELPING HAND OF ADVANCED COUNTRIES

How can poor countries escape the vicious circle of poverty? Low GDP per capita leads to low savings and investment, which lead, in turn, to low growth. Although there is no easy way for poor countries to become richer, the United States and other advanced countries can be an instrument of growth. The necessary funds can come from the LDCs' own domestic savings, or it can come from external sources that include foreign private investment, foreign aid, and foreign loans.

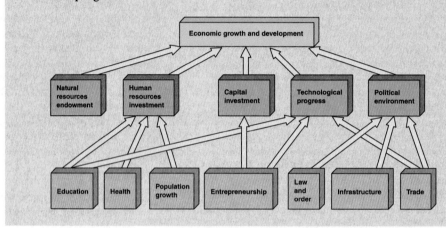

EXHIBIT 6 Key Categories That Determine Economic Growth and Development

There are five basic categories that interact to determine the economic growth and development of countries: natural resources, human resources, capital, technological progress, and the political environment. The exhibit also indicates important factors that influence the five factors. LDCs are faced with a formidable task. Because economic growth and development are multidimensional, LDCs must improve many factors in order to achieve economic progress.

Exhibit 7 illustrates how external funds can shift a country's production possibilities curve outward. Here you should look back and review Exhibit 5. Suppose country Alpha is trapped in poverty and produces only enough capital (K_a) to replace the existing capital being worn out. Alpha's consumption level is at C_a, corresponding to point A on production possibilities curve PPC_1. Because C_a is at the subsistence level, Alpha cannot save and invest by substituting capital for current consumption and move upward along PPC_1. This inability to increase capital means Alpha cannot use internal sources of funds to increase its production possibilities curve in the future. There is a way out of the trap using external sources. Now assume Alpha receives an inflow of funds from abroad and buys capital goods that increase its rate of investment from K_a to K_b. At K_b, the rate of capital formation exceeds the value of capital depreciated, and Alpha's production possibilities curve shifts rightward to PPC_1. Economic growth made possible by external investment means Alpha can improve its standard of living by increasing its consumption level from C_a at point A on PPC_1 to C_b at point B on PPC_2.

20-3a Foreign Private Investment

Many countries' development benefits from private-sector foreign investment from private investors. For example, Microsoft might finance construction of a plant in the Philippines to manufacture software, or Bank of America may make loans to the

EXHIBIT 7 The Effect of External Financing on an LDC's Production Possibilities Curve

The poor country of Alpha is initially operating at point A on production possibilities curve PPC_1, with only enough capital (K_a) to replace depreciation. If C_a is the consumption level of subsistence, Alpha's economy cannot grow by reducing consumption. An inflow of external funds from abroad permits the LDC to increase its capital from K_a to K_b and its production possibilities curve shifts outward to PPC_2. At PPC_2, Alpha is able to increase its production of consumer goods from C_a to C_b.

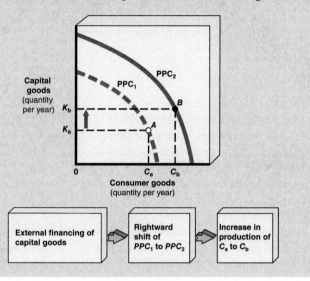

government of Haiti. These large multinational corporations and commercial banks supply scarce capital to the LDCs. A multinational corporation is a firm with headquarters in one country and one or more branch or plants in other countries. Multinational firms often seek new investment opportunities in LDCs because these poor countries offer abundant supplies of low-wage labor and raw materials. But the political environment in the LDCs must be conducive to investment. Multinational corporations often become the largest employers, largest taxpayers, and largest exporters in the LDCs.

20-3b Foreign Aid

About 1 percent of the U.S. federal budget is spent on foreign aid. **Foreign aid** is the transfer of money or resources from one government to another with no repayment required. These transfers may be made as outright grants, technical assistance, or food supplies. Foreign aid flows from country to country through governments and voluntary agencies, such as the Red Cross, CARE, and Church World Relief. The United States distributes most of its official development assistance through the Agency for International Development, established in 1961. The **Agency for International Development (AID)** is the agency of the U.S. State Department that is in charge of U.S. aid to foreign countries.

   One reason that countries such as the United States provide foreign aid to LDCs is the belief that it is a moral responsibility of richer countries to share their wealth with

Foreign aid
The transfer of money or resources from one government to another with no repayment required.

Agency for International Development (AID)
The agency of the U.S. State Department that is in charge of U.S. aid to foreign countries.

poorer countries. A second reason is that it is in the best economic interest of the IACs to help the LDCs. When these countries become more prosperous, the IACs have more markets for their exports, and thereby all countries benefit from trade.

The LDCs often complain that foreign aid comes with too many economic and political strings attached. The aid is often offered on a take-it-or-leave-it basis, tied to policies other than basic trade policies, such as human rights, politics, or the military. Consequently, many LDCs argue for "trade, not aid." If the IACs would simply buy more goods from the LDCs, the LDCs could use their gains in export earnings to purchase more capital and to invest in other ingredients needed for growth. Many people in the United States believe that most foreign aid is a waste of money because it is misused by the recipient countries. This belief has caused Congress to grow increasingly reluctant to send taxpayers' money abroad except in the clearest cases of need or for reasons of national security.

20-3c Foreign Loans

A third source of external funds that can be used to finance LDCs' domestic investment is loans from abroad. Governments, international organizations, and private banks all make loans to LDCs. Like foreign private investment and foreign aid, loans give LDCs the opportunity to shift their production possibilities curves outward. There are various types of loan sources for LDCs. Bilateral loans are made directly from one country to another. The principal agent for official U.S. bilateral loans is the U.S. Agency for International Development, introduced earlier.

World Bank
The lending agency that makes long-term low interest loans and provides technical assistance to less developed countries.

One prominent multilateral lending agency is the World Bank. The 189-member **World Bank** is the lending agency affiliated with the United Nations that makes long-term low-interest loans and provides technical assistance to LDCs. Loans are made only after a planning period lasting a year or more. The World Bank was established in 1944 by major nations meeting in Bretton Woods, New Hampshire. Its first charge was to assist with reconstruction after World War II. Today, the World Bank is located in Washington, D.C., and its main purpose is to channel funds from rich countries to poor countries. Voting shares are in proportion to the money provided by the members. The World Bank makes "last resort" loans to LDCs that are limited to financing basic infrastructure projects, such as schools, health centers, dams, irrigation systems, and transportation facilities, for which private financing is not available. In addition, the World Bank helps LDCs get loans from private lenders by insuring the loans. Thus, the poor countries are able to complete projects and use the economic returns to pay off the lender with interest.

International Monetary Fund (IMF)
The lending agency that makes short-term conditional low-interest loans to developing countries.

The World Bank is not the only multilateral lending agency making loans to LDCs. The World Bank's partner institution is the International Monetary Fund. The **International Monetary Fund (IMF)** is the lending agency that makes short-term conditional low-interest loans to developing countries. The IMF was also established at Bretton Woods in 1944. Its purpose is to help countries overcome short-run financial difficulties. Typically, the IMF makes conditional loans that require the debtor countries to implement fiscal and monetary policies that will alleviate balance-of-payments deficit problems and promote noninflationary economic growth. The 189-member IMF is not a charitable institution. It operates like a credit union with funding quotas that earn interest on the loans. The United States is the IMF's largest shareholder and thus has effective veto power over IMF decisions.

The IMF has performed a major role in providing short-term loans to developing countries and to economies making the transition to capitalism. In the late 1990s, the IMF provided multibillion-dollar bailouts to Russia, several Asian countries, Brazil, and other countries experiencing economic turmoil. In recent years, the IMF and some of the

EU countries made rescue loans to debt-plagued Greece with the condition of deep cutbacks in government spending and tax hikes. Critics argue that as long as governments believe the IMF will bail them out, they will fail to correct their own problems. IMF supporters counter that if the IMF does not intervene, troubled economies will default on outstanding loans and cause a worldwide financial ripple effect. Critics respond that a flood of low-cost short-term loans from the IMF encourages bad government policies and excessive risk taking by banks. Consequently, a bailout in a crisis generates new financial crises and reduces world economic growth.

CHECKPOINT

Is the Minimum Wage an Antipoverty Solution for Poor Countries?
Imagine you are an economic adviser to the president of a poor LDC. The president is seeking policies to promote economic growth and a higher standard of living for citizens of this country. You are asked whether adopting a minimum wage equal to the average of the IACs' average hourly wages would achieve these goals. Recall the discussion of the minimum wage from Chapter 4 and evaluate this policy.

Key Concepts

GDP per capita

Industrially advanced countries (IACs)

Less-developed countries (LDCs)

Vicious circle of poverty

Infrastructure

Foreign aid

Agency for International Development (AID)

World Bank

International Monetary Fund (IMF)

Summary

- **GDP per capita** provides a general index of a country's standard of living. Countries with low GDP per capita and slow growth in GDP per capita are less able to satisfy basic needs for food, shelter, clothing, education, and health.

- **Industrially advanced countries (IACs)** are countries with high GDP per capita, and output is produced by technologically advanced capital. Countries that have high incomes without widespread industrial development, such as the oil-rich Arab countries, are not included in the IAC list.

- **Less-developed countries (LDCs)** are countries with low production per person. In these countries, output is produced without large amounts of technologically advanced capital and without well-educated labor. The LDCs account for about three-fourths of the world's population.

- The *Four Tigers of the Pacific Rim* are Hong Kong, Singapore, South Korea, and Taiwan. These recently industrialized countries have achieved high growth rates and standards of living.

- **GDP per capita comparisons** are subject to three problems: (1) the accuracy of LDC data is questionable, (2) GDP per capita ignores income distribution, (3) fluctuations in exchange rates affect GDP per capita gaps between countries.

- **Economic growth** and **economic development** are related, but somewhat different, concepts. Economic growth is measured *quantitatively* by

GDP per capita, while economic development is a broader concept that includes *qualitative* factors. In addition to GDP per capita, economic development includes quality-of-life measures, such as life expectancy at birth, adult literacy rate, and per capita energy consumption. Economic growth and development are the result of a complex process that is determined by five major factors: (1) natural resources, (2) human resources, (3) capital, (4) technological progress, and (5) the political environment. There is no single correct strategy for economic development and a lack of strength in one or more of the five areas does not prevent growth.

- The **vicious circle of poverty** is a trap in which an LDC is too poor to save and therefore it cannot invest and shift its production possibilities curve outward. As a result, the LDC remains poor. One way for a poor country to gain savings, invest, and grow is to use funds from external sources such as foreign private investment, foreign aid, and foreign loans.

Summary of Conclusion Statements

- LDCs' GDP per capita is subject to greater measurement errors than data for IACs.

- GDP per capita comparisons among nations can be misleading because GDP per capita does not measure income distribution.

- A conversion problem may widen or narrow the GDP per capita gap between nations because the fluctuations in exchange rates do not reflect actual differences in the value of goods and services produced.

- In general, GDP per capita is highly correlated with alternative measures of quality of life.

- Natural resource endowment can promote economic growth, but a country can develop without a large natural resource base.

- Investment in human capital generally results in increases in GDP per capita.

- Rapid population growth combined with low human capital investment explains why many countries are LDCs.

- There is a significant positive relationship between investment and economic growth and development.

- Many LDCs continue to experience low growth rates even though IACs have developed advanced technologies that the world can utilize.

- By fixing its exchange rates and by imposing trade barriers, a country will lower its economic growth rate.

- There is no single strategy for economic growth and development.

Study Questions and Problems

Please see Appendix A for answers to the odd-numbered questions. Your instructor has access to the answers for even-numbered questions.

1. What is the difference between industrially advanced countries (IACs) and less-developed countries (LDCs)? List five IACs and five LDCs.

2. Explain why GDP per capita comparisons among nations are not a perfect measure of differences in economic well-being.

3. Assume you are given the following data for country Alpha and country Beta:

Country	GDP per capita
Alpha	$25,000
Beta	15,000

a. Based on the GDP per capita data given here, in which country would you prefer to live?

b. Now assume you are given the following additional quality-of-life data. In which country would you prefer to reside?

Country	Life expectancy at birth (years)	Daily per capita calorie supply	Per capita energy consumption*
Alpha	65	2,500	3,000
Beta	70	3,000	4,000

*Kilograms of oil equivalent.

4. What is the difference between economic development and economic growth? Give examples of how each of these concepts can be measured.

5. Do you agree with the argument that the rich nations are getting richer and the poor nations are getting poorer? Is this an oversimplification? Explain.

6. Explain why it is so difficult for poor LDCs to generate investment in capital in order to increase productivity and growth and, therefore, improve their standard of living.

7. Why is the quest for economic growth and development complicated?

8. Indicate whether each of the following is associated with a high or low level of economic growth and development:

	High	Low
a. Overpopulation	____	____
b. Highly skilled labor	____	____
c. High savings rate	____	____
d. Political stability	____	____
e. Low capital accumulation	____	____
f. Advanced technology	____	____
g. Highly developed infrastructure	____	____
h. High proportion of agriculture	____	____
i. High degree of income inequality	____	____

9. Without external financing from foreign private investment, foreign aid, and foreign loans, poor countries are caught in the vicious circle of poverty. Explain. How does external financing help poor countries achieve economic growth and development?

10. What are some of the problems for LDCs of accepting foreign aid?

11. Why would an LDC argue for "trade, not aid"?

12. Explain the differences among the Agency for International Development (AID), the World Bank, and the International Monetary Fund (IMF).

 ## CHECKPOINT ANSWERS

Does Rapid Growth Mean a Country Is Catching Up?

GDP growth alone does not measure the standard of living. You must also consider population. Even though Beta experienced a greater GDP growth rate, its GDP per capita might be less than Alpha's because its population growth rate is greater. Of course, the reverse is also possible, but without population data, we cannot say. If you said which country's people are better off cannot be determined because the GDP must be divided by the population to measure the average standard of living, **YOU ARE CORRECT**.

Is the Minimum Wage an Antipoverty Solution for Poor Countries?

An important source of foreign investment for LDCs is multinational corporations that locate plants and other facilities in these countries. LDCs compete with each other for the economic growth and development benefits that these multinational corporations can provide. For an LDC to win the competition, it must offer political stability, adequate infrastructure, a favorable business climate, and a cheap labor force. If you said you would not support the president's proposal to raise the minimum wage because it would place the LDC at a competitive disadvantage in the labor market, thereby reducing foreign private investment and growth, **YOU ARE CORRECT**.

Sample Quiz

Please see Appendix B for answers to Sample Quiz questions.

1. Which of the following is a problem when comparing GDP per capita between nations?
   a. GDP per capita fails to measure income distribution.
   b. Fluctuations in exchange rates affect differences in GDP per capita.
   c. GDP per capita is subject to greater measurement errors for LDCs compared to IACs.
   d. All of the above answers are correct.

2. GDP per capita is a relatively good measurement of
   a. the distribution of income.
   b. purchasing power.
   c. household production.
   d. the standard of living.

3. Which of the following is infrastructure?
   a. Police
   b. Training and education
   c. Highways
   d. All of the answers above answers are correct.

4. Which of the following statements explains the vicious circle of poverty?
   a. By investing in education and infrastructure at the same time, the country can overcome the problems of poverty.
   b. Poverty arises out of the lack of investment, but countries cannot invest because they are poor.
   c. A nation can shift its production possibilities curve inward by shifting more resources into the production of capital goods.
   d. A nation can shift its production possibilities curve outward by shifting more resources into the production of consumer goods.

5. Which of the following is not a characteristic of most less-developed countries?
   a. Inadequate human capital
   b. Inadequate capital goods
   c. High population growth rate
   d. Inadequate water supplies
   e. High productivity

6. Compared to IACs, LDCs are often characterized by
   a. lower life expectancy.
   b. lower adult literacy.
   c. lower per capita energy consumption.
   d. All of the above answers are correct.

7. Real GDP per capita and other alternative measures of the quality of life are
   a. independent.
   b. directly correlated.
   c. poorly correlated.
   d. inversely related.

8. Economic development encompasses which of the following measures?
   a. Economic growth
   b. The political environment
   c. Education
   d. All of the above answers are correct.

9. Which of the following is a characteristic of an LDC?
   a. Capital flight
   b. Vicious circle of poverty
   c. Lack of entrepreneurs
   d. All of the answers are correct.

10. Economic growth and development in LDCs are low because many of them lack
    a. savings.
    b. infrastructure.

c. a political environment favorable to growth.
d. All of the answers are correct.

11. Which of the following is a *true* statement?
   a. The LDC classification is of questionable accuracy.
   b. GDP per capita ignores the degree of income distribution.
   c. GDP per capita is affected by exchange rate changes.
   d. GDP per capita does not account for the difference in the cost of living among nations.
   e. All of the answers are correct.

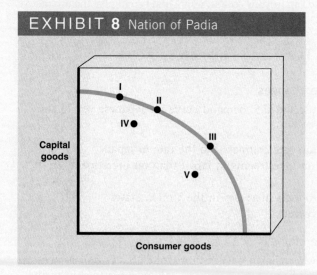

EXHIBIT 8 Nation of Padia

Capital goods

Consumer goods

12. Exhibit 8 shows the production possibilities curve of the nation of Padia. Based only on this information, which point would produce the highest rate of growth?
   a. I
   b. II
   c. III
   d. IV
   e. V

13. Exhibit 8 shows the production possibilities curve of the nation of Padia. Based only on this information, the point which would produce the lowest rate of growth would be
   a. I
   b. II
   c. III
   d. IV
   e. V

14. Which of the following is in charge of U.S. aid to foreign countries?
   a. Agency for International Development (AID)
   b. World Bank
   c. International Monetary Fund (IMF)
   d. New International Economic Order (NIEO)

15. Which of the following makes long-term low-interest loans to LDCs?
   a. Agency for International Development (AID)
   b. World Bank
   c. International Monetary Fund (IMF)
   d. New International Economic Order (NIEO)

16. Which of the following makes short-term conditional low-interest loans to LDCs?
   a. World Bank
   b. Agency for International Development (AID)
   c. Agency for International Finance (AIF)
   d. International Monetary Fund (IMF)

17. Which of the following is *not* an example of a country's infrastructure?
   a. Transportation system
   b. Communications system
   c. Political system
   d. Educational system

18. Which of the following *best* defines the vicious circle of poverty?
   a. Countries are poor because they cannot afford to save and invest.
   b. Countries are poor because of high population growth.
   c. Countries are poor because of lack of education and training for workers.
   d. Countries are poor because of poor international credit.

19. If a country's population grows at the same rate as its real GDP, then real per capita GDP
   a. grows at an increasing rate.
   b. grows at a constant rate.
   c. doesn't change.
   d. decreases at a decreasing rate.

20. In order for Ethiopia to increase its future economic growth, it must choose a point that is
   a. below its production possibilities curve.
   b. further along on its production possibilities curve toward the capital goods axis.
   c. further along on its production possibilities curve toward the consumption goods axis.
   d. above its production possibilities curve.

PART 6
The International Economy

This road map feature helps you tie together material in the part as you travel the Economic Way of Thinking Highway. The following are review questions listed by chapter from the previous part. The key concept in each question is given for emphasis, and each question or set of questions concludes with an interactive game to reinforce the concepts. The correct answers to the multiple choice questions are given in Appendix C. If your instructor has included MindTap in your course, visit MindTap to play the interactive Causation Chain Game.

Chapter 18: International Trade and Finance

1. Key Concept: Exchange rate changes

Which of the following would cause the U.S. demand curve for Japanese yen to shift to the right?

a. An increase in the U.S. inflation rate compared to the rate in Japan.
b. A higher real rate of interest on investments in Japan than on investments in the United States.
c. The popularity of Japanese products increases in the United States.
d. All of the answers above are correct.

2. Key Concept: Exchange rate changes

In the foreign exchange market, where Japanese Yen and United States dollars are traded, which of the following would cause the supply of dollars curve to shift to the right?

a. Japanese imports become less popular.
b. The value of the dollar falls.
c. The supply of dollars decreases.
d. Japanese imports become more popular.

CAUSATION CHAIN GAME
Changes in the Supply and Demand Curves for Dollars—Exhibit 10

3. Key Concept: Impact of relative price level changes

An increase in inflation in the United States relative to the rate in France would make

a. U.S. goods relatively less expensive in the United States and in France.
b. French goods relatively less expensive in the United States, and U.S. goods relatively more expensive in France.

c. French goods relatively more expensive in the United States and in France.
d. French goods relatively more expensive in the United States, and U.S. goods relatively less expensive in France.

4. Key Concept: Impact of relative price level changes

If the Japanese price level falls relative to the price level in the United States, then

a. Japanese buy U.S. exports.
b. the demand for dollars decreases.
c. the supply of dollars increases.
d. the value of the dollar falls.
e. All of the answers above are correct.

CAUSATION CHAIN GAME
The Impact of Relative Price Level Changes on Exchange Rates—Exhibit 11

Chapter 19: Economies in Transition

5. Key Concept: Command economy

Which of the following statements is *true* about a command economy?

a. Shortages occur because of complexities in the planning process.
b. Planners determine what, how many, and for whom goods and services are to be produced.
c. Planners often allocate goods and services using a rationing system.
d. The quality of produced goods and services tends to be inferior.
e. All of the answers are correct.

6. Key Concept: Command economy

Which of the following statements *best* describes the role played by prices in a command economy such as the former Soviet Union?

a. Prices were used to allocate resources.
b. Prices played the same role as in a market economy.
c. Prices and queuing were used to ration final goods and services.
d. None of the statements are true.

CAUSATION CHAIN GAME
Central Planners Fixing Prices—Exhibit 2

Chapter 20: Growth and the Less-Developed Countries

7. Key Concept: Economic growth

An outward shift of an economy's production possibilities curve is caused by an

a. increase in capital.
b. increase in labor.

c. advance in technology.
d. All of the answers are correct.

8. Key Concept: Economic growth

Which of the following statements are *correct*?

a. Economic development is more quantitative than economic growth.
b. A country cannot achieve economic growth with a limited base of natural resources.
c. Infrastructure is capital provided by the private sector.
d. All of the above are correct.
e. All of the above are incorrect.

CAUSATION CHAIN GAME
Economic Growth—Exhibit 4

9. Key Concept: Achieving economic growth

Which of the following can be a barrier to an LDC's economic growth and development?

a. Low population growth
b. A low level of human capital
c. Faster capital accumulation
d. More infrastructure

10. Key Concept: Economic growth and development

To grow and prosper, less-developed countries must *not*

a. invest in human capital.
b. build a strong infrastructure.
c. shift resources out of the production of consumer goods and into the production of capital goods.
d. shift resources out of the production of capital goods and into the production of consumer goods.
e. improve the quality of the water supply.

CAUSATION CHAIN GAME
The Effect of External Financing on an LDC's Production Possibilities Curve—Exhibit 7

Answers to Odd-Numbered Study Questions and Problems*

CHAPTER 1
INTRODUCING THE ECONOMIC WAY OF THINKING

1. A poor nation with many people who lack food, clothing, and shelter certainly experiences wants beyond the availability of goods and services to satisfy these unfulfilled wants. On the other hand, no wealthy nation has all the resources necessary to produce everything everyone in the nation wants to have. Even if you had $1 million and were completely satisfied with your share of goods and services, other desires would be unfulfilled. There is never enough time to accomplish all the things that you can imagine would be worthwhile.

3. Macroeconomics applies an overview perspective to an economy by examining economy-wide variables, such as inflation, unemployment, and growth of the economy. Microeconomics examines individual economic units, such as the market for corn, gasoline, or ostrich eggs.

5. The real world is full of complexities that make it difficult to understand and predict the relationships between variables. For example, the relationship between changes in the price of gasoline and changes in consumption of gasoline requires abstraction from the reality that variables such as weather and the fuel economy of cars often change at the same time as the price of gasoline.

7. The two events are associated because the first event (cut in military spending) is followed by the second event (higher unemployment in the defense industry). The point is that association does not necessarily mean causation, but it might. For example, the economy could be in recession.

APPENDIX TO CHAPTER 1
APPLYING GRAPHS TO ECONOMICS

1. a. The probability of living is *inversely* related to age. This model could be affected by improvements in diet, better health care, reductions in hazards to health in the workplace, or changes in the speed limit.

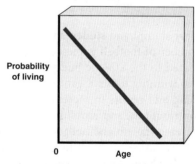

   b. Annual income and years of formal education are *directly* related. This relationship might be influenced by changes in such human characteristics as intelligence, motivation, ability, and family background. An example of an institutional change that could affect this relationship over a number of years is the draft.

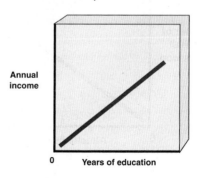

---

*Note: Answers to even-numbered questions are in the Instructor's Manual.

c. Inches of snow and sales of bathing suits are *inversely* related. The weather forecast and the price of travel to sunny vacation spots can affect this relationship.

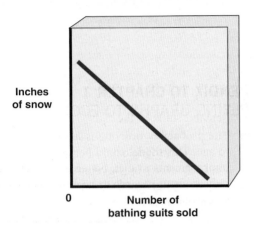

d. Most alumni and students will argue that the number of football games won is *directly* related to the athletic budget. They reason that winning football games is great advertising and results in increased attendance, contributions, and enrollment that, in turn, increase the athletic budget. Success in football can also be related to other factors, such as school size, age and type of institution, number and income of alumni, and quality of the faculty and administrators.

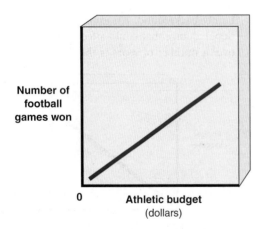

CHAPTER 2
PRODUCTION POSSIBILITIES, OPPORTUNITY COST, AND ECONOMIC GROWTH

1. Because the wants of individuals and society exceed the goods and services available to satisfy these desires, choices must be made. The consumption possibilities of an individual with a fixed income are limited, and as a result, additional consumption of one item necessarily precludes an expenditure on another next-best choice. The forgone alternative is called the opportunity cost, and this concept also applies to societal decisions. If society allocates resources to the production of guns, then those same resources cannot be used at the same time to make butter.

3. Regardless of the price of a lunch, economic resources—land, labor, and capital—are used to produce the lunch. These scarce resources are no longer available to produce other goods and services.

5. Using marginal analysis, students weigh the benefits of attending college against the costs. There is an incentive to attend college when the benefits (improved job opportunities, income, improvement, social life, and so on) outweigh the opportunity costs.

7.

Flower boxes	Opportunity cost (pies forgone)
0	—
1	4 (30 − 26)
2	5 (26 − 21)
3	6 (21 − 15)
4	7 (15 − 8)
5	8 (8 − 0)

9. Movements along the curve are efficient points and conform to the well-known "free lunch" statement. However, points inside the curve are exceptions because it is possible to produce more of one output without producing less of another output.

11.

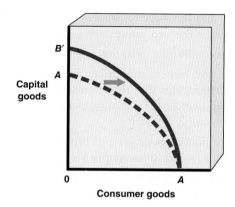

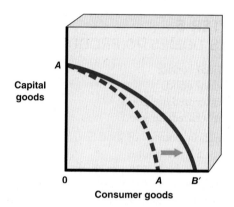

CHAPTER 3
MARKET DEMAND AND SUPPLY

1. If people buy a good or service because they associate higher quality with higher price, this is a violation of the ceteris paribus assumption. An increase in the quantity demanded results only from a decrease in price. Quality and other nonprice determinants of demand, such as tastes and preferences and the price of related goods, are held constant in the model.

3. a. Demand for cars decreases; oil and cars are *complements*.
    b. Demand for insulation increases; oil and home insulation are *substitutes*.
    c. Demand for coal increases; oil and coal are *substitutes*.
    d. Demand for tires decreases; oil and tires are *complements*.

5. One reason that the demand curve for word processing software shifted to the right might be that people desire new, higher-quality output features. The supply curve can shift to the right when new technology makes it possible to offer more software for sale at different prices.

7. a. Demand shifts to the right.
    b. Supply shifts to the left.
    c. Supply shifts to the right.
    d. Demand shifts to the right.
    e. Demand shifts to the right.
    f. Supply of cotton shifts to the right.

9. a. The supply of Blu-ray players shifts rightward.
    b. The demand for Blu-ray players is unaffected.
    c. The equilibrium price falls, and the equilibrium quantity increases.
    d. The demand for Blu-ray discs increases because of the fall in the price of Blu-ray players (a complementary good).

11. The number of seats (quantity supplied) remains constant, but the demand curve shifts because tastes and preferences change according to the importance of each game. Although demand changes, the price is a fixed amount, and to manage a shortage, colleges and universities use amount of contributions, number of years as a contributor, or some other rationing device.

APPENDIX TO CHAPTER 3
CONSUMER SURPLUS, PRODUCER SURPLUS, AND MARKET EFFICIENCY

1. $50

3.

Price	$30	$15
Consumer surplus	$50	$105
Producer surplus	$25	$5
Total surplus	$75	$110

The lower price results in higher total surplus because in this case the rise in consumer surplus exceeds fall in producer surplus.

CHAPTER 4
MARKETS IN ACTION

1.

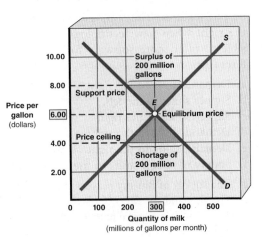

a. The equilibrium price is $6.00 per gallon, and the equilibrium quantity is 300 million gallons per month. The price system will restore the market's $6.00 per gallon price because a surplus will either drive prices down or a shortage will drive prices up.

b. The support price results in a persistent surplus of 200 million gallons of milk per month, which the government purchases with taxpayers' money. Consequently, taxpayers who do not drink milk are still paying for milk. The purpose of the support price is to bolster the incomes of dairy farmers.

c. The ceiling price will result in a persistent shortage of 200 million gallons of milk per month, but 200 million gallons are purchased by consumers at the low price of $4.00 per gallon. The shortage places a burden on the government to ration milk in order to be fair and to prevent black markets. The government's goal is to keep the price of milk below the equilibrium price of $6.00 per gallon, which would be set by a free market.

3. The labor market can be divided into two separate markets, one for skilled union workers and one for unskilled workers. If the minimum wage is above the equilibrium wage rate and is raised, the effect will be to increase the demand for, and the wage of, skilled union workers because the two groups are substitutes.

5. The equilibrium price rises.

7. The government can reduce emissions by (a) regulations that require smoke-abatement equipment or (b) imposing pollution taxes that shift supply leftward.

9. Pure public goods are not produced in sufficient quantities by private markets because there is no feasible method to exclude free riders.

CHAPTER 5
GROSS DOMESTIC PRODUCT

1. a. final service
   b. final good
   c. intermediate good
   d. intermediate good

3. 3 million pounds of food
× $1 per pound	= $3 million
50,000 shirts × $20 per shirt	= 1 million
20 houses × $50,000 per house	= 1 million
50,000 hours of medical services × $20 per hour	= 1 million
1 automobile plant × $1 million per plant	= 1 million
2 tanks × $500,000 per tank	= 1 million
Total value of output	= $8 million

5. Capital is not excluded from being a final good. A final good is a finished good purchased by an ultimate user and not for resale. The ultimate user is the warehouse, so the sale would be included in GDP and there would be no double-counting problem.

7. Using the expenditure approach, net exports are exports minus imports. If the expenditures by foreigners for U.S. products exceed the expenditures by U.S. citizens for foreign products, net exports will be a positive contribution to GDP. If foreigners spend less for U.S. products than U.S. citizens spend for foreign products, GDP is reduced.

9. NI = GDP − depreciation
   4,007 = 4,486 − 479

The depreciation charge is not a measure of newly produced output. It is an estimate, subject to error, of the value of capital worn out in the production of final goods and services. Errors in the capital consumption allowance overstate or understate GDP.

11. When the price level is rising, nominal GDP overstates the rate of change between years. Dividing nominal GDP by the GDP chain price index results in real GDP by removing the distortion from inflation. Comparison of real GDP changes between years reflects only changes in the market value of all final products and not changes in the price level.

13. GDP does not tell the mix of output in two nations, say, between military and consumer goods. GDP also does not reveal whether GDP is more equally distributed in one nation compared to another.

CHAPTER 6
BUSINESS CYCLES AND UNEMPLOYMENT

1. The generally accepted theory of business cycles is that they are the result of changes in the level of total spending, or aggregate demand. Total spending includes spending for final goods by households, businesses, government, and foreign buyers. Expressed as a formula, $GDP = C + I + G + (X - M)$.

3. *Civilian unemployment rate*

$$= \frac{\text{unemployed}}{\text{civilian labor force}} \times 100$$

where the civilian labor force = unemployed + employed. Therefore,

$$7.7\% = \frac{10 \text{ million persons}}{130 \text{ million persons}} \times 100$$

5. The official unemployment rate is overstated when respondents to the BLS falsely report that they are seeking employment. The unemployment rate is understated when *discouraged* workers who want to work have given up searching for a job.

7. Structural unemployment occurs when those seeking jobs do not possess the skills necessary to fill the available jobs. Cyclical unemployment is caused by a recession (deficient total spending). In this case, there are not enough available jobs.

9. The increasing participation of women and teenagers in the labor force has increased the rate of unemployment. Women take more time out of the labor force than do men for childbearing and child rearing.

11. The GDP gap is the difference between potential real GDP and actual real GDP. Because potential real GDP is estimated on the basis of the full-employment rate of unemployment, the GDP gap measures the cost of *cyclical* unemployment in terms of real GDP.

CHAPTER 7
INFLATION

1. This statement is incorrect. The price of a single good or service can rise while the average price of all goods and services falls. In short, the inflation rate rises when the average price of consumer goods and services rises.

3. First, the CPI is based on a typical market basket purchased by the urban family. Any group not buying the same market basket, such as retired persons, is not experiencing the price changes measured by changes in the CPI. Second, the CPI fails to adjust for quality changes. Third, the CPI ignores the law of demand and the substitution effect as prices of products change.

5. If the percentage increase in the CPI exceeds the salary increase, a person's purchasing power declines in a given year.

7. The loan is advantageous to you because the real interest rate is −5 percent (5 percent nominal interest rate minus 10 percent inflation). In one year, you must repay $105. If prices rise by 10 percent during the year, the real value of the $105 will be only $95; therefore, you have borrowed $100 worth of purchasing power and are repaying $95 worth of purchasing power.

9. At full employment, the economy operates at full capacity and produces the maximum output of goods and services. As buyers try to outbid one another for the fixed supply of goods and services, prices rise rapidly.

11. If buyers think prices will be higher tomorrow, they may buy products today and cause demand-pull inflation. If businesses believe prices for inputs will be higher in the future, many will raise prices today and cause cost-push inflation.

CHAPTER 8
THE KEYNESIAN MODEL

1. Classical economists argued that underconsumption and unemployment could not exist in the long run because of price-wage flexibility. Unsold merchandise would force firms to compete and lower product prices, and unemployed workers would accept a lower wage rate.

3. Consumers have only two options for any extra disposable income they receive. The MPC and MPS must add up to one because the portion of extra income that is not spent must be saved.

5. a. The consumption schedule downshifts, and the saving schedule downshifts.
   b. The consumption schedule upshifts, and the saving schedule downshifts.
   c. The consumption schedule downshifts, and the saving schedule upshifts.
   d. The consumption schedule downshifts, and the saving schedule downshifts.
   e. Both the consumption and the saving schedules downshift.

7. Changes in the nonincome determinants of the consumption and saving schedules tend to offset each other, and people are reluctant to change their consumption and saving habits. On the other hand, Keynes considered the volatility of businesses' decisions to invest as a major cause of the business cycle. The potentially unstable determinants of investment spending include expectations, technological change, the stock of capital goods, and business taxes.

9. a.

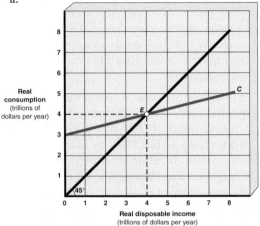

b. The autonomous consumption is $3 trillion where real disposable income is 0. The MPC = 0.25 because each $1 trillion increase in real disposable income results in a $0.25 trillion increase in consumption. Since MPS = (1 − MPC), MPS = (1 − 0.25) = 0.75.

c. The break-even income of real disposable income equals $4 trillion where the C line intersects the 45° line.

d. At $2 trillion real GDP on the 45° line, consumption is $3.5 trillion, so dissavings is $1.5 trillion. At $7 trillion real GDP on the 45° line, consumption is $4.75 trillion, so savings is $2.5 trillion.

CHAPTER 9
THE KEYNESIAN MODEL IN ACTION

1.

Employment, Output, Consumption, and Unplanned Inventory			
Possible levels of employment (millions)	Real GDP (output) equals disposable income (billions of dollars)	Consumption (billions of dollars)	Unplanned inventory (billions of dollars)
40	325	300	−75
45	375	325	−50
50	425	350	−25

55	475	375	0
60	525	400	25
65	575	425	50
70	625	450	75

a. Answers are given in the previous table.

b.

$$\text{MPC} = \frac{\text{change in consumption}}{\text{change in disposable income}}$$

$$= \frac{\$25 \text{ billion}}{\$50 \text{ billion}} = \frac{1}{2} = 0.50$$

c. At an employment level of 40 million workers, $75 million in unplanned inventory investment encourages businesses to expand output, and GDP increases toward the equilibrium real GDP of $475 billion.

3.

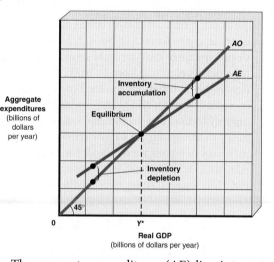

The aggregate expenditures (AE) line intersects the aggregate output (AO) line at the equilibrium level of real GDP, Y*. Below Y*, an unplanned inventory depletion causes businesses to expand output, which pushes the economy toward equilibrium output. Above Y*, an unintended inventory accumulation pushes the economy toward Y* by pressuring businesses to reduce production.

5. Multiplier $= \dfrac{1}{1 - \text{MPC}} = \dfrac{1}{\text{MPS}}$

The greater the MPC, the smaller the MPS and the greater the size of the multiplier.

a. 1, 1.5, 10

b. Y = M × I = 5 × $10 billion = $50 billion

c. Y = M × I = 3 × $10 billion = $30 billion

7. a.

Round	Component of total spending	New consumption spending (billions of dollars)
1	Investment	$100
2	Consumption	75
3	Consumption	56
4	Consumption	42
	Total spending	$273

b. The spending multiplier is

$$\frac{1}{(1 - \text{MPC})} = \frac{1}{(1 - 0.75)} = \frac{1}{0.25} = 4$$

Therefore, change in investment spending × spending multiplier = change in aggregate spending ($100 billion × 4 = $400 billion).

Note: This problem demonstrates how useful the spending multiplier formula is because it avoids working through individual steps in the multiplier process.

9. Spending multiplier

$$= \frac{\text{change in GDP}}{\text{change in government spending}} = \frac{\Delta Y}{\Delta G}$$

Since MPC = 0.75,

$$\text{Spending multiplier} = \frac{1}{(1 - \text{MPC})} = \frac{1}{0.25} = 4$$

rewritten as

$$4 = \frac{\$100 \text{ billion}}{\Delta G}$$

Therefore,

$$\Delta G = \frac{\$100 \text{ billion}}{4} = \$25 \text{ billion}$$

Given that the MPC is 0.75, this means households spend only $18.75 billion of the additional $25 billion of disposable income from the tax cut. Therefore,

$$\Delta C \times \text{spending multiplier} = \text{change in GDP}$$
$$\$18.75 \text{ billion} \times 4 = \$75 \text{ billion}$$

Because GDP must increase by $100 billion, a tax cut of $25 billion would not be enough to restore full-employment GDP.

CHAPTER 10
AGGREGATE DEMAND AND SUPPLY

1. There are three reasons why the aggregate demand curve is downward sloping:
   a. The *real balances effect* means that a lower price level increases the purchasing power of money and other financial assets. The result is an increase in consumption, which increases the quantity of real GDP demanded.
   b. The *interest-rate effect* assumes a fixed money supply, and, therefore, a lower price level reduces the demand for borrowing and the interest rate. The lower rate of interest increases spending for consumption and investment.
   c. The *net exports effect* encourages foreign customers to buy more of an economy's domestic exports relative to its domestic purchases of imports when the price level falls. An increase in net exports increases aggregate expenditures.
   Rationales for the downward-sloping demand curve for an individual market are the income effect, the substitution effect, and the law of diminishing marginal utility, which are quite different from the three effects that determine the aggregate demand curve.

3. a. A leftward shift occurs because of a decrease in the consumption schedule.
   b. A rightward shift occurs because of an increase in autonomous investment spending.
   c. A rightward shift occurs because of an increase in government spending.
   d. A rightward shift occurs because of an increase in net exports.

5. This statement may not be correct. The equilibrium GDP is not necessarily the same as the full-employment GDP. Equilibrium GDP refers to the equality between the aggregate demand and the aggregate supply curves, which does not necessarily equal the full capacity of the economy to produce goods and services.

7. a. Leftward because of an increase in resource prices
   b. Rightward because of a decrease in resource prices
   c. Rightward because technological change reduces the cost of production
   d. Leftward because an increase in taxes means the price must cover the tax at each possible quantity supplied

9. a. Aggregate demand increases.
   b. Aggregate supply increases.
   c. Aggregate demand decreases.
   d. Aggregate supply decreases.
   e. Aggregate demand decreases along the classical range.
   f. Aggregate demand increases along the Keynesian range.

11. Assuming the aggregate supply curve remains constant, a rightward shift of the aggregate demand curve from AD_1 to AD_2 in the upward-sloping range of the aggregate supply curve causes the price level to rise from P_1 to P_2. In addition to demand-pull inflation, the level of real GDP increases from Q_1 to Q_2 and provides the economy with new jobs. In the classical or vertical range of the aggregate supply curve, any further increases in aggregate demand, for example from AD_2 to AD_3, will result in only demand-pull inflation. Real GDP remains unaffected at Q_2.

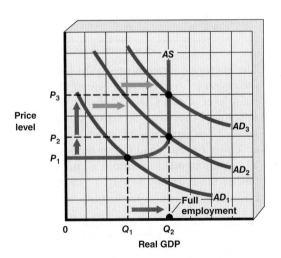

APPENDIX TO CHAPTER 10
THE SELF-CORRECTING AGGREGATE DEMAND AND SUPPLY MODEL

1. a.–c.

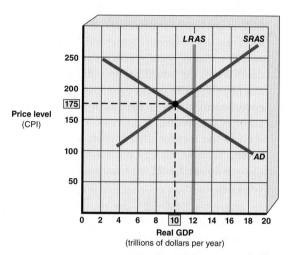

Real GDP
(trillions of dollars per year)

3.

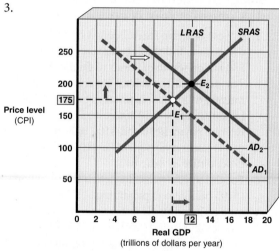

Real GDP
(trillions of dollars per year)

5. Nominal incomes of workers in the short run are fixed. In response to the fall in aggregate demand, firms' profits decline, and they cut output and employment. As a result, the economy moves downward along SRAS to temporary equilibrium at E_2. When workers lower their nominal incomes because of competition from unemployed workers, the short-run aggregate supply curve shifts rightward to E_3 and returns to long-run equilibrium. Profits rise and firms increase output and employment while the price level falls.

CHAPTER 11
FISCAL POLICY

1. *Expansionary* fiscal policy refers to increasing government spending and/or decreasing taxes in order to increase aggregate demand and eliminate a GDP gap. *Contractionary* fiscal policy is designed to cool inflation by decreasing aggregate demand. This result is accomplished by decreasing government spending and/or increasing taxes.

3. a. Contractionary fiscal policy
   b. Contractionary fiscal policy
   c. Expansionary fiscal policy

5. The spending multiplier is

$$\frac{1}{1 - \text{MPC}} = \frac{1}{0.25} = \frac{1}{1/4} = 4$$

The spending multiplier (SM) times the change in government spending (ΔG) equals the change in aggregate demand (ΔAD). Therefore,

$$\Delta G \times SM = \Delta AD$$
$$\Delta G \times 4 = \$500 \text{ billion}$$
$$\Delta G = \$125 \text{ billion}$$

The government must increase government spending by \$125 billion in order to eliminate the GDP gap.

7. The tax multiplier equals the spending multiplier minus 1. Thus, the impact of the expansion in government spending exceeds the impact of an equal amount of tax cut.

9. As a supply-side economist, you would argue that the location of the aggregate supply curve is related to the tax rates. Ceteris paribus, if the tax rates are cut, there will be strong incentives for workers to supply more work, households to save more, and businesses to invest more in capital goods. Thus, cutting tax rates shifts the aggregate supply curve rightward, the level of real GDP rises, and the price level falls.

11. a. Rightward shift in the aggregate demand curve
    b. Leftward shift in the aggregate demand curve
    c. Rightward shift in the aggregate supply curve
    d. Rightward shift in the aggregate demand curve
    e. Leftward shift in the aggregate supply curve

CHAPTER 12
THE PUBLIC SECTOR

1. Transfer payments account for the difference between total government expenditures, or outlays, and total government spending. Transfers do not "use up" resources; they reallocate purchasing power by collecting taxes from one group and paying benefits to other groups.

3. Between 1970 and 2016, income security became the largest category of federal expenditures. During the same period, national defense declined from the largest spending category to the third largest. Income security and national defense combined accounted for 69 percent of federal outlays in 2016.

5. The marginal tax rate is the percentage of additional income paid in taxes. The average tax rate is the amount of taxes paid as a percentage of income.

7. a. More than $6,000
   b. Less than $6,000
   c. $6,000

9. Sales tax paid as a percentage of income:

   10 percent

   7 percent

   6 percent

   4 percent

   Because the sales tax paid as a percentage of income falls as income rises, the tax is regressive.

11. A profit-maximizing firm follows the marginal rule that units will be produced so long as the marginal benefit exceeds or equals the marginal cost. Dollars can measure the intensity of benefits in relation to costs. A "one-person, one-vote" system does not necessarily measure benefits in proportion to the dollar value of benefits among individual voters. Thus, a majority of voters can approve projects for which costs exceed benefits and reject projects for which benefits exceed costs.

CHAPTER 13
FEDERAL DEFICITS, SURPLUSES, AND THE NATIONAL DEBT

1. The national debt is the sum of past federal budget deficits. When budget deficits are large, the national debt increases at a rapid rate. When budget deficits are small, the national debt increases at a lower rate.

3. The statement makes the argument that most of the debt is internal national debt that one U.S. citizen owes to another U.S. citizen. Suppose the federal government finances a deficit by having the Treasury sell government bonds to one group of U.S. citizens, thereby increasing the national debt. When the bonds mature, the government can pay the interest and principal by issuing new government bonds (rolling over the debt) to another group of U.S. citizens. This argument ignores the income distribution problem that results because interest payments go largely to those who are better off financially.

5. When the government makes interest payments on internally held debt, the money remains in the hands of U.S. citizens. External debt is very different. Repayment of interest and principal to foreigners withdraws purchasing power from U.S. citizens in favor of citizens abroad.

7. a. In year one, the federal deficit begins at $50 billion and the U.S. Treasury issues $50 billion worth of bonds to finance the deficit.
   b. The next year the federal government must pay interest of $5 billion to service the debt ($50 billion bonds × 0.10 interest rate). Adding the interest payment to the $100 billion spent for goods and services yields a $105 billion expenditure in year two.
   c. For the second year, the deficit is $55 billion ($105 billion in expenditures − $50 billion in taxes), and the U.S. Treasury borrows this amount by issuing new bonds. The new national debt is $105 billion, consisting of the $50 billion in bonds issued in the first year and the $55 billion in bonds issued in the second year.

9. During a depression, tax hikes and/or expenditure cuts would only reduce aggregate demand and, in turn, real GDP, jobs, and income. Because the economy is operating in the Keynesian segment of the aggregate demand curve, this fiscal policy would have no impact on the price level.

11. This answer should be logical and supported by a thoughtful explanation. For example, the federal deficit might be the result of a recession and you

argue that the deficit is correct fiscal policy. When the recession ends, the deficit will decline. Other arguments include some combinations of cutting spending or increasing taxes.

CHAPTER 14
MONEY AND THE FEDERAL RESERVE SYSTEM

1. Money is worthless in and of itself. The value of money is to serve as a medium of exchange, a unit of account, and a store of value.

3. a. The quantity of credit cards can be controlled. Credit card funds are portable, divisible, and uniform in quality.
   b. The quantity of Federal Reserve notes is controlled by the U.S. government. These notes are portable, divisible, and uniform in quality.
   c. Debit cards can be controlled. Debit card funds are portable, divisible, and uniform in quality.
   d. Although Picasso paintings are scarce, they are not so portable, divisible, or uniform.

5. The narrowest definition of money in the United States is M1. M1 = currency (coins + paper bills) + checkable deposits.

7. The Fed's most important function is to regulate the U.S. money supply. The *Board of Governors* is composed of seven persons who have the responsibility to supervise and control the money supply and the U.S. banking system. The *Federal Open Market Committee (FOMC)* controls the money supply by directing the buying and selling of U.S. government securities.

9. Banks that belong to the Fed must join the FDIC. Banks chartered by the states may affiliate with the FDIC. There are relatively few nonmember, noninsured state banks.

CHAPTER 15
MONEY CREATION

1. At first, the goldsmiths followed Shakespeare's advice and gave receipts only for gold on deposit in their vaults. They then realized that at any given time new deposits were coming in that could offset old deposits people were drawing down. The conclusion is that banking does not require a 100 percent required reserve ratio; therefore, loans can be made, which stimulate the economy.

3. Banks can and do create money by granting loans to borrowers. These loans are deposited in customers' checking accounts, and, therefore, banks are participants in the money supply creation process.

5. There is no impact on the money supply. A check deposited in bank *A*, drawn on bank *B*, increases deposits, reserves, and lending at bank *A*. However, bank *B* experiences an equal reduction in deposits, reserves, and lending.

7.

First National Bank			
Balance Sheet			
Assets		**Liabilities**	
Reserves	−$1,000	Checkable deposits	−$1,000
Required	−$200		
Excess	−$800		
Total assets	−$1,000	Total liabilities	−$1,000

Negative excess reserves mean that loans must be reduced by $1,000.

9. Some customers may hold cash, rather than writing a check for the full amount of the loan. Some banks may hold excess reserves, rather than using these funds to make loans.

11. The decision of the public to hold cash and the willingness of banks to use excess reserves for loans affect the money multiplier. Variations in the money multiplier can cause unexpected changes in the money supply. Nonbanks can make loans and offer other financial services that are not under the direct control of the Federal Reserve. Finally, the public can decide to transfer funds from M1 to M2 or other definitions of the money supply.

CHAPTER 16
MONETARY POLICY

1. a. Transactions and precautionary balances increase.

b. Speculative balances decrease.
c. Transactions and precautionary balances decrease.
d. Speculative balances increase.
e. Transactions and precautionary balances decrease.

3.

Bond price	Interest rate
$ 800	10%
1,000	8
2,000	4

There is an inverse relationship between the price of a bond and the interest rate.

5. a. The price level declines slightly. Real GDP and employment fall substantially.
   b. The price level, real GDP, and employment rise.
   c. The price level declines slightly. Real GDP and employment fall substantially.

7. In the monetarist view, the velocity of money, V, and the output, Q, variables in the equation of exchange are constant. Therefore, the quantity theory of money is stated as

$$M \times V = P \times Q$$

Given this equation, changes in the money supply, M1, yield proportionate changes in the price level, P.

9. In the Keynesian view, an increase in the money supply decreases the interest rate and causes investment spending, which increases aggregate demand through the multiplier effect and causes demand-pull inflation. In the monetarist view, money supply growth gives people more money to spend. This direct increase in aggregate demand causes demand-pull inflation.

11. Under such conditions, the Keynesian view is correct. The Fed would have no influence on investment because changes in the interest rate failed to alter the quantity of investment goods demanded.

APPENDIX TO CHAPTER 16
POLICY DISPUTES USING THE SELF-CORRECTING AGGREGATE DEMAND AND SUPPLY MODEL

1. a. See Exhibit A-1. The economy starts with a real GDP of $8 trillion and a price level of 150 at macro equilibrium E_1. Since full-employment real GDP is $12 trillion,

EXHIBIT A-1

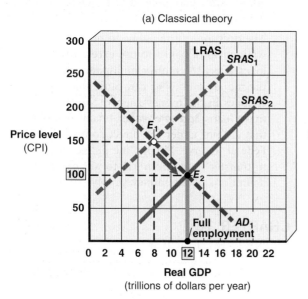

(a) Classical theory

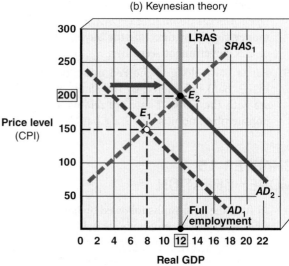

(b) Keynesian theory

there is a recessionary gap. In part (a) of Exhibit A-1, the economy closes the gap through the classical self-correction process. The key classical assumption is that nominal wages are flexible and fall as a result of competition among unemployed workers for jobs.

b. Over time, the result is that the short-term aggregate supply curve ($SRAS_1$) shifts rightward to $SRAS_2$ and the economy automatically adjusts to long-run macro full-employment equilibrium at E_2. Real GDP has expanded over time but with a lower price level.

3. a. See Exhibit A-2. The economy starts with a real GDP of $16 trillion and a price level of 150 at macro equilibrium E_1. Since full-employment real GDP is $12 trillion, there is an inflationary gap. In part (b) of Exhibit A-2, Keynesian contractionary fiscal policy aims at decreasing AD_1 to AD_2 using cuts in government spending or tax hikes. According to Keynesians, monetary policy can also be used to shift the aggregate demand curve leftward. In this case, the Federal Reserve could follow a contractionary policy and decrease the money supply, resulting in a higher interest rate, and firms respond by decreasing their investment spending. Consequently, AD_1 decreases to AD_2.

b. Working through the multiplier process, the inflationary gap is eliminated, and the economy moves from point E_1 to E_2 where the price level falls from 150 to 100 and full-employment real GDP of $12 trillion is achieved.

CHAPTER 17
THE PHILLIPS CURVE AND EXPECTATIONS THEORY

1. The short-run Phillips curve shows an inverse relationship between the inflation rate and the unemployment rate. An increase in aggregate demand would cause the inflation rate to increase and the unemployment rate to decrease.

3. In the 1970s and early 1980s, the economy experienced supply shocks from skyrocketing oil and food prices. The result was a leftward shift in the aggregate supply curve and stagflation.

5. a. The inflation rate is 6 percent, and the unemployment rate is 6 percent.
   b. The inflation rate rises to 10 percent, and the employment rate falls in the short run. In the long run, the unemployment rate returns to 6 percent.

EXHIBIT **A-2**

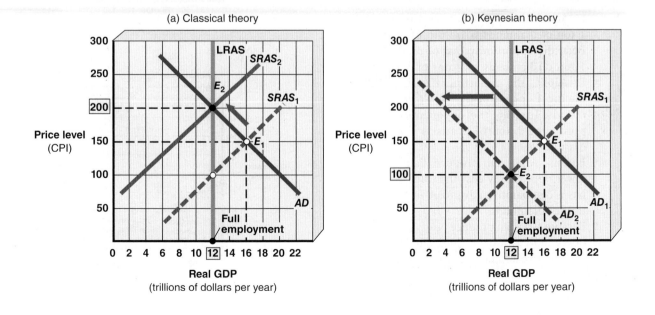

(a) Classical theory

(b) Keynesian theory

Real GDP
(trillions of dollars per year)

c. The inflation rate rises to 12 percent, and the unemployment rate falls in the short run. In the long run, the unemployment rate returns to 6 percent.

7. The economy is stimulated prior to an election, and there is a boom. After the election, the strategy is to contract the economy, causing recession until the next election approaches. Thus, political policies are counter to Keynesian policies because political policies cause the business cycle instead of stabilizing it.

9. a. Both prices and nominal wages will rise immediately, causing the inflation rate to rise from 4 percent to 6 percent. The unemployment rate remains unchanged at the 4 percent natural rate.
   b. Both prices and nominal wages will rise immediately, causing the inflation rate to rise from 6 percent to 8 percent. The unemployment rate remains unchanged at the 4 percent natural rate.
   c. Both prices and nominal wages will fall immediately, causing the inflation rate to fall from 8 percent to 4 percent. The unemployment rate remains unchanged at the 4 percent natural rate.

CHAPTER 18
INTERNATIONAL TRADE AND FINANCE

1. a. In Alpha, the opportunity cost of producing 1 ton of diamonds is 1/2 ton of pearls. In Beta, the opportunity cost of producing 1 ton of diamonds is 2 tons of pearls.
   b. In Alpha, the opportunity cost of producing 1 ton of pearls is 2 tons of diamonds. In Beta, the opportunity cost of producing 1 ton of pearls is 1/2 ton of diamonds.
   c. Because Alpha can produce diamonds at a lower opportunity cost than Beta can, Alpha has a comparative advantage in the production of diamonds.
   d. Because Beta can produce pearls at a lower opportunity cost than Alpha can, Beta has a comparative advantage in the production of pearls.

e.

	Diamonds (tons per year)	Pearls (tons per year)
Before specialization		
Alpha (at point B)	100	25
Beta (at point C)	30	120
Total output	130	145
After specialization		
Alpha (at point A)	150	0
Beta (at point D)	0	180
Total output	150	180

As shown in the previous table, specialization in each country increases total world output per year by 20 tons of diamonds and 35 tons of pearls.

f.

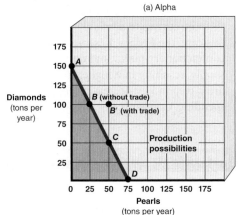

(a) Alpha

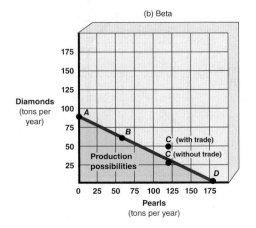

(b) Beta

Without trade, Alpha produces and consumes 100 tons of diamonds and 25 tons of pearls at point *B* on its production possibilities curve. Without trade, Beta produces and consumes 30 tons of diamonds and 120 tons of pearls (point *C*). Now assume Alpha specializes in producing diamonds at point *A* and imports 50 tons of pearls in exchange for 50 tons of diamonds. Through specialization and trade, Alpha moves its consumption possibility to point *B′*, outside its production possibilities curve.

3. The principle of specialization and trade according to comparative advantage applies to both nations and states in the United States. For example, Florida grows oranges, and Idaho grows potatoes. Trade between these states, just like trade between nations, increases the consumption possibilities.

5. U.S. industries (and their workers) that compete with restricted imports would benefit. Consumers would lose from the reduced supply of imported goods from which to choose and from higher prices for domestic products, resulting from lack of competition from imports.

7. Although some domestic jobs may be lost, new ones are created by international trade. Stated differently, the economy as a whole gains when nations specialize and trade according to the law of comparative advantage, but imports will cost jobs in some specific industries.

9. Although each nation's balance of payments equals zero, its current and capital account balances usually do not equal zero. For example, a current account deficit means a nation purchased more in imports than it sold in exports. On the other hand, this nation's capital account must have a surplus to offset the current account deficit. This means that foreigners are buying more domestic capital (capital inflow) than domestic citizens are buying foreign capital (capital outflow). Thus, net ownership of domestic capital stock is in favor of foreigners.

11. a.

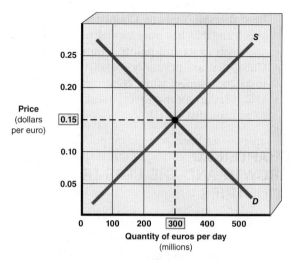

b. $0.15 per euro
c. An excess quantity of 200 million euros would be demanded.

CHAPTER 19
ECONOMIES IN TRANSITION

1. Americans prefer large cars and canned soup. Europeans predominantly buy small cars and dry soup. The role of women and minorities in the workplace is an excellent example of how culture relates to the labor factor of production.

3. Such a program would provide additional economic security for the elderly, but higher taxes could reduce the incentive to work, and economic efficiency might be reduced.

5. In a traditional agricultural system, a benefit would be that members of society would cooperate by helping to build barns, harvest, and so on. Under the command system, worrying about errors and crop failures would be minimized because the state makes the decisions and everyone in society has a basic income. In a market economy, a bumper crop would mean large profits and the capacity to improve one's standard of living.

7. Because most economies are mixed systems, this term is too broad to be very descriptive. The terms *capitalism* and *communism* are

more definitive concerning the role of private ownership, market allocations, and decentralized decision making. Countries fall along a spectrum that has pure capitalism and pure socialism as its end points. Countries, such as Cuba, that are primarily socialist are referred to as communist, while countries, such as the U.S., that are primarily capitalist are referred to as capitalist.

CHAPTER 20
GROWTH AND THE LESS-DEVELOPED COUNTRIES

1. The difference between IACs and LDCs is based on GDP per capita. This classification is somewhat arbitrary. A country with a high GDP per capita and narrow industrial development based on oil, such as the United Arab Emirates, is excluded from the IAC list. There are 27 economies listed in the text as IACs, including Switzerland, Japan, the United States, Singapore, and Hong Kong. The following countries are considered to be LDCs: Argentina, Sudan, South Africa, Jordan, and Bangladesh.

3. a. Based only on GDP per capita, you would conclude that Alpha is a better place to live because this country produces a greater output of goods and services per person.
   b. Based on the additional evidence, you would change your mind and prefer to live in Beta because the quality-of-life data indicate a higher standard of living in this country.

5. The average growth rate of GDP per capita for IACs exceeds the GDP per capita growth rate for LDCs. This evidence is consistent with the argument. The argument is oversimplified because there is considerable diversity among the LDCs. In a given year, a LDC may have a GDP per capita growth rate greater than many IACs.

7. Economic growth and development are complicated because there is no single prescription that a country can follow. The chapter presents a multidimensional model with five basic categories: natural resources, human resources, capital, technological progress, and political environment. Because an LDC is weak in one or more of the key factors, such as natural resources, does not necessarily mean that the LDC cannot achieve economic success.

9. Because they are poor countries with low GDP per capita, they lack domestic savings to invest in capital; and lacking investment, they remain poor. The rich in these poor countries often put their savings abroad because of the fear of political instability. An inflow of external funds from abroad permits the LDC to increase its capital without reducing its consumption and to shift its production possibilities curve outward.

11. Poor countries are too poor to save enough to finance domestic capital formation. International trade is a way LDCs can generate savings from abroad. Exports provide the LDCs with foreign exchange to pay for imports of capital stock that is necessary for economic growth and development. LDCs often prefer trade to aid since they feel that aid comes with too many political and economic strings attached.

APPENDIX B

Answers to Sample Quizzes

Chapter 1 Introducing the Economic Way of Thinking

1. d 2. c 3. a 4. c 5. b 6. d 7. d 8. d 9. b
10. d 11. a 12. c 13. a 14. b 15. c 16. d
17. d 18. b 19. a 20. d

Appendix 1 Applying Graphs to Economics

1. d 2. d 3. b 4. c 5. a 6. a 7. d 8. c
9. a 10. c 11. d 12. a. 13. b 14. d 15. d 16. c
17. c 18. c 19. d 20. c

Chapter 2 Production Possibilities, Opportunity Cost, and Economic Growth

1. d 2. b 3. a 4. c 5. c 6. e 7. b 8. a 9. c
10. d 11. d 12. b 13. a 14. b 15. a 16. a
17. a 18. d 19. a 20. c

Chapter 3 Market Demand and Supply

1. b 2. a 3. d 4. c 5. d 6. c 7. c 8. d
9. b 10. a 11. b 12. e 13. d 14. a 15. b
16. c 17. d 18. a 19. a 20. b 21. c 22. e
23. d 24. a 25. e

Appendix to Chapter 3 Consumer Surplus, Producer Surplus and Market Efficiency

1. c 2. c 3. c 4. d 5. e 6. d 7. d 8. d
9. a 10. d 11. d 12. d 13. a 14. b 15. d
16. a 17. b 18. d 19. d 20. d

Chapter 4 Markets in Action

1. b 2. c 3. a 4. c 5. b 6. b 7. a 8. d
9. b 10. a 11. b 12. b 13. b 14. c 15. a
16. a 17. b 18. c 19. d 20. c

Chapter 5 Gross Domestic Product

1. b 2. e 3. b 4. d 5. c 6. a 7. a 8. c 9. c
10. c 11. a 12. d 13. d 14. c 15. d 16. a
17. b 18. a 19. a 20. c

Chapter 6 Business Cycles and Unemployment

1. c 2. b 3. d 4. b 5. d 6. c 7. b 8. c
9. d 10. b 11. c 12. d 13. c 14. d 15. e
16. b 17. d 18. b 19. b 20. c

Chapter 7 Inflation

1. c 2. c 3. a 4. d 5. d 6. b 7. a 8. d
9. c 10. c 11. d 12. b 13. a 14. e 15. d
16. b 17. b 18. d 19. a 20. a

Chapter 8 The Keynesian Model

1. c 2. c 3. b 4. d 5. c 6. c 7. c 8. c 9. a
10. b 11. d 12. b 13. c 14. b 15. b 16. b
17. d 18. a 19. c 20. a

Chapter 9 The Keynesian Model in Action

1. c 2. c 3. a 4. d 5. c 6. a 7. c 8. a 9. b
10. b 11. a 12. d 13. d 14. a 15. b 16. d
17. b 18. c 19. d 20. d

Chapter 10 Aggregate Demand and Supply

1. c 2. e 3. a 4. b 5. a 6. a 7. d 8. a 9. c
10. b 11. c 12. c 13. d 14. b 15. b 16. a
17. a 18. e 19. c 20. c

Appendix to Chapter 10 The Self-Correcting Aggregate Demand and Supply Model

1. c 2. e 3. a 4. d 5. b 6. a 7. d 8. d
9. b 10. b 11. b 12. a 13. b 14. b 15. c
16. a 17. a 18. c 19. d 20. c

Chapter 11 Fiscal Policy

1. c 2. c 3. d 4. a 5. d 6. d 7. d 8. a
9. c 10. c 11. b 12. a 13. d 14. d 15. d
16. b 17. a 18. c 19. b 20. a

Chapter 12 The Public Sector

1. a 2. a 3. a 4. a 5. b 6. d 7. c 8. a 9. a
10. b 11. c 12. c 13. b 14. d 15. b 16. d
17. a 18. c 19. d 20. b

Chapter 13 Federal Deficits, Surpluses, and the National Debt

1. a 2. d 3. c 4. c 5. d 6. b 7. d 8. d
9. d 10. d 11. a 12. d 13. a 14. d 15. a
16. d 17. d 18. a 19. a 20. e

Chapter 14 Money and the Federal Reserve System

1. a   2. b   3. c   4. d   5. b   6. d   7. d   8. b
9. d   10. d   11. d   12. a   13. c   14. c   15. d
16. d   17. b   18. d   19. a   20. a

Chapter 15 Money Creation

1. c   2. b   3. a   4. b   5. e   6. b   7. a   8. b
9. a   10. c   11. c   12. c   13. b   14. a   15. d
16. e   17. b   18. b   19. b   20. a

Chapter 16 Monetary Policy

1. a   2. c   3. e   4. b   5. b   6. b   7. d   8. a
9. b   10. d   11. a   12. c   13. d   14. a   15. a
16. b   17. d   18. e   19. d   20. e

Appendix to Chapter 16 Policy Disputes Using the Self-Correcting Aggregate Demand and Supply Model

1. a   2. d   3. d   4. c   5. b   6. b   7. a   8. b
9. a   10. d   11. a   12. c   13. b   14. c   15. d

Chapter 17 The Phillips Curve and Expectations Theory

1. a   2. a   3. c   4. a   5. a   6. c   7. b   8. b   9. b
10. b   11. a   12. b   13. a   14. b   15. d   16. d
17. d   18. d   19. b   20. a

Chapter 18 International Trade and Finance

1. c   2. a   3. c   4. b   5. b   6. d   7. d   8. a
9. e   10. a   11. d   12. a   13. a   14. c   15. c
16. a   17. d   18. b   19. c   20. b

Chapter 19 Economies in Transition

1. d   2. a   3. c   4. a   5. c   6. d   7. d   8. a
9. c   10. a   11. a   12. d   13. a   14. b   15. d
16. b   17. d   18. c   19. d   20. c

Chapter 20 Growth and the Less-Developed Countries

1. d   2. d   3. c   4. b   5. e   6. d   7. b   8. d
9. d   10. d   11. e   12. a   13. e   14. a   15. b
16. d   17. c   18. a   19. c   20. b

Answers to Road Map Questions

Part 1 Introduction to Economics

1. e   2. c   3. c   4. d   5. a   6. e   7. d   8. d
9. d   10. b

Part 2 Microeconomics Fundamentals

1. b   2. c   3. a   4. a   5. d   6. d   7. d   8. c

Part 3 Macroeconomics Fundamentals

1. e   2. a   3. a   4. c   5. c   6. b   7. b   8. c   9. c
10. a   11. c   12. d

Part 4 Macroeconomics Theory and Policy

1. d   2. a   3. a   4. d   5. b   6. c   7. e   8. b
9. a   10. a   11. d   12. b   13. e   14. d   15. d

Part 5 Money, Banking, and Monetary Policy

1. d   2. d   3. d   4. e   5. c   6. b   7. a   8. d
9. d   10. a   11. e   12. d   13. a   14. a

Part 6 The International Economy

1. d   2. d   3. b   4. e   5. e   6. c   7. d   8. e
9. b   10. d

GLOSSARY

A

Ability-to-pay principle The concept that those who have higher incomes can afford to pay a greater proportion of their income in taxes, regardless of benefits received.

Absolute advantage The ability of a country to produce a good using the same or fewer resources than another country.

Adaptive expectations theory The concept that people believe the best indicator of the future is recent information. As a result, people persistently underestimate inflation when it is accelerating and overestimate it while it is slowing down.

Adjustable-rate mortgage (ARM) A home loan that adjusts the nominal interest rate to changes in an index rate, such as rates on Treasury securities that reflect changes in inflation.

Agency for International Development (AID) The agency of the U.S. State Department that is in charge of U.S. aid to foreign countries.

Aggregate demand curve (AD) The curve that shows the level of real GDP purchased by households, businesses, government, and foreigners (net exports) at different possible price levels during a time period, ceteris paribus.

Aggregate expenditures function (AE) The total spending in an economy at different levels of real GDP.

Aggregate expenditures model The model that determines the equilibrium level of real GDP by the intersection of the aggregate expenditures and aggregate output and income (real GDP) curves.

Aggregate supply curve (AS) The curve that shows the level of real GDP produced at different possible price levels during a time period, ceteris paribus.

Appreciation of currency A rise in the price of one currency relative to another.

Arbitrage The practice of earning a profit by buying a good at a low price and reselling the good at a higher price.

Automatic stabilizers Federal expenditures and tax revenues that automatically change levels in order to stabilize an economic expansion or contraction; sometimes referred to as nondiscretionary fiscal policy.

Autonomous consumption Consumption spending that is independent of the level of real disposable income.

Autonomous expenditure Spending that does not vary with the level of real disposable income.

Average fixed cost (AFC) Total fixed cost divided by the quantity of output produced.

Average tax rate The tax divided by the income.

Average total cost (ATC) Total cost divided by the quantity of output produced.

Average variable cost (AVC) Total variable cost divided by the quantity of output produced.

B

Balance of payments A bookkeeping record of all the international transactions between a country and other countries during a given period of time.

Balance of trade The value of a nation's imports subtracted from its exports. Balance of trade can be expressed in terms of goods, services, or goods and services.

Balanced budget multiplier An equal change in government spending and taxes, which changes aggregate demand by the amount of the change in government spending.

Barrier to entry Any obstacle that makes it difficult for a new firm to enter a market.

Barter The direct exchange of one good or service for another good or service, rather than for money.

Base year A year chosen as a reference point for comparison with some earlier or later year.

Benefit-cost analysis The comparison of the additional rewards and costs of an economic alternative.

Benefits-received principle The concept that those who benefit from government expenditures should pay the taxes that finance their benefits.

Board of Governors of the Federal Reserve System The seven members appointed by the president and confirmed by the U.S. Senate who serve for one nonrenewable 14-year term. Their responsibility is to supervise and control the money supply and the banking system of the United States.

Budget deficit A budget in which government expenditures exceed government revenues in a given time period.

Budget line A line that shows the different combinations of two goods a consumer can purchase with a given amount of money and at given prices.

Budget surplus A budget in which government revenues exceed government expenditures in a given time period.

Business cycle Alternating periods of economic growth and contraction, which can be measured by changes in real GDP.

C

Capital A human-made good used to produce other goods and services.

Capitalism An economic system characterized by private ownership of resources and markets.

Cartel A group of firms that formally agree to reduce competition by coordinating the price and output of a product.

Celler–Kefauver Act of 1950 An amendment to the Clayton Act that prohibits one firm from merging with a competitor by purchasing its physical assets if the effect is to substantially lessen competition.

Ceteris paribus A Latin phrase that means while certain variables change, all other things remain unchanged.

Change in demand An increase or a decrease in the quantity demanded at each possible price. An increase in demand is a rightward shift in the entire demand curve. A decrease in demand is a leftward shift in the entire demand curve.

Change in quantity demanded A movement between points along a stationary demand curve, ceteris paribus.

Change in quantity supplied A movement between points along a stationary supply curve, ceteris paribus.

Change in supply An increase or a decrease in the quantity supplied at each possible price. An increase in supply is a rightward shift in the entire supply curve. A decrease in supply is a leftward shift in the entire supply curve.

Checkable deposits The total money in financial institutions that can be withdrawn on demand by writing a check.

Circular flow model A diagram showing the exchange of money, products, and resources between households and businesses.

Civilian labor force The number of people 16 years of age and older who are employed or who are actively seeking a job, excluding armed forces, homemakers, discouraged workers, and other persons not in the labor force.

Classical economics The theory that free markets will restore full employment without government intervention.

Classical economists A group of economists whose theory dominated economic thinking from the 1770s to the Great Depression. They believed recessions would naturally cure themselves because the price system would automatically restore full employment.

Classical range The vertical segment of the aggregate supply curve, which represents an economy at full-employment output.

Clayton Act of 1914 An amendment that strengthens the Sherman Act by making it illegal for firms to engage in certain anticompetitive business practices.

Coase Theorem The proposition that private market negotiations can achieve social efficiency regardless of the initial definition of property rights.

Coincident indicators Variables that change at the same time real GDP changes.

Collective bargaining The process of negotiating labor contracts between the union and management concerning wages and working conditions.

Command economy An economic system that answers the What, How, and For Whom questions by a dictator or central authority.

Command-and-control regulations Government regulations that set an environmental goal and dictate how the goal will be achieved.

Commodity money Anything that serves as money while having market value based on the material from which it is made.

Communism A stateless, classless economic system in which all the factors of production are owned by the workers and people share in production according to their needs. In Marx's view, this is the highest form of socialism toward which the revolution should strive.

Comparable worth The principle that employees who work for the same employer must be paid the same wage when their jobs, even if different, require similar levels of education, training, experience, and responsibility. A nonmarket wage-setting process is used to evaluate and compensate jobs according to point scores assigned.

Comparative advantage The ability of a country to produce a good at a lower opportunity cost than another country.

Complementary good A good that is jointly consumed with another good. As a result, there is an inverse relationship between a price change for one good and the demand for its "go together" good.

Conglomerate merger A merger between firms in unrelated markets.

Constant returns to scale A situation in which the long-run average cost curve does not change as the firm increases output.

Constant-cost industry An industry in which the expansion of industry output by the entry of new firms has no effect on the individual firm's average total cost curve.

Consumer equilibrium A condition in which total utility cannot increase by spending more of a given budget on one good and spending less on another good.

Consumer Financial Protection Bureau (CFPB) An independent bureau within the Federal Reserve that helps consumers make financial decisions.

Consumer price index (CPI) An index that measures changes in the average prices of consumer goods and services.

Consumer sovereignty The freedom of consumers to cast their dollar votes to buy, or not to buy, at prices determined in competitive markets.

Consumer surplus The value of the difference between the price consumers are willing to pay for a product on the demand curve and the price actually paid for it.

Consumption function The graph or table that shows the amount households spend for goods and services at different levels of real disposable income.

Cost-push inflation An increase in the general price level resulting from an increase in the cost of production, and illustrated by a leftward shift of the aggregate supply curve.

Cross-elasticity of demand The ratio of the percentage change in the quantity demanded of a good or service to a given percentage change in the price of another good or service.

Crowding-in effect An increase in private-sector spending as a result of federal budget deficits financed by U.S. Treasury borrowing. At less than full employment, consumers hold more Treasury securities, and this additional wealth causes them to spend more. Business investment spending increases because of optimistic profit expectations.

Crowding-out effect A reduction in private-sector spending as a result of federal budget deficits financed by U.S. Treasury borrowing. When federal government borrowing increases interest rates, the result is lower consumption spending by households and lower investment spending by businesses.

Currency Money, including coins and paper money.

Cyclical unemployment Unemployment caused by the lack of jobs during a recession.

D

Deadweight loss The net loss of consumer and producer surplus from underproduction or overproduction of a product.

Debt ceiling A legislated legal limit on the national debt.

Decreasing-cost industry An industry in which the expansion of industry output by the entry of new firms decreases the individual firm's average total cost curve (cost curve shifts downward).

Deflation A decrease in the general (average) price level of goods and services in the economy.

Demand curve for labor A curve showing the different quantities of labor employers are willing to hire at different wage rates in a given time period, ceteris paribus. It is equal to the marginal revenue product of labor.

Demand for money curve A curve representing the quantity of money that people hold at different possible interest rates, ceteris paribus.

Demand A curve or schedule showing the various quantities of product consumers are willing to purchase at possible prices during a specified period of time, ceteris paribus.

Demand-pull inflation A rise in the general price level resulting from an excess of total spending (demand); illustrated by a rightward shift of the aggregate demand curve.

Depreciation of currency A fall in the price of one currency relative to another.

Deregulation The elimination or phasing out of government restrictions on economic activity.

Derived demand The demand for labor and other factors of production that depends on the consumer demand for the final goods and services the factors produce.

Direct relationship A positive association between two variables. When one variable increases, the other variable increases, and when one variable decreases, the other variable decreases.

Discount rate The interest rate the Fed charges on loans of reserves to banks.

Discouraged worker A person who wants to work, but who has given up searching for work because he or she believes there will be no job offers.

Discretionary fiscal policy The deliberate use of changes in government spending or taxes to alter aggregate demand and stabilize the economy.

Diseconomies of scale A situation in which the long-run average cost curve rises as the firm increases output.

Disinflation A reduction in the rate of inflation.

Disposable personal income (DI) The amount of income that households actually have to spend or save after payment of personal taxes.

Dissaving The amount by which real personal consumption expenditures exceed real disposable income.

E

Economic growth The ability of an economy to produce greater levels of output, represented by an outward shift of its production possibilities curve. An expansion in national output measured by the annual percentage increase in a nation's real GDP.

Economic profit Total revenue minus explicit and implicit costs.

Economic system The organizations and methods used to determine what goods and services are produced, how they are produced, and for whom they are produced.

Economics The study of how society chooses to allocate its scarce resources to the production of goods and services to satisfy unlimited wants.

Economies of scale A situation in which the long-run average cost curve declines as the firm increases output.

Effluent tax A tax on the pollutant.

Elastic demand A condition in which the percentage change in quantity demanded is greater than the percentage change in price.

Embargo A law that bars trade with another country.

Emissions trading Firms buying and selling the right to pollute.

Entrepreneurship The creative ability of individuals to seek profits by taking risks and combining resources to produce innovative products.

Equation of exchange An accounting identity that states the money supply times the velocity of money equals total spending.

Equilibrium A market condition that occurs at any price and quantity at which the quantity demanded and the quantity supplied are equal.

Excess reserves Potential loan balances held in vault cash or on deposit with the Fed in excess of required reserves.

Exchange rate The number of units of one nation's currency that equals one unit of another nation's currency.

Expansion An upturn in the business cycle during which real GDP rises. Also called a recovery.

Expenditure approach The national income accounting method that measures GDP by adding all the spending for final goods during a period of time.

Explicit costs Payments to nonowners of a firm for their resources.

External national debt The portion of the national debt owed to foreign citizens.

Externality A cost or benefit imposed on people other than the consumers and producers of a good or service.

F

Federal Deposit Insurance Corporation (FDIC) A government agency established in 1933 to insure customer deposits up to a limit if a bank fails.

Federal funds market A private market in which banks lend reserves to each other for less than 24 hours.

Federal funds rate The interest rate banks charge for overnight loans of reserves to other banks.

Federal Open Market Committee (FOMC) The Federal Reserve's committee that directs the buying and selling of U.S. government securities, which are major instruments for controlling the money supply. The FOMC consists of the 7 members of the Federal Reserve's Board of Governors, the president of the New York Federal Reserve Bank, and the presidents of 4 other Federal Reserve District Banks.

Federal Reserve System The central bank of the United States that consists of 12 Federal Reserve District Banks that service banks and other financial institutions within each of the Federal Reserve districts; popularly called the Fed.

Federal Trade Commission Act of 1914 The federal act that in 1914 established the Federal Trade Commission (FTC) to investigate unfair competitive practices of firms.

Fiat money Money accepted by law and not because of its redeemability or intrinsic value.

Final goods Finished goods and services produced for the ultimate user.

Fiscal policy The use of government spending and taxes to influence the nation's output, employment, and price level.

Fixed input Any resource for which the quantity cannot change during the period of time under consideration.

Flow A rate of change in a quantity during a given time period, such as dollars per year. For example, income and consumption are flows that occur per week, per month, or per year.

Foreign aid The transfer of money or resources from one government to another with no repayment required.

Fractional reserve banking A system in which banks keep only a percentage of their deposits on reserve as vault cash and deposits at the Fed.

Free rider An individual who enjoys benefits without paying the costs.

Free trade The flow of goods between countries without restrictions or special taxes.

Free-rider problem The problem that if some individuals benefit, while others pay, few will be willing to pay for improvement of the environment or other public goods. As a result, these goods are under produced.

Frictional unemployment Temporary unemployment caused by the time required of workers to move from one job to another.

Full employment The situation in which an economy operates at an unemployment rate equal to the sum of the frictional and structural unemployment rates. Also called the natural rate of unemployment.

G

Game Theory A model of the strategic moves and countermoves of rivals.

GDP chain price index A measure that compares changes in the prices of all final goods during a given time period relative to the prices of those goods in a base year. This index is also called GDP price index or simply GDP deflator.

GDP gap The difference between actual real GDP and potential or full-employment real GDP.

GDP per capita The value of final goods produced (GDP) divided by the total population.

Government expenditures Federal, state, and local government outlays for goods and services, including transfer payments.

Government failure Government intervention or lack of intervention that fails to correct market failure.

Gross domestic product (GDP) The market value of all final goods and services produced in a nation during a period of time, usually a year.

H

Homogeneous product A good or service that is identical regardless of which firm produces it.

Horizontal merger A merger of firms that compete in the same market.

Hot spot problem For emissions that do not disperse uniformly, emissions may be higher in locations where firms buy permits that allow them to increase emissions.

Human capital The accumulation of education, training, experience, and the level of good health that enables a worker to enter an occupation and be productive.

Hyperinflation An extremely rapid rise in the general price level.

I

Implicit costs The opportunity costs of using resources owned by a firm.

Incentive-based regulations Government regulations that set an environmental goal, but are flexible as to how buyers and sellers achieve the goal.

Income approach The national income accounting method that measures GDP by adding all incomes during a period of time, including compensation of employees, rents, net interest, and profits.

Income effect The change in quantity demanded of a good or service caused by a change in real income (purchasing power).

Income elasticity of demand The ratio of the percentage change in the quantity demanded of a good or service to a given percentage change in income.

Incomes policies Federal government policies designed to affect the real incomes of workers by controlling nominal wages and prices. Such policies include presidential jawboning, wage–price guidelines, and wage–price controls.

Increasing-cost industry An industry in which the expansion of industry output by the entry of new firms increases the individual firm's average total cost curve (cost curve shifts upward).

Independent relationship A zero association between two variables. When one variable changes, the other variable remains unchanged.

Indifference curve A curve showing the different combinations of two products that yield the same satisfaction or total utility to a consumer.

Indifference map A selection of indifference curves with each curve representing a different level of satisfaction or total utility.

Indirect business taxes Taxes levied as a percentage of the prices of goods sold and therefore collected as part of the firm's revenue. Firms treat such taxes as production costs. Examples include general sales taxes, excise taxes, and customs duties.

Industrially advanced countries (IACs) High-income nations that have market economies based on large stocks of technologically advanced capital and well-educated labor. The United States, Canada, Australia, New Zealand, Japan, and most of the countries of Western Europe are IACs.

Inelastic demand A condition in which the percentage change in quantity demanded is less than the percentage change in price.

Inferior good Any good for which there is an inverse relationship between changes in income and its demand curve.

Inflation An increase in the general (average) price level of goods and services in the economy.

Inflationary gap The amount by which the aggregate expenditures exceed the amount required to achieve full-employment equilibrium.

Infrastructure Capital goods usually provided by the government, including highways, bridges, waste and water systems, and airports.

In-kind transfers Government payments in the form of goods and services, rather than cash, including such government programs as food stamps, Medicaid, and housing.

Interest-rate effect The impact on total spending (and therefore real GDP) caused by the direct relationship between the price level and the interest rate.

Intermediate goods Goods and services used as inputs for the production of final goods.

Intermediate range The rising segment of the aggregate supply curve, which represents an economy as it approaches full employment output.

Internal national debt The portion of the national debt owed to a nation's own citizens.

International Monetary Fund (IMF) The lending agency that makes short-term conditional low-interest loans to developing countries.

Inverse relationship A negative association between two variables. When one variable increases, the other variable decreases, and when one variable decreases, the other variable increases.

Investment demand curve The curve that shows the amount businesses spend for investment goods at different possible rates of interest.

Investment The accumulation of capital, such as factories, machines, and inventories, used to produce goods and services.

Invisible hand A phrase that expresses the belief that the best interests of a society are served when individual consumers and producers compete to achieve their own private interests.

J

Jawboning Oratory intended to pressure unions and businesses to reduce wage and price increases.

K

Keynesian economics The theory, first advanced by John Maynard Keynes, that the role of the federal government is to increase or decrease aggregate demand to achieve economic goals.

Keynesian range The horizontal segment of the aggregate supply curve, which represents an economy in a severe recession.

Kinked demand curve A demand curve facing an oligopolist that assumes rivals will match a price decrease, but ignore a price increase.

L

Labor The mental and physical capacity of workers to produce goods and services.

Laffer curve A graph depicting the relationship between tax rates and total tax revenues.

Lagging indicators Variables that change after real GDP changes.

Land Any natural resource provided by nature that is used to produce a good or service.

Law of demand The principle that there is an inverse relationship between the price of a good and the quantity buyers are willing to purchase in a defined time period, ceteris paribus.

Law of diminishing marginal utility The principle that the extra satisfaction provided by a good or service declines as people consume more in a given period.

Law of diminishing returns The principle that beyond some point the marginal product decreases as additional units of a variable factor are added to a fixed factor.

Law of increasing opportunity costs The principle that the opportunity cost increases as production of one output expands.

Law of supply The principle that there is a direct relationship between the price of a good and the quantity sellers are willing to offer for sale in a defined time period, ceteris paribus.

Leading indicators Variables that change before real GDP changes.

Less-developed countries (LDCs) Nations without large stocks of technologically advanced capital and without well-educated labor. LDCs are economies based on agriculture, such as most countries of Africa, Asia, and Latin America.

Long run A period of time so long that all inputs are variable.

Long-run aggregate supply curve (LRAS) The curve that shows the level of real GDP produced at different possible price levels during a time period in which nominal incomes change by the same percentage as the price level changes.

Long-run average cost curve (LRAC) The curve that traces the lowest cost per unit at which a firm can produce any level of output when the firm can build any desired plant size.

Lorenz curve A graph of the actual cumulative distribution of income compared to a perfectly equal cumulative distribution of income.

M

M1 The narrowest definition of the money supply. It includes currency and checkable deposits.

M2 The definition of the money supply that equals M1 plus near monies, such as savings deposits and small time deposits of less than $100,000.

Macroeconomics The branch of economics that studies decision making for the economy as a whole.

Marginal analysis An examination of the effects of additions to or subtractions from a current situation.

Marginal cost (MC) The change in total cost when one additional unit of output is produced.

Marginal cost pricing A system of pricing in which the price charged equals the marginal cost of the last unit produced.

Marginal factor cost (MFC) The additional total cost resulting from a one-unit increase in the quantity of a factor.

Marginal product The change in total output produced by adding one unit of a variable input, with all other inputs used being held constant.

Marginal propensity to consume (MPC) The change in consumption resulting from a given change in real disposable income.

Marginal propensity to save (MPS) The change in saving resulting from a given change in real disposable income.

Marginal rate of substitution (MRS) The rate at which a consumer is willing to substitute one good for another without a change in total utility. The MRS equals the slope of the indifference curve at any point on the curve.

Marginal revenue (MR) The change in total revenue from the sale of one additional unit of output.

Marginal revenue product (MRP) The increase in a firm's total revenue resulting from hiring an additional unit of labor or other variable resource.

Marginal tax rate The fraction of additional income paid in taxes.

Marginal utility The change in total utility from one additional unit of a good or service.

Marginal-average rule The rule that states when marginal cost is below average cost, average cost falls. When marginal cost is above average cost, average cost rises. When marginal cost equals average cost, average cost is at its minimum point.

Market economy An economic system that answers the What, How, and For Whom questions using prices determined by the interaction of the forces of supply and demand.

Market failure A situation in which market equilibrium results in too few or too many resources being used in the production of a good or service. This inefficiency may justify government intervention.

Market structure A classification system for the key traits of a market, including the number of firms, the similarity of the products they sell, and the ease of entry into and exit from the market.

Market Any arrangement in which buyers and sellers interact to determine the price and quantity of goods and services exchanged.

Means test A requirement that a family's income not exceed a certain level to be eligible for public assistance.

Medium of exchange The primary function of money to be widely accepted in exchange for goods and services.

Microeconomics The branch of economics that studies decision making by a single individual, household, firm, industry, or level of government.

Mixed economy An economic system that answers the What, How, and For Whom questions through a mixture of traditional, command, and market systems.

Model A simplified description of reality used to understand and predict the relationship between variables.

Monetarism The theory that changes in the money supply directly determine changes in prices, real GDP, and employment.

Monetary Control Act A law, formally titled the Depository Institutions Deregulation and Monetary Control Act of 1980, that gave the Federal Reserve System greater control over nonmember banks and made all financial institutions more competitive.

Monetary policy The Federal Reserve's use of open market operations, changes in the discount rate, and changes in the required reserve ratio to change the money supply (M1).

Money multiplier The maximum change in the money supply (checkable deposits) due to an initial change in the excess reserves held by banks. The money multiplier is equal to 1 divided by the required reserve ratio.

Money Anything that serves as a medium of exchange, unit of account, and store of value.

Monopolistic competition A market structure characterized by many small sellers, a differentiated product, and easy market entry and exit.

Monopoly A market structure characterized by a single seller, a unique product, and impossible entry into the market.

Monopsony A labor market in which a single firm hires labor.

Mutual interdependence A condition in which an action by one firm may cause a reaction from other firms.

N

National debt The total amount owed by the federal government to owners of government securities.

National income (NI) The total income earned by resource owners, including wages, rents, interest, and profits. NI is calculated as gross domestic product minus depreciation of the capital worn out in producing output.

Nationalization The act of transforming a private enterprise's assets into a government enterprise.

Natural monopoly An industry in which the long-run average cost of production declines throughout the entire market. As a result, a single firm can supply the entire market demand at a lower cost than two or more smaller firms.

Natural rate hypothesis The concept that argues that the economy will self-correct to the natural rate of unemployment. The long-run Phillips curve is therefore a vertical line at the natural rate of unemployment.

Negative income tax (NIT) A plan under which families below a certain breakeven level of income would receive cash payments that decrease as their incomes increase.

Net exports effect The impact on total spending (and therefore real GDP) caused by the inverse relationship between the price level and the net exports of an economy.

Net public debt National debt minus all government interagency borrowing.

Network good A good that increases in value to each user as the total number of users increases. As a result, a firm can achieve economies of scale. Examples include Facebook and Match.com.

New-source bias Bias that occurs when regulations provide an incentive to keep assets past the efficient point.

Nominal GDP The value of all final goods based on the prices existing during the time period of production.

Nominal income The actual number of dollars received over a period of time.

Nominal interest rate The actual rate of interest without adjustment for the inflation rate.

Nonprice competition The situation in which a firm competes using advertising, packaging, product development, better quality, and better service, rather than lower prices.

Normal good Any good for which there is a direct relationship between changes in income and its demand curve.

Normal profit The minimum profit necessary to keep a firm in operation. A firm that earns normal profits earns total revenue equal to its total opportunity cost.

Normative economics An analysis based on subjective value judgments.

O

Offset A reduction in an existing pollution source to counteract pollution from a new source.

Offshoring The practice of work for a company performed by the company's employees located in another country.

Oligopoly A market structure characterized by few large sellers, either a homogeneous or a differentiated product, and difficult market entry.

Open market operations The buying and selling of government securities by the Federal Reserve System.

Opportunity cost The best alternative sacrificed for a chosen alternative.

Outsourcing The practice of a company having its work done by another company in another country.

P

Peak The phase of the business cycle in which real GDP reaches its maximum after rising during a recovery.

Per se rule The antitrust doctrine that the existence of monopoly alone is illegal, regardless of whether or not the monopoly engages in illegal business practices.

Perfect competition A market structure characterized by a large number of small firms; a homogeneous product; and very easy entry into or exit from the market. Perfect competition is also referred to as pure competition.

Perfectly competitive firm's short-run supply curve A firm's marginal cost curve above the minimum point on its average variable cost curve.

Perfectly competitive industry's long-run supply curve The curve that shows the quantities supplied by the industry at different equilibrium prices after firms complete their entry and exit.

Perfectly competitive industry's short-run supply curve The supply curve derived from horizontal summation of the marginal cost curves of all firms in the industry above the minimum point of each firm's average variable cost curve.

Perfectly elastic demand A condition in which a small percentage change in price brings about an infinite percentage change in quantity demanded.

Perfectly inelastic demand A condition in which the quantity demanded does not change as the price changes.

Personal income (PI) The total income received by households that is available for consumption, saving, and payment of personal taxes.

Phillips curve A curve showing an inverse relationship between the inflation rate and the unemployment rate.

Political business cycle A business cycle caused by policy-makers to improve politicians' reelection chances.

Positive economics An analysis limited to statements that are verifiable.

Poverty line The level of income below which a person or a family is considered to be poor.

Precautionary demand for money The stock of money people hold to pay unpredictable expenses.

Predatory pricing The practice of one or more firms temporarily reducing prices in order to eliminate competition and then raising prices.

Price ceiling A legally established maximum price a seller can charge.

Price discrimination The practice of a seller charging different prices for the same product that are not justified by cost differences.

Price elasticity of demand The ratio of the percentage change in the quantity demanded of a product to a percentage change in its price.

Price elasticity of supply The ratio of the percentage change in the quantity supplied of a product to the percentage change in its price.

Price floor A legally established minimum price a seller can be paid.

Price leadership A pricing strategy in which a dominant firm sets the price for an industry and the other firms follow.

Price maker A firm that faces a downward-sloping demand curve, and therefore it can choose among price and output combinations along the demand curve.

Price system A mechanism that uses the forces of supply and demand to create an equilibrium through rising and falling prices.

Price taker A seller that has no control over the price of the product it sells.

Private benefits and costs Benefits and costs to the decision maker, ignoring benefits and costs to third parties. Third parties are people outside the market transaction who are affected by the product.

Privatization The process of turning a government enterprise into a private enterprise.

Producer surplus The value of the difference between the actual selling price of a product and the price producers are willing to sell it for on the supply curve.

Product differentiation The process of creating real or apparent differences between goods and services.

Production function The relationship between the maximum amounts of output a firm can produce and various quantities of inputs.

Production possibilities curve A curve that shows the maximum combinations of two outputs an economy can produce in a given period of time with its available resources and technology.

Progressive tax A tax that charges a higher percentage of income as income rises.

Proportional tax A tax that charges the same percentage of income, regardless of the size of income. Also called a flat tax rate or simply a flat tax.

Protectionism The government's use of embargoes, tariffs, quotas, and other trade restrictions to protect domestic producers from foreign competition.

Public choice theory The analysis of the government's decision-making process for allocating resources.

Public good A good or service with two properties: users collectively consume benefits; and there is no way to bar people who do not pay (free riders) from consuming the good or service.

Q

Quantity theory of money The theory that changes in the money supply are directly related to changes in the price level.

Quota A limit on the quantity of a good that may be imported in a given time period.

R

Rational expectations theory The belief that people use all available information to predict the future, including the future impact of predictable expansionary monetary and fiscal policies. Predictable expansionary macroeconomic policies can therefore be negated by immediately flexible wages and prices when businesses and workers anticipate the effects of these policies on the economy.

Rational ignorance The voter's choice to remain uninformed because the marginal cost of obtaining information is higher than the marginal benefit from knowing it.

Real balances effect The impact on total spending (and therefore real GDP) caused by the inverse relationship between the price level and the real value of financial assets with fixed nominal value.

Real GDP The value of all final goods produced during a given time period based on the prices existing in a selected base year.

Real income The actual number of dollars received (nominal income) adjusted for changes in the CPI.

Real interest rate The nominal rate of interest minus the inflation rate.

Recession A downturn in the business cycle during which real GDP declines, and the unemployment rate rises. Also called a contraction.

Recessionary gap The amount by which the aggregate expenditures fall short of the amount required to achieve full-employment equilibrium.

Regressive tax A tax that charges a lower percentage of income as income rises.

Required reserve ratio The percentage of deposits that the Fed requires a bank to hold in vault cash or on deposit with the Fed rather than being loaned.

Required reserves The minimum balance that the Fed requires a bank to hold in vault cash or on deposit with the Fed.

Resources The basic categories of inputs used to produce goods and services. Resources are also called factors of production. Economists divide resources into three categories: land, labor, and capital.

Robinson--Patman Act of 1936 An amendment to the Clayton Act that strengthens the Clayton Act's provision against price discrimination.

Rule of reason The antitrust doctrine that the existence of monopoly alone is not illegal unless the monopoly engages in illegal business practices.

S

Saving The part of disposable income households do not spend for consumer goods and services.

Say's Law The theory that supply creates its own demand.

Scarcity The condition in which human wants are forever greater than the available supply of time, goods, and resources.

Sherman Act of 1890 The federal antitrust law enacted that prohibits monopolization and conspiracies to restrain trade.

Short run A period of time so short that there is at least one fixed input.

Shortage A market condition existing at any price at where the quantity supplied is less than the quantity demanded.

Short-run aggregate supply curve (SRAS) The curve that shows the level of real GDP produced at different possible price levels during a time period in which nominal incomes do not change in response to changes in the price level.

Slope The ratio of the change in the variable on the vertical axis (the rise or fall) to the change in the variable on the horizontal axis (the run).

Social benefits and costs The sum of benefits to everyone in society, including both private benefits and external benefits. Social costs are the sum of costs to everyone in society, including both private costs and external costs.

Socialism An economic system characterized by government ownership of resources and centralized decision making.

Speculative demand for money The stock of money people hold to take advantage of expected future changes in the price of bonds, stocks, or other nonmoney financial assets.

Spending multiplier (SM) The change in aggregate demand (total spending) resulting from an initial change in any component of aggregate expenditures, including consumption, investment, government spending, and net exports. As a formula, spending multiplier equals $1/(1 - MPC)$ or $1/MPS$.

Stagflation The condition that occurs when an economy experiences the twin maladies of high unemployment and rapid inflation simultaneously.

Stock A quantity measured at one point in time. For example, an inventory of goods or the amount of money in a checking account

Store of value The ability of money to hold value over time.

Structural unemployment Unemployment caused by a mismatch of the skills of workers out of work and the skills required for existing job opportunities.

Subprime mortgage loan A home loan made to borrowers with poor or less than ideal credit scores.

Substitute good A good that competes with another good for consumer purchases. As a result, there is a direct relationship between a price change for one good and the demand for its competitor good.

Substitution effect The change in quantity demanded of a good or service caused by a change in its price relative to substitutes.

Supply curve of labor A curve showing the different quantities of labor workers are willing to offer employers at different wage rates in a given time period, ceteris paribus.

Supply A curve or schedule showing the various quantities of a product sellers are willing to produce and offer for sale at possible prices during a specified period of time, ceteris paribus.

Supply-side fiscal policy A fiscal policy that emphasizes government policies that increase aggregate supply in order to achieve long-run growth in real output, full employment, and a lower price level.

Surplus A market condition existing at any price where the quantity supplied is greater than the quantity demanded.

Sustainability Meeting the needs of the present generation without compromising the ability of future generations to meet their needs.

T

Tariffs A tax on an import.

Tax incidence The share of a tax ultimately paid by consumers and sellers.

Tax multiplier The change in aggregate expenditures (total spending) resulting from an initial change in taxes. As a formula, the tax multiplier equals 1 − spending multiplier.

Technology The body of knowledge applied to how goods are produced.

Total cost (TC) The sum of total fixed cost and total variable cost at each level of output.

Total fixed cost (TFC) Costs that do not vary as output varies and that must be paid even if output is zero. These are payments that the firm must make in the short run, regardless of the level of output.

Total revenue (TR) The total number of dollars a firm earns from the sale of a good or service, which is equal to its price multiplied by the quantity demanded.

Total utility The amount of satisfaction received from all the units of a good or service consumed.

Total variable cost (TVC) Costs that are zero when output is zero and vary as output varies.

Traditional economy An economic system that answers the What, How, and For Whom questions the way they have always have been answered.

Tragedy of the Commons Individuals will use an open access resource to the point of exhaustion, basing their use on private benefits while disregarding external costs to others.

Transactions costs The costs of negotiating and enforcing a contract.

Transactions demand for money The stock of money people hold to pay everyday predictable expenses.

Transfer payment A government payment to individuals not in exchange for goods or services currently produced.

Trough The phase of the business cycle in which real GDP reaches its minimum after falling during a recession.

Trust A combination or cartel consisting of firms that place their assets in the custody of a board of trustees.

U

Unemployment compensation The government insurance program that pays income for a short time period to unemployed workers.

Unemployment rate The percentage of people in the civilian labor force who are without jobs and are actively seeking jobs.

Unit of account The function of money to provide a common measurement of the relative value of goods and services.

Unitary elastic demand A condition in which the percentage change in quantity demanded is equal to the percentage change in price.

Utility The satisfaction, or pleasure, that people receive from consuming a good or service.

V

Variable input Any resource for which the quantity can change during the period of time under consideration.

Velocity of money The average number of times per year a dollar of the money supply is spent on final goods and services.

Vertical merger A merger of a firm with its suppliers.

Vicious circle of poverty The trap in which countries are poor because they cannot afford to save and invest, and they cannot save and invest because they are poor.

W

Wage and price controls Legal restrictions on wage and price increases. Violations can result in fines and imprisonment.

Wage and price guidelines Voluntary standards set by the government for permissible wage and price increases.

Wage-price spiral A situation that occurs when increases in nominal wage rates are passed on in higher prices, which, in turn, result in even higher nominal wage rates and prices.

Wealth effect A shift in the consumption function caused by a change in the value of real and financial assets.

Wealth The value of the stock of assets owned at some point in time.

World Bank The lending agency affiliated with the United Nations that makes long-term low-interest loans and provides technical assistance to less developed countries.

World Trade Organization (WTO) An international organization of member countries that oversees international trade agreements and rules on trade disputes.

INDEX